STRE

Cheshire

First published in 1995 by

Philip's, a division of
Octopus Publishing Group Ltd
2-4 Heron Quays, London E14 4JP

Third colour edition 2005
First impression 2005

ISBN-10   0-540-08749-1 (pocket)
ISBN-13   978-0-540-08749-5 (pocket)

© Philip's 2005

Ordnance Survey

This product includes mapping data licensed from
Ordnance Survey® with the permission of the
Controller of Her Majesty's Stationery Office.
© Crown copyright 2005. All rights reserved.
Licence number 100011710.

Printed and bound in Spain
by Cayfosa-Quebecor

Contents

III **Key to map symbols**

IV **Key to map pages**

VI **Route planning**

VIII **Administrative and Postcode boundaries**

1 **Street maps** at 2⅔ inches to 1 mile

237 **Street map of Chester city centre**
at 5⅓ inches to 1 mile

238 **Index** of towns and villages

241 **Index** of streets, hospitals, industrial estates, railway
stations, schools, shopping centres, universities
and places of interest

Digital Data

The exceptionally high-quality mapping found in this atlas is available as digital data in TIFF
format, which is easily convertible to other bitmapped (raster) image formats.

The index is also available in digital form as a standard database table. It contains all the details
found in the printed index together with the National Grid reference for the map square in which
each entry is named.

For further information and to discuss your requirements, please contact Philip's on
020 7644 6932 or james.mann@philips-maps.co.uk

III

(22a)	**Motorway** with junction number
	Primary route – dual/single carriageway
	A road – dual/single carriageway
	B road – dual/single carriageway
	Minor road – dual/single carriageway
	Other minor road – dual/single carriageway
	Road under construction
	Tunnel, covered road
	Rural track, private road or narrow road in urban area
	Gate or obstruction to traffic (restrictions may not apply at all times or to all vehicles)
	Path, bridleway, byway open to all traffic, road used as a public path
	Pedestrianised area
DY7	**Postcode boundaries**
	County and unitary authority boundaries
	Railway, tunnel, railway under construction
	Tramway, tramway under construction
	Miniature railway
≷ Walsall	**Railway station**
⊕	**Private railway station**
● South Shields	**Metro station**
⊕ ⊕	**Tram stop, tram stop under construction**
●	**Bus, coach station**

◆	**Ambulance station**
◆	**Coastguard station**
◆	**Fire station**
◆	**Police station**
✚	**Accident and Emergency entrance to hospital**
H	**Hospital**
✚	**Place of worship**
i	**Information Centre** (open all year)
🛒	**Shopping Centre**
P P&R	**Parking, Park and Ride**
PO	**Post Office**
⛺ 🚐	**Camping site, caravan site**
▶ ✕	**Golf course, picnic site**
Prim Sch	**Important buildings, schools, colleges, universities and hospitals**
	Built up area
	Woods
River Medway	**Water name**
	River, weir, stream
	Canal, lock, tunnel
	Water
	Tidal water
Church	**Non-Roman antiquity**
ROMAN FORT	**Roman antiquity**
87	**Adjoining page indicators and overlap bands** The colour of the arrow and the band indicates the scale of the adjoining or overlapping page (see scales below)
237	

Enlarged mapping only

	Railway or bus station building
	Place of interest
	Parkland

Acad	**Academy**	Inst	**Institute**	Recn Gd	**Recreation Ground**
Allot Gdns	**Allotments**	Ct	**Law Court**		
Cemy	**Cemetery**	L Ctr	**Leisure Centre**	Resr	**Reservoir**
C Ctr	**Civic Centre**	LC	**Level Crossing**	Ret Pk	**Retail Park**
CH	**Club House**	Liby	**Library**	Sch	**School**
Coll	**College**	Mkt	**Market**	Sh Ctr	**Shopping Centre**
Crem	**Crematorium**	Meml	**Memorial**	TH	**Town Hall/House**
Ent	**Enterprise**	Mon	**Monument**	Trad Est	**Trading Estate**
Ex H	**Exhibition Hall**	Mus	**Museum**	Univ	**University**
Ind Est	**Industrial Estate**	Obsy	**Observatory**	W Twr	**Water Tower**
IRB Sta	**Inshore Rescue Boat Station**	Pal	**Royal Palace**	Wks	**Works**
		PH	**Public House**	YH	**Youth Hostel**

■ The small numbers around the edges of the maps identify the 1 kilometre National Grid lines
■ The dark grey border on the inside edge of some pages indicates that the mapping does not continue onto the adjacent page

The scale of the maps on the pages numbered in blue is 4.2 cm to 1 km • 2⅔ inches to 1 mile • 1: 23810	0 ¼ ½ ¾ 1 mile 0 250m 500m 750m 1 kilometre
The scale of the maps on pages numbered in red is 8.4 cm to 1 km • 5⅓ inches to 1 mile • 1: 11900	0 220 yards 440 yards 660 yards ½ mile 0 125m 250m 375m ½ kilometre

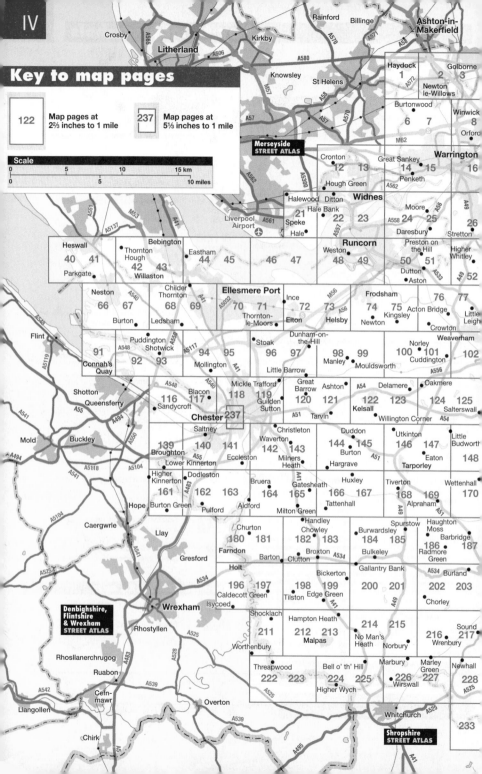

IV

Key to map pages

122	Map pages at 2⅔ inches to 1 mile
237	Map pages at 5⅓ inches to 1 mile

Scale

0   5   10   15 km
0   5   10 miles

Rainford Billinge **Ashton-in-Makerfield**

Crosby Kirkby

Litherland

Knowsley St Helens

Haydock **1** Golborne **2 3**

Newton le-Willows

Burtonwood

6 7 Winwick **8** Orford

Merseyside STREET ATLAS

Cronton **12 13** Great Sankey **14 15** **Warrington 16**

Hough Green Penketh

Halewood Ditton **Widnes**

Liverpool Airport Hale Bank **21** Moore **24 25**

Speke **22 23** **26**

Hale Daresbury Stretton

Weston **Runcorn** Preston on the Hill

Heswall **40 41** Bebington Eastham **44 45 46 47** **48 49** **50 51** Higher Whitley

Thornton Hough **42 43** Dutton Aston **52**

Parkgate Willaston

Neston **66 67** Childer Thornton **68 69** **Ellesmere Port 70 71** Ince **72 73** Frodsham **74 75 76 77**

Burton Ledsham Thornton-le-Moors Elton Helsby Newton Kingsley Acton Bridge Little Leigh

Crowton

Flint Puddington Shotwick **94 95 96 97** Stoak Dunham-on-the-Hill **98 99 100 101 102** Norley Weaverham

91 **92 93** Mollington Little Barrow Manley Mouldsworth Cuddington

Connah's Quay

Shotton Blacon **116 117 118 119 120 121 122 123 124 125** Mickle Trafford Great Barrow Ashton Delamere Oakmere

Queensferry Sandycroft Guilden Sutton Kelsall Salterswall

Chester 237 Tarvin Willington Corner

Mold Saltney Christleton Duddon Utkinton Little Budworth

Buckley **139 140 141 142 143 144 145 146 147 148**

Broughton Waverton Burton Eaton

Lower Kinnerton Eccleston Milners Heath Hargrave **Tarporley**

Higher Kinnerton Dodleston **161 162 163** Bruera **164 165** Huxley Tiverton **168 169** Wettenhall **170**

Hope Burton Green Gatesheath **166 167** Alpraham

Caergwrle Pulford Aldford Tattenhall

Llay Milton Green

Gresford Churton **180 181** Handley Chowley **182 183** Burwardsley **184 185** Spurstow Haughton Moss Barbridge **186 187**

Farndon Broxton Bulkeley Radmore Green

Barton Clutton **A534**

Holt Bickerton Gallantry Bank Burland

196 197 198 199 200 201 202 203

Caldecott Green Tilston Edge Green Chorley

Wrexham Isycoed

Rhostyllen Shocklach **211** Hampton Heath **212 213** **214 215** Marbury Marley Green Newhall

Worthenbury **Malpas** No Man's Heath Norbury **216 217** **228**

Rhosllanerchrugog Wrenbury Sound

Denbighshire, Flintshire & Wrexham STREET ATLAS

Ruabon Threapwood **222 223** Bell o' th' Hill **224 225** **226 227** Wirswall

Cefn-mawr Higher Wych

Llangollen Overton

Chirk Whitchurch **233**

Shropshire STREET ATLAS

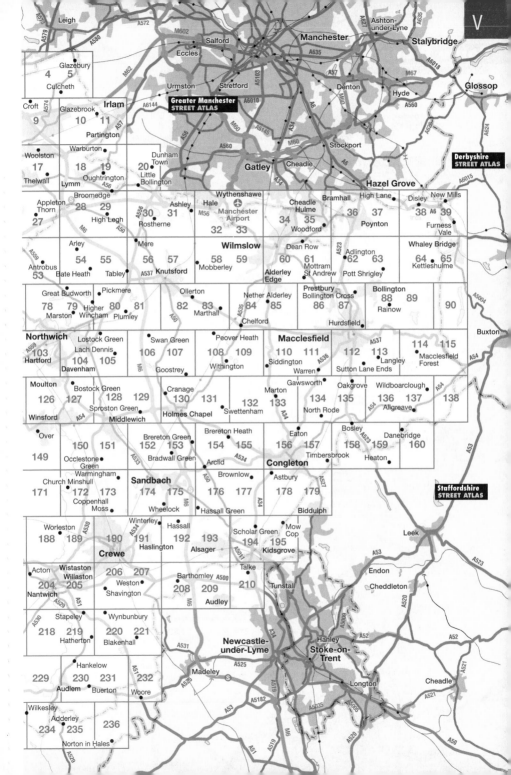

Route Planning

Scale

0   5   10 km

0   5 miles

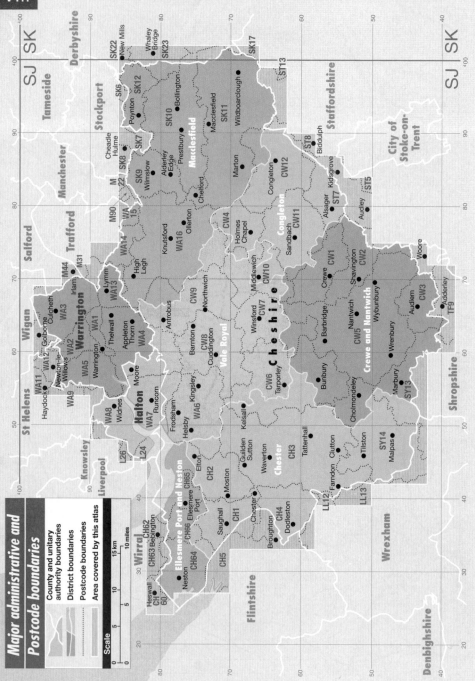

Major administrative and Postcode boundaries

- County and unitary authority boundaries
- District boundaries
- Postcode boundaries
- Area covered by this atlas

Scale

0   5   10   15 km
0   5   10 miles

Derbyshire

Tameside

Stockport

Manchester

Salford

Trafford

Wigan

St Helens

Warrington

Halton

Knowsley

Liverpool

Wirral

Ellesmere Port and Neston

Chester

Flintshire

Denbighshire

Wrexham

Cheshire

Vale Royal

Macclesfield

Congleton

Crewe and Nantwich

Staffordshire

City of Stoke-on-Trent

Shropshire

SJ | SK

SK22   New Mills
Whaley Bridge   SK23
SK17
SK6   Poynton   SK12
Cheadle Hulme   SK8
SK7
SK9   Alderley Edge   Prestbury
Wilmslow   Chelford
SK10   Bollington   Macclesfield   SK11   Wildboarclough   ST13
Marton
Congleton   CW12
ST8   Biddulph
Kidsgrove   ST7
Alsager   CW11   ST5
Audley   Woore
WA15   M90   WA   15
WA14   Knutsford   WA16   Ollerton
M   22   SK8
M90
M31   High Legh
Lymm   WA13
Irlam   M44
Culcheth   WA3
Golborne
Haydock   WA12   WA2   WA1
Newton-le-Willows   WA5   Warrington   WA4
Thelwall   Appleton Thorn
WA11   WA9
WA8   Widnes
Runcorn   WA7   Moore
Frodsham   WA6
Helsby   Kingsley
L26   Elton
L24   CH2
CH1   Moston
Saughall   Waverton
Guilden Sutton   CH3
CH4   Dodleston
Broughton   CH5
CH64
CH66   Ellesmere Port   CH65
CH63   Bebington   CH62   CH60
Neston   Heswall   CH60
CW9   Northwich
Antrobus
CW8   Cuddington   Barnton
CW6   Tarporley
Kelsall   Tattenhall
Bunbury   Cholmondeley
Tilston   SY14   Malpas
Farndon   Clutton
LL12   LL13
Holmes Chapel   CW4
Middlewich   CW10   CW7   Winsford
Sandbach
Crewe   CW1
Barbridge   Nantwich   CW5   Shavington   CW2
Wybunbury   Wrenbury   CW3   Audlem
Marbury   SY13
SY14
Adderley   TF9

SJ | SK

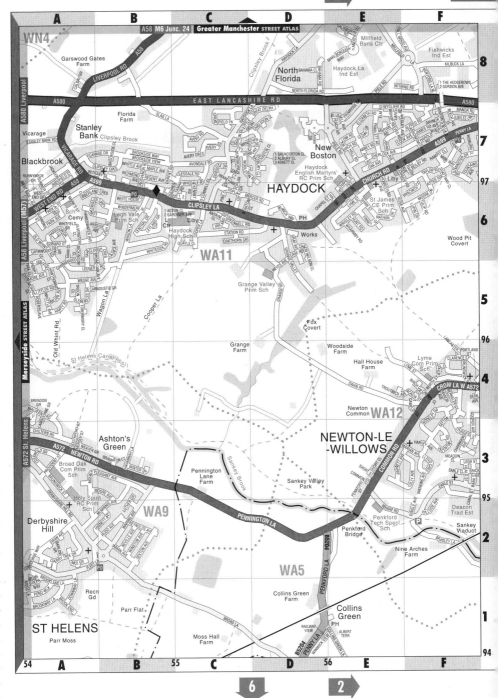

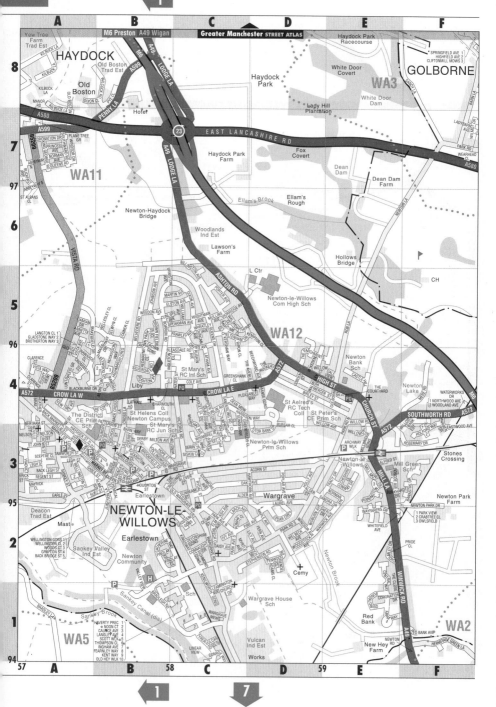

1

Greater Manchester STREET ATLAS

HAYDOCK

Yew Tree
Farm
Trad Est

KILBUCK LA

KILBUCK

M6 Preston   A49 Wigan

Old Boston
Trad Est

Old
Boston

KILBUCK LA

MANOR
RD

AUL BUCK LA

DIXON CL

PENNY LA

Hotel

Haydock Park Racecourse

Springfield Ave 1
Highfield Ave 2
Cliffonmill Mdws 3

GOLBORNE

WA3

White Door
Covert

Haydock
Park

Haydock
Park

White Door
Dam

LADYBARROW
AVE

A580

B5209

CORONATION DR

PLANE TREE
GR

23

EAST LANCASHIRE RD

A599

LADY HILL
AVE

PARK RD
WEARHEAD
CL

A580

WA11

Haydock Park
Farm

Fox
Covert

Lady Hill
Plantation

Dean
Dam

Dean Dam
Farm

NEWTON LA

VISTA RD

ST ALBANS LA

Newton-Haydock
Bridge

Ellam's Brook

Ellam's
Rough

Hollows
Bridge

CH

Woodlands
Ind Est

Lawson's
Farm

L Ctr

Newton-le-Willows
Com High Sch

ASHTON RD

WA12

Newton
Bank
Sch

Newton
Lake

WATERWORKS RD
1 Northwood Ave
2 Woodland Ave

M6

Langton Cl 1
Gladstone Way 2
Brotherton Way 3

CLARENCE

VISTA WAY

B5209

BLACKBURNE DR

CROW LA W

A572

Liby

CROW LA E

HIGH ST

Newton
Lake

EASTWOOD AVE

ROSEMARY DR

A572

SOUTHWORTH RD

St Mary's
RC Inf Sch

COLE AVE

Greenshank
Way

PLEASANCE
WAY

St Aelred's
RC Prim
Coll

St Peter's
CE Prim Sch

CHURCH ST

Stones
Crossing

Mill Green
Sch

The District
CE Prim
Sch

St Helens Coll
Newton Campus

St Mary's
RC Jun Sch

DERBY

MILTON AVE

Newton-le-Willows
Prim Sch

ARCHWAY
WLK

Newton-le-
Willows

MILL LA

Newton Park
Farm

SCEPTRE CL

BACK LEGH ST

REGENT ST

RAILWAY

HOUGHTON
CT

Earlestown

WARGRAVE

ACORN ST

OAK AVE

ALFRED ST

P

1 Park View
2 Crabtree Cl
3 Owlsfield

DEACON
TRAD EST

Mast

NEWTON-LE-
WILLOWS

Earlestown

ALDER

LAUREL DR

Wargrave

WAYFARERS DR

WHITEFIELD
AVE

PRIDE
CL

WA2

Wellington Gdns 1
Wellington Cl 2
Woods Ct 3
Grafton St 4
Back Bridge St 5

Sankey Valley
Ind Est

Newton
Community

H

Sch

Cemy

THE CLOSE

WARWICK RD

Red
Bank

Sankey Canal (dis)

Wargrave House
Sch

NEWTON
RD

A49

RED BANK AVE

HERMITAGE GREEN LA

Haverty Prec 1
Noon Ct 2
Caunce Ave 3
Langley Ave 4
Scott Wlk 5
Thompson Cl 6
Ingham Ave 7
Fearnley Way 8
Kent Way 9
Old Hey Wlk 10

WA5

Sankey Brook

LINEAR
VIEW

Vulcan
Ind Est

Works

New Hey
Farm

WA2

57   A   B   58   C   D   59   E   F

94

1   7

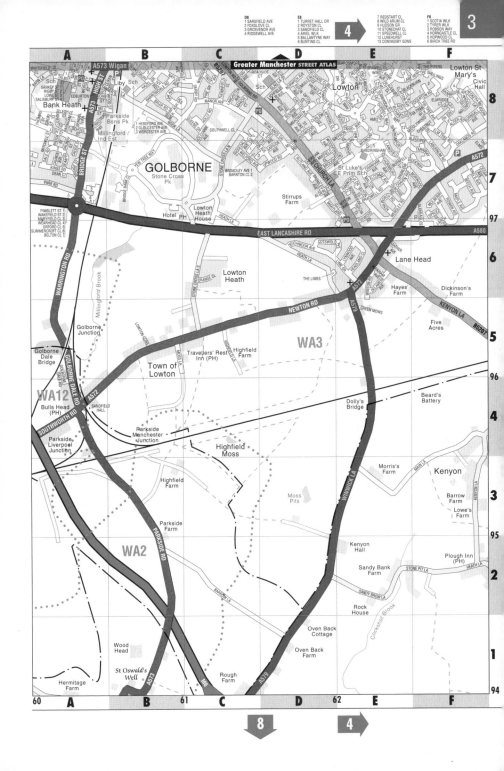

Greater Manchester STREET ATLAS

D8
1 SARSFIELD AVE
2 FOXGLOVE CL
3 GROSVENOR AVE
4 RIDGEWELL AVE

E8
1 TURRET HALL DR
2 ROYSTON CL
3 SANDFIELD CL
4 ARIEL WLK
5 BALLANTYNE WAY
6 BUNTING CL

7 REDSTART CL
8 WILD ARUM CL
9 HUDSON GR
10 STONECHAT CL
11 SPEEDWELL CL
12 LUNEHURST
13 CONINGSBY GDNS

F8
1 SCOTIA WLK
2 TYRER WLK
3 ROBSON WAY
4 HORNCASTLE CL
5 HOPWOOD CL
6 BIRCH TREE RD

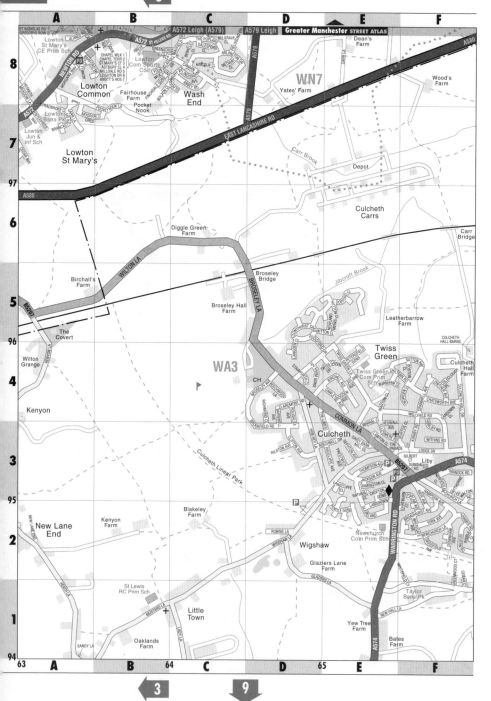

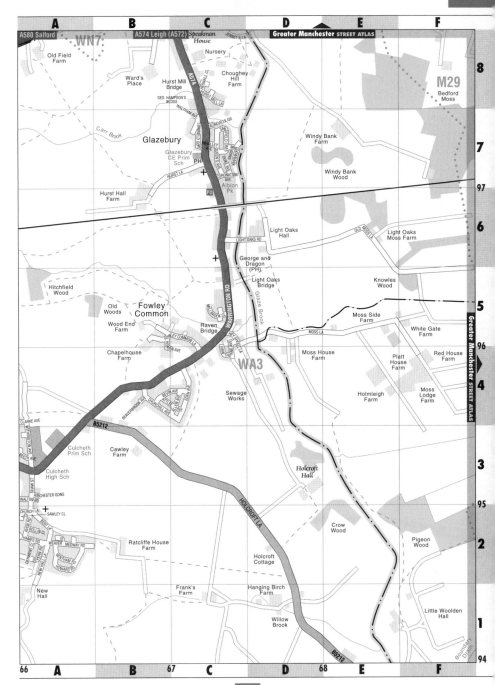

A580 Salford

WN7

A574 Leigh (A572)

Speakman House

Jennet's La

Nursery

Old Field Farm

Ward's Place

Hurst Mill Bridge

GEO. HAMPSON'S BLDGS

Choughey Hill Farm

WALTHAM AVE

Carr Brook

Glazebury

AGNEVILLE GR

ANFIELD CRES

Windy Bank Farm

Glazebury CE Prim Sch

PH

WHALLEY

QUEEN'S AVE

HURST LA

CORONATION AVE

Windy Bank Wood

Albion Pk

Hurst Hall Farm

PO

97

Light Oaks Hall

LIGHT OAKS RD

OLD MOSS LA

Light Oaks Moss Farm

6

George and Dragon (PH)

Hitchfield Wood

Light Oaks Bridge

Glaze Brook

Knowles Wood

Old Woods

Fowley Common

WARRINGTON RD

MILL BROOK LA

Moss Side Farm

White Gate Farm

5

Wood End Farm

Raven Bridge

FOWLEY COMMON LA

MOSS LA

Moss House Farm

Platt House Farm

Red House Farm

96

Chapelhouse Farm

FEN AVE

WA3

Holmleigh Farm

Moss Lodge Farm

4

REAVENBROOK AVE

BEVIN AVE

CHURCHILL AVE

ATTLEE AVE

EDEN AVE

Sewage Works

CLARKE AVE

B5212

Holcroft Hall

3

WITHINGTON AVE

BEECH AVE

Culcheth Prim Sch

Cawley Farm

Culcheth High Sch

RIBCHESTER GDNS

WALTON RD

95

CHURCH LA

SAWLEY CL

BENT LA

DR ROLLIN CL

THAMES RD

WEAVER

MEDWAY RD

Ratcliffe House Farm

Crow Wood

Pigeon Wood

2

ST MARIE'S RD

ST WERBURGH

HOWARD ST

WELTHAM RD

Holcroft Cottage

New Hall

Frank's Farm

Hanging Birch Farm

Little Woolden Hall

1

Willow Brook

B5212

Boundary Drain

94

66

67

68

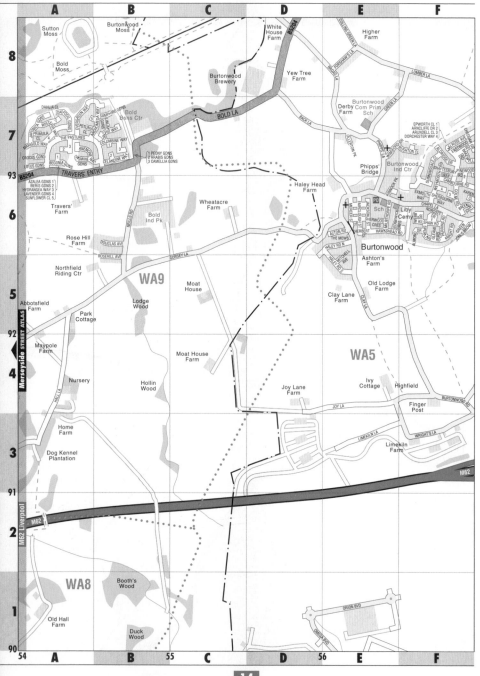

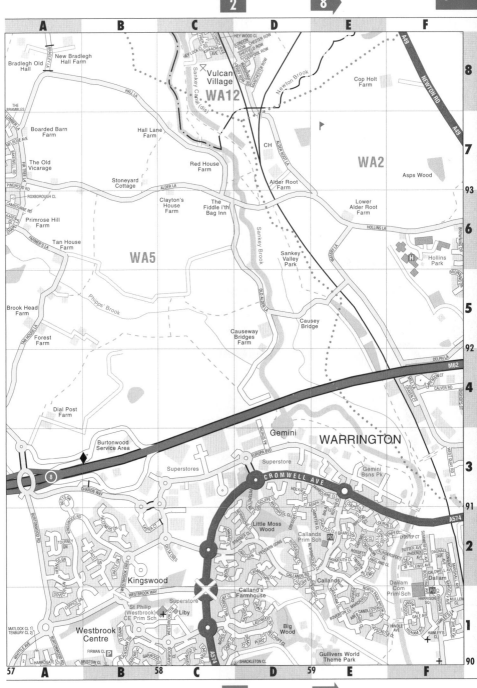

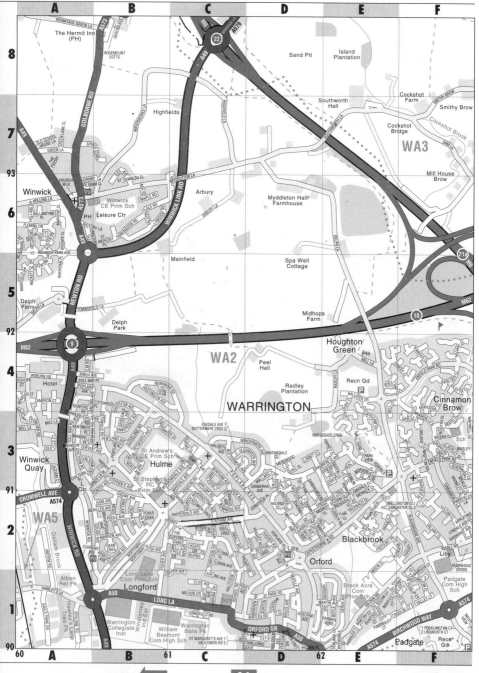

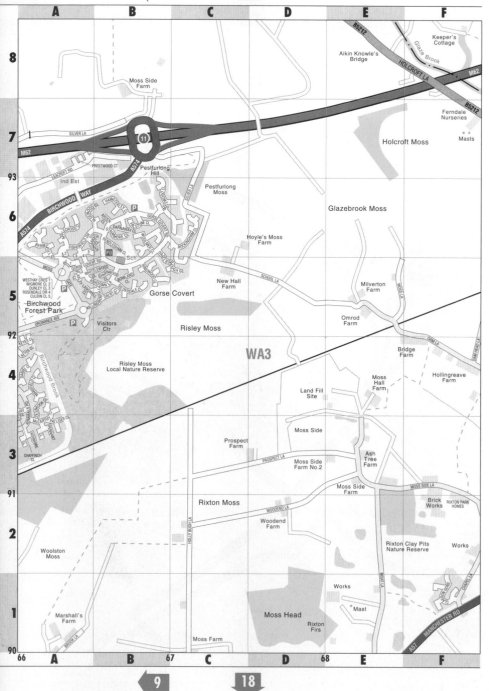

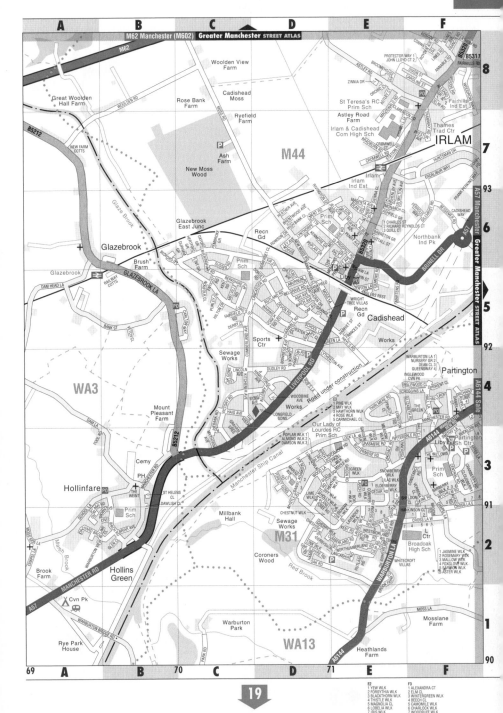

A B C D E F

M62

B5212

Woolden View Farm

Great Woolden Hall Farm

Rose Bank Farm

Cadishead Moss

Ryefield Farm

PROTECTOR WAY 1
JOHN LLOYD CT 2

B5319
B5317
FAIRHILLS RD

ZINNIA DR

St Teresa's RC Prim Sch

Astley Road Farm

Irlam & Cadishead Com High Sch

CROMWELL

Thames Trad Ctr

Fairhills Ind Est

IRLAM

8

NEW FARM COTTS

Ash Farm

New Moss Wood

M44

Irlam Ind Est

A57 Manchester Greater Manchester STREET ATLAS

7

93

Glaze Brook

RAILWAY COTTS

Glazebrook East Junc

Recn Gd

Prim Sch

CHARLES ST
RICHARD REYNOLDS CT
QUILL CT

CADISHEAD WAY

Northbank Ind Pk

BRINELL DR

6

Glazebrook

Glazebrook

DAM HEAD LA

GLAZEBROOK LA

BANK ST

Brush Farm

Prim Sch

BERKSHIRE

Lib

Recn Gd

WRIGHT TREE VILLAS

Cadishead

5

Sports Ctr

Works

92

WA3

Mount Pleasant Farm

B5212

Sewage Works

LINCOLN AVE
DUDLEY RD

LIVERPOOL RD

Road under construction

WARBURTON LA
NURSERY GR 2
DEAN CL 3
QUEENSWAY 4
INGLEWOOD
INGLEWOOD CVN PK

Partington

A6144 Sale

4

Works

Our Lady of Lourdes RC Prim Sch

PINE WLK
MAY WLK
HAWTHORN WLK
ROSE WLK
CARMICHAEL CL

POPLAR WLK 1
ALMOND WLK 2
DAMSON WLK 3

MANCHESTER RD

THE WILLOWS

Partington Sh Ctr

Lib

Prim Sch

3

Hollinfare

Cemy

PH

THE WEINT

St HELENS CL
DAWLISH CL

Prim Sch

Manchester Ship Canal

SNOWBERRY WLK
LILAC WLK
ELDERBERRY WLK
CEDAR RD

GREEN WLK

HANKINSON WY

CROSS LA

91

Millbank Hall

Chestnut Wlk

Sewage Works

M31

JASMINE WLK 1
ROSEMARY WLK 2
MALLOW WLK 3
FOXGLOVE WLK 4
SAFFRON WLK 5
ASTER WLK 6

Broadoak High Sch

WHITECROFT VILLAS

WARBURTON LA

2

MOSS DE LA

Brook Farm

Hollins Green

MANCHESTER RD

A57

Cvn Pk

WARBURTON BRIDGE RD

Coroners Wood

Red Brook

Warburton Park

A6144

NORTHUMBERLAND RD

Mosslane Farm

1

Rye Park House

PARK RD

Warburton Park

WA13

Heathlands Farm

90

69 A B 70 C D 71 E F

19

E2
1 YEW WLK
2 FORSYTHIA WLK
3 BLACKTHORN WLK
4 THISTLE WLK
5 MAGNOLIA CL
6 LOBELIA WLK
7 IRIS WLK
8 THORN WLK
9 HYACINTH WLK

F3
1 ALEXANDRA CT
2 ELM CL
3 WINTERGREEN WLK
4 BEECH CL
5 CAMOMILE WLK
6 CHARLOCK WLK
7 WOODRUFF WLK
8 COLUMBINE WLK
9 WORTHINGTON AVE

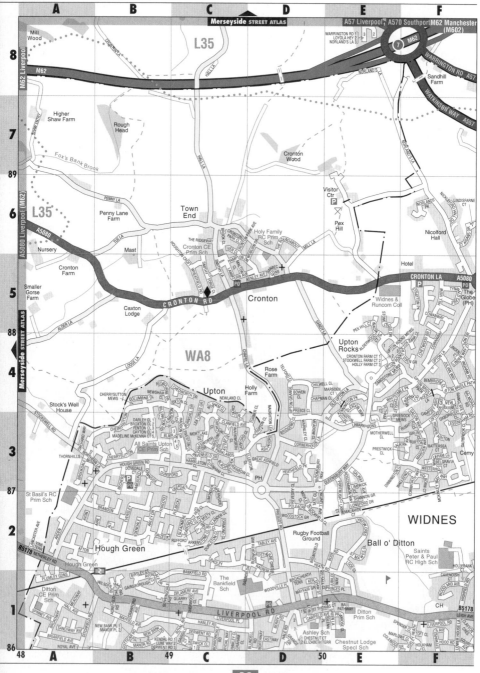

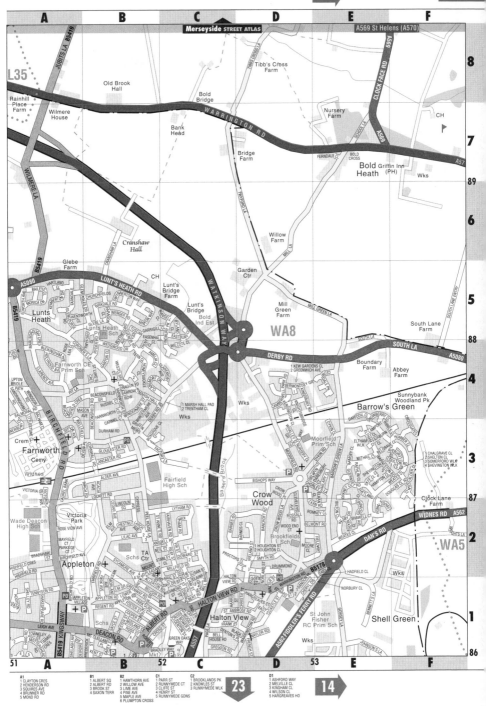

Merseyside STREET ATLAS

A1
1 CLAYTON CRES
2 HENDERSON RD
3 SQUIRES AVE
4 BRUNNER RD
5 MOND RD

B1
1 ALBERT SQ
2 ALBERT RD
3 BROOK ST
4 SAXON TERR

B2
1 HAWTHORN AVE
2 WILLOW AVE
3 LIME AVE
4 PINE AVE
5 MAPLE AVE
6 PLUMPTON CROSS

C1
1 PARR ST
2 RUNNYMEDE CT
3 CLIFFE ST
4 HENRY ST
5 RUNNYMEDE GDNS

C2
1 BROOKLANDS PK
2 KNOWLES ST
3 RUNNYMEDE WLK

D1
1 ASHFORD WAY
2 MELVILLE CL
3 KINGHAM CL
4 WILSON CL
5 HARGREAVES HO

23

14

8

Eccles
Plantation

Finch's
Plantation

Lingley Mere
Bsns Pk

Lingley
Mere

L Ctr

Great Sankey
High Sch

South Park
Plantation

Whittle Brook

Barrow Hall
Com Prim Sch

Brow
Farm

7

Park
Farm

ALVERSTONE CL

Bargyloo

89 WARRINGTON RD

A57

Dawson
House

Lingley
Green

Park Road
Com Prim Sch

Sankey
For Penketh

A57

6

Hayfield
Farm

SANDY LA

The
Trigger
Pond
(PH)

Laburnum
Farm

LIVERPOOL RD

Greenside
Farm

LABURNUM

Sandy Lane
Farm

WA8

WARRINGTON

5

BRIGHTWELL

Sch

Sch

88

Camp
(dis)

A5080

SUNNY BANK
COTTS

Penketh Com
Prim Sch

Recn
Gd

Liby

4

SOUTH LA

Four Top'd
Oak

Brook
Farm

FARNWORTH RD

Penketh

A5080

WARRINGTON RD

A562

3

Fowl
Farm

MOWCROFT LA

WIDNES RD

Doe
Green

BEECH AVE

St Vincent's
RC Prim Sch

Penketh South
Com Prim Sch

LC

87

Cuerdley
Cross

A562

PH

WRIGHTS LA

Cross Lane Farm
Cottages

CH

WA5

NEWSPAPER
HQ

LC

Trans Pennine Trail

2

Marsh End
Farm

WABER LA

River Mersey

Ferry Inn
(PH)

Swing
Bridge

LC

Riverside
Trad Est

Fiddler's
Ferry

1

Power
Station

Fiddler's Ferry

St Helens Canal
(disused)

WA4

86

54 A B 55 C D 56 E F

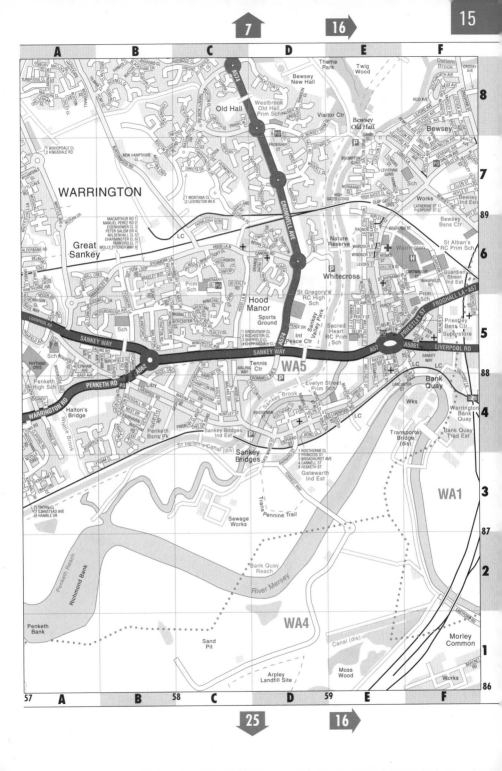

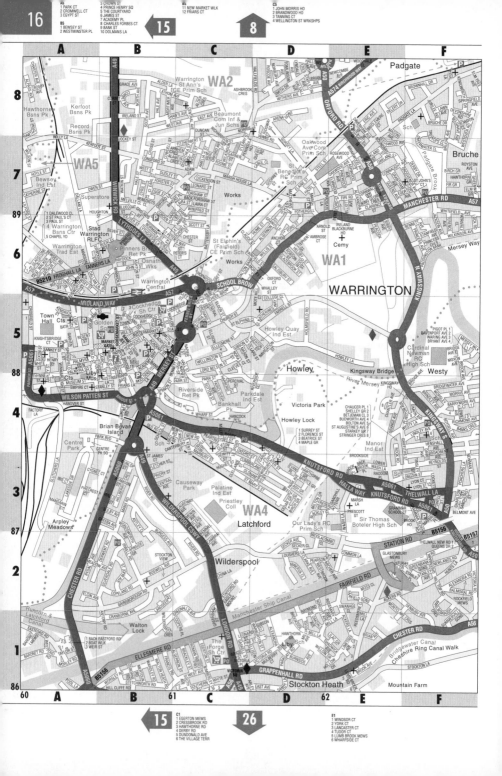

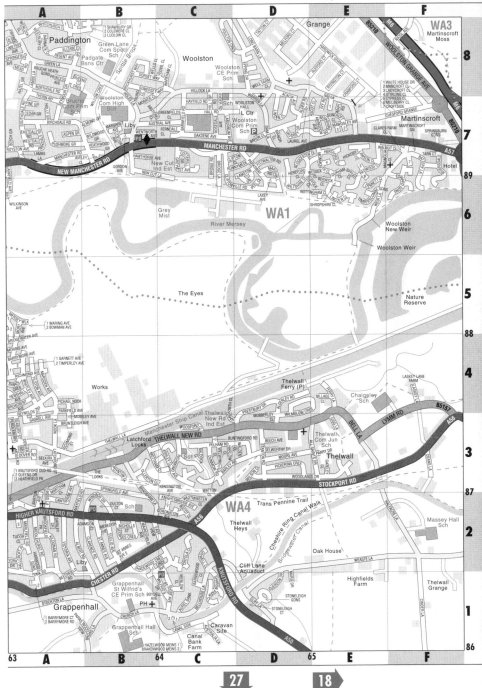

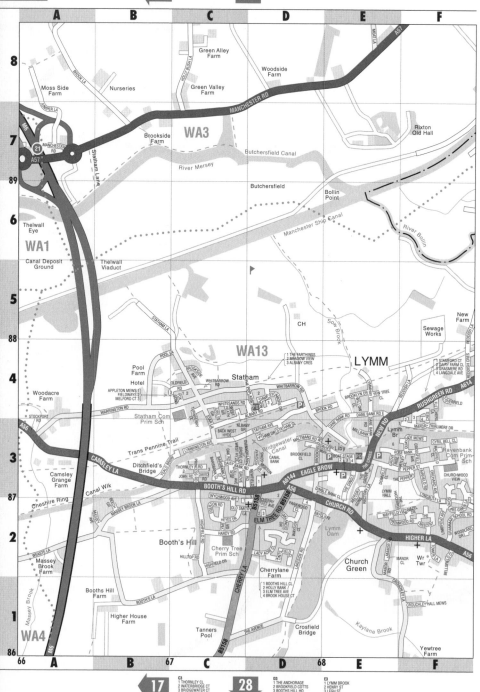

A   B   C   D   E   F

8

Green Alley Farm

Woodside Farm

Moss Side Farm

Nurseries

Green Valley Farm

7
MANCHESTER RD

Brookside Farm

WA3

Rixton Old Hall

Butchersfield Canal

River Mersey

89

Butchersfield

Bollin Point

6

Thelwall Eye

WA1

River Bollin

Manchester Ship Canal

Canal Deposit Ground

Thelwall Viaduct

5

STATHAM LA

New Farm

88

CH

Sow Brook

Sewage Works

WA13

1 THE FARTHINGS
2 MEADOW VIEW
3 ALBANY CRES

1 STAMFORD CT
2 DAIRY FARM CL
3 GRASMERE CL
4 LANGDALE AVE

LYMM

4

Pool Farm Hotel

Statham

OLDFIELD RD

WHITBARROW RD

WHITBARROW RD

Woodacre Farm

APPLETON MEWS 1
FIELDWAYS 2
MELFORD CT 3

WHITESANDS RD

P

BROOK RD

RUSHGREEN RD   A614

YEW TREE CL

Coverfield

Ravenbank Com Prim Sch

STOCKPORT RD

WARRINGTON RD

Statham Com Prim Sch

ALBANY

STATHAM AVE

DANE BANK RD

NEW RD

Lymm Br

JOE MEWS

CYRIL BELL CL

Churchwood View

3
CAMSLEY LA

Trans Pennine Trail

Ditchfield's Bridge

BACK WEST HYDE

BOOTH'S HILL RD

Bridgewater Canal

BROOKFIELD LA

Liby

BOAT STAGE

P

P

A6144

EAGLE BROW

A56

CANAL BANK

P

THE CROSS

DINGLE BANK CL

Lymm Hall

THE PEPPER ST

87

Cheshire Ring

Canal Wlk

Camsley Grange Farm

THORNLEY RD

JOHN RD

DAVID

ST

CHERRY TREE AVE

CHURCH RD

THE DINGLE

CHURCHILL

WOODLAND VIEW

2

MASSEY BROOK LA

Booth's Hill

WYCHWOOD AVE

B5158

HARDY RD

ELM TREE RD

B5158

PARKWOOD

BAYLIFFE

Lymm Dam

Church Green

HIGHER LA

A56

Massey Brook Farm

WEASTE LA

HILLFOR RD

HILLFIELD DR

Cherry Tree Prim Sch

CHERRYLANE FM

Cherrylane Farm

1 BOOTHS HILL CL
2 HOLLY BANK
3 ELM TREE AVE
4 BROOK HOUSE CT

MANOR CL

Wr Twr

1

WA4

M6

Massey Brook

Booths Hill Farm

Higher House Farm

BOOTH'S LA

Tanners Pool

THE AVENUE

B5158

Crosfield Bridge

Kaylane Brook

Yewtree Farm

86
66   A   B   67   C   D   68   E   F

C3
1 THORNLEY CL
2 WATERBRIDGE CT
3 BRIDGEWATER CT

D3
1 THE ANCHORAGE
2 BROOKFIELD COTTS
3 BOOTHS HILL HO

E3
1 LYMM BROOK
2 HENRY ST
3 LEGH ST
4 BRIDGEWATER ST
5 THIRLMERE LODGE
6 THE SQUARE

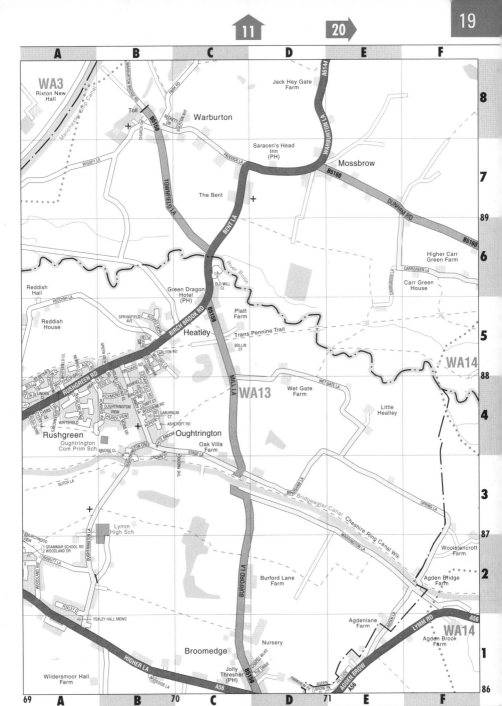

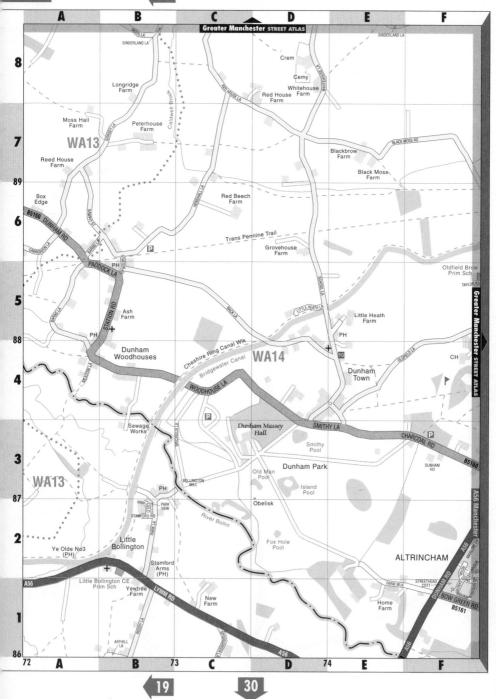

Greater Manchester STREET ATLAS

A B C D E F

8

Sinderland La

Sinderland La

Crem

Cemy

Longridge Farm

Moss La

Whitehouse Farm

Red House Farm

7

WA13

Moss Hall Farm

Peterhouse Farm

Caldwell Brook

Red House La

Blackbrow Farm

Black Moss Rd

89

Reed House Farm

Black Moss Farm

6

B5160 DUNHAM RD

Box Edge

Swift La

Red Beech Farm

Trans Pennine Trail

Grovehouse Farm

Oldfield Brow Prim Sch

TAYLOR RD

Carrhouse La

P

Paddock La

PH

Station Rd

Back La

School La

5

Barns La

Saddle La

Ash Farm

Little Heath La

Little Heath Farm

PH

Greater Manchester STREET ATLAS

88

PH

McDonna La

Dunham Woodhouses

Cheshire Ring Canal Wlk

WA14

PO

CH

4

Bridgewater Canal

Woodhouse La

Dunham Town

Brookvilla La

P

Dunham Massey Hall

Smithy La

Charcoal Rd

P

B5160

A56 Manchester

3

Sewage Works

Smithy Pool

Dunham Park

Dunham Ho

PH

87

Bollington Mill

Old Man Pool

Island Pool

Park View

High Elm

Stamford Rd

Obelisk

WA13

Park La

River Bollin

2

Ye Olde No3 (PH)

Little Bollington

Fox Hole Pool

ALTRINCHAM

Stamford Arms (PH)

Dunham Rd

Bow Green Rd

A56

Little Bollington CE Prim Sch

Yewtree Farm

Lymm Rd

Bessey La

New Farm

Farm Wlk

Streethead Cott

Home Farm

B5161

1

86

Arthill La

A56

A 72 B 73 C D 74 E F

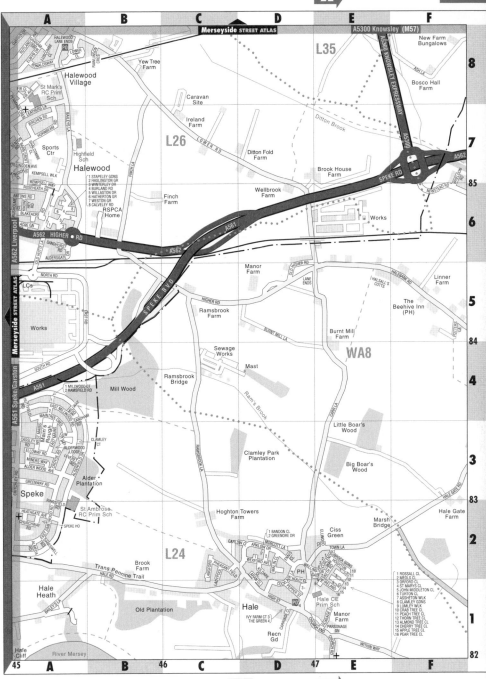

Merseyside STREET ATLAS

A5300 Knowsley (M57)

L35

A5300 KNOWSLEY EXPRESSWAY

New Farm Bungalows

A5611 LA

Bosco Hall Farm

8

Halewood Lane Ends

PO

LOWER CL

Yew Tree Farm

Halewood Village

St Mark's RC Prim Sch

Caravan Site

Ireland Farm

L26

LOWER RD

Ditton Brook

A5300

A562

7

Halewood

Ditton Fold Farm

Brook House Farm

SPEKE RD

85

1 STAPELEY GDNS
2 HASLINGTON GR
3 WINTERLEY DR
4 BURLAND RD
5 WILLASTON DR
6 HATHERTON GR
7 WESTON GR
8 CALVELEY RD

Finch Farm

Wellbrook Farm

Works

6

Liverpool A562

A562 HIGHER RD

RSPCA Home

A561

Manor Farm

OLD HIGHER RD

LANE ENDS

HALSALL'S COTTS

HALEBANK RD

Linner Farm

5

SPEKE BLVD

NORTH RD

LCs

HIGHER RD

Ramsbrook Farm

BURNT MILL LA

Burnt Mill Farm

The Beehive Inn (PH)

POTTERS LA

84

Works

WA8

4

SOUTH RD

A561 Speke/Garston

A561

1 MILLWOOD CT
2 RAMSFIELD RD

Mill Wood

Ramsbrook Bridge

Sewage Works

Mast

Ram's Brook

RAMSBROOK LA

CABB LA

Little Boar's Wood

Big Boar's Wood

3

Speke

CLAMLEY CT

Alder Plantation

Clamley Park Plantation

HALE GATE RD

83

St Ambrose RC Prim Sch

SPEKE HO

Hoghton Towers Farm

Marsh Bridge

Hale Gate Farm

Ciss Green

2

L24

Brook Farm

Trans Pennine Trail

HALE RD

1 BANDON CL
2 GREENORE DR

CARLOW CL

ARKLOW LA

MORCOTT LA

TOWN LA

ELLWOOD...

WELLINGTON...

1 ROSSALL CL
2 MEOLS CL
3 ORFORD CL
4 ST MARYS CL
5 JOHN MIDDLETON CL
6 TURTON CL
7 ASSHETON WLK
8 CLAMLEY GDNS
9 LUMLEY WLK
10 CRAB TREE CL
11 PEACH TREE CL
12 THORN TREE CL
13 ALMOND TREE CL
14 CHERRY TREE CL
15 APPLE TREE CL
16 PEAR TREE CL

Hale Heath

Old Plantation

WEXFORD AVE

PH

HOLLY RD

Hale CE Prim Sch

Manor Farm

PO

1

BAILEYS LA

Hale

IVY FARM CT 3
THE GREEN 4

HIGH ST

CARRIAGE DR

PARSONAGE GN

WITHIN WAY

Recn Gd

82

Hale Cliff

River Mersey

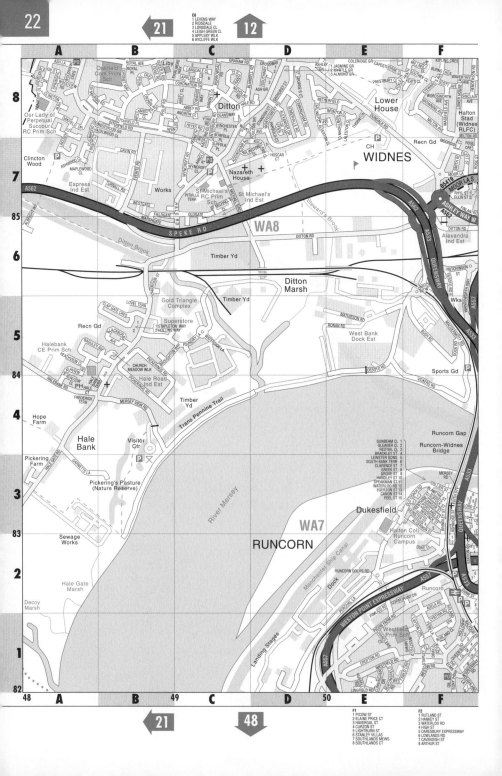

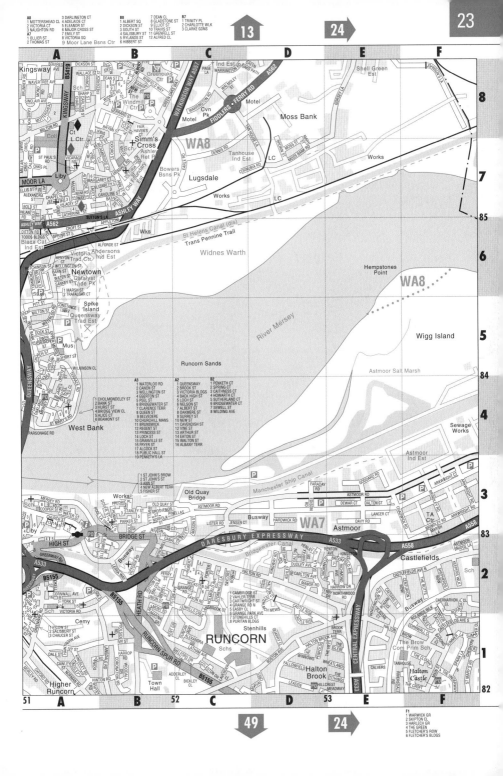

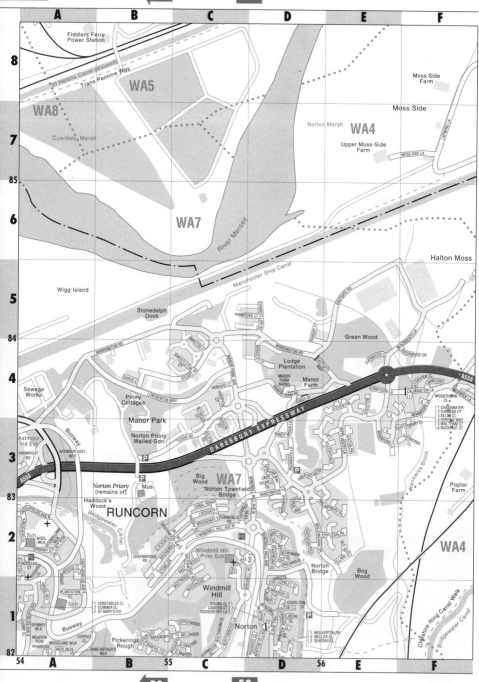

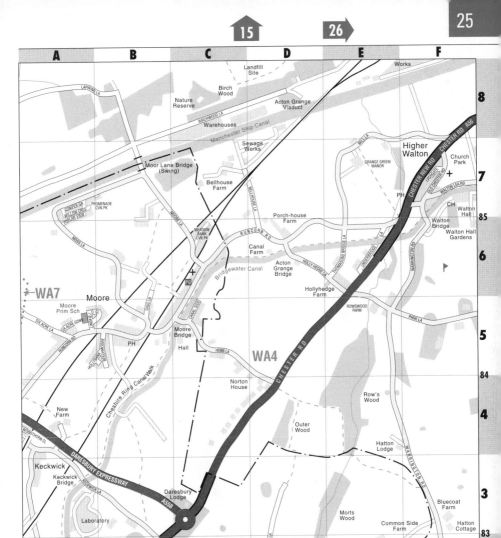

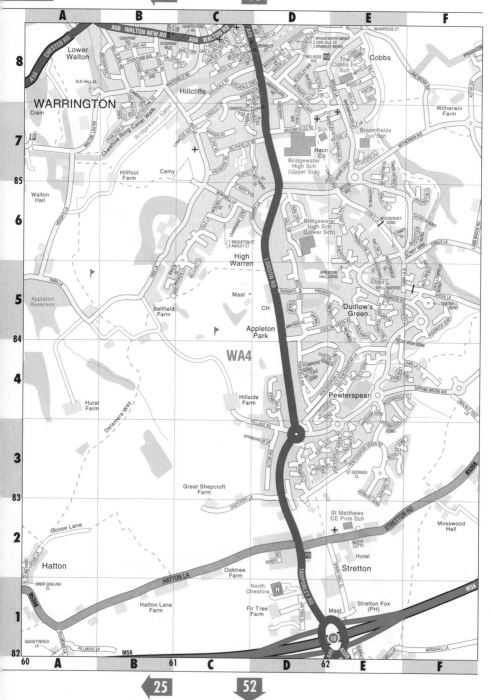

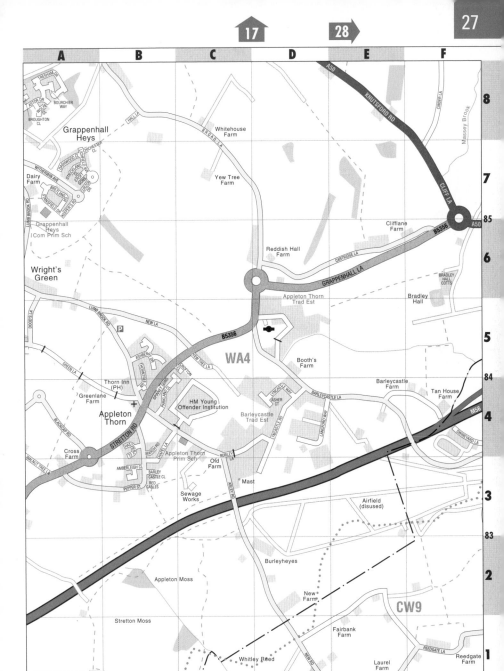

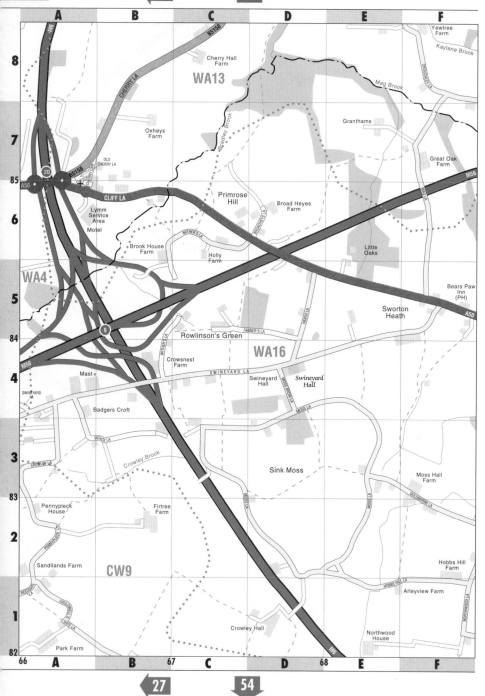

WA13

Cherry Hall Farm

Oxheys Farm

OLD CHERRY LA

CLIFF LA

Lymm Service Area

Motel

WA4

Brook House Farm

Holly Farm

Primrose Hill

Broad Heyes Farm

Granthams

Great Oak Farm

Little Oaks

Bears Paw Inn (PH)

Sworton Heath

Rowlinson's Green

FANNER'S LA

WA16

Crowsnest Farm

Mast

SWINEYARD LA

Swineyard Hall

Swineyard Hall

SWINEYARD LA

Badgers Croft

INTACK LA

Crowley Brook

CROWLEY LA

Sink Moss

Moss Hall Farm

Pennypleck House

Firtree Farm

Sandilands Farm

CW9

Hobbs Hill Farm

HOBBS HILL LA

Arleyview Farm

NORTHWOOD LA

GOLBORNE LA

Crowley Hall

Northwood House

Park Farm

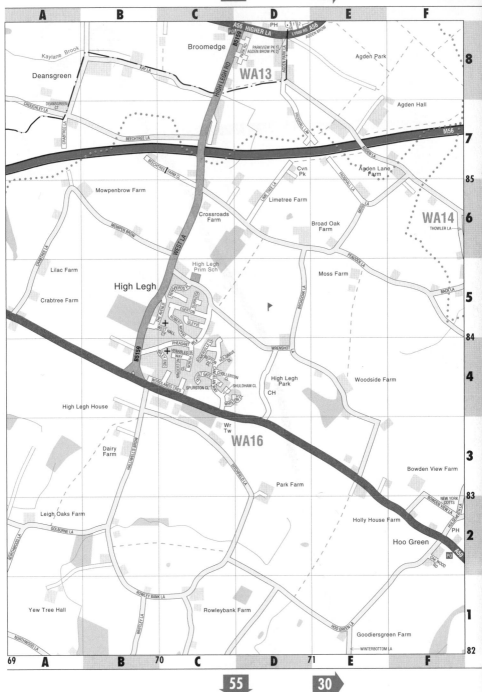

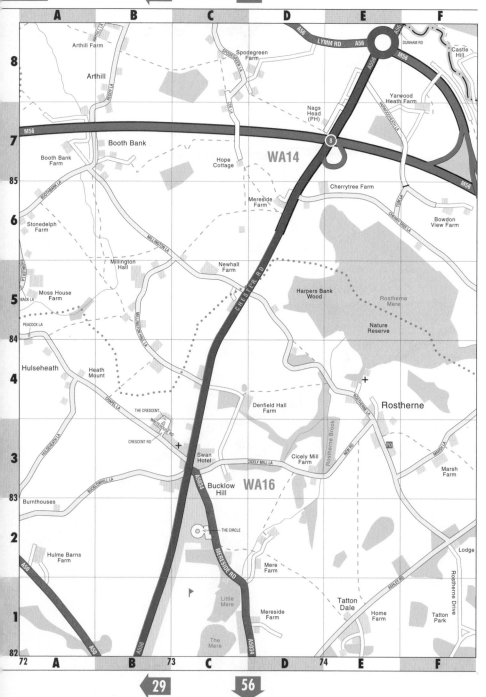

32

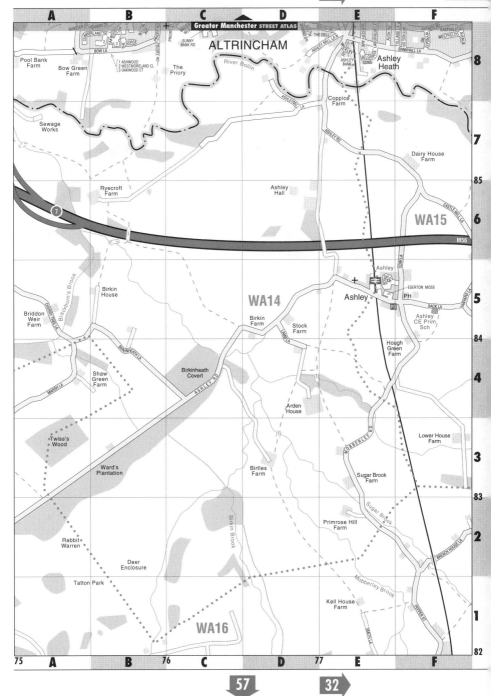

Greater Manchester STREET ATLAS

ALTRINCHAM

8

Pool Bank Farm

Bow Green Farm

CUMBERLAND DR

BOW LA

1 ASHWOOD
2 WESTMORELAND CL
3 OAKWOOD CT

PRIORY RD

SUNNY BANK RD

The Priory

MINSTER DR

CANONS RD

GORSE

ASHBURY RD

SOUTH RD

THE DELL

SOUTH RD

River Bollin

ASHLEY MILL LA

NURSERY AVE

BELGRAVE
GDNS

ASHLEY
BANK RD

ST ANTHONY'S RD

ARTHOG RD

ARTHOG DR

BANKHALL LA

EASTDALE RD

WYNDALE RD

WESTFIELDS
AVENUE

Ashley
Heath

Sewage
Works

7

ASHLEY MILL LA

Coppice
Farm

ASHLEY RD

Dairy House
Farm

85

Ryecroft
Farm

Ashley
Hall

WA15

CASTLE MILL LA

6

M56

7

Birkin
House

WA14

Blackburn's Brook

COW LA

Ashley

PH

HILLSIDE GR

EGERTON MOSS

BACK LA

Ashley
CE Prim
Sch

VANTYKE LA

5

CHERRY TREE LA

Briddon
Weir
Farm

BIRKINHEATH LA

Birkin
Farm

Stock
Farm

CRAIG LA

Hough
Green
Farm

PO

84

MARSH LA

Shaw
Green
Farm

Birkinheath
Covert

ASHLEY RD

Arden
House

4

Twiss's
Wood

Ward's
Plantation

Birtles
Farm

MOBBERLEY RD

Sugar Brook
Farm

Sugar Brook

Lower House
Farm

3

83

Rabbit
Warren

Deer
Enclosure

Birkin Brook

Primrose Hill
Farm

BREACH HOUSE LA

2

Tatton Park

Mobberley Brook

Kell House
Farm

SMITH LA

FERRIS DR

1

WA16

82

57   32

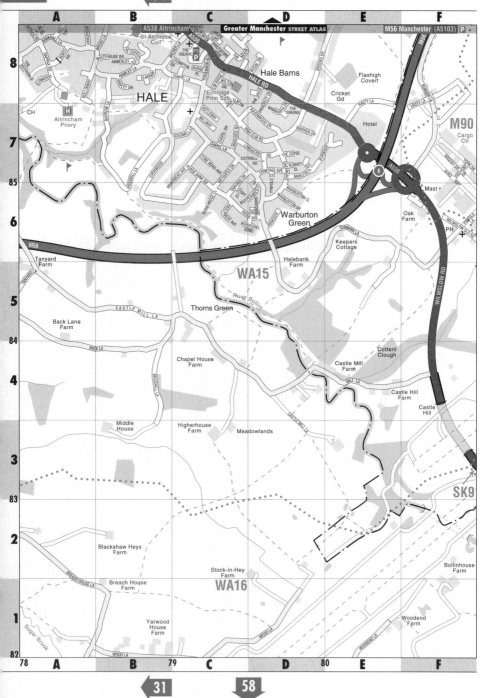

31

A B C D E F

8

St Ambrose Coll

THE SQUARE

Hale Barns

HALE RD

Flaxhigh Covert

Cricket Gd

Hotel

M90

Cargo Ctr

HALE

Elmridge Prim Sch

Altrincham Priory

CH

7

Warren Dr

Mast

85

Warburton Green

Oak Farm

PH

6

M56

Keepers Cottage

Tanyard Farm

Halebank Farm

WA15

SUNBANK LA

5

CASTLE MILL LA

Thorns Green

River Bollin

Back Lane Farm

84

BACK LA

Cotteril Clough

Castle Mill Farm

4

Chapel House Farm

Castle Hill Farm

CASTLE MILL

Castle Hill

Middle House

Higherhouse Farm

Meadowlands

3

83

SK9

2

Blackshaw Heys Farm

Stock-in-Hey Farm

WA16

Bollinhouse Farm

BREACH HOUSE LA

Breach House Farm

1

Sugar Brook

Yarwood House Farm

Woodend Farm

WOOD LA

WOODLA

82

78 A B 79 C D 80 E F

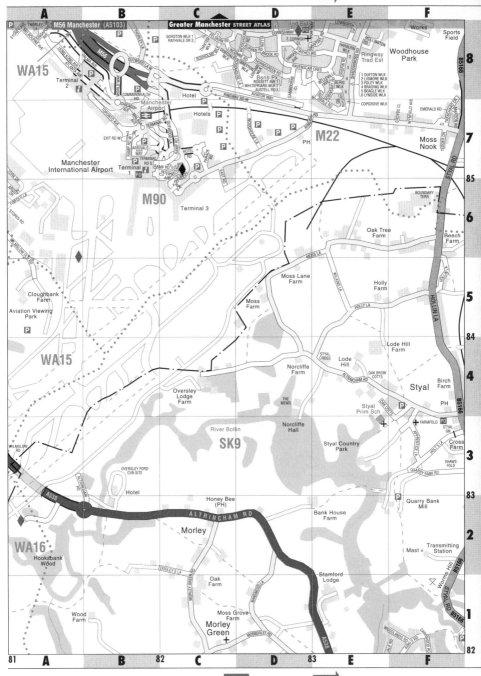

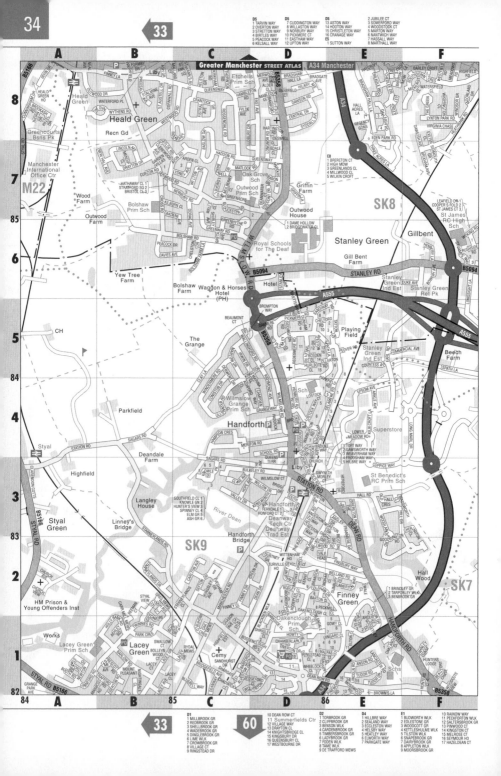

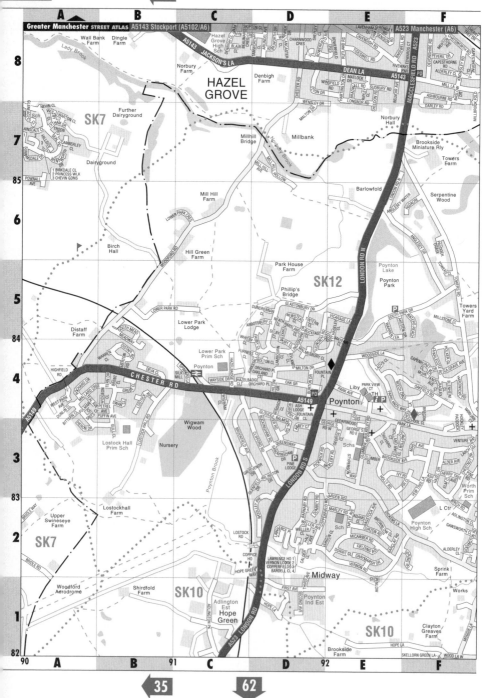

Greater Manchester STREET ATLAS A5143 Stockport (A5102/A6) A523 Manchester (A6)

A **B** **C** **D** **E** **F**

8

A5143
JACKSON'S LA
DEAN LA
A5143

Wall Bank
Farm
Dingle
Farm

Lady Brook

Norbury
Farm

HAZEL
GROVE

Denbigh
Farm

SK7

Further
Dairyground

Millhill
Bridge

Millbank

Norbury
Hall

Brookside
Miniature Rly

Towers
Farm

7

1 BIRKDALE CL
2 PRINCESS WLK
3 CHEVIN GDNS

Dairyground

85

Mill Hill
Farm

Barlowfold

Serpentine
Wood

6

Birch
Hall

Hill Green
Farm

Park House
Farm

Poynton
Lake

Poynton
Park

Towers
Yard
Farm

5

Distaff
Farm

Lower Park
Lodge

Phillip's
Bridge

SK12

Millstone

84

Lower Park
Prim Sch

Poynton

Lower Park

CHESTER RD

Highfield
RD

SILK
MILL

Wayside Dr

Hazelbadge

Liby
TH
P

Park View
Ct

4

A5149

West Park
Ave

Wigwam
Wood

Nursery

A5149

Poynton

Schs

Worth
Prim
Sch

3

Lostock Hall
Prim Sch

Poynton Brook

L Ctr

Poynton
High Sch

83

Upper
Swineseye
Farm

Lostockhall
Farm

LOSTOCK
RD

SK7

2

Sprink
Farm

Woodford
Aerodrome

Shirdfold
Farm

SK10

Adlington
Est
Hope
Green

LAWRENCE HO 1
VERNON LODGE 2
COPPERFIELDS 3
BARDELL CL 4

Midway

Works

1

Hope Green
Way

Poynton
Ind Est

SK10

Clayton
Greaves
Farm

82

Brookside
Farm

A 90 **B** 91 **C** 92 **D** **E** **F**

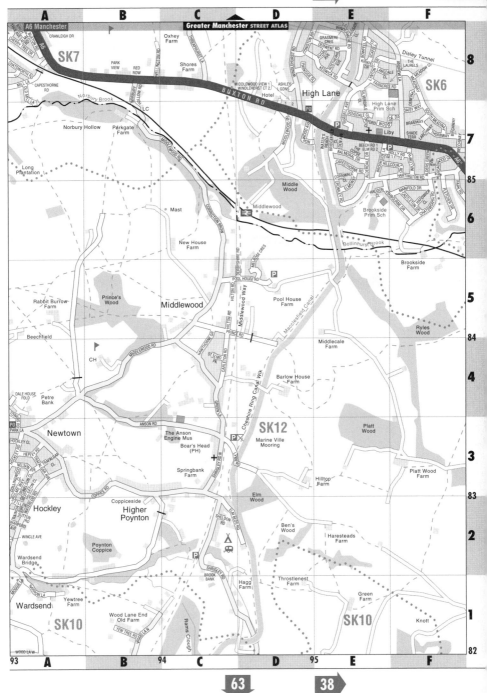

A   B   C   D   E   F

A6 Manchester

Greater Manchester STREET ATLAS

CRANLEIGH DR

SK7

8

Oxhey Farm

CHATSWORTH DR
CHERRY TREE DR

PARK VIEW

RED ROW

Shores Farm

Disley Tunnel

GRASMERE CRES

DERWENT RD

KESWICK RD

The Laurels

SK6

7

CAPESTHORNE RD
MILL LA

Norbury Brook

BUXTON RD

MIDDLEWOOD VIEW 1
WINDLEHURST CT 2

ASHLEY GDNS

Hotel

High Lane

High Lane Prim Sch

DAISY RD

LC

Norbury Hollow

Parkgate Farm

DOVEDALE CL

P

Liby

BRAMWAY

85

Long Plantation

CORNWALL

WATER'S REACH

BRIDGEEND

BALMORAL DR

Middle Wood

CAPESTHORNE RD

Brookside Prim Sch

MANIFOLD DR

7

Mast

Middlewood

HARTINGTON RD

6

New House Farm

DERBYSHIRE RD

MELROSE CRES

POOL HOUSE RD

P

Pool House Farm

Macclesfield Canal

Bollinhurst Brook

Brookside Farm

Rabbit Burrow Farm

Prince's Wood

Middlewood

HILTON DR

Middlewood Way

PRINCE RD

Middlecale Farm

Ryles Wood

5

Beechfield

HARTINGTON GR

ST LEMO PK

CARLTON RD

Barlow House Farm

84

CH

MIDDLEWOOD RD

Platt Wood

4

DALE HOUSE FOLD

Petre Bank

ANSON RD

GREEN LA

Cheshire Ring Canal Wlk

SK12

Marine Ville Mooring

Platt Wood Farm

3

PARK LA

Newtown

The Anson Engine Mus

Boar's Head (PH)

SHEPLEY RD

Hilltop Farm

83

HOCKLEY CL

Springbank Farm

Elm Wood

Ben's Wood

Haresteads Farm

2

WINCLE AVE

Hockley

Coppiceside

Higher Poynton

SHELDON RD

ELM TREE RD

Wardsend Bridge

Poynton Coppice

P

Throstlenest Farm

Green Farm

1

Wardsend

Yewtree Farm

SK10

Wood Lane End Old Farm

BROOK BANK

SHRIGLEY RD

Hagg Farm

Rams Clough

SK10

Knott

82

WOOD LA W

93   A   B   94   C   D   95   E   F

37

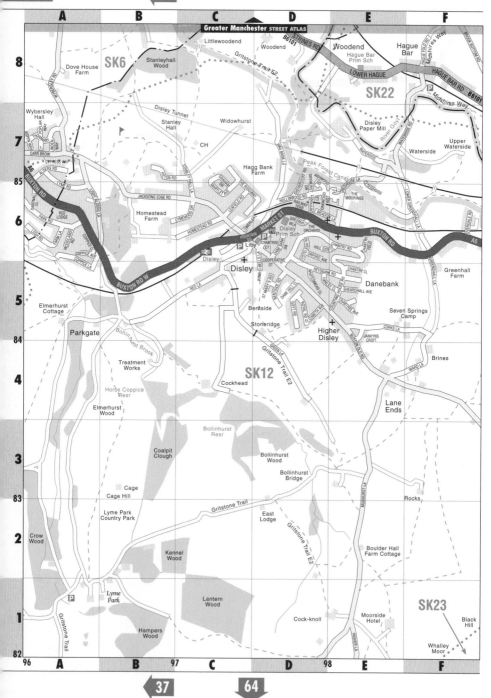

Greater Manchester STREET ATLAS

37
64

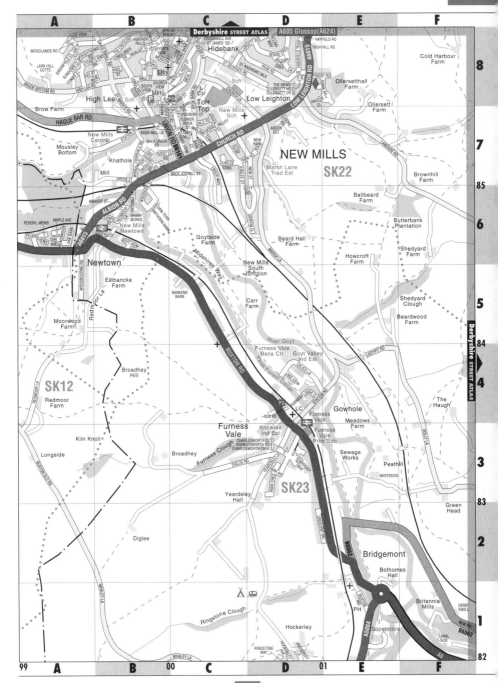

Derbyshire STREET ATLAS A605 Glossop(A624)

NEW MILLS

SK22

SK12

SK23

Bridgemont

99 A   B   00 C   D   01 E   F

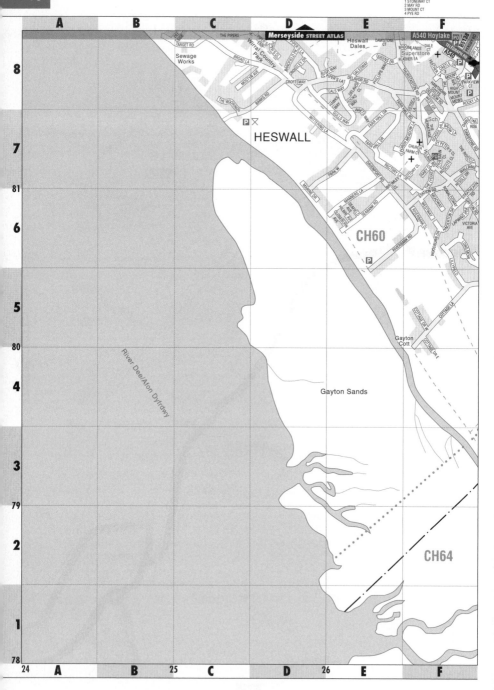

Merseyside STREET ATLAS

A540 Hoylake

HESWALL

CH60

River Dee/Afon Dyfrdwy

Gayton Sands

Gayton Cott

CH64

Sewage Works

Wirral County Park

Heswall Dales

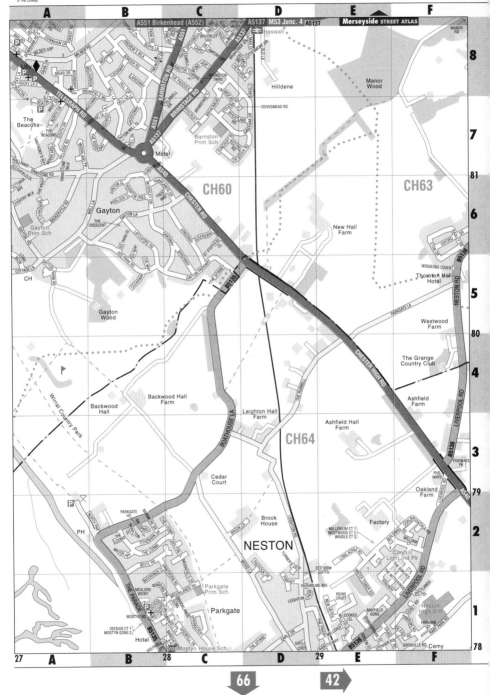

42

All
1 DOWNHAM CT
2 BIRCHES HO
3 CHERRY TREE MEWS
4 BEACON CT
5 THE CHASE

A551 Birkenhead (A552) A5137 M53 Junc. 4 A5137

Merseyside STREET ATLAS

MANOR RD

Hilldene

Manor Wood

DOVESMEAD RD

The Beacons

Motel

Barnston Prim Sch

CH60

CH63

Gayton

New Hall Farm

WIDGEONS COVERT

Thornton Hall Hotel

The Crescent

Gayton Prim Sch

CH

Gayton Wood

Westwood Farm

The Grange Country Club

Backwood Hall Farm

Backwood Hall

Leighton Hall Farm

Ashfield Farm

Wirral Country Park

Ashfield Hall Farm

CH64

FIVEWAYS PK

FIVE WAYS

Oakland Farm

Cedar Court

PH

Brook House

Factory

MILLENNIUM CT 1
WESTWOOD CT 2
WINDLE CT 3

Clayhill Light Ind Pk

NESTON

Parkgate Prim Sch

DEE VIEW COTTS

FAIRHOLME AVE

REINS CROFT

Neston High Sch

Parkgate

MEALORS WEINT

DEESIDE CT 1
MOSTYN GDNS 2

COOKES CL

MAYFIELD GDNS

HOWARD CT

Hotel

Mostyn House Sch

THE SPINNEY

EAGLE CRES

GRENVILLE RD

Cemy

42

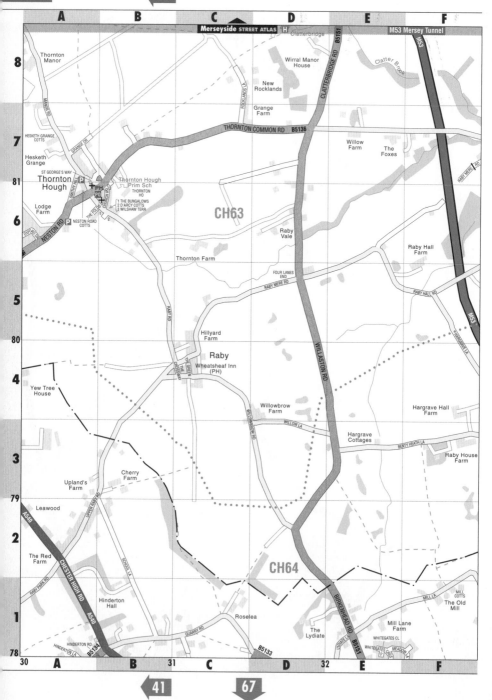

Merseyside STREET ATLAS

M53 Mersey Tunnel

Clatterbridge

Wirral Manor House

New Rocklands

Grange Farm

THORNTON COMMON RD B5136

Thornton Manor

HESKETH GRANGE COTTS

Hesketh Grange

St George's Way

Thornton Hough

Thornton Hough Prim Sch

THORNTON HO

1 THE BUNGALOWS
2 D'ARCY COTTS
3 WILSHAW TERR

Lodge Farm

NESTON ROAD COTTS

NESTON RD

CH63

Raby Vale

Willow Farm

The Foxes

Raby Hall Farm

RABY HALL RD

Thornton Farm

FOUR LANES END

RABY MERE RD

Hillyard Farm

Raby

Wheatsheaf Inn (PH)

THE GREEN CROSSWAY

Willowbrow Farm

WILLOW LA

Hargrave Hall Farm

Yew Tree House

Hargrave Cottages

BENTY HEATH LA

Raby House Farm

Upland's Farm

Cherry Farm

Leawood

The Red Farm

CHESTER HIGH RD

A540

Hinderton Hall

CH64

BIRKENHEAD RD B5151

MILL LA

MILL COTTS

The Old Mill

Mill Lane Farm

WHITEGATES CL

Roselea

The Lydiate

QUARRY RD

B5133

WHITEGATES CTRS

MEADOW

HINDERTON LA

HINDERTON RD

B5134

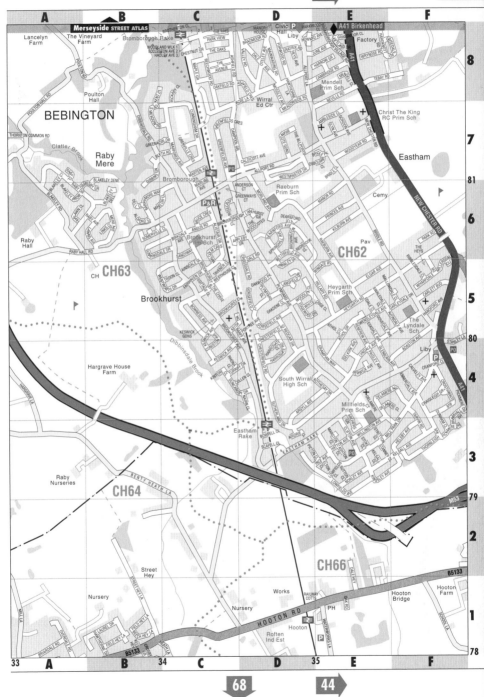

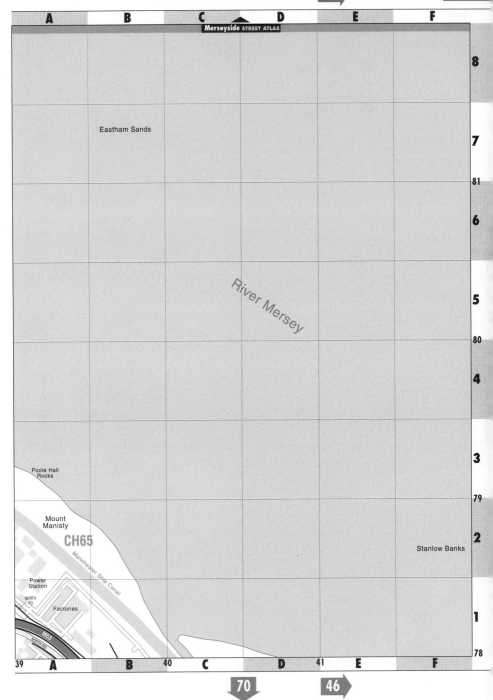

Merseyside STREET ATLAS

A   B   C   D   E   F

8

7

81

6

5

80

4

3

79

2

1

78

Eastham Sands

River Mersey

Poole Hall
Rocks

Mount
Manisty

CH65

Manchester Ship Canal

Power
Station

NORTH
RD

Factories

M53

NORTH RD

Stanlow Banks

45

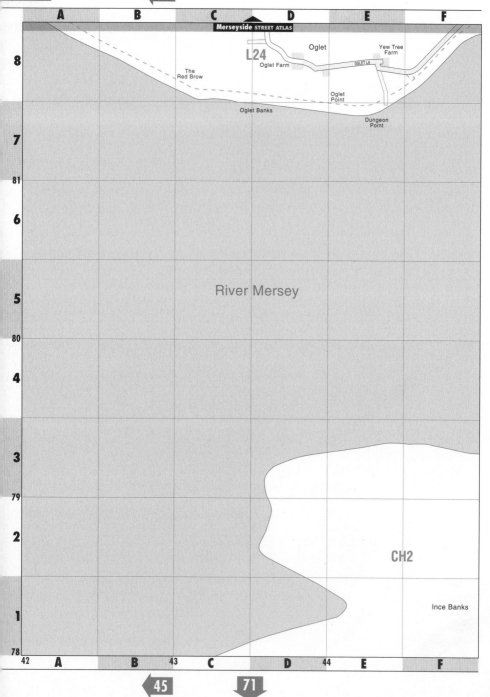

8

Oglet

Yew Tree
Farm

L24

Oglet Farm

OGLET LA

The
Red Brow

Oglet
Point

81

Oglet Banks

Dungeon
Point

7

6

River Mersey

5

80

4

3

79

CH2

2

Ince Banks

1

78

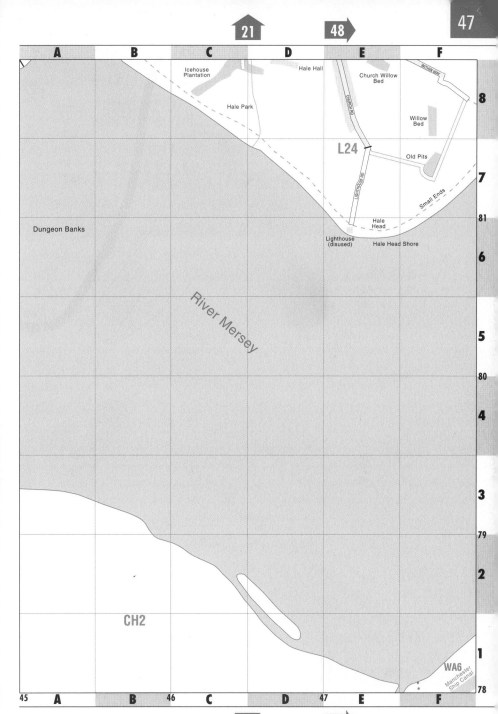

| | A | B | C | D | E | F | |

Icehouse
Plantation

Hale Hall

Church Willow
Bed

WITHIN WAY

8

Hale Park

CHURCH RD

Willow
Bed

L24

Old Pits

7

LIGHT HOUSE RD

Small Ends

81

Dungeon Banks

Hale
Head

6

Lighthouse
(disused)

Hale Head Shore

River Mersey

5

80

4

3

79

2

CH2

1

WA6

*Manchester
Ship Canal*

78

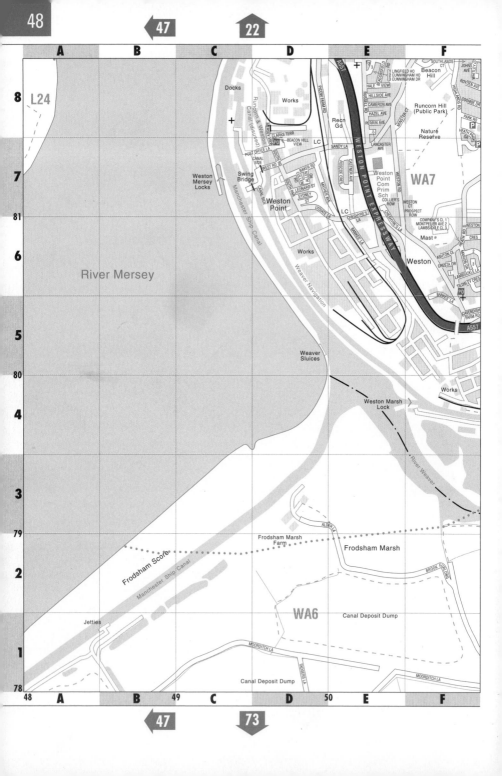

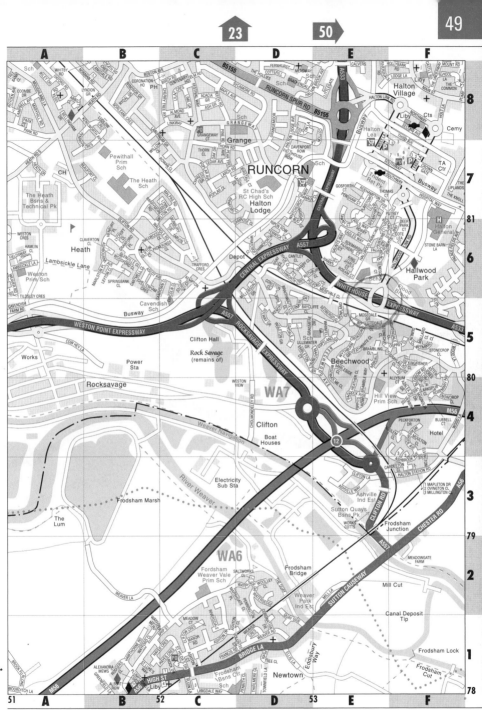

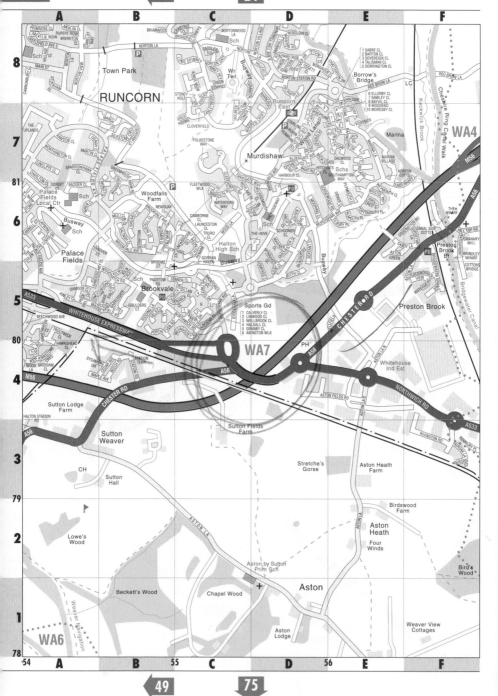

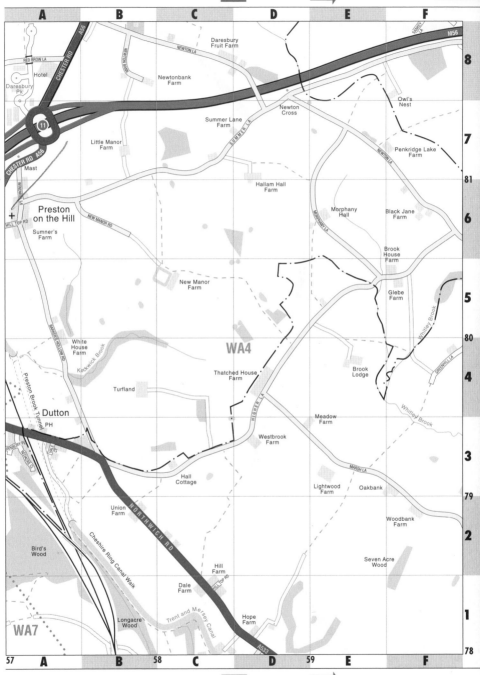

25
52
76
52

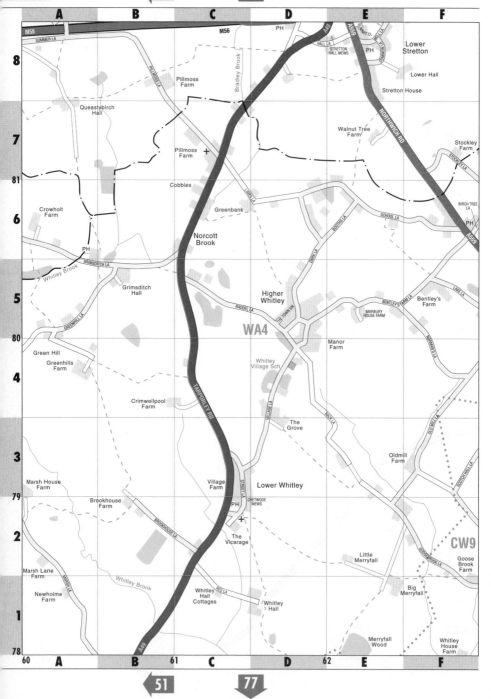

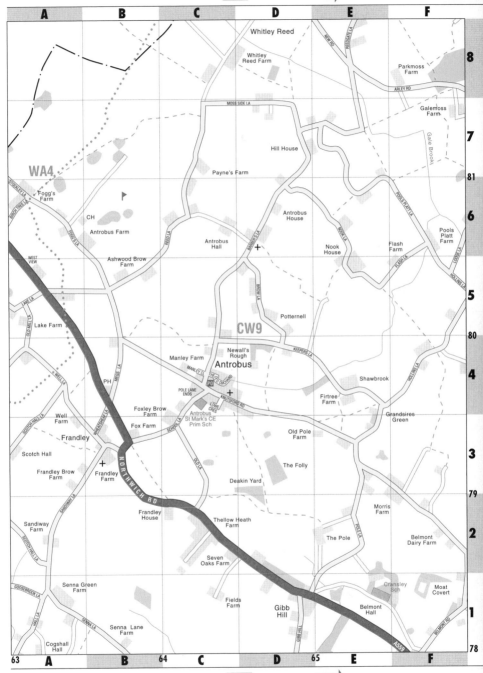

Whitley Reed

Whitley Reed Farm

Parkmoss Farm

ARLEY RD

Galemoss Farm

MOSS SIDE LA

Gale Brook

Hill House

Payne's Farm

WA4

Fogg's Farm

Antrobus House

Pools Platt Farm

Antrobus Farm

Antrobus Hall

Nook House

Flash Farm

Ashwood Brow Farm

WEST VIEW

Lake Farm

Potternell

CW9

Manley Farm

Newall's Rough

Antrobus

Shawbrook

KEEPERS LA

PH

Foxley Brow Farm

POLE LANE ENDS

KNUTSFORD RD

Antrobus St Mark's CE Prim Sch

Firtree Farm

Grandsires Green

Well Farm

Fox Farm

Frandley

Old Pole Farm

Scotch Hall

The Folly

Frandley Brow Farm

Frandley Farm

NORTHWICH RD

Deakin Yard

Morris Farm

Sandiway Farm

Frandley House

Thellow Heath Farm

The Pole

Belmont Dairy Farm

Seven Oaks Farm

Senna Green Farm

Cransley Sch

Moat Covert

Fields Farm

Gibb Hill

Belmont Hall

Senna Lane Farm

Cogshall Hall

A550

53
28

A B C D E F

8

The Firs

WA16

M6

Crowley Grange

CALDWELL'S GATE LA

Stockley Farm

7

Garland Hall

ARLEY RD

Arley

BACK LA

81

LOORE LA

Home Farm

Arley Hall & Gardens

Lady Park

Arley Green

The Ashes

6

Crowley Lodge

SACK LA

5

HOLLINS LA

Hollins Farm

Big Wood

80

Arley Park

The Belts

CW9

Alderhedge Wood

4

Reed House Farm

The Kennels

CANL LA

Cannlane Farm

Arley Brook

New Farm

3

Willowbed Wood

Willow Lodge

The Slacks

Bate Heath

79

ARLEY MOSSEND

BUDWORTH RD

CHELFORD LA

Arley Moss Farm

2

Kays Farm

KNUTSFORD RD

KNUTSFORD RD

Hilltop Farm

Moss End

Yewtree Farm

Fields Farm

George's Lane Farm

GEORGE'S LA

1

Budworth Heath

HEATH LA

BUDWORTH HEATH LA

Wathall Farm

Aston Park

Gravestones Farm

78

66 A B 67 C D 68 E F

29

56

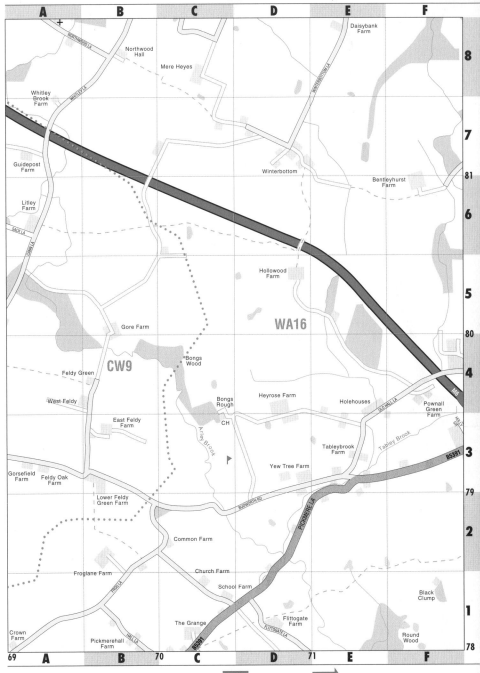

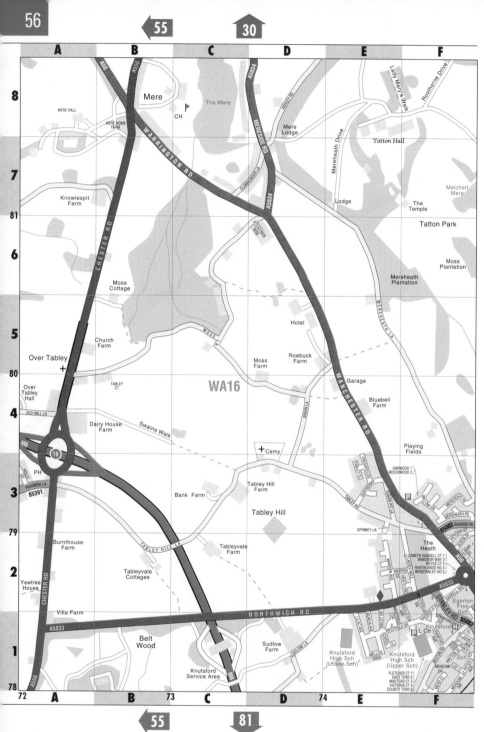

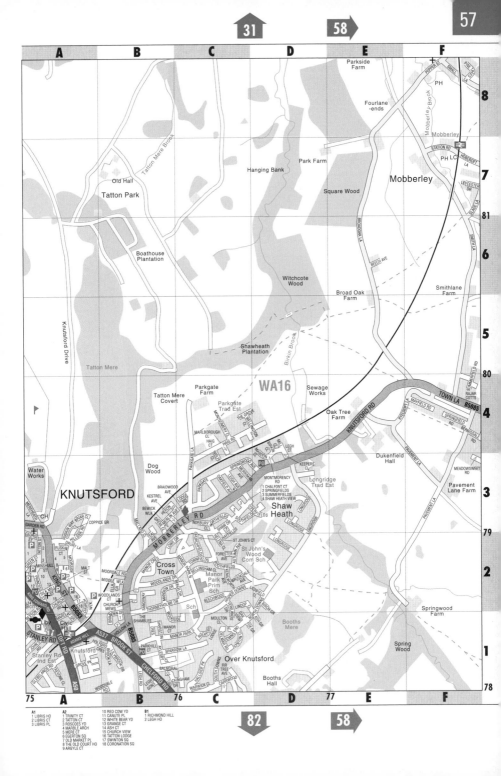

8

7

81

6

5

80

4

3

79

2

1

78

A B C D E F

Parkside Farm

Fourlane -ends

PEPPER ST SMALL LA PINE TREE LA

PH

Mobberley

STATION RD ABERCROFT LA

PH LC

LEYCESTER DR

RAJAR CTTS

SMITH LA

LYME DRIVE

Park Farm

Hanging Bank

Square Wood

Mobberley

Mobberley Brook

BROADOAK LA

BEECH AVE

Broad Oak Farm

Smithlane Farm

Old Hall

Tatton Park

Tatton Mere Brook

Boathouse Plantation

Witchcote Wood

Knutsford Drive

Tatton Mere

Shawheath Plantation

Birkin Brook

WA16

Sewage Works

Oak Tree Farm

KNUTSFORD RD

SPRINGFIELD RD

TOWN LA B5085

MAYFIELD RD

SPRINGFIELD RD

BERKSDALE RD

Parkgate Farm

Tatton Mere Covert

Parkgate Trad Est

THE GROVE

FIELD VIEW

MARLBOROUGH CL

HAIG CT

LEGH CT

Dukenfield Hall

MEADOWSWEET RD

Pavement Lane Farm

Dog Wood

SPRINGWOOD AVE

MONTMORENCY RD

1 CHALFONT CT
2 SPRINGFIELDS
3 SUMMERFIELDS
4 SHAW HEATH VIEW

Shaw Heath

KEEPERS CL

Longridge Trad Est

LONGRIDGE

PASSMETT LA

KNUTSFORD

BRAIDWOOD AVE

KESTREL AVE

BEWICK WLK

MOBBERLEY RD

NORBURY CL

SHAWFIELDS

St John's CT

PARKGATE LA

Cross Town

St John's Wood Com Sch

FORESTER AVE

OUTFIELDS

LONGRIDGE

Manor Park Prim Sch

Water Works

GARDEN RD

CH

COPPICE GR

MOORDALE RD

MIDDLE WLK

WOODLANDS DR

BELLINGHAM CL

THE DOWNS

Springwood Farm

MINSHULL ST

KING ST

MALT ST

WOODLANDS CHURCH MEWS

THORNEYHOLME DR

Sch

REECHWOOD

LINECOT

SHEFIELD DR

Booths Mere

Spring Wood

STANLEY RD

TOFT RD

ADAMS HILL

A537 BROOK ST B5085

THE SHAMBLES

MANOR PK

MOULTON CT

Civic Hall

Stanley Rd Ind Est

Knutsford Cres

CHELFORD RD

PARKHILL RD

SPARROW LA

BALMORAL

Over Knutsford

FIR TREE AVE

CARRWOOD

Booths Hall

BUCKINGHAM

WARWICK CT

A50

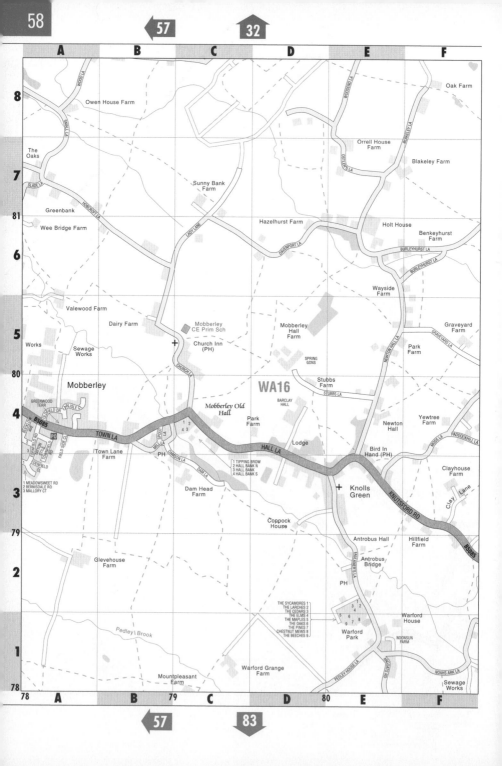

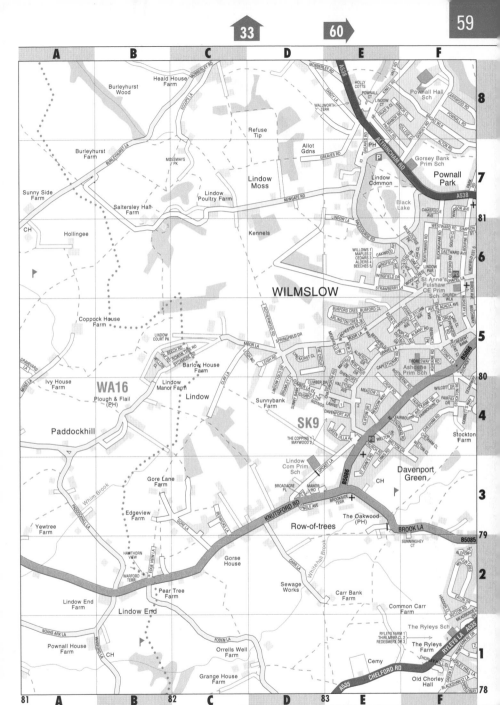

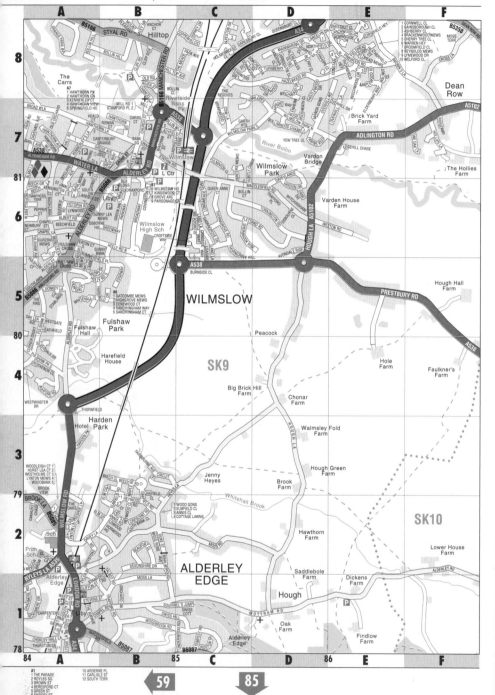

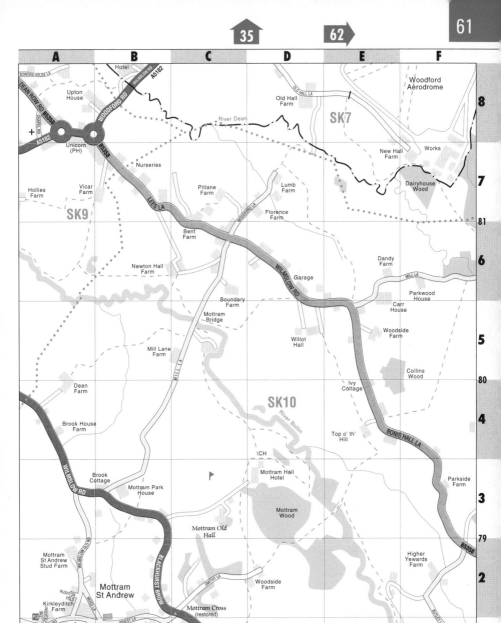

A B C D E F

Bowden House La
Upton House
Hotel
WILMSLOW RD
WOODFORD RD
A5102
Old Hall La
Old Hall Farm
Woodford Aerodrome
SK7
8
DEAN ROW RD B5358
CHAPEL RD
A5102
+
Unicorn (PH)
B5358
River Dean
New Hall Farm
Works
Nurseries
7
Hollies Farm
Vicar Farm
SK9
LEES LA
Pitlane Farm
Lumb Farm
Dairyhouse Wood
WOODFORD LA
81
Florence Farm
Bent Farm
WILMSLOW RD
Garage
Newton Hall Farm
Dandy Farm
MILL LA
6
Boundary Farm
Parkwood House
Carr House
Mottram Bridge
Woodside Farm
5
Mill Lane Farm
Willot Hall
MILL LA
Collins Wood
Dean Farm
SK10
Ivy Cottage
80
Brook House Farm
River Bollin
Top o' th' Hill
BONIS HALL LA
4
WILMSLOW RD
Brook Cottage
Parkside Farm
Mottram Park House
CH
Mottram Hall Hotel
3
Mottram Old Hall
Mottram Wood
B5358
79
Mottram St Andrew Stud Farm
WILMSLOW OLD RD
BLACKHURST BROW
Higher Yewards Farm
2
RUSHTON FOLD
Kirkleyditch Farm
Mottram St Andrew
MOSS LA
SMITHY LA
Woodside Farm
BUTLEY LANES
ALDERLEY RD
MOOR RD
PRIEST LA
+
Mottram St Andrew Prim Sch
PH
Mottram Cross (restored)
Sewage Works
Brook House Farm
WILMSLOW RD
A538
Legh Hall
1
78

87 A B 88 C D 89 E F

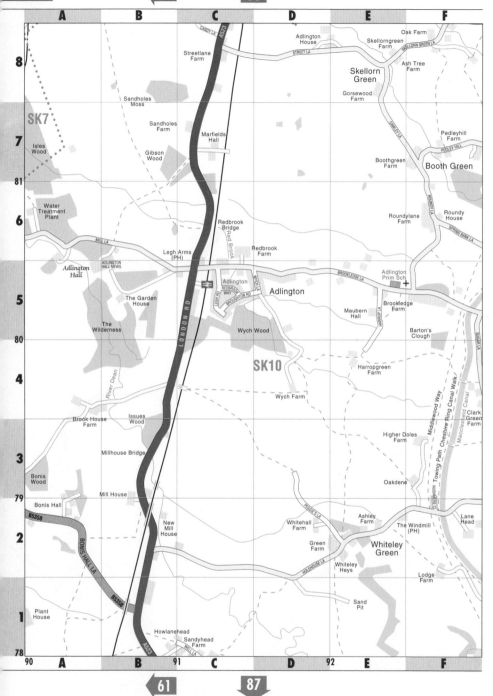

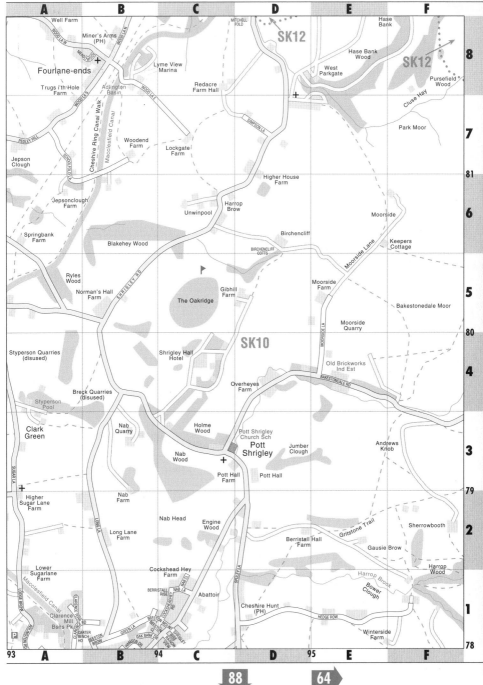

A **B** **C** **D** **E** **F**

Well Farm

Miner's Arms (PH)

Fourlane-ends

Lyme View Marina

MITCHELL FOLD

SK12

Hase Bank

Hase Bank Wood

West Parkgate

SK12

Pursefield Wood

8

Trugs i'th'Hole Farm

Adlington Basin

Redacre Farm Hall

Cluse Hay

Park Moor

Pedley Hill

Woodend Farm

Lockgate Farm

SIMPSON LA

7

Jepson Clough

Higher House Farm

81

Jepsonclough Farm

Unwinpool

Harrop Brow

Birchencliff

Moorside

6

Springbank Farm

Blakehey Wood

BIRCHENCLIFF COTTS

Moorside Lane

Keepers Cottage

Ryles Wood

SHRIGLEY RD

Norman's Hall Farm

The Oakridge

Gibhill Farm

Moorside Farm

Bakestonedale Moor

5

Moorside Quarry

80

Styperson Quarries (disused)

Shrigley Hall Hotel

SK10

MOORSIDE LA

Old Brickworks Ind Est

BAKESTONEDALE RD

4

Breck Quarries (disused)

Overheyes Farm

Styperson Pool

Clark Green

Nab Quarry

Holme Wood

Pott Shrigley Church Sch

Pott Shrigley

Jumber Clough

Andrews Knob

3

SUGAR LA

Nab Wood

Pott Hall Farm

Pott Hall

79

Higher Sugar Lane Farm

Nab Farm

Nab Head

Engine Wood

Gritstone Trail

Sherrowbooth

2

LONG LA

Long Lane Farm

Berristall Hall Farm

SHRIGLEY RD

Gausie Brow

Harrop Wood

Lower Sugarlane Farm

Cockshead Hey Farm

Harrop Brook

Bower Clough

1

Macclesfield Canal

Clarence Mill Bsns Pk

BERRISTALL RISE

NAB LA

GREEN LA

COCKSHEAD RD

Abattoir

SHRIGLEY RD

Cheshire Hunt (PH)

HEDGE ROW

Winterside Farm

78

93 **A** **94** **B** **C** **D** **95** **E** **F**

63
38

A   B   C   D   E   F

Lyme Park

Higher Moor

Whaley Moor

SK12

Knightslow
Wood

Handleybarn
Farm

Cliff

Knights
Low

8

Bow
Stones

Bailey's
Farm

Bowstonegate

7

Park Moor

Browside
Farm

Holme Wood   Cornfield
Farm

81

Hale
House

Sweet Hill

6

Handley Fold
Farm

Sponds
Hill

Lower Cliff
Farm

Griffstone Trail

5

Hollow
Sponds

Higher Cliff
Farm

HIGHER LA

Sponds

Reed Hill

SK23

KISHFIELD LA

80

PADDOCK CL

B5470

4

Back Sponds

Kettleshulme

Spout House
Farm

St James
CE Prim
Sch

PH

Manor
Farm

SK10

Brink
Farm

The Reed
Farm

Ellis
Bank

BAKESTONEDALE RD

MACCLESFIELD RD

Slaters Green
Farm

SIDE END LA

Side
End
Farm

3

Gnathole Brook

Brink
Brow

Charles
Head

Midfield

Thorneycroft
Farm

79

Whitelands

Neighbourway
Farm

2

Charles Head
Farm

Carr
Clough

Near Carr
Farm

Todd Brook

Further Harrop
Farm

Harrop
Wood

Harrop House
Farm

Tunstead
Knoll
Farm

Harrop Brook

1

Black Brook

B5470

Dunge Clough

Harrop Fold
Farm

78

96   A   B   97   C   D   98   E   F

63
89

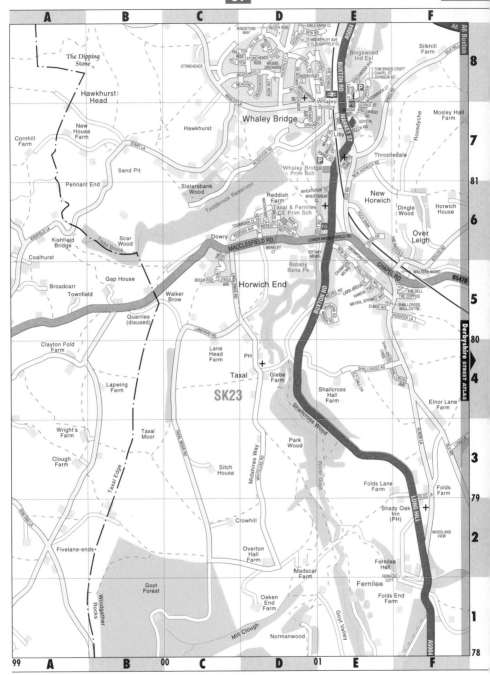

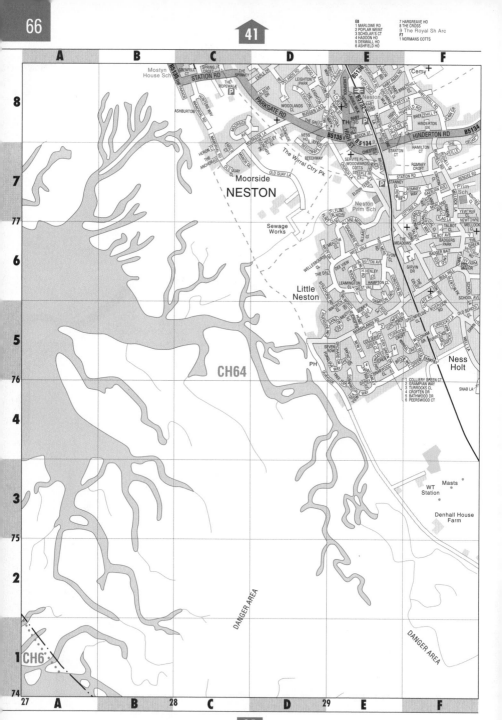

E8
1 MARLOWE RD
2 POPLAR WEINT
3 SCHOLAR'S CT
4 HADDON HO
5 DENWALL HO
6 ASHFIELD HO

7 HARGREAVE HO
8 THE CROSS
9 The Royal Sh Arc
F7
1 NORMANS COTTS

CH64

Moorside
NESTON

Little
Neston

Ness
Holt

1 COLLIERY GREEN CT
2 GRAMPIAN WAY
3 TURROCKS CL
4 CROFTEN DR
5 BATHWOOD DR
6 PEERSWOOD CT

SNAB LA

WT
Station

Masts

Denhall House
Farm

DANGER AREA

DANGER AREA

CH6

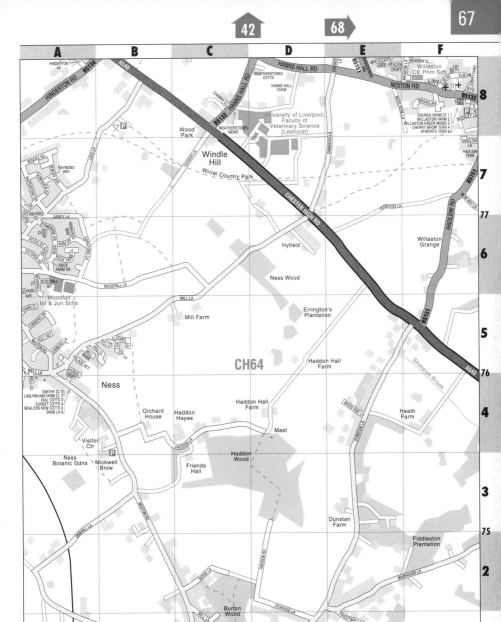

67 43

8

BRIARDALE RD
B5133
HOOTON RD
B5133
THE MEWS
CHANGE LA
CROSBY GRANGE
ORFORD GRANGE
ORME CL
OLD LYCHGATE RD
B5151
HADLOW RD
BENNET CL
PLATINUM CL
INTAKE CL
ASHTREE FARM CT
OAKTREE CROFT
SMITHY LA
HALLCROFT

Willaston

Works

THE OLD PUMP HO
WATERWORKS LA

The Oaklands

Hotel

OAKFIELD TERR
OAKFIELD RD

Wirral Country Park
Wirral Way

Heath Farm

Mayfield

Heath Lodge

ADFALENT LA

7

77

The Grange

HEATH LA

MARGARET'S LA

NEW HEY LA

6

Leaswood Farm

Oaks Farm

BERWICK RD
STIPERSTONES CL
Dehon House Youth Centre
Hotel
KELSYS DR
LULLAPOOL CL
LOCARNO
PEEBLES CL
OSTREAM DR

5

CH64

CH66

PH
LEDSHAM RD
B5463
JEDBURGH AVE 1
SELKIRK CL 2
HOWGILL CL 3

76

A540
CHESTER HIGH RD

Ledsham Hall Farm

BADGERSRAKE LA

Hallwood Farm
HALLWOOD DR
Inglewood

LEDSHAM HALL LA

WELSH RD

4

Foxes Farm

Cross Lanes Farm

Bank Farm

Garden Centre

BADGERSRAKE LA

Badger's Rake House

3

Badgersrake Covert

MUDHOUSE LA

75

PARKGATE RD

LEDSHAM LA

2

Aviary Farm

Manor House Farm

Daisy Bank Farm

Ledsham

Court Farm

1

Hotel

The Tudor Rose

CHAPEL LA
LEDSHAM GRANGE
NEWBOLD LA

Heath Hey

PARKGATE LA

Whitegates Farm

PIPER'S LA

A550
A540

Millhey Farm

CH1

74

33 A B 34 C D 35 E F

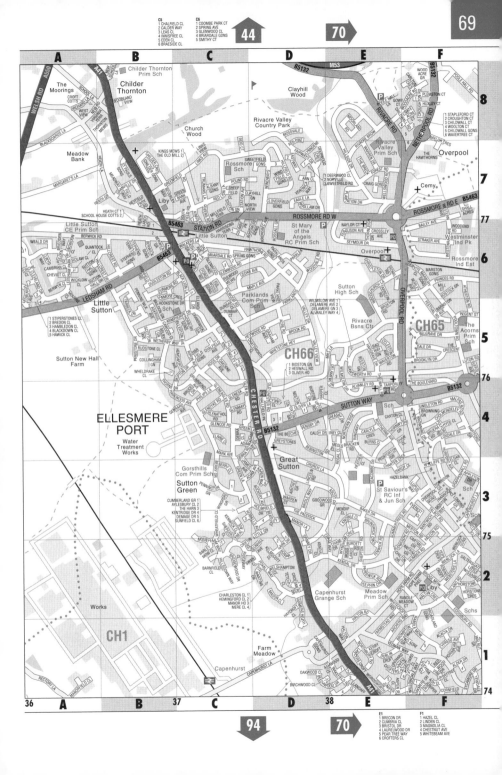

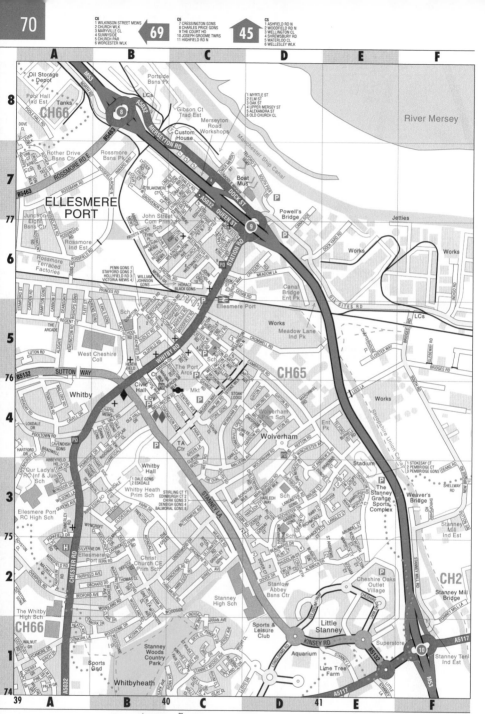

C6
1 WILKINSON STREET MEWS
2 CHURCH WLK
3 MARYVILLE CL
4 SUNNYSIDE
5 CHURCH PAR
6 WORCESTER WLK

69

C6
7 CRESSINGTON GDNS
8 CHARLES PRICE GDNS
9 THE COURT HO
10 JOSEPH GROOME TWRS
11 HIGHFIELD RD N

45

C5
1 ASHFIELD RD N
2 WOODFIELD RD N
3 WELLINGTON CL
4 SHREWSBURY RD
5 WATERLOO CL
6 WELLESLEY WLK

D2
1 BUCKINGHAM GDNS
2 SANDRINGHAM GDNS
3 FOTHERINGAY CT
4 CAERNARVON CT

C1
1 BARDSEY CL
2 ANGLESEY CL
3 ORKNEY CL
4 CUMBRAE DR

69

95

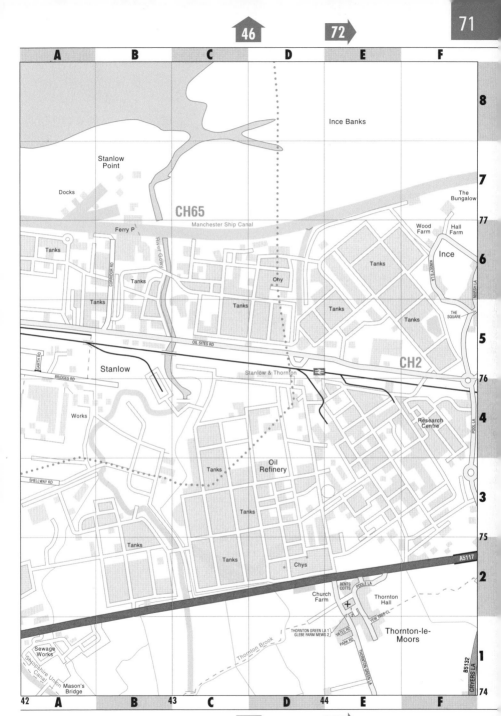

46
72

A B C D E F

8

7

The Bungalow

77

Ince Banks

Stanlow
Point

Docks

CH65

Manchester Ship Canal

Ferry P

Wood
Farm

Hall
Farm

Ince

6

Tanks

Tanks

Tanks

THE
SQUARE

Tanks

Tanks

Tanks

Tanks

OIL SITES RD

5

CH2

76

Stanlow

Stanlow & Thornton

Works

Research
Centre

4

SHELLWAY RD

Tanks

Oil
Refinery

3

75

Tanks

Tanks

A5117

2

Tanks

Tanks

Chys

BENTS
COTTS

POOLE LA

Thornton
Hall

Church
Farm

Thornton Green La 1
Glebe Farm Mews 2

Thornton-le-
Moors

Sewage
Works

Thornton Brook

YATES RD

PARK RD

B5132

1

Mason's
Bridge

CRYERS LA

74

42 A B 43 C D 44 E F

CORRIDOR RD

River Gowy

GARTH RD

BRIDGES RD

KINSEY'S LA

MARSH LA

POOLE LA

YEW TREE CL

THORNTON GREEN LA

Shropshire Union Canal

Ohy

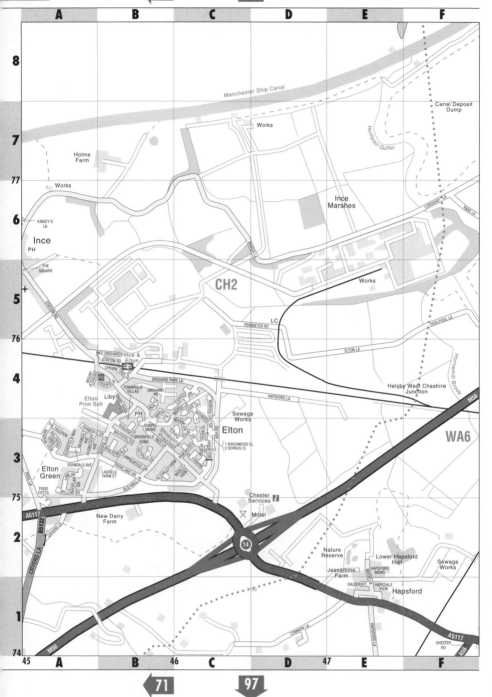

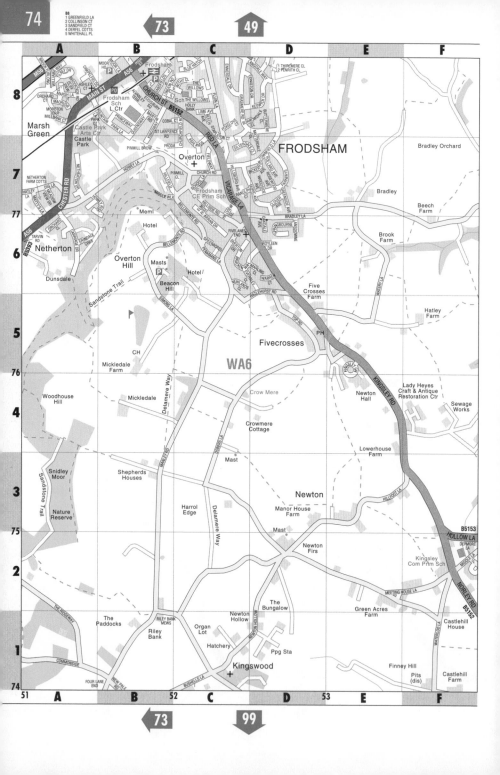

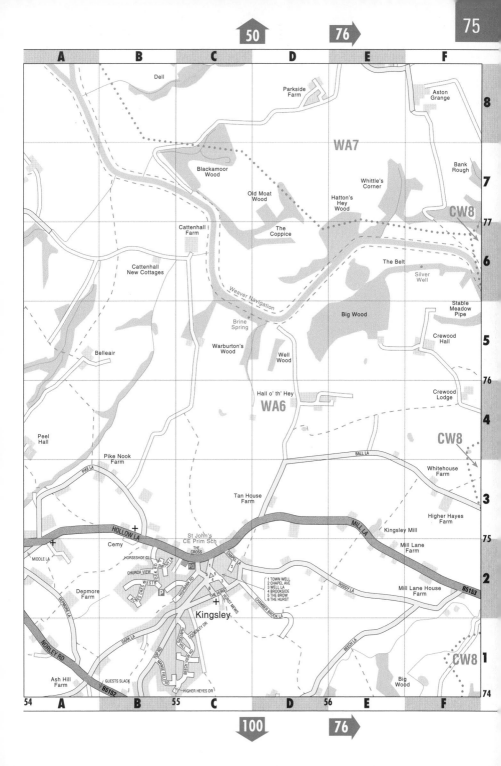

A   B   C   D   E   F

8

WA7

7

Dell

Parkside
Farm

Aston
Grange

Bank
Rough

CW8

77

Blackamoor
Wood

Old Moat
Wood

Whittle's
Corner

Hatton's
Hey
Wood

The
Coppice

6

Cattenhall
Farm

The Belt

Silver
Well

Cattenhall
New Cottages

Weaver Navigation

Stable
Meadow
Pipe

Crewood
Hall

5

Brine
Spring

Warburton's
Wood

Well
Wood

Big Wood

76

Belleair

Hall o' th' Hey

WA6

Crewood
Lodge

4

Peel
Hall

CW8

Pike Nook
Farm

BALL LA

Whitehouse
Farm

3

PIKE LA

Tan House
Farm

Higher Hayes
Farm

MILL LA

Kingsley Mill

75

HOLLOW LA

St John's
CE Prim Sch

THE CROSS

Mill Lane
Farm

Cemy

Middle La

MIDDLE LA

HORSESHOE CL

RODDY LA

Mill Lane House
Farm

B5153

2

CHURCH VIEW

WEST'S

P

Depmore
Farm

DEPMORE LA

HIGHLAND RD

THE HURST

SPRING MEADS

CHAPEL LA

1 TOWN WELL
2 CHAPEL AVE
3 WELL LA
4 BROOKSIDE
5 THE BROW
6 THE HURST

Kingsley

CHAMBER BROOK LA

NORLEY RD

DARK LA

TOP RD

BRITISH LA

RODSLEY DR

GRANGE FIELD

BEECH HILL RD

BEECH LA

Big
Wood

CW8

1

Ash Hill
Farm

B5152

GUESTS SLACK

HIGHER HEYES DR

74

54   A   B   55   C   D   56   E   F

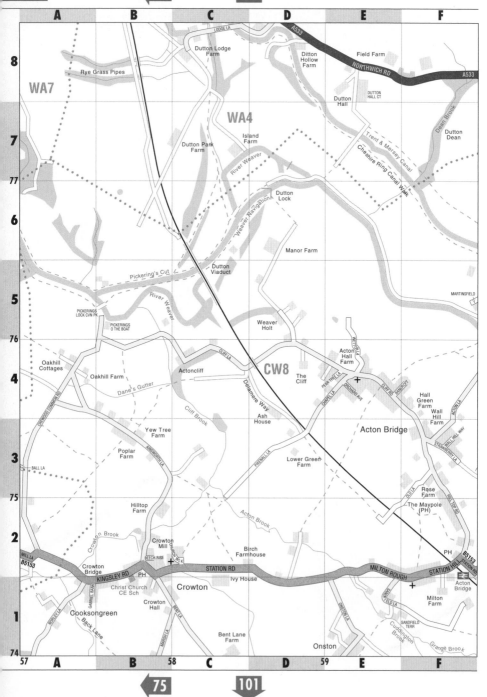

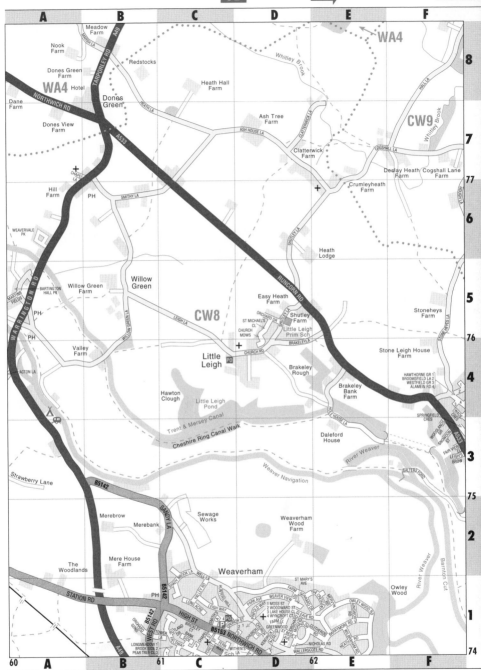

52
78
78

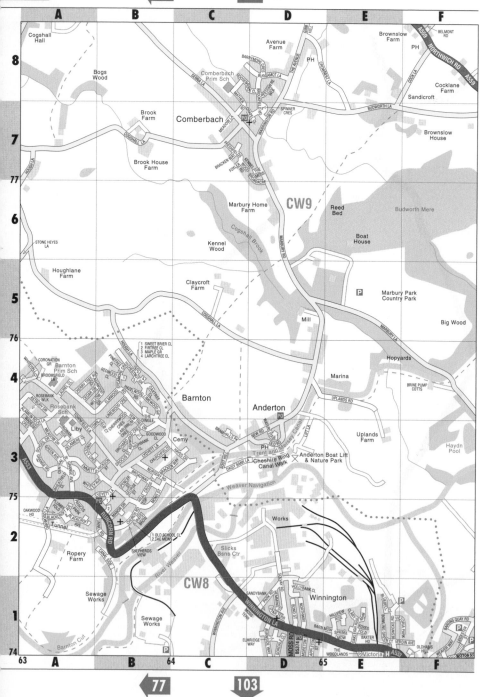

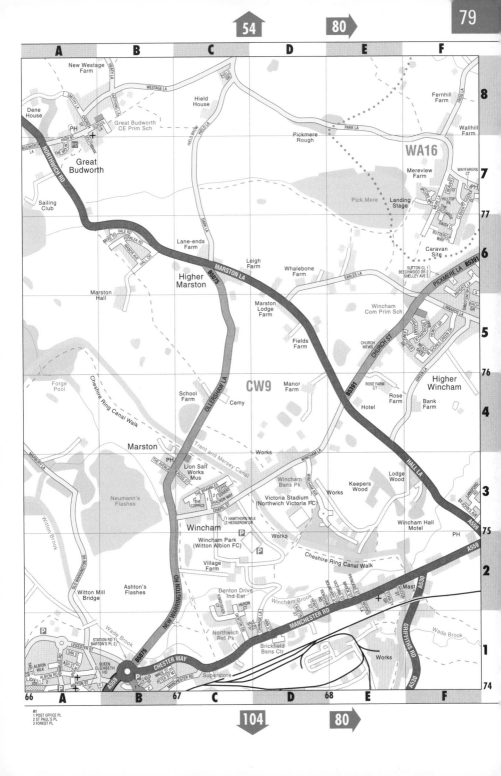

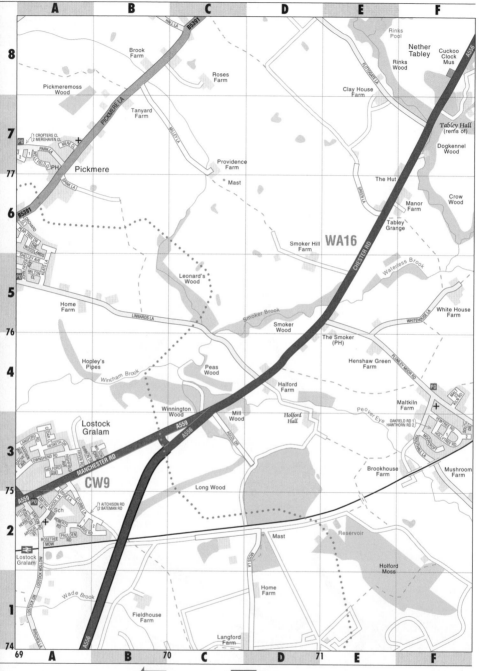

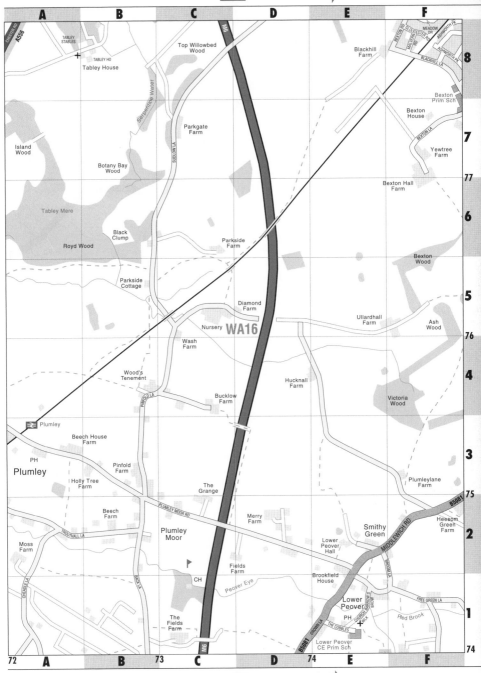

A   B   C   D   E   F

A556
CHESTER RD
TABLEY STABLES
TABLEY HO
Tabley House
Top Willowbed Wood
M6
Blackhill Farm
BEXTON RD
GLOUCESTER RD
MEADOW DR
ASHWORTH DR
MAXWELL
BLACKHILL LA
8

Serpentine Water
Parkgate Farm
Bexton Prim Sch
Bexton House
BEXTON LA
7

Island Wood
SUDLOW LA
Yewtree Farm
77

Tabley Mere
Botany Bay Wood
Bexton Hall Farm

Black Clump
Parkside Farm
Bexton Wood
6

Royd Wood
Parkside Cottage
Diamond Farm
Ullardhall Farm
Ash Wood
5

Nursery **WA16**
76

Wash Farm
Wood's Tenement
PINFOLD LA
Bucklow Farm
Hucknall Farm
Victoria Wood
4

Plumley
Beech House Farm
Pinfold Farm
Plumleylane Farm
3

PH
Plumley
Holly Tree Farm
The Grange
PLUMLEY MOOR RD
Merry Farm
Smithy Green
B5081
Heesom Green Farm
MIDDLEWICH RD
75
2

Beech Farm
TROUTHALL LA
Plumley Moor
BACK LA
Lower Peover Hall
Brookfield House
BROOK LA

Moss Farm
CHEADLE LA
CH
Fields Farm
Peover Eye
Lower Peover
FREE GREEN LA
Red Brook
1

The Fields Farm
M6
B5081
JODRELL LA
THE COBBLES
CHURCH WALK
PH
Lower Peover CE Prim Sch
74

72   A   B   73   C   D   74   E   F

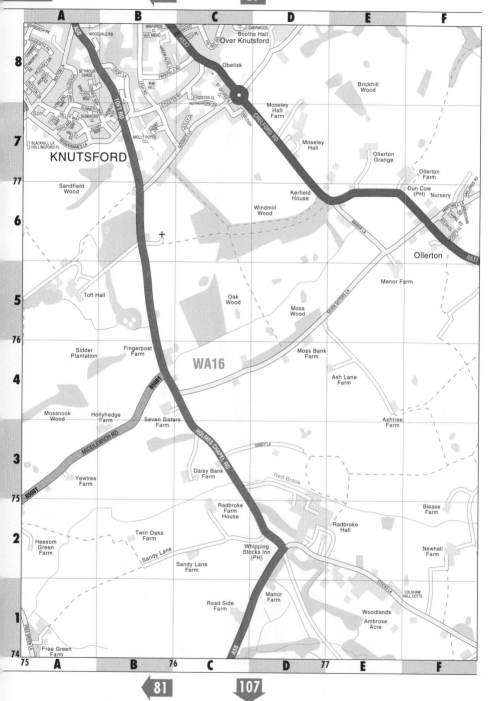

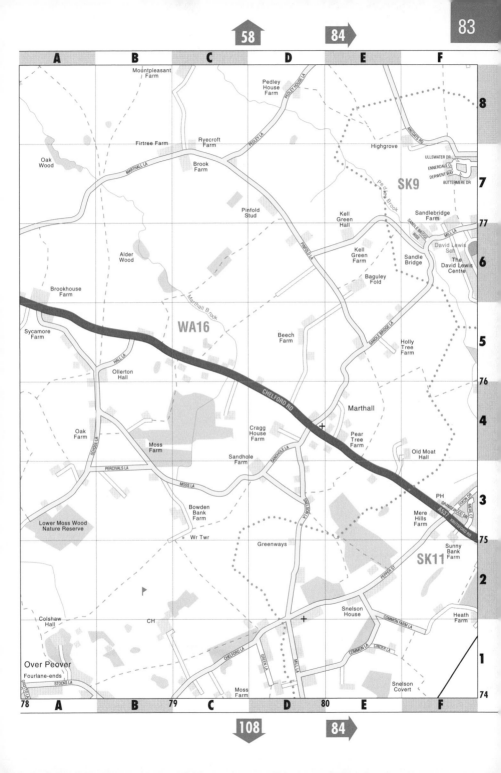

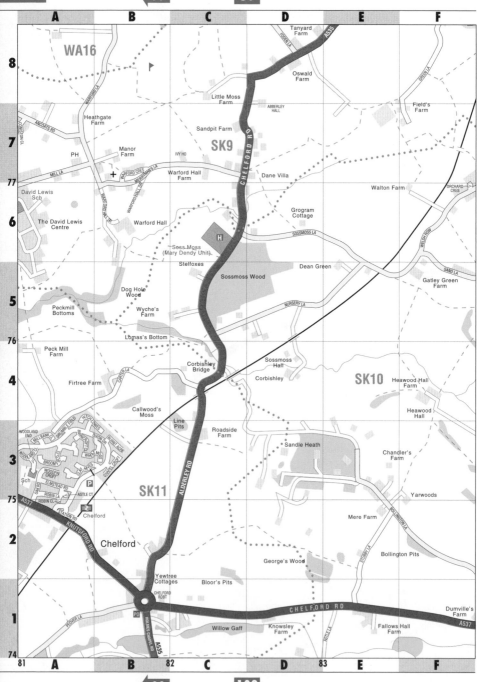

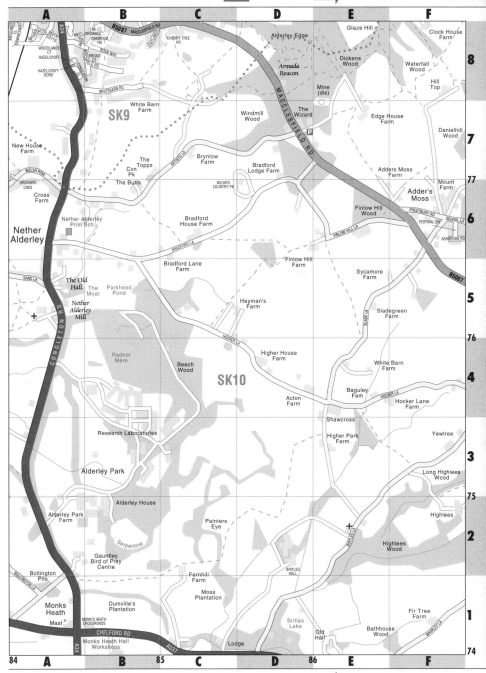

A B C D E F

84 A B 85 C D 86 E F

8
7
77
6
5
76
4
3
75
2
1
74

SK9

SK10

Nether
Alderley

Alderley Edge

Glaze Hill

Clock House
Farm

Dickens
Wood

Waterfall
Wood

Hill
Top

*Armada
Beacon*

Mine
(dis)

The Wizard

Edge House
Farm

Danielhill
Wood

Windmill
Wood

New House
Farm

Brynlow
Farm

Bradford
Lodge Farm

Adders Moss
Farm

Mount's
Moss

Adder's
Moss

The
Topps
Cvn
Pk

The Butts

WIZARD
COUNTRY PK

Finlow Hill
Wood

White Barn
Farm

Nether Alderley
Prim Sch

Bradford
House Farm

Finlow Hill
Farm

Sycamore
Farm

Cross
Farm

The Old
Hall

The
Moat

Parkhead
Pond

*Nether
Alderley
Mill*

Bradford Lane
Farm

Hayman's
Farm

Higher House
Farm

Sladegreen
Farm

White Barn
Farm

Radnor
Mere

Beech
Wood

Acton
Farm

Baguley
Fam

Hocker Lane
Farm

Research Laboratories

Shawcross

Higher Park
Farm

Yewtree

Alderley Park

Long Highlees
Wood

Alderley House

Highlees

Alderley Park
Farm

Serpentine

Painters
Eye

Highlees
Wood

Gauntley
Bird of Prey
Centre

Fernhill
Farm

Birtles
Hall

Bollington
Pits

Moss
Plantation

Birtles
Lake

Fir Tree
Farm

Monks
Heath

Mast

Dumville's
Plantation

Old
Hall

Bathhouse
Wood

Monk's Heath
Crossroads

Monks Heath Hall
Workshops

CHELFORD RD

Lodge

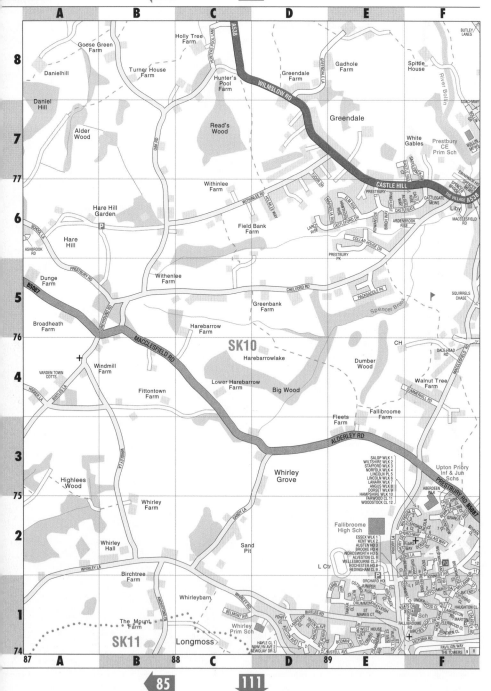

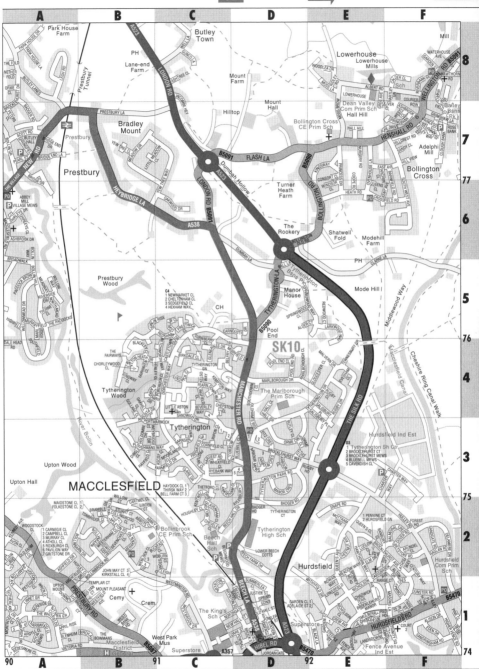

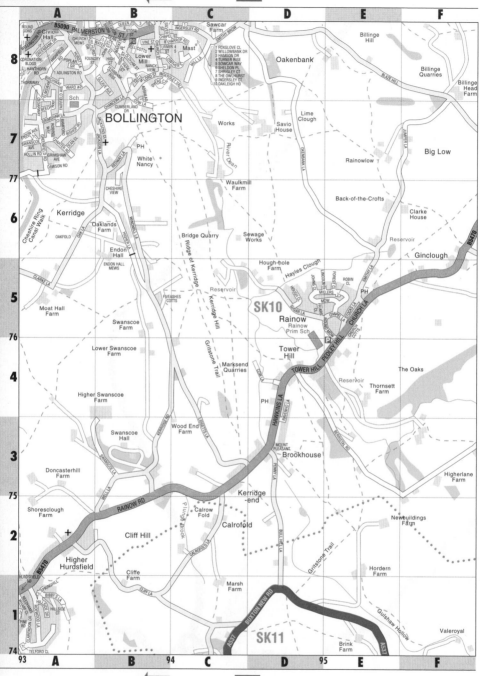

	A	B	C	D	E	F

8

Round
Gons
Civic
Hall
B5090 PALMERSTON ST QUEEN ST
CHURCH
MEWS
Sawcar
Farm
SMITHY BROW
INGERSLEY RD
HARROP RD
Lower
Mill
Mast
CHAPEL ST
VINE ST
COTTS
VALE RD

1 FOXGLOVE CL
2 WILLOWBANK DR
3 HAAGON DR
4 TURNER RISE
5 SOWCAR WAY
6 SHELDON PL
7 SHRIGLEY CT
8 THE OWL HURST
9 INGERSLEY CT
10 OAKLEIGH HO

Oakenbank
Billinge
Hill
Billinge
Quarries
Billinge
Head
Farm

CORONATION
BLDGS
HAWTHORN
RD
THORNWAY
FOUNDRY
1 ADLINGTON RD
NANCY
VIEW
Works
Savio
House
Lime
Clough
BLAZE HILL

7

ENDON AVE
SWANSCOE
AVE
HOLLIN RD
GRIMSHAW
AVE
DAWSON RD
Sch
PH
White
Nancy
River Dean
Rainowlow
Big Low

BOLLINGTON
CUMBERLAND
DR

77

CHESHIRE
VIEW
Waulkmill
Farm
Back-of-the-Crofts
Clarke
House

6

Kerridge
Oaklands
Farm
WINDMILL CL
Bridge Quarry
Sewage
Works
Ridge of Kerridge
Reservoir
Ginclough
B5470

OAKFOLD
Endon
Hall
ENDON HALL
MEWS
Hough-hole
Farm
Hayles Clough
MILLERS
HOUSE CL
LINDOW CL
FOREST CL
ROBIN
CL
PH

5

CLARKE LA
Reservoir
FIVEASHES
COTTS
Kerridge Hill
SK10
SUGAR LA
JOHNS CL
MDW
FRANS
CLOSE
ROBIN LA
CHURCH LA
PH
CHURCH COTTS

Moat Hall
Farm
Swanscoe
Farm
Rainow
Rainow
Prim Sch
P
SMITH LA

76

Lower Swanscoe
Farm
Gritstone Trail
Marksend
Quarries
Tower
Hill
TOWER HILL
PEDLEY HILL
Reservoir
The Oaks
Thornsett
Farm

4

Higher Swanscoe
Farm
Wood End
Farm
LIDGETTS LA
DON LA
PH
HAWKINS LA
LAUGHLIN LA
BRIDGE RD

3

Swanscoe
Hall
OAKENCLOUGH RD
MOUNT
PLEASANT
Brookhouse
Higherlane
Farm

Doncasterhill
Farm
WILLA
RAINOW RD
PENNY LA

75

Shoresclough
Farm
Kerridge-
end
Calrow
Fold
Calrofold
CALROFOLD LA
BULL HILL LA
Newbuildings
Farm

2

Cliff Hill
Plunge Brook
Gritstone Trail
Hordern
Farm
Valeroyal

Higher
Hurdsfield
HURDSFIELD RD
Cliffe
Farm
CLIFF LA
Marsh
Farm
BUXTON NEW RD
Guishaw Hollow
A537

SPRINGHILL
BIBBY LA
HILLSIDE
CT
PINE
RD
TELFORD CL
B5470

1

SK11
A537
Brink
Farm

74

93	A	B	94	C	D	95	E	F

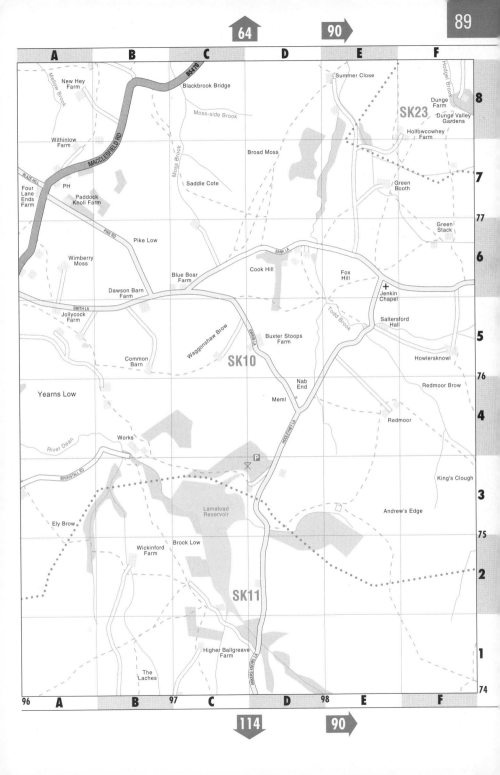

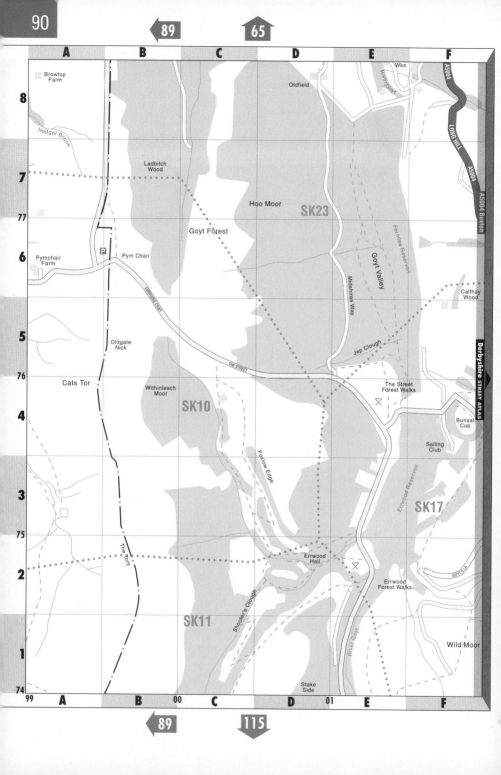

89
65

A   B   C   D   E   F

Browtop
Farm

8

Wks

River Goyt

Oldfield

A5004

Hodget Brook

LONG HILL

7

Ladbitch
Wood

A5004

77

Hoo Moor

SK23

Goyt Forest

Fernilee Reservoir

A5004 Buxton

6

Pymchair
Farm

P

Pym Chair

Midshires Way

Goyt Valley

Calfhay
Wood

Derbyshire STREET ATLAS

ERRWOOD RD

5

Oldgate
Nick

THE STREET

Jep Clough

76

Cats Tor

Withinleach
Moor

The Street
Forest Walks

SK10

Bunsal
Cob

4

Foxlow Edge

Sailing
Club

75

SK17

3

Errwood Reservoir

The Tors

Errwood
Hall

Errwood
Forest Walks

2

Stoaper's Clough

GOYT'S LA

SK11

River Goyt

Wild Moor

1

74

Stake
Side

99   A   B   00   C   D   01   E   F

89
115

A B C D E F

CH6

CH6

CH6

CH64

DANGER AREA

DANGER AREA

DANGER AREA

CH5

White
Sands

CH5

FLINT/
Y FFLINT

A548 Flint

Nature Study
Ctr

River Dee/
Afon Dyfrdwy

Power
Sta

Beacon

A548

Power
Sta

A548

CHESTER RD

KELSTERTON RD

B5129

Kelsterton
Farm

Kelsterton

CH6

Park
Farm

Coleg Glannau
Dyfrdwy/
Deeside
Coll

CONNAH'S
QUAY

Top-y-fron

Sports
Ctr

Connah's Quay
High Sch

KELSTERTON RD

CH5

Golftyn

CHURCH ST

PO

B5129

WEIGHBRIDGE RD

WEIGHBRIDGE RD

NORTH RD

COATINGS
TWO

KING RD

COATINGS BY PASS RD

RIVER RD

1 COLEHILL PL
2 LLYS SANT IAGG/ST JAMES CT
3 CLIFTON PARK AVE
4 TALFRYN CL
5 QUEEN'S AVE
6 ROCK COTTS
7 KINGS CROFT
8 KINGS RD
9 WILLOW CT
10 ROCK RD

8

7

73

6

5

72

4

3

71

2

1

70

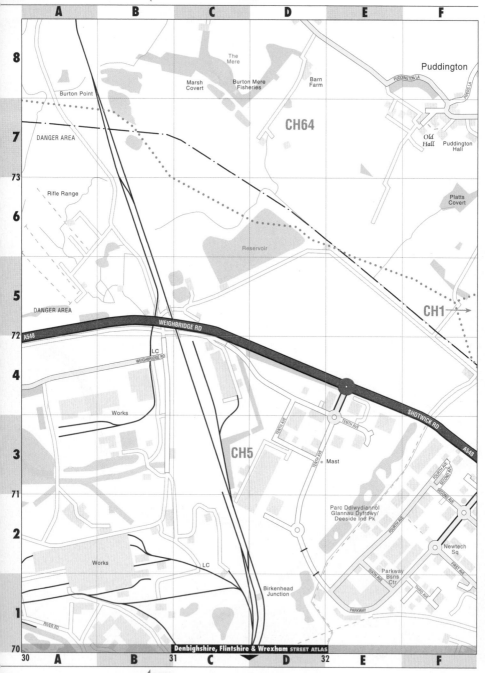

8

The Mere

Puddington

Marsh Covert

Burton Mere Fisheries

Barn Farm

PUDDINGTON LA

Burton Point

CH64

Old Hall

Puddington Hall

7

DANGER AREA

73

Rifle Range

Platts Covert

6

Reservoir

5

DANGER AREA

CH1

72 A548

WEIGHBRIDGE RD

LC

WEIGHBRIDGE RD

SHOTWICK RD

4

A548

Works

TENTH AVE

TENTH AVE

3

CH5

Mast

FOURTH AVE

SECOND AVE

71

Parc Ddiwydiannol Glannau Dyfrdwy/ Deeside Ind Pk

Newtech Sq

2

Works

LC

FOURTH AVE

Parkway Bsns Ctr

FIRST AVE

SIXTH AVE

THIRD AVE

SECOND AVE

Birkenhead Junction

1

RIVER RD

PARKWAY

70

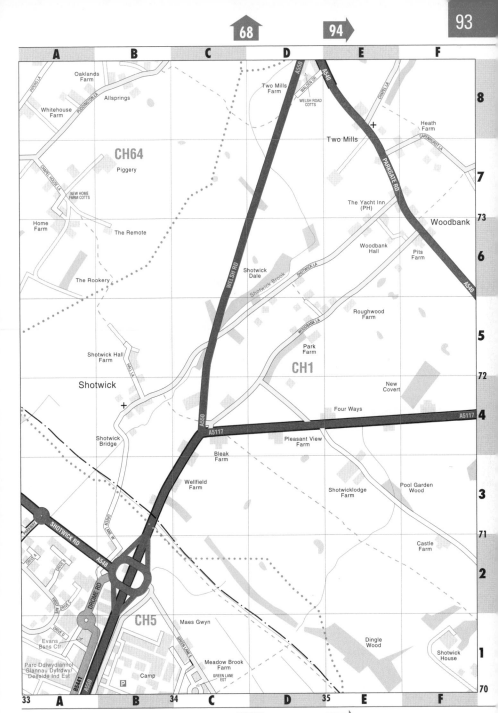

68

94

A B C D E F

8
7
73
6
5
72
4
3
71
2
1
70

Oaklands Farm
Allsprings
Whitehouse Farm
PICTON LA
PUDDINGTON LA

CH64
Piggery
CHASE HOUSE LA
NEW HOME FARM COTTS
Home Farm
The Remote
The Rookery

Two Mills Farm
WALDEN DR
A550
A540
WELSH ROAD COTTS
CHAPEL LA
Two Mills
Heath Farm
CAPENHURST LA

The Yacht Inn (PH)
PARKGATE RD
Woodbank
Woodbank Hall
Pits Farm
A540

WELSH RD
Shotwick Dale
Shotwick Brook
SHOTWICK LA
WOODBANK LA
Park Farm
Roughwood Farm
CH1
New Covert

Shotwick Hall Farm
HALL LA
Shotwick
Shotwick Bridge
A550
Four Ways
A5117
A5117
Bleak Farm
Pleasant View Farm
Wellfield Farm
Shotwicklodge Farm
Pool Garden Wood

GREEN LANE W.
SHOTWICK RD
A548
Castle Farm

BROOKDALE
DROVE RD
A550
CH5
Maes Gwyn
GREEN LANE
Meadow Brook Farm
GREEN LANE EST
Dingle Wood
Shotwick House

DRIVE 4
DRIVE D.
FIRST AVE.
DRIVE C.
Evans Bsns Ctr
Parc Ddiwydiannol Glannau Dyfrdwy/ Deeside Ind Est
B5441
Camp
P

33 A 34 B C 35 D E F

116

94

93
69

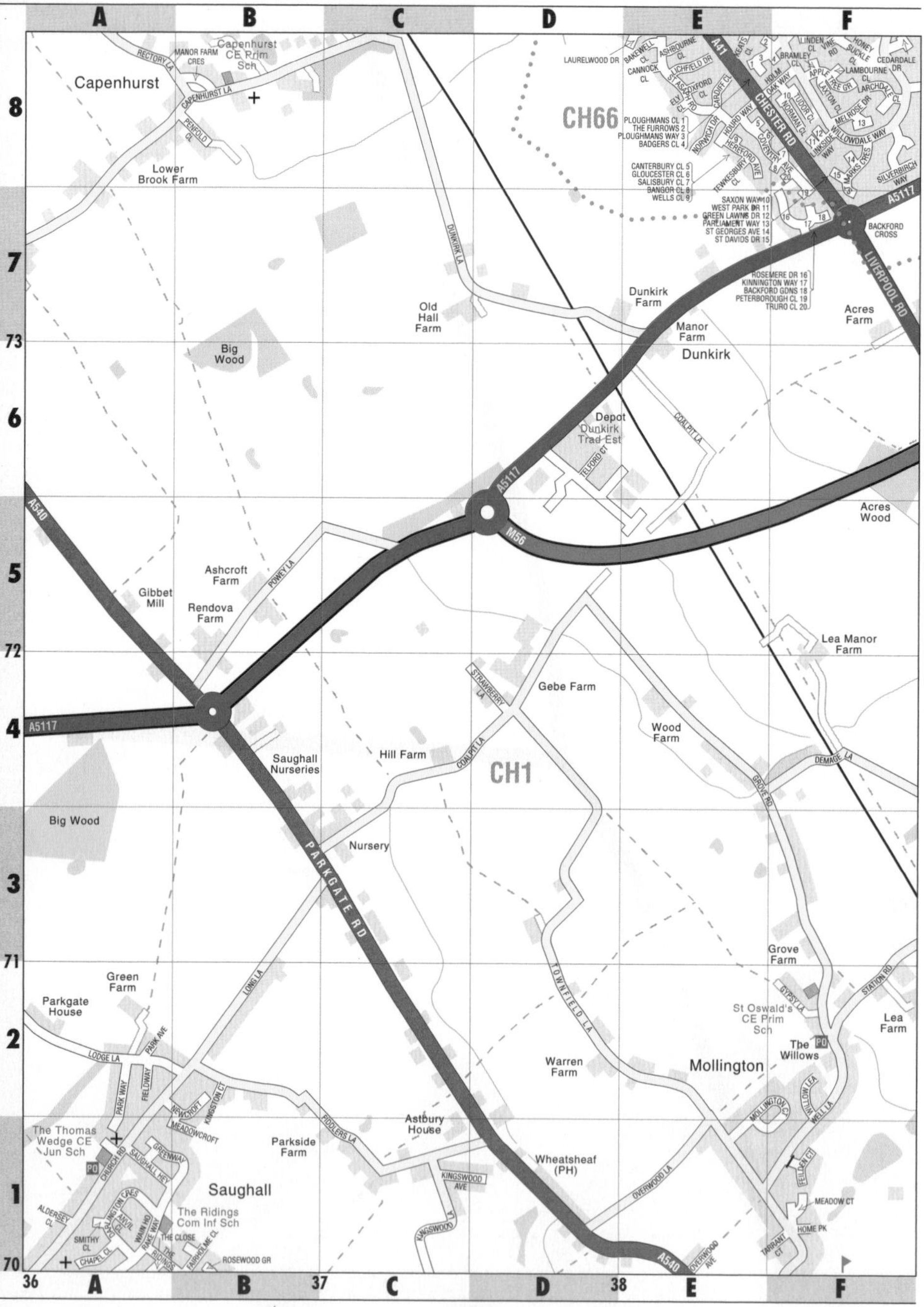
A
B
C
D
E
F
8
7
73
6
5
72
4
3
71
2
1
70
36
37
38
Capenhurst
Capenhurst CE Prim Sch
RECTORY LA
MANOR FARM CRES
CAPENHURST LA
PENFOLD CL
Lower Brook Farm
DUNKIRK LA
Old Hall Farm
Big Wood
CH66
LAURELWOOD DR
BAKEWELL
ASHBOURNE CL
CANNOCK CL
LICHFIELD DR
OXFORD CL
CARDIFF CL
KEATS CL
HOLM OAK WAY
BRAMLEY CL
LINDEN CL
VINE RD
HONEY SUCKLE CL
CEDARDALE DR
APPLE TREE GR
LAMBOURNE CL
LAXTON CL
LARCHDALE CL
MELROSE DR
WILLOWDALE WAY
MARKS CRES
SILVERBIRCH WAY
TUDOR CL
NORMAN CL
CHESTER RD
A41
NORWICH DR
HEREFORD AVE
COVENTRY AVE
TEWKESBURY CL
LINKSIDE WAY
PLOUGHMANS CL 1
THE FURROWS 2
PLOUGHMANS WAY 3
BADGERS CL 4
CANTERBURY CL 5
GLOUCESTER CL 6
SALISBURY CL 7
BANGOR CL 8
WELLS CL 9
SAXON WAY 10
WEST PARK DR 11
GREEN LAWNS DR 12
PARLIAMENT WAY 13
ST GEORGES AVE 14
ST DAVIDS DR 15
ROSEMERE DR 16
KINNINGTON WAY 17
BACKFORD GDNS 18
PETERBOROUGH CL 19
TRURO CL 20
A5117
BACKFORD CROSS
LIVERPOOL RD
Dunkirk Farm
Manor Farm
Dunkirk
Acres Farm
Depot
Dunkirk Trad Est
TELFORD CT
COALPIT LA
A5117
M56
Acres Wood
A540
Ashcroft Farm
POWEY LA
Gibbet Mill
Rendova Farm
Lea Manor Farm
STRAWBERRY LA
Gebe Farm
A5117
Saughall Nurseries
Hill Farm
COALPIT LA
CH1
Wood Farm
DEMAGE LA
GROVE RD
Big Wood
Nursery
PARKGATE RD
Grove Farm
Green Farm
Parkgate House
LONG LA
TOWNFIELD LA
GYPSY LA
STATION RD
St Oswald's CE Prim Sch
Lea Farm
LODGE LA
PARK AVE
PARK WAY
FIELDWAY
NEWCROFT
KINGSTON CT
MEADOWCROFT
The Willows
Warren Farm
Mollington
MOLLINGTON CT
WILLOW LEA
WELL LA
The Thomas Wedge CE Jun Sch
CHURCH RD
GREENWAY
SAUGHALL HEY
FIDDLERS LA
Parkside Farm
Astbury House
Wheatsheaf (PH)
KINGSWOOD AVE
FEILDEN CT
Saughall
ALDERSEY CL
ANVIL CL
WAIN HO
RAKE WAY
The Ridings Com Inf Sch
THE CLOSE
FAIRHOLME CL
SMITHY CL
CHAPEL CL
THE RIDINGS
ROSEWOOD GR
KINGSWOOD LA
OVERWOOD LA
OVERWOOD AVE
A540
MEADOW CT
HOME PK
TARRANT CT

93
117

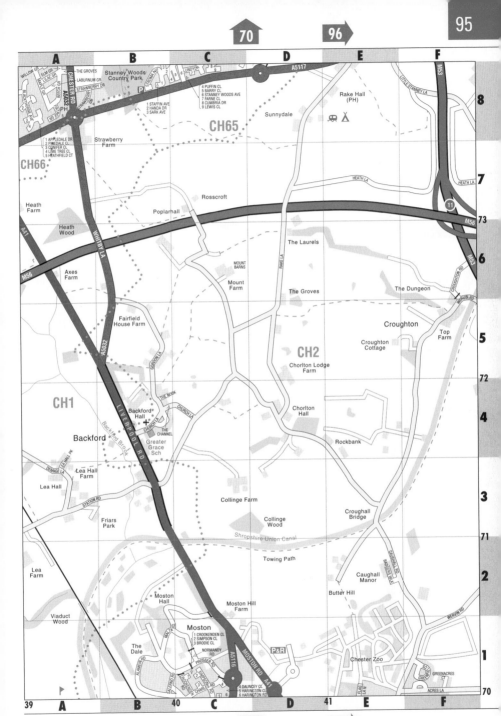

95
71

A B C D E F

8 Stoak Grange

Shropshire Union Canal

Cryers Farm

B5132

Dension's Bridge

Thornton Green Farm

THORNTON GREEN LA

CRYERS LA

7 PH Stoak
HEATH LA CHURCH LA
CROUGHTON RD
BUNBURY CL

Spring Farm

HALLSGREEN LA

HOB LA

Stoke Bridge

73 M56 M56

Heath Farm

6 15

Wimbolds Trafford

ASHWOOD FARM CT

INCE LA

M53

Ashwood House

Hall Farm

5 Ash Wood

ASHWOOD LA

River Gowy

CH2

72 B5132

Park Farm

Mill Brook

4 Wervin

Landfill Site

PICTON LA

Wervin New Hall

3 Woodside Farm

Picton

Hill Far

GREEN LA

Picton Hall

PH

Trafford Bridge

A56

Ashton House

71

The Shrewsbury Arms (PH)

2 New House Farm

Green La

ASH HEY LA

Sewage Works

WARRINGTON RD

Saw Mill

Ash Hey Farm

1 HURLESTONE CL
2 WEAVER GR
3 DANE GR
4 ALYN RD
5 WOODLAND BANK
6 ST PETERS WAY
7 ST ANDREWS WLK

Cvn Site

FOX COVERT LA

1 M53

PLEMSTALL LA
GLEBE MEWS
LINDEN

70 ACRES LA

TIE STREET

DEE RD
TOWN LA

LYDIA RD

A56

PLEMSTALL WAY

42 A 43 B C 44 D E F

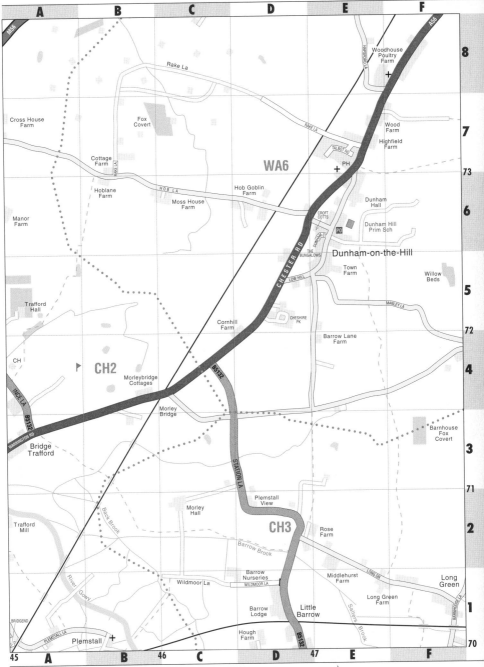

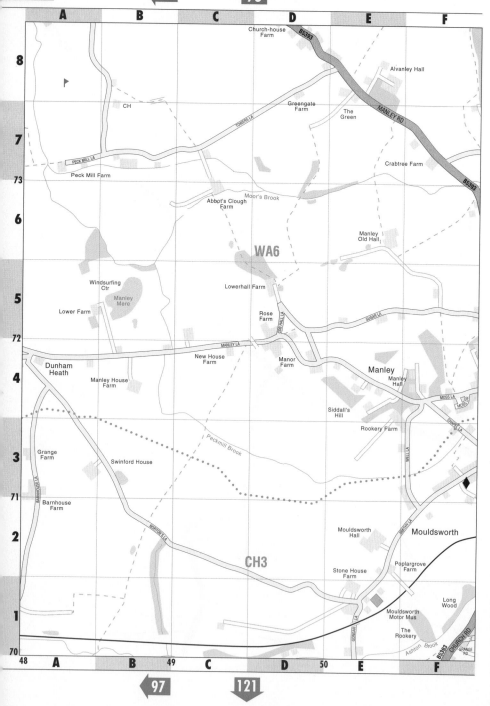

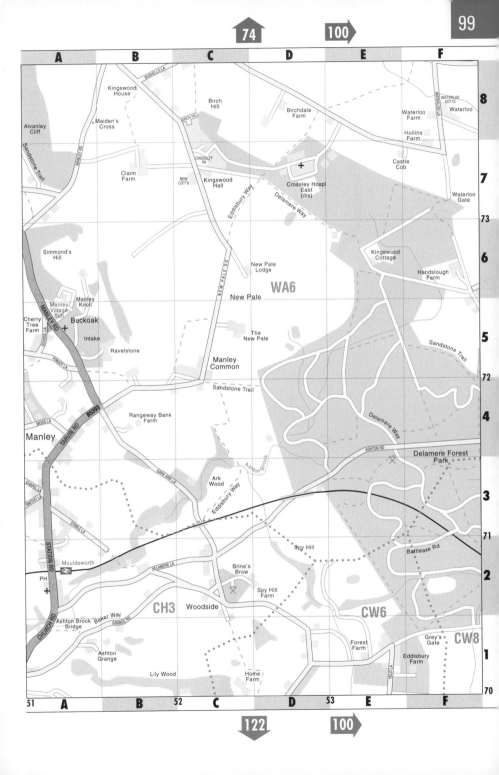

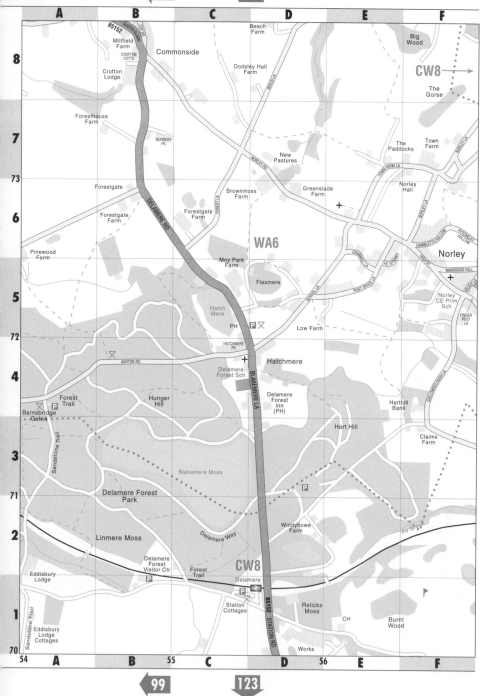

8

7

73

6

5

72

4

3

71

2

1

70

A B 54 B 55 C D 56 E F

Big Wood

CW8→

The Gorse

Beech Farm

Commonside

Millfield Farm
CROFTON COTTS
Crofton Lodge

B5152

Dodsley Hall Farm

Foresthouse Farm

NURSERY PK

New Pastures

The Paddocks

Town Farm

NORLEY LA

Forestgate

Brownmoss Farm

Greenslade Farm

Norley Hall

Norley

Forestgate Farm

Forestgate Farm

WA6

DELAMERE RD

FOREST LA

NORLEY RD

BEECH LA

TOWN FARM LA

HAMBLETTS HOLLOW

PITCHELLS HOLLOW

Pinewood Farm

Moy Park Farm

Flaxmere

Hatch Mere

Low Farm

PH

HATCHMERE PK

Hatchmere

CRABB LA

POST OFFICE LA

SCHOOL LA

THE SPINNEY

HIGH ST

MADDOCKS HILL

Norley CE Prim Sch

FINGER POST LA

Delamere Forest Sch

Delamere Forest Inn (PH)

Harthill Bank

ASHTON RD

Hunger Hill

Hart Hill

Claims Farm

Barnsbridge Gates

Forest Trail

Sandstone Trail

BLAKEMERE LA

Blakemere Moss

Delamere Forest Park

Windyhowe Farm

Fir Br...

P

P

Linmere Moss

Delamere Way

Delamere Forest Visitor Ctr

Forest Trail

CW8

Delamere

B5152

STATION RD

Relicks Moss

Burnt Wood

Eddisbury Lodge

Station Cottages

Works

CH

Sandstone Trail

Eddisbury Lodge Cottages

SALTERSFORD HALL LA

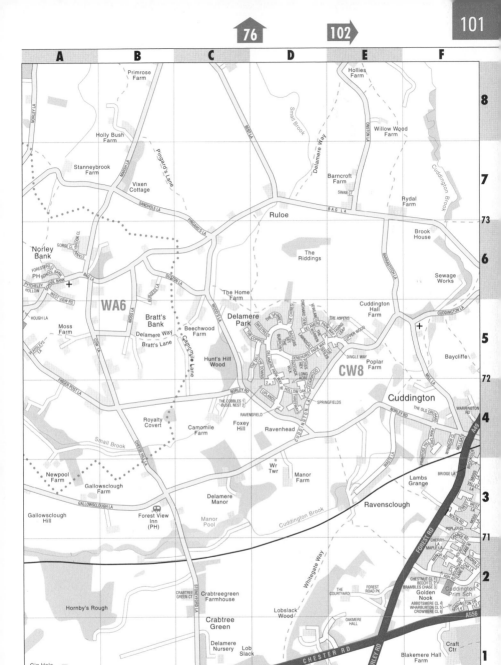

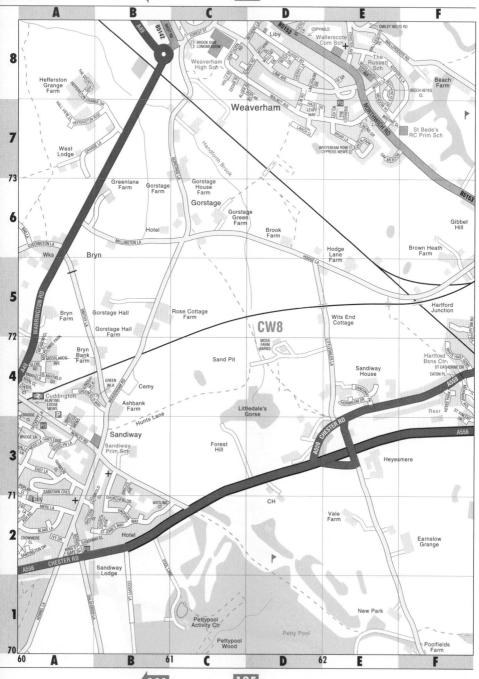

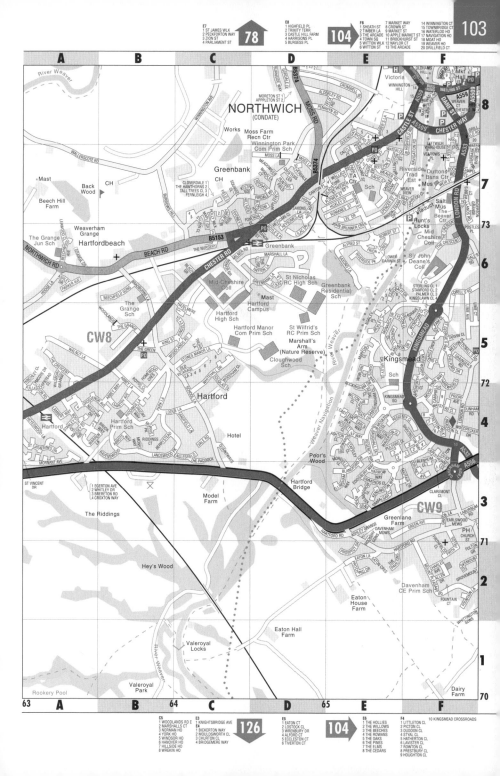

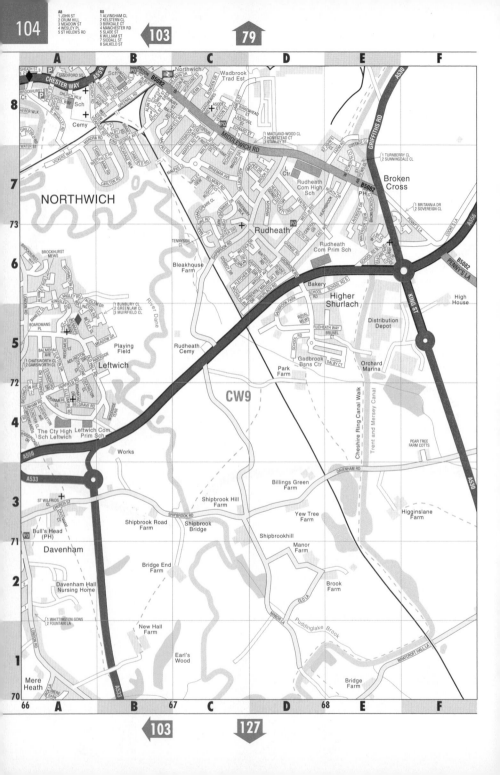

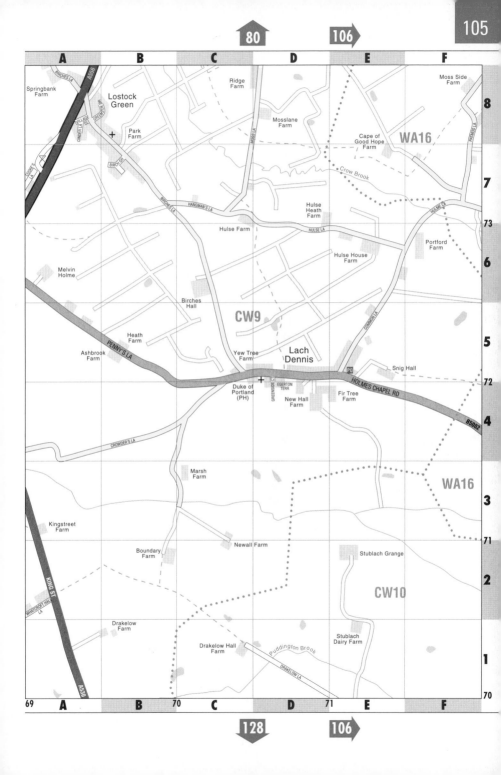

A **B** **C** **D** **E** **F**

8

Springbank
Farm

BIRCHES LA

A556

CHURCH VILLAGE CL

GREENACRE DR

Lostock
Green

Ridge
Farm

Mosslane
Farm

MOSS LA

Moss Side
Farm

Cape of
Good Hope
Farm

WA16

FLATTERS LA

Park
Farm

BIRCHS

COOKE'S LA

Crow Brook

7

HOLME LA

BIRCHES LA

HANGMAN'S LA

Hulse Heath
Farm

73

Hulse Farm

HULSE LA

Hulse House
Farm

Portford
Farm

6

Melvin
Holme

Birches
Hall

CW9

Heath
Farm

COMMON LA

5

Ashbrook
Farm

PENNY'S LA

Yew Tree
Farm

Lach
Dennis

Snig Hall

72

Duke of
Portland
(PH)

GREENSIDE CL

EGERTON
TERR

HOLMES CHAPEL RD

New Hall
Farm

Fir Tree
Farm

4

CROWDER'S LA

B5082

Marsh
Farm

3

Kingstreet
Farm

WA16

71

KING ST

Boundary
Farm

Newall Farm

Stublach Grange

CW10

2

WHATCROFT HALL
LA

A530

Drakelow
Farm

Drakelow Hall
Farm

Puddington Brook

DRAKELOW LA

Stublach
Dairy Farm

1

69

70

71

70

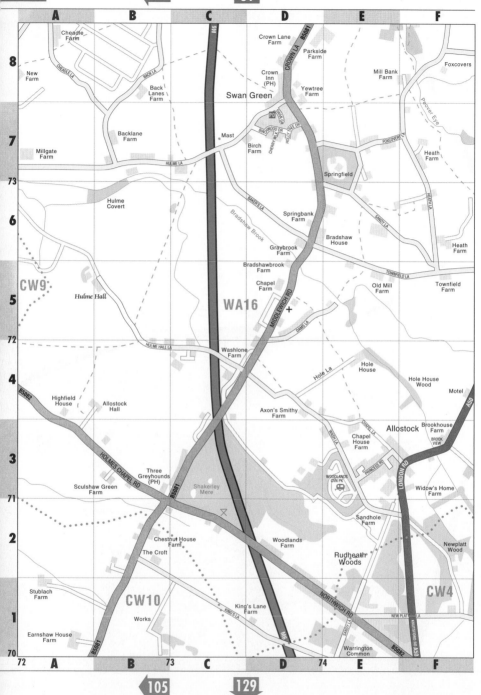

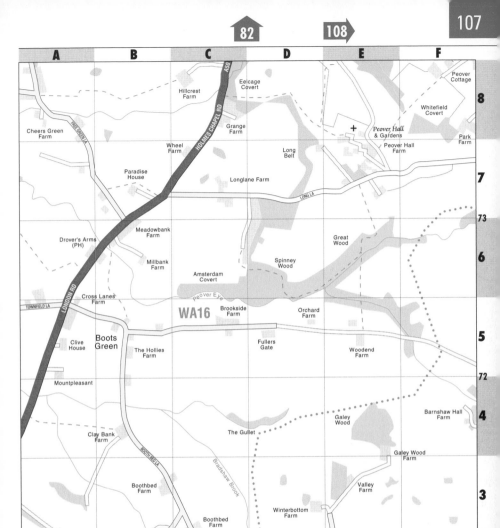

A   B   C   D   E   F

Peover
Cottage

Hillcrest
Farm

Eelcage
Covert

Whitefield
Covert

8

Cheers Green
Farm

Grange
Farm

Peover Hall
& Gardens

Park
Farm

Wheel
Farm

HOLMES CHAPEL RD

A50

FREE GREEN LA

Long
Belt

Peover Hall
Farm

7

Paradise
House

Longlane Farm

LONG LA

73

Meadowbank
Farm

Great
Wood

6

Drover's Arms
(PH)

Millbank
Farm

Spinney
Wood

Amsterdam
Covert

Peover Eye

LONDON RD

Cross Lanes
Farm

WA16

Brookside
Farm

Orchard
Farm

TOWNFIELD LA

Boots
Green

Fullers
Gate

Woodend
Farm

5

Clive
House

The Hollies
Farm

72

Mountpleasant

Barnshaw Hall
Farm

4

Clay Bank
Farm

The Gullet

Galey
Wood

Galey Wood
Farm

BOOTH BED LA

Bradshaw Brook

3

Boothbed
Farm

Valley
Farm

Boothbed
Farm

Winterbottom
Farm

CW4

71

Hales
Pasture

Meadow Bank
Farm

Barnshaw Bank
Farm

2

BRICK BANK LA

Shear Brook

MILL LA

Millbank
Farm

Brickbank
Farm

Swanwick Hall
Farm

The
Bongs

Newplatt
Wood

Newplatt
Farm

Goostrey

1

HARRISON DR

BIRCH TREE LA

LEA AVE

FOREST AVE

MEADOW AVE

WOOD LA

EATON LA

SWANWICK CL

DANE LA

WILLOW LA

SHEARBROOK LA

FREE PEASE DR

MAIN RD

MANOR
AVE

BROWNFIELD CRES

CHURCH BANK

Sch

NEW PLATT LA

70

75   A   B   76   C   D   77   E   F

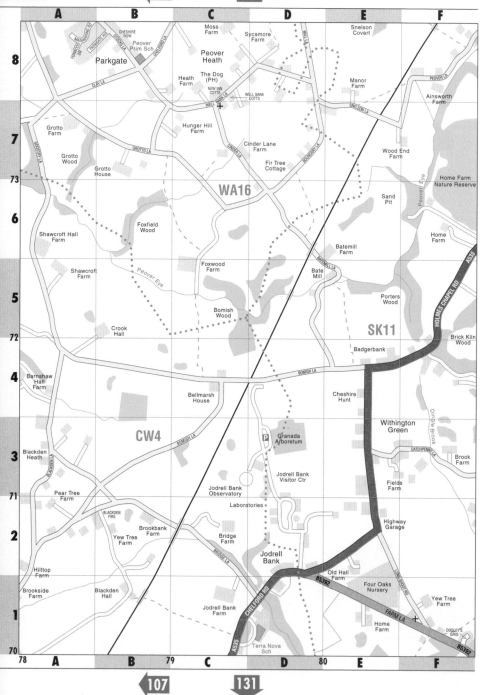

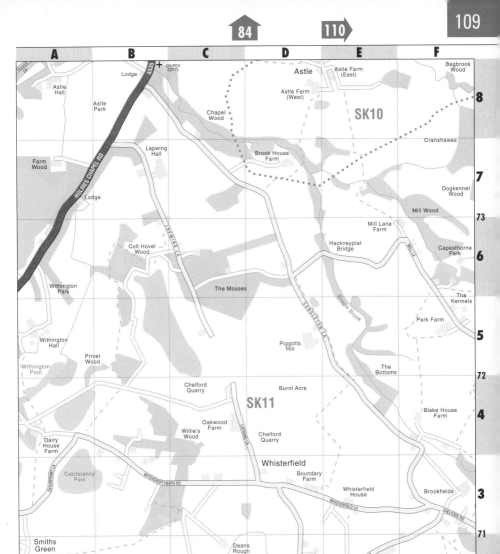

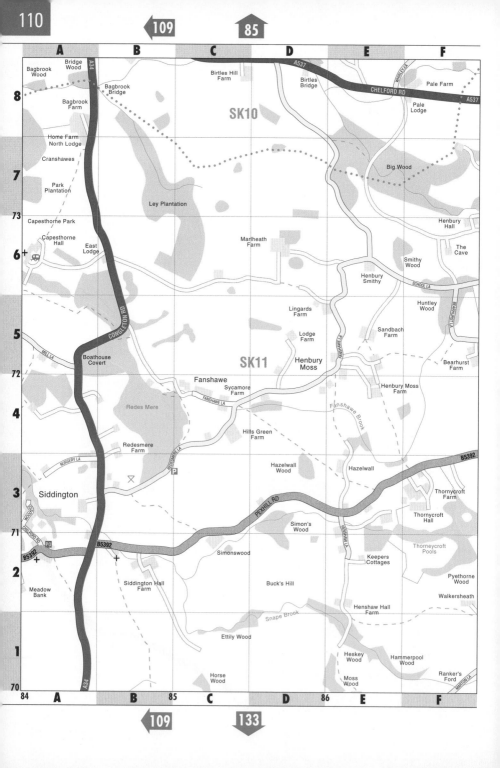

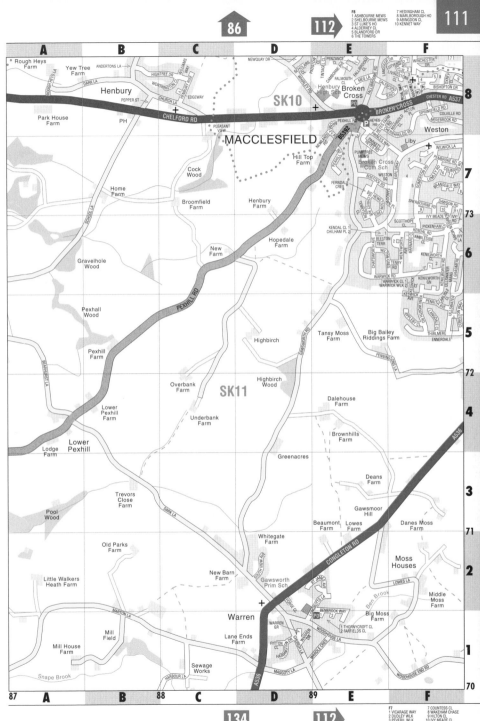

86

112

111

F8
1 ASHBOURNE MEWS
2 SHELBOURNE MEWS
3 ST LUKE'S HO
4 ALDERNEY CL
5 BLANDFORD DR
6 THE TOWERS

7 HEDINGHAM CL
8 MARLBOROUGH HO
9 ABINGDON CL
10 KENNET WAY

MACCLESFIELD

SK10

SK11

Henbury

Broken Cross

Weston

Warren

Moss Houses

F7
1 VICARAGE WAY
2 DUDLEY WLK
3 PEVERIL WLK
4 PORTLAND WLK
5 SOMERTON CL
6 WARDOUR CL

7 COUNTESS CL
8 WAKEHAM CHASE
9 HILTON CL
10 IVY MEADE CL
11 DAWSON CL

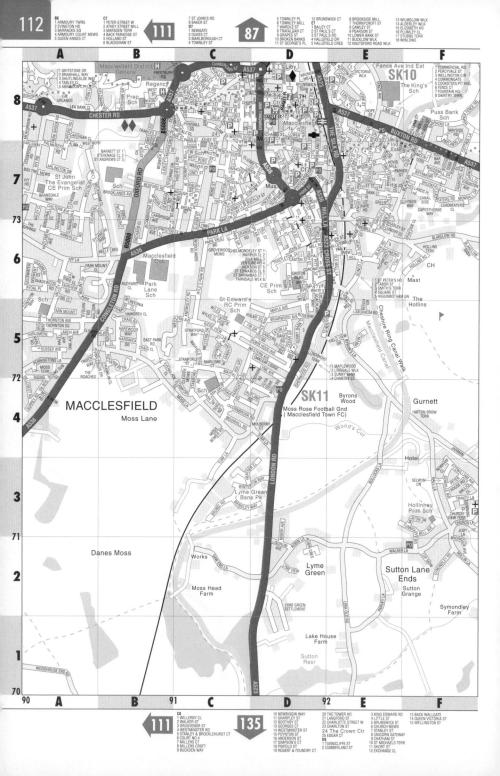

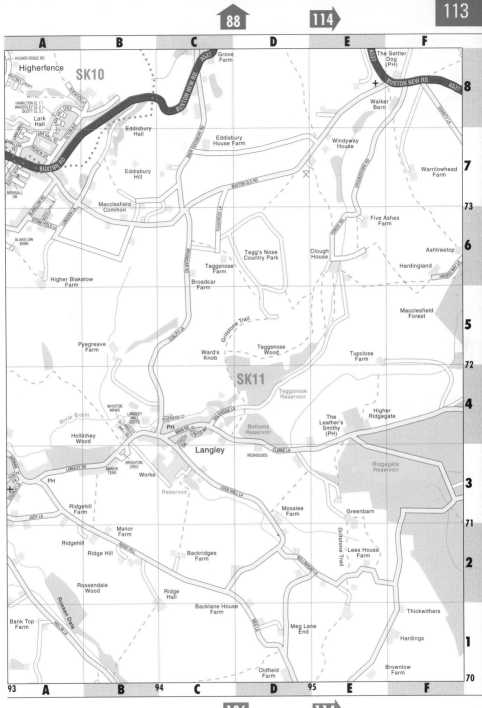

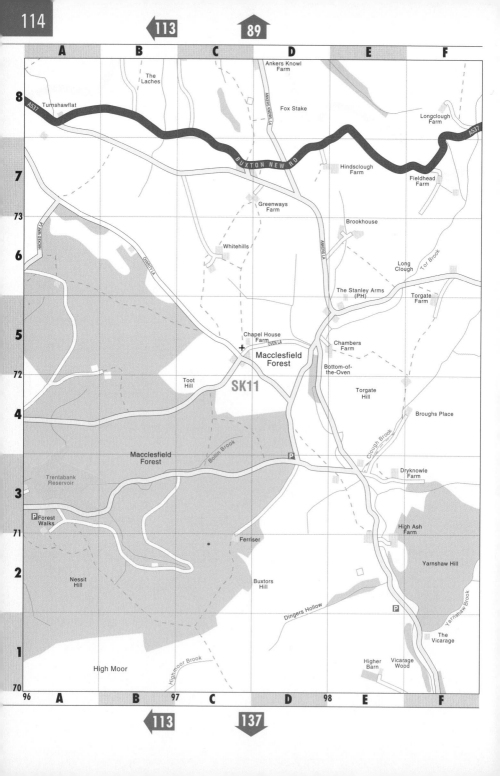

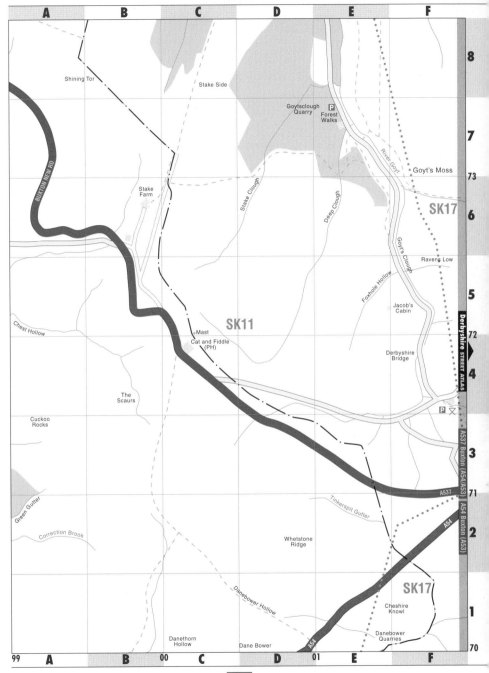

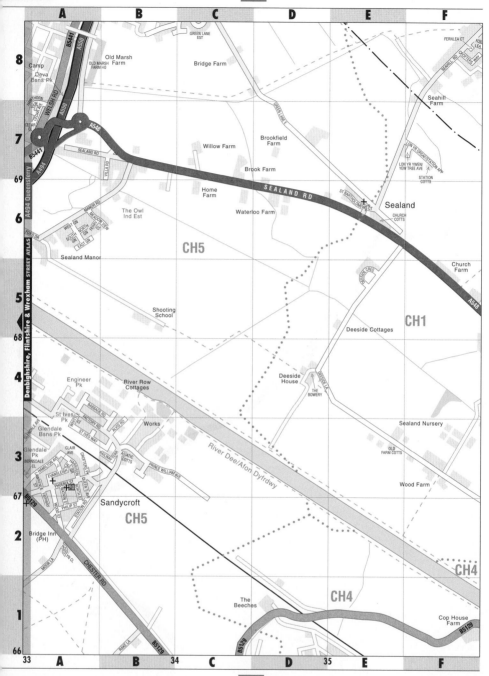

Denbighshire, Flintshire & Wrexham STREET ATLAS

94
118
140
118

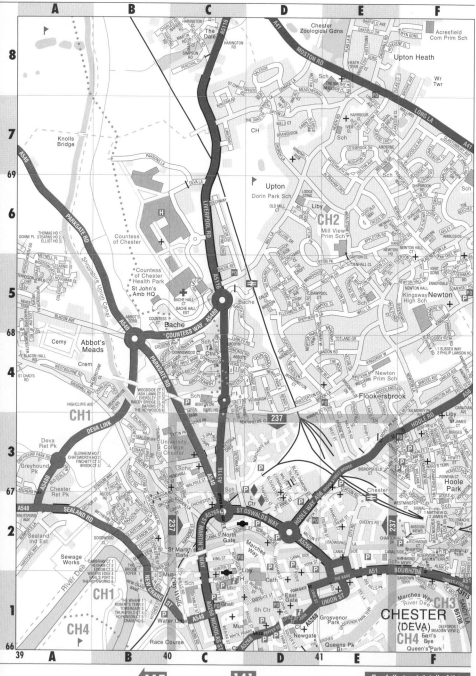

For full street detail of the highlighted area see page 237.

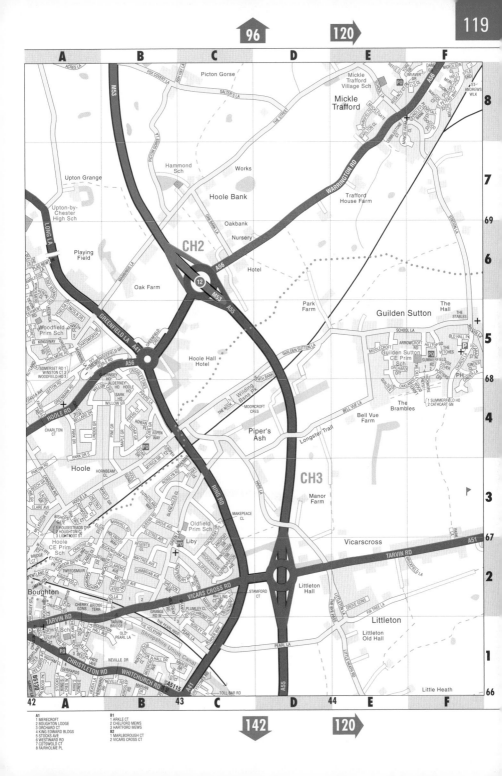

A1
1 MERECROFT
2 BOUGHTON LODGE
3 ORCHARD CT
4 KING EDWARD BLDGS
5 STOCKS AVE
6 WESTWARD RD
7 COTSWOLD CT
8 FAIRHOLME PL

B1
1 ARKLE CT
2 CHELFORD MEWS
3 HARTFORD MEWS
B2
1 MARLBOROUGH CT
2 VICARS CROSS CT

119
97

A B C D E F

8

LC

Holme Farm

Broomhill La

Broomhill

Salters Brook

Ardmore

Broom Hill

The Avenue

CH2

7

The Croft

Ferma La

Barrow Hill

Beddingtons La

Barrowmore Est

Heath Farm

69

Hollowmoor Heath

6

Greysfield

Long Looms

Hawkins Way

Lakepits La

Great Barrow

Glebe Rd

Manor Pk

Heath La

Barrow CE Prim Sch

Greenfields Lodge

Ferma La

Longster Trail

Old Stack Yd

New Farm

Barrow Hall Farm

Manor Dr

Farm Ct

Mill La

+

Barrow Mill

Mill Lane Cotts

5

Oxen Bridge

Barrow La

Hill Farm House

Cinder La

Milton Brook Lodge

Milton Brook

Barrow Mill

68

The Steadings

The Byatts

Weaver La

Hillview Farm

CH3

4

River Gowy

Stamford Bridge

Stamford Bridge Inn (PH)

B5132

Lansdowne Rd

3

Tarvin Rd

CH

The Limes

Holme Bank

A51

67

Nursery

Stamford Heath

Gowy Bank Farm

Holme St

Green La

Stamford Mill

Mill Lane

Abbeyfield

A51

2

Stamford Hollows Farm

Cotton La

Holme-street Hall

Hollows Farm

1

Stamford La

Birch Bank Farm

Cotton Hall

66

45 A B 46 C D 47 E F

119
143

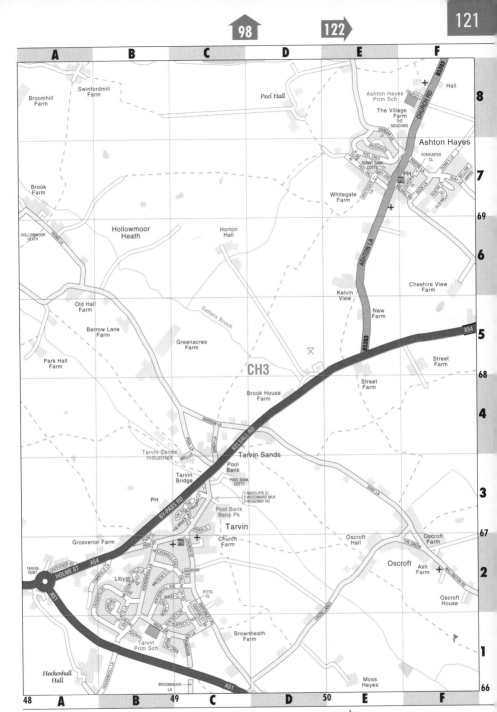

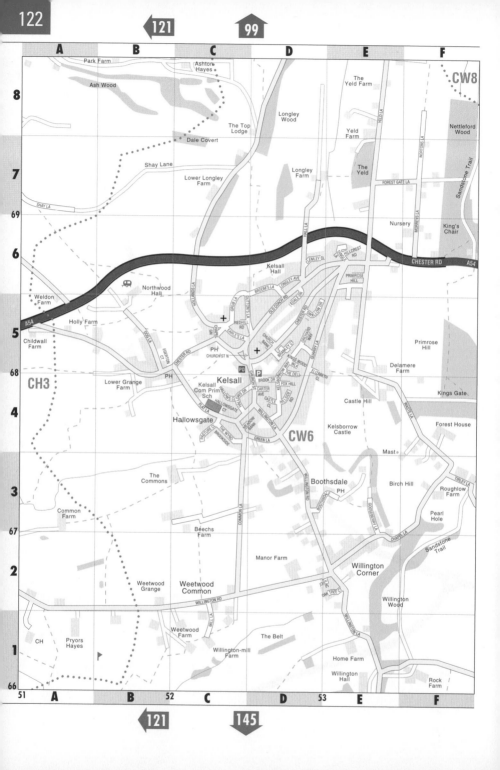

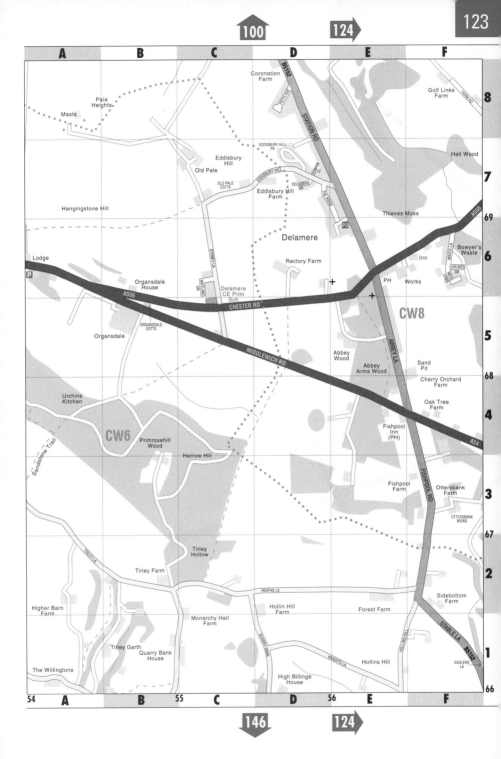

100 →
124 →

A B C D E F

8

Coronation
Farm

Golf Links
Farm

FARM RD

B5152

Pale
Heights

Masts

7

Eddisbury
Hill
Old Pale

EDDISBURY HILL
PK

Hall Wood

STATION RD

EDDISBURY HILL

Eddisbury Hill
Farm

DELAMERE
DR

TOWMAN
CL.

THE RISE

A556

69

Hangingstone Hill

OLD PALE
COTTS

Thieves Moss

PO

Delamere

Bowyer's
Waste

6

Lodge

Rectory Farm

Inn

KAYSITE
CRES

CHIMES
DR

P

Organsdale
House

+

PH

Works

STONEY LA

MILL RD

Delamere
CE Prim
Sch

+

A556

Organsdale

CHESTER RD

CW8

ORGANSDALE
COTTS

5

Organsdale

MIDDLEWICH RD

Abbey
Wood

Abbey
Arms Wood

Sand
Pit

ABBEY LA

Cherry Orchard
Farm

68

Urchins
Kitchen

Oak Tree
Farm

4

Sandstone Trail

CW6

Primrosehill
Wood

Harrow Hill

Fishpool
Inn
(PH)

A54

Fishpool
Farm

Ottersbank
Farm

3

FISHPOOL RD

OTTERSBANK
MEWS

67

Tirley
Hollow

Tirley Farm

TIRLEY LA

2

HEATHS LA

Higher Barn
Farm

Monarchy Hall
Farm

Hollin Hill
Farm

Forest Farm

Sidebottom
Farm

STABLE LA

1

Tirley Garth

Quarry Bank
House

DUSTY BANK

THE OLD PD RD

B5152

The Willingtons

KNIGHTS LA

High Billinge
House

Hollins Hill

SADLERS
LA

66

54   A   B   55   C   D   56   E   F

146 →
124 →

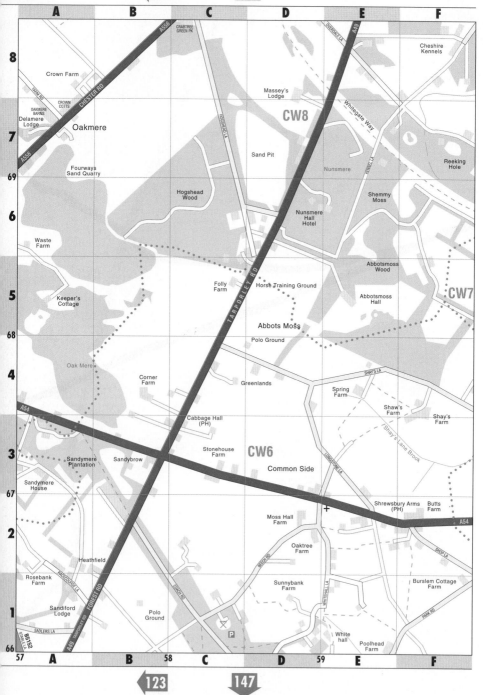

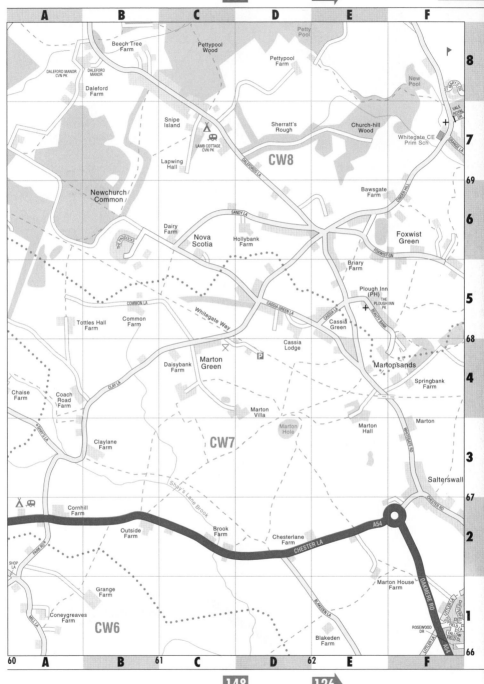

102
126

A B C D E F

8
7
69
6
5
68
4
3
67
2
1
66

Petty Pool

Beech Tree Farm

Pettypool Wood

Pettypool Farm

DALEFORD MANOR CVN PK
DALEFORD MANOR

Daleford Farm

New Pool

Snipe Island

Sherratt's Rough

Church-hill Wood

VALE ROYAL DR

Whitegate CE Prim Sch

GRANGE LA

LAMB COTTAGE CVN PK

Lapwing Hall

CW8

DALEFORDS LA

Newchurch Common

Bawsgate Farm

SANDY LA

Dairy Farm

Nova Scotia

Hollybank Farm

Foxwist Green

FOXWIST GN

ORDER HILL

THE PADDOCKS

Briary Farm

Plough Inn (PH)
THE PLOUGH INN PK

BEAUTY BANK

COMMON LA

Whitegate Way

CASSIA GREEN LA

CASSIA LA

Cassia Green

Tottles Hall Farm

Common Farm

Cassia Lodge

Martonsands

Chaise Farm

Coach Road Farm

CLAY LA

Daisybank Farm

Marton Green

P

Springbank Farm

SHAY LA

Claylane Farm

Marton Villa

Marton Hole

Marton Hall

Marton

WHITEGATE RD

CW7

Salterswall

CHESTER RD

Shay's Lane Brook

67

Cornhill Farm

Outside Farm

Brook Farm

Chesterlane Farm

A54

CHESTER LA

PARK RDW

SHOP LA

Marton House Farm

DARNHERE RD

Grange Farm

CW6

Coneygreaves Farm

MILL LA

Blakeden Farm

BLAKEDEN LA

ROSEWOOD DR

LITTLE LA

A54

60 A 61 B C 62 D E F 66

148
126

125
103

	A	B	C	D	E	F

8

CH

Vale Royal

VALE ROYAL CTYD

Monk's Well

Eaton Bank Wood

Moulton Sch

P.O.

CW8

Valeroyal Park

CW9
Moulton

Whitegate

ABBEY CL

7

Quesse Wood

Moultonbank Farm

GRANGE LA

69

Mill Lane Cottages

MILL LA

Parkside Farm

Newbridge Wood

MEADOW HOME PK

VALE ROYAL RIVER PARK CVN SITE

Hillside Farm

NI DDRIES CT

6

Bark House

Bradford Mill

Foxwist Green Farm

Pettypool Brook

Bradford Wood Farm

Salt Mine

5

Meadow House Farm

P.O.

SCHOOL RD

Meadowbank

68

Brook House

GRANGE LA

Works

4

Gale Green Farm

Whitegate Way

CW7

Weaver Navigation

3

Bradfordwood

Catsclough

Cat's Clough

Sewage Works

BRADFORD RD

Wharton Ret Pk

HELMDON CL 1
DOULTON CL 2

Mills

KNIGHT'S GRANGE (Sports Complex)

CH

SANDRINGHAM CL

WADES LA

SHEPHERDS FOLD DR

ENNERDALE

A5018

67

MEADOW CL 1
AMBLESIDE CL 2
ESK DALE CL 3
TURNBERRY CL 4
PRESTWICK CL 5
DALMAHOY CL 6
MUIRFIELD MEWS 7

Roehurst Lane

VERDIN'S CUT

Nat Lane Ret Pk

Wharton Ind Est
Superstore

WELLFIELD
BEAULIEU AVE

2

Littler

NIXON DR

KINGSLEY WLK

ASTON AVE

The Verdin High Sch

1 LANGDALE CL
2 KESWICK CL
3 STAVELEY DR
4 CARTMEL CL
5 KENTMERE AVE
6 ARNSIDE CL

WINSFORD

WHARTON PARK RD

A5018

Barton Stadium

1

WOODCOTT AVE

Sch

SANDYMERE CL

Mid Cheshire Coll

Sch

Guildhall

Civic Hall

Lib

Winsford Cross Sh Ctr

HIGH ST

A54

CORONATION AVE

HIGH ST

Jun Sch

CURZON GR

66

CHIRK

SPRINGBANK CRES 1
GENEVA RD 2

Mkt

THE DRUMBER

CONINGSBY DR

RIVER WEAVER

Cvn Pk

STATION RD

A54

	A					

63 · A · B · **64** · C · D · **65** · E · F

125
149

A1
1 BADGERS CL
2 OTTERS BANK
3 REDSTONE DR
4 BECKENHAM GR
5 FINSBURY WLK

D1
1 QUEEN'S PAR
2 FOUNTAIN CT
3 THE ROW
4 DINGLE WLK
5 JUBILEE WAY

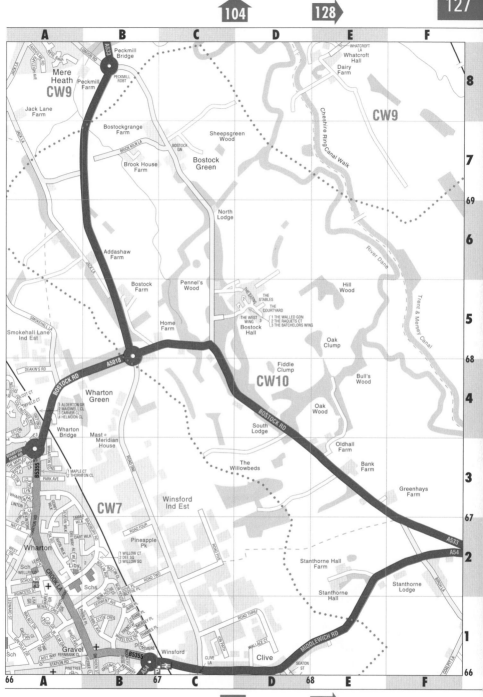

104

128

150

128

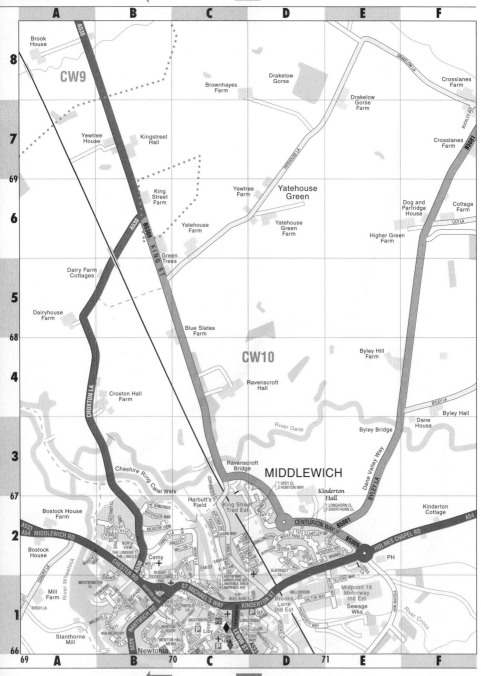

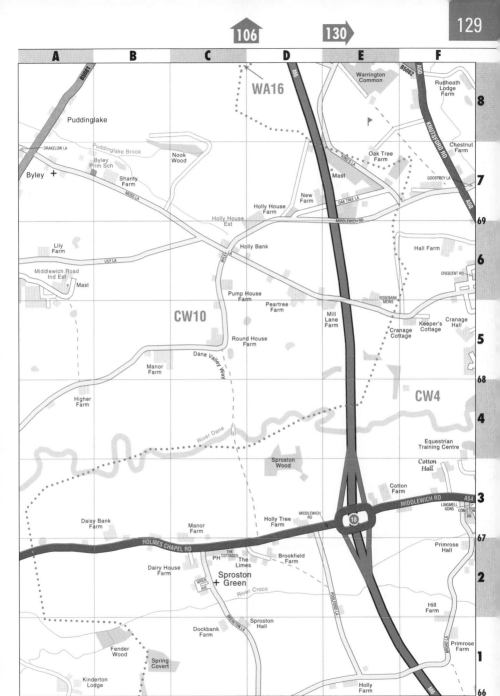

A   B   C   D   E   F

8
7
69
6
68
5
4
3
67
2
1
66

Puddinglake

DRAKELOW LA

Byley

Byley Prim Sch

Shanty Farm

Nook Wood

Puddinglake Brook

MOSS LA

WA16

Warrington Common

Oak Tree Farm

Mast

Rudheath Lodge Farm

Chestnut Farm

GOOSTREY LA

Lily Farm

LILY LA

Middlewich Road Ind Est

Mast

Holly House Est

Holly Bank

New Farm

Holly House Farm

Oak Tree Farm

OAK TREE LA

MIDDLEWICH RD

Hall Farm

CRESCENT RD

CW10

Pump House Farm

Peartree Farm

Mill Lane Farm

ROSEBANK MEWS

Cranage Cottage

Keeper's Cottage

Cranage Hall

Round House Farm

Dane Valley Way

Manor Farm

Higher Farm

River Dane

CW4

Equestrian Training Centre

Sproston Wood

Cotton Hall

Cotton Farm

Daisy Bank Farm

Manor Farm

Holly Tree Farm

MIDDLEWICH RD

18

MIDDLEWICH RD   A54

LINGMELL GDNS

CONISTON DR

Primrose Hall

HOLMES CHAPEL RD

Dairy House Farm

PH

THE COTTAGES

The Limes

Sproston Green

Brookfield Farm

River Croco

FOOLROOD LA

Hill Farm

Dockbank Farm

Sproston Hall

Fender Wood

Spring Covert

Kinderton Lodge

Holly Farm

Primrose Farm

72   A   B   73   C   D   74   E   F

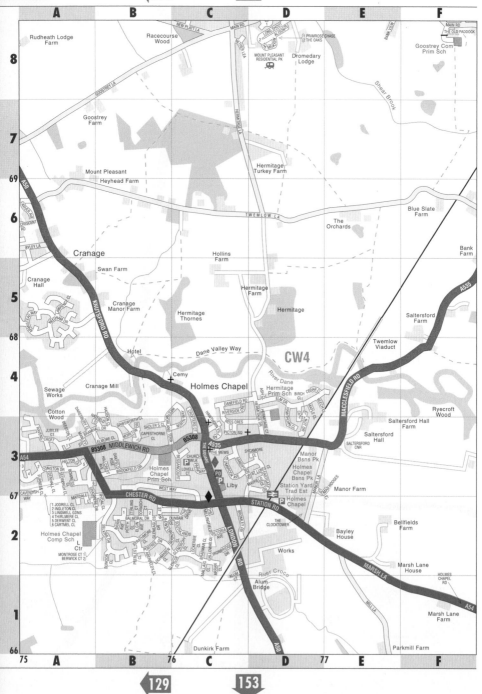

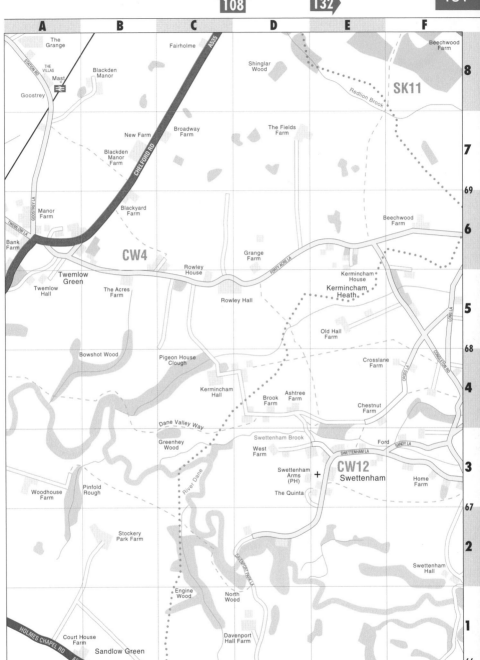

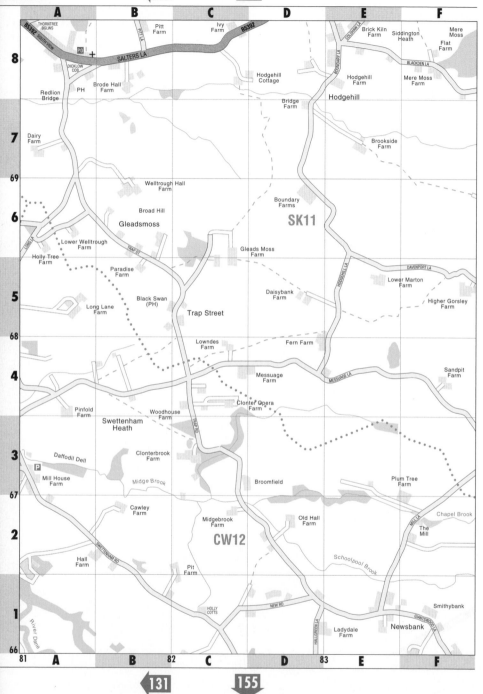

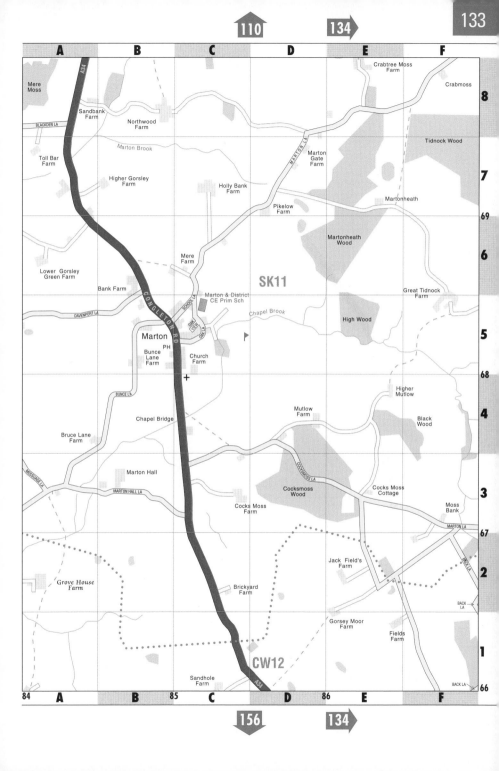

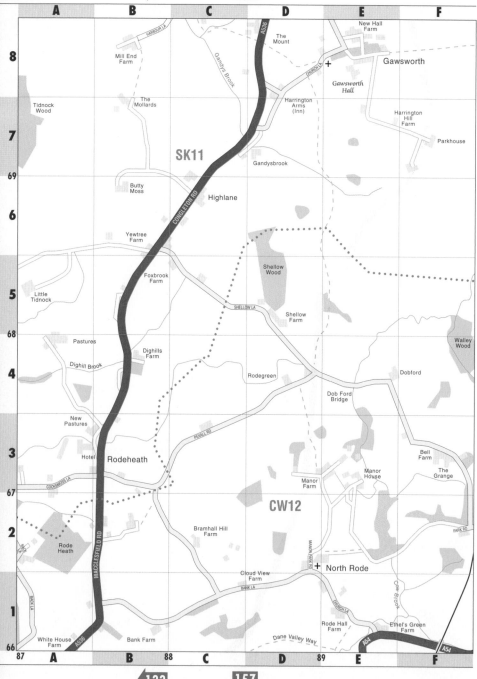

| A | B | C | D | E | F |

8

Mill End
Farm

HARBOUR LA

The Mount

New Hall
Farm

A536

Gandys Brook

Gawsworth

Harrington
Arms
(Inn)

CHURCH LA

Gawsworth
Hall

Tidnock
Wood

The
Mollards

7

SK11

Harrington
Hill
Farm

Parkhouse

69

Gandysbrook

Butty
Moss

CONGLETON RD

Highlane

6

Yewtree
Farm

Shellow
Wood

Foxbrook
Farm

5

Little
Tidnock

SHELLOW LA

Shellow
Farm

68

Pastures

Dighills
Farm

Walley
Wood

Dighill Brook

4

New
Pastures

Rodegreen

Dob Ford
Bridge

Dobford

Bell
Farm

Hotel

Rodeheath

3

PEXALL RD

Manor
House

The
Grange

COCKSMOSS LA

67

CW12

Manor
Farm

Rode
Heath

2

Bramhall Hill
Farm

MACCLESFIELD RD

MANOR PARK RD

PARK RD

North Rode

Cow Brook

1

Cloud View
Farm

BANK LA

BACK LA

Rode Hall
Farm

Ethel's Green
Farm

A54

A536

66

White House
Farm

Bank Farm

Dane Valley Way

A54

87

| A | B | C | D | E | F |
| | 88 | | 89 | |

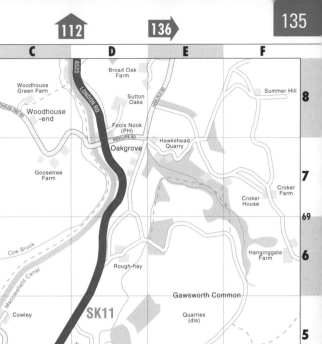

| | A | B | C | D | E | F |

8

Mount Farm
Fodens Farm
Woodhouse Green Farm
Woodhouse -end
Broad Oak Farm
Sutton Oaks
Summer Hill

WOODHOUSE END RD

7

Woodlands Farm
Brereton Farm
Goosetree Farm
Fools Nook (PH)
RADCLIFFE RD
Oakgrove
Hawkshead Quarry
Croker Farm
Croker House

LONDON RD
A523
LEEK OLD RD

69

Cowbrook Farm
Cow Brook
Cowbrook La
Rough-hay
Hanginggate Farm

6

Macclesfield Canal
Cowley
Whitemoor
SK11
Gawsworth Common
Quarries (dis)

5

Cheshire Ring Canal Wlk
Crowholt
Whitemoor Hollow
Whitemoor Hill

68

4

Stonyfold

Bosley Brook

3

Warehouse
Marshhead
The Hollins
Brooks Farm

BROOKS LA

67

Bull Gate
CW12
Gibbons Farm
Primrose Bank
Dawsons Farm

2

FELTON RD
Smithygreen
FOLD LA
BOARS LEIGH PK
Bosley Locks
Greatoak Farm
Broadoak
Pyeash
Bosley Reservoir
Sourbutts Farm
DUMBERS A54

1

Wheatsheaf
Blakefield Farm
A523
LAKESIDE
A54
Ladder Stile

66

| 90 | A | B | 91 | C | D | 92 | E | F |

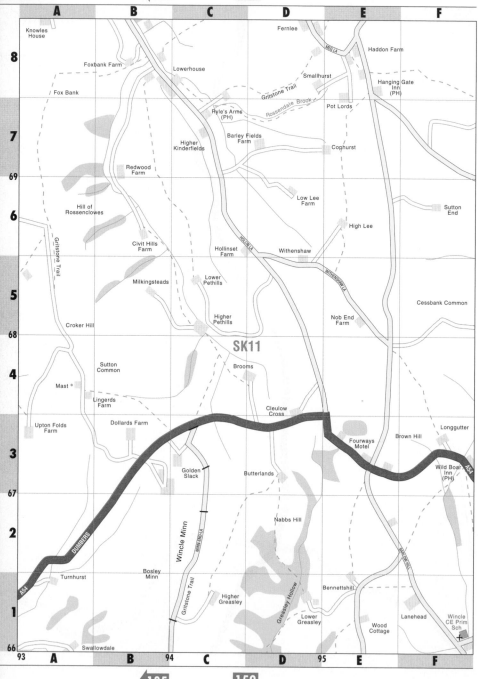

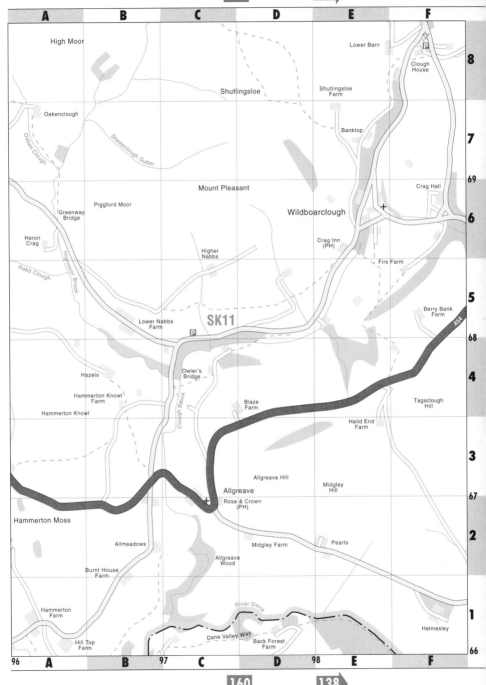

A B C D E F

8

High Moor

Lower Barn

Clough
House

P

Oakenclough

Shutlingsloe

Shutlingsloe
Farm

7

Banktop

Oaken Clough

Sheepclough Gutter

69

Crag Hall

Mount Pleasant

Wildboarclough

6

Piggford Moor

Greenway
Bridge

Crag Inn
(PH)

Heron
Crag

Higher
Nabbs

Firs Farm

Highmoor Brook

Rabb Clough

5

Berry Bank
Farm

Lower Nabbs
Farm

SK11

A54

P

68

Hazels

Owler's
Bridge

4

Hammerton Knowl
Farm

Blaze
Farm

Tagsclough
Hill

Hammerton Knowl

Clough Brook

Heild End
Farm

3

Allgreave Hill

Midgley
Hill

Allgreave

67

Hammerton Moss

Rose & Crown
(PH)

Allmeadows

Midgley Farm

Pearls

2

Burnt House
Farm

Allgreave
Wood

Hammerton
Farm

River Dane

1

Helmesley

Hill Top
Farm

Dane Valley Way

Back Forest
Farm

66

96 A B 97 C D 98 E F

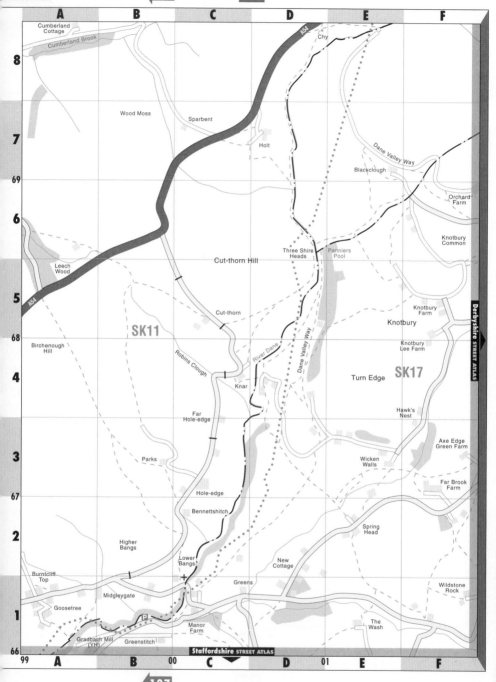

Cumberland Cottage

Cumberland Brook

Wood Moss

Sparbent

Holt

A54

Chy

Dane Valley Way

Blackclough

Orchard Farm

Leech Wood

Cut-thorn Hill

Three Shire Heads

Panniers Pool

Knotbury Common

A54

Cut-thorn

River Dane

Dane Valley Way

Knotbury Farm

Knotbury

SK11

Birchenough Hill

Robins Clough

Knar

Turn Edge

Knotbury Lee Farm

SK17

Far Hole-edge

Hawk's Nest

Axe Edge Green Farm

Parks

Wicken Walls

Far Brook Farm

Hole-edge

Bennettshitch

Higher Bangs

Lower Bangs

Spring Head

Burntcliff Top

Midgleygate

New Cottage

Greens

Wildstone Rock

Goosetree

P

The Wash

Manor Farm

Gradbach Mill (YH)

Greenstitch

Derbyshire STREET ATLAS

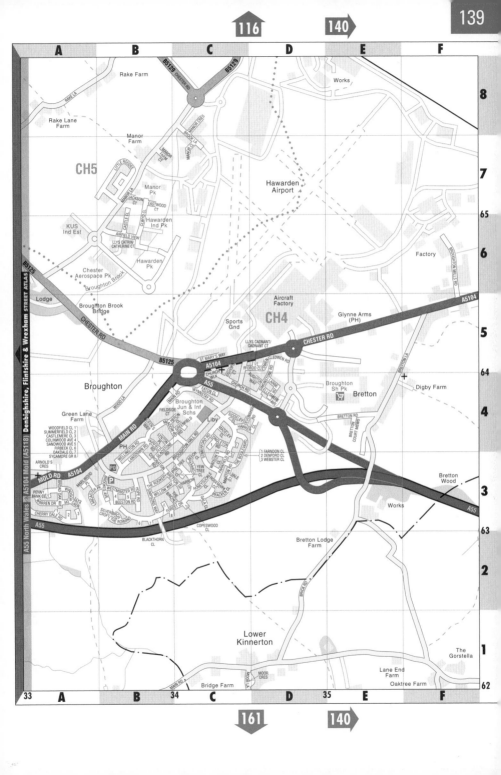

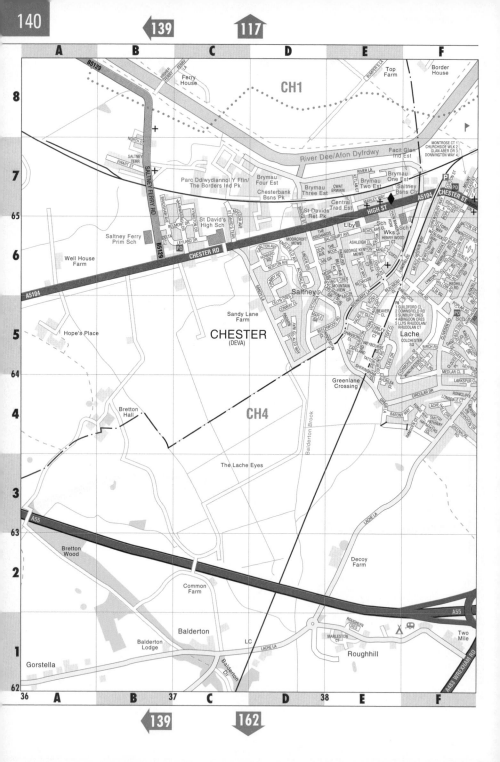

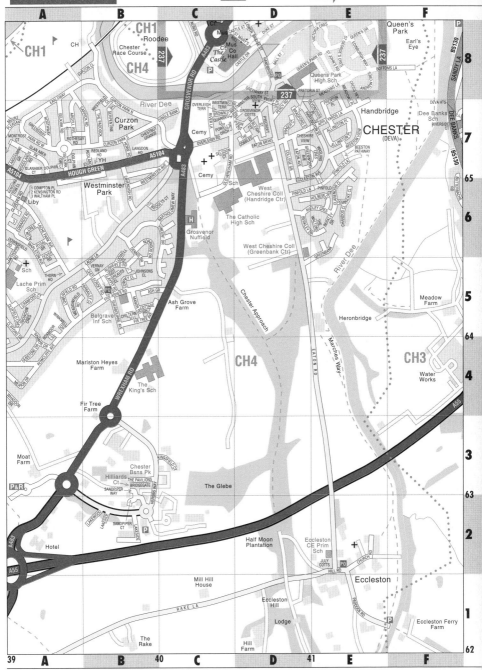

For full street detail of the highlighted area see page 237.

118

142

CH1

CH1

CH

CH1
Roodee
Chester Race Course

CH4

Queen's Park

Earl's Eye

B5130

8

Mus
Co
Hall

The Castle

237

GROSVENOR RD

A483

NURSERY LA

CASTLE ST

LOWER BRIDGE ST

DUKE ST

ST MARY'S HILL

CASTLE DR

MILL ST

Queens Dr

ST OLAVE ST

EDINBURGH WAY

BOTTOMS LA

237

Queens Park High Sch

237

River Dee

OVERLEIGH TERR

WESTMINSTER TERR

GREENWAY ST

SOUTH VIEW

GROSVENOR COTTS

PRETORIA ST

PIERLTON

Handbridge

Deva Hts

Dee Banks Sch

DEVA HTS

B5130

Curzon Park

EAST SWAY

CURZON PARK N

WESTMINSTER

THE PADDOCK

ARGYLL AVE

SELKIRK RD

CURZON PARK S

RINGLE BANK

INGLE BANK

OVERLEIGH RD

BROWN'S

DIAMOND

POWELL

THE COBBLES

EATON MEWS

CHESHIRE VIEW

COLLEGE DR

PIERLTON

BRANDFILL

APPLEYARDS LA

ALLINGTON PL

COLLEGE AVE

PILGRIM

CHESTER (DEVA)

Riverside Dr

BEESTON PATHWAY

DEE BANKS

BUTTERBACH

RD

7

MOUNT PLEASANT

GREENBURY

OVERYWAY

ROTHESAY RD

REDLAND HO

DOLPHIN CT

LANGDON

A5104

HOUGH GREEN

A5104

WESTMINSTER AVE

A483

WREXHAM WAY

SELDON CT

Cemy

Cemy

Sch

WEXHAM RD

West Cheshire Coll (Handridge Ctr)

PINFOLD LA

HOLBEIN

PEMBS

GREENBANK

65

1 COMPTON PL
2 KENSINGTON RD
3 WALTHAM PL

Liby

Westminster Park

CAVENDISH DR

BARTHOLOMEW WAY

The Catholic High Sch

AUDLEY CRES

BRISTOL

6

Sch

DOVER

THORN HO

JOHNSONS CL

ASH GR

H

Grosvenor Nuffield

West Cheshire Coll (Greenbank Ctr)

River Dee

VERNAY GN

FIVE ASHES RD

FIR TREES

Meadow Farm

5

Lache Prim Sch

Belgrave Inf Sch

CHILTERN

COTTAGE

Ash Grove Farm

Chester Approach

Heronbridge

64

Marlston Heyes Farm

WREXHAM RD

CH4

CH3

Water Works

4

The King's Sch

EATON RD

Marches Way

A55

Fir Tree Farm

3

Moat Farm

Chester Bsns Pk
THE PAVILIONS
BRIDGEGATE

KINGSFIELD CT

SANDPIPER WAY

The Glebe

63

P&R

Hilliards Ct

LAKEWOOD

LAKESIDE

SANDPIPER CT

LAKESIDE

P

Half Moon Plantation

Eccleston CE Prim Sch

JULY COTTS

HILL RD

CHURCH RD

PADDOCK RD

2

A483

Hotel

Mill Hill House

RAKE LA

Eccleston

Eccleston Hill

PO

Eccleston Ferry Farm

1

A55

Lodge

Hill Farm

P

The Rake

62

39

40

41

163

142

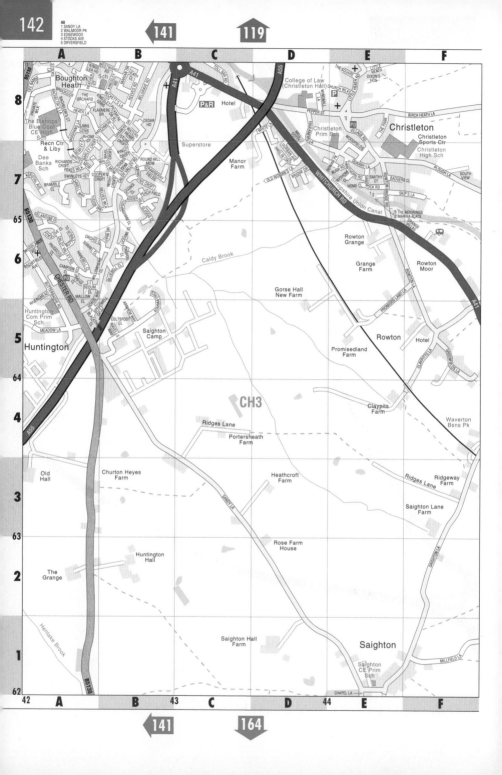

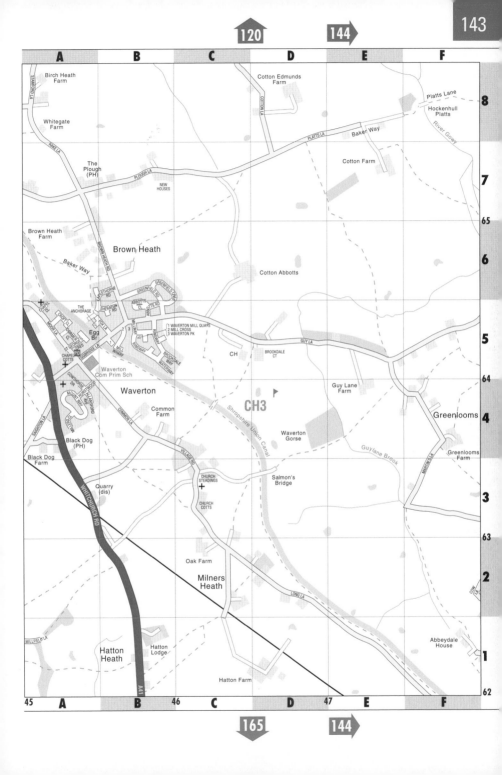

8
7
65
6
5
64
4
3
63
2
1
62

A　B　C　D　E　F

Platts Lane
Baker Way
HOCKENHILL LA
Broom Bank
AUSTINES HILL
PLATTS LA
Sheaf Farm
CROSS LANES
BIRCHENHEATH LA
A51
TARPORLEY RD
Duddon Hall
Old Moss
TARPORLEY RD
PLATTS LA
Duddon Heath
Cross Lanes Farm
Old Moss Farm
OLD MOSS LA
RYECROFT LA
Moss Lane Farm
The Moss
SIDE LA
Warren House Farm
BURTON LA
A51
Smithy Farm
GULF LA
Stapleford Hall
BROOKHOUSE LA
CW6
DUDDON HOOK LA
Ford Farm
Brookhouse Farm
CH3
Burton
Burton Hall
River Gowy
Waterless Brook
Upper Brookhouse Farm
Waterless Wood
MARTIN'S LA
COW LA
Upper Brereton Park Farm
PARK LA
Lane End Farm
LEADGATE LA
Brereton Park Farm
Leadgate Farm
Hargrave Hall
Church Farm
Hargrave
Mill Lane Farm
MILL LA
FISH LA
CHURCH LA
Lower Huxley Hall
Southley Brook
CHAPEL LA
Hargrave Farm

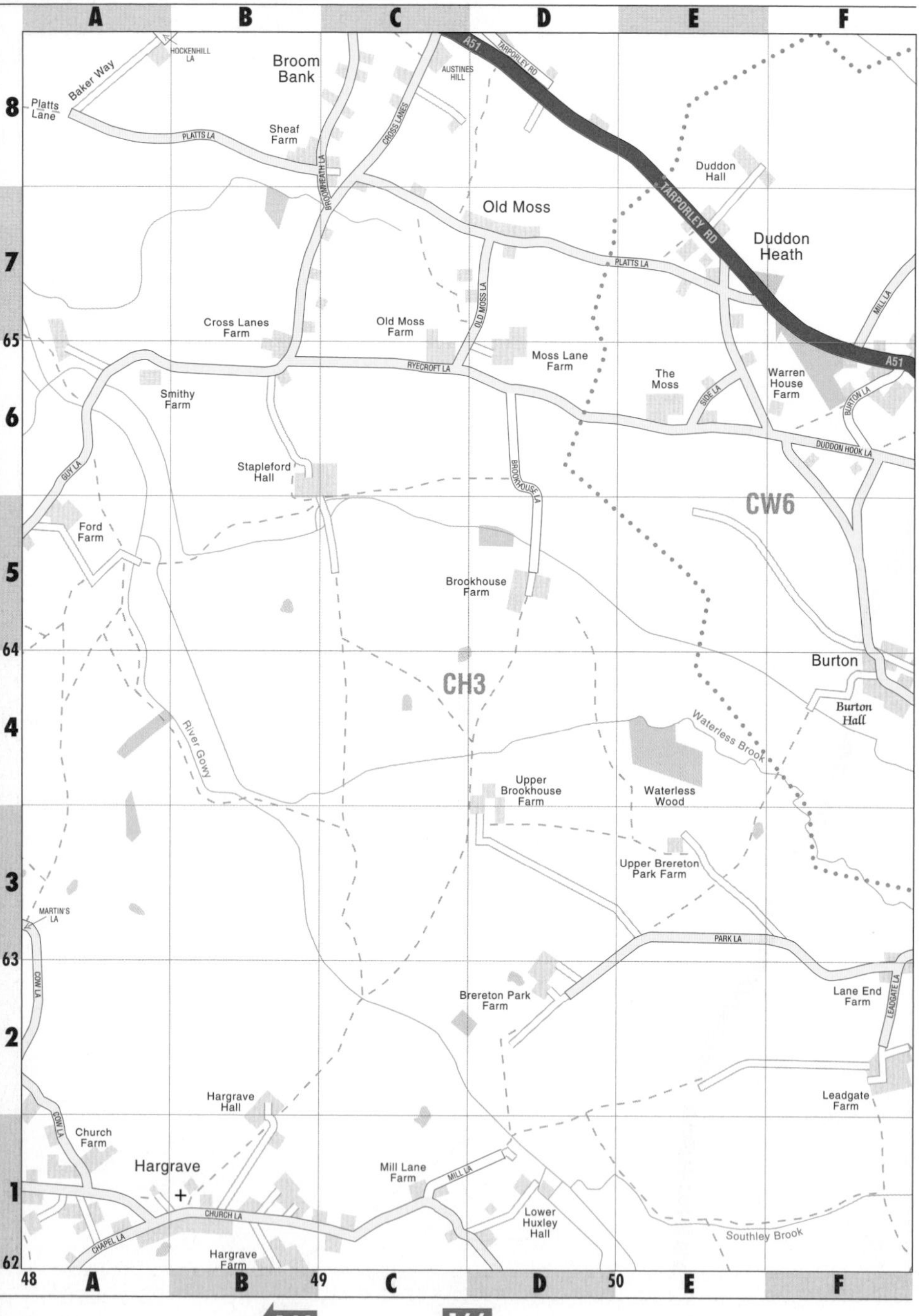

48　A　B　49　C　D　50　E　F

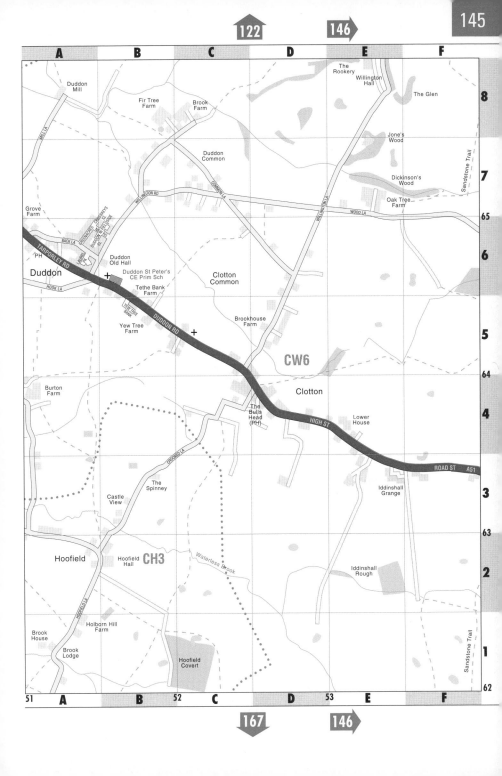

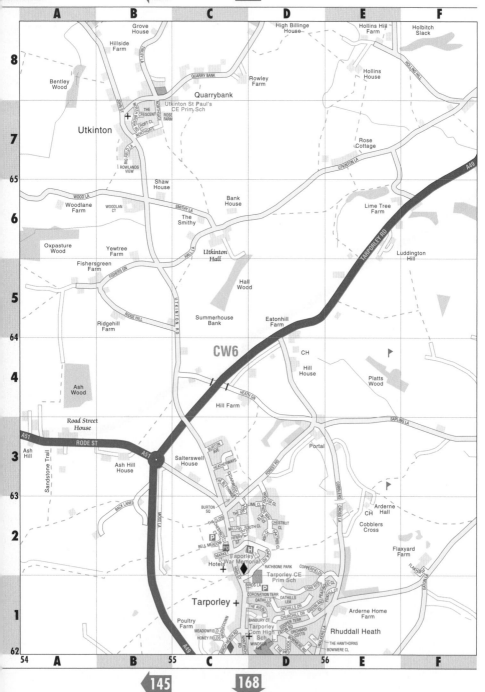

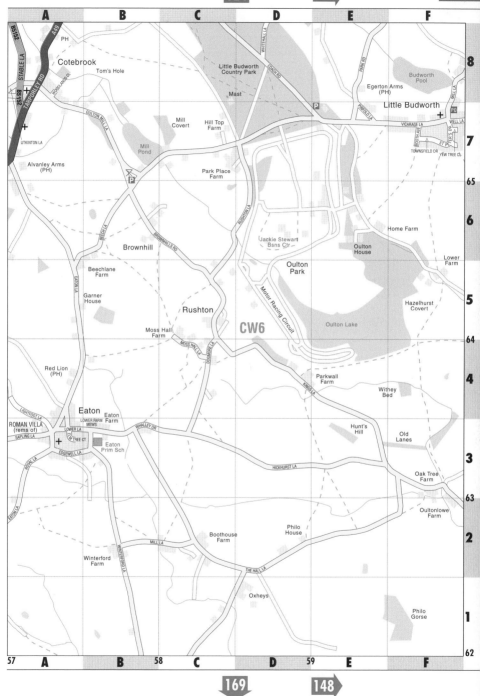

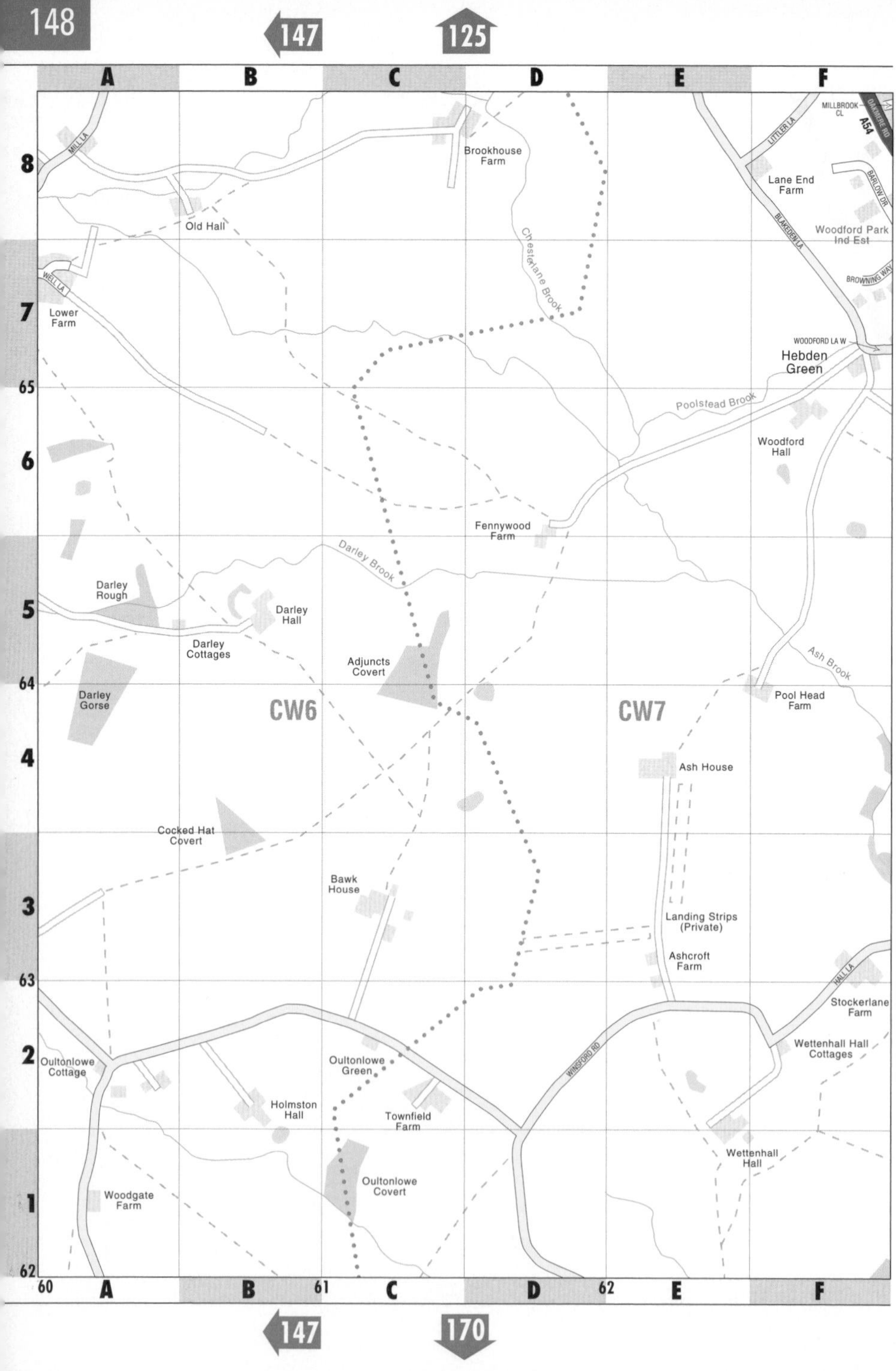

147
125

A B C D E F

8

Brookhouse
Farm

MILL LA

MILLBROOK
CL
A54
LITTLER LA
GRANGE RD
Lane End
Farm
Woodford Park
Ind Est
BARTON DR
BLAKEMERE LA
BROWNING WAY

Old Hall

Chesterlane Brook

7

WELL LA

Lower
Farm

WOODFORD LA W
Hebden
Green

65

Poolstead Brook

6

Woodford
Hall

Fennywood
Farm

Darley Brook

Ash Brook

Darley
Rough

5

Darley
Hall

Darley
Cottages

Adjuncts
Covert

CW6

CW7

Pool Head
Farm

64

Darley
Gorse

4

Ash House

Cocked Hat
Covert

Bawk
House

3

Landing Strips
(Private)

Ashcroft
Farm

MILL LA

Stockerlane
Farm

63

Oultonlowe
Cottage

2

Oultonlowe
Green

Holmston
Hall

Townfield
Farm

WINSFORD RD

Wettenhall Hall
Cottages

1

Woodgate
Farm

Oultonlowe
Covert

Wettenhall
Hall

62

60 A B 61 C D 62 E F

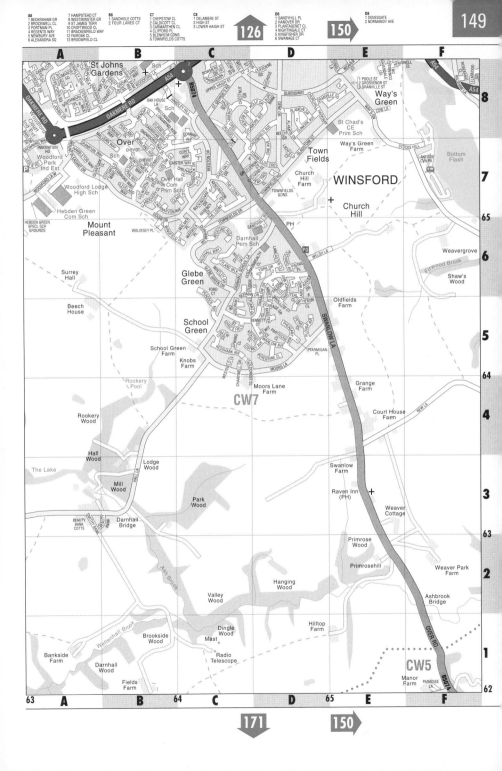

149
127

A   B   C   D   E   F

Clive

8

ACORN CL
ROOKERY RISE
WOODLARK CL

Weaver
Lodge

Clive Hall
Farm

TRAVELLERS
REST
CVN PK

BEECHFIELDS 1
DIERDEN ST 2
FIRTREE CL 3
PINETREE CL 4
ELMWOOD GR 5

RILSHAW LA

A54

Dairy
House
Farm

Yew-Tree
Farm

Rilshaw
Farm

Clive Farm

7

Clive House

The
Wallange
Farm

Park Farm

COLMITT LA

Double
Wood

Mole House
Farm

Pear Tree
Farm

CLIVE LA

CLIVE BACK LA

OLIVEGREEN LA

65

Bottom Flash

Clive
Green

Clive
Farm

6

Weaver
Dairy House

Dairy
House

A530

NANTWICH RD

Lea
House
Farm

CW7

Wimboldsley
Wood

5

Weaver
Hall

Top Flash

Middlewich Branch

WEAVERHALL LA

64

Lea Hall

Stove Room
Wood

NEW LA

Hop Yard
Wood

Shropshire Union Canal

CW10

4

Weaverwood
Farm

Rookery
Wood

SCHOOL
COTTS

Wimboldsley

Wimboldsley
Com Prim Sch

Rookery
Wood

River Weaver

Twelve
Acres

YEW TREE
CT

3

Trelfa's Wood

The
Dingle

Yewtree
Farm

63

Boundary
Wood

Owen's
Wood

2

Weaver
Bank Wood

Lea Green
Villa Farm

Weaver
Bank

A530

CW5

Wimboldsley
Hall

RAILWAY
COTTS

1

Lea Green
Hall

LEE GREEN LA

Verdin Arms
(PH)

NANTWICH RD

CW1

MIDDLEWICH
RD

62

66   A   B   67   C   D   68   E   F

149
172

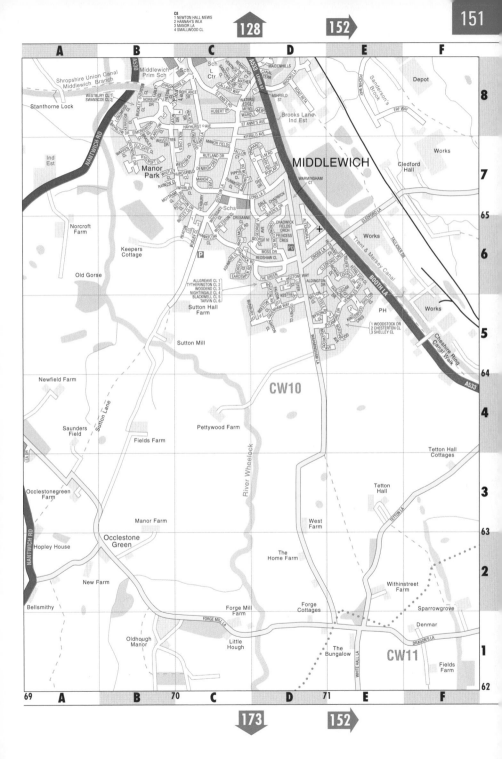

128
152

C8
1 NEWTON HALL MEWS
2 HANNAH'S WLK
3 MANOR LA
4 SMALLWOOD CL

MIDDLEWICH

Shropshire Union Canal
Middlewich Branch

Stanthorne Lock

Westbury Cl 1
Swanscoe Cl 2

Middlewich
Prim Sch

Ind Est

Manor Park

Norcroft Farm

Keepers Cottage

Old Gorse

Sutton Hall Farm

Sutton Mill

Newfield Farm

Saunders Field

Fields Farm

Occlestonegreen Farm

Hopley House

Occlestone Green

Manor Farm

New Farm

Bellsmithy

Oldhough Manor

Little Hough

Forge Mill Farm

Forge Cottages

The Bungalow

Pettywood Farm

The Home Farm

West Farm

Tetton Hall

Tetton Hall Cottages

Withinstreet Farm

Sparrowgrove

Denmar

Fields Farm

CW10

CW11

River Wheelock

Sutton Lane

NANTWICH RD

NANTWICH RD

A530

A533

A533

BOOTH LA

Trent & Mersey Canal

Cheshire Ring Canal Walk

Sanderson's Brook

Depot

Works

Cledford Hall

Works

Works

Brooks Lane Ind Est

ALLGREAVE CL 1
TYTHERINGTON CL 2
WOODEND CL 3
NIGHTINGALE CL 4
BLACKWELL CL 5
TARVIN CL 6

1 WOODSTOCK DR
2 CHESTERTON CL
3 SHELLEY CL

FORGE MILL LA

WHITE HALL LA

DRAGONS LA

TETTON LA

CLEDFORD LA

MAIDENHILLS

LEA DR

A B C D E F

8 7 65 6 5 64 4 3 63 2 1 62

Parkside Farm

Rookery Wood

BROAD LA

Broadlane Farm

CW4

M6

BRERETON LA

Dawfields

Brierley Hulme Farm

Pool Farm

Walkers Green

Briar Pool Farm

CLEDFORD LA

Lodge La

KINDERTON MOBILE HOME PK

Sanderson's Brook

Parme Farm

Knightshulme Farm

Curtishulme Farm

CW10

New Farm

Tetton Bridge

A533

Union Gorse

Higher Deleacre Farm

Fousley Farm

Hollinsgreen

Bridge Farm

BRIDGE FARM CT

TETTON LA

LC

Hollins Green Farm

Wood Lane Farm

Bridge Farm

Trent & Mersey Canal

Cheshire Ring Canal Wlk

BOOTH LA

Small Brook

Hollinswood Farm

Works

Barlow Wood

Bridge Cottage

Hollins Wood

The Cottage

CW11

Hilltop Cottage

Woodville Farm

DRAGON'S LA

PLANT LA

Stud Green

Flowcrete Bsns Pk

WARMINGHAM LA

Ivy Cottage Farm

Crow Nest Bridge

MILL LA

A533

MARSH GREEN RD

Beech Tree Farm

72 A B 73 C D 74 E F

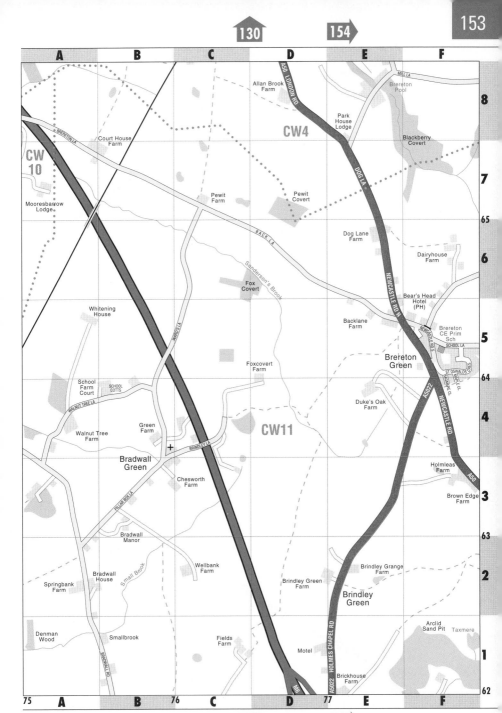

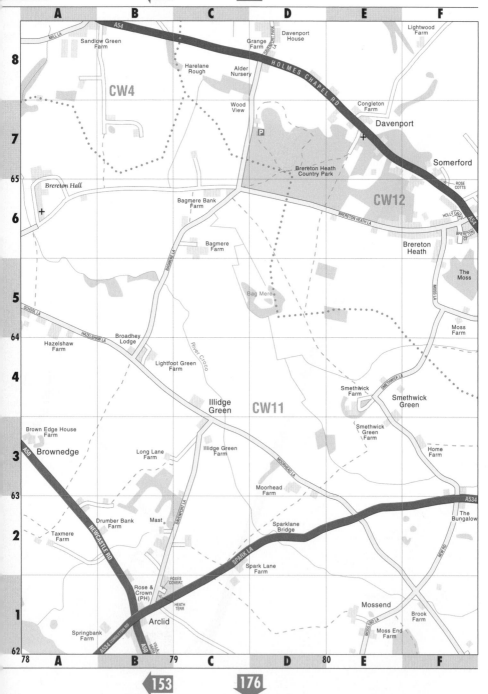

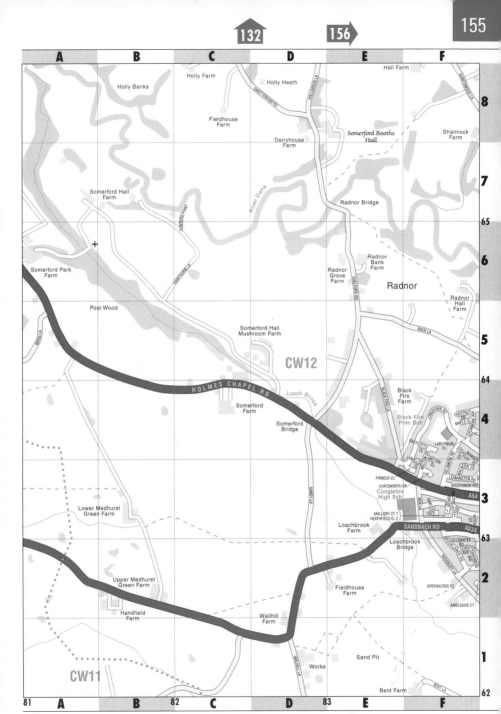

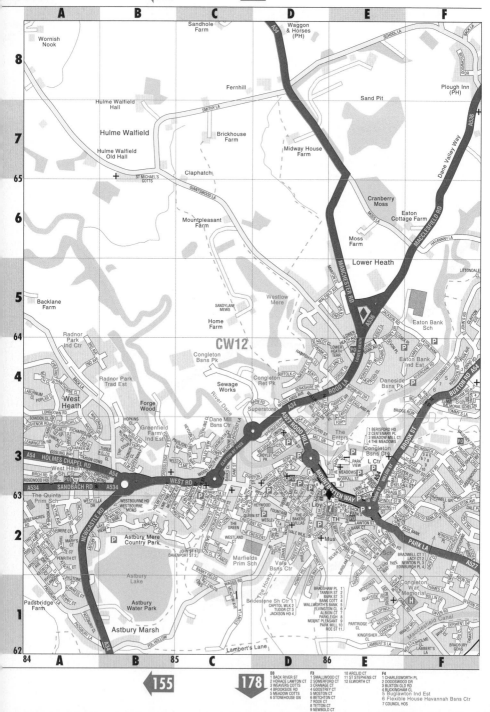

D3
1 BACK RIVER ST
2 HORACE LAWTON CT
3 WEAVERS COTTS
4 BROOKSIDE RD
5 MEADOW COTTS
6 STONEHOUSE GN

F3
1 SMALLWOOD ST
2 SOMERFORD CT
3 CRANAGE CT
4 GODSTREY CT
5 MOSTON CT
6 BETCHTON CT
7 RODE CT
8 TETTON CT
9 NEWBOLD CT

10 ARCLID CT
11 ST STEPHENS CT
12 ELWORTH CT

F4
1 CHARLESWORTH PL
2 DODDSWOOD DR
3 BUXTON OLD RD
4 BUCKINGHAM CL
5 Buglawton Ind Est
6 Flexible House Havannah Bsns Ctr
7 COUNCIL HOS

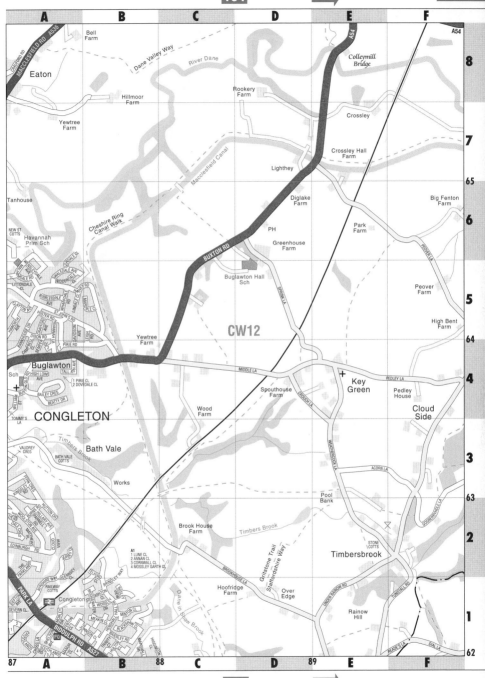

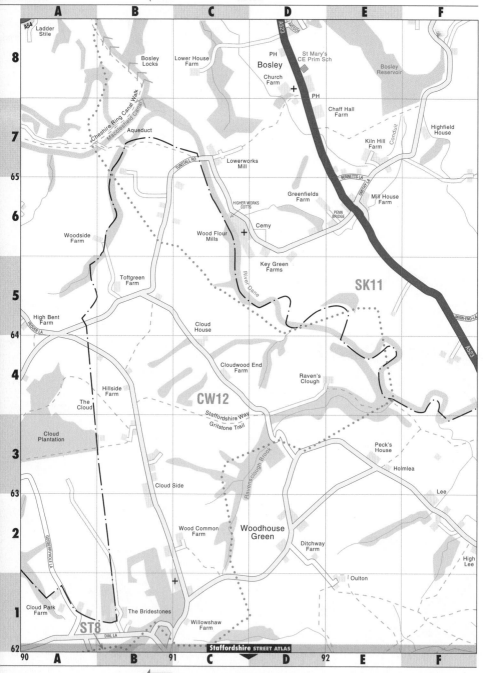

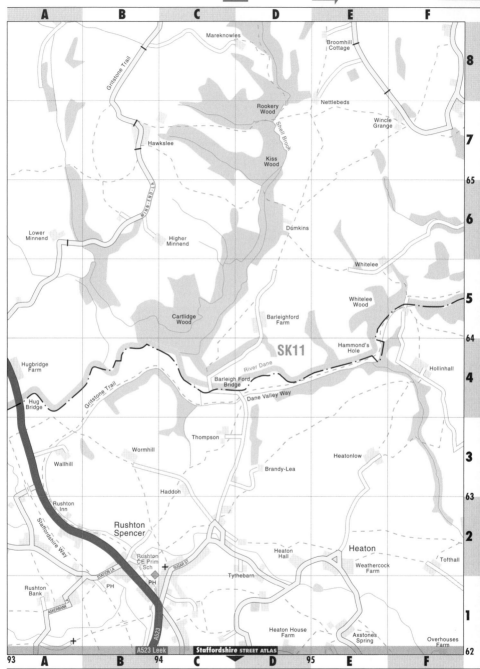

A   B   C   D   E   F

8

Mareknowles

Broomhill
Cottage

Gritstone Trail

Nettlebeds

Rookery
Wood

Wincle
Grange

7

Hawkslee

Shell Brook

Kiss
Wood

65

MINN END LA

6

Lower
Minnend

Dumkins

Higher
Minnend

Whitelee

Whitelee
Wood

5

Cartlidge
Wood

Barleighford
Farm

64

SK11

Hammond's
Hole

Hollinhall

Hugbridge
Farm

River Dane

Gritstone Trail

4

Hug
Bridge

Barleigh Ford
Bridge

Dane Valley Way

Thompson

Staffordshire Way

Wormhill

Heatonlow

3

Wallhill

Brandy-Lea

63

Haddon

Rushton
Inn

Rushton
Spencer

Heaton

2

Rushton
CE Prim
Sch

SUGAR ST

Heaton
Hall

Weathercock
Farm

Tofthall

STATION LA

PH

PH

Tythebarn

Rushton
Bank

ASKERBANK

1

A523

Heaton House
Farm

Axstones
Spring

Overhouses
Farm

62

A523 Leek   Staffordshire STREET ATLAS

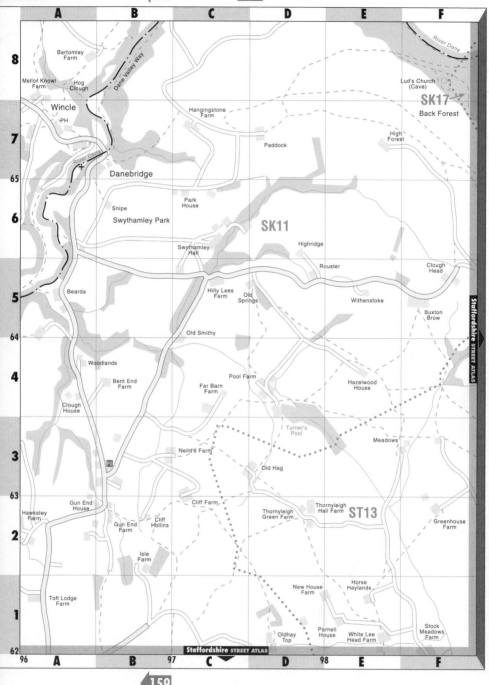

	A	B	C	D	E	F

8

Bartomley Farm

Mellor Knowl Farm

Hog Clough

Dane Valley Way

River Dane

Lud's Church (Cave)

SK17

Back Forest

Wincle

PH

Hangingstone Farm

High Forest

7

Paddock

River Dane

Danebridge

65

Park House

Swythamley Hall

Highridge

6

Snipe

Swythamley Park

SK11

Rouster

Clough Head

Bearda

Hilly Lees Farm

Old Springs

Withenstoke

Buxton Brow

5

Old Smithy

64

Woodlands

Pool Farm

Hazelwood House

4

Bent End Farm

Far Barn Farm

Clough House

Turner's Pool

Meadows

Neild's Farm

3

Old Hag

63

Gun End House

Cliff Farm

Thornyleigh Hall Farm

ST13

Greenhouse Farm

Hawksley Farm

Gun End Farm

Cliff Hollins

Thornyleigh Green Farm

2

Isle Farm

Horse Haylands

New House Farm

1

Toft Lodge Farm

Parnell House

Stock Meadows Farm

Oldhay Top

White Lee Head Farm

62

96	A	B	97	C	D	98	E	F

Staffordshire STREET ATLAS

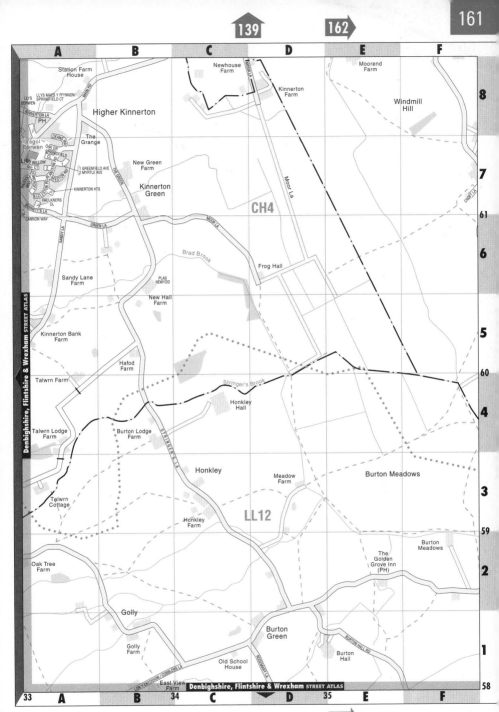

Station Farm House

Newhouse Farm

Moorend Farm

Kinnerton Farm

LLYS DERWEN
KINNERTON LA
PH

Higher Kinnerton

Windmill Hill

8

LLYS MAES Y FFYNNON/ SPRINGFIELD CT

MAIN RD

DEANS WAY

The Grange

Ysgol Derwen
Lib
WILLOW

OAK DR SPRINGFIELD
CL

New Green Farm

THE GREEN

Moor La

1 GREENFIELD AVE
2 MYRTLE AVE

Kinnerton Green

CH4

7

PADOG
MC CT
ECCLESTON RD
EATON CT
BRYN LA

FAULKNERS CL

KINNERTON HTS

61

BENNET'S LA
CANNON WAY

SANDY LA

GREEN LA

MOOR LA

6

Sandy Lane Farm

Brad Brook

Frog Hall

PLAS NEWYDD

New Hall Farm

Kinnerton Bank Farm

5

Hafod Farm

Stringer's Brook

60

Talwrn Farm

Honkley Hall

4

Talwrn Lodge Farm

STRINGER'S LA

Burton Lodge Farm

Honkley

Meadow Farm

Burton Meadows

3

Talwrn Cottage

LL12

59

Honkley Farm

Oak Tree Farm

Burton Meadows

The Golden Grove Inn (PH)

2

Golly

Burton Green

BURTON HALL RD

Golly Farm

ROSEMARY LA

Burton Hall

1

LON Y GRYDDION/ COBBLERS LA

East View Farm

Old School House

58

33 A 34 B C D 35 E F

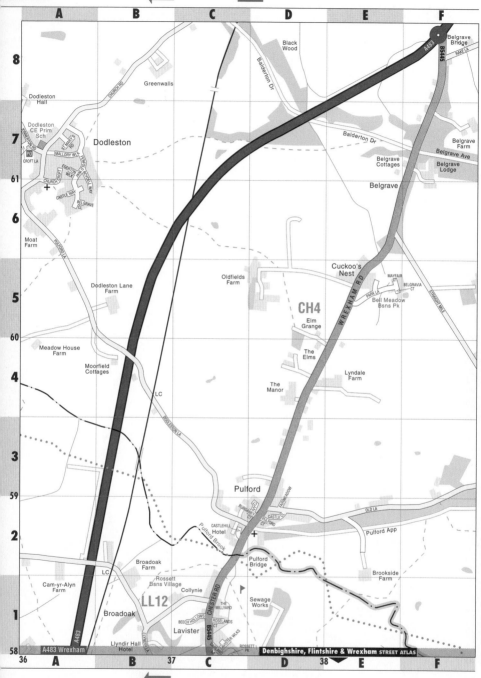

161
140
161

A B C D E F

8

7

61

6

5

60

4

3

59

2

1

58

36 A B 37 C D 38 E F

Black Wood

Balderton Dr

A483
B5445
RAKE LA

Belgrave Bridge

Belgrave Farm

Belgrave Ave

Belgrave Lodge

Belgrave Cottages

Balderton Dr

Belgrave

Greenwalls

Dodleston Hall

CHURCH RD

Dodleston CE Prim Sch

ST MARY'S RD

KINNERTON RD

PO

CROFT LA

MALLORY WLK

CASTLE WAY

CHURCH

EGERTON WLK

TRYGARN CL

STICKLE WAY

BELGRAVE PL

Dodleston

Moat Farm

PULFORD LA

Dodleston Lane Farm

Oldfields Farm

CH4

Elm Grange

Cuckoo's Nest

WREXHAM RD

MAYFAIR CT

PARK LA

BELGRAVIA CT

Bell Meadow Bsns Pk

STRAIGHT MILE

Meadow House Farm

Moorfield Cottages

LC

DODLESTON LA

The Elms

The Manor

Lyndale Farm

Pulford

FAIR MEADOW

BURGANEY

CASTLE CROFT

PULFORD

OLD LA

Pulford App

Castlehill Hotel

Brookside Farm

Cam-yr-Alyn Farm

LC

Broadoak Farm

Pulford Brook

Pulford Bridge

Sewage Works

Rossett Bsns Village

Collynie

LL12

Broadoak

CHESTER RD

B5445

THE MILLYARD

BEECH HOLLOWS

ROSELANDS CT

WALTER WLKS

ROSSETT PK

Lavister

Llyndir Hall Hotel

A483

A483 Wrexham

Denbighshire, Flintshire & Wrexham STREET ATLAS

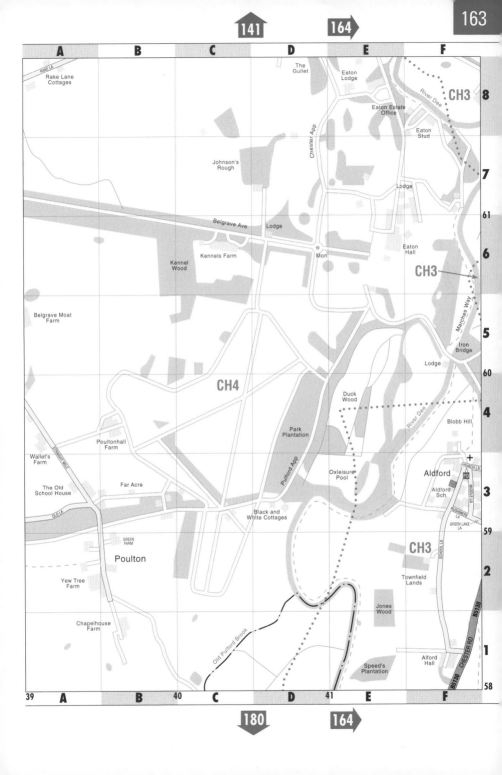

141
164
180
164

A B C D E F

8 7 61 6 5 60 4 3 59 2 1 58

39 40 41

RAKE LA

Rake Lane
Cottages

The
Gullet

Eaton
Lodge

River Dee

CH3

Eaton Estate
Office

Eaton
Stud

Johnson's
Rough

Chester App

Lodge

Belgrave Ave

Lodge

Eaton
Hall

CH3

Kennel
Wood

Kennels Farm

Mon

Marches Way

Belgrave Moat
Farm

Iron
Bridge

Lodge

CH4

Duck
Wood

River Dee

Blobb Hill

Park
Plantation

Pulford App

Oxleisure
Pool

Aldford

Poultonhall
Farm

Wallet's
Farm

STRAIGHT MILE

CHURCH LA

PO

Aldford
Sch

MIDDLE LA

The Old
School House

Far Acre

OLD LA

Black and
White Cottages

RUSHMERE LA

GREEN LAKE
LA

GREEN
FARM

CH3

SCHOOL LA

Poulton

Townfield
Lands

Yew Tree
Farm

Jones
Wood

B5130

Chapelhouse
Farm

Old Pulford Brook

Speed's
Plantation

Alford
Hall

CHESTER RD

B5130

163
142

A   B   C   D   E   F

8

Cheaveley Bridge

B5130

Cheaveleyhall Farm

Crook of Dee

River Dee

Saighton Grange

Abbey Gate Coll

Powsey Brook

7

CH4

Horse Pasture

Smithy Farm

Powseybrook Bridge

61

Lodge

WAVERTON APP

6

Sooty Fields Plantation

Chapelhouse Farm

Platt's Rough

Bruera

BUERTON APP

Buerton Kennels

CHAPEL LA

Coldharbour Farm

PLATT'S LA

Coldharbour

5

Churton Heath Farm

60

CH3

Newbold

Penlington's Wood

CH4

HILL COTTS

Lea Newbold Farm

4

CHURCH LA

Brickyard Farm

PH

Bank Farm

Brickyard Plantation

3

GREEN LAKE LA

LEA LA

Lea Cottages

59

B5130

CHESTER RD

Leahall Farm

Wim Bridge

2

LOW LA

Maches Way

Aldford Brook

Bishop Bennet Way

Glebe Farm

1

The Ponderosa

Ford La

Ford Lane Farm

58

42   A   B   43   C   D   44   E   F

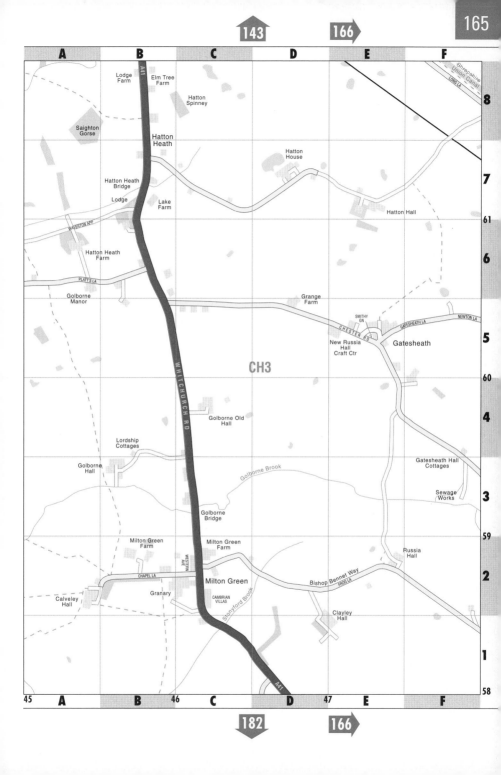

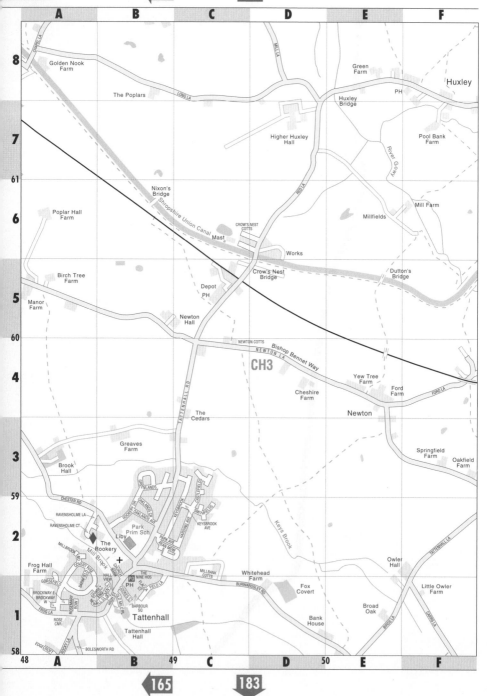

165
144

A   B   C   D   E   F

8

Golden Nook Farm

Green Farm

PH

Huxley

The Poplars

LONG LA

MILL LA

Huxley Bridge

7

Higher Huxley Hall

Pool Bank Farm

River Gowy

61

Nixon's Bridge

Shropshire Union Canal

ROT LA

Mill Farm

6

Poplar Hall Farm

CROW'S NEST COTTS

Mast

Millfields

Works

Birch Tree Farm

Crow's Nest Bridge

Dutton's Bridge

5

Manor Farm

Depot
PH

Newton Hall

60

NEWTON COTTS

Bishop Bennet Way

NEWTON LA

CH3

4

TATTENHALL RD

Yew Tree Farm

Ford Farm

FORD LA

Cheshire Farm

Newton

The Cedars

3

Greaves Farm

Springfield Farm

Oakfield Farm

Brook Hall

59

CHESTER RD

RAVENSHOLME LA

GREENLANDS

Park Prim Sch

Keys Brook

RAVENSHOLME CT

Liby

KEYSBROOK

KEYSBROOK AVE

2

MILLBROOK

Mill Brook

The Rookery

PARK AVE

Owler Hall

TATTENHALL LA

Frog Hall Farm

COVERT RISE

HALL VIEW

THE NINE HOS

Millbank Cotts

Whitehead Farm

Fox Covert

Little Owler Farm

GORSEFIELD

PO
PH

BURWARDISLEY RD

BROCKWAY E
BROCKWAY W

BARBOUR SQ

Broad Oak

BRIDGE LA

FROG LA

ROSE CNR

Tattenhall

Bank House

1

EDGECROFT

BOLESWORTH RD

Tattenhall Hall

CARRS LA

58

48   A   B   49   C   D   50   E   F

165
183

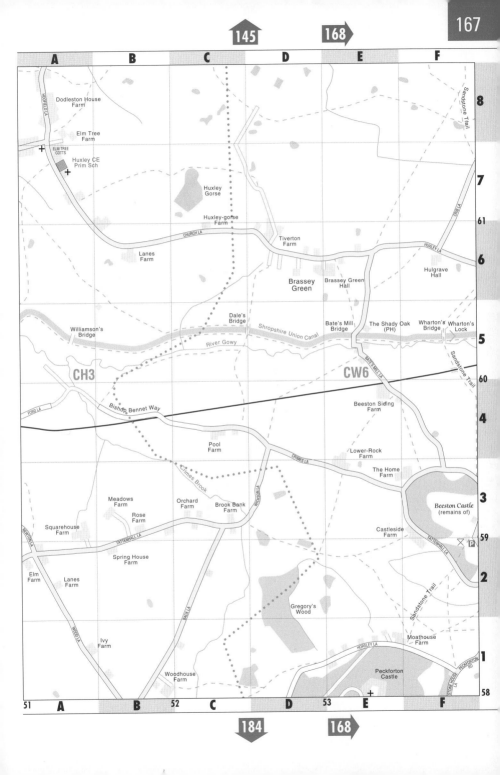

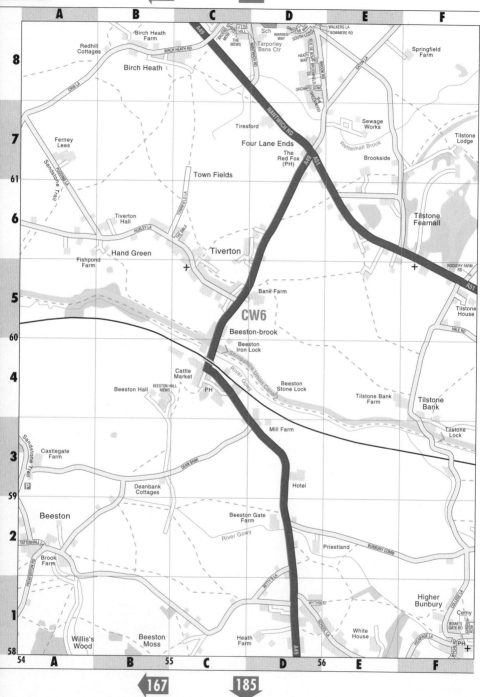

167 146

A B C D E F

8

7

61

6

5

60

4

3

59

2

1

58

54 A B 55 C D 56 E F

167 185

Birch Heath Farm
Redhill Cottages
Birch Heath
Birch Heath Rd
Ferney Lees
Crib La
Sandstone Trail
Tiresford
Four Lane Ends
The Red Fox (PH)
Town Fields
Tiverton Hall
Hand Green
Fishpond Farm
Hoofield La
Huxley La
The Dale
Townsend La
Tiverton
Bank Farm
CW6
Beeston-brook
Beeston Iron Lock
Shropshire Union Canal
River Gowy
Cattle Market
Beeston Hall Mews
PH
Beeston Hall
Beeston Stone Lock
Mill Farm
Castlegate Farm
Sandstone Trail
Dean Bank
Deanbank Cottages
Beeston
Tattenhall La
Brook Farm
Peckforton Rd
Beeston Gate Farm
River Gowy
Priestland
Hotel
Betty's La
Willis's Wood
Beeston Moss
Heath Farm
Wythin St
School La
White House
Higher Bunbury
Bunbury Comm
A49
Nantwich Rd
Spring Hill
The Mews
Tarporley Bsns Ctr
Oakdene Way
Warren Way
South Lodge
Walkers La
Bowmere Rd
Sch
Heath Way
Rue de Bois
Broom Rd
Brook Rd
Orchard Gdns
The Greenwood
Eaton La
Springfield Farm
Sewage Works
Wettenhall Brook
Brookside
Tilstone Lodge
Tilstone Fearnall
Rockery Farm Rd
A51
A49
A51
Tilstone House
Vale Rd
Tilstone Bank Farm
Tilstone Bank
Tilstone Lock
Cemy
Bowe's Gate Rd
College La
Vicarage La
Hitcher Rd
PH
Church Row

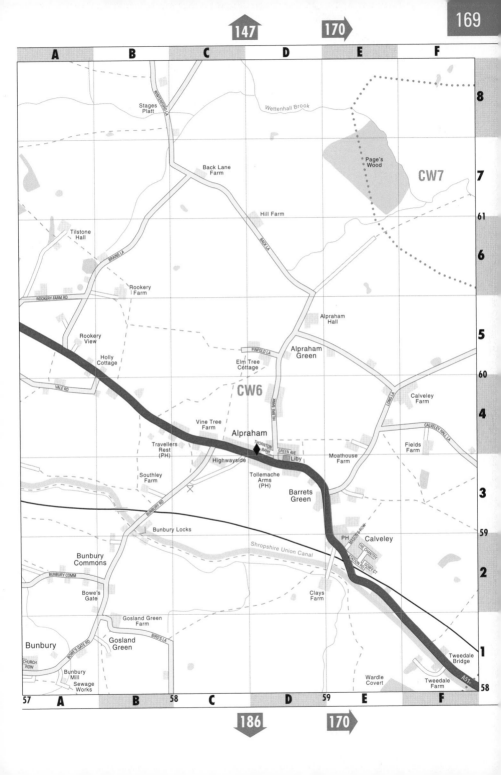

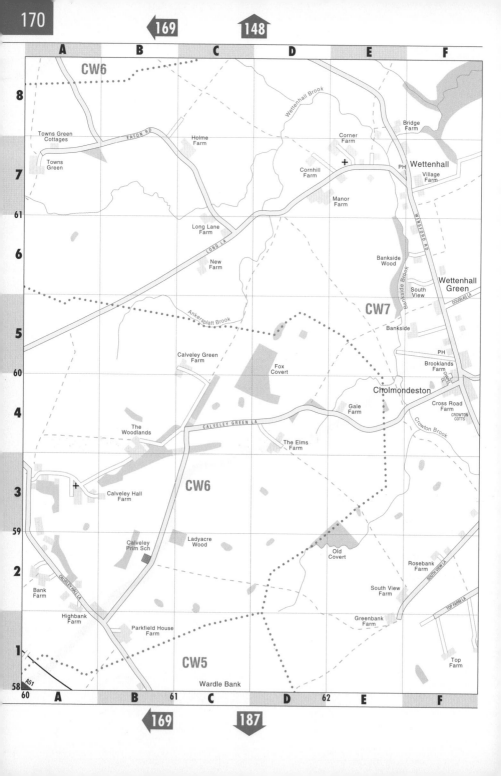

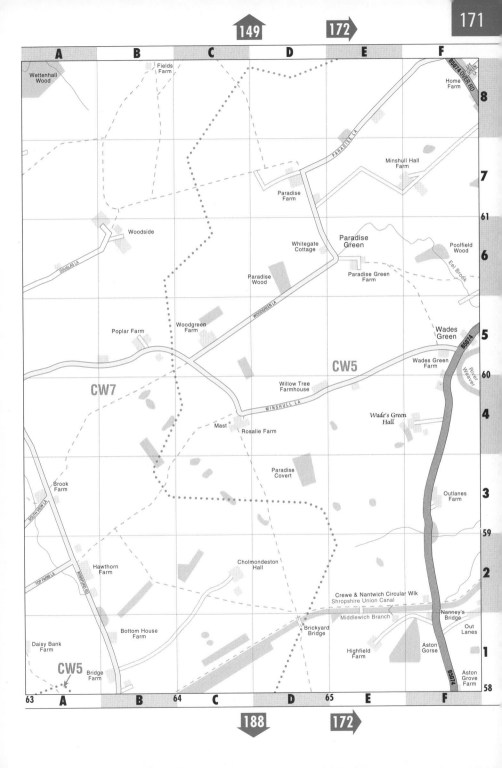

171
150

A B C D E F

8

Lea Green

HOME FARM PK
LEA GREEN LA
Sandicroft Wood

B5074

River Weaver

Newfield

Newfield Hall Farm

CW10

Weaver Wood Rookery

Woodside Farm

Walley's Green

7

Lower Elms

Higher Elms

Mast

Brook House Farm

OVER RD

The Woodlands

61

Ivy Cottage

WEAVER BANK

Weir

Worsley Covert

Moat House Farm

6

Church Minshull

PH

CROSS LA

Minshullhill

Cross Lane

Minshull Vernon

Dairy Farm Cottage

THE STREET VILLAGE FARM
HORSE TRAM

Eardswick Wood

MIDDLEWICH RD

Dairy Farm

Shropshire Union Canal Middlewich Branch

Crewe & Nantwich Circular Wlk

5

B5074

Eardswick Hall Bridge

Eardswick Hall

EARDSWICK LA

60

Old Hoolgrave

CW5

CW1

4

River Weaver

Crewe & Nantwich Circular Wlk

High Farm

Church Farm

3

Bradfield Green

59

Prescott's Bridge

PH

MOSS LA

QUEENS CRES

2

Hoolgrave Manor

Bradfield Green Farm

B5076

FLOWERS LA

1

Red Hall Wood

Red Hall

A530

South Cheshire

H H

Leighton

Leighton Lodge

B5076

58

66 A B 67 C D 68 E SMITHY LA F

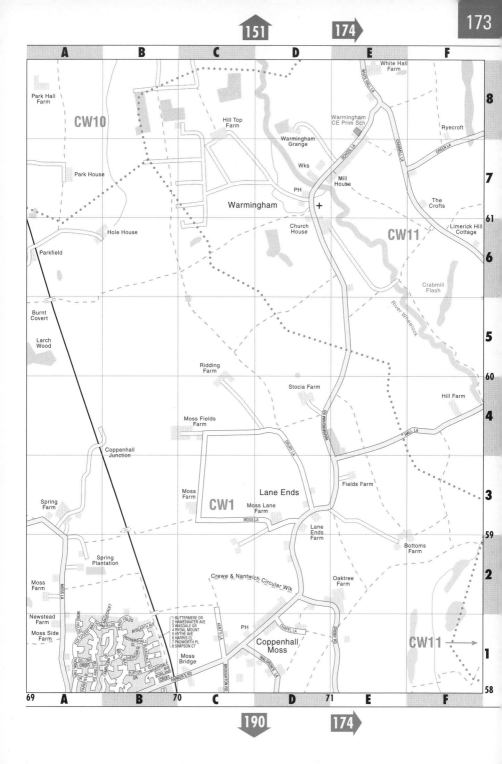

151
174

8

Park Hall
Farm

CW10

7

Park House

61

Hole House

6

Parkfield

Burnt
Covert

Larch
Wood

5

Coppenhall
Junction

Spring
Farm

Moss
Farm

Spring
Plantation

Newstead
Farm

Moss Side
Farm

Moss
Bridge

Hill Top
Farm

Warmingham
Grange

Wks

PH

Warmingham

Church
House

Ridding
Farm

Moss Fields
Farm

Moss
Farm

CW1

Moss Lane
Farm

Crewe & Nantwich Circular Wlk

White Hall
Farm

Warmingham
CE Prim Sch

Mill
House

Ryecroft

The
Crofts

Limerick Hill
Cottage

CW11

Crabmill
Flash

River Wheelock

Stocia Farm

Lane Ends

Fields Farm

Lane
Ends
Farm

Oaktree
Farm

PH

Coppenhall
Moss

Hill Farm

60

4

Bottoms
Farm

59

2

CW11 →

1

58

1 BUTTERMERE DR
2 HAWESWATER AVE
3 WASDALE GR
4 RYDAL MOUNT
5 HYTHE AVE
6 HARRIS CL
7 PADWORTH PL
8 SIMPSON CT

69 A   B   70 C   D   71 E   F

190
174

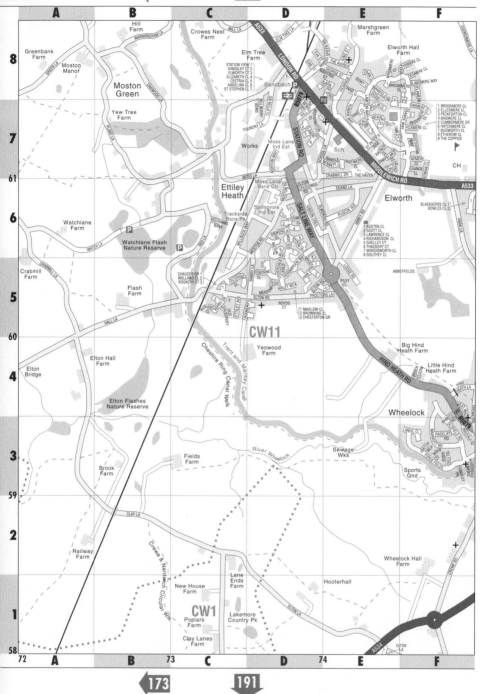

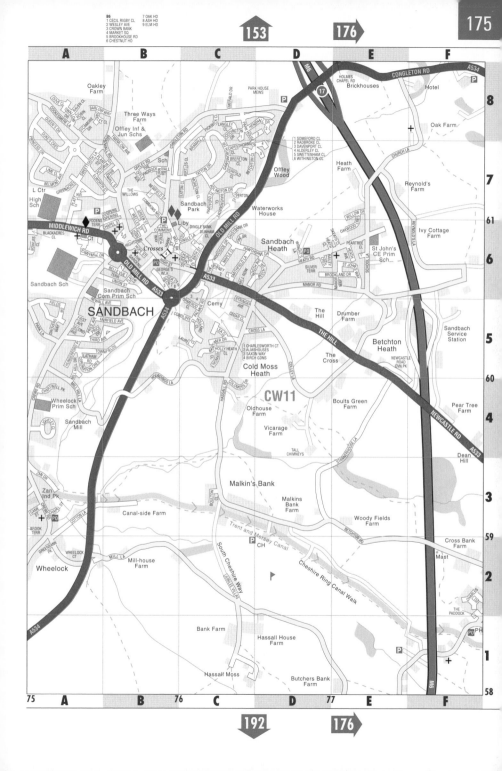

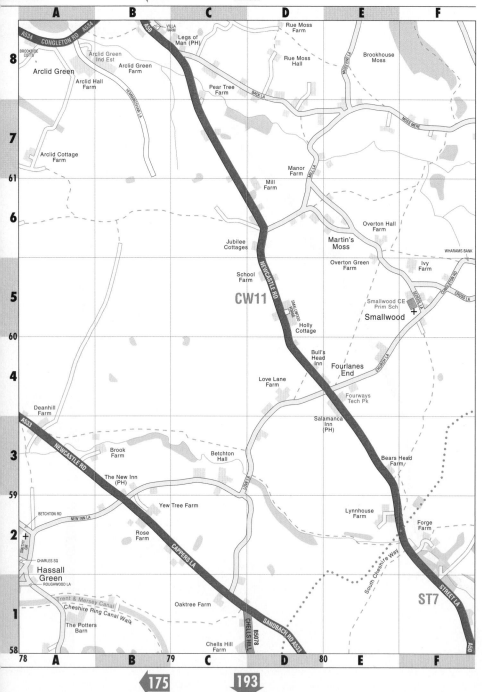

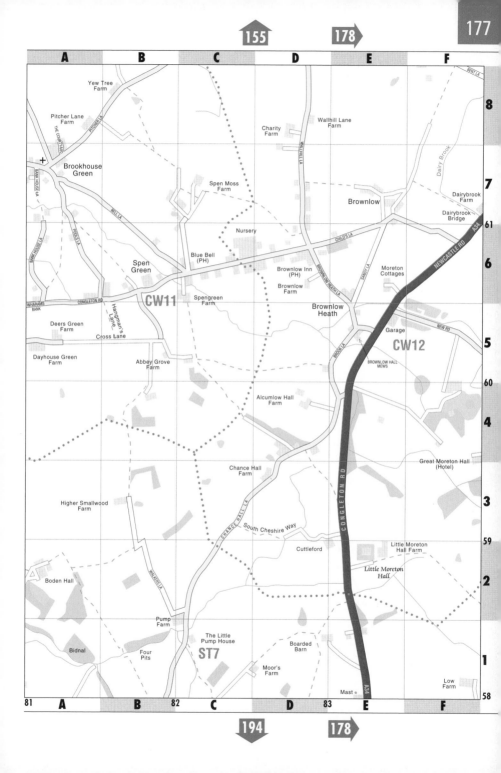

155
178
194
178

A   B   C   D   E   F

Yew Tree Farm

Pitcher Lane Farm

Brookhouse Green

THE COMPTARD

PITCHER LA

BANK HOUSE LA

Charity Farm

Wallhill Lane Farm

WALLHILL LA

Dairy Brook

BENT LA

8

Spen Moss Farm

Brownlow

Dairybrook Farm

Dairybrook Bridge

7

BELL LA

POOL LA

BANK HOUSE LA

Nursery

Blue Bell (PH)

Spen Green

CHILD'S LA

NEWCASTLE RD

A34

61

Brownlow Inn (PH)

Brownlow Farm

BROWNLOW HEATH LA

Moreton Cottages

6

CW11

Spengreen Farm

Brownlow Heath

FAIRS LA

WHARAMS BANK

CONGLETON RD

Hangman's Lane

Deers Green Farm

Cross Lane

Garage

NEW RD

CW12

5

Dayhouse Green Farm

Abbey Grove Farm

BROWNLOW HALL MEWS

BROOK LA

60

Alcumlow Hall Farm

4

Chance Hall Farm

Great Moreton Hall (Hotel)

Higher Smallwood Farm

CHANCE HALL LA

South Cheshire Way

CONGLETON RD

3

Cuttleford

Little Moreton Hall Farm

59

Boden Hall

Little Moreton Hall

WALKERS LA

2

Pump Farm

Bidnal

Four Pits

The Little Pump House

ST7

Moor's Farm

Boarded Barn

1

Mast

A34

Low Farm

58

81   A   B   82   C   D   83   E   F

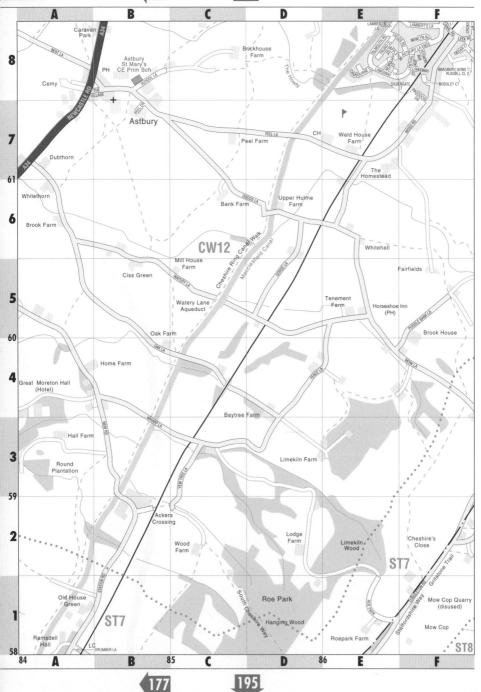

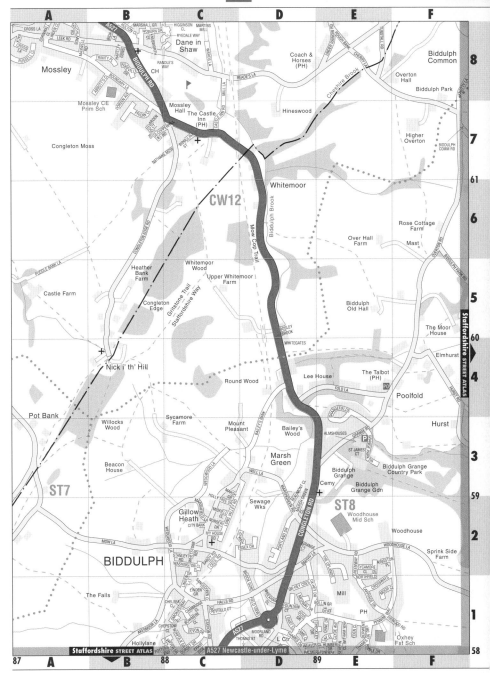

A B C D E F

8
7
61
6
5
60
4
3
59
2
1
58

A527 Newcastle-under-Lyme

Staffordshire STREET ATLAS

Mossley
Cross La
Leek Rd
Russell Cl
A527
Hulton Cl
Marshall Gr
Higginson Cl
Martins Mill
Woburn Dr
Ryedale Way
Randle's Way
Dane in Shaw
Reade's La
Coach & Horses (PH)
Biddulph Common
Overton Hall
Biddulph Park
Trinity Pl
CH
Mossley CE Prim Sch
Mossley Hall
The Castle Inn (PH)
Mill La
Hineswood
Cheshire Brook
Higher Overton
Congleton Moss
Biddulph Comm Rd
Whitemoor
CW12
Biddulph Brook
Rose Cottage Farm
Mast
Puddle Bank La
Heather Bank Farm
Whitemoor Wood
Upper Whitemoor Farm
Over Hall Farm
Castle Farm
Congleton Edge
Gritstone Trail
Staffordshire Way
Mow Cop Trail
Biddulph Old Hall
The Moor House
Bosley Brook
Whitegates
Elmhurst
Nick i' th' Hill
Round Wood
Lee House
The Talbot (PH)
Poolfold
Pot Bank
Willocks Wood
Sycamore Farm
Mount Pleasant
Bailey's Wood
Fold La
Grangefields
Almshouses
Hurst
Beacon House
Marsh Green
Biddulph Grange
Biddulph Grange Country Park
St James Ct
ST7
Gillow Heath
City Bank
Sewage Wks
Biddulph Grange Gdn
ST8
Woodhouse Mid Sch
Woodhouse
BIDDULPH
Mow La
Cemy
Woodhouse La
Sprink Side Farm
Congleton Rd
The Falls
Essex Dr
Mill
PH
Oxhey Fst Sch
Hollylane
L Ctr
Moorland Rd
Thomas St

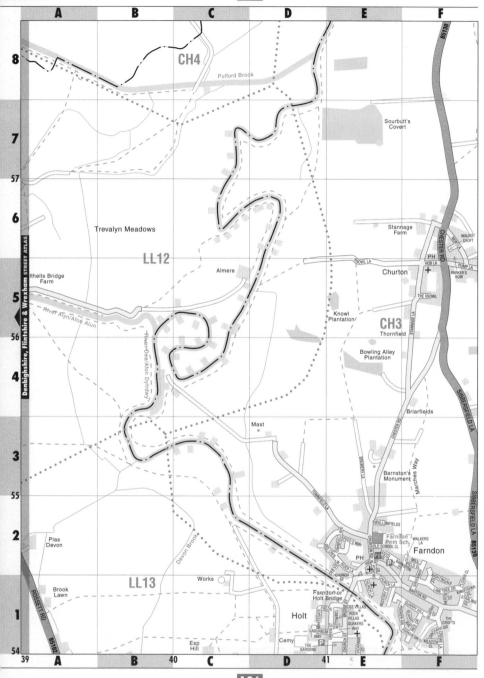

Denbighshire, Flintshire & Wrexham STREET ATLAS

8

CH4

Pulford Brook

Sourbutt's Covert

7

57

Trevalyn Meadows

6

LL12

Stannage Farm

WALNUT CROFT

CHESTER RD

KNOWL LA

PUMP LA

Almere

PH

HOB LA

PARKER'S ROW

Churton

THE KNOWL

Ithells Bridge Farm

5

River Alyn/Afon Alun

Knowl Plantation

CH3

Thornfield

STANNAGE LA

56

River Dee/Afon Dyfrdwy

Bowling Alley Plantation

4

Briarfields

CHESTER RD

SIBBERSFIELD LA

Mast

Barnston's Monument

3

Marches Way

BREWERY LA

BS5130

SWALLOWFIELDS

Farndon Prim Sch

WALKERS LA

55

SPEED S WAY

OLD SCHOOL CL

Farndon

TOWNFIELD

CHURTON RD

PH

MILL

NIGHTINGALE

Plas Devon

2

DANNELL DANE

CHURCH ST

P

LIME TREE DR

KINGFISHER

DUNLING

DEE CL

Brook Lawn

Works

CHURCH

BARTON RD

QUAKERS WAY

QUARRY HILL

THE CROFTS

ORCHARD DR

MEADOW

1

LL13

Farndon or Holt Bridge

DEE VILLAS

ROCK VILLAS

FIELDS

CHURCH LA

VICARAGE

CHERRY

ROSSETT RD

LABURNUM WAY

WHITEGATE

Holt

Cemy

Esp Hill

54

BS102

THE GARDENS

P

39

40

41

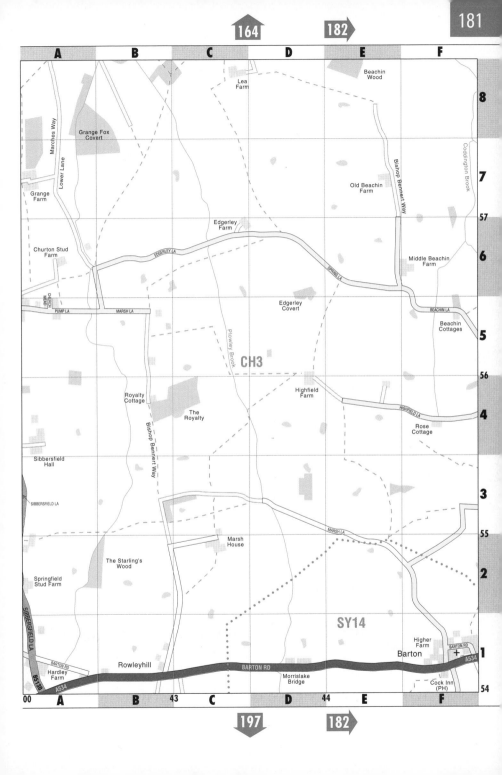

164 182

197 182

8
7
57
6
5
56
4
3
55
2
1
54

A B C D E F

Beachin Wood

Lea Farm

Grange Fox Covert

Marches Way

Lower Lane

Grange Farm

Old Beachin Farm

Bishop Bennert Way

Coddington Brook

Edgerley Farm

Churton Stud Farm

EDGERLEY LA

Middle Beachin Farm

SPRING LA

CHURCH VIEW

PUMP LA   MARSH LA

Edgerley Covert

BEACHIN LA

Beachin Cottages

Plowley Brook

CH3

Royalty Cottage

The Royalty

Highfield Farm

HIGHFIELD LA

Rose Cottage

Bishop Bennert Way

Sibbersfield Hall

SIBBERSFIELD LA

MARSH LA

Marsh House

The Starling's Wood

Springfield Stud Farm

SY14

Higher Farm

Barton

BARTON RD

A534

SIBBERSFIELD LA

BARTON RD

Rowleyhill

BARTON RD

Morrislake Bridge

Cock Inn (PH)

B5130

A534

Hardley Farm

00   43   44   A   B   C   D   E   F

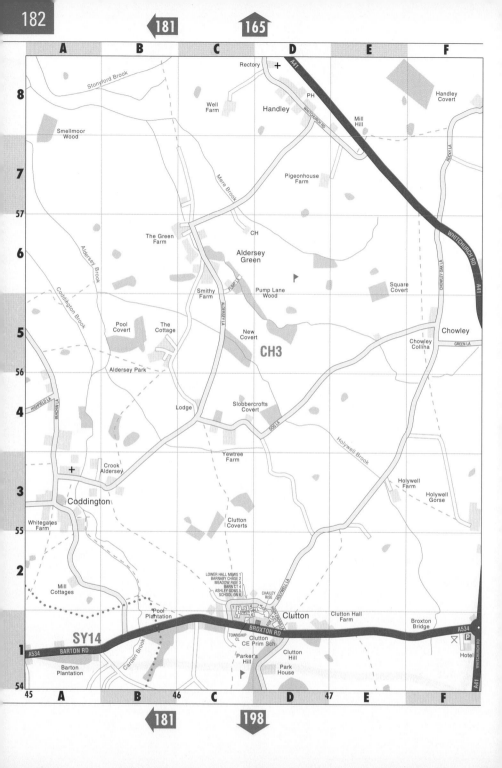

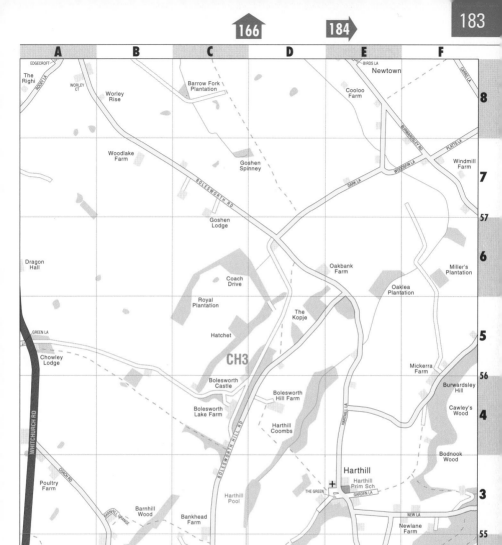

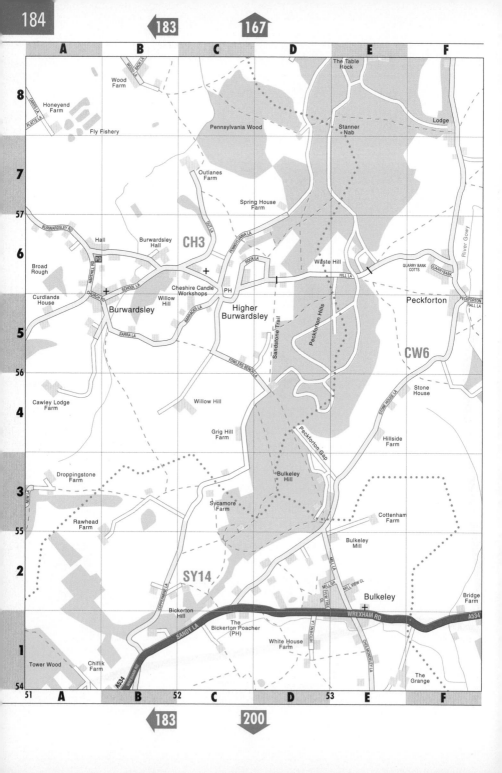

A B C D E F

8

Honeyend
Farm

Wood
Farm

Fly Fishery

Pennsylvania Wood

The Table
Rock

Stanner
Nab

Lodge

7

Outlanes
Farm

Spring House
Farm

57

BURWARDSLEY RD

Broad
Rough

Hall

Burwardsley
Hall

CH3

6

Curdlands
House

Burwardsley

Cheshire Candle
Workshops

Willow
Hill

PH

Higher
Burwardsley

Waste Hill

HILL LA

QUARRY BANK
COTTS

QUARRYBANK

Peckforton

PECKFORTON
HALL LA

River Gowy

5

FOWLERS BENCH LA

Sandstone Trail

Peckforton Hills

CW6

56

Cawley Lodge
Farm

Willow Hill

STONE HOUSE LA

Stone
House

4

Grig Hill
Farm

Peckforton Gap

Hillside
Farm

3

Droppingstone
Farm

Sycamore
Farm

Bulkeley
Hill

Cottenham
Farm

55

NEW LA

Rawhead
Farm

Bulkeley
Mill

2

COTTENHAM LA

SY14

MILL LA

MILL VIEW CL

Bulkeley

Bridge
Farm

Bickerton
Hill

The
Bickerton Poacher
(PH)

White House
Farm

HITCHENS LA

WREXHAM RD

A534

1

Tower Wood

Chiflik
Farm

SANDY LA

A534

WREXHAM RD

The
Grange

54

51 A B 52 C D 53 E F

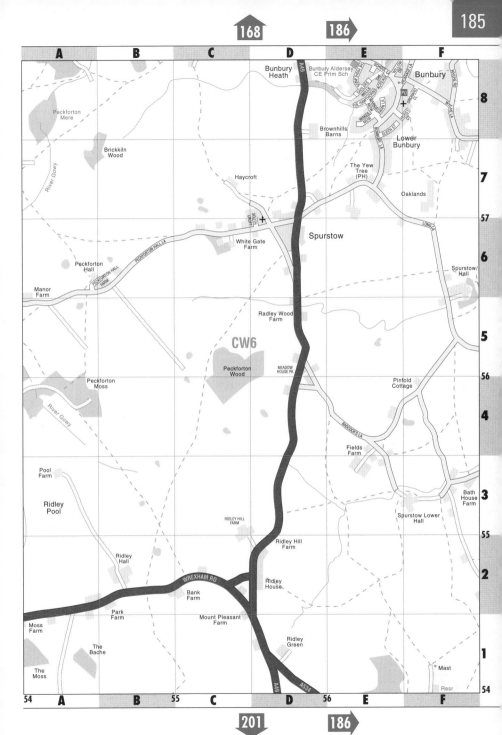

168   186

Bunbury
Heath

Bunbury Aldersey
CE Prim Sch

Bunbury

Brownhills
Barns

Lower
Bunbury

Peckforton
Mere

Brickkiln
Wood

Haycroft

The Yew
Tree
(PH)

Oaklands

River Gowy

SOUTH
CROFT

Spurstow

White Gate
Farm

PECKFORTON HALL LA

LONG LA

Peckforton
Hall

Spurstow
Hall

PECKFORTON HALL
FARM

Manor
Farm

Radley Wood
Farm

CW6

Peckforton
Wood

MEADOW
HOUSE PK

Pinfold
Cottage

Peckforton
Moss

River Gowy

BADDOCK'S LA

Fields
Farm

Pool
Farm

Bath
House
Farm

Ridley
Pool

RIDLEY HILL
FARM

Spurstow Lower
Hall

Ridley Hill
Farm

Ridley
Hall

WREXHAM RD

Bank
Farm

Ridley
House

Park
Farm

Mount Pleasant
Farm

Moss
Farm

The
Bache

Ridley
Green

Mast

The
Moss

A49   A534

Resr

8
7
57
6
5
56
4
3
55
2
1
54

A   B   C   D   E   F

54   55   56

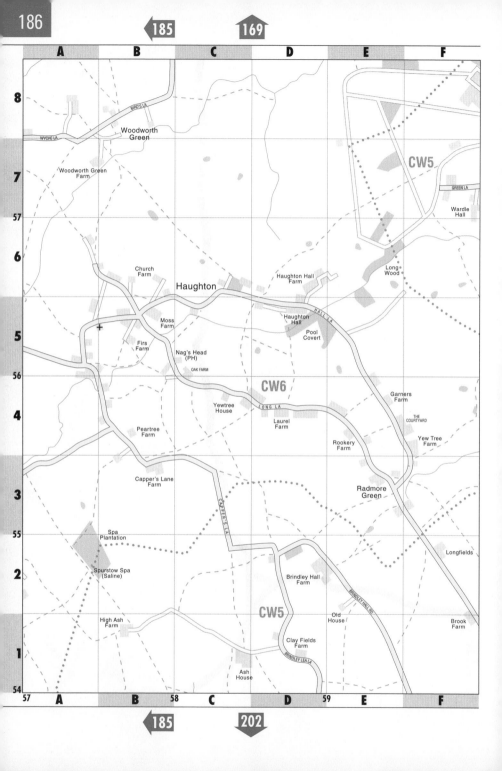

185
169

A B C D E F

8

185

CW5

7

Woodworth
Green

GREEN LA

Woodworth Green
Farm

Wardle
Hall

57

6

Church
Farm

Haughton

Haughton Hall
Farm

Long
Wood

WYCHE LA

BIRD'S LA

Moss
Farm

Haughton
Hall

HALL LA

5

Firs
Farm

Nag's Head
(PH)

Pool
Covert

OAK FARM

56

CW6

Garners
Farm

4

Yewtree
House

LONG LA

Laurel
Farm

THE
COURTYARD

Peartree
Farm

Rookery
Farm

Yew Tree
Farm

3

Capper's Lane
Farm

CAPPER'S LA

Radmore
Green

55

Spa
Plantation

2

Spurstow Spa
(Saline)

Brindley Hall
Farm

Longfields

BRINDLEY HALL RD

CW5

Old
House

Brook
Farm

High Ash
Farm

1

Clay Fields
Farm

BRINDLEY LEA LA

Ash
House

54

57 A B 58 C D 59 E F

185
202

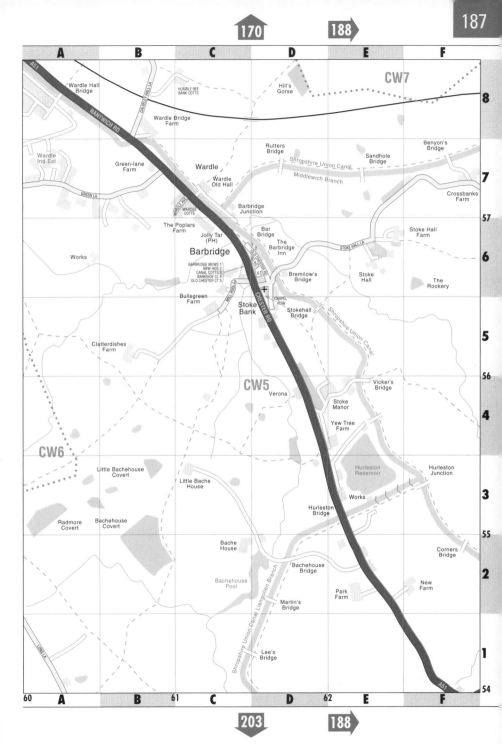

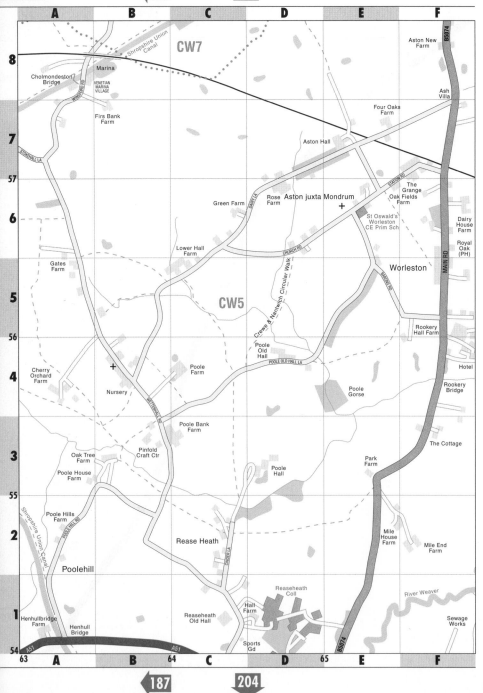

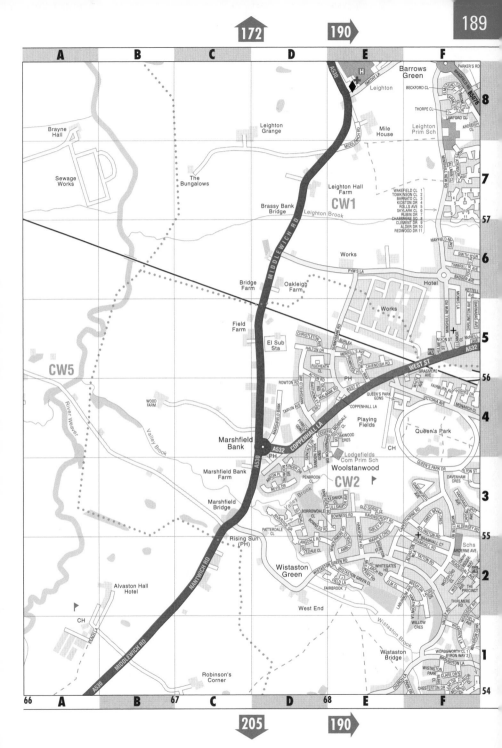

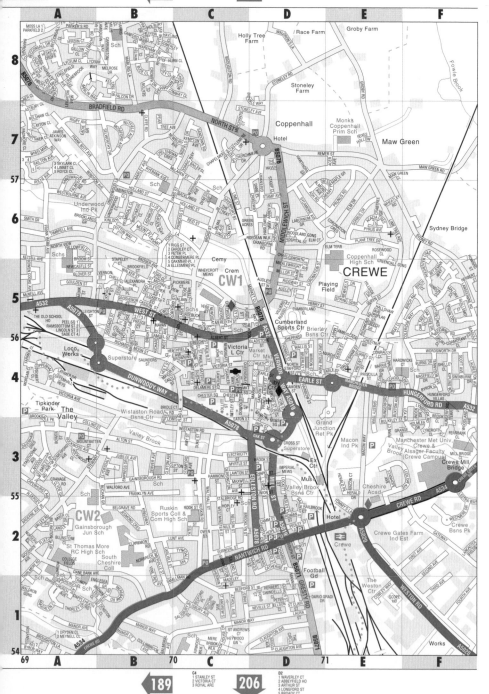

C4
1 STANLEY ST
2 VICTORIA CT
3 ROYAL ARC

D4
1 WAVERLEY CT
2 ABBEYFIELD HO
3 ARTHUR ST
4 LONGFORD ST
5 BROADY CT

A B C D

CW11

Haslington House Farm

WESTERN PK 1
MILLCROFT 2
COPPICE RD 3

WOOD-COTE PL

Winterley

Foxholme Farm

Crewe & Nantwich Circular Wlk

MAW LA

Clayhanger Hall Farm

Yew Tree Farm

CLAY LA

NEWTONS LA

NEWTONS LA

NESFIELD CL

NEWTONS DEPT

POOL LA

7

Brook House Farm

Holly Bush Farm

KENTS GREEN LA

FISHERMANS

Winterley Pool

Kent's Green Farm

57

Thorney Fields Farm

Fox Covert

Winterley House

6

Works

The Dingle Prim Sch

Fowle Brook

Sandfield House Farm

HOLMSHAW LA

Bradeley Hall

DELVES BROUGHTON CT 1
PALMERSTON CL 2

ASQUITH

NEPTON DR

LYNTON GR

Park Farm

Sydney

BRADELEY RD

Bradeley Abattoir

ASH BROOKFIELD

Hall Farm

5

RHODES ST

HERBERT ST

PENDLE

LAVON

CL

Bradeley Hall

SKELBURNE DR

CHATHAM WAY

WELLS FM

GUTTERSCROFT

MULCASTER CT

56

PELICAN CL

Field Farm

THE BRAEBLES

PRIMROSE AV

CAMPBELL CT

CHAMBERLAIN

ROAD

ORCHARD

BRADELEY RD

SCHOOL ST

MERE ST

THE CREW

PAIN RD

Haslington Hall

BENTLEY CL

1 TREVITHICK CL
2 RENAISSANCE CT

POOL MEADOWS RD

KINGSLEY RD

CLIFFORD

HAMES CL

MERE CL

MATTHEW

Haslington

4

SHAKESPEARE WAY

STANIER ST

JENSON DR

VICTORIA AVE

VICTORIA

GOLD ST

HOBBS GR

TATE DR

WALKER CL

MORE PLEASANT

SYDNEY RD

SANDRINGHAM

WENTWORTH

VERITY ST

CROSS LA

CROSS ST

FIELDER

HUNGERFORD RD

WELLESLEY AVE

CREWE GREEN AVE

BREACE CL

TELFORD

55

B5077

Tollgate Farm

CREWE GREEN RD

Crewe Green

NARROW LA

Haslington Prim Sch

HEATH VIEW

WALDRON RD

The Bank

Clapgates Farm

South Cheshire Way

3

Springfield Sch

ARTHUR MILL WAY

CW1

Slaughter Hill

CH

A5020

UNIVERSITY WAY

ELECTRA WAY

COPPICEMERE DR

SALFORD CT

MALLARD WAY

Crewe Bsns Pk

Park Farm

Valley Brook

55

Temple of Peace Wood

2

LANCASTER

HAZELS

QUAKERS

Quaker's Coppice Nature Reserve

Englesea Brook

GATEWAY

FOURTH AVE

Rookery Wood

B5077

Crewe Gates Farm Ind Est

Crewe Hall (Hotel)

BUTTERTON LA

BARTHOMLEY RD

Englesea House

1

72 A B 73 C D 74 E F 54

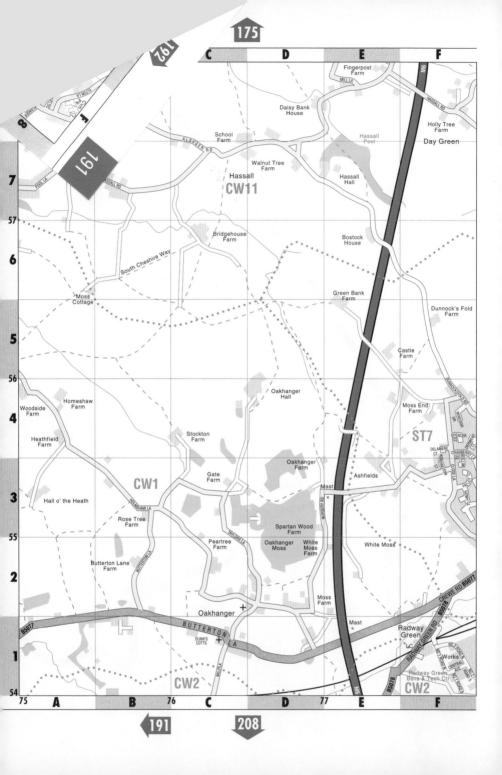

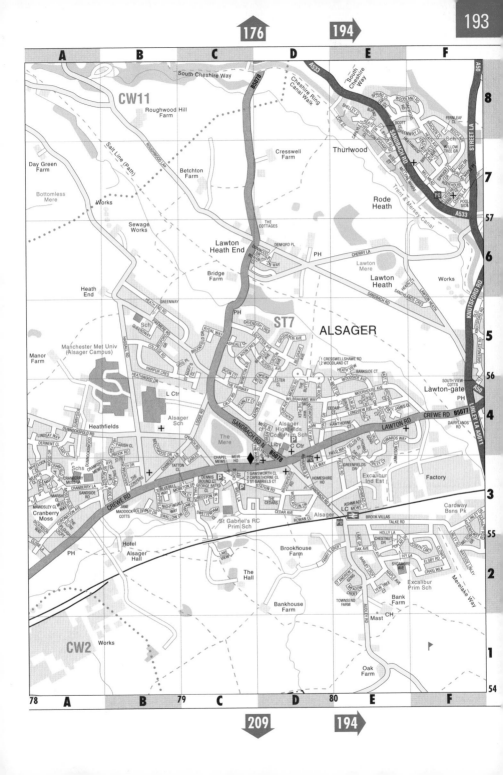

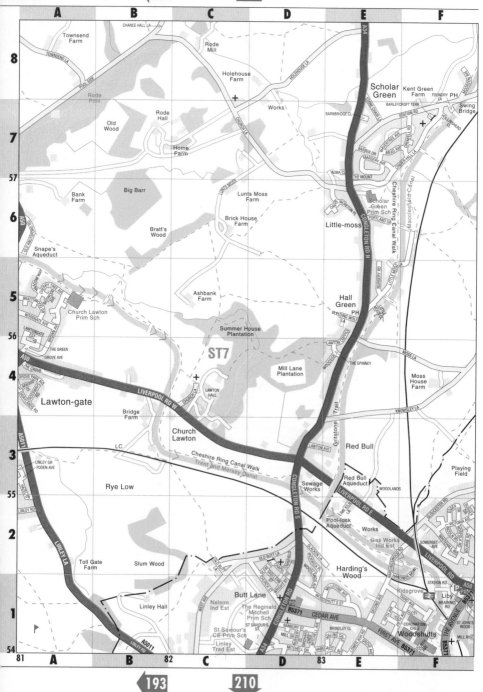

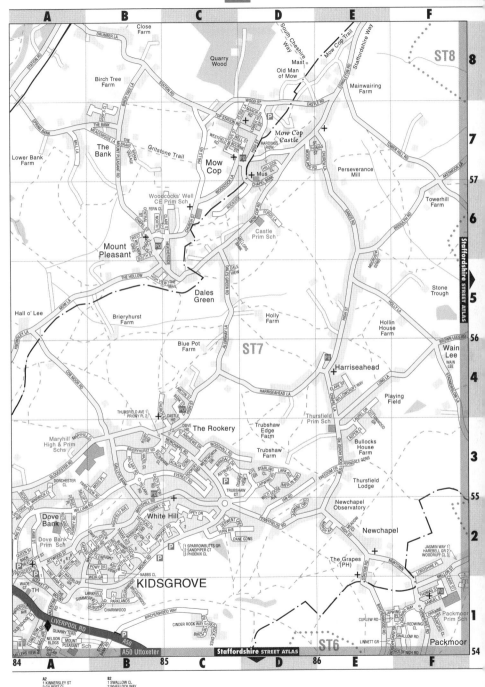

KIDSGROVE

Packmoor

Newchapel

ST7

ST8

ST6

180

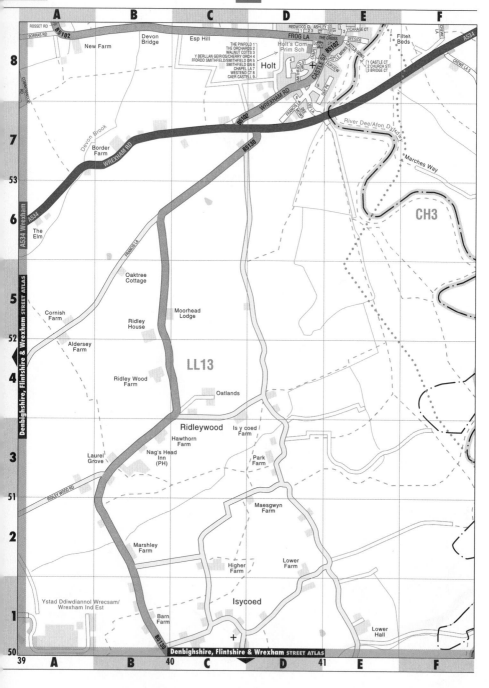

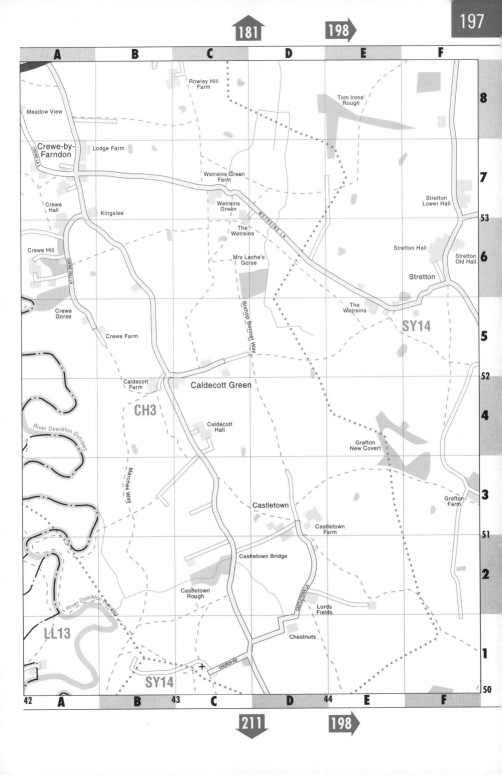

181 198

211 198

8

7

53

6

5

52

4

3

51

2

1

50

Meadow View

Rowley Hill Farm

Tom Irons' Rough

Crewe-by-Farndon

Lodge Farm

Wetreins Green Farm

Stretton Lower Hall

Crewe Hall

Kingslee

Wetreins Green

Crewe Hill

The Wetreins

Stretton Hall

Stretton Old Hall

Mrs Leche's Gorse

Stretton

Crewe Gorse

The Wetreins

SY14

Crewe Farm

Bishop Bennet Way

Caldecott Farm

CH3

Caldecott Green

Caldecott Hall

Marches Way

Grafton New Covert

Castletown

Grafton Farm

River Dee/Afon Dyfrdwy

Castletown Farm

Castletown Bridge

Castletown Rough

Lords Fields

River Dee/Afon Dyfrdwy

LL13

Chestnuts

SY14

CHURCH RD

CASTLETOWN LA

42   A   B   43   C   D   44   E   F   50

A B C D E F

CH3

8

The Birches

Golborne's Wood

Moor Gorse

Round Hill

Garden Plantation

The Quarries

Cliffe Bank

7

Mill Coppice

Home Farm

Hotel

Carden Marsh

Stretton Mill

Higher Carden

53

Laurel Grove

6

Lower Carden

Lower Farm

Hook's Rough

Hook's Brook

5

Lower Carden Hall

Stone House

52

Grafton Lodge

4

SY14

Isle Farm

The Heir's Wood

Hobb Hill Farm

Hobb Hill

3

Carden Arms Inn (PH)

Tilston

Finsdale Farm

Lowcross Hill

Grange La

Grafton Farm

Ford

Edge Grange

Tilston CE Prim Sch

51

Yewtree Farm

2

Frog Hall

The Old Rectory

Quarry (dis)

The Cape

Lowcross Gorse

Lowcross Farm

Dyer's Farm

Scar La

1

Church Croft

Lower Wood

50

45 A B 46 C D 47 E F

CARDEN BROOK

HIGHER CARDEN LA

HOLLY LEM

RIVER LA

LONGCROSS LA

LONG LA

CHURCH RD

WYNTER LA

ROOKERY RD

GREENWAY

A41 WHITCHURCH RD

A41

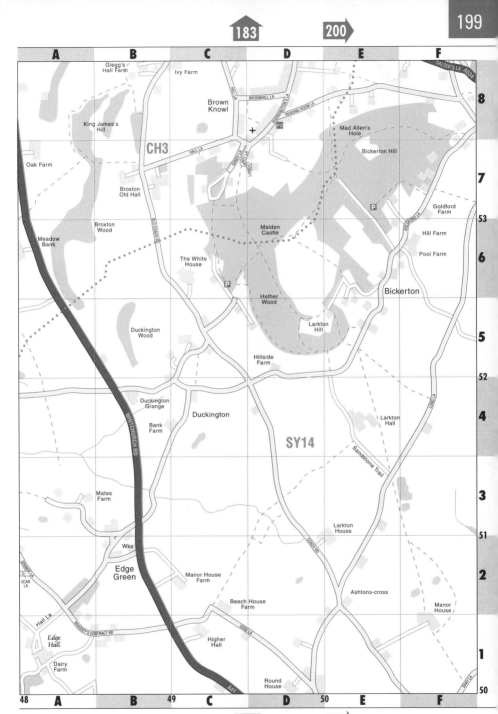

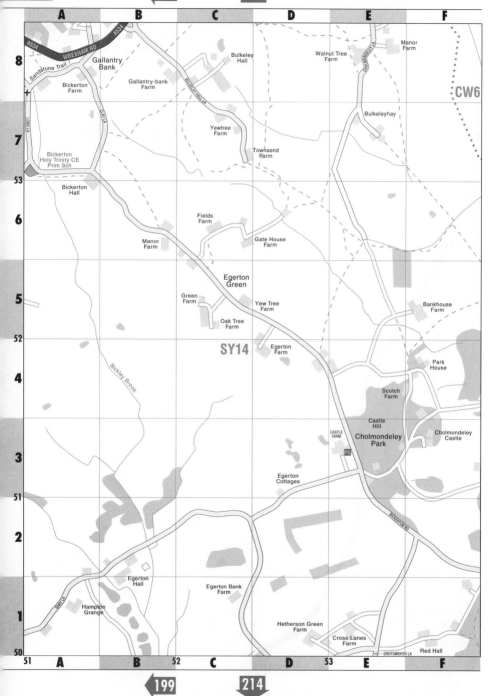

A   B   C   D   E   F

8

Sandstone Trail
A534 WREXHAM RD
A534
Gallantry Bank
Bickerton Farm
Gallantry-bank Farm
Bulkeley Hall
Walnut Tree Farm
Manor Farm
CW6

7

LONG LA
BULKELEY HALL LA
GYLL LA
CHOLMONDELEY LA
Yewtree Farm
Townsend Farm
Bulkeleyhay

53

Bickerton Holy Trinity CE Prim Sch
Bickerton Hall

6

Manor Farm
Fields Farm
Gate House Farm

Egerton Green

5

Green Farm
Oak Tree Farm
Yew Tree Farm
Bankhouse Farm

52

Bickley Brook
SY14
Egerton Farm
Park House

4

Scotch Farm

Castle Hill
CASTLE FARM
PO
Cholmondeley Park
Cholmondeley Castle

3

Egerton Cottages

51

BICKERTON RD

2

GYLL LA
Egerton Hall
Egerton Bank Farm

1

Hampton Grange
Hetherson Green Farm
Cross Lanes Farm
Red Hall

50

GROTSWORTH LA

51   A   B   52   C   D   53   E   F

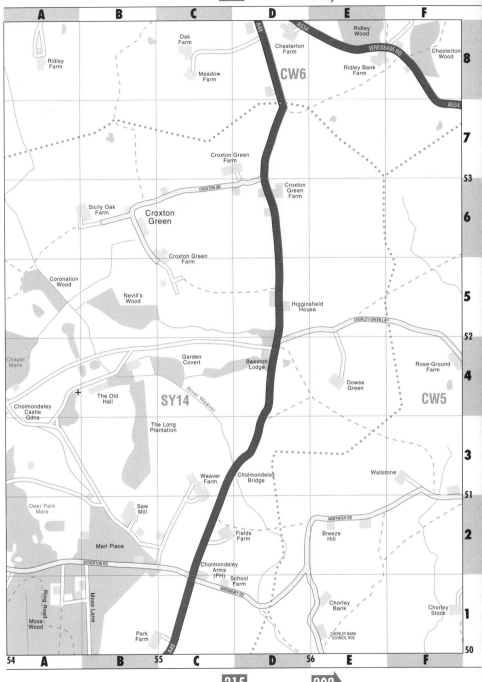

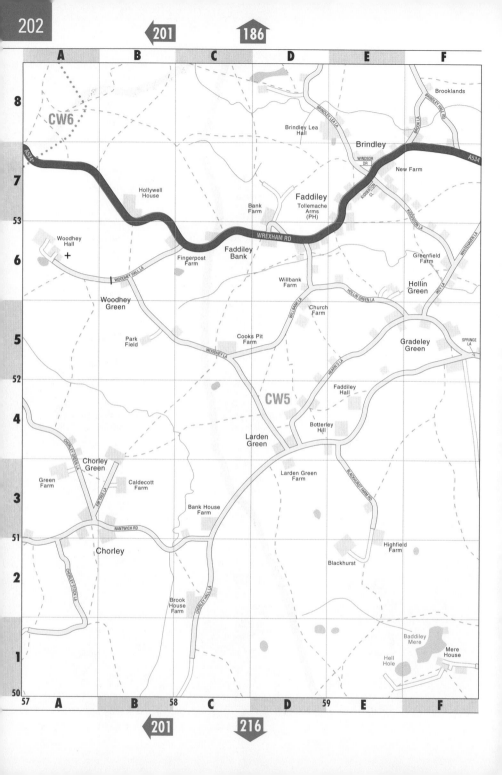

201
186

A **B** **C** **D** **E** **F**

8

CW6

7

53

6

Woodhey
Hall

Hollywell
House

Bank
Farm

Fingerpost
Farm

Faddiley
Bank

Woodhey
Green

Park
Field

Cooks Pit
Farm

Willbank
Farm

Church
Farm

5

52

CW5

Larden
Green

Botterley
Hill

Faddiley
Hall

Gradeley
Green

SPRINGE
LA

4

Chorley
Green

Green
Farm

Caldecott
Farm

Larden Green
Farm

3

Bank House
Farm

51

Chorley

NANTWICH RD

Blackhurst

Highfield
Farm

2

Brook
House
Farm

Baddiley
Mere

Mere
House

1

Hell
Hole

50

WOODHEY HALL LA

WREXHAM RD

WOODHEY LA

HEARNS LA

WILLMARK LA

HOLLIN GREEN LA

BLACKHURST FARM RD

CHORLEY HALL LA

CHORLEY STOCK LA

OAK TREE LA

CHORLEY GREEN LA

Brooklands

BRINDLEY HALL RD

BROOK LA

BRINDLEY LEA LA

Brindley Lea
Hall

Brindley

WINDSOR
DR

New Farm

Faddiley

Tollemache
Arms
(PH)

KIDDINGTON
CL

KIDDINGTON LA

WHITEMOOR LA

MILL LA

Greenfield
Farm

Hollin
Green

A534

A534

57   **A**   **B**   58   **C**   **D**   59   **E**   **F**

201
216

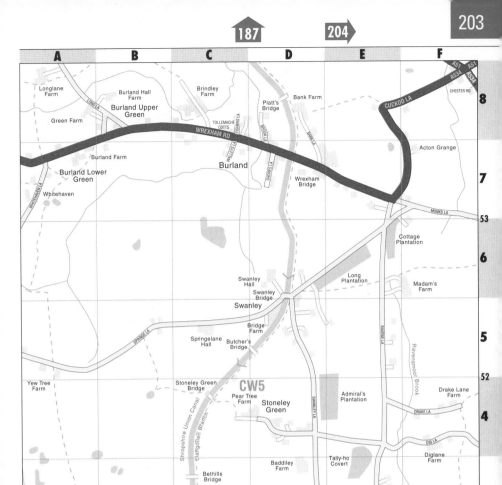

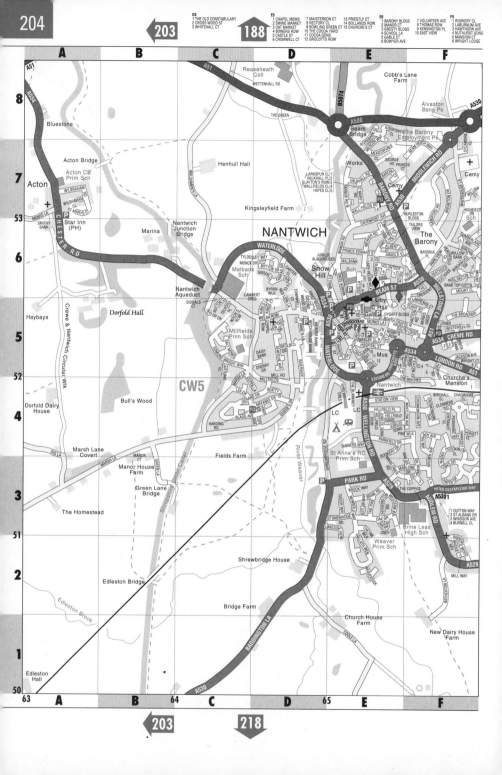

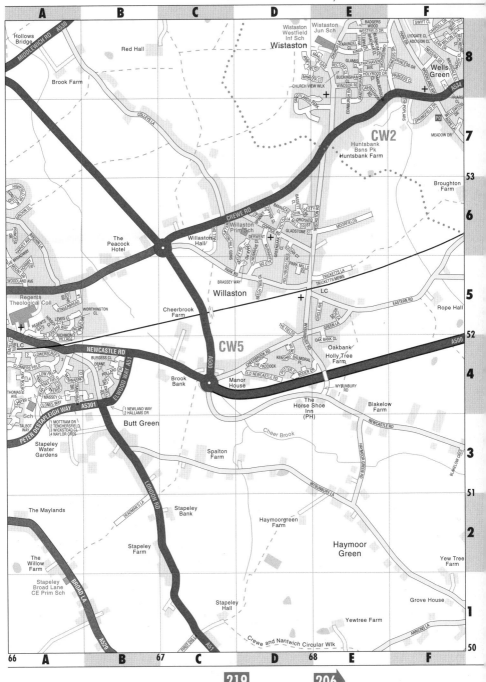

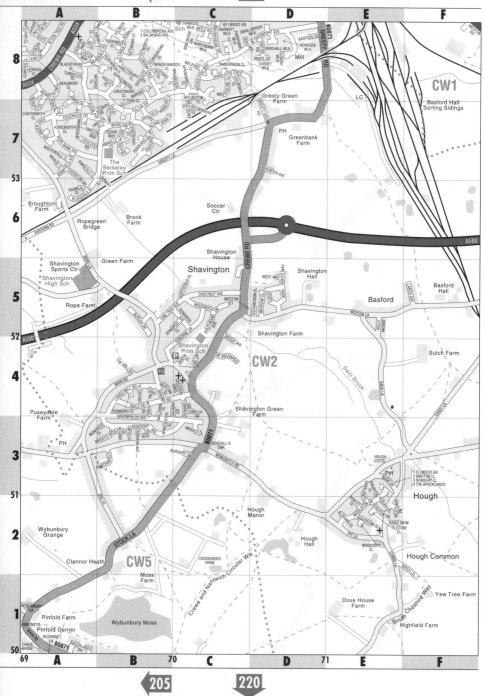

205
190

	A	B	C	D	E	F

8

CREWE RD

A534

1 COLLINSBROOK AVE
2 BALMORAL AVE

Firwood Sch
FIRWOOD WLK
ARTLE RD
HEYWOOD GN
BARNETT CL
SMALLBROOK
BIRCHALL WLK
HOWBECK WLK

NORTHBANK

B5071 GRESTY

BASFORD RD

Mill

CW1

Basford Hall
Sorting Sidings

A534

BLACKTHORN

CHATSWORTH CL
EDGEWOOD DR
KENILWORTH CL

WIGTERSDALE CL

Gresty Green Farm

Gresty La

The Berkeley Prim Sch

LC

7

53

Broughton Farm

Ropegreen Bridge

Brook Farm

Soccer Ctr

Greenbank Farm

PH

Eastern Rd

6

Shavington Sports Ctr

Green Farm

Shavington High Sch

Rope Farm

A500

Shavington House

CREWE RD

Shavington

Shavington Hall

Basford

A500

5

52

ROPE LA

CHESTNUT AVE

WESTON CT

BUCKLA

Shavington Prim Sch

WOODNOTH DR

BROOK AVE

Shavington Farm

RICHARDSON CL
WEST WAY
MEADOW CL
NORTH WAY

WESTON LA

Basford Hall

LARCH AVE

LYMM

Sutch Farm

BACK LA

CASEY LA

4

Puseydale Farm

PH

THE HOLLIES

MAIN RD

LORDS MILL RD
CAWLS RD
HEAWARD CL
GREENFIELDS AVE

PO

CAMELOT GR

WEBBEX CL

Shavington Green Farm

Swill Brook

CW2

3

MONTROSE CL
WRIGHTS AVE
ASHCROFT AVE
HUNTERS

NURSERY CL

B5071

GOODALL'S CNR

NEWCASTLE RD

HOUGH COTTS

PH

BUCKLA

1 ELLWOOD GN
2 MARTON CL
3 NORBURY CL
4 THE BROOKLANDS

Hough

51

BUCKLA

BUCKLEY TON
WOODCOTT CL
ALDERN CL
WAVERTON CL
PIT LA

KINGS MDW
TILSTONE CL

2

Wybunbury Grange

STOCK LA

Clannor Heath

CW5

Moss Farm

COCKSHADES FARM

Hough Manor

Hough Hall

WOODCOTT CL

COBBS LA

BIRCH LA

Hough Common

Hough

1

WYBUNBURY LA

Pinfold Farm

ANNIONS LA

MAIN RD

Pinfold Corner

CHADS GREEN

B5071

RIDDINGS LA

MOORLANDS DR

Wybunbury Moss

Crewe and Nantwich Circular Wlk

Dove House Farm

South Cheshire Way

Highfield Farm

Yew Tree Farm

50

69	A		B	70	C		D	71	E		F

205
220

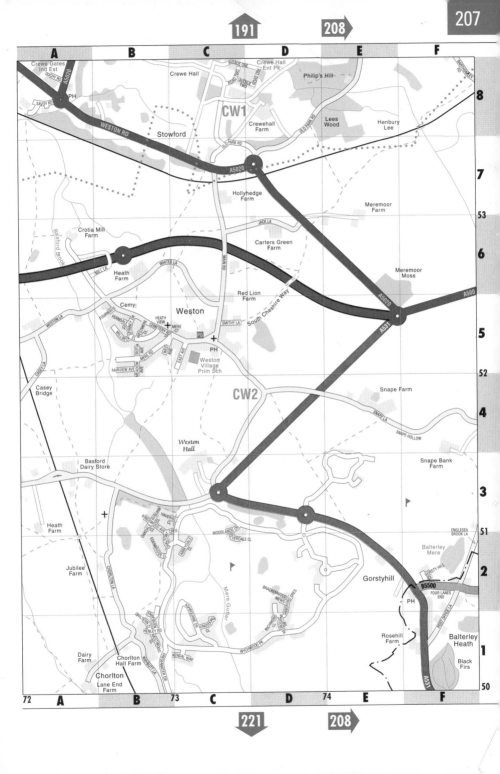

207
192

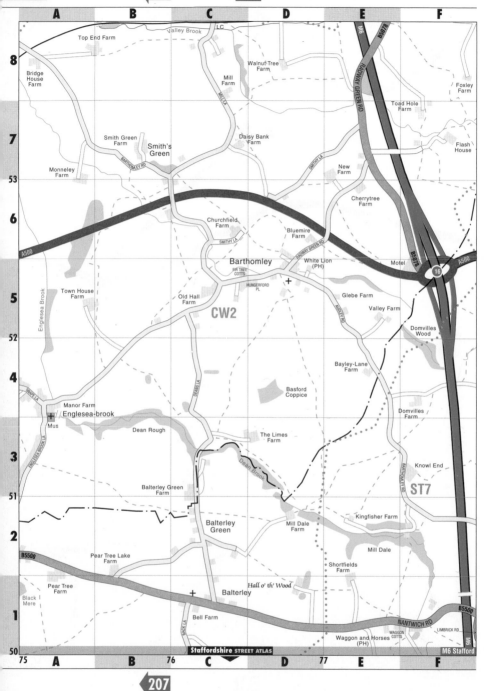

207

Staffordshire STREET ATLAS

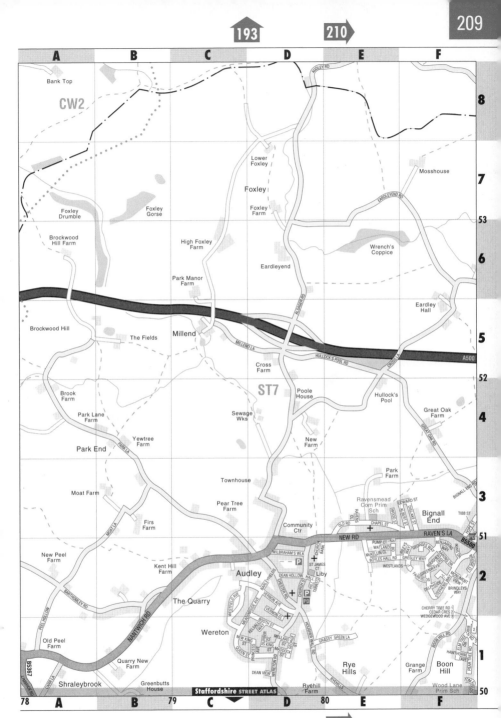

CW2

Bank Top

Lower Foxley

Foxley

Mosshouse

Foxley Gorse

Foxley Farm

Foxley Drumble

High Foxley Farm

EARDLEYEND RD

Wrench's Coppice

Brockwood Hill Farm

Eardleyend

Park Manor Farm

Eardley Hall

Brockwood Hill

Millend

The Fields

MILLEND LA

HULLOCK S POOL RD

A500

Cross Farm

ST7

Poole House

Hullock's Pool

Brook Farm

Great Oak Farm

Park Lane Farm

Sewage Wks

Yewtree Farm

Park End

New Farm

Park Farm

PARK LA

Moat Farm

Townhouse

Ravensmead Com Prim Sch

EDWARD ST

Bignall End

TIBB ST

Pear Tree Farm

Community Ctr

CHAPEL ST

RAVEN'S LA

B5500

FIRS Farm

OLD RD

NEW RD

PUMP CT

New Peel Farm

WILBRAHAM'S WLK

ST JAMES CT

McKELLIN CL

BOYLES HALL RD

GRESLEY WAY

BENJAMINS

Kent Hill Farm

WESTLANDS

NANTWICH RD

DEAN HOLLOW

Liby

Audley

BARTHOMLEY RD

The Quarry

VERNON AV

BOOTH ST

MELLARD RD

GRASSY GREEN LA

CHERRY TREE RD 1
CEDAR CRES 2
WEDGEWOOD AVE 3

PEEL HOLLOW

Wereton

NEW KING ST

KING ST

MADDOCK ST

HUGGER WALL RD

BOON HILL RD

HAWTHORNE AVE

FEATHER RD

Old Peel Farm

QUEEN ST

DEAN VIEW

Rye Hills

Grange Farm

Boon Hill

Quarry New Farm

Greenbutts House

Staffordshire STREET ATLAS

Ryehill Farm

RYEHILLS

Wood Lane Prim Sch

Shraleybrook

B5367

CARR LA

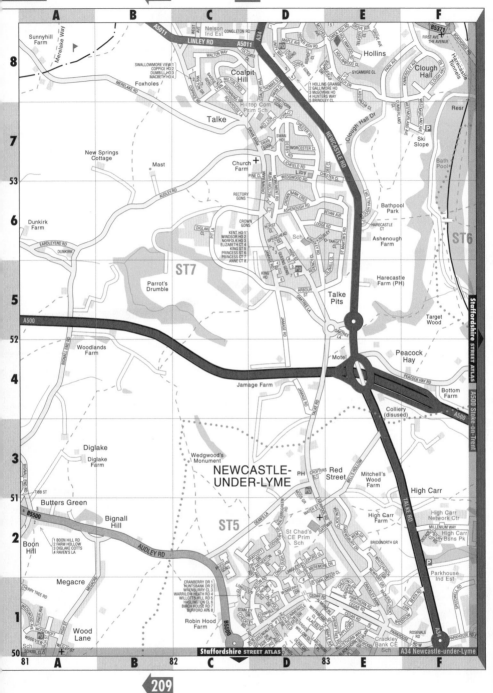

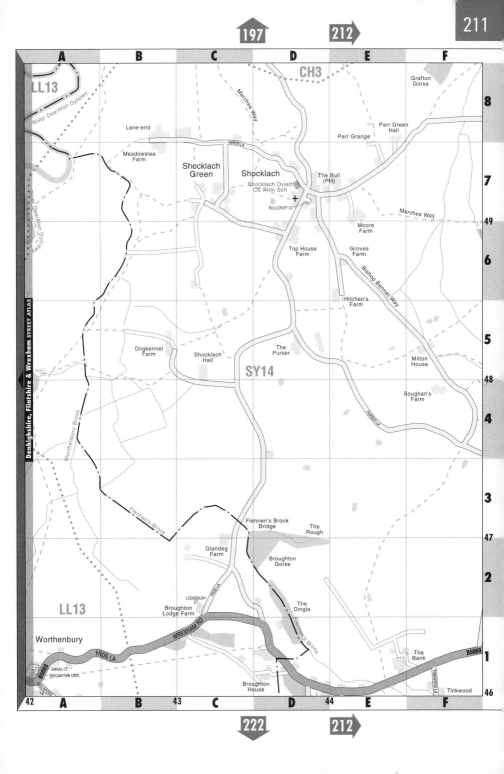

LL13

River Dee/Afon Dyfrdwy

River Dee/Afon Dyfrdwy

Denbighshire, Flintshire & Wrexham STREET ATLAS

CH3

Grafton Gorse

Lane-end

Marches Way

Parr Green Hall

Meadowslea Farm

GREEN LA

Parr Grange

Shocklach Green

Shocklach

The Bull (PH)

Shocklach Oviatt CE Prim Sch

BULLCROFT CL

Marches Way

Moore Farm

Top House Farm

Groves Farm

Bishop Bennet Way

Hitchen's Farm

Dogkennel Farm

Shocklach Hall

The Purser

SY14

Milton House

Soughan's Farm

PURSER LA

Worthenbury Brook

Flennen's Brook

Flennen's Brook Bridge

The Rough

Glandeg Farm

Broughton Gorse

LODGEBURY CT

FROG LA

Broughton Lodge Farm

LL13

The Dingle

Flennen's Brook

Worthenbury

WREXHAM RD

FROG LA

The Bank

B5069

B5069

EMRAL CT

BROUGHTON CRES

Broughton House

TINKWOOD LA

Tinkwood

8 7 49 6 5 48 4 3 47 2 1 46

42 A B 43 C D 44 E F

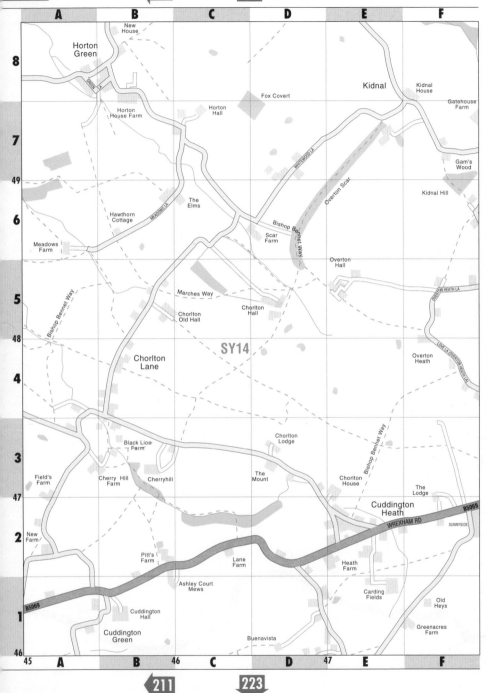

211
198

A B C D E F

8

New House

Horton Green

BREEN LA

Horton House Farm

Fox Covert

Horton Hall

Kidnal

Kidnal House

Gatehouse Farm

7

WHITEWOOD LA

Gam's Wood

49

The Elms

MEADOWS LA

Overton Scar

Kidnal Hill

6

Hawthorn Cottage

Bishop Bennet Way

Scar Farm

Overton Hall

Meadows Farm

OVERTON HEATH LA

5

Bishop Bennet Way

Marches Way

Chorlton Old Hall

Chorlton Hall

48

SY14

Overton Heath

LOVE LA (OVERTON HEATH LA)

4

Chorlton Lane

3

Black Lion Farm

Chorlton Lodge

Bishop Bennet Way

Chorlton House

The Lodge

Field's Farm

Cherry Hill Farm

Cherryhill

The Mount

47

Cuddington Heath

B5069

New Farm

WREXHAM RD

SUNNYSIDE

2

Pitt's Farm

Lane Farm

Heath Farm

B5069

Ashley Court Mews

Carding Fields

Old Heys

1

Cuddington Hall

Cuddington Green

Buenavista

Greenacres Farm

46

45 A B 46 C D 47 E F

211
223

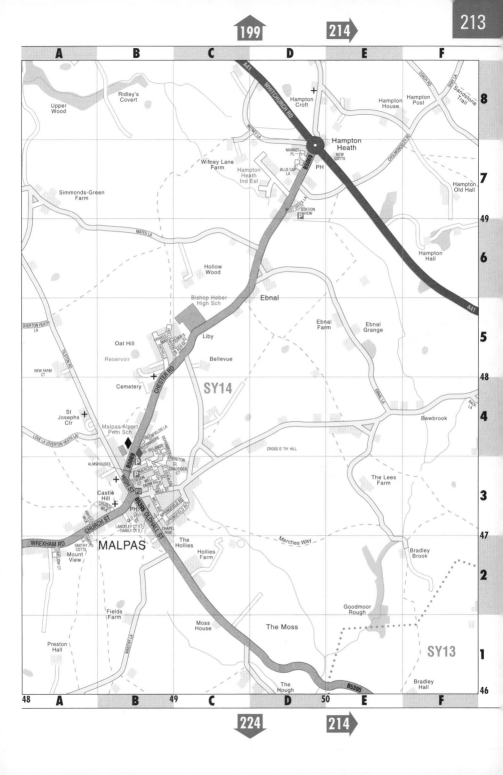

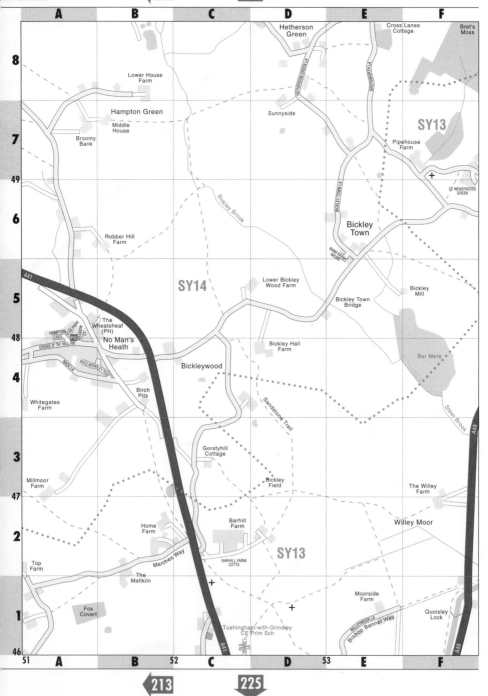

8

Hetherson
Green

Cross Lanes
Cottage

Bret's
Moss

Lower House
Farm

Hampton Green

Sunnyside

SY13

7

Middle
House

Broomy
Bank

Pipehouse
Farm

49

ST WENEFREDES
GREEN

Bickley Brook

6

Robber Hill
Farm

Bickley
Town

BANK FARM
MEWS

5

SY14

Lower Bickley
Wood Farm

Bickley Town
Bridge

Bickley
Mill

The
Wheatsheaf
(PH)

48

HAMPTON
CRES

MEADOW
CT

No Man's
Heath

CROSS O' TH' HILL RD

Bickley Hall
Farm

Bar Mere

4

Bickleywood

BACK LA

CHOLMONDELEY RISE

Birch
Pits

Whitegates
Farm

Steer Brook

A49

Sandstone Trail

3

Gorstyhill
Cottage

Millmoor
Farm

Bickley
Field

The Willey
Farm

47

Home
Farm

Barhill
Farm

Willey Moor

2

Marches Way

BARHILL FARM
COTTS

SY13

Top
Farm

The
Maltkiln

Moorside
Farm

1

Fox
Covert

Bishop Bennet Way

WILLEYMOOR LA

Quoisley
Lock

Tushingham-with-Grindley
CE Prim Sch

OLD CHESTER RD

A41

A49

46

51

A

B

52

C

D

53

E

F

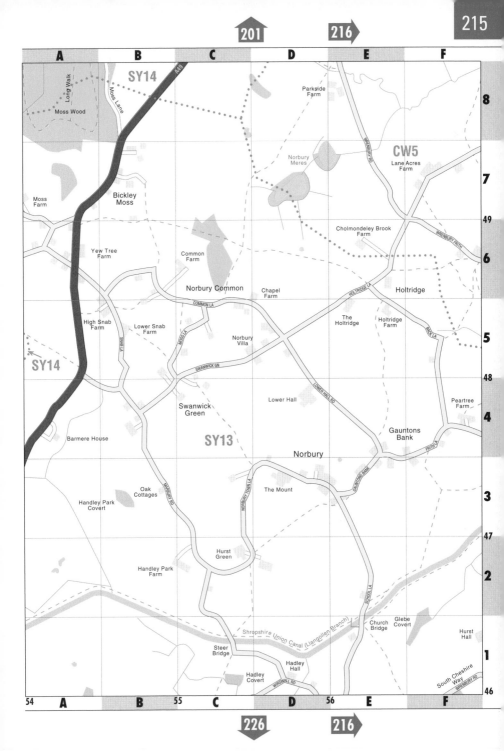

201
216
226
216

SY14

Long Walk

Moss Wood

Moss Lane

A49

SY14

Parkside Farm

CW5

Lane Acres Farm

WRENBURY RD

Norbury Meres

Moss Farm

Bickley Moss

Cholmondeley Brook Farm

WRENBURY FRITH

Yew Tree Farm

Common Farm

Norbury Common

Chapel Farm

Holtridge

HOLTRIDGE LA

The Holtridge

Holtridge Farm

BACK LA

COMMON LA

High Snab Farm

Lower Snab Farm

SNAB LA

MOSS LA

Norbury Villa

SWANWICK GN

LOWER HALL RD

Lower Hall

Peartree Farm

Swanwick Green

SY13

Barmere House

Oak Cottages

MARBURY RD

Norbury

The Mount

NORBURY TOWN LA

Gauntons Bank

GAUNTONS BANK

FRITH LA

Handley Park Covert

Handley Park Farm

Hurst Green

SCHOOL LA

Shropshire Union Canal (Llangollen Branch)

Church Bridge

Glebe Covert

Hurst Hall

Steer Bridge

Hadley Covert

Hadley Hall

WIRSWALL RD

South Cheshire Way

WRENBURY RD

54   55   56

8   7   49   6   5   48   4   3   47   2   1   46

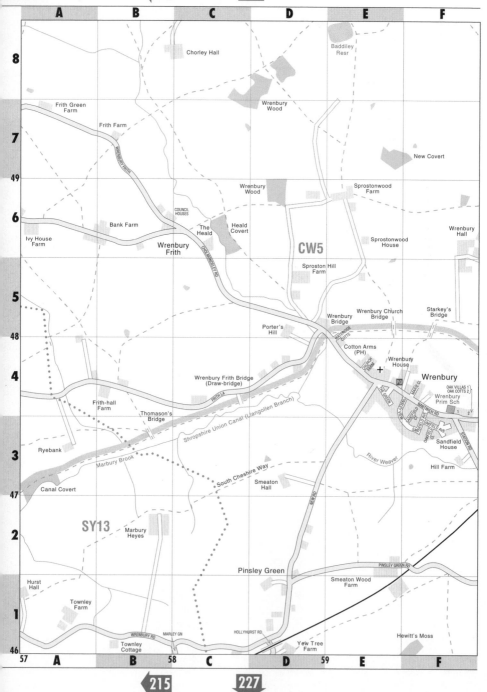

215
202

A B C D E F

8

Chorley Hall

Baddiley
Resr

Wrenbury
Wood

7

Frith Green
Farm

Frith Farm

New Covert

49

Wrenbury
Wood

Sprostonwood
Farm

6

COUNCIL
HOUSES

Bank Farm

The
Heald

Heald
Covert

Sprostonwood
House

Wrenbury
Hall

Ivy House
Farm

Wrenbury
Frith

CW5

Sproston Hill
Farm

5

Porter's
Hill

Wrenbury
Bridge

Wrenbury Church
Bridge

Starkey's
Bridge

48

Cotton Arms
(PH)

Wrenbury
House

4

Wrenbury Frith Bridge
(Draw-bridge)

FRITH LA

Wrenbury

OAK VILLAS 1
OAK COTTS 2

Wrenbury
Prim Sch

Frith-hall
Farm

Thomason's
Bridge

Shropshire Union Canal (Llangollen Branch)

Sandfield
House

3

Ryebank

Marbury Brook

South Cheshire Way

River Weaver

Hill Farm

47

Canal Covert

Smeaton
Hall

2

SY13

Marbury
Heyes

Pinsley Green

Smeaton Wood
Farm

PINSLEY GREEN RD

1

Hurst
Hall

Townley
Farm

Hewitt's Moss

46

Townley
Cottage

WRENBURY RD

MARLEY GN

HOLLYHURST RD

Yew Tree
Farm

57 A B 58 C D 59 E F

215
227

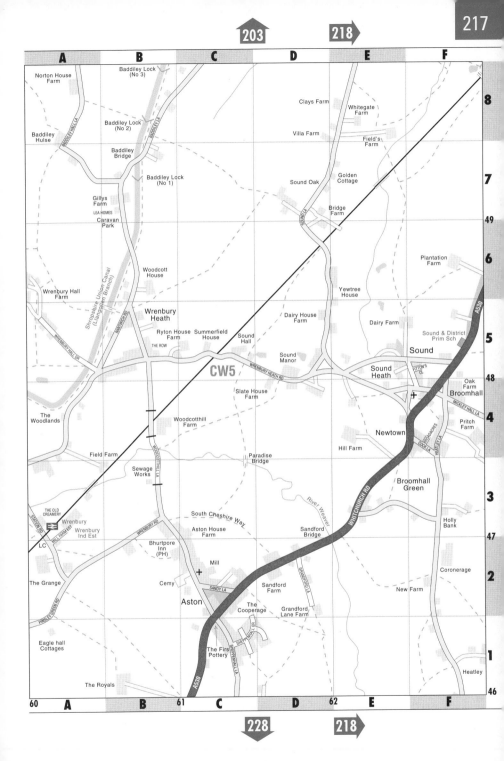

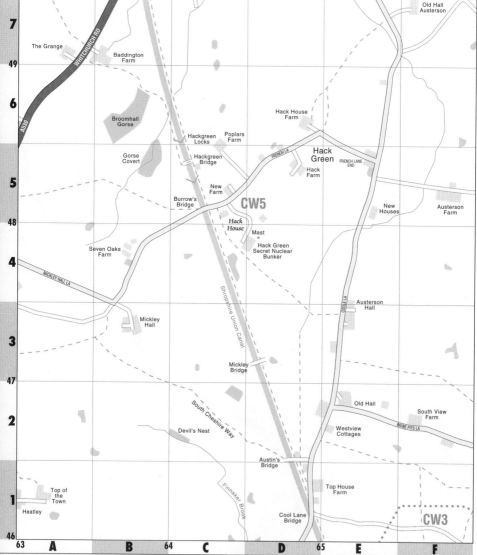

	A	B	C	D	E	F

8
The Brooklands
Baddington Lane Bridge
Baddington Bank Farm
Batherton Hall
Crewe and Nantwich Circular Walk
ATCHERLEY CL
CRISHAM AVE

7
Old Hall Austerson

49
The Grange
Baddington Farm

6
A530
Broomhall Gorse
Hack House Farm
WHITCHURCH RD
BADDINGTON LA
A530

5
Gorse Covert
Hackgreen Locks
Poplars Farm
Hackgreen Bridge
FRENCH LA
Hack Green
FRENCH LANE END
Hack Farm
New Houses
Austerson Farm
New Farm
Burrow's Bridge
CW5
Hack House

48
Mast
Hack Green Secret Nuclear Bunker
Seven Oaks Farm

4
MICKLEY HALL LA
Shropshire Union Canal
Austerson Hall
COOL LA

3
Mickley Hall
Mickley Bridge
Old Hall
South View Farm

47
South Cheshire Way
Westview Cottages
BRINE PITS LA

2
Devil's Nest
Austin's Bridge
Top House Farm

1
Top of the Town
Heatley
Finnaker Brook
Cool Lane Bridge
CW3

46

63	A	B	64	C	D	65	E	F

205
220
230
220

Crewe and Nantwich Circular Walk

White Cottage

Oakfield

Oak Farm

Stapeley

Crewe and Nantwich Circular Walk

Howbeck Bank

Five Oaks Farm

Hollies Farm

Grove Farm

Artle Brook Farm

Artlebrook Bridge

Artle Brook

Lodge Farm

Howbeck Farm

Howbeck Brook

Bridge House

Howbeck Bridge

Ashtree Farm

Acton's Rough

Chapel Farm

Oat Eddish Farm

Hatherton House

Dairy House Farm

River Weaver

CW5

GREENHAVEN CT

Hatherton Farm

Park House

Heathfield

Fields Farm

The Hollies

Motorcross Race Track

PARK LA

SANDY LA

B5071

LODGE LA

Hatherton

CREWE RD

HUNSTERSON RD

Hatherton Lodge Farm

OAKES CNR

B5071

Laurels Farm

Hatherton Hall

Chestnut Wood

Gorse Wood

Hatherton Manor

Brinepits Farm

BRINE PITS LA

Brinepits Wood

Blackthorn Wood

CW3

Broomlands

Oak Wood

Hankelow Hall

The Dell

Rookery Wood

Lodge Wood

South Cheshire Way

A529

BROOMLANDS COTTS

BIRCHALL MOSS LA

Birchall Moss

Birchall Moss

Woodside

BRIDGEMERE LA

Broomlands Lodge

A529

BROAD LA

FIRST DIG LA

SECOND DIG LA

PENMAN'S LA

A51

LONDON RD

ANNION LA

A51

AUDLEM RD

66   67   68

49   48   47   46

8   7   6   5   4   3   2   1

A   B   C   D   E   F

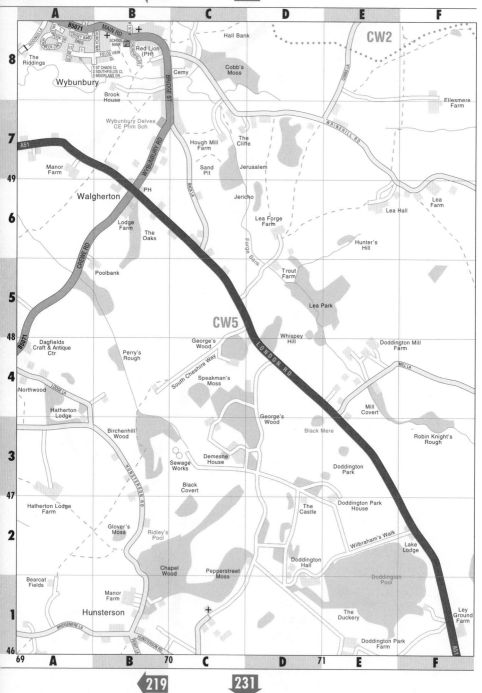

219
206
219
231

CW2

CW5

Wybunbury

Walgherton

Hunterston

The Riddings

Manor Farm

Lodge Farm

The Oaks

Poolbank

Dagfields Craft & Antique Ctr

Northwood

Hatherton Lodge

Hatherton Lodge Farm

Birchenhill Wood

Glover's Moss

Ridley's Pool

Bearcat Fields

Manor Farm

Chapel Wood

Perry's Rough

Sewage Works

Black Covert

Demesne House

Pepperstreet Moss

George's Wood

South Cheshire Way

Speakman's Moss

George's Wood

Black Mere

Whispey Hill

Doddington Mill Farm

Mill Covert

Robin Knight's Rough

Doddington Park

Doddington Park House

The Castle

Doddington Hall

Wilbraham's Walk

Lake Lodge

Doddington Pool

The Duckery

Doddington Park Farm

Ley Ground Farm

Hall Bank

Cobb's Moss

Ellesmere Farm

The Cliffe

Hough Mill Farm

Sand Pit

Jerusalem

Jericho

Lea Forge Farm

Lea Hall

Lea Farm

Hunter's Hill

Trout Farm

Lea Park

Forge Bank

Brook House

Wybunbury Delves CE Prim Sch

Red Lion (PH)

Cemy

Main Rd

School Bank

Fields View

St Chads Cl

Southfields Cl

Moorlans Dr

B5071

Bridge St

Wybunbury Rd

Back La

Crewe Rd

London Rd

Hunsterson Rd

Lodge La

Mill La

Bridgemere La

Wrinehill Rd

Cobbs La

A51

B5071

PH

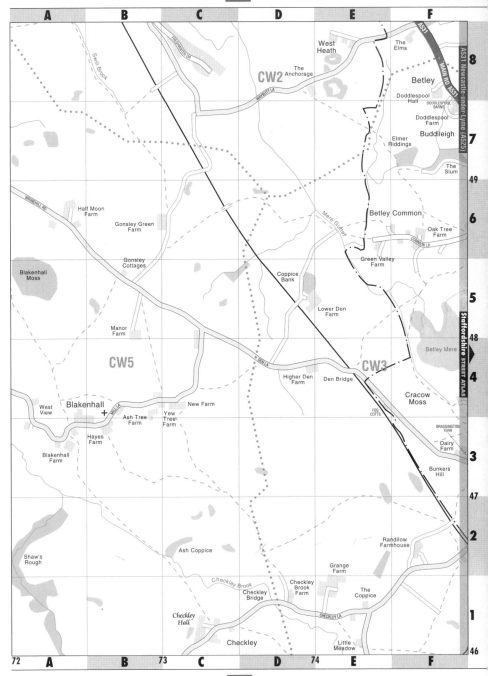

211

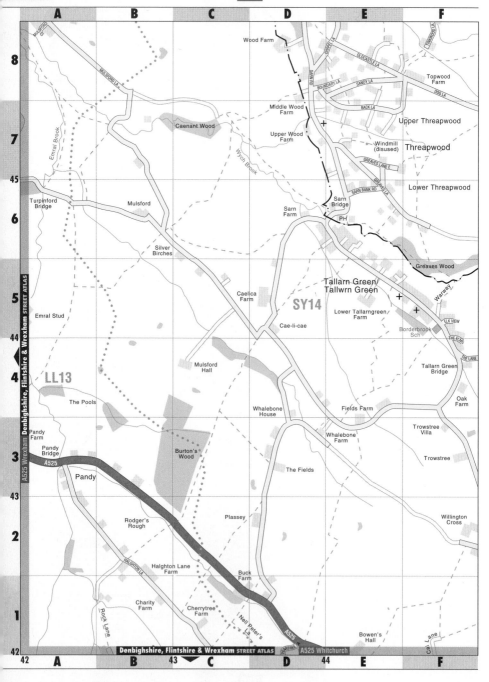

8

MILLSFORD CT

MILLSFORD LA

Wood Farm

CHAPEL LA

OLDCASTLE LA

SANDY LA

Topwood
Farm

TRWMDD LA

7

Emral Brook

Caenant Wood

Wych Brook

Middle Wood
Farm

Upper Wood
Farm

SARN RD

BOUNDARY LA

BACK LA

Upper Threapwood

Windmill
(disused)

GREAVES LANE E

Threapwood

DOG LA

45

Turpinford
Bridge

Mulsford

Sarn
Farm

SARN BANK RD

GREAVES LA

Lower Threapwood

6

Silver
Birches

Sarn
Bridge

PH

Greaves Wood

Warway

5

Emral Stud

Caelica
Farm

Cae-li-cae

SY14

Tallarn Green/
Tallwrn Green

Lower Tallarngreen
Farm

Borderbrook
Sch

ELK VIEW

THE ELMS

THE LANE

44

LL13

Mulsford
Hall

The Pools

Whalebone
House

Fields Farm

Tallarn Green
Bridge

Oak
Farm

4

Pandy
Farm

Pandy
Bridge

A525

Pandy

Burton's
Wood

Whalebone
Farm

Trowstree
Villa

Trowstree

3

The Fields

43

Rodger's
Rough

Plassey

Willington
Cross

2

HALGHTON LA

Halghton Lane
Farm

Buck
Farm

A525

1

Charity
Farm

Rock Lane

Cherrytree
Farm

Neil Peter's
La

Bowen's
Hall

Cal Lane

42

A525 Wrexham **Denbighshire, Flintshire & Wrexham** STREET ATLAS

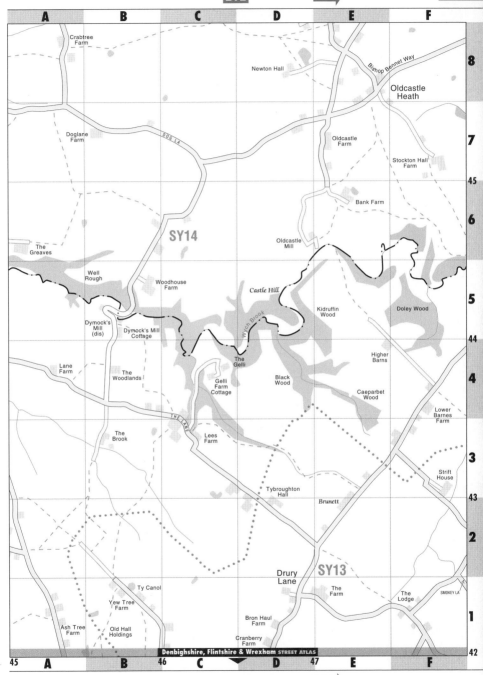

A   B   C   D   E   F

8

Crabtree Farm

Newton Hall

Bishop Bennet Way

Oldcastle Heath

7

Doglane Farm

DOG LA

Oldcastle Farm

Stockton Hall Farm

45

Bank Farm

6

SY14

The Greaves

Oldcastle Mill

Well Rough

Woodhouse Farm

Castle Hill

Kidruffin Wood

Doley Wood

5

Wytch Brook

Dymock's Mill (dis)

Dymock's Mill Cottage

The Gelli

Higher Barns

44

Lane Farm

The Woodlands

Gelli Farm Cottage

Black Wood

Caeparbet Wood

4

THE LANE

The Brook

Lees Farm

Lower Barnes Farm

3

Tybroughton Hall

Strift House

Brunett

43

2

SY13

Drury Lane

Ty Canol

Yew Tree Farm

The Farm

The Lodge

SMOKEY LA

1

Ash Tree Farm

Old Hall Holdings

Bron Haul Farm

Cranberry Farm

42

45   A   B   46   C   D   47   E   F

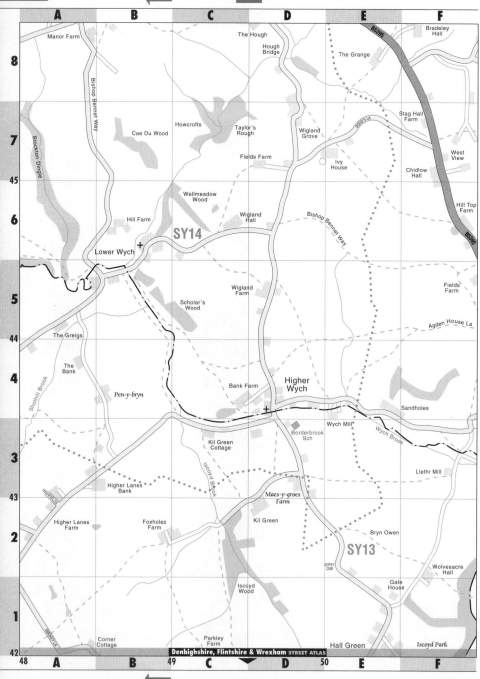

A B C D E F

8

Manor Farm

The Hough

Hough
Bridge

The Grange

B5395

Bradeley
Hall

Bishop Bennet Way

7

Stockton Dingle

Cae Du Wood

Howcrofts

Taylor's
Rough

Wigland
Grove

DODD'S LA

Stag Hall
Farm

West
View

Chidlow
Hall

45

Fields Farm

Ivy
House

6

Hill Farm

SY14

Wellmeadow
Wood

Wigland
Hall

Bishop Bennet Way

Hill Top
Farm

B5395

Lower Wych

5

Scholar's
Wood

Wigland
Farm

Fields
Farm

44

The Greigs

Agden House La

4

Snothill Brook

The
Bank

Pen-y-bryn

Bank Farm

Higher
Wych

Sandholes

Wych Brook

3

Kil Green
Cottage

Iscoyd Brook

Borderbrook
Sch

Wych Mill

Llethr Mill

43

HIGHERLOS

Higher Lanes
Bank

Maes-y-groes
Farm

2

Higher Lanes
Farm

Foxholes
Farm

Kil Green

Bryn Owen

SY13

Wolvesacre
Hall

GIPSY
CNR

Gate
House

1

Iscoyd
Wood

42

Corner
Cottage

Parkley
Farm

Hall Green

Iscoyd Park

48 A B 49 C D 50 E F

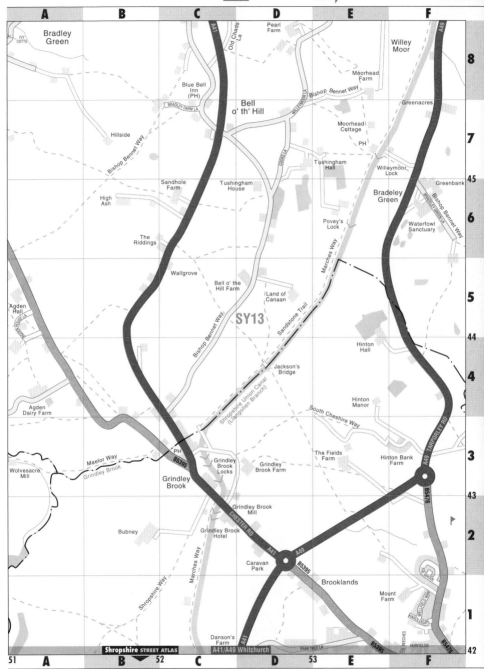

A   B   C   D   E   F

Bradley
Green

IVY
COTTS

Hillside

Bishop Bennet Way

High
Ash

Sandhole
Farm

The
Riddings

Wallgrove

Agden
Hall

Bell o' the
Hill Farm

Bishop Bennet Way

SY13

Land of
Canaan

Agden
Dairy Farm

Shropshire Union Canal
(Llangollen Branch)

Jackson's
Bridge

Maelor Way

Grindley Brook

Wolvesacre
Mill

PH
B5395

Grindley
Brook

Grindley
Brook
Locks

Grindley
Brook Farm

The Fields
Farm

South Cheshire Way

Hinton
Manor

Hinton Bank
Farm

Bubney

Grindley Brook
Mill

Grindley Brook
Hotel

CHESTER RD

Marches Way

Caravan
Park

A41

A49

B5395

Brooklands

Mount
Farm

Shropshire Way

Danson's
Farm

PEAR TREE LA

B5395

THE BREECHES

FAIRFIELDS

A5476

Blue Bell
Inn
(PH)

BRADLEY FARM LA

Bell
o' th' Hill

Old Chads La

A41

Pearl
Farm

Bishop Bennet Way

WELLSMOOR LA

COOKS LA

Moorhead
Farm

Moorhead
Cottage

PH

Tushingham
Hall

Tushingham
House

Povey's
Lock

Marches Way

Sandstone Trail

Willey
Moor

A49

Greenacres

Willeymoor
Lock

Bradeley
Green

Greenbank

BRADELEY GREEN LA

Bishop Bennet Way

Waterfowl
Sanctuary

Hinton
Hall

A49 TARPORLEY RD

A49

B5476

THE BIRCHES

WELLFIELD WK

FAIRFIELDS

A5476

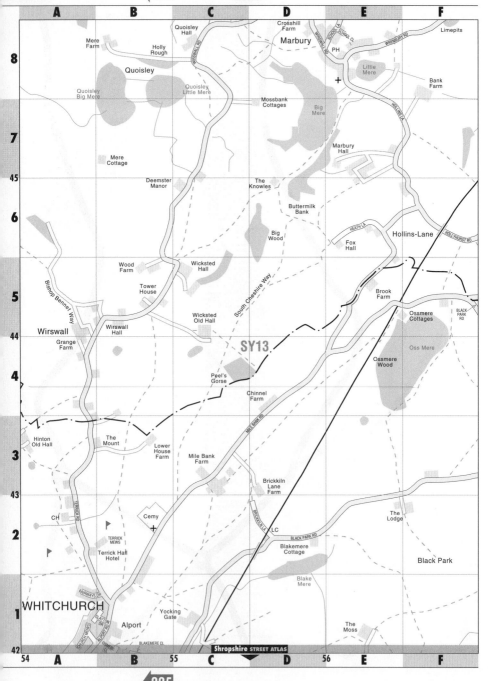

Shropshire STREET ATLAS

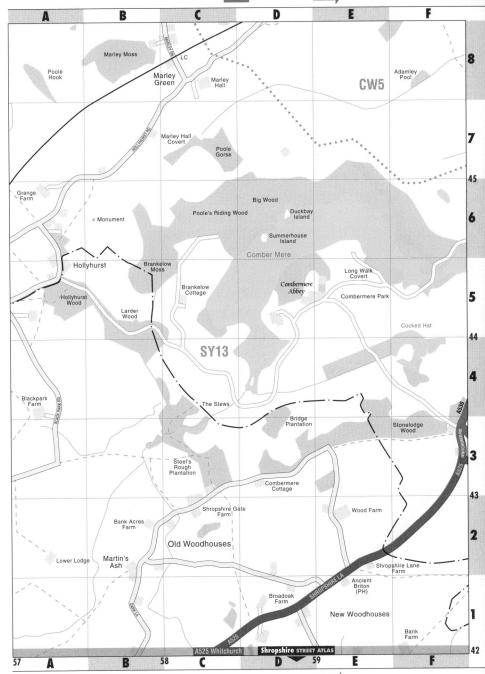

216
228

A   B   C   D   E   F

8

Marley Moss

Poole
Hook

MARLEY DR

LC

Marley
Green

Marley
Hall

CW5

Adamley
Pool

7

HOLLYHURST RD

Marley Hall
Covert

Poole
Gorse

45

Grange
Farm

Monument

Big Wood

Poole's Riding Wood

Duckbay
Island

6

Summerhouse
Island

Comber Mere

Hollyhurst

Brankelow
Moss

Brankelow
Cottage

Combermere
Abbey

Long Walk
Covert

Combermere Park

5

Hollyhurst
Wood

Larder
Wood

Cocked Hat

44

SY13

The Stews

Bridge
Plantation

Stonelodge
Wood

A530

WHITCHURCH RD

4

Blackpark
Farm

BLACK PARK RD

Steel's
Rough
Plantation

Combermere
Cottage

43

3

Shropshire Gate
Farm

Wood Farm

2

Bank Acres
Farm

Old Woodhouses

Lower Lodge

Martin's
Ash

DARK LA

Shropshire Lane
Farm

A525

Broadoak
Farm

SHROPSHIRE LA

Ancient
Briton
(PH)

New Woodhouses

1

Bank
Farm

42

A525 Whitchurch

Shropshire STREET ATLAS

57   A   B   58   C   D   59   E   F

228

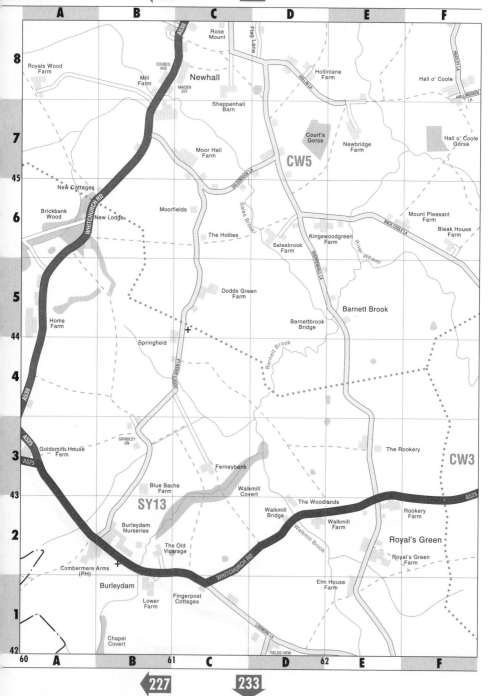

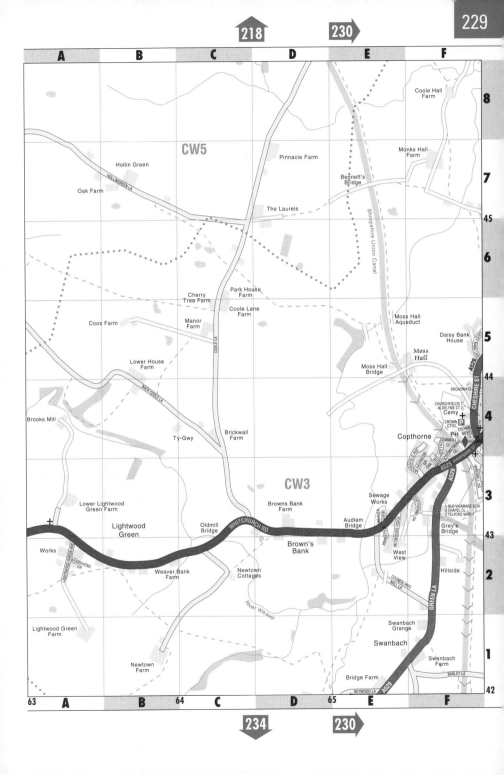

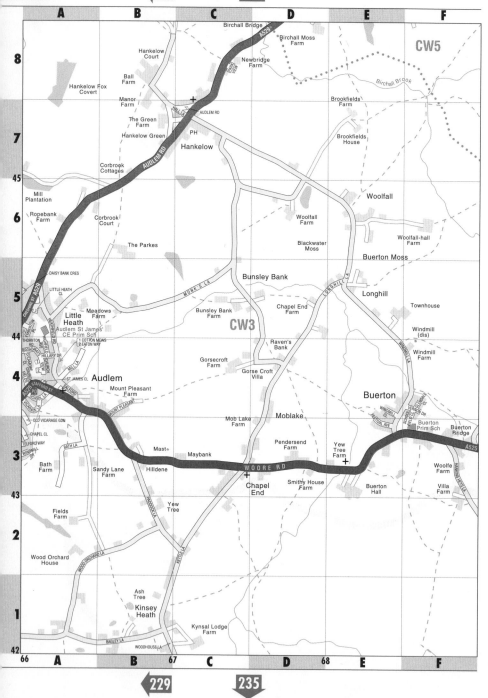

229

219

A B C D E F

8

CW5

Birchall Bridge

Birchall Moss
Farm

Newbridge
Farm

Hankelow
Court

Birchall Brook

Ball
Farm

Hankelow Fox
Covert

Manor
Farm

Brookfields
Farm

7

The Green
Farm

AUDLEM RD

PH

Brookfields
House

Hankelow Green

Hankelow

45

Corbrook
Cottages

Woolfall

6

Mill
Plantation

Ropebank
Farm

Corbrook
Court

Woolfall
Farm

Woolfall-hall
Farm

The Parkes

Blackwater
Moss

Buerton Moss

DAISY BANK CRES

Bunsley Bank

LONGHILL LA

Longhill

5

CHURCH ST A529

LITTLE HEATH
CL

MONK'S LA

Meadows
Farm

Bunsley Bank
Farm

Chapel End
Farm

Townhouse

Little
Heath

HEATHFIELD RD

Audlem St James'
CE Prim Sch

CW3

Windmill
(dis)

44

THORNTON
RD

1 COTTON MEWS
2 EATON WAY

WINDMILL LA

Windmill
Farm

BROADLANDS

HILLARY DR

Raven's
Bank

Gorsecroft
Farm

BELL LA

ST JAMES CL

Audlem

Gorse Croft
Villa

Buerton

4

A529

ST STAFFORD ST

SCHOOL LA

Mount Pleasant
Farm

MOUNT PLEASANT

Mob Lake
Farm

Moblake

SCHOOL LA
FIELDS RD

FESTIVAL AVE

WINDMILL

Buerton
Prim Sch

Buerton
Bridge

OLD VICARAGE GDN

Pendersend
Farm

Yew
Tree
Farm

A525

CHAPEL CL

Mast

Maybank

WOORE RD

Smithy House
Farm

Woolfe
Farm

3

TELFORD WAY

WIGNALL DR

BATH LA

Bath
Farm

Sandy Lane
Farm

Hilldene

Buerton
Hall

Villa
Farm

HANKINS HEYS LA

43

Fields
Farm

Yew
Tree

Chapel
End

PRODCOCK LA

KETTEL LA

2

Wood Orchard
House

WOOD ORCHARD LA

1

Ash
Tree

Kinsey
Heath

Kynsal Lodge
Farm

BAGLEY LA

WOODHOUSE LA

42

66 A B 67 C D 68 E F

229

235

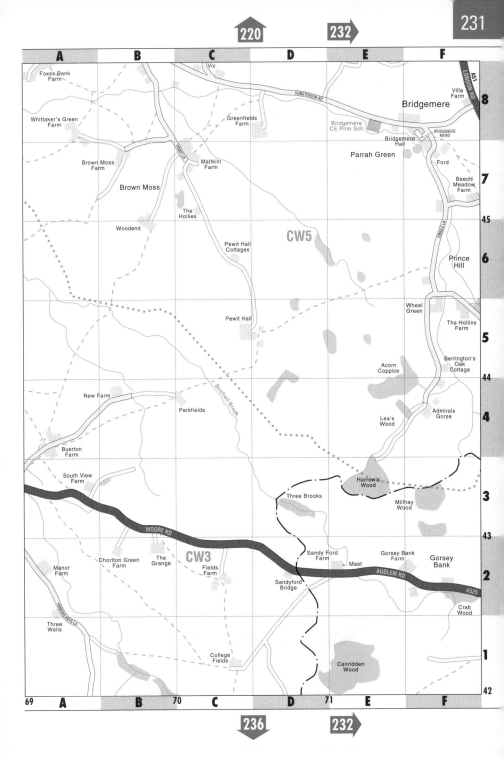

Foxes Bank Farm

Vic

Whittaker's Green Farm

Greenfields Farm

HUNSTERSON RD

Bridgemere

Villa Farm

A51 LONDON RD

Bridgemere CE Prim Sch

BRIDGEMERE MEWS

Bridgemere Hall

Parrah Green

Ford

Brown Moss Farm

PEWIT LA

Maltkiln Farm

Beech Meadow Farm

Brown Moss

The Hollies

7

45

Woodend

Pewit Hall Cottages

CW5

Prince Hill

6

Pewit Hall

Wheel Green

The Hollins Farm

5

44

Acorn Coppice

Berrington's Oak Cottage

DINKLE LA

New Farm

Birchall Brook

Parkfields

Lea's Wood

Admirals Gorse

4

Buerton Farm

South View Farm

Harrow's Wood

Three Brooks

Millhay Wood

3

43

WOORE RD

Choriton Green Farm

The Grange

CW3

Fields Farm

Sandy Ford Farm

Mast

Gorsey Bank Farm

Gorsey Bank

Manor Farm

Sandyford Bridge

AUDLEM RD

A525

2

Three Wells

HARKERS LA

Crab Wood

College Fields

Canridden Wood

1

42

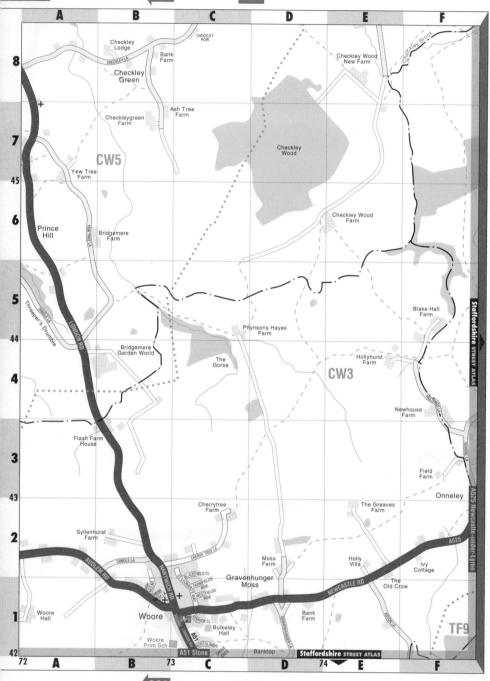

A B C D E F

8

Checkley
Lodge

Checkley
Row

Bank
Farm

Checkley Wood
New Farm

Checkley Brook

CHECKLEY LA

Checkley
Green

7

Ash Tree
Farm

Checkleygreen
Farm

CW5

Checkley
Wood

45

Yew Tree
Farm

6

Prince
Hill

Bridgemere
Farm

Checkley Wood
Farm

YEW TREE LA

LONDON RD

5

Threapers Drumble

Blake Hall
Farm

JINGLE LA

44

Phynsons Hayes
Farm

Bridgemere
Garden World

Hollyhurst
Farm

Staffordshire STREET ATLAS

4

The
Gorse

CW3

HOLDINGS LA

Newhouse
Farm

Flash Farm
House

3

Field
Farm

SCHOOL LA

A525 Newcastle-under-Lyme

43

Onneley

Cherrytree
Farm

The Greaves
Farm

2

Syllenhurst
Farm

A525

AUDLEM RD

CANDLE LA

CHERRY TREE LA

Holly
Villa

Ivy
Cottage

BLAIZEFIELD CL

ST LEONARDS
RISE

NANTWICH RD

Moss
Farm

Gravenhunger
Moss

NEWCASTLE RD

The
Old Crow

ASTON LA

WESTFIELDS
RISE

1

Woore
Hall

Bank
Farm

GRAVENHUNGER LA

TF9

Bulkeley
Hall

Woore

DORRICK CL

LONDON RD

42

Woore
Prim Sch

NORTHLANDS

Banktop

72 A B 73 C D 74 E F

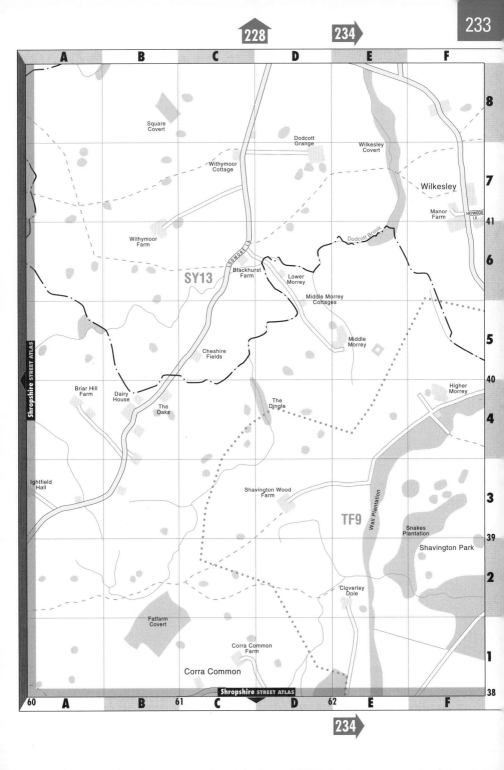

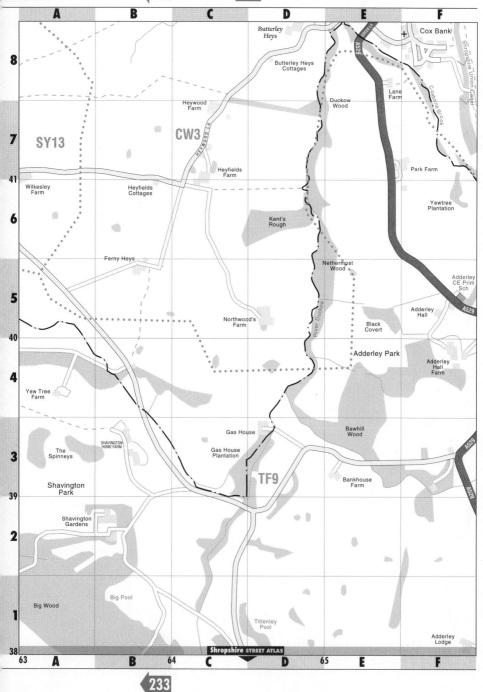

8

7

SY13

CW3

41

6

5

40

4

3

39

2

1

38

A B C D E F

Butterley
Heys

Butterley Heys
Cottages

Heywood
Farm

Duckow
Wood

Cox Bank

GREEN LA

A529

Lane
Farm

Shropshire Union Canal

Coxbank Brook

Park Farm

Heyfields
Farm

Wilkesley
Farm

Heyfields
Cottages

Yewtree
Plantation

Kent's
Rough

Ferny Heys

Nethermost
Wood

Adderley
CE Prim
Sch

A529

Northwood's
Farm

River Duckow

Black
Covert

Adderley
Hall

40

Adderley Park

Adderley
Hall
Farm

Yew Tree
Farm

Gas House

Bawhill
Wood

A529

The
Spinneys

SHAVINGTON
HOME FARM

Gas House
Plantation

TF9

Bankhouse
Farm

Shavington
Park

39

Shavington
Gardens

Big Wood

Big Pool

Tittenley
Pool

Adderley
Lodge

63 A B 64 C D 65 E F

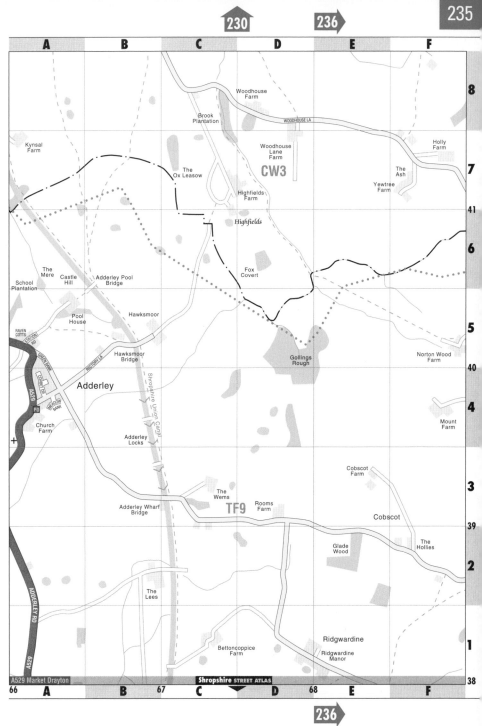

A B C D E F

8

Woodhouse Farm

Brook Plantation

WOODHOUSE LA

Kynsal Farm

Woodhouse Lane Farm

Holly Farm

The Ox Leasow

CW3

The Ash

7

Yewtree Farm

Highfields Farm

41

Highfields

The Mere

School Plantation

Castle Hill

Adderley Pool Bridge

Fox Covert

6

Pool House

Hawksmoor

RAVEN COTTS

STATION RD

GREEN BANK

RECTORY LA

Hawksmoor Bridge

Gollings Rough

Norton Wood Farm

5

40

Adderley

A529

CORBET DR

MEADOW BANK

PO

Shropshire Union Canal

Mount Farm

4

Church Farm

Adderley Locks

+

Cobscot Farm

3

Adderley Wharf Bridge

The Wems

TF9

Rooms Farm

Cobscot

39

Glade Wood

The Hollies

2

ADDERLEY RD

A529

The Lees

Bettoncoppice Farm

Ridgwardine

Ridgwardine Manor

1

38

66 A 67 B C 68 D E F

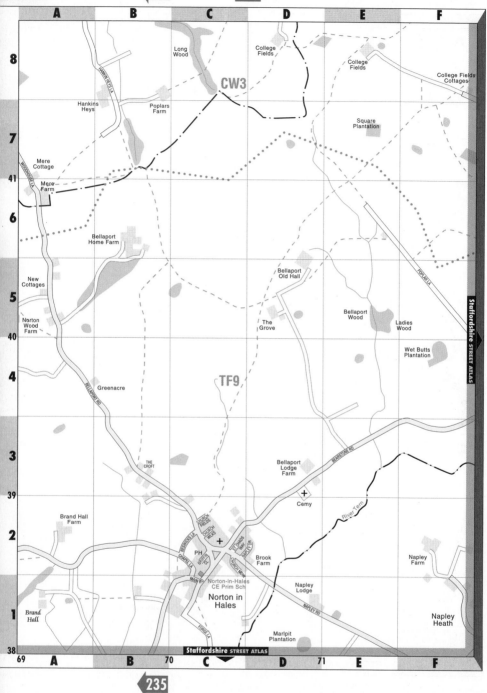

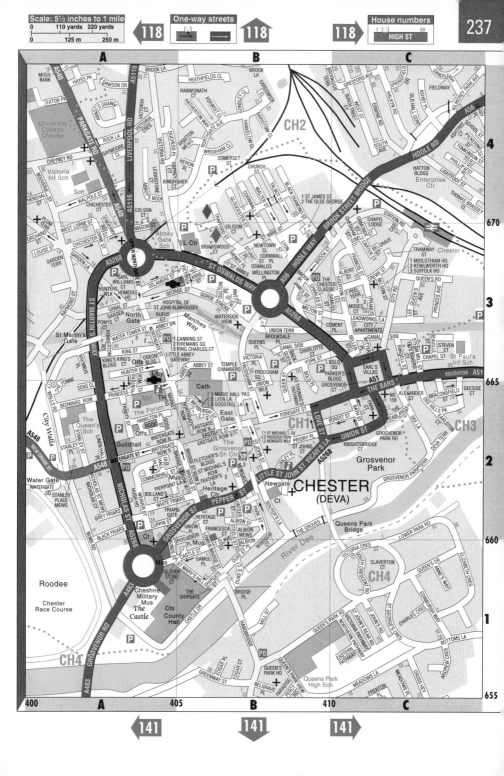

Index

Church Rd **6** Beckenham BR2......... **53** C6

Place name
May be abbreviated
on the map

Location number
Present when a number
indicates the place's
position in a crowded area
of mapping

Locality, town or village
Shown when more than one
place has the same name

Postcode district
District for the indexed place

Page and grid square
Page number and grid
reference for the standard
mapping

Public and commercial buildings are highlighted in magenta   **Places of interest** are highlighted in blue with a star ✶

Abbreviations used in the index

Acad	Academy	Comm	Common	Gd	Ground	L	Leisure	Prom	Promenade
App	Approach	Cott	Cottage	Gdn	Garden	La	Lane	Rd	Road
Arc	Arcade	Cres	Crescent	Gn	Green	Liby	Library	Recn	Recreation
Ave	Avenue	Cswy	Causeway	Gr	Grove	Mdw	Meadow	Ret	Retail
Bglw	Bungalow	Ct	Court	H	Hall	Meml	Memorial	Sh	Shopping
Bldg	Building	Ctr	Centre	Ho	House	Mkt	Market	Sq	Square
Bsns, Bus	Business	Ctry	Country	Hospl	Hospital	Mus	Museum	St	Street
Bvd	Boulevard	Cty	County	HQ	Headquarters	Orch	Orchard	Sta	Station
Cath	Cathedral	Dr	Drive	Hts	Heights	Pal	Palace	Terr	Terrace
Cir	Circus	Dro	Drove	Ind	Industrial	Par	Parade	TH	Town Hall
Cl	Close	Ed	Education	Inst	Institute	Pas	Passage	Univ	University
Cnr	Corner	Emb	Embankment	Int	International	Pk	Park	Wk, Wlk	Walk
Coll	College	Est	Estate	Intc	Interchange	Pl	Place	Wr	Water
Com	Community	Ex	Exhibition	Junc	Junction	Prec	Precinct	Yd	Yard

Index of localities, towns and villages

A

Abbot's Meads 118 A4
Acton 204 A7
Acton Bridge 76 E3
Adderley 235 B4
Adder's Moss 85 F6
Adlington 62 D5
Alderley Edge 60 C2
Aldersey Green 182 C6
Aldford 163 F3
Allgreave 137 C3
Allostock 106 E3
Alport 226 B1
Alpraham 169 C4
Alsager 193 E5
Altrincham 31 C8
Alvanley 73 C1
Anderton 78 D4
Antrobus 53 C4
Appleton 13 A2
Appleton Park 26 D5
Appleton Thorn 27 B4
Arclid 154 B1
Arclid Green 176 A8
Arley 54 C7
Arley Green 54 E6
Ashley 31 E5
Ashley Heath 31 E8
Ashton Hayes 121 F7
Ashton's Green 1 B3
Astbury 178 B7
Astbury Marsh 156 B1
Astle 109 D8
Astmoor 23 E3
Aston Nantwich 217 C2
Aston Heath 50 E2
Aston juxta Mondrum ..188 E6
Audlem 230 B4
Audley 209 D2

B

Bache 118 C5
Backford 95 A4

Baddiley 203 B1
Balderton 140 C1
Ball o' Ditton 12 E2
Balterley 208 C1
Balterley Green 208 C2
Balterley Heath 207 F1
Bank Heath 3 A8
Bank Quay 14 F4
Barbridge 187 C6
Barnett Brook 228 E5
Barnhill 183 B1
Barnton 78 C4
Barrets Green 169 D3
Barrows Green 189 F8
Barrow's Green 13 E4
Barthomley 208 D5
Barton 181 F1
Basford 206 E5
Bate Heath 54 F3
Bath Vale 157 B3
Bebington 43 A7
Beechwood 49 E5
Beeston 168 A2
Beeston-brook 168 C5
Belgrave 162 E6
Bell o' th' Hill 225 D7
Betchton Heath 175 E5
Betley 221 F8
Betley Common 221 E6
Bewsey 15 F8
Bickerton 199 E6
Bickley Moss 215 B7
Bickley Town 214 E6
Bickleywood 214 C4
Biddulph 179 B2
Biddulph Common 179 F8
Bignall End 209 F3
Birchall Moss 219 E1
Birch Heath 168 B8
Birchwood 9 E5
Blackbrook Haydock ...1 A7
Blackbrook Warrington .8 E2
Blacon 117 F3
Blakenhall 221 A4
Bold Heath 13 E7
Bollington 88 B7
Bollington Cross 87 F7

Boon Hill 209 F1
Booth Bank 30 B7
Booth Green 62 F7
Boothsdale 122 E3
Booth's Hill 18 C2
Bosley 158 D8
Bostock Green 127 C7
Boughton 119 A2
Boughton Heath 142 A8
Bradeley Green 225 F6
Bradfield Green 172 E3
Bradley Green 225 A8
Bradley Mount 87 B7
Bradwall Green 153 B3
Bramhall 35 D8
Brassey Green 167 D6
Bratt's Bank 101 B5
Brereton Green 153 F5
Brereton Heath 154 F6
Bretton 139 E4
Bridgemere 231 F8
Bridgemont 39 E2
Bridge Trafford 97 A3
Brindley 202 E7
Brindley Green 153 E2
Broadoak 162 B1
Broken Cross Macclesfield 111 E8
Broken Cross Northwich .104 E7
Brookhouse 88 D3
Brookhouse Green 177 A7
Brookhurst 43 C5
Brooklands 225 E1
Brookvale 50 B5
Broom Bank 144 B8
Broomedge 19 C1
Broomhall 217 F4
Broomhall Green 217 E3
Broomhill 120 F8
Broughton 139 B4
Brownedge 154 A3
Brown Heath 143 B6
Brownhill 147 B6
Brown Knowl 199 C8
Brownlow 177 E7
Brownlow Heath 177 E5
Brown Moss 231 B7

Brown's Bank 229 D2
Broxton 183 A1
Bruche 16 F7
Bruera 164 D6
Bryn 102 A6
Bucklow Hill 30 C3
Buckoak 99 A5
Buddileigh 221 F7
Budworth Heath 54 A1
Buerton 230 E4
Buglawton 157 A4
Bulkeley 184 E2
Bunbury 185 F8
Bunbury Commons 169 A2
Bunbury Heath 185 D8
Bunsley Bank 230 C5
Burland 203 C7
Burland Lower Green ..203 A7
Burland Upper Green ..203 B8
Burleydam 228 B1
Burton Duddon 144 F4
Burton Neston 67 D1
Burton Green 161 D1
Burtonwood 6 E6
Burwardsley 184 B5
Butley Town 87 C8
Butters Green 210 A2
Butt Green 205 B3
Butt Lane 194 D1
Byley 129 A7

C

Cadishead 11 E5
Caldecott Green 197 C4
Calrofold 88 C2
Calveley 169 E2
Capenhurst 94 A8
Castlefields 23 F2
Castletown 197 D3
Chapel End 230 D3
Cheadle Hulme 35 A8
Checkley 221 C1
Checkley Green 232 B8
Chelford 84 B2
Chester 237 B2

Childer Thornton 69 B8
Cholmondeston 170 F4
Chorley 202 B2
Chorley Green 202 A3
Chorlton 207 B1
Chorlton Lane 212 B4
Chowley 182 F5
Christleton 142 F8
Church Green 18 E2
Church Hill 149 F7
Church Lawton 194 C5
Church Minshull 172 A6
Churton 180 E5
Cinnamon Brow 8 F4
Clark Green 63 A3
Clifton 49 D4
Clive 150 C8
Clive Green 150 D6
Clotton 145 D4
Cloud Side 157 F4
Clough Hall 210 F8
Clutton 182 D1
Coalpit Hill 210 C8
Cobbs 26 E8
Cobscot 235 E3
Coddington 182 A3
Coldharbour 164 F5
Cold Moss Heath 175 D5
Collins Green 1 E1
Comberbach 78 C2
Commonside 100 B8
Common Side 124 D3
Congleton 157 A4
Connah's Quay 91 B1
Cooksongreen 76 A1
Coppenhall 190 D7
Coppenhall Moss 173 D1
Copthorne 229 F4
Cotebrook 147 A8
Cox Bank 234 F8
Crabtree Garden 101 C1
Cranage 130 E5
Crewe 190 C5
Crewe-by-Farndon ...197 A7
Crewe Green 191 B3
Croft 9 B8
Cronton 12 D5

Cross Lane 172 D6
Cross Town 57 B2
Croughton 95 F5
Crowton 76 C1
Crow Wood 13 D3
Croxton Green 201 B6
Cuckoo's Nest 162 E5
Cuddington 101 F4
Cuddington Green 212 B1
Cuddington Heath 212 E2
Cuerdley Cross 14 A2
Culcheth 4 E3
Culcheth Carrs 4 E6
Curzon Park 141 B7

D

Dales Green 195 C5
Danebank 38 E5
Danebridge 160 B7
Dane in Shaw 179 C8
Daresbury 25 B2
Daresbury Delph 25 B1
Davenham 104 A2
Davenport 154 E7
Davenport Green 59 F3
Day Green 192 F8
Dean Row 60 F8
Delamere 123 D6
Delamere Park 101 C5
Derbyshire Hill 1 A2
Diglake 210 A3
Disley 38 C5
Ditton 22 C8
Ditton Marsh 22 D6
Dodleston 162 A7
Dones Green 77 B8
Dove Bank 195 A2
Drury Lane 223 D2
Duckington 199 C4
Duddon 145 A6
Duddon Heath 144 E7
Dudlow's Green 26 E5
Dukesfield 4 E6
Dunham Heath 98 A4
Dunham-on-the-Hill 97 E5
Dunham Town 20 E4
Dunham Woodhouses . . .20 B4
Dunkirk 94 E6
Dutton 51 A4

E

Earlestown 2 B2
Eastham 43 F7
Eastham Ferry 44 B8
Eaton Congleton 157 A8
Eaton Tarporley 147 B4
Ebnal 213 D6
Eccleston 141 E1
Edge Green 199 B2
Egerton Green 200 C5
Ellesmere Port 70 A7
Elton 72 C3
Elworth 174 E6
Englesea-brook 208 A4
Ettiley Heath 174 C6

F

Faddiley 202 D7
Faddiley Bank 202 C6
Fanshawe 110 C4
Farndon 180 F2
Farnworth 13 A3
Fearnhead 9 A3
Fernilee 65 E1
Finney Green 34 E2
Fivecrosses 74 D5
Flint/Y Fflint 91 A3
Flookersbrook 118 E4
Fourlane-ends 63 A8
Four Lane Ends 168 D7
Fourlanes Ends 176 E4
Fowley Common 5 B5
Foxley 209 D7
Foxwist Green 125 F6
Frandley 53 A3
Frodsham 74 D7
Frodsham Marsh 48 E2
Fuller's Moor 183 D1
Fulshaw Park 60 B5
Furness Vale 39 C3

G

Gallantry Bank 200 A8
Gatesheath 165 E5
Gauntons Bank 215 E4
Gawsworth 134 E8
Gayton 41 B6
Gemini 7 D3
Gibb Hill 53 D1
Gillbent 34 F6
Gillow Heath 179 C2
Ginclough 88 A6
Glazebrook 11 B6

Glazebury 5 B7
Gleadsmoss 132 B6
Glebe Green 149 C6
Golborne 3 B7
Golly 161 B1
Goostrey 107 D1
Gorse Covert 10 B5
Gorstage 102 C6
Gorstella 140 A1
Gorstyhill 207 E2
Gosland Green 169 B1
Gowhole 39 E4
Gradeley Green 202 F5
Grange Runcorn 49 D7
Grange Warrington 17 E8
Grappenhall 17 A1
Grappenhall Heys 27 A8
Gravel 127 A1
Great Barrow 120 E6
Great Budworth 79 A7
Great Sankey 15 A6
Great Sutton 69 D3
Greenbank 103 C7
Greendale 86 E7
Greenlooms 143 F4
Grindley Brook 225 C3
Guilden Sutton 119 E5
Gurnett 112 F4

H

Hack Green 218 D8
Hague Bar 38 F8
Hale Altrincham 32 B8
Hale Speke 21 D1
Hale Bank 22 A4
Hale Barns 32 D8
Hale Heath 21 A1
Halewood Village 21 A8
Hall Green Kidsgrove 194 E5
Hall Green Whitchurch . . .224 E1
Hallowsgate 122 C4
Hallwood Park 49 F6
Halton Brook 23 D1
Halton Lodge 49 D7
Halton Moss 24 F6
Halton View 13 C1
Halton Village 49 F8
Hampton Green 214 B7
Hampton Heath 213 E7
Handbridge 141 E7
Handforth 34 C4
Hand Green 168 B6
Handley 182 D8
Hankelow 230 C7
Hapsford 72 E1
Harden Park 60 A3
Harding's Wood 194 E2
Hargrave 144 A1
Harriseahead 195 E4
Hartford 103 C4
Hartfordbeach 103 B6
Harthill 183 E3
Haslington 191 D4
Hassall 192 C7
Hassall Green 176 A1
Hatchmere 100 D4
Hatherton 219 E3
Hatton 26 A2
Hatton Heath 143 B1
Haughton 186 C6
Haydock 1 D6
Haymoor Green 205 E2
Heald Green 34 B8
Heath 49 B6
Heatley 19 C5
Hebden Green 148 F7
Helsby 73 C3
Henbury 111 B8
Heswall 40 D7
Hetherson Green 214 D8
Hidebank 39 C8
High Carr 210 F3
Higher Bunbury 168 F1
Higher Burwardsley 184 C5
Higher Carden 198 D7
Higher Disley 38 D5
Higherference 113 A8
Higher Hurdsfield 88 A2
Higher Kinnerton 161 B8
Higher Marston 79 C6
Higher Poynton 37 B2
Higher Runcorn 23 A1
Higher Shurlach 104 E6
Higher Walton 25 F7
Higher Whitley 52 D5
Higher Wincham 79 F4
Higher Wych 224 D4
Highlane 134 C6
High Lane 37 F5
High Lee 39 B8
High Legh 29 B5
High Warren 26 C6
Hillcliffe 26 C8
Hilltop 60 B8
Hobb Hill 198 D3
Hockley 37 A2
Hodgehill 132 E8
Hollinfare 11 A3

Hollin Green 202 F6
Hollins 210 E8
Hollinsgreen 152 D4
Hollins Green 11 B2
Hollins-Lane 226 E6
Hollyhurst 227 A5
Holmes Chapel 130 C4
Holt 196 D8
Holtridge 215 E6
Honkley 161 C3
Hood Manor 15 D5
Hoofield 145 A2
Hoo Green 29 F2
Hoole 119 A3
Hoole Bank 119 C7
Hoole Park 118 F3
Hooton 44 A1
Hooton Park 44 C4
Hope Green 36 C1
Horton Green 212 A8
Horwich End 65 D5
Hough Alderley Edge 60 D1
Hough Crewe 206 F3
Hough Green 12 B2
Houghton Green 8 E4
Howbeck Bank 219 E8
Howley 16 D5
Hulme 8 B3
Hulme Walfield 156 B7
Hulseheath 30 A4
Hunsterson 220 B1
Huntington 142 A5
Hurdsfield 87 E2
Hurst 179 F3
Huxley 166 F8

I

Illidge Green 154 C4
Ince .72 A6
Irlam 11 F7
Isycoed 196 C1

J

Jodrell Bank 108 D2

K

Keckwick 25 A3
Kelsall 122 C4
Kelsterton 91 B2
Kenyon 3 F3
Kermincham Heath 131 E5
Kerridge 88 A6
Kerridge-end 88 C3
Kettleshulme 64 F4
Key Green 157 E4
Kidnal 212 E8
Kidsgrove 195 B1
Kingsley 75 C2
Kingsmead 103 E5
Kingsway 23 A8
Kingswood Frodsham 74 C1
Kingswood Warrington 7 B7
Kinnerton Green 161 B7
Kinsey Heath 230 B1
Kitt's Moss 35 D6
Knolls Green 58 E3
Knotbury 138 F5
Knutsford 57 A3

L

Lacey Green 34 B1
Lach Dennis 105 D3
Lache 140 F5
Lane Ends Crewe 173 D3
Lane Ends Disley 38 E4
Lane Head 3 C6
Langley 113 C3
Larden Green 202 D4
Latchford 16 D3
Lavister 162 C1
Lawton-gate 194 A4
Lawton Heath 193 E6
Lawton Heath End 193 C6
Lea Green 172 A8
Ledsham 68 F2
Leftwich 104 B5
Lightwood Green 229 B3
Lindow 59 C4
Lindow End 59 B2
Lindow Moss 59 D7
Lingley Green 14 C7
Little Barrow 97 F7
Little Bollington 20 B2
Little Budworth 147 F7
Little Heath 230 A5
Little Leigh 77 C4
Little-moss 194 E6
Little Neston 66 D6
Littler 126 A2
Little Stanney 70 E1
Little Sutton 69 B5
Littleton 119 E1
Little Town 4 C1

Locking Stumps 9 C3
Longbarn 9 B1
Longford 8 B1
Long Green 97 F1
Longhill 230 E5
Longmoss 86 C1
Lostock Gralam 80 A3
Lostock Green 105 B8
Lowcross Hill 198 D3
Lower Bunbury 185 E7
Lower Carden 198 C6
Lower Heath 156 E5
Lowerhouse 87 E8
Lower House 22 E8
Lower Kinnerton 139 D1
Lower Peover 81 E1
Lower Pexhill 111 A4
Lower Stretton 52 F8
Lower Threapwood 222 F6
Lower Walton 26 A8
Lower Whitley 52 D3
Lower Withington 109 A1
Lower Wych 224 B6
Low Leighton 39 D8
Lowton 3 E8
Lowton Common 4 A8
Lowton Heath 3 C6
Lowton St Mary's 3 F8
Lugsdale 23 C7
Lunts Heath 13 A5
Lyme Green 112 D2
Lymm 18 E4

M

Macclesfield 112 B4
Macclesfield Forest 114 D5
Malkin's Bank 175 C3
Malpas 213 B2
Manley 99 A4
Manor Park Middlewich . .151 B7
Manor Park Runcorn 24 B3
Marbury 226 D8
Marley Green 227 C8
Marshfield Bank 189 C4
Marsh Green Biddulph . . .179 D3
Marsh Green Frodsham . .74 A8
Marston 79 B4
Marthall 83 E4
Martin's Ash 227 B2
Martinscroft 17 F7
Martin's Moss 176 E6
Marton 133 B5
Marton Green 125 C4
Martonsands 125 F4
Maw Green 190 E7
Meadowbank 126 E5
Megacre 194 E2
Mere 56 B8
Mere Heath 104 A1
Mickle Trafford 119 E8
Middlewich 128 D3
Middlewood 37 C5
Midway 36 D2
Millend 209 C5
Milners Heath 143 C2
Milton Green 165 C2
Minshull Vernon 172 E5
Mobberley 57 F7
Moblake 230 D4
Mollington 94 E2
Monks Heath 85 A1
Moore 25 B6
Moorside 65 C7
Morley 33 C2
Morley Common 15 F1
Morley Green 33 C1
Moss Bank 23 D8
Mossbrow 19 E7
Mossend 154 E1
Moss End 54 C2
Moss Houses 111 F2
Moss Lane 112 B4
Mossley 179 A8
Moss Nook 33 F7
Moston 95 C1
Moston Green 174 E8
Mottram St Andrew 61 B2
Mouldsworth 98 C3
Moulton 126 E4
Mount Pleasant Kidsgrove 195 B6
Mount Pleasant Winsford 149 B6
Mow Cop 195 C7
Murdishaw 50 D7

N

Nantwich 204 D6
Ness 67 B4
Ness Holt 66 F5
Neston 66 C7
Nether Alderley 85 A6
Nether Tabley 80 F8
Netherton 74 A6
New Boston 1 E7
Newcastle-under-Lyme . .210 D3
Newchapel 195 E2
New End Lane 4 A2
Newfield 172 E8

New Horwich 65 E6
New Mills 39 D7
New Pale 99 C6
Newsbank 132 F1
Newton Chester 118 F5
Newton Frodsham 74 D3
Newton Tattenhall 166 E4
Newtonia 128 B1
Newton-le-Willows 2 B2
Newtown Frodsham 49 D1
Newtown New Mills 39 B6
Newtown Poynton 37 A3
Newtown Sound 217 E4
Newtown Widnes 23 A6
New Woodhouses 227 E1
Nick i' th' Hill 179 B4
No Man's Heath 214 B4
Norbury 215 D4
Norbury Common 215 C6
Norcott Brook 52 C6
Norley 100 F6
Norley Bank 101 A6
North Florida 1 D8
North Rode 134 E2
Northwich 103 D8
Norton in Hales 236 C1
Nova Scotia 125 C6

O

Oakenbank 88 D8
Oakgrove 135 D7
Oakhanger 192 C2
Oakmere 124 A7
Oakwood 9 F4
Occlestone Green 151 B2
Oglet 46 D8
Old Boston 2 A8
Oldcastle Heath 223 F8
Old Hall 15 C8
Old Moss 144 D7
Old Woodhouses 227 C2
Ollerton 82 F6
Onneley 232 F3
Orford 8 D2
Oscroft 121 E2
Oughtrington 19 C4
Over 149 B7
Over Knutsford 57 C1
Over Leigh 65 F6
Over Peover 83 A1
Overpool 69 F7
Over Tabley 56 A5
Overton 74 C7

P

Packmoor 195 F1
Paddington 17 A8
Paddockhill 59 A4
Padgate 8 F1
Palace Fields 50 A6
Pandy 222 A3
Paradise Green 171 E6
Park End 209 A4
Parkgate Chelford 108 B8
Parkgate Disley 38 A5
Parkgate Neston 41 C1
Partington 11 F4
Peacock Hay 210 F4
Peckforton 184 F5
Penketh 14 D4
Peover Heath 108 C6
Pewterspear 26 E4
Pickmere 80 A7
Picton 96 C3
Pinsley Green 216 D2
Piper's Ash 119 D4
Plemstall 97 A1
Plumley 81 C2
Plumley Moor 81 C2
Podehill 188 A2
Poolfold 179 F4
Pot Bank 179 A4
Pott Shrigley 63 D3
Poulton 163 B2
Pownall Green 35 E6
Pownall Park 59 F7
Poynton 36 C4
Prestbury 87 B7
Preston Brook 50 F5
Preston on the Hill 51 A6
Primrose Hill 28 C6
Puddinglake 129 B8
Puddington 92 F8
Pulford 162 D3

Q

Quarrybank 146 C8
Queen's Park 141 F8
Quoisley 226 B8

R

Raby 42 C4
Raby Mere 43 B7

Radmore Green 186 E3
Radnor 155 E6
Radway Green 192 F1
Rainow...............88 D5
Ravensclough 101 E3
Ravensmoor 203 E2
Rease Heath 188 C2
Red Bull 194 E3
Red Street 210 E3
Rhuddall Heath 146 E1
Ridgwardine 235 E1
Ridleywood 196 C3
Risley 9 E6
Rocksavage 49 B4
Rodeheath 134 B3
Rode Heath 193 E7
Roodee 141 B8
Rostherne 30 E4
Roughhill 140 E1
Rowleyhill 181 B1
Rowlinson's Green ...28 C5
Row-of-trees 59 D3
Rowton 142 E5
Royal's Green 228 E2
Rudheath 104 D6
Rudheath Woods 106 E2
Ruloe 101 D7
Runcorn 23 C1
Rushgreen 19 A4
Rushton 147 C5
Rushton Spencer 159 B2
Rye Hills 209 E1

S
Saighton 142 E1
St Johns Gardens 149 B8
Salterswall 125 F3
Saltney 140 D6
Sandbach 175 B5
Sandbach Heath 175 D6
Sandiway 102 B3
Sandlow Green 131 B1
Sandycroft 116 B2
Sankey Bridges 15 C4
Saughall 94 B1
Scholar Green 194 E8
School Green 149 C5
Sealand 116 E6
Shavington 206 C5
Shaw Heath 57 D3
Shell Green 13 E1
Shocklach 211 D7
Shocklach Green 211 C7
Shotwick 93 B4
Shraleybrook 209 A1

Siddington 110 A3
Siddington Heath 109 E1
Simm's Cross 23 B7
Skellorn Green 62 E8
Slaughter Hill 191 D3
Smallwood 176 E5
Smethwick Green 154 F4
Smith's Green 208 B7
Smithy Green Bramhall ..35 B7
Smithy Green Knutsford ..81 E2
Snow Hill 204 D6
Somerford 154 F7
Sound 217 F5
Sound Heath 217 E5
Spen Green 177 B6
Sproston Green 129 C2
Spurstow 185 D6
Stamford Bridge 120 D4
Stanley Bank 1 A7
Stanley Green 34 E6
Stanlow 71 B5
Stapeley 219 D8
Stoak 96 A7
Stockton Heath 16 D1
Stoke Bank 187 C5
Stoneley Green 203 D4
Stowford 207 B8
Stretton 197 F6
Stretton 26 E2
Stud Green 152 C1
Styal 33 F4
Styal Green 34 A3
Sutton Green 69 C3
Sutton Lane Ends 112 F2
Sutton Weaver 50 B3
Swanbach 229 E1
Swan Green 106 D8
Swanley 203 C5
Swanwick Green 215 C4
Swettenham 131 E3
Swettenham Heath 132 B3
Sworton Heath 28 E5
Sydney 191 A5

T
Tabley Hill 56 D3
Talke 210 C7
Talke Pits 210 E5
Tallarn Green/Tallwrn
   Green 222 E5
Tarporley 146 C1
Tarvin 121 C3
Tarvin Sands 121 C4
Tattenhall 166 B1
Tatton Dale 30 E1

Taxal 65 D4
The Bank 195 B7
The Barony 204 F6
Thelwall 17 E3
The Quarry 209 C2
The Rookery 195 C3
The Valley 190 A3
Thorns Green 32 C5
Thornton Hough 42 A7
Thornton-le-Moors ...71 F1
Threapwood 222 F7
Thurlwood 193 E7
Tilston 198 B3
Tilstone Bank 168 F4
Tilstone Fearnall ...168 F6
Timbersbrook 157 E2
Tiverton 168 C6
Torr Top 39 C8
Town End 12 C6
Town Fields 149 D7
Town of Lowton 3 B5
Trap Street 132 C5
Twemlow Green 131 A5
Twiss Green 4 E4
Two Mills 93 E8
Tytherington 87 C3

U
Upper Threapwood 222 F7
Upton Chester 118 D6
Upton Widnes 12 C4
Upton Heath 118 F8
Upton Rocks 12 E4
Utkinton 146 B7

V
Vicarscross 119 E2
Vulcan Village 7 C8

W
Wades Green 171 F5
Wain Lee 195 F4
Walgherton 220 B6
Walkers Green 152 D7
Walley's Green 172 E7
Warburton 19 C8
Warburton Green 32 D6
Wardle 187 C7
Wardsend 37 A1
Wargrave 2 D3
Warmingham 173 D7

Warren 111 D1
Warrington 16 E6
Wash End 4 C8
Waverton 143 B4
Way's Green 149 E8
Weaverham 77 C2
Weetwood Common 122 C2
Wells Green 205 F8
Wereton 209 C1
Wervin 96 A4
West Bank 23 A4
Westbrook Centre 7 B1
West Heath Betley ...221 E8
West Heath Congleton ..156 A4
Westminster Park 141 B6
Weston Crewe 207 C5
Weston Macclesfield ..111 F8
Weston Runcorn 48 F6
Weston Point 48 D7
Westy 16 F5
Wettenhall 170 F7
Wettenhall Green 170 F6
Whaley Bridge 65 D7
Wharton 127 A2
Wharton Green 127 B4
Wheelock 174 F4
Wheelock Heath 192 A8
Whirley Grove 86 D3
Whisterfield 109 D3
Whitby 70 A4
Whitchurch 226 A1
Whitecross 15 E6
Whitegate 126 A7
White Hill 195 B2
Whiteley Green 62 E2
Whitley Reed 53 D8
Widnes 22 E7
Wigshaw 4 D2
Wildboarclough 137 E6
Wilderspool 16 C2
Wilkesley 233 F7
Willaston Ellesmere Port ..68 A8
Willaston Nantwich ..205 C5
Willington Corner ...122 E2
Willow Green 77 B5
Wilmslow 60 C5
Wilmslow Park 60 D7
Wimboldsley 150 F4
Wimbolds Trafford ...96 F6
Wincham 79 C3
Wincle 160 A7
Windle Hill 67 C7
Windmill Hill 24 C1
Windyharbour 109 D1
Winnington 78 D1
Winsford 126 E2
Winterley 191 F7

Winwick 8 A6
Winwick Quay 8 A3
Wirswall 226 A5
Wistaston 205 D8
Wistaston Green 189 D2
Withington Green 108 E3
Wolverham 70 D4
Woodbank 93 F6
Woodend 38 E8
Woodford 35 E2
Woodhey Green 202 B6
Woodhouse-end 135 C8
Woodhouse Green 158 D2
Woodhouse Park 33 F8
Woodhouses 73 E4
Wood Lane 210 A1
Woodshutts 194 F1
Woodworth Green 186 B8
Woolfall 230 E6
Woolstanwood 189 E3
Woolston 17 C8
Woore 232 B1
Worleston 188 F5
Worthenbury 211 A1
Wrenbury 216 F4
Wrenbury Frith 216 C6
Wrenbury Heath 217 B5
Wright's Green 27 A6
Wybunbury 220 A8

Y

Yatehouse Green 128 D6

2

2nd Ave CW12 ....156 A4

3

3rd Ave CW12 ....156 A4

1

1875 Bakers Ct CH1, CH3 ....237 C3

A

Aarons Dr ST7 ....209 F2
Abberley Hall SK9 ......84 D7
Abbey Cl Croft WA3 ......9 A8
Whitegate CW8 ......126 A7
Widnes WA8 ......22 C8
Winsford CW7 ......149 D5
Abbey Ct SK12 ......36 D3
Abbey Fields CW2 ......205 E8
Abbey Gate Coll CH3 ......164 E8
Abbey Gate Sch CH2 ......237 A3
Abbey Gn CH1 ......237 A3
Abbey Hey WA7 ......50 C8
Abbey La Delamere CW8 ......123 E5
Hartford CW8 ......103 B4
Abbey Mill SK10 ......87 A6
Abbey Pl CW1 ......190 D6
Abbey Rd Golborne WA3 ......4 C8
Haydock WA11 ......1 E7
Macclesfield SK10 ......87 B2
Sandbach CW11 ......174 E6
Widnes WA8 ......22 C8
Abbey Sq CH1 ......237 B3
Abbey St CH1 ......237 B3
Abbey Way CW8 ......103 B4
Abbeydale Cl CW2 ......207 C2
Abbeyfield Ho
 2 Crewe CW2 ......190 D2
Ellesmere Port CH65 ......70 A3
Abbeyfields WA11 ......174 F5
Abbeyway N WA11 ......2 A7
Abbeyway S WA11 ......2 A7
Abbot's Dr CH2 ......118 C8
Abbot's Grange CH2 ......237 A4
Abbot's Nook CH2 ......237 A4
Abbot's Terr CH1 ......118 B5
Abbots Cl SK10 ......87 B2
Abbots Ct CH2 ......118 C4
Abbots Knoll CH2 ......118 C4
Abbots Mews CH65 ......70 B6
Abbots Pk CH2 ......118 C4
Abbots Way
Hartford CW8 ......103 B4
Neston CH64 ......41 E1
Abbotsbury Cl
Poynton SK12 ......36 D5
Wistaston CW2 ......206 B8
Abbotsfield Cl WA4 ......26 E6
Abbotsmere Cl CW8 ......101 F2
Abbott's Cl CW12 ......179 B8
Abbotts Cl Runcorn WA7 ......49 A8
Waverton CH3 ......143 B5
Abbotts Rd CH3 ......143 B5
Abbotts Way CW7 ......126 B2
Aberdare Cl WA5 ......7 E1
Aberdaron Dr CH1 ......117 E3
Aberdeen Wlk SK10 ......86 F3
Aberfeldy Cl CW4 ......130 B8
Abingdon Ave WA1 ......17 E7
Abingdon 9 SK11 ......111 F8
Abingdon Cres 8 WA4 ......17 A3
Abington Wlk WA7 ......50 C5
Abstone Cl WA1 ......17 B7
Acacia Ave
Knutsford WA16 ......56 E1
Warrington WA1 ......17 A7
Widnes WA8 ......13 B3
Wilmslow SK9 ......59 F5
Acacia Cl CH2 ......72 C3
Acacia Cres CW1 ......190 E6
Acacia Dr
Ellesmere Port CH66 ......69 D1
Sandbach CW11 ......174 E7
Acacia Gdns ST7 ......195 C3
Acacia Gr WA7 ......49 C8
Acacia St WA12 ......1 F4
Academy Pl 7 WA1 ......16 B5
Academy St WA1 ......16 B5
Academy Way WA1 ......16 B5
Acer Ave CW1 ......190 E7
Achilles Ave WA2 ......8 B2
Achilles Ct WA7 ......24 A2
Ack La E SK7 ......35 D7
Ack La W SK7 ......35 C7
Ackerley Cl WA2 ......8 F3
Ackers La WA4 ......16 E1
Ackers Rd WA4 ......16 E2
Ackersley Ct SK8 ......35 B8
Acorn Bank Cl CW12 ......206 B7
Winsford CW7 ......150 A8
Acorn Dr CH65 ......70 B1
Acorn La CW12 ......157 E3
Acorn St WA12 ......2 D3
Acorn Terr SK22 ......39 B6
Acorns Prim Sch The CH65 ......69 F5
Acre Gn L26 ......21 A6
Acre La Bebington CH62 ......43 D8

Acre La continued
Cheadle Hulme SK8 ......35 C6
Heswall CH60 ......41 C8
Acre Rd CH66 ......69 D5
Acreage The
Bunbury CW6 ......185 E8
Goostrey CW4 ......107 E1
Acrefield Rd WA8 ......12 B1
Acres Cres WA6 ......75 B2
Acres La CH2 ......119 A8
Acresfield Com Prim Sch CH2 ......118 F8
Acreville Gr WA3 ......5 C7
Acton Ave WA4 ......26 D3
Acton Bridge Sta CW8 ......76 F1
Acton CE Prim Sch CW5 ......204 A7
Acton Cl WA11 ......1 C6
Acton La CW8 ......76 F4
Acton Rd Burtonwood WA5 ......6 E6
Crewe CW2 ......189 D4
Acton Way ST7 ......193 D6
Adam Ave
Ellesmere Port CH66 ......69 D3
Ellesmere Port,Great Sutton CH66 ......69 C4
Adam Cl CH66 ......69 D4
Adam St WA4 ......16 C7
Adams Cl
Newton-le-W WA12 ......2 D2
Poynton SK12 ......36 E2
Adams Hill WA16 ......57 A1
Adamson Ct WA4 ......17 B2
Adamson St WA4 ......16 B3
Adaston Ave CH62 ......43 F4
Adder Hill CH3 ......142 B7
Adderley CE Prim Sch TF9 ......234 F5
Adderley Rd TF9 ......235 A2
Addingham Ave WA8 ......22 C7
Addison Cl CW2 ......205 F8
Addison Sq WA8 ......13 A1
Adela Rd WA7 ......22 F2
Adelaide Ct 4 WA8 ......23 A7
Adelaide Rd Blacon CH1 ......117 D4
Bramhall SK7 ......35 F7
Adelaide Sch CW1 ......190 C5
Adelaide St Crewe CW1 ......190 C5
Macclesfield SK10 ......87 E1
Adey Rd WA13 ......19 A5
Adfalent La CH64 ......68 A7
Adlington Cl SK12 ......36 F2
Adlington Ct WA3 ......9 F6
Adlington Dr
Northwich CW9 ......104 A5
Sandbach CW11 ......175 C7
Adlington Est SK10 ......36 C1
Adlington Hall Mews SK10 ......62 B5
Adlington Pk SK10 ......62 C5
Adlington Prim Sch SK10 ......62 E5
Adlington Rd
Bollington SK10 ......63 A1
Crewe CW2 ......189 F3
Runcorn WA7 ......24 D2
Wilmslow SK9 ......60 E7
Adlington St SK10 ......112 C8
Adlington Sta SK10 ......62 C5
Admirals Rd WA3 ......9 F4
Adshead Ct SK10 ......88 B7
Adwell Cl WA3 ......4 A8
Afton WA8 ......12 A2
Agden Brow WA13 ......19 E1
Agden Brow Pk
Broomedge WA13 ......19 D1
Lymm WA13 ......29 D8
Agden House La SY13 ......225 A5
Agden La
Broomedge WA13 ......19 E1
Little Bollington WA13 ......29 C7
Agden Park La WA13 ......29 D8
Agecroft Rd CW9 ......104 C7
Ainley Cl WA7 ......50 A5
Ainscough Rd WA3 ......9 E3
Ainsdale Cl
Bebington CH63 ......43 C5
Bramhall SK7 ......36 A7
Warrington WA5 ......14 F4
Ainsworth La CW8 ......76 B3
Ainsworth Rd CW8 ......77 E1
Aintree Gr CH66 ......69 D3
Airdrie Cl CH62 ......43 D3
Aire WA8 ......12 A2
Aire Cl CH65 ......70 A7
Aire Pl CW7 ......127 B1
Airedale Cl WA5 ......14 F7
Airfield View WA15 ......139 B6
Aitchison Rd CW9 ......80 A2
Ajax Ave WA2 ......8 B2
Akesmoor La
Biddulph ST8 ......179 B1
Kidsgrove ST7 ......195 F7
Alamein Cres WA2 ......16 C7
Alamein Dr CW7 ......149 D8
Alamein Rd Barnton CW8 ......78 A4
Chester CH2 ......95 B1
Alan Dr WA15 ......32 A8
Alan St CW9 ......104 B8
Alban Ret Pk WA2 ......8 C2
Alban St CW1 ......190 C5
Albany Cres WA13 ......18 D4
Albany Gdns CH66 ......69 C7
Albany Rd Bramhall SK7 ......35 F4
Lymm WA13 ......18 D4
Wilmslow SK9 ......59 F5

Albany Terr 16 WA7 ......23 A2
Albert Dr Neston CH64 ......66 D8
Warrington WA5 ......14 D6
Albert Pl Congleton CW12 ......156 E2
Northwich CW9 ......104 B8
Albert Rd Bollington SK10 ......87 E8
Warrington WA4 ......17 A2
2 Widnes WA8 ......13 B1
Wilmslow SK9 ......60 A6
Albert Row WA6 ......49 B1
Albert Sq 4 WA8 ......23 B8
Albert St Audley ST7 ......209 F3
Chester CH1 ......237 C3
Crewe CW1 ......190 C5
Irlam M44 ......11 C6
Knutsford WA16 ......56 F2
Macclesfield SK11 ......112 C8
Nantwich CW5 ......204 E6
7 Runcorn WA7 ......23 A2
Albert Terr WA5 ......1 E1
Albion Cl CW12 ......156 E2
Albion Mews CH1 ......237 B2
Albion Pl CH1 ......237 B2
Albion Rd New Mills SK22 ......39 B6
Northwich CW9 ......79 A1
Albion St Chester CH1 ......237 B2
Crewe CW2 ......190 A3
Albion Wlk CW9 ......79 A1
Albright Rd WA8 ......22 A6
Albury Cl WA11 ......1 D7
Alcock St Audley ST7 ......209 F4
Alconbury Cl WA5 ......15 B6
Alcott Pl WA2 ......8 A6
Aldelyme Ct CW3 ......229 F4
Alder Ave Poynton SK12 ......36 F3
Widnes WA8 ......13 B3
Alder Cl SK8 ......34 D8
Alder Cres WA2 ......16 C8
Alder Ct SK10 ......87 E5
Alder Dr CH2 ......69 F1
Alder Gr CH2 ......119 B4
Alder La
Burtonwood WA2,WA5 ......7 C7
Cronton WA8,L35 ......12 A5
Frodsham WA6,WA7 ......49 D7
Warrington WA2 ......16 B8
Alder Rd Golborne WA3 ......3 F8
Warrington WA1 ......17 D7
Weaverham CW8 ......102 D8
Alder Rise SK23 ......65 D8
Alder Root La WA2 ......7 D7
Alder St WA12 ......2 C3
Alder Wood Ave L24 ......21 A3
Alderbank Rd WA5 ......15 A6
Alderdale Dr SK6 ......37 E7
Alderdale Gr SK9 ......59 E5
Alderfield Dr L24 ......21 A3
Alderhay La ST7 ......195 C4
Alderley Ave WA3 ......3 D7
Alderley Cl
Hazel Grove SK7 ......36 F8
Poynton SK12 ......36 F2
Sandbach CW11 ......175 D7
Alderley Edge Prim Sch SK9 ......60 A2
Alderley Edge Sch for Girls SK9 ......60 A2
Alderley Edge Sta SK9 ......60 A2
Alderley Lodge SK9 ......60 A2
Alderley Pk CH1 ......117 E6
Alderley Rd
Alderley Edge SK10,SK9 ......60 F2
Chelford SK10 ......84 C3
Northwich CW8 ......103 E8
Prestbury SK10 ......86 E3
Warrington WA4 ......17 D4
Wilmslow SK9 ......60 A6
Alderley Wlk 14 SK11 ......112 E7
Alderman Bolton Prim Sch WA4 ......16 F3
Alderney Cl
Ellesmere Port CH65 ......70 C1
4 Macclesfield SK11 ......111 F8
Alderney Ho CH2 ......119 B4
Alders Green Ave SK6 ......37 F7
Alders Rd SK12 ......38 A7
Alders Way SK10 ......86 E6
Aldersey Cl Runcorn WA7 ......24 D1
Saughall CH1 ......94 A1
Aldersey La CH3 ......182 C5
Aldersey Rd CW2 ......190 A2
Aldersgate SK22 ......39 B8
Aldersgate Ave WA7 ......50 D7
Aldersgate Dr L26 ......21 A6
Aldersgate Rd SK8 ......35 C5
Alderton Gr CW7 ......127 A4
Alderwood Cl WA8 ......12 E4
Alderwood Lodge L24 ......21 A3
Aldewood Cl WA3 ......10 B6
Aldford Cl Bebington CH63 ......43 B6
Hough CW2 ......206 E2
Aldford Pl SK9 ......59 F2
Aldford Rd CH66 ......118 F6
Aldford Sch CH3 ......163 F3
Aldford Way CW7 ......126 B2
Aldgate CH65 ......70 A5
Aldington Dr CW10 ......151 D5
Aldridge Dr WA5 ......15 A6
Aled Way CH4 ......140 D5
Alexander Ct CH3 ......237 C2
Alexander Dr WA8 ......22 D8
Alexandra 5 1 M31 ......11 F3
Alexandra Ind Est WA8 ......22 F7

Alexandra Mews WA6 ......49 B1
Alexandra Pl CW1 ......190 B5
Alexandra Rd
Middlewich CW10 ......151 D6
Warrington WA4 ......16 F2
Warrington, Stockton Heath WA4 ......16 D1
Alexandra Sq 6 CW7 ......149 A8
Alexandra St
Ellesmere Port CH65 ......70 C7
Warrington WA1 ......16 E7
Widnes WA8 ......23 A7
Winsford CW7 ......126 C1
Alford Ct 4 CW9 ......103 E5
Alforde St WA8 ......23 A7
Alfred Cl 7 WA8 ......23 B8
Alfred Rd Golborne WA3 ......4 A8
Haydock WA11 ......1 F7
Alfred St Irlam M44 ......11 E6
Newton-le-W WA12 ......2 E3
Northwich CW9 ......103 E6
Widnes WA8 ......23 B8
Algernon St Runcorn WA7 ......22 F3
Warrington WA1 ......16 D6
Warrington, Stockton Heath WA4 ......16 C1
Alice Ct WA8 ......23 A4
Alison Dr Goostrey CW4 ......130 D8
Macclesfield SK10 ......87 F1
Alistair Dr CH63 ......43 C6
All Hallows RC High Sch SK11 ......112 B7
All Saints Dr WA4 ......17 E3
All Saints RC Prim Sch WA3 ......3 A8
All Saints Upton CE Prim Sch CH2 ......118 E4
Allans Cl CH64 ......66 C6
Allans Mdw CH64 ......66 E7
Allansford Ave CH3 ......143 A4
Allcard St WA5 ......15 F7
Allen Ave WA13 ......5 C4
Allen Dr CW9 ......103 F2
Allen Pl CW1 ......190 C6
Allen St WA7 ......48 D7
Allen St Bollington SK10 ......88 B8
Macclesfield SK11 ......112 E7
Allenby Rd M44 ......11 D4
Allendale WA7 ......50 B6
Allerby Way WA3 ......3 E8
Allerton Rd WA8 ......13 B1
Allgreave Cl CW10 ......151 C6
Allington Pl CH4 ......141 C5
Allman Cl CW1 ......189 F7
Allotment Rd M44 ......11 D6
Allport La CH62 ......43 D8
Allport Rd CH62,CH63 ......43 D7
Allports The CH62 ......43 D7
Allysum Cl WA7 ......49 F4
Alma Ave CW1 ......190 C6
Alma Cl
Macclesfield SK11 ......112 A7
Scholar Green ST7 ......194 E7
Alma La SK9 ......60 A7
Alma Rd SK7 ......37 A8
Alma St Chester CH2 ......118 F2
Newton-le-W WA12 ......2 B3
Almeda Rd L24 ......21 A2
Almer Dr WA5 ......15 C5
Almond Ave Crewe CW1 ......190 D6
Runcorn WA7 ......49 C8
Almond Dr WA5 ......6 F6
Almond Gr
Warrington WA1 ......17 B7
Weaverham CW8 ......102 E7
Widnes WA8 ......22 D8
Almond Tree Cl L24 ......21 E1
Almond Wlk M31 ......11 D3
Almshouses
Biddulph ST8 ......179 D3
Malpas SY14 ......213 B3
Sandbach CW11 ......175 C6
Alnwick Dr CH65 ......70 D2
Alpass Ave WA5 ......14 D6
Alpine St SK9 ......2 A3
Alport Rd SY13 ......226 B1
Alpraham Cres CH2 ......118 E6
Alpraham Gn CW6 ......169 E5
Alric Wlk M22 ......33 E8
Alsager Highfields Com Prim Sch ST7 ......193 D4
Alsager Rd Audley ST7 ......209 D5
Haslington CW11 ......192 C7
Alsager Sch ST7 ......193 B4
Alsager Sta ST7 ......193 E3
Alsfeld Way SK22 ......39 A8
Alt WA8 ......12 B2
Alt Wlk CW7 ......127 A2
Alton Dr SK10 ......87 F1
Alton St CW9 ......59 F7
Alton St CW2 ......190 B3
Altrincham Priory Hospl WA15 ......32 A7
Altrincham Rd Styal SK9 ......33 E4
Wilmslow SK9 ......33 C2
Alum Ct WA4 ......130 C2
Alumbrook Ave CW4 ......130 C3
Alun Cres CW4 ......141 A6
Alundale Rd CW7 ......126 C3
Alvanley Dr WA6 ......73 C2
Alvanley Prim Sch WA6 ......73 D1
Alvanley Rd
Ellesmere Port CH66 ......69 E4
Helsby WA6 ......73 C2
Alvanley Rise WA9 ......104 A6
Alvanley Terr WA6 ......74 B8

Alvanley View CH2 ......72 B3
Alvanley Way CH66 ......69 E4
Alvaston Bsns Pk CW5 ......204 F8
Alvaston Rd CW5 ......204 F5
Alvaston Wlk CW2 ......189 F2
Alverstone Cl WA5 ......14 C7
Alverton Cl WA8 ......22 D8
Alveston Cl SK10 ......86 F1
Alveston Dr WA9 ......6 A7
Alvingham Cl 1 CW9 ......104 B8
Alvis Rd CH5 ......116 B3
Alwyn Gdns CH2 ......118 F8
Alwyn Rd CW2 ......96 F1
Alyndale Rd CH4 ......140 D6
Amberleigh Cl WA4 ......27 B3
Amberley Dr WA15 ......32 B8
Amberley Rd SK11 ......112 A6
Ambleside CH2 ......119 A6
Ambleside Cl
Bebington CH62 ......43 E7
Crewe CW2 ......189 E2
Macclesfield SK11 ......111 F6
Runcorn WA7 ......49 E5
Winsford CW7 ......126 C3
Ambleside Cres WA2 ......8 C3
Ambleside Ct CW12 ......156 A2
Ambleside Rd CH65 ......70 C2
Ambrose Cl WA1 ......17 A8
Ambuscade Cl CW1 ......190 E5
Amelia Cl WA8 ......13 B4
Amelia St WA2 ......16 D7
Amersham Cl SK10 ......87 C3
Amis Gr WA3 ......3 E8
Amy St CW2 ......190 C3
Anchor Cl WA7 ......50 D6
Anchor Ct
Warrington WA1 ......16 D6
Wilmslow SK9 ......60 B8
Anchorage The
1 Lymm WA13 ......18 D3
Neston CH64 ......66 C7
Waverton CH3 ......143 A5
Ancoats Rd WA14,SK9 ......83 F8
Anderson Cl Crewe CW1 ......191 A4
Warrington WA2 ......9 B2
Anderson Ct CH42 ......23 D6
Anderson St 16 SK10 ......112 C8
Andersons Ind Est WA8 ......23 A6
Anderton Boat Lift & Nature Pk* CW9 ......78 D2
Anderton Grange CW9 ......103 F7
Anderton Way SK9 ......34 D3
Andertons La SK10,SK11 ......86 B1
Andover Cl WA2 ......8 E1
Andover Rd WA11 ......1 C8
Andrew Cl WA8 ......22 C8
Andrew Cres CH4 ......237 C1
Andrew Gr SK10 ......113 A7
Andrew La SK6 ......37 F8
Andrew's Cl CH3 ......121 B2
Andrew's Wlk CH60 ......41 B8
Andromeda Way WA9 ......6 B7
Anemone Way WA9 ......6 A7
Angelina Cl CW11 ......174 F7
Anglers Rest M44 ......11 E5
Anglesey Cl 2 CH65 ......70 C2
Anglesey Dr SK12 ......36 F6
Anglesey Water SK12 ......36 F6
Angus Gr CW10 ......128 D2
Angus Rd CH63 ......43 C6
Angus Wlk SK10 ......86 F2
Ankers Knowl La SK11 ......114 D8
Ankers La SK11 ......114 D6
Ann Cl CH66 ......69 D7
Ann St W Northwich CW9 ......79 D1
Runcorn WA7 ......23 B3
Ann St W WA8 ......23 B7
Annable Rd M44 ......11 F8
Annan Cl 2 CW12 ......157 A1
Anne Ct ST7 ......210 D6
Anne's Way CH4 ......237 C1
Annette Ave WA12 ......2 A5
Annie St WA2 ......16 C6
Annions La CW5 ......205 F1
Annis Cl SK9 ......60 B2
Annis Rd SK9 ......60 B2
Ansdell Rd WA8 ......13 C2
Anson Cl Bramhall SK7 ......35 F5
Warrington WA3 ......8 E2
Anson Engine Mus The* SK12 ......37 C3
Anson Rd Handforth SK9 ......34 E1
Poynton SK12 ......37 B3
Anthony Dr CW9 ......126 F7
Anthony's Way CH60 ......41 A7
Antons Rd L26 ......21 A6
Antony Rd WA6 ......16 B1
Antrim Cl WA11 ......1 C6
Antrim Dr CH66 ......69 F2
Antrim Rd WA2 ......8 A2
Antrobus St CW12 ......156 D3
Anvil Cl Elton CH2 ......72 B4
Haslington CW11 ......174 F3
Saughall CH1 ......94 A1
Apple Market St 10 CW9 ......103 F8
Apple Tree Cl L24 ......21 E1
Apple Tree Gr CH66 ......94 F8
Appleby Cl
Macclesfield SK11 ......111 F5
Widnes WA8 ......22 C8
Appleby Gr CH62 ......43 D6
Appleby Rd WA2 ......8 D2
Appleby Wlk 5 WA8 ......22 C8
Applecroft ST5 ......210 E1

Applecross Cl WA3 10 A6
Appledale Dr CH66 95 A8
Applefield CW8 103 D7
Appleford Cl WA4 26 E7
Appleton Cl CW12 178 E8
Appleton Dr CH65 69 F3
Appleton Hall Gdns WA4 26 E5
Appleton Mews WA13 18 C4
Appleton Rd
Chester CH2 118 E6
Widnes WA8 13 B1
Appleton St Widnes WA8 23 B7
Winnington CW8 78 D1
Appleton Thorn Prim Sch WA4 27 C4
Appleton Thorn Trad Est WA4 27 D5
Appleton Village WA8 13 B1
Appleton Wlk 8 SK9 34 E1
Appletree Gr WA2 8 F2
Appleyards La CH4 141 E7
April Rise SK10 87 A1
Arabis Gdns WA9 6 B7
Aragon Ct WA7 24 C3
Aragon Gn CH1 117 E6
Aran Cl L24 21 D1
Arbour Cl
Macclesfield SK10 87 D3
Northwich CW9 104 C8
Arbour Cres SK10 87 D3
Arbour Mews SK10 87 D3
Arbour St ST7 210 D5
Arbourhay St SK10 87 E1
Arbury La WA2 8 C6
Arcade The
Ellesmere Port CH65 70 A5
13 Northwich CW8 103 F8
Archer Ave WA4 16 E2
Archer Cl SK10 87 E7
Archers Gn CH62 43 E3
Archers Way Blacon CH1 118 A2
Ellesmere Port CH66 69 E1
Archway Wlk WA12 2 E3
Arclid Cl SK9 34 E1
Arclid Ct 10 CW12 156 F3
Arclid Green Ind Est CW11 176 A8
Arden WA8 12 A2
Arden Cl Heald Green SK8 34 C7
Tarvin CH3 121 C3
Warrington WA3 10 B6
Arden Ct CW12 179 B7
Arden Dr CH64 66 E6
Arden Est SK22 39 D7
Arden St SK22 39 C7
Ardenbrook Rise SK10 86 F6
Ardens Mdw CW6 168 C8
Ardern Lea WA6 73 D1
Arderne Ave CW2 190 A2
Arderne Ho CH2 118 F7
Arderne Pl 10 SK9 60 A1
Ardleigh Cl CW1 189 F8
Arena Gdns WA2 16 D8
Argosy Dr M90 32 F7
Argyle Ct 9 WA16 57 A2
Argyll Ave Bebington CH62 43 D4
Chester CH4 141 A7
Argyll Cl SK10 87 A1
Ariel Wlk 4 WA3 3 E8
Arizona Cres WA5 15 B7
Arkenshaw Rd WA3 9 A8
Arkenstone Cl WA8 12 C2
Arkle Ave SK9 34 E4
Arkle Ct 1 CH3 119 B1
Arklow Dr L24 21 D2
Arkwright Cl CW7 149 A8
Arkwright Ct WA7 23 F3
Arkwright Rd WA7 23 F3
Arley Ave WA4 26 D8
Arley Cl Alsager ST7 193 C3
Chester CH2 118 F6
Macclesfield SK11 112 A7
Arley Dr WA8 12 B2
Arley End WA16 29 C4
Arley Hall & Gdns* CW9 54 D6
Arley Mossend La CW9 54 D2
Arley Pl CW2 206 A8
Arley Rd Antrobus CW9 54 B7
Appleton Thorn WA4 27 C3
Northwich CW9 104 C8
Arley Wlk CW11 174 D5
Arlington Cl CW2 206 C8
Arlington Cres SK9 59 E5
Arlington Dr Golborne WN7 4 C8
Macclesfield SK11 112 A7
Poynton SK12 36 D3
Warrington WA5 14 E4
Arlington Way SK9 59 E5
Armistead Way CW4 130 A5
Armitstead Rd CW11 174 F4
Armitt St SK11 112 C7
Armour Ave WA2 8 B2
Armoury Court Mews 4 SK11 112 B6
Armoury Twrs 1 SK11 112 B6
Armstrong Cl
Audlem CW3 229 F4
Warrington WA3 9 D4
Armthorpe Dr CH66 69 C5
Arncliffe Dr WA5 6 F6
Arndale WA7 49 E5
Arnhem Cres WA2 16 C7
Arnhem Way CH3 142 B5
Arnold Pl WA8 22 C7
Arnold St Nantwich CW5 204 E6
Arnold St *continued*
Warrington WA1 16 D6
Arnold's Cres CH4 139 A3
Arnside Ave
Congleton CW12 156 A2
Haydock WA11 1 B6
Arnside Cl High Lane SK6 37 E8
Winsford CW7 126 D2
Arnside Gr WA4 16 B2
Arpley Rd WA1 16 B4
Arpley St WA1 16 A4
Arradon Ct CH2 118 E5
Arran Ave CH65 70 C1
Arran Cl
Holmes Chapel CW4 130 C2
Warrington WA2 9 A2
Arran Dr WA6 74 C6
Arrivals Way M90 33 B7
Arron Pl CW2 189 D3
Arrowcroft Rd CH3 119 F5
Arrowsmith Dr ST7 193 B3
Arrowsmith Rd WA11 1 F7
Arthill La
Little Bollington WA14 20 B1
Rostherne WA14 30 B8
Arthog Dr WA15 31 F8
Arthog Rd WA15 31 F8
Arthur Ave CH65 70 C5
Arthur St Chester CH1 118 A2
3 Crewe CW2 190 D2
Lostock Gralam CW9 80 A2
13 Runcorn WA7 23 A2
Warrington WA2 16 A6
Artists La SK10 85 C7
Artle Rd CW2 206 C8
Arundel Ave SK7 36 D8
Arundel Cl
Knutsford WA16 82 A8
Macclesfield SK10 87 F2
Wistaston CW2 205 E8
Arundel Ct CH65 70 E3
Arundel Rd SK8 35 A6
Arundell Cl WA5 6 F6
Ascol Dr WA16 80 C3
Ascot Ave WA7 49 B6
Ascot Cl Congleton CW12 156 D4
Macclesfield SK10 87 C3
Warrington WA4 17 C2
Warrington, Martinscroft WA1 17 E7
Ascot Ct CW9 104 C8
Ascot Dr CH66 69 E3
Ascot Ho CH1 118 B2
Ash Ave Irlam M44 11 D5
Newton-le-W WA12 2 C2
Ash Cl Ellesmere Port CH66 69 F1
Holmes Chapel CW4 130 D4
Malpas SY14 213 C5
Tarporley CW6 146 D2
Ash Ct 14 WA16 57 A2
Ash Gr Chester CH4 141 B5
Congleton CW12 156 A3
Ellesmere Port CH66 69 C6
Golborne WA3 3 B8
Handforth SK9 34 C3
Heald Green SK8 34 B8
Knutsford WA16 57 D1
Macclesfield SK11 112 C4
Middlewich CW10 151 D7
Nantwich CW5 204 F3
Rode Heath ST7 193 F7
Runcorn WA7 49 C8
Warrington WA4 16 D3
Weaverham CW8 102 E7
Widnes WA8 22 D8
Ash Grove Prim Sch SK11 112 C4
Ash Hay La
Hoole Bank CH2 119 C8
Picton CH2 96 C2
Ash Ho 8 CW11 175 B6
Ash House La CW8 77 D7
Ash La Warrington WA4 26 E8
Widnes WA8 22 A8
Ash Lawn Ct CH2 118 C4
Ash Lodge SK12 36 D4
Ash Mount CW3 232 B1
Ash Priors WA8 12 D3
Ash Rd Crewe CW1 190 D6
Cuddington CW8 101 F2
Elton CH2 72 C3
Haydock WA11 1 E7
Hollinfare WA3 11 A2
Lymm WA13 18 C3
Partington M31 11 D3
Poynton SK12 36 F3
Warrington WA5 14 F4
Winwick WA2 8 B6
Ash St CW9 79 A1
Ash Terr SK11 112 C4
Ash View ST7 195 B2
Ash Way CH60 41 B6
Ashbank CW9 104 D7
Ashberry Cl SK9 60 D8
Ashberry Dr WA4 27 B5
Ashbourne Ave WA7 49 B6
Ashbourne Cl CH66 94 E8
Ashbourne Dr
Chorlton CW2 207 C1
High Lane SK6 37 F6
Ashbourne Mews 1 SK10 111 F8
Ashbourne Rd
Hazel Grove SK7 36 F8
Warrington WA5 15 B5
Ashbrook Ave WA7 49 F3
Ashbrook Cres WA2 16 D8
Ashbrook Dr SK10 87 A6
Ashbrook Rd
Bollington SK10 87 F7
Nether Alderley SK10 85 F6
Ashburton CH64 66 C8
Ashbury Cl WA7 24 D2
Ashbury Dr WA11 1 D7
Ashby Dr CW11 174 C5
Ashby Pl CH2 237 C4
Ashcroft SK9 59 F5
Ashcroft Ave CW2 206 B3
Ashcroft Rd WA13 19 B4
Ashdale Cl ST7 193 C5
Ashdene Prim Sch SK9 59 F5
Ashdene Rd SK9 59 F5
Ashdown La WA3 10 B5
Ashdown Rd WA16 82 F6
Ashenhurst Rd ST7 193 F3
Ashenough Rd ST7 210 D6
Asher Ct WA4 27 D4
Ashfield Cl WA13 19 B4
Ashfield Cres
Bebington CH62 43 D8
Blacon CH1 117 D5
Ashfield Dr SK10 87 A2
Ashfield Gr M44 11 E6
Ashfield Ho 6 CH64 66 E8
Ashfield Rd
Bebington CH62 43 C8
Ellesmere Port CH65 70 C5
Ashfield Rd N 1 CH65 70 C5
Ashfield St CW10 151 D8
Ashford Cl SK9 34 C4
Ashford Dr WA4 26 E3
Ashford Rd SK9 60 A4
Ashford Way 1 WA8 13 D1
Ashgate La CW9 79 F6
Ashgrove CW7 149 D8
Ashlands WA6 74 C7
Ashlea Dr CW5 205 E5
Ashleigh Cl CH4 140 E6
Ashley Bank WA14 31 E8
Ashley CE Prim Sch WA15 31 F5
Ashley Cl WA4 17 C3
Ashley Ct Frodsham WA6 74 A8
Holt LL13 196 D8
Warrington WA4 26 C6
Ashley Dr Bramhall SK7 35 C6
Hartford CW8 103 A6
Ashley Gdns Clutton CH3 182 C1
High Lane SK6 37 D8
Ashley Gn WA8 22 D8
Ashley Grange CW9 103 E3
Ashley Mdw CW1 191 D5
Ashley Mill La N WA14 31 E8
Ashley Rd
Ashley WA14,WA15,WA16 31 C4
Ashley,Ashley Heath WA14, WA15 31 E7
Handforth SK9 34 B1
Mere WA16 56 D8
Runcorn WA7 23 D2
Ashley Ret Pk WA8 23 B7
Ashley Sch WA8 12 D1
Ashley Sta WA15 31 E5
Ashley Way WA8 23 B7
Ashley Way W WA8 22 F7
Ashleymill La WA14 31 D7
Ashmead Cl ST7 193 E3
Ashmead Mews ST7 193 E3
Ashmore Cl
Middlewich CW10 151 C6
Warrington WA3 10 A3
Ashmore's La ST7 193 D3
Ashmuir Cl Blacon CH1 117 E3
Crewe CW1 190 B6
Ashness Dr SK7 35 E8
Ashridge St WA7 22 F3
Ashton Ave SK10 86 D1
Ashton Cl Bebington CH62 43 E3
Congleton CW12 157 B1
Frodsham WA6 49 C1
Middlewich CW10 151 D5
Northwich CW9 103 E4
Runcorn WA7 48 F6
Ashton Ct WA6 49 C1
Ashton Dr WA6 49 C1
Ashton Hayes Prim Sch CH3 121 F8
Ashton La CH3 121 E6
Ashton Rd Manley WA6 99 E4
Newton-le-W WA12 2 C5
Norley WA6 100 B4
Ashton St WA2 16 B6
Ashtree Cl Neston CH64 67 A7
Prestbury SK10 87 C8
Ashtree Croft CH64 68 A7
Ashtree Ct CH2 237 C4
Ashtree Dr CH64 67 A7
Ashtree Farm Ct CH64 68 A7
Ashville Ct CW2 206 B7
Ashville Ind Est WA7 49 E3
Ashville Way WA7 49 E3
Ashwood WA14 31 B8
Ashwood Ave
Golborne WA3 3 D8
Warrington WA1 16 E7
Ashwood Cl Barnton CW8 78 B4
Ellesmere Port CH66 69 D1
Widnes WA8 22 A7
Ashwood Cres CW8 78 B3
Ashwood Ct CH2 119 A3
Ashwood Farm Ct CH2 96 B6
Ashwood La CH2 96 B5
Ashwood Rd SK12 38 D6
Ashworth Pk WA16 81 F8
Asiatic Cotts CH5 116 B3
Askerbank La SK11 159 A1
Askett Cl WA11 1 C7
Askrigg Ave CH66 69 B5
Aspen Cl
Ellesmere Port CH66 69 E1
Heswall CH60 41 D8
Kidsgrove ST7 195 E3
Aspen Gr Saughall CH1 117 B7
Warrington WA1 17 A7
Aspen Way Chester CH2 119 B4
High Lane SK6 38 A7
Aspens The CW8 101 E5
Aspinall Cl WA2 9 A3
Aspull Cl WA3 9 C4
Asquith Cl CW1 191 C5
Assheton Cl WA12 2 B4
Assheton Wlk L24 21 E2
Astbury Cl Crewe CW1 190 A7
Golborne WA3 4 B8
Kidsgrove ST7 195 C3
Astbury Dr CW8 78 A4
Astbury Lane Ends CW12 178 F8
Astbury Mere Ctry Pk* CW12 156 B2
Astbury St CW12 156 C2
Astbury St Mary's CE Prim Sch CW12 178 B8
Aster Cres WA7 49 F5
Aster Rd WA11 1 F7
Aster Wlk M31 11 F2
Astle Cl CW10 151 C7
Astle Ct SK11 84 A3
Astle La SK10 84 E1
Astley Cl Knutsford WA16 82 C7
Warrington WA4 16 B3
Widnes WA8 12 C3
Astley Ct M44 11 E8
Astley Rd M44 11 E8
Astmoor Bridge La WA7 23 F2
Astmoor East Intc WA7 24 A3
Astmoor Ind Est WA7 23 F3
Astmoor La WA7 23 F1
Astmoor Prim Sch WA7 23 F2
Astmoor Rd Runcorn WA7 23 C3
Runcorn WA7 23 E3
Aston Ave Warrington WA3 9 F4
Winsford CW7 126 B2
Aston by Sutton Prim Sch WA7 50 C2
Aston Ct WA1 9 C1
Aston Fields Rd WA7 50 E4
Aston Gn WA7 50 E6
Aston La Runcorn WA7 50 F5
Sutton WA7 50 C2
Woore CW3 232 E1
Aston La N WA7 50 E4
Aston La S WA7 50 E3
Aston Rd ST5 210 D1
Aston Way
13 Handforth SK9 34 D5
Middlewich CW10 128 E1
Astor Dr WA4 26 F8
Atcherley Cl CW5 218 E8
Athelbrae Cl CW8 103 F7
Atherton La M44 11 E5
Atherton Rd CH65 69 F6
Athey St SK11 112 C8
Athey Street Mill 2 SK11 112 C7
Athlone Rd WA2 8 A1
Athol Cl Bebington CH62 43 E5
Newton-le-W WA12 1 F4
Athol Dr CH62 43 E5
Athol Rd SK7 35 D5
Atholl Ave CW2 190 C1
Atholl Cl SK10 87 A1
Atkin Cl CW12 156 A3
Atlanta Ave M90 33 A8
Atterbury Cl WA8 12 C2
Attlee Ave WA3 5 C4
Attwood Cl CW1 191 C4
Attwood St ST7 195 A2
Atworth Terr CH64 67 F8
Aubourn Cl WA8 12 C3
Auckery Ave CH66 69 D3
Auckland Rd CH1 117 D4
Audlem Cl WA7 49 F4
Audlem Dr CW9 104 A6
Audlem Rd
Hankelow CW3 230 C7
Hatherton CW5 219 D3
Nantwich CW5 204 F3
Audlem St James' CE Prim Sch CW3 230 A5
Audley Cres CH4 141 E6
Audley Rd Alsager ST7 193 E1
Barthomley CW2 208 E5
Newcastle-u-Lyme ST7, ST5 210 B2
Talke ST7 210 B6
Audley St CW1 190 D5
Audley St W CW1 190 D5
Audre Cl WA5 14 D6
Aughton Way CH4 139 D4
Augusta Dr SK10 87 B4
Augusta Ho CH1 117 F6
Austell Rd M22 33 D8
Austen Cl 1 CW11 174 D6
Austen Dr WA2 8 A6
Austen Ho SK10 86 F1
Austin Cl CW7 149 C6
Austin St CW9 79 D1
Austins Hill CH3 144 C8
Austral Ave WA1 17 C7
Australia La WA4 17 C1
Autumn Ave WA16 57 C2
Avebury Cl Golborne WA3 3 E8
Widnes WA8 13 F3
Aveley Cl WA1 17 B7
Avens Rd M31 11 F3
Avenue One CW1 207 C8
Avenue The
Alderley Edge SK9 60 A1
Alsager ST7 193 D4
Altrincham WA15 31 F8
Bebington CH62 43 C8
Comberbach CW9 78 D8
Great Barrow CH3 120 F7
High Legh WA16 29 C5
Kidsgrove ST7 194 F1
Lymm WA13 18 D1
Marston CW9 79 B3
Newton-le-W WA12 2 D4
Sandbach CW11 174 E8
Tarporley CW6 146 D1
Avenue Two CW1 207 C8
Avery Cl WA2 8 E2
Avery Cres WA11 1 C7
Avery Rd WA11 1 C7
Avery Sq WA11 1 C7
Aviator Way M22 33 D8
Aviemore Dr WA2 9 A3
Avocet Cl
Newton-le-W WA12 2 C4
Warrington WA2 8 D3
Avocet Dr CW7 149 D6
Avon WA8 12 A2
Avon Ave WA5 14 F4
Avon Cl Kidsgrove ST7 195 B2
Macclesfield SK10 87 A2
Neston CH64 66 E6
Avon Ct ST7 193 C5
Avon Dr Congleton CW12 156 F1
Crewe CW1 191 A5
Avon Rd Altrincham WA15 31 E8
Culcheth WA3 5 A2
Heald Green SK8 34 C7
Avon Wlk CW7 127 A2
Avondale CH65 70 B2
Avondale Ave CH62 43 F5
Avondale Dr WA8 12 B1
Avondale Rd WA11 1 C7
Avondale Rise SK9 60 D6
Avonlea Cl CH4 140 E4
Avonside Way SK11 112 C5
Avro Way M90 32 F7
Axminster Wlk SK7 35 E7
Aycliffe Wlk 6 WA8 22 C8
Aylesbury Cl
Ellesmere Port CH66 69 C3
Macclesfield SK10 87 D3
Aylesby Cl WA16 57 B1
Aylsham Cl WA8 12 C4
Ayrshire Cl CW10 128 D2
Ayrshire Way CW12 157 A1
Aysgarth Ave CW1 173 B1
Azalea Gdns WA9 6 A7
Azalea Gr WA7 49 F4

B

Babbacombe Rd WA5 14 E4
Babbage Rd CH5 116 A4
Bache Ave CH2 118 C5
Bache Dr CH2 118 D5
Bache Hall Ct CH2 118 C5
Bache Hall Est CH2 118 C5
Bache Sta CH2 118 D5
Bachefield Ave CH3 142 A6
Bachelor's Ct CH3 142 A8
Bachelor's La CH3 142 A8
Back Bridge St WA12 2 B3
Back Brook Pl WA4 16 E3
Back Coole La CW3 229 B4
Back Crosland Terr WA6 73 B2
Back Cross La
Congleton CW12 179 A8
Newton-le-W WA12 2 B4
Back Eastford Rd WA4 16 A1
Back Eddisbury Rd SK11 113 C7
Back Forshaw St WA2 16 C7
Back Heathcote St ST7 195 A2
Back High St 4 WA7 23 A2
Back Jodrell St SK22 39 B7
Back La Alpraham CW6 169 D6
Altrincham WA15 32 B4
Bate Heath CW9 54 D7
Betley CW2 208 C1
Brereton Green CW11 153 D6
Burtonwood WA5 6 D7
Congleton CW12 156 A4
Duddon CW6 145 A6
Helsby WA6 73 D2
High Legh WA14 29 F5
Higher Whitley WA4 52 E4
Marton CW12,SK11 133 F2
No Man's Heath SY14 214 A4
Norbury SY13 215 F5
Partington WA14 20 C5
Plumley WA16 81 B1
Shavington CW2 206 E4
Smallwood CW11 176 D8
Swan Green WA16 106 B8
Tattenhall CH3 167 C2
Threapwood SY14 222 E7
Warrington WA5 14 A3
Wybunbury CW5 220 C6
Back Lanes CW6 146 B2
Back Legh St WA12 2 A3
Back Market St WA12 2 A3
Back Paradise St 4 SK11 112 C7
Back Park St CW12 156 E2
Back Queen St CH1 237 B3

Back Rathbone St WA12 ....2 A3
Back River St 🔢 CW12 ..156 D3
Back Union Rd SK22 ....39 C7
Back Wallgate 🔢 SK11 ..112 D8
Backford Cl WA7 ....50 C5
Backford Cross CH66 .....94 F7
Backford Gdns CH1 ......94 F7
Backlands CW1 ....190 C6
Badbury Cl WA11 ....1 D7
Badcock's La CW6 ......185 E4
Baddiley Cl CW5 ....203 D2
Baddiley Hall La CW5 ...217 A8
Baddiley La CW5 ....203 D1
Baddington La CW5 .....204 C1
Badger Ave CW1 ....190 B5
Badger Bait CH64 ....66 F6
Badger Cl WA7 ....50 A6
Badger Ho SK10 ....87 D2
Badger Rd
 Macclesfield SK10 ....87 D2
 Prestbury SK10 ....87 A7
Badgers Cl
 Christleton CH3 ....142 E7
 Ellesmere Port CH66 ....94 F8
 🔢 Winsford CW7 ......126 A1
Badgers Croft ST5 ......210 E1
Badgers Pk CH64 ....66 F6
Badgers Set CW8 ....101 D5
Badgers Wlk CH2 ....95 E2
Badgersrake La CH66 ....68 D3
Bag La
 Cuddington CW8,WA6 ...101 E7
 Norley WA6 ....101 A6
Bagley La CW3 ....230 B1
Bagmere Cl
 Brereton Green CW11 ..153 F4
 Sandbach CW11 ....174 F7
Bagmere La CW11 ......154 B5
Bagnall Cl WA5 ....15 C5
Bagot Ave WA5 ....15 F8
Bagstock Ave SK12 ......36 E2
Baguley Ave WA8 ....22 A5
Bahama Cl WA11 ....1 D8
Bahama Rd WA11 ....1 D8
Baildon Gn CH66 ....69 B5
Bailey Ave CW5 ....204 F6
Bailey Bridge Cl CW2 ...118 D4
Bailey Bsns Pk SK10 .....87 F7
Bailey Cl CW1 ....190 C7
Bailey Cres
 Congleton CW12 ....157 A4
 Sandbach CW11 ....175 D6
Bailey Ct Alsager ST7 ..193 E3
 🔢 Macclesfield SK10 ..112 E7
Bailey La M31 ....11 F3
Bailey Wlk WA14 ....31 C8
Bailey's Bank ST8 .....179 D3
Bailey's La L24 ....21 A1
Baileys Cl WA8 ....13 A5
Baileys La L26 ....21 A7
Bainbridge Ave WA3 ......3 F8
Bainbridge Cres WA5 ...14 E8
Baines Ave M44 ....11 F8
Baker Cl CW2 ....190 A2
Baker Dr CH66 ....69 E3
Baker St 🔢 SK11 ....112 C7
Baker's Ct CW7 ....126 E1
Baker's La
 Swan Green WA16 .....106 D6
 Winsford CW7 ....126 E1
Bakers Pl WA2 ....16 B7
Bakers Villas The CW12 ..156 D2
Bakestonedale Rd SK10 ..63 E4
Bakewell Cl CH66 ....94 E8
Bakewell Rd
 Burtonwood WA5 ....7 A7
 Hazel Grove SK7 ....36 E8
Bala Cl WA5 ....7 E2
Baldock Cl WA4 ....17 C3
Balfour Cl WA3 ....191 C4
Balfour St WA7 ....22 F1
Balham Cl WA8 ....13 A4
Balharry Ave WA11 ....1 E7
Ball La Bollington SK10 ..87 D5
 High Lane SK6 ....37 E7
Ball Pathway WA8 ....12 E1
Ballantyne Pl WA2 ....8 A6
Ballantyne Way 🔢 WA3 ..3 E8
Ballater Cres CH3 ......119 B2
Ballater Dr WA2 ....8 E4
Ballerat Cl CH1 ....117 D4
Balliol Cl SK11 ....112 F3
Balmoral Ave
 Crewe CW2 ....190 B1
 Northwich CW9 ....104 A5
Balmoral Cl
 Knutsford WA16 ....57 B1
 Winsford CW7 ....126 C3
Balmoral Cres SK10 .....87 F2
Balmoral Dr Helsby WA6 ..73 B4
 High Lane SK6 ....37 E7
 Holmes Chapel CW4 ...130 B2
 Poynton SK12 ....36 D3
Balmoral Gdns
 Congleton CW12 ....156 F4
 Ellesmere Port CH65 ....70 D3
Balmoral Pk CH1 ....118 B3
Balmoral Pl CW5 ....205 D4
Balmoral Rd
 Warrington WA4 ....16 F2
 Widnes WA8 ....13 A4
Balmoral Way SK10 ......60 A6
Bamburgh Ct CH65 ......70 E3
Bamford Cl
 Bollington SK10 ....88 A7
 Heald Green SK8 ....34 D8

Bamford Cl continued
 Runcorn WA7 ....49 C7
Bamford St SK10 ....87 E1
Banastre Dr WA12 ....2 F3
Banbury Cl SK10 ....87 E2
Banbury Ct CW6 ....146 D1
Banbury Dr WA5 ....15 C5
Banbury St ST7 ....194 D1
Bancroft CW8 ....76 F4
Bancroft Rd WA8 ....13 D2
Bandon Cl L24 ....21 D2
Banff Ave CH63 ....43 D5
Bangor Cl CH66 ....94 F8
Bank Cl Chester CH2 ...118 E5
 Sandbach CW11 ....112 E7
 Neston CH64 ....67 A6
Bank Cott CW12 ....156 E2
Bank Ct CW12 ....156 E2
Bank Farm Mews SY14 ..214 E6
Bank Gdns WA5 ....14 C4
Bank Ho CW7 ....126 C1
Bank House La
 Helsby WA6 ....73 C4
 Smallwood CW11 ......177 A6
Bank La Burland CW5 ...203 D7
 Congleton CW12 ....134 C1
 Rainow SK10 ....89 D6
Bank Mews WA6 ....73 C4
Bank Quay Trad Est WA1 ..15 F4
Bank Rd CH5 ....91 D1
Bank Side CW8 ....97 D1
Bank Sq SK9 ....60 B7
Bank St Congleton CW12 ..156 E2
 Hollinfare WA3 ....11 B5
 Kidsgrove ST7 ....195 C4
 Macclesfield SK11 .....112 E7
 Newton-le-W WA12 ......1 F3
 🔢 Warrington WA1 .....16 B5
Bank The ST7 ....195 B7
Bank Top Cotts CW5 ...204 F6
Bank View CW4 ....107 E1
Bankend Barn SK23 .....39 C5
Bankes' La
 Runcorn,Weston WA7 ...48 F5
 Runcorn,Weston Point WA7 ..48 D4
Bankfield Ave Irlam M44 ..11 D5
 Wistaston CW2 ....206 A7
Bankfield Rd WA8 ......12 C1
Bankfield Sch The WA8 ..12 D1
Bankfields Dr CH62 .....44 B5
Bankhall La WA14,WA15 ..31 F8
Bankhall Pk WA1 ....16 C4
Bankhey CH66 ....69 F5
Bankhouse Dr CW12 ....157 A5
Banklands Cl M44 ....11 D5
Banks Cl CW12 ....156 C3
Banks Cres WA4 ....16 F4
Banks Rd CH60 ....40 B8
Bankside Altrincham WA15 ..32 D6
Bankside Cl
 Barbridge CW5 ....187 D6
 Handforth SK9 ....34 D1
Bankside Ct ST7 ....193 E5
Banky Fields CW12 .....156 C1
Banky Fields Cres
 CW12 ....156 C1
Bannacks Cl CW5 ......205 D6
Barbauld St WA1 ....16 B5
Barber Dr ST7 ....194 E7
Barber St SK11 ....112 E6
Barber's La Antrobus CW9 ..53 D6
 Northwich CW8 ....101 A5
Barberry Wlk WA11 .....11 F3
Barbondale Cl WA5 .....14 F7
Barbour Sq CH3 ....166 B1
Barbridge Mews CW5 ..187 D6
Barbridge Rd ST5 .....210 D2
Barclay Hall WA16 ......58 D4
Barclay Rd SK12 ....36 E3
Bardell Cl SK12 ....36 E2
Bardsey Cl 🔢 CH65 ....70 C1
Bardsley Ave WA5 ....7 F1
Barford Cl WA5 ....7 B1
Barford Dr Golborne WA3 ..4 A8
 Handforth SK9 ....34 E2
Barford Grange CH64 ...68 B8
Barham Ct WA3 ....9 D4
Barhill Farm Cotts SY13 ..214 C2
Barington Dr WA7 ....50 E7
Baristow Cl CH2 ....237 B4
Bark St CW12 ....156 E2
Barker St Crewe CW2 ..190 D1
 Nantwich CW5 ....204 E5
Barker's Hollow Rd WA4 ..51 A5
Barkhill Rd CH3 ....119 B3
Barley Castle Cl WA4 ....27 B3
Barley Croft Alsager ST7 ..193 E2
 Cheadle Hulme SK8 ....34 F8
 Chester CH3 ....142 A7
Barley Dr SK7 ....35 C7
Barley Mow Cl CH66 ....69 C2
Barley Rd WA4 ....17 C3
Barleycastle La WA4 .....27 D4
Barleycastle Trad Est
 WA4 ....27 A7
Barleycroft Terr ST7 ...194 F7
Barleyfields ST7 ....209 D2
Barleywood Cl CW7 ....206 B8
Barlow Dr CW7 ....148 F8
Barlow Gr WA9 ....1 A2
Barlow Hill SK11 ....136 F2
Barlow Rd Handforth SK9 ..34 B1
 Moulton CW9 ....126 F7
Barlow Way CW11 ......174 E7
Barmouth Cl WA5 ....7 E3
Barn Croft WA6 ....73 C4

Barn Croft Rd L26 ......21 A7
Barn Ct CH3 ....182 C2
Barn La WA3 ....2 F8
Barn Mdw CW8 ....78 E1
Barn Rd CW12 ....156 D4
Barn St WA8 ....23 A6
Barn Way WA12 ....2 B3
Barnabas Ave CW1 ....189 F5
Barnaby Chase CH3 ...182 C2
Barnaby Rd SK12 ....36 D2
Barnack Cl WA1 ....17 A8
Barnacre Dr CH64 ......41 B2
Barnard Cl SK11 ....111 F6
Barnard St WA5 ....15 D3
Barnato Cl CW1 ....189 F7
Barnbridge Cl ST7 ....194 E7
Barnbrook Cl CW7 ....126 A1
Barncroft ST5 ....210 E1
Barncroft Cl SK11 ......84 A3
Barnes Ave WA2 ....9 B2
Barnes Cl Blacon CH1 ..117 F6
 Haslington CW1 ....191 C4
 Warrington WA5 ....15 A5
 Widnes WA8 ....13 D2
Barnes Rd WA8 ....13 C2
Barneston Rd WA8 ......13 E3
Barnett Ave WA12 ....1 E3
Barnett Gr CW12 ......156 A3
Barnett St SK11 ....112 B7
Barnett Wlk CW2 ......206 F8
Barnfield CH3 ....166 A2
Barnfield Ave WA7 .....50 D7
Barnfield Cl CH66 ......69 C2
Barnfield Rd
 Bollington SK10 ....87 F6
 Warrington WA1 ....17 C7
Barnham Cl WA3 ....3 A8
Barnhill Grange CH3 ...183 B3
Barnhill Rd CH3 ....183 A1
Barnhouse La
 Great Barrow CH3 .....120 E7
 Mouldsworth CH3 ......98 A3
Barnmoore Cl SY14 ....213 B4
Barns La WA13,WA14 ...20 A5
Barns Pl WA15 ....32 C8
Barns The CW10 ......127 D5
Barnside Way
 Macclesfield SK10 ......87 C3
 Moulton CW9 ....126 F8
Barnstaple Way WA5 ...14 E4
Barnston Ave CH65 .....69 F5
Barnston Ct CW5 ......180 C2
Barnston Prim Sch CH60 ..41 C7
Barnston Rd CH60 ......41 C8
Barnston Towers Cl
 CH60 ....41 C8
Barnston Twrs CH60 ....41 C8
Barnswood Cl WA4 .....17 C1
Barnton Cl WA3 ....3 D7
Barnton Prim Sch CW8 ..78 A4
Barnwell Ave WA3 ....3 E7
Barnwell Cl CW2 ......206 B8
Baron Cl WA1 ....17 D7
Baron Gn SK8 ....34 D7
Baron's Cl WA7 ....22 C8
Baronet Mews WA4 .....16 A1
Baronet Rd WA4 ....16 A1
Baronia Pl CW5 ....204 F6
Barons Cl Frodsham WA6 ..74 C8
 Runcorn WA7 ....49 D1
Barons Quay Rd CW9 ...78 F1
Barons Rd
 Shavington CW2 ......206 B4
 Worleston CW5 ....188 E5
Barony Bldgs 🔢 CW5 ...204 E6
Barony Ct CW5 ....204 E7
Barony Employment Pk The
 CW5 ....204 E8
Barony Rd CW5 ....204 E7
Barony Terr CW5 ......204 E6
Barony Way CH4 ....140 E4
Barracks La
 Burwardsley CH3 ......184 C5
 Macclesfield SK10 .....112 F8
 Ravensmoor CW5 .....203 E1
Barracks Sq 🔢 SK11 ..112 B8
Barrastitch La CW8 ....101 E6
Barratt Rd ST7 ....193 F3
Barrel Well Hill CH2 ...118 F1
Barrie Gdns ST7 ......210 C8
Barrie Gr CW1 ....190 E4
Barrington Dr CW10 ...151 C7
Barrow Ave WA2 ....8 E2
Barrow CE Prim Sch
 CH3 ....120 D6
Barrow Hall Com Prim Sch
 WA5 ....14 E2
Barrow Hall Farm CH3 ..120 D5
Barrow Hall La WA5 ....14 E2
Barrow La
 Altrincham WA15 ....32 B7
 Golborne WA2 ....3 C2
 Great Barrow CH3 .....120 C5
 Tarvin CH3 ....121 C4
Barrow Mdw SK8 ....34 E8
Barrow's Brow WA16 ...81 E1
Barrow's Row WA8 .....13 E4
Barrowdale Rd WA3 .....3 B8
Barrowmore Est CH3 ..120 F7
Barrows Cl CW1 ....190 A8
Barrule Cl WA4 ....26 E5
Barry St WA4 ....16 F4
Barrymore Ave WA4 .....16 F4
Barrymore Cres CW9 ...78 D8
Barrymore Ct WA4 ......17 A1

Barrymore Rd
 Runcorn WA7 ....49 B7
 Warrington WA4 ....17 A1
 Weaverham CW8 ....77 E1
Barrymore Way CH63 ...43 B6
Bars The CH1,CH3 ....237 C2
Barsbank Cl WA13 ......18 C3
Barsbank La WA13 ......18 C3
Barshaw Gdns WA4 .....26 E4
Bartholomew Way CH4 ..141 C6
Bartholomey Cres CW2 ..189 D4
Barthomley Rd
 Barthomley CW2 ......208 B7
 Betley ST7 ....208 F3
Bartington Hall Pk CW8 ..77 A5
Bartlegate WA7 ....50 B5
Barton Ave WA4 ....17 A2
Barton Cl Handforth SK9 ..34 D2
 Runcorn WA7 ....50 D7
Barton Ct CW7 ....126 F1
Barton Rd
 Barton CH3,SY14 .....181 D1
 Congleton CW12 ......156 F3
 Farndon CH3 ....180 F1
Barton St SK11 ....112 C7
Barton Stad CW7 ......126 F1
Barton's Pl CW9 ....79 B1
Barwood Ave ST7 .....194 A5
Barwoods Dr CH4 .....140 F6
Basford Rd CW2 ......206 D8
Basford Way CW7 .....126 B2
Baskervyle Cl CH60 ....41 A6
Baskervyle Rd CH60 ...41 A6
Baslow Dr Hazel Grove SK7 ..36 F8
 Heald Green SK8 ......34 C8
Bassett Cl CW5 ....205 D6
Batchelors Wing The
 CW10 ....127 D5
Bate's Mill La CW6 ....167 E5
Bateman Rd CW9 ....80 B2
Batemans Ct CW2 ....206 B8
Batemill Cl WA16 ......86 F1
Batemill La WA16,SK11 ..108 E5
Bates La WA6 ....73 D4
Bath Cres SK8 ....34 B6
Bath La CW3 ....230 A3
Bath St Chester CH1 ...237 C2
 Sandbach CW11 ....175 C6
 Warrington WA1 ....16 A5
Bath Vale Cotts CW12 ..157 A3
Batherton Cl WA8 ......23 B7
Batherton La CW5 .....204 F4
Battlewood Dr CH64 ....66 E5
Batterbee Ct CW1 .....191 D5
Battersby La WA2 ......16 C6
Battersea Ct WA8 ......12 F3
Battery La WA1 ....17 F7
Bawtry Rd WA2 ....8 E1
Baxter Cl WA7 ....50 D7
Baxter Ho WA8 ....78 E1
Baxter St WA5 ....15 F5
Baycliffe WA13 ....18 D2
Baycliffe Cl WA7 ....49 D5
Bayley Rd CW5 ....205 D6
Bayswater Cl WA7 ......24 F4
Baytree Cl CH66 ....69 F1
Bayvil Cl WA7 ....50 E7
Beach Gr CW8 ....103 C6
Beach La WA16 ....58 A4
Beachin La CH3 ....182 A4
Beachin Cl 🔢 WA7 ......48 E1
Beacon Hill View WA7 ..48 D7
Beacon La CH60 ....41 A7
Beacons The
 Heswall CH60 ....41 A7
 Warrington WA3 ....9 D5
Beaconsfield Cres WA8 ..13 A4
Beaconsfield Gr WA8 ...13 B4
Beaconsfield Rd
 Runcorn WA7 ....22 C1
 Widnes WA8 ....13 B4
Beaconsfield St CH3 ...237 C2
Beadnell Dr WA5 ....14 F3
Beagle Point CW7 .....126 A1
Beagle Wlk M22 ....33 E8
Beam Heath Way CW5 ..204 F7
Beam St CW5 ....204 E6
Beamish Cl WA7 ....26 D3
Beamont St WA8 ....23 A4
Beardsmore Dr WA3 .....3 E8
Bearhurst La SK11 .....111 A5
Bearstone Rd TF9 .....236 C6
Beasley Cl CW6 ....69 D3
Beata Rd ST5 ....210 F1
Beatrice St WA4 ....16 C4
Beatty Ave WA2 ....8 C1
Beatty Dr CW12 ....157 A4
Beatty Rd CW5 ....204 D4
Beaufort Chase SK9 ....34 F1
Beaufort Cl
 Alderley Edge SK9 .....60 B2
 Warrington WA3 ....9 D7
 Widnes WA8 ....22 A8
Beaufort St WA5 ....15 E4
Beaulieu Ave CW7 ....126 F2
Beaumaris Cres SK7 ...36 C8
Beaumaris Dr CW7 .....126 D2
Beaumont Cl
 Biddulph ST8 ....179 D3
 Chester CW2 ....140 E6
 Wistaston CW2 ....205 F8
Beaumont Com Inf & Jun
 Schs WA2 ....16 C7
Beaumont Ct WA5 ......34 C5
Beauty Bank
 Whitegate CW7 ....125 E5

Beauty Bank continued
 Winsford CW7 ....149 A3
Beauty Bank Cotts CW7 ..149 A3
Beaver Cl Chester CH4 ..140 E5
 Pickmere WA16 ....79 F7
Beaver Ctr The CW9 ...103 F7
Beaverbrook Ave WA5 ...5 B4
Bebington Rd CH66 .....69 D4
Becconsall Cl CW1 ....190 A8
Becconsall Dr CW1 ....190 A8
Bechers WA8 ....12 B3
Beckenham Gr 🔢 CW7 ..126 A1
Beckett Ave CW7 .....150 D8
Beckett Dr Lymm WA13 ..19 B8
 Winwick WA2 ....8 A5
Beckett's La CH3 ......142 B8
Beckford Cl CW1 ......189 F8
Becks La SK10 ....86 F2
Bedells La SK9 ....60 A6
Bedford Ave CH65 ......70 A2
Bedford Ave E CH65 ....70 B2
Bedford Ct CW2 ....190 D1
Bedford Gdns CW2 ....190 C1
Bedford Gn M44 ....11 B6
Bedford Gr ST7 ....193 B5
Bedford Pl CW2 ....190 C1
Bedford Rd
 Kidsgrove ST7 ....195 A3
 Macclesfield SK11 .....112 B7
Bedford Rise CW7 .....149 C6
Bedford St Crewe CW2 ..190 C1
 Warrington WA4 ....26 C8
Bedward Row CH1 .....237 A2
Beech Ave Culcheth WA3 ..5 A3
 Frodsham WA6 ....74 C8
 Golborne WA3 ....3 F7
 Haydock WA11 ....1 F7
 Mobberley WA16 ....57 E6
 Rode Heath ST7 ......193 F8
 Warrington WA5 ....14 C3
Beech Bank Beech SK10 ..87 F1
Beech Cl
 Alderley Edge SK9 .....85 A8
 Stretton WA4 ....26 E3
 Beech Cres SK12 ....36 E4
Beech Ct
 Alderley Edge SK9 .....85 A8
 Congleton CW12 ......156 A4
 Cuddington CW8 ......101 F2
 Holmes Chapel CW4 ...130 D4
 Newton-le-W WA12 ......2 C2
 Ollerton WA16 ....82 F6
 🔢 Partington M31 .....11 F3
Beech Farm Dr SK10 ...87 D2
Beech Gr Chester CW2 ..119 A3
 Crewe CW1 ....190 E5
 Ellesmere Port CH66 ...95 A8
 Lymm WA13 ....18 B2
 Macclesfield SK11 .....112 E5
 Sandbach CW11 ....175 D6
 Warrington WA1 ....17 C7
 Warrington,Latchford WA4 ..16 D3
 Weaverham CW8 ......102 D8
 Wilmslow SK9 ....60 A6
 Winsford CW7 ....149 D8
Beech Hall Dr SK10 ....87 C2
Beech Hall Sch SK10 ...87 C2
Beech Hey La CH64 ....43 B1
Beech Heyes Cl CW8 ..102 E8
Beech Heyes Dr CW8 ..102 E8
Beech Hollows LL12 ...162 C1
Beech La Barnton CW8 ..78 A3
 Eaton CW6 ....147 B6
 Macclesfield SK10 .....87 D1
 Norley WA6 ....75 C3
 Wilmslow SK9 ....60 A6
Beech Rd
 Alderley Edge SK9 .....60 B3
 Haslington CW1 ....91 C8
 High Lane SK6 ....37 F7
 Little Budworth CW6 ..124 D2
 Morley Green WA16 ....59 C5
 Runcorn WA7 ....50 B4
 Sutton WA7 ....50 B4
 Warrington WA3 ....9 E7
 Whaley Bridge SK23 ...65 E7
Beech Rise Crowton CW8 ..76 B2
 Whaley Bridge SK23 ...65 C5
Beech St Crewe CW1 ..190 C4
 Middlewich CW10 .....128 C1
Beech Tree Cl CW5 ...205 D5
Beech View Rd WA6 ....75 C1
Beechcroft Ave CW2 ..206 B7
Beechcroft Dr CH65 ...70 D2
Beeches SK9 ....60 A7
Beeches The
 Chester CH2 ....119 A6
 Ellesmere Port CH66 ...69 D4
 Helsby WA6 ....73 C3
 Mobberley WA16 ....58 E1
 Nantwich CW5 ....204 F5
 🔢 Northwich CW9 ....103 F8
 Whitchurch SY13 .....225 F1
Beechfield Moulton CW9 ..126 E8
 Wilmslow SK9 ....60 A6
Beechfield Ave SK9 .....59 E5
Beechfield Cl CH60 .....41 A8
Beechfield Dr CW10 ...128 B2
Beechfield Gdns CH66 ..103 B6
Beechfield Rd
 Alderley Edge SK9 .....85 B8

Beechfield Rd continued
Cheadle Hulme SK8 ....35 B8
Ellesmere Port CH65 ......70 B5
Warrington WA4 ....17 A2
Beechfields CW7 ....150 B8
Beechlands Ave CH3 .....119 A1
Beechmill Dr WA3 ....4 E3
Beechmoore WA4 ....25 B5
Beechmuir CH1 ....117 E3
Beechtree Farm CI WA16 ..29 C7
Beechtree La WA13 ....29 B7
Beechway Bollington SK10 .88 A7
 Chester CH2 ....118 C6
 High Lane SK6 ....37 F7
 Neston CH64 ....66 D7
 Wilmslow SK9 ....59 F5
Beechways WA4 ....26 D5
Beechways Dr CH64 ....66 D7
Beechwood
 Knutsford WA16 ....56 F3
 Knutsford,Cross Town
 WA16 ....57 C2
Beechwood Ave
 Hartford CW8 ....103 A6
 Newton-le-W WA12 ....2 D4
 Runcorn WA7 ....49 E5
 Warrington WA5 ....14 F5
 Warrington,Padgate WA1 ..16 E7
Beechwood Dr
 Alsager ST7 ....193 B4
 Eaton (nr Congleton)
 CW12 ....156 F8
Beechwood La WA3 ....4 D4
Beechwood Mews SK10 ...87 C2
Beechwood Prim Sch
 WA7 ....49 E5
Beechwood Rd
 Bebington CH62 ....43 C8
 Saltney CH4 ....140 E5
Beechwood Sch CW1 ....190 C5
Beecroft CI WA5 ....7 D1
Beehive La CW9 ....126 F8
Beeston Brow SK10 ....88 B8
Beeston Castle* CW6 ....167 F3
Beeston Ct Aldington SK10 .63 C1
 Holmes Chapel CW4 ...130 A3
 Middlewich CW10 ....151 D5
 Warrington WA3 ....9 D4
Beeston Ct WA7 ....24 C4
Beeston Dr Alsager ST7 .193 C3
 Knutsford WA16 ....82 A8
 Winsford CW7 ....149 C7
Beeston Gn CW6 ....69 E5
Beeston Hall Mews
 CW6 ....168 B4
Beeston Mount SK10 ......63 C1
Beeston Pathway CH4 ...141 E7
Beeston Rd
 Broughton CH4 ....139 B3
 Handforth SK9 ....34 D5
 Higher Kinnerton CH4 ..161 A7
Beeston St CW8 ....103 E7
Beeston Terr SK11 ....111 E6
Beeston View CH4 ....117 E5
Beggarman's La WA16 .....82 A7
Begonia Gdns WA9 ....6 A7
Beilby Rd WA11 ....5 E3
Belfry CI SK9 ....60 D8
Belfry Dr SK10 ....87 C4
Belgrave Ave
 Alsager ST7 ....193 D5
 Congleton CW12 ....156 D3
 Saltney CH4 ....140 E6
 Warrington WA1 ....16 F8
Belgrave CI
 Dodleston CH4 ....162 A6
 Golborne WN7 ....4 C8
 Widnes WA8 ....13 E3
Belgrave Dr CH65 ....69 F5
Belgrave Inf Sch CH4 ....141 B5
Belgrave PI CH4 ....237 B1
Belgrave Rd Chester CH3 .142 B8
 Crewe CW2 ....190 B2
 Irlam M44 ....11 D5
 Macclesfield SK11 ......112 C4
 Northwich CW9 ....104 A4
Belgrave St CH1 ....237 C3
Belgravia Ct Pulford CH4 .162 E5
 Widnes WA8 ....12 F3
Belgravia Gdns WA15 .....31 E8
Bell Ave SK11 ....112 F3
Bell Farm Ct SK10 ....87 C3
Bell House Rd WA8 ....13 C1
Bell La Smallwood CW11 ..177 B7
 Warrington WA4 ....17 E3
Bell Meadow Bsns Pk
 CH4 ....162 E5
Bell Meadow Ct CW6 .....146 C2
Bell's Hollow ST5 ....210 E3
Bellaport Rd TF9 ....236 A4
Bellard Dr CH2 ....118 F5
Bellcast CI WA4 ....26 C5
Belle Vue Terr CW11 .....175 B6
Bellemonte Rd WA6 ....74 C6
Belleville Ave M22 ....33 E8
Bellevue La CH3 ....119 E4
Bellhouse La
 Higher Walton WA4 ......25 D7
 Warrington WA4 ....17 C1
Bellingham CI WA16 ......57 C2
Bellingham Dr WA7 ....49 A8

Bellsfield CI WA13 ....18 F2
Belmont Ave
 Macclesfield SK10 ....86 C1
 Sandbach CW11 ....175 A7
 Warrington WA4 ....16 F3
Belmont Cres WA5 ....15 A6
Belmont Dr CH4 ....140 C6
Belmont Rd Bramhall SK7 .35 F5
 Great Budworth CW9 .....53 F1
 Northwich CW9 ....104 C7
 Widnes WA8 ....13 E2
Belton CI WA3 ....3 E2
Beltony Dr CW1 ....173 A1
Belvedere 9 WA7 ....23 A3
Belvedere La CH4 ....117 E4
Belvedere Rd WA12 ....2 B5
Belvedere Terr ST7 ......193 F7
Belvoir Ave SK7 ....36 E8
Belvoir Rd
 Warrington WA4 ....26 B8
 Widnes WA8 ....13 B1
Bembridge CI
 Widnes WA8 ....12 F4
 Warrington WA5 ....14 C7
Bembridge Ct CW10 .....151 C8
Bembridge Dr CW10 .....151 C8
Ben Nevis Dr CH66 ....68 F6
Benbrook Gr SK9 ....34 E2
Benbrook Way SK11 .....111 E1
Bendee Ave CH64 ....67 A7
Bendee Rd CH64 ....67 A7
Benjamins Way ST7 ......209 F2
Bennet CI CH64 ....68 A8
Bennet Rd CW9 ....104 B6
Bennet Ave WA1 ....16 F6
Bennett CI CW1 ....190 E4
Bennett Ct CW7 ....149 D5
Bennett St WA1 ....16 B5
Bennett's La
 Higher Kinnerton CH4 ...161 A7
 Widnes WA8 ....13 E1
Bennetts La SK11 ....158 E7
Benson Rd WA3 ....3 E8
Benson Wlk 3 SK9 ....34 D2
Bent La Astbury CW12 ...178 A8
 Culcheth WA3 ....5 A2
 Lymm WA13 ....19 C6
 Norley CW8 ....101 C8
Bentham Ave WA2 ....8 C3
Bentham Rd WA3 ....5 E7
Bentinck St WA7 ....22 F3
Bentley Dr CW1 ....191 A5
Bentley Gr CW7 ....149 C6
Bentley's Farm La WA4 ...52 E5
Benton Dr CH2 ....118 C4
Bents Cotts CH2 ....71 E2
Bentside Rd SK12 ....38 D5
Benty Heath La CH64,
 CH66 ....43 B3
Beresford Ct 4 SK9 ......60 A1
Beresford St WA1 ....16 F7
Berisford Ho CW12 ......156 F3
Berkeley Ave ST7 ....193 D5
Berkeley Cres CW2 .....206 A8
Berkeley Ct
 Newton-le-W WA12 ....1 F4
 Runcorn WA7 ....24 D4
Berkeley Prim Sch The
 CW2 ....206 B7
Berkeley Rise CW7 ......149 A8
Berkley Ct SK23 ....65 D6
Berkley Dr CW7 ....141 E6
Berkshire Dr SK10 ....86 E2
Berkshire Dr
 Congleton CW12 ....156 D4
 Irlam M44 ....11 C5
Bermondsey Gr WA8 .....13 D4
Bernard Ave WA4 ....26 D8
Bernisdale Rd CH66 ......57 F4
Bernsdale CI CH5 ....116 A3
Berristal Rd SK10 ....88 E3
Berristall Rise SK10 ......63 C1
Berry CI
 Ellesmere Port CH66 ....69 C3
 Wilmslow SK9 ....60 A5
Berry Rd WA8 ....12 D1
Berrystead CW8 ....103 B4
Bertram St WA12 ....2 A4
Berwick Ave CH62 ....43 E4
Berwick CI
 Macclesfield SK10 ....86 F2
 Warrington WA4 ....17 E6
Berwick Ct WA4 ....130 B2
Berwick Gdns CH66 ......69 B6
Berwick Gr CH66 ....69 B6
Berwick Rd CH66 ....69 B6
Berwyn CI CH66 ....69 A6
Bessancourt CW4 ....130 C3
Bessemer Rd M44 ....11 F6
Beswick St SK11 ....112 B7
Beswicks La
 Norton in Hales TF9 ....236 C2
 Row-of-trees SK9 ....59 C3
Beswicks Rd CW8 ....78 E1
Betchton CI CW11 ....175 C7
Betchton CI 6 CW12 ....156 F3
Betchton Rd CW11 ......175 E3
Betchworth Cres WA7 ....49 D6
Betchworth Way SK10 ....87 C4
Bethany CI WA11 ....1 B7
Betjeman CI WA4 ....16 B7
Betjeman Way CW1 .....190 F5
Betley CI CW9 ....104 A5
Betley St CW1 ....190 C4

Betsyfield Dr WA3 ....9 A8
Bettisfield Ave CH62 .....43 D6
Betty's La CW6 ....168 D1
Bevan Ave ST7 ....210 E6
Bevan CI WA5 ....15 D6
Bevan CI WA5 ....15 D6
Beverley Ave WA4 ....26 D8
Beverley Dr CH60 ....41 B6
Beverley Rd WA5 ....15 C6
Beverley Way
 Ellesmere Port CH66 ....69 B7
 Macclesfield SK10 ....87 C4
Bevin Ave WA3 ....3 A8
Bevyl Rd CH64 ....41 B2
Bewick Wlk WA16 ....57 B3
Bewley Ct CH3 ....142 A7
Bewsey Bsns Ctr WA5 ....15 F6
Bewsey Farm CI WA5 .....15 D8
Bewsey Ind Est WA5 .....16 A7
Bewsey Lodge Prim Sch
 WA5 ....15 F7
Bewsey Park CI WA5 .....15 F7
Bewsey Rd WA2,WA5 .....16 A6
Bewsey St 1 WA1 ....16 B5
Bexhill Ave WA4 ....8 B4
Bexington Dr CW1 ....190 B8
Bexton Ave CW7 ....126 A2
Bexton La WA16 ....82 A8
Bexton Prim Sch WA16 ...81 F7
Bexton Rd WA16 ....56 F1
Bibby Ave WA1 ....16 E6
Bibby St ST7 ....193 E7
Bibby's La CW5 ....88 A1
Bickerton Ave WA6 ....74 D7
Bickerton CI WA3 ....9 D4
Bickerton Holy Trinity CE
 Prim Sch SY14 ....200 A7
Bickerton Rd SY14 ......201 B2
Bickerton Way 1 CW9 ...103 E4
Bickley CI Hough CW2 ...206 E2
 Northwich CW9 ....103 E5
 Runcorn WA7 ....23 C1
Bickley Town La SY14 ...214 E6
Bicknell CI WA5 ....15 B8
Bida La CW12 ....179 B8
Biddulph Common Rd
 ST8 ....179 F7
Biddulph Grange Ctry Pk*
 ST8 ....179 F5
Biddulph Grange Gdn*
 ST8 ....179 E3
Biddulph Park Rd ST8 ...179 F5
Biddulph Rd
 Biddulph ST7 ....195 F6
 Congleton CW12 ....179 B8
Biddulph St CW12 ......179 C7
Bideford Rd WA5 ....14 E4
Bidston CI CH2 ....118 D5
Bidston Dr SK9 ....34 E2
Bidston Gn CH66 ....69 D4
Bidvale Way CW1 ....190 D7
Big Field La CW6 ....146 B7
Biggin CI WA2 ....8 E1
Bignall End Rd
 Audley ST7 ....210 A3
 Newcastle-u-Lyme ST7 ..210 A4
Billingion Ave WA12 ....2 C5
Billington CI Crewe CW2 .190 A2
 Warrington WA5 ....14 E8
Billington Rd WA8 ....12 B3
Bilton CI WA8 ....13 E2
Bilton Way CW7 ....189 E5
Bings Rd SK23 ....65 F8
Bingswood Ave SK23 .....65 E8
Bingswood Ind Est SK23 .65 E8
Bingswood Rd SK23 ......65 E7
Binney Rd CW9 ....104 B8
Binyon Way CW1 ....191 A4
Birch Ave Alsager ST7 ..193 E2
 Crewe CW1 ....190 E6
 Irlam M44 ....11 D5
 Macclesfield SK10 ....87 B1
 Warrington WA2 ....8 A4
 Wilmslow SK9 ....59 F6
 Winsford CW7 ....127 A1
Birch Brook Rd WA13 ....19 C5
Birch CI Crewe CW1 .....190 F5
 Holmes Chapel CW4 ...130 D3
Birch Cres WA12 ....1 F4
Birch Ct CW12 ....155 F3
Birch Fold CW4 ....107 B1
Birch Gdns CW11 ....175 C5
Birch Gr
 Ellesmere Port CH66 ....70 A1
 Higher Wincham CW9 ....79 F5
 Knutsford WA16 ....57 D2
 Lostock Green CW9 ....105 B7
 Warrington, Bruche WA1 ..16 F7
 Warrington, Latchford WA4 .16 D3
Birch Heath La CH3 .....142 F8
Birch Heath Rd CW6 ....168 C8
Birch Hill WA6 ....99 C8
Birch Ho SK7 ....35 E5
Birch House Rd ST5 ....210 D1
Birch La Hough CW2 ....206 F2
Birch Rd Audley ST7 ...210 D1
 Chester CH4 ....140 F5
 Congleton CW12 ....155 F3
 Haydock WA11 ....1 E7
 Hollinfare WA3 ....11 B2
 Partington M31 ....11 D3
 Poynton SK12 ....36 F2
 Runcorn WA7 ....49 C8
 Widnes WA8 ....13 D6
Birch Rise CW8 ....103 B4
Birch Tree Ave SK7 ......37 A8
Birch Tree Ct CH2 ......237 C4

Birch Tree La
 Antrobus WA4 ....53 A6
 Goostrey CW4 ....107 C1
 The Bank ST7 ....195 B8
Birch Tree Rd 6 WA3 .....3 F8
Birch Valley Rd ST7 ....195 C1
Birch Way SK10 ....86 E6
Birchall Ave WA3 ....4 E4
Birchall Moss La CW5 ...219 E1
Birchall St WA3 ....9 A7
Birchall Wlk CW2 ....206 D8
Birchdale Cres WA4 .....26 C8
Birchdale Rd
 Warrington WA4 ....26 C8
 Warrington,Paddington
 WA1 ....17 A7
Birchen Rd L26 ....21 A7
Birchencliff Cotts SK10 ..63 D6
Birchenwood Rd ST6,
 WA5 ....15 F7
Birchenwood Way ST7 ...195 B1
Birches CI CH60 ....41 A8
Birches Croft Dr SK10 ...86 F1
Birches Ho 2 CH60 ....41 A8
Birches La CW9 ....105 B7
Birches The
 Broughton CH4 ....139 B3
 Crewe CW2 ....206 C8
 Neston CH64 ....41 F2
Birches Way 7 ST7 .....195 B2
Birchfield Ave
 Rode Heath ST7 ....193 F7
 Widnes WA8 ....13 A2
Birchfield Rd Lymm WA13 .19 B4
 Warrington WA5 ....15 B5
 Widnes,Appleton WA8 ...13 A2
 Widnes,Farnworth WA8 ..13 A3
Birchgate CI SK10 ....86 E1
Birchhall CI CW5 ....204 F4
Birchin CI CW5 ....205 A6
Birchin La CW5 ....205 A6
Birchinall CI SK11 ......112 A7
Birchmuir CH1 ....117 E3
Birchmuir CI CW1 ....190 B6
Birchway Bollington SK10 .88 A8
 Bramhall SK7 ....35 D3
 Heswall CH60 ....41 C5
 High Lane SK6 ....37 F7
Birchways WA4 ....26 E5
Birchwood Bvd WA3 ......9 D2
Birchwood CE Prim Sch
 WA3 ....9 F3
Birchwood CI
 Ellesmere Port CH66 ....69 D1
 Elton CH2 ....72 C3
Birchwood Com High Sch
 WA3 ....9 D5
Birchwood Dr
 Nantwich CW5 ....204 F6
 Sawn Green WA16 .....106 D7
 Wilmslow SK9 ....60 C7
Birchwood Forest Pk
 WA3 ....10 A5
Birchwood La WA4 ....25 C8
Birchwood Office Pk WA2 .9 B3
Birchwood One Bsns Pk
 WA3 ....9 E2
Birchwood Park Ave WA3 .9 D5
Birchwood Science Pk
 WA3 ....9 D5
Birchwood Sh Ctr WA3 ...9 D2
Birchwood Sta WA3 ....9 E2
Birchwood Tech Pk WA3 ..9 E5
Birchwood Way WA2,WA3 .9 D3
Bird's La CW6 ....186 B8
Birds La Tarporley CW6 .146 C1
 Tattenhall CH3 ....166 E1
Birdwell Dr WA5 ....15 A5
Birkdale Ave CH63 ....43 C6
Birkdale CI Bramhall SK7 .36 A7
 Macclesfield SK10 ....87 C4
Birkdale CI 8 CW9 ......104 B8
Birkdale Gdns CW7 .....126 A2
Birkdale Rd
 Warrington WA5 ....14 F4
 Widnes WA8 ....13 A1
Birkenhead Rd CH64 .....42 E1
Birkenhead St CW9 .....104 B8
Birkett Ave CH65 ....70 C2
Birkin CI CW12 ....156 F4
Birkinheath La WA14 .....31 B4
Birley St WA12 ....2 D4
Birstall Ct WA7 ....49 D6
Birtles CI CW11 ....175 C7
Birtles Hall SK10 ....85 D2
Birtles La SK10 ....85 E2
Birtles Rd
 Macclesfield SK10 ....86 D1
 Warrington WA2 ....8 A3
Birtles Way 4 SK9 ....34 D5
Birtley Ct WA8 ....13 A2
Birtwistle Rd CW9 ....79 D8
Bisham Pk WA7 ....24 D2
Bishop Heber High Sch
 SY14 ....213 C5
Bishop Reeves Rd WA11 ..1 E7
Bishop St CH2 ....118 F3
Bishop Wilson CE Prim Sch
 CH64 ....67 D1
Bishop's CI ST7 ....210 D8
Bishopdale CI WA5 ....14 F7
Bishopgates Dr CW9 ....103 E4
Bishops Ct
 Broughton CH4 ....139 C4
 Warrington WA2 ....8 A4
Bishops Gate CH2 ......119 A3

Bishops Gdns CH65 ....70 A5
Bishops Way WA8 ....13 D3
Bishops Wood CW5 .....204 F2
Bishops' Blue Coat CE High
 Sch The CH3 ....142 A8
Bishopsfield Ct CH2 ....118 F3
Bishopton Dr SK11 .....111 F8
Bispham Rd WA5 ....15 B4
Bittern CI Poynton SK12 .36 A4
 Runcorn WA7 ....50 D8
 Warrington WA2 ....8 A8
Black Bear Rd CH3 ....87 A1
Black Cat Ind Est WA8 ...23 A6
Black Denton's PI WA8 ...13 C1
Black Diamond St CH1 ..237 B4
Black Firs La CW12 .....155 E4
Black Firs Prim Sch
 CW12 ....237 A2
Black Friars CH1 ....237 A2
Black La CW10 ....87 E1
Black Lion La CH66 ......69 C6
Black Moss Rd WA14 .....20 F7
Black Park Rd SY13 ....226 D2
Black Rd SK11 ....112 F7
Blackacres CI CW11 ....174 F6
Blackbird Way ST7 .....195 F1
Blackboards La CH66 .....69 A8
Blackbrook Ave WA2 .....8 F2
Blackbrook CI WA8 ......12 C3
Blackburn CI WA3 ....3 E8
Blackburne Ave WA8 ....22 B5
Blackburne CI WA2 ....9 C2
Blackburne Dr WA12 ......2 A4
Blackcap Rd WA4 ....27 A4
Blackcap Wlk WA3 ....9 E3
Blackden CI CW4 ....78 A2
Blackden Firs CW4 ......108 B2
Blackden La
 Goostrey CW4 ....108 A3
 Siddington SK11 ....132 F8
Blackden Wlk SK9 ....34 D1
Blackdown CI CH66 ......69 A5
Blackeys La CH64 ....66 E8
Blackheath La WA7 .....24 F5
Blackhill La WA16 ....81 F8
Blackhurst Brow SK10 ...61 B2
Blackhurst Farm Rd
 CW5 ....202 E3
Blackhurst St WA1 ....16 B5
Blackledge CI WA2 ....9 A3
Blackley CI
 Macclesfield SK10 ....87 B4
 Warrington WA4 ....16 D3
Blackshaw CI CW12 ....157 B1
Blackshaw Dr WA5 ....7 B1
Blackshaw La SK9 ....59 F1
Blackshaw St 6 SK11 ...112 C7
Blackthorn CI
 Broughton CH4 ....139 B3
 Huntington CH3 ....142 A5
 Wistaston CW2 ....206 B8
Blackthorn PI ST5 ......210 E1
Blackthorne Ave CH66 ...95 A8
Blackwell CI CW10 .....151 D6
Blacon Ave CH1 ....118 A5
Blacon Hall Jun Sch
 CH1 ....117 E5
Blacon Hall Rd CH1 .....117 E5
Blacon High Sch CH1 ...117 D4
Blacon Inf Sch CH1 .....117 E5
Blacon Point Rd CH1 ...117 E3
Bladon CI Crewe CW5 ...204 C4
Bladon Cres ST7 ....193 C5
Blair CI SK7 ....36 C8
Blair Dr WA8 ....12 C3
Blairgowrie Dr SK10 .....87 B4
Blaizefield CI CW3 ......232 C2
Blake CI Blacon CH1 .....117 F6
 Crewe CW2 ....189 F1
Blake La CW8 ....102 A2
Blakeacre Rd L26 ....21 A6
Blakelow CI WA16 ....58 F8
Blakelow Dell CW5 ......113 A6
Blakelow Dene CW5 .....113 A6
Blakeley La WA16 ....58 F8
Blakeley Bank SK11 ....112 F6
Blakelow CI CW10 ......151 B8
Blakelow Cres CW5 ....205 F3
Blakelow Rd SK11 ......112 F6
Blakemere CI SY13 .....226 B1
Blakemere Ct CH65 ......70 C7
Blakemere Dr CW9 .....103 E5
Blakemere La WA6 ......100 D4
Blakemere Way CW11 ...174 F8
Blandford CI
 3 Macclesfield SK10 ...111 F8
 Northwich CW9 ....103 E3
Blandford Rd WA5 ....15 B5
Blankney The CW5 .....204 E4
Blantern Rd CH4 ....161 A7
Blantyre St WA7 ....22 F3
Blaze Hill SK10 ....88 B8
Bleadale CI SK9 ....34 D1
Bleasdale Rd
 Crewe CW1 ....173 B1
 Newton-le-W WA12 ......1 F3
Bleeding Wolf La ST7 ...194 C5
Blenheim CI
 3 Macclesfield SK10 ....87 A1
 Northwich CW9 ....103 E3
 Poynton SK12 ....36 F4
 Warrington WA2 ....8 F2

Blenheim Cl *continued*
Wilmslow SK9 . . . . .60 D7
Wistaston CW2 . . . . .205 E8
Blenheim Ct ST7 . . . . .193 D5
Blenheim Gdns ⑤ CW7 . .149 C7
Blenheim Ho CH1 . . . . . . .118 B3
Bloomsbury Way WA8 . .12 D3
Blossom Hts CW8 . . . . . . .103 D7
Blossom Rd M31 . . . . .11 E2
Blossoms La SK7 . . . . .35 B2
Blue Bridge La WA6 . . . . .73 C5
Blue Cap La SY14 . . . . . . .213 D7
Blue Hatch WA6 . . . . .74 C8
Blue Planet Aquarium*
  CH65 . . . . .70 D1
Blue Ridge Cl WA5 . . . . . .14 E7
Bluebell Ave WA11 . . . . . . .1 E7
Bluebell Cl
  Huntington CH3 . . . . .142 B6
  Macclesfield SK10 . . . . . . .87 D3
  Winnington CW8 . . . . .78 E1
Bluebell Ct WA7 . . . . .49 F4
Bluebell La SK10 . . . . .87 D3
Bluebell Mews ④ SK10 . .87 D3
Bluebell Way
  Alsager ST7 . . . . .193 B3
  Northwich CW9 . . . . .34 C1
Bluecoat St WA2 . . . . .16 B7
Blundell Rd WA8 . . . . .22 D8
Blunstone Cl CW2 . . . . . . .190 A4
Blyth Cl Macclesfield SK10 .86 E1
  Runcorn WA7 . . . . .50 D5
Blyth Rd CH63 . . . . .43 C7
Blythe Ave Bramhall SK7 . .35 C6
  Congleton CW12 . . . . .156 A2
  Widnes WA8 . . . . .13 B5
Blythe Pl CW7 . . . . .127 B2
Blythings The CW6 . . . . . .146 C3
Boardmans Pl CW9 . . . . . .104 A5
Boars Leigh Pk SK11 . . . .135 D1
Boat Mus The* CH65 . . . . .70 C7
Boat Stage WA13 . . . . .18 E3
Boat Wlk WA4 . . . . .16 A8
Boathorse Rd ST7 . . . . . . .210 F8
Boathouse La CH64 . . . . . .41 C3
Bob's La WA4 . . . . .11 D4
Boden Dr CW5 . . . . .205 D4
Boden St SK11 . . . . .112 D8
Bodiam Ct CH65 . . . . .70 E2
Bodmin Ave SK10 . . . . .86 E1
Bodmin Cl WA7 . . . . .50 B6
Bodmin Dr SK7 . . . . .35 E7
Bodnant Cl CW1 . . . . .190 A8
Bold Bsns Ctr WA9 . . . . .6 B7
Bold Cross WA8 . . . . .13 E7
Bold Ind Est WA8 . . . . .13 C5
Bold Ind Park WA9 . . . . .6 B6
Bold La WA5,WA9 . . . . .6 C7
Bold Pl CH1 . . . . .237 B3
Bold Sq CH1 . . . . .237 C3
Bold St Haslington CW1 . .191 C4
  Runcorn WA7 . . . . .23 B3
  Sandbach CW11 . . . . .175 B6
  Warrington WA1 . . . . .16 A5
  Widnes WA8 . . . . .23 A7
Bolesworth Hill Rd CH3 .183 C4
Bolesworth Rd
  Chester CH2 . . . . .118 F6
  Tattenhall CH3 . . . . .183 C7
Boleyn Cl CH1 . . . . .117 E6
Boleyn Ct WA7 . . . . .24 C3
Bolland's Ct CH1 . . . . .237 A2
Bollands Row ⑭ CW5 . . .204 E5
Bolleyn Wood Ct SK9 . . . .34 B1
Bollin Ave
  Altrincham WA14 . . . . .31 B8
  Winsford CW7 . . . . .127 B2
Bollin Cl Alsager ST7 . . . .192 F3
  Culcheth WA3 . . . . .5 A2
  Lymm WA13 . . . . .19 A4
  Sandbach CW11 . . . . .174 E2
Bollin Ct Lymm WA13 . . . . .19 A4
  Wilmslow SK9 . . . . .60 B8
  Winsford CW7 . . . . .127 B2
Bollin Ct Lymm WA13 . . . . .19 A4
  Wilmslow SK9 . . . . .60 C6
Bollin Dr Congleton CW12 .156 F1
  Lymm WA13 . . . . .19 A4
Bollin Gr Biddulph ST8 . .179 E1
  Prestbury SK10 . . . . .87 A2
Bollin Hill Prestbury SK10 .87 A5
  Wilmslow SK9 . . . . .60 C7
Bollin Mews SK10 . . . . .86 F7
Bollin Way SK10 . . . . .87 A6
Bollin Wlk SK9 . . . . .60 C7
Bollinbrook Rd SK10 . . . . .87 B2
Bollinbarn Dr SK10 . . . . . .87 A2
Bollinbrook CE Prim Sch
  SK10 . . . . .87 B2
Bollinbrook Rd SK10 . . . . .87 B2
Bollington Ave CW9 . . . . .104 A5
Bollington Cross CE Prim Sch
  SK10 . . . . .87 E7
Bollington La SK10 . . . . . . .84 E2
Bollington Mill WA14 . . . . .20 C3
Bollington Old Rd SK10 . .87 D6
Bollington Rd SK10 . . . . . .87 E6
Bollinhead La SK11 . . . . .113 C2
Bollinway WA15 . . . . .32 A8
Bollinwood Chase SK9 . . .60 D7
Bolshaw Cl CW1 . . . . .190 A7
Bolshaw Farm La SK8 . . . .34 C6
Bolshaw Prim Sch SK8 . . .34 C6
Bolshaw Rd SK8 . . . . .34 C6
Bolton Ave
  Cheadle Hulme SK8 . . . . . .35 B6
  Warrington WA4 . . . . .16 F4
Bolton Cl Golborne WA3 . . . .4 B8
  Poynton SK12 . . . . .36 D4

Bomish La CW4,SK11 . . . .108 C3
Bond Cl WA5 . . . . .15 D4
Bond St
Bond St
  Macclesfield SK11 . . . . . . .112 C7
  Winnington CW8 . . . . .78 D1
Bonis Hall La SK10 . . . . . . .61 F4
Boon Hill Rd ST7 . . . . .209 F1
Booth Ave
  Ashton Hayes CH3 . . . . . .121 E7
  Little Budworth CW6 . . . . .147 F7
  Sandbach CW11 . . . . .175 C6
Booth Bed La WA16,
  CW4 . . . . .107 B4
Booth La
  Middlewich CW10 . . . . . . .151 E6
  Middlewich,Stud Green
  CW10,CW11 . . . . .152 B3
Booth Rd Handforth SK9 . .34 A1
  Hartford CW8 . . . . .209 D1
Booth St Audley ST7 . . . .209 D1
  Congleton CW12 . . . . .156 C2
  Warrington WA5 . . . . .15 E4
Booth's Hill Rd WA13 . . . .18 C3
Booth's La WA13 . . . . .18 B1
Boothbank La WA14 . . . . .30 A6
Boothby St ⑫ SK10 . . . . .112 C8
Boothfields CW6 . . . . .57 C2
Booths Hill Cl WA13 . . . . .18 C2
Booths Hill Ho ⑤ WA13 . .18 D3
Booths La WA4 . . . . .52 E6
Boothsdale CW6 . . . . .122 D3
Boothsmere Cl CW11 . . . .174 F8
Border Rd CH60 . . . . .41 B8
Border Way CH4 . . . . .119 C1
Borderbrook Sch
  Drury Lane SY14 . . . . .224 D3
  Tallarn Green/Tallwrn Green
  SY14 . . . . .222 F5
Borders Ind Pk The/Parc
  Ddiwydiannol Y Ffin
  CH4 . . . . .140 C7
Borough Rd CW12 . . . . . .156 F3
Borras Rd LL13 . . . . .196 A8
Borron Rd WA12 . . . . .2 B5
Borrowdale Ave WA2 . . . . .8 C3
Borrowdale Cl
  Crewe CW2 . . . . .189 E3
  Frodsham WA6 . . . . .74 D8
Borrowdale Rd WA8 . . . . .22 C8
Bosden Cl SK9 . . . . .34 E2
Bosley Brook CW12 . . . . .179 D5
Bosley Cl Handforth SK9 . .34 D2
  Middlewich CW10 . . . . . . .151 C6
Bosley Dr SK12 . . . . .37 A3
Bosley View CW12 . . . . . .157 B1
Bostock Gn
  Bostock Green CW9 . . . . .127 C7
  Ellesmere Port CH65 . . . . .69 F6
Bostock Hall CW10 . . . . . .127 D5
Bostock Rd
  Macclesfield SK11 . . . . . . .111 E7
  Winsford CW7 . . . . .127 A4
Bostock St WA5 . . . . .15 E6
Boston Ave WA7 . . . . .23 D1
Boston Bvd WA5 . . . . .15 B7
Boston Cl Bramhall SK7 . . .35 D7
  Culcheth WA3 . . . . .4 F4
Boswell Ave WA4 . . . . .16 B2
Botany Bsns Pk SK23 . . . .65 D5
Botany Mews CW7 . . . . . . .65 E6
Boteler Ave WA5 . . . . .15 F7
Bottoms La CH4 . . . . .141 F8
Boughey Rd ST7 . . . . .209 F2
Boughton CH2,CH3 . . . . .118 F2
Boughton Hall Ave CH3 .119 A1
Boughton Hall Dr CH3 . .119 B1
Boughton Heath Prim Sch
  CH3 . . . . .142 B8
Boughton Lodge ②
  CH3 . . . . .119 A1
Boulevard The
  Broughton CH4 . . . . .139 C3
  Ellesmere Port CH65 . . . . .69 F4
Boulting Ave WA5 . . . . .7 F1
Boulton Cl CH1 . . . . .175 C3
Boundary La
  Chester CH4 . . . . .140 C5
  Congleton CW12 . . . . .179 B8
  Heswall CH60 . . . . .41 A8
  Over Peover WA16,SK11 . .108 D7
  Siddington SK11 . . . . .132 E8
  Threapwood SY14 . . . . . . .222 E8
Boundary Lane N CW8 . .101 F2
Boundary Lane S CW8 . .101 F2
Boundary Pk CH64 . . . . . . .66 D7
Boundary St
  Northwich CW9 . . . . .79 E2
  Warrington WA4 . . . . .16 B4
Boundary Terr SK9 . . . . . . .33 F6
Bourchier Way WA4 . . . . .27 A8
Bourne Ave WA3 . . . . .3 D8
Bourne Cl CW8 . . . . .102 E7
Bourne Rd ST7 . . . . .194 F2
Bourne St Mow Cop ST7 .195 C7
  Wilmslow SK9 . . . . .59 F6
Bournemouth Cl WA7 . . . .50 D6
Bouverie St CH1 . . . . .237 A3
Boverton Cl WA5 . . . . .7 E1
Bow Green Rd WA14 . . . . .20 F1
Bow La WA14 . . . . .31 B8
Bowden Cl
  Congleton CW12 . . . . .156 A3
  Culcheth WA3 . . . . .4 F4
Bowden Dr CW9 . . . . .104 C8
Bowden House La SK9 . . .61 A8
Bowden View La WA16 . . .29 F2
Bowden Cl WA1 . . . . .16 F8

Bowe's Gate Rd CW6 . . . .169 A1
Bowen Cl Bramhall SK7 . . .35 F5
  Widnes WA8 . . . . .12 D4
Bowen Cooke Ave CW1 . .190 A5
Bowen Cl CW2 . . . . .190 A3
Bower Cres WA4 . . . . .26 D2
Bower Rd CH60 . . . . .41 C8
Bower St WA8 . . . . .13 C1
Bowerfield Ave SK7 . . . . . .36 E8
Bowerfield Cres SK7 . . . . .36 E8
Bowers Bsns Pk WA8 . . . .23 B7
Bowers Row ⑧ CW5 . . . .204 E5
Bowery Ave SK8 . . . . .34 F6
Bowery The CH1 . . . . .116 D4
Bowfell Cl CH62 . . . . .43 D3
Bowfell Dr SK6 . . . . .37 E8
Bowkers Croft CW1 . . . . .191 F8
Bowland Cl Runcorn WA7 . .49 F5
Bowland Cl WA9 . . . . .10 B5
Bowland Croft CW1 . . . . .173 B1
Bowland Rise CW7 . . . . . .149 B7
Bowles Cl CW11 . . . . .175 A6
Bowling Green Ct
  ⑨ Nantwich CW5 . . . . . .204 E5
  Winnington CW8 . . . . .78 E1
Bowman Ave WA4 . . . . . . .17 A5
Bowmans The SK10 . . . . . .87 B1
Bowmere Cl
  Biddulph ST8 . . . . .179 C1
  Tarporley CW6 . . . . .146 D1
Bowmere Dr CW7 . . . . . . .149 C8
Bowmere Rd CW6 . . . . . . .146 D1
Bowness Ave
  Bebington CH63 . . . . .43 C5
  Irlam M44 . . . . .11 D4
  Warrington WA2 . . . . .8 C2
  Winsford CW7 . . . . .126 D2
Bowness Cl CW4 . . . . .130 A3
Bowness Ct ⑫ WA7 . . . . .50 D5
Bowness Rd WA2 . . . . . . .189 E3
Bowood Cl WA4 . . . . .8 A4
Bowring Dr CH64 . . . . .41 B1
Bowyer Ave ⑧ SK9 . . . . .204 E6
Bowyer Way SK10 . . . . . . .151 C4
Box La CW12 . . . . .155 F3
Box Tree Mews SK11 . . . .112 A7
Box Wlk M31 . . . . .11 E2
Boxgrove Cl WA8 . . . . .13 B3
Boxmoor Cl CH4 . . . . .141 A5
Boydell Ave
  Warrington WA4 . . . . .17 B2
  Warrington,Westy WA4 . . .16 F4
Boydell Way CW4 . . . . . . .162 A6
Boyle Ave WA2 . . . . .8 E1
Boyles Hall Rd ST7 . . . . . .209 E2
Bracken Cl
  Broughton CH4 . . . . .139 C3
  Macclesfield SK10 . . . . . . .86 F1
  Rode Heath ST7 . . . . .193 F8
  Warrington WA3 . . . . .9 C5
Bracken Rd CH66 . . . . .69 E4
Bracken Way
  Barnton CW8 . . . . .78 B3
  Comberbach CW9 . . . . . . .78 C7
  Frodsham WA6 . . . . .74 C6
  Knutsford WA16 . . . . .82 A8
  Wincham CW9 . . . . .79 C3
Brackenfield Way ⑪
  CW7 . . . . .149 A8
Brackenwood Cl CW2 . . .206 B8
Brackenwood Dr WA8 . . .22 A8
Brackenwood Mews
  Chorlton CW2 . . . . .207 D2
  Wilmslow SK9 . . . . .60 E8
Brackley Ave WA4 . . . . .11 D6
Brackley St Runcorn WA7 . .22 F3
  Warrington WA4 . . . . .16 A1
Bradburn Rd M44 . . . . .11 E7
Bradburns La CW8 . . . . . .103 B6
Bradbury Gdns CW12 . . .156 F1
Bradbury Rd CW7 . . . . . . .149 A8
Braddon Cl CW9 . . . . .103 F4
Bradeley Green La SY13 .225 F2
Bradeley Hall Rd CW1 . . .191 B5
Bradeley Rd CW1 . . . . . . .191 C4
Bradfield Rd CW1 . . . . . . .190 B7
Bradford La SK10 . . . . .85 C6
Bradford Rd CW7 . . . . . . .126 E4
Bradford St CH4 . . . . .141 D7
Bradgate Ave SK8 . . . . . . .34 D8
Brading Wlk M22 . . . . .33 E8
Bradlegh Rd WA12 . . . . . . .2 B1
Bradley Bvd WA5 . . . . .15 E5
Bradley Cl CW10 . . . . .151 B7
Bradley Farm La SY13 . . .225 C7
Bradley Hall Cotts WA4 . .27 F6
Bradley La Frodsham WA6 .74 D2
  Newton-le-W WA5,WA12 . . .2 A1
Bradley St SK11 . . . . .112 E6
Bradley Way WA8 . . . . . . .13 A1
Bradmoor Rd CH62 . . . . . .43 D8
Bradshaw Ave WA14 . . . .140 B7
Bradshaw Com Prim Sch
  WA4 . . . . .17 B2
Bradshaw Hall La
  Cheadle Hulme SK8 . . . . . .34 E8
  Heald Green SK8 . . . . .34 D8
Bradshaw La Lymm WA13 .19 D3
  Warrington WA4 . . . . .17 B2
Bradshaw Pl CW12 . . . . .156 C2
Bradshaw St WA8 . . . . . . .13 A2
Bradwall Rd CW11 . . . . . .175 B7
Bradwall Cl CW11 . . . . . . .175 B7
Bradwell Ct CW12 . . . . . .156 F2
Bradwell Dr SK8 . . . . .34 C7
Bradwell Gr CW2 . . . . . . .156 F2

Bradwell Rd Golborne WA3 . .3 E7
  Hazel Grove SK7 . . . . .36 E8
Braemar Ave CW9 . . . . . . .103 C7
Braemar Cl Chester CH3 .119 C3
  Holmes Chapel CW4 . . . . .130 C2
  Warrington WA2 . . . . .9 A3
  Wistaston CW2 . . . . .205 E8
Braemar Ct CH65 . . . . .70 E3
Braeside Cl
  ⑥ Ellesmere Port CH66 . .69 C5
  Macclesfield SK11 . . . . . . .112 F6
Braidwood Ave WA16 . . . .57 C3
Brains La CW6 . . . . .169 B6
Braintree Rd M22 . . . . .33 E8
Braithwaite Cl WA7 . . . . . .49 D5
Braithwaite Rd WA3 . . . . . .3 D8
Brake The ST7 . . . . .195 B7
Brake Village ST7 . . . . . . .195 B7
Brakeley La CW8 . . . . .101 C7
Brakenwood Mews WA4 . .17 C1
Bramall Cl CW11 . . . . .175 C7
Bramble Cl Chester CH3 . .142 A7
  Macclesfield SK10 . . . . . . .87 B2
  Middlewich CW10 . . . . . . .128 C2
  Warrington WA5 . . . . .14 E3
  Winsford CW7 . . . . .126 C3
Bramble Way WA7 . . . . . . .49 E4
Brambles Chase CW8 . . .101 F2
Brambles The
  Burtonwood WA5 . . . . .7 A7
  Haslington CW1 . . . . .191 B4
  Wincham CW9 . . . . .79 C3
Brambling Cl WA7 . . . . . . .49 F5
Brambling Way WA3 . . . . . .3 E7
Bramhall Cl CW7 . . . . .126 B1
Bramhall Ct CW2 . . . . . . .189 F2
Bramhall Ctr The* SK7 . . .35 E6
Bramhall St WA5 . . . . .15 E5
Bramhall Sta SK7 . . . . .35 E6
Bramhall Way WA16 . . . .112 A8
Bramhall Dr
  Bebington CH62 . . . . .43 F4
  Holmes Chapel CW4 . . . . .130 A3
Bramhall High Sch SK7 . . .35 F8
Bramhall La S SK7 . . . . . . .35 E7
Bramhall Pk Rd SK7 . . . . .35 E7
Bramhall St WA5 . . . . .15 E5
Bramhall Wlk SK8 . . . . . . .112 A8
Bramhalls Pk CW9 . . . . . . .78 C3
Bramley Cl Bramhall SK7 . .35 E6
  Ellesmere Port CH66 . . . . .94 F8
  Wilmslow SK9 . . . . .59 D4
Bramley Ct CW6 . . . . .122 D5
Bramley Dr SK7 . . . . .35 E6
Bramley Mews WA4 . . . . .26 C8
Bramley Rd SK7 . . . . .35 E6
Bramley Wlk WA6 . . . . .73 A1
Brampton Ave SK10 . . . . . .87 A2
Brampton Cl WA9 . . . . .1 B3
Brancaster Cl WA3 . . . . .4 A7
Brancaster Dr WA3 . . . . .4 A7
Brancepeth Ct CH65 . . . . .70 E3
Branch Way WA11 . . . . .1 A5
Brancote Gdns CH62 . . . . .43 D7
Brandon Dr WA16 . . . . . . .57 B2
Brandon Wlk
  Lymm WA13 . . . . .19 B4
  Wistaston CW2 . . . . .206 A7
Brandwood Ave WA2 . . . . .8 A3
Brandwood Ho ② WA1 . .16 C5
Bransdale Cl WA5 . . . . .14 F7
Bransdale Way SK11 . . . .111 F7
Brantfield Cl WA2 . . . . .8 E2
Brassey St CH3 . . . . .118 F1
Brassey Way CW5 . . . . . . .205 D5
Brassey's Contract Rd
  SY14 . . . . .199 A1
Brassington Terr CW3 . . .221 F3
Brathay Cl WA2 . . . . .8 C3
Bratton Dr SK11 . . . . .194 A5
Bray Cl Crewe CW2 . . . . . .190 E5
  Warrington WA7 . . . . .49 D6
Bray Rd CH4 . . . . .140 F6
Breach House La WA16 . . .32 A1
Bread St SK11 . . . . .112 C7
Breck Rd WA8 . . . . .13 B1
Breck The CH66 . . . . .69 E7
Brecon Cl SK12 . . . . .36 F4
Brecon Ct WA5 . . . . .7 B2
Brecon Dr CH66 . . . . .69 E1
Brecon Way CW7 . . . . . . .206 A7
Breconway CW7 . . . . .149 B8
Bredon Cl CH66 . . . . .69 A6
Breen Cl CH3 . . . . .166 B8
Breezehill Cl CH64 . . . . . . .66 F8
Breezehill Pk CH64 . . . . . .66 F8
Breezehill Rd CH64 . . . . . .66 F8
Brendon Ave WA2 . . . . .8 C3
Brendon Gr WA9 . . . . .1 A4
Brennus Pl CH1 . . . . .237 A3
Brent Cl SK12 . . . . .36 B4
Brentfield WA8 . . . . .12 D2
Brentnall Cl WA5 . . . . .7 C2
Brentwood Ave M44 . . . . .11 D6
Brentwood Rd CH1 . . . . .117 E5
Brereton CE Prim Sch
  CW11 . . . . .153 F5
Brereton Cl Crewe CW2 . .189 F2
  Malpas SY14 . . . . .213 B3
  Runcorn WA7 . . . . .50 A8
  Sandbach CW11 . . . . .175 C7
Brereton Dr
  Brereton Green CW12 . . .154 F6
  ❶ Cheadle Hulme SK8 . . .34 E8
Brereton Dr CW5 . . . . .204 F7
Brereton Gr M44 . . . . .11 E6
Brereton Heath Ctry Pk*
  CW12 . . . . .154 D7

Brereton Heath La
  CW11,CW12 . . . . .154 E6
Brereton La CW4 . . . . .152 E8
Brereton Rd
  Handforth SK9 . . . . .34 E3
  Hartford CW8 . . . . .103 A4
Bretland Dr WA4 . . . . .27 A7
Breton Cl CH2 . . . . .118 E5
Bretton Court Mews
  CH4 . . . . .139 E4
Bretton Dr CH4 . . . . .139 B3
Bretton La CH4 . . . . .139 E3
Bretton Rd CH4 . . . . .139 E5
Bretton Wlk M22 . . . . .33 D8
Brewery La CH3 . . . . .180 E3
Brewery La CH4 . . . . .118 B3
Brian Ave Warrington WA2 .16 D8
  Warrington,Stockton Heath
  WA4 . . . . .16 E1
Briar Ave WA3 . . . . .11 B2
Briar Cl WA16 . . . . .57 A3
Briar Dr CH60 . . . . .41 A8
Briar La CW8 . . . . .102 E7
Briar Rd WA3 . . . . .3 B8
Briar Wlk WA3 . . . . .3 B8
Briardale Cl CW2 . . . . .205 F8
Briardale Gdns ④ CH66 . .69 C6
Briardale Rd
  Ellesmere Port CH66 . . . . .69 C6
  Willaston CH64 . . . . .43 A1
Briarfield Ave WA8 . . . . . . .12 A1
Briarfield Rd
  Ellesmere Port CH65 . . . . .70 B5
  Heswall CH60 . . . . .41 B8
Briarlands Cl SK7 . . . . .35 D6
Briarstead Cl SK7 . . . . .35 D7
Briarswood CT 195 B1
Briarswood Ct CH1 . . . . . .237 B3
Briarwood Runcorn WA7 . .50 B8
  Wilmslow SK9 . . . . .60 C7
Briarwood Ave
  Macclesfield SK11 . . . . . . .112 D5
  Warrington WA1 . . . . .16 E7
Brick Bank CW5 . . . . .204 F5
Brick Bank La WA16,
  CW4 . . . . .107 B2
Brick Kiln La CW10 . . . . .127 B7
Brick Rd CH4 . . . . .139 C2
Brick St Newton-le-W WA12 . .1 F3
  Warrington WA1 . . . . .16 C5
Brickfield Bsns Ctr CW9 . .79 D1
Brickfield La CH3 . . . . .119 F2
Brickhill La WA15 . . . . .32 B4
Brickhurst Way WA1 . . . . .17 B8
Brickiln La
  Little Bollington WA14 . . . .20 C3
  Whitchurch SY13 . . . . . . .226 D2
Brickley Ct CW8 . . . . .77 C1
Bridestone Sh Ctr
  CW12 . . . . .156 D2
Bridge Ave WA4 . . . . .16 F4
Bridge Ave E WA4 . . . . . . .16 F5
Bridge Bank Cl WA3 . . . . . .3 B7
Bridge Cl Audley ST7 . . . .209 F2
  Cuddington CW8 . . . . . . .102 A3
  Lymm WA13 . . . . .19 B4
  Wistaston CW2 . . . . .206 A7
Bridge Ct Chester CH2 . . .119 A2
  Holt LL13 . . . . .196 E8
  Neston CH64 . . . . .66 E7
Bridge Dr
  Christleton CH3 . . . . .142 D7
  Handforth SK9 . . . . .34 D3
Bridge End Dr SK10 . . . . . .87 A7
Bridge End La SK10 . . . . . .87 A7
Bridge Farm Ct CW10 . . .152 A4
Bridge Foyer The CH1 . . .118 B2
Bridge Gn SK10 . . . . .87 A7
Bridge La
  Cuddington CW8 . . . . . . .101 F3
  Frodsham WA6 . . . . .49 D1
  Goostrey CW4 . . . . .108 C2
  Warrington WA4 . . . . .26 E7
  Warrington WA4 . . . . .26 E8
  Warrington,Woolston WA1 .17 C7
Bridge Mdw CH66 . . . . . . .69 F2
Bridge Pl CH1 . . . . .237 B2
Bridge Rd WA1 . . . . .17 C7
Bridge Row CW12 . . . . . .156 F4
Bridge Side Dr WA4 . . . . . .73 B4
Bridge St Chester CH1 . . .237 B2
  Congleton CW12 . . . . .156 D3
  Golborne WA3 . . . . .3 A7
  Holt LL13 . . . . .180 E1
  Macclesfield SK11 . . . . . . .112 C7
  Newton-le-W WA12 . . . . . .2 B3
  Northwich CW9 . . . . .79 E2
  Runcorn WA7 . . . . .23 B2
  Saltney CH4 . . . . .140 D7
  Warrington WA1 . . . . .16 B4
  Warrington WA1 . . . . .16 B5
  Whaley Bridge SK23 . . . . .65 F7
  Wybunbury CW5 . . . . .220 B8
Bridge St Row E CH1 . . . .237 B2
Bridge St Row W CH1 . . .237 B2
Bridge Terr CH3 . . . . .119 B2
Bridge View Vil WA8 . . . . .23 A4
Bridge Wlk ❼ WA7 . . . . . .49 F7
Bridgedown CW5 . . . . . . .146 C1
Bridgefield Ave SK9 . . . . .34 D1
Bridgefield Cl WA4 . . . . . . .37 E7
Bridgegate CH4 . . . . .141 B3
Bridgeman Rd CH1 . . . . .117 C3
Bridgeman St WA5 . . . . . .15 D4

Bridgemere CE Prim Sch
CW5 ....231 E8
Bridgemere CI CW11 ...174 F8
Bridgemere Garden World*
CW5 ....232 B4
Bridgemere La CW5 ...219 E1
Bridgemere Mews CW5 .231 F8
Bridgemere Way 4
CW9 ....103 E4
Bridgend CH2 ....97 A1
Bridgend CI WA8 ....12 D3
Bridges Rd CH65 ....70 F5
Bridgewater Ave WA4 ..16 F4
Bridgewater CI
Congleton CW12 ....157 B1
Heald Green SK8 ....34 D7
Bridgewater Ct
3 Lymm WA13 ....18 C3
6 Runcorn WA7 ....23 B2
Bridgewater Dr CH3 ...119 C2
Bridgewater Grange
WA7 ....50 F5
**Bridgewater High Sch (Lower
Sch)** WA4 ....26 D6
**Bridgewater High Sch (Upper
Sch)** WA4 ....26 D6
Bridgewater Mews WA4 .26 C8
Bridgewater St
1 Lymm WA13 ....18 E3
6 Runcorn WA7 ....23 A3
Bridgeway E WA7 ....24 C2
Bridgeway W WA7 ......24 C2
Bridgewood Dr CH66 ....69 F2
Bridgnorth Gr ST5 .....210 E2
Bridle CI CH62 ....43 E7
Bridle CI Bramhall SK7 ..35 F2
Crewe CW2 ....190 B4
Bridle Hey CW5 ....204 F2
Bridle Pk CH62 ....43 E7
Bridle Rd Bebington CH62 .43 E6
Crewe CW2 ....190 B4
Woodford SK7 ....35 F2
Bridle Way
Ellesmere Port CH66 .....69 D3
Woodford SK7 ....36 A2
Bridlemere Ct WA1 ......16 E8
Briedden Way CH66 ......69 A6
Brierley Bsns Ctr CW1 .190 D4
Brierley Prim Sch CW1 .190 C4
Brierley Rd CW12 ......157 B1
Brierley St CW1 ....190 D4
Briers CI WA2 ....8 F3
Brieryhurst Rd ST7 ....195 B3
Briggs Ave CW2 ....190 D1
Bright St CW1 ....190 B5
Brighton Cres SK11 ....113 B3
Brighton St WA5 ....15 E6
Brights Ave 6 ST7 ....195 B2
Brightwell CI WA5 ......14 E5
Brimelow Cres WA5 ......14 E3
Brimstage CI CH60 ......41 C8
Brimstage Gn CH60 ......41 D8
Brimstage Rd CH60 .....41 C7
Brindley Ave
Warrington WA4 ....16 F4
Winsford CW7 ....126 C1
Brindley CI
Kidsgrove ST7 ....194 E1
Talke ST7 ....210 E8
Brindley Ct WA4 ....26 D8
Brindley Gr SK9 ....34 E2
Brindley Hall Rd CW5 ..186 E2
Brindley La CW11 ......153 C4
Brindley Lea La CW5 ..186 D1
Brindley PI CW5 ....174 F3
Brindley Rd WA7 ....23 F3
Brindley St WA7 ....22 F3
Brindley Way
Congleton CW12 ....157 B1
Macclesfield SK11 ....112 C3
Brindley Wharf WA4 .....50 F6
Brights Way ST7 ....209 F2
Brine Leas High Sch
CW5 ....204 F3
Brine Pits La CW5 .....218 F2
Brine Pump Cotts CW9 ..78 F4
Brine Rd CW5 ....204 E3
Brinell Dr M44 ....11 F6
Brinley CI CH62 ....43 D5
Brinton CI WA8 ....22 D8
Brisbane CI SK7 ....35 F5
Brisbane Rd CH1 ....117 C4
Bristol Ave WA7 ....50 E6
Bristol CI Blacon CH1 ..117 C4
Heald Green SK12 ....34 C7
Bristol Dr 3 CH66 ......69 E1
Britannia Dr CW9 ......104 E7
Britannia Gdns WA6 .....73 B1
Britannia Rd WA6 ....73 B2
Brixham Ave SK8 ....34 F7
Brixham Wlk SK7 ....35 E7
Broad CI SK9 ....85 B8
Broad La Altrincham WA15 .32 B8
Appleton Thorn WA4 ....27 C8
Burtonwood WA5 ....9 E1
Haydock WA5,WA9 ....1 C1
Heswall CH60 ....40 C8
Holmes Chapel CW4 .....129 F1
Stapeley CW5 ....205 A1
Broad Oak Ave
Broughton CH4 ....139 A3
Haydock WA11 ....1 A6
Warrington WA4 ....14 E4

Broad Oak Com Prim Sch
WA9 ....1 A3
Broad St CW1 ....190 C6
Broad Street Inf Sch
CW1 ....190 C6
Broad Wlk SK9 ....59 F8
Broadacre CW9 ....78 D6
Broadacre PI SK9 ....59 D3
Broadacres CW5 ....217 F4
Broadbent Ave WA4 ......16 F4
Broadcar Rd SK11 ......113 C6
Broadfields WA7 ....50 C8
Broadheath Terr WA8 ....12 D1
Broadheys La WA16 .....28 D6
Broadhurst Ave
Culcheth WA3 ....4 F2
Warrington WA5 ....15 D4
Broadhurst La CW12 ....156 C3
Broadlake CH64 ....67 F8
Broadland Gdns CH66 ....69 F2
Broadland Rd CH66 ......69 F2
Broadleigh Way CW2 ....206 C8
Broadley Ave WA3 ....3 C7
Broadmead Chester CH3 .119 C2
Heswall CH60 ....41 C7
Broadoak High Sch M31 .11 F2
Broadoak La
High Legh WA16 ....29 D5
Mobberley WA16 ....57 E6
Broadwalk SK10 ....87 A5
Broadway
Altrincham WA15 ....32 A8
Barnton CW8 ....78 B3
Widnes WA8 ....12 A1
Wilmslow SK9 ....60 B6
Broadway E CH2 ....118 E5
Broadway The CW5 .....204 F5
Broadway W CH2 ....118 D5
Broadways CW3 ....230 A4
Broadwood CI SK6 ....37 F7
Broady Ct 5 CW2 ....190 D2
Brock Dr SK8 ....35 B8
Brock Gdns L24 ....21 E2
Brock Hollow CW11 .....174 F4
Brock Rd WA3 ....9 D3
Brock St
Macclesfield SK10 ....112 D8
Macclesfield SK10 ....87 D1
Brockhurst Mews CW9 ..104 A8
Brockhurst St CW9 .....104 A8
Brockhurst Way CW9 ...104 A6
Brocklebank Dr CW8 ....103 E7
Brocklehurst Ave SK10 ..87 F2
Brocklehurst Ct 2 SK10 .87 D3
Brocklehurst St SK10 ...87 A7
Brocklehurst Manor
SK10 ....87 E1
Brocklehurst Mews 3
SK10 ....87 D3
Brocklehurst Way SK10 .87 D3
Brockton Ct WA4 ....26 C6
Brockway E CH3 ....166 A1
Brockway W CH3 ....166 A1
Brockwell CI 2 CW7 ....149 A8
Brodie CI CH2 ....95 C1
Brogden Ave WA3 ....4 E4
Broken Banks 10 SK11 .112 D7
Broken Cross SK11 .....111 E7
Broken Cross Com Sch
SK11 ....111 E7
Brokencross PI CW9 ....104 E7
Bromborough Rake Sta
CH62 ....43 C8
Bromborough Sta CH63 ..43 C7
Bromborough Village Rd
CH62 ....43 E8
Bromley Ave WA3 ....3 D7
Bromley CI Crewe CW1 ..189 F8
Heswall CH60 ....40 E7
Warrington WA3 ....8 F3
Bromley Dr CW4 ....130 C2
Bromley Rd
Congleton CW12 ....156 F3
Macclesfield SK10 ....111 E8
Brompton Gdns WA5 .....15 F7
Brompton Way
Ellesmere Port CH66 .....69 E1
Handforth SK9 ....34 C5
Bronington Ave CH62 ....43 D6
Bronte CI WA2 ....8 A6
Brook Acre Com Prim Sch
WA2 ....8 E1
Brook Ave
Shavington CW2 ....206 C5
Warrington, Stockton Heath
WA4 ....16 E1
Warrington, Westy WA4 ..16 F5
Brook Bank SK12 ....37 C2
Brook CI Crewe CW1 ....190 F4
Cronton WA8 ....12 C6
Brook Ct Chester CH1 ..118 B3
Sandbach CW11 ....175 B6
Brook Dr Kelsall CW6 ..122 D4
Warrington WA5 ....15 A5
Brook End WA9 ....1 A1
Brook Farm M31 ....11 E2
Brook Furlong WA6 ......48 F2
Brook Gdns ST8 ....179 D1
Brook Hey CH64 ....41 B2
Brook Ho WA9 ....16 F3
Brook House Ct WA13 ...18 D7
Brook La Alderley Edge SK9 .59 F3
Astbury CW12 ....177 E5
Broughton CH5 ....139 C7
Burland CW5 ....203 D8
Chester CH2 ....118 E4
Faddiley CW5 ....202 F8

Brook La continued
Knutsford WA16 ....57 B1
Neston CH64 ....41 C2
Northwich CW9 ....104 D7
Warrington WA3 ....18 B8
Brook PI Chester CH1 ...237 B3
Warrington WA4 ....16 E3
Brook Rd
Ellesmere Port CH66 .....69 D5
Lymm WA13 ....18 E4
Tarporley CW6 ....168 D8
Brook Side CW8 ....102 C8
Brook St Chester CH1 ..237 B3
Congleton CW12 ....156 F3
Crewe CW2 ....190 D3
Golborne,Bank Heath WA3 ..3 A8
Knutsford WA16 ....57 B1
Macclesfield SK11 ....112 E7
Neston CH64 ....66 E8
Northwich CW9 ....79 A1
Northwich, Lostock Gralam
CW9 ....79 E2
2 Runcorn WA7 ....23 A2
3 Widnes WA8 ....13 B1
Brook Street Bridge
CH1,CH2 ....237 C4
Brook Terr Runcorn WA7 .23 F1
Sandbach CW11 ....175 A3
Brook View
Alderley Edge SK9 ......60 A3
Allostock WA16 ....106 F3
Brook Villas ST7 ......193 E3
Brook Way Hartford CW8 .103 B4
Nantwich CW5 ....204 E3
Warrington WA5 ....15 A5
Brook Well CH64 ....66 F5
Brookash Rd M22 ....34 A8
Brookdale WA8 ....12 A3
Brookdale Ave WA16 ....57 C2
Brookdale Ct CH3 ......143 D5
Brookdale PI CH1 ......237 B3
Brookdale Way CH3 ....143 D5
Brooke Ave Chester CH2 .118 F8
Handforth SK9 ....34 D4
Brooke Dean Com Sch
SK9 ....34 D4
Brooke Dr SK9 ....34 D4
Brooke Ho SK10 ....86 F1
Brooke Way SK9 ....34 D4
Brookes Ave CH4 ....139 B3
Brookfield CI WA1 .....191 D5
Brookfield Ave
Poynton SK12 ....36 C3
Runcorn WA7 ....23 E2
Brookfield CI Lymm WA13 .18 D3
Tarporley CW6 ....168 D8
Brookfield Cotts 2
WA13 ....18 D3
Brookfield Cres CW4 ...107 F1
Brookfield Ct CW1 .....190 B5
Brookfield Dr
Alsager ST7 ....193 C5
Chester CH2 ....118 E4
Holmes Chapel CW4 .....130 B3
Brookfield La SK11 ....112 F7
Brookfield Pk WA4 ......17 A2
Brookfield Rd
Comberbach CW9 ....78 D3
Culcheth WA3 ....4 D3
Lymm WA13 ....18 D3
Brookfield St WA12 ......2 B3
Brookfields SK WA8 ....13 D2
Brookhouse CI SK10 .....86 F1
Brookhouse Dr CW2 ....206 C8
Brookhouse La
Church Minshull CW1,
CW10 ....172 D7
Congleton CW12 ....157 C2
Duddon CH3 ....144 D6
Lower Whitley WA4 ....52 B2
Brookhouse Rd
Alsager ST7 ....193 D3
5 Congleton CW12 .....156 F3
Brookhurst Ave CH63 ....43 C5
Brookhurst CI CH63 .....43 C5
Brookhurst Prim Sch
CH63 ....43 C6
Brookhurst Rd CH63 ....43 C5
Brookland Ave WA4 ....205 F8
Brookland Dr CW11 .....175 E6
Brookland La WA9 ....1 A1
Brookland St WA1 ....16 E7
Brooklands Ave SK11 ..112 B7
Brooklands Dr
Goostrey CW4 ....107 F1
Northwich CW9 ....104 A4
Brooklands Gdns CH64 ..41 C1
Brooklands Gr CW1 .....190 A6
Brooklands Pk 1 WA8 ..13 C2
Brooklands Rd
Congleton CW12 ....155 F2
Neston CH64 ....41 C1
Brooklands The CW2 ...206 E3
Brookledge La SK10 ....62 E3
Brooklet Rd CH60 ......41 C8
Brooklyn Dr
Ellesmere Port CH65 .....70 C5
Lymm WA13 ....18 E4
Brooklyn St CW2 ....190 C2
Brookmere CI CW11 ....174 E8
Brooks Dr WA15 ....32 C8
Brooks La Bosley SK11 .135 E2
Middlewich CW10 ....128 D1
Brooks Lane Ind Est
Middlewich CW10 ....128 D1
Middlewich CW10 ....151 D8

Brookside
Ashton Hayes CH3 ....121 E7
Chester CH3 ....142 A8
Cuddington CW8 ....101 F3
Kelsall CW6 ....122 C4
Kingsley WA6 ....75 C2
Warrington WA3 ....16 E3
Brookside Ave
Lymm WA13 ....18 C4
Poynton SK12 ....36 E3
Sutton Lane Ends SK11 ..112 F2
Warrington, Stockton Heath
WA4 ....15 A4
Brookside CI WA11 ....1 B7
Brookside Cotts CT1 ...176 A8
Brookside Ct SK10 ......87 A1
Brookside Gn CW2 .....206 C8
Brookside La SK6 ....37 E7
Brookside Mill 6 SK11 .112 E7
Brookside Miniature Rly*
SK12 ....36 F7
Brookside Prim Sch
Ellesmere Port CH66 .....69 E4
High Lane SK6 ....37 E6
Brookside Rd
4 Congleton CW12 .....156 D3
Frodsham WA6 ....74 A8
Brookside Terr
Chester CH2 ....237 C4
Wilmslow SK9 ....59 E3
Brookside View WA11 ....1 B7
Brookvale Ave N WA7 ...50 B6
Brookvale Ave S WA7 ...50 B6
Brookview CI CW2 ......206 C8
Brookway La WA9 ....1 A1
Brookwood CI WA4 ......26 B8
Broom Ave WA4 ....26 E6
Broom Cres CH3 ....121 B1
Broom La WA16 ....81 F2
Broom Rd M31 ....11 E2
Broom St CW1 ....190 A6
Broom's La CW6 ....122 D6
Broome Ct WA7 ....50 B5
Broomehouse Ave M44 ...11 E8
Broomfield CI
Chelford SK11 ....84 A3
Wilmslow SK9 ....60 E8
10 Winsford CW7 ......149 A8
Broomfield La WA4 ......26 E7
Broomfields Jun Sch
WA4 ....26 E7
Broomfields Rd WA4 ....26 D7
Broomheath La
Tarvin CH3 ....121 C1
Tarvin CH3 ....144 C7
Broomhill La
Brown Knowl CH3 ....199 D8
Great Barrow CH3 ....120 E8
Broomlands CH60 ....40 E8
Broomlands Cotts CW5 ..219 E1
Broomsfield La CW8 .....78 A4
Broseley Ave WA3 ....4 D4
Broseley La WA3 ....4 D5
Brotherton CI CH62 .....43 C8
Brotherton Way WA12 ....2 B3
Brough St W SK11 ......112 C7
Broughton Ave WA3 ......3 D7
Broughton CI WA4 ....26 F8
Broughton Cres SY14 ..211 A1
Broughton Hall Rd CH4 .139 C4
Broughton Inf Sch CH4 .139 C4
Broughton Jun Sch
CH4 ....139 C4
Broughton La CW2 .....189 F1
Broughton Mills Rd
CH4 ....139 F6
Broughton Rd
Adlington SK10 ....62 C5
Crewe CW1 ....190 C8
Broughton Sh Pk CH4 ..139 E4
Broughton Way WA8 .....22 D5
Brow Com Prim Sch The
WA7 ....23 E1
Brow La Antrobus CW9 ...53 D5
Heswall CH60 ....40 F7
Brow The WA6 ....75 C2
Browmere Dr WA3 ....9 A7
Brown Ave
Lawton-gate ST7 ....194 A5
Nantwich CW5 ....204 F4
Brown Heath Rd CH3 ...143 B6
Brown Lees CI CW2 ....190 B1
Brown Lees Rd ST7 ....195 F4
Brown St
8 Alderley Edge SK9 ...60 A1
Congleton CW12 ....156 E3
Macclesfield SK11 ....112 C7
Widnes WA8 ....12 D2
Brown's La Chester CH4 .141 C7
Wilmslow SK9 ....60 D3
Brownhill Dr WA1 ....16 F8
Brownhills Rd CW6 .....147 C6
Browning Ave WA8 ......22 F8
Browning CI 2 Blacon CH1 .117 F6
Sandbach CW11 ....174 D5
Browning Dr
Ellesmere Port CH65 .....69 F4
Winwick Way3 ....8 A6
Browning Gn CH65 ....69 F4
Browning Gr ST7 ....210 C8
Browning St CW1 ......190 C4
Browning Way CW7 .....149 A7
Brownlow CI SK12 ....36 E2

Brownlow Hall Mews
CW12 ....177 E5
Brownlow Heath CW12 ..177 E5
Brownlow Heath La
CW12 ....177 D6
Broxton Ave CW9 ....151 D6
Broxton CI WA8 ....12 C3
Broxton Rd Clutton CH3 .182 D3
Ellesmere Port CH66 .....69 E5
Bruce Ave WA2 ....8 D1
Bruce Cres CH63 ....43 C6
Bruce Dr CH66 ....69 C4
Bruche Ave WA1 ....16 F8
Bruche Com Prim Sch
WA1 ....17 A7
Bruche Dr WA1 ....16 F8
Bruche Heath Gdns WA1 .17 A8
Bruen The CH3 ....121 C3
Bruera Rd CH65 ....69 F4
Brunel Ct CW9 ....104 E5
Brunel Rd SK11 ....112 C3
Brunner Gr CW5 ....205 A5
Brunner Rd WA8 ....23 A8
Brunsborough CI CH62 ..43 C6
Brunswick CH1 ....23 A3
Brunswick Cres CH66 ...69 E3
Brunswick Hill SK11 ...112 D7
Brunswick Hill SK10 ...112 D8
Brunswick Rd WA12 ......1 F4
Brunswick St
Congleton CW12 ....156 F3
5 Macclesfield SK10 ..112 D8
St Helens WA9 ....1 A3
Brunswick Terr SK10 ...112 D8
Bruntleigh Ave WA4 ....17 A3
Bryant Ave WA4 ....16 F5
Brymau Four Est CH4 ..140 D7
Brymau One Est CH4 ...140 D7
Brymau Three Est CH4 .140 D7
Brymau Two Est CH4 ...140 E7
Brynlow Dr CW10 ....151 B8
Brynmore Dr SK11 ......112 F7
Brynn St WA8 ....23 B8
Brynton CI SK10 ....87 C1
Brynton Rd SK10 ....87 C1
Buchan CI WA5 ....15 B8
Buchan Gr CW2 ....190 B3
Buck La CW2 ....206 E3
Buckbean Way CW4 .....107 E1
Buckden Way 9 SK10 ...112 C8
Buckfast Ave WA11 ......2 A7
Buckfast CI
Cheadle Hulme SK8 ....35 B6
Macclesfield SK10 ....87 C2
Poynton SK12 ....36 D5
Warrington WA5 ....14 E3
Buckfast Ct WA7 ....24 E3
Buckfast Way CW10 ....128 B1
Buckingham Ave
Chester CH3 ....119 B2
Widnes WA8 ....13 A4
Buckingham CI
4 Congleton CW12 .....156 F4
Wistaston CW2 ....205 E8
Buckingham Dr
Knutsford WA16 ....57 B1
Northwich CW9 ....103 E4
Warrington WA5 ....15 C4
Winsford CW7 ....149 C7
Buckingham Gdns 1
CH65 ....70 D2
Buckingham Rd
Irlam M44 ....11 C6
Poynton SK12 ....36 D3
Wilmslow SK9 ....59 F6
Buckland CI WA8 ....22 D7
Buckley Ave CW10 ......128 F7
Buckley CI CW10 ....151 B8
Buckley St
Macclesfield SK11 ....112 D7
Warrington WA2 ....16 B6
Bucklow Ave
Mobberley WA16 ....58 A4
Partington M31 ....11 F3
Bucklow Gdns WA13 ....19 D4
Bucklow View 11 SK11 .112 E7
Bucklowhill La WA16 ...30 B3
Buckton St WA1 ....16 D7
Bude CI Alsager ST7 ...193 B3
Bramhall SK7 ....35 F7
Crewe CW1 ....190 B8
Bude Rd WA8 ....12 E2
Budworth Ave
Warrington WA4 ....16 F4
Widnes WA8 ....12 D2
Budworth CI
Runcorn WA7 ....49 D7
Sandbach CW11 ....174 F7
Budworth Heath La CW9 .54 C1
Budworth La CW9 ....78 E7
Budworth Rd
Bate Heath CW9 ....54 E2
Ellesmere Port CH66 .....69 E2
Over Tabley WA16 ....55 C2
Budworth Wlk 1 SK9 ....34 E1
Buerton App CH3 ....164 B6
Buerton Prim Sch CW3 .230 F3
Buffs La CH60 ....41 B8
Buggen La CH64 ....66 D8
Buglawton Hall Sch
CW12 ....157 D5
Buglawton Ind Est 5
CW12 ....156 F4
Buglawton Prim Sch
CW12 ....157 A4
Buildwas Rd CH64 ....41 F2
Bulkeley Hall La SY14 .200 C8

Bulkeley Rd
Handforth SK9 .....34 D3
Poynton SK12 .....36 E3
Bulkeley St Chester CH3 ..119 A1
Crewe CW1 .....190 E3
Bull Hill CH4 .....66 F6
Bull Hill La SK10 .....88 D2
Bull Ring CW9 .....103 F8
Bull Ring The CW10 .....128 C1
Bullcroft Cl SY14 .....211 D7
Bullocks House Rd ST7 .195 E3
Bullocks La SK11 .....112 E3
Bumper's La CH1 .....117 F1
Bunbury Aldersey CE Prim Sch CW6 .....185 E8
Bunbury Cl
Middlewich CW10 .....151 D5
Northwich CW9 .....104 A5
Stoak CH2 .....96 A7
Bunbury Comm CW6 ..168 E2
Bunbury Dr WA7 .....49 C6
Bunbury Gn CH65 .....70 D2
Bunbury La CW6 .....185 E8
Bunbury Mill* CW6 ..169 A1
Bunbury Rd CH65 .....169 B3
Bunce La SK11 .....133 B4
Bunce St CH1 .....237 A1
Bungalow Rd WA12 .....2 E1
Bungalows The
Dunham-on-t-H WA6 .....97 E6
Thornton Hough CH63 .42 B6
Bunting Cl [6] WA3 .....3 E8
Buntingford Rd WA4 .....17 C3
Bunts La CW12 .....156 E1
Burdett Rd CH66 .....69 E2
Burfield Dr WA4 .....26 D7
Burford Ave Bramhall SK7 .35 D5
Newcastle-u-Lyme ST5 .210 D1
Burford Cl SK9 .....59 E5
Burford Cres SK9 .....59 E5
Burford La WA13 .....19 C2
Burgamot La CW9 .....78 D8
Burganey Ct CH4 .....162 D2
Burges St CH2 .....118 F3
Burgess Ave WA4 .....16 D8
Burgess Cl CW5 .....205 B4
Burgess Dr CH1 .....117 A5
Burgess La WA6 .....101 B6
Burgess Pl [5] CW8 .....103 E8
Burgess St SK10 .....112 F8
Burjen Way CW1 .....190 B6
Burkhardt Dr WA12 .....2 E3
Burland Cl WA7 .....22 F1
Burland Gr CW7 .....126 A2
Burland Rd Halewood L26 .21 A6
Newcastle-u-Lyme ST5 .210 D2
Burlea Cl CW2 .....189 E5
Burlea Dr CW2 .....206 B5
Burley La WA4 .....27 C4
Burleyhurst La SK9,WA16 .59 B7
Burnell Cl CW5 .....204 F3
Burnell Rd CH65 .....70 C4
Burnet Cl WA2 .....9 C2
Burnfell WA3 .....3 E7
Burnham Cl Culcheth WA3 .4 F4
Warrington WA5 .....14 F5
Widnes WA8 .....12 C3
Burnham Rd CH4 .....140 F6
Burns Cl
Ellesmere Port CH66 .....69 E4
Rode Heath ST7 .....193 E8
Burns Cres WA8 .....22 F8
Burns Dr CW1 .....190 F4
Burns Gr WA2 .....8 C2
Burns Rd CW12 .....157 A2
Burns Way CH1 .....117 E6
Burnsall Ave WA3 .....3 F8
Burnsall Dr WA8 .....12 C3
Burnside WA15 .....32 D7
Burnside Ave WA4 .....16 D1
Burnside Cl SK9 .....60 C6
Burnside Way
Northwich CW8 .....103 D8
Winnington CW8 .....78 D1
Burnt Acre SK11 .....84 B3
Burnt Mill La WA8 .....21 D5
Burnwood Gr ST7 .....195 B2
Burran Rd M22 .....33 D8
Burrough Cl WA3 .....9 F3
Burrows Hill CW8 .....103 B7
Burrows La WA6 .....73 F2
Burrows St WA11 .....1 A6
Burrows The CW8 .....101 D5
Bursar Cl WA12 .....2 C1
Burslam St CW12 .....156 E2
Burton Ave CW6 .....146 C3
Burton Cl Culcheth WA3 .4 F3
Widnes WA8 .....12 F3
Burton Dr SK12 .....36 D4
Burton Gn CH66 .....69 D4
Burton Gr CW1 .....173 B1
Burton Hall Rd LL12 .....161 E1
Burton La CW6 .....144 F6
Burton Manor Coll CH64 .67 F8
Burton Rd Blacon CH1 .....117 E5
Neston CH64 .....66 F6
Warrington WA2 .....8 D1
Burton Sq CW6 .....146 C2
Burtonwood Com Prim Sch WA5 .....6 F7
Burtonwood Ind Ctr WA5 .6 E7
Burtonwood Rd WA5 .....6 F7
Burwardsley Rd CH3 .....166 D1
Burwardsley Way CW9 ..103 E4
Bush Rd Christleton CH3 .142 E7
Widnes WA8 .....22 F5
Bush Way CH60 .....40 D8
Bushell Cl CH64 .....66 F7

Bushell Rd CH64 .....66 F7
Bushells La WA6 .....99 B8
Butler Way CW5 .....204 E3
Butley Cl
Macclesfield SK10 .....87 D3
Middlewich CW10 .....151 C7
Butley Hall SK10 .....87 A7
Butley Lanes SK10 .....61 F1
Butterbache Rd CH3 .....142 A6
Butterbur Cl CH3 .....142 A6
Buttercup Way WA16 .....79 F6
Buttermarket St WA1 ..16 B5
Buttermere Ave
Ellesmere Port CH65 .....70 C3
Warrington WA2 .....8 C3
Buttermere Cl WA6 .....74 D8
Buttermere Cres WA2 .....8 C3
Buttermere Ct CW12 ..156 A2
Buttermere Dr WA7 .....49 D5
Buttermere Rd
Partington M31 .....11 E3
Winsford CW7 .....126 C2
Butterton La Crewe CW1 .192 C1
Oakhanger CW1 .....192 B2
Button Field CW8 .....126 A7
Butts Gn WA5 .....7 A3
Butts The Alsager ST7 ..193 D4
Runcorn WA7 .....23 F2
Buxton Ave CW1 .....190 E4
Buxton Cl WA5 .....15 A8
Buxton New Rd
Macclesfield SK11 .....88 E1
Macclesfield Forest SK11 .114 D7
Buxton Old Rd
Congleton CW12 .....157 A4
Disley SK12 .....38 E4
Macclesfield SK11 .....113 D7
Buxton Rd
Congleton CW12 .....157 C6
Disley SK12 .....38 E6
High Lane SK6,SK7,SK12 ..37 D8
Macclesfield SK10,SK11 ..113 A7
New Mills SK22,SK23 .....39 C4
Whaley Bridge SK23 .....65 E8
Whaley Bridge, New Horwich SK23 .....65 E5
Buxton Rd W SK12 .....38 B5
By-Pass Rd CH3 .....121 B3
Bye Pass The CH3 .....119 E2
Byland Ave SK8 .....35 B6
Byland Cl WA8 .....13 C5
Bylands Cl SK12 .....36 D4
Byley La
Cranage CW4,CW10 ....129 C6
Middlewich CW10 .....128 E3
Byley Prim Sch CW10 ..128 F7
Byley Way CW7 .....126 B1
Byng Ave M44 .....11 D4
Byron Cl Blacon CH1 .....117 F6
Crewe CW1 .....190 F4
Middlewich CW10 .....151 D5
Rode Heath ST7 .....193 E7
Sandbach CW11 .....174 D6
Byron Ct WA2 .....8 C2
Byron St WA7 .....23 A1
Byron Way CW2 .....190 A1
Byron Wlk CW5 .....204 D6
Byron's La SK11 .....112 E5
Byrons St SK11 .....112 D6
Bythom Cl CH3 .....142 E7

C

Cabot Cl WA5 .....7 C1
Cabul Cl WA2 .....16 D7
Cadishead Prim Sch M44 .11 E6
Cadishead Way M44 .....11 F6
Cadnant Cl CH1 .....117 E5
Cadnant Ct/Llys Cadnant CH4 .....139 D5
Cadshaw Cl WA3 .....9 D5
Caer Castell LL13 .....196 D8
Caerleon Cl CW7 .....149 A8
Caerllew LL13 .....180 E1
Caernarvon Ave CW7 ..149 B7
Caernarvon Cl
Caernarvon Ct [4] CH65 ..70 D2
Caernarvon Rd CW2 .....205 E8
Caesars Cl WA7 .....23 E2
Cairns Cres CH1 .....117 D4
Cairo St WA1 .....16 B5
Caister Way CW7 .....149 C7
Caithness Ct [3] WA7 .....23 B7
Calamine St SK11 .....112 E6
Calday Gr WA11 .....1 A8
Caldbeck Ave WA2 .....8 D2
Caldene Terr SK23 .....65 E7
Calder Ave CW1 .....191 A5
Calder Cl Bollington SK10 .87 F8
Poynton SK12 .....36 D2
Widnes WA8 .....13 F5
Calder Way [2] CH66 .....69 C5
Calderfield Cl WA4 .....26 D5
Caldicott Ave CH62 .....43 D7
Caldicott Cl [2] CW7 .....149 C7
Caldwell Ave WA5 .....7 F2
Caldwell Cl CW5 .....205 B4
Caldwell Rd WA8 .....23 A7
Caldwell's Gate La CW9 .54 B8
Caldy Cl CH2 .....118 D5
Caldy Dr CH66 .....69 D4
Caldy Rd Alsager ST7 ..193 C4
Handforth SK9 .....34 D3

Caldy Valley Rd
Chester CH3 .....142 B7
Huntington CH3 .....142 A6
Caldy Way CW7 .....126 C1
Cale Rd SK22 .....39 D8
Calico La SK23 .....39 D4
California Cl WA8 .....15 C8
Callands Prim Sch WA5 ..7 E2
Callands Rd WA5 .....7 D2
Calmington La WA7 .....24 F4
Calrofold Dr ST5 .....210 D1
Calrofold La SK10 .....88 C2
Calstock Cl WA5 .....14 E3
Calveley Ave CH62 .....43 F4
Calveley Cl CW9 .....103 E5
Calveley Green La CW6, CW7 .....170 A2
Calveley Hall La CW5, CW6 .....170 A2
Calveley Prim Sch CW6 .170 B2
Calveley Rd Halewood L26 .21 A6
Macclesfield SK10 .....88 C2
Calveley Way CW7 .....126 B1
Calver Rd WA2 .....8 C2
Calverley Cl [3] SK9 .....60 C8
Calverly Cl WA7 .....50 C5
Calvers WA7 .....23 E1
Camberley Cl WA7 .....50 C5
Camberwell Park Rd WA4 .....13 D4
Camborne Ave SK10 ..111 E8
Camborne Cl
Congleton CW12 .....178 E8
Runcorn WA7 .....50 C6
Cambourne Rd WA5 .....6 F6
Cambrai Ave WA4 .....16 C2
Cambrian Ave CH3 .....119 B2
Cambrian Cl CH66 .....69 A6
Cambrian Ct CH1 .....118 B2
Cambrian Rd CH1 .....118 B2
Cambrian Villas CH3 ..165 C2
Cambrian Way CW7 .....149 B8
Cambridge Ave
Macclesfield SK11 .....112 B7
Wilmslow SK9 .....59 F7
Winsford CW7 .....126 A1
Cambridge Cl
Biddulph ST8 .....179 C1
Warrington WA4 .....26 B7
Cambridge Gdns
Helsby WA6 .....73 D4
Warrington WA4 .....26 C6
Cambridge Rd
Bebington CH62 .....43 E8
Chester CH2 .....118 F5
Ellesmere Port CH65 ..70 D2
Macclesfield SK11 .....112 B7
Cambridge Road Com Prim Sch CH65 .....70 C5
Cambridge St
Runcorn WA7 .....23 C2
Widnes WA8 .....23 B7
Camden Cl WA1 .....24 D1
Camden Rd CH65 .....70 A5
Camden St CW1 .....190 D4
Camellia Gdns WA9 .....6 B7
Camelot Cl WA1 .....24 D1
Camelot Gr CW2 .....206 C4
Camelot Way WA7 .....50 D8
Cameron Ave
Runcorn WA7 .....48 E8
Shavington CW2 .....206 B3
Cameron Rd WA8 .....23 A8
Camm St CW2 .....190 D2
Camomile Wlk [5] M31 ..11 F3
Campbell Ave WA7 .....49 A8
Campbell Cl
Congleton CW12 .....157 A4
Haslington CW1 .....191 C4
Macclesfield SK10 .....87 A1
Northwich CW9 .....103 F4
Campbell Cres WA5 .....14 F6
Campden Way SK9 .....34 D4
Campion Cl
Huntington CH3 .....142 A6
Warrington WA3 .....9 C4
Campsey Ash WA8 .....12 F4
Camrose Cl WA7 .....49 C6
Camsley La WA13 .....18 B3
Canaan WA3 .....4 C8
Canada Cl WA2 .....8 C2
Canadian Ave CH2 .....119 A3
Canal Bank WA13 .....18 D1
Canal Bridge Ent Pk CH65 .....70 D6
Canal Cotts CW12 .....187 D6
Canal Rd CW12 .....156 F1
Canal Reach WA7 .....24 C2
Canal Side Barnton CW8 .78 B2
Chester CH1 .....237 C3
Macclesfield SK11 .....112 F7
Moore WA4 .....25 C5
Runcorn WA7 .....48 D7
Whaley Bridge SK23 .....39 F1
Canal Side Cotts WA7 ..50 F6
Canal St
Chester CH1 .....237 A3
Congleton CW12 .....179 C8
Macclesfield SK11 .....112 E8
Newton-le-W WA12 .....1 F7
Runcorn WA7 .....23 B2
Whaley Bridge SK23 .....65 F8
Canal Terr CW10 .....151 D8
Canalside 70 D6
Canberra Rd WA2 .....8 D2
Canberra Sq WA2 .....8 D2

Canberra Way CH1 .....117 D4
Candelan Way WA16 .....29 C4
Candle La CW3 .....232 B2
Candleston Cl WA3 .....3 E7
Candy La SK10 .....62 C8
Canford Cl Crewe CW1 .190 B8
Warrington WA5 .....15 C6
Cann La N WA4 .....26 E5
Cann La N WA4 .....26 E5
Cann La N WA4 .....26 F4
Cannell Ct WA7 .....50 A6
Cannell St WA5 .....15 C6
Canning St CH1 .....237 A3
Canniswood Rd WA11 .....1 A6
Cannock Cl CH66 .....94 E8
Cannon St CH65 .....70 A5
Cannon Way CH4 .....161 A7
Cannonbury Cl WA7 .....50 A8
Canon Dr WA14 .....31 B8
Canon St WA7 .....22 F3
Canon Wilson Cl WA11 ..1 D6
Canons Rd WA5 .....15 D6
Canterbury Cl CH66 .....94 E8
Canterbury Grange SK9 .60 B7
Canterbury Rd
Blacon CH1 .....117 F5
Widnes WA8 .....22 C8
Canterbury St WA4 .....16 C4
Cantilever Gdns WA4 ..26 E5
Cantley Cl WA7 .....49 D6
Canton Pl CW8 .....103 D7
Canton St SK11 .....112 D6
Canton Wlks SK11 .....112 D6
Canute Pl [1] WA16 .....57 A2
Capeland Cl CH4 .....140 E5
Capenhurst Ave
Crewe CW2 .....190 A3
Warrington WA2 .....9 A2
Capenhurst CE Prim Sch CH1 .....94 B8
Capenhurst Cl SK11 .....112 D6
Capenhurst Gdns CH66 .69 D1
Capenhurst Grange Sch CH66 .....69 E2
Capenhurst La
Capenhurst CH1 .....94 B8
Ellesmere Port CH65 .....70 A3
Woodbank CH1 .....93 F7
Capenhurst Sta CH1 .....69 C1
Capesthorne Cl
Alsager ST7 .....193 C3
Hazel Grove SK7 .....36 F8
Holmes Chapel CW4 .....130 B3
Northwich CW9 .....103 F4
Sandbach CW11 .....175 C7
Widnes WA8 .....22 B8
Capesthorne Hall* SK11 .....110 A6
Capesthorne Rd
Crewe CW2 .....189 F3
Hazel Grove SK7 .....36 F8
High Lane SK6 .....37 E7
Warrington WA2 .....8 D2
Waverton CH3 .....143 B6
Wilmslow SK9 .....59 E5
Capesthorne Way [8] SK11 .....112 F7
Capital Wlk CW12 .....156 D2
Capper's Cl ST7 .....195 A2
Capper's La CW5,Crewe .186 C3
Cappers La CW11 .....176 C2
Car St CH1 .....237 C3
Carden Ave CW7 .....126 B1
Carden Cl WA3 .....9 D4
Cardenbrook Gr [4] SK9 .34 D2
Cardeston Cl WA7 .....49 D7
Cardiff Cl CH66 .....94 E8
Cardigan Cl
Macclesfield SK11 .....112 A8
Warrington WA5 .....7 E1
Cardinal Newman RC High Sch WA4 .....16 C4
Cardway Bsns Pk ST7 ..193 F3
Carey St WA8 .....13 B1
Cargo Ctr M90 .....32 E7
Carisbrook Ave SK10 .....87 E2
Carisbrook Dr CW7 .....149 C7
Carisbrooke Cl CW2 ..205 E8
Carleton Rd SK12 .....37 C4
Carlett Bvd CH62 .....43 F5
Carlingford Rd WA4 .....26 C8
Carlisle Cl
Macclesfield SK11 .....111 F5
Mobberley WA16 .....58 A4
Winsford CW7 .....126 A1
Carlisle Rd CH1 .....117 E5
Carlisle St
[1] Alderley Edge SK9 .....60 A1
Crewe CW1 .....190 B2
Warrington WA5 .....14 D6
Widnes WA8 .....23 A8
Carlton Ave
Mickle Trafford CH2 .....119 E8
Neston CH64 .....41 C2
Carlton Cres CH66 .....69 F8
Carlton Pl CH2 .....119 A4
Carlton Rd Lymm WA13 ..19 B5
Northwich CW9 .....104 B7
Carlton St
Warrington WA4 .....26 C8
Widnes WA8 .....23 A8
Carlton Way M44 .....11 C5
Carlyle Cl ST7 .....193 E8
Carlyle Cres CH66 .....69 E4

Bul – Cas 247

Carmarthen Cl
Warrington WA5 .....7 D1
[3] Winsford CW7 .....149 C7
Carmel Cl CH1 .....117 D3
Carmel Ct WA8 .....13 B4
Carmenna Dr SK7 .....35 F7
Carmichael Cl [5] M31 ..11 E3
Carnegie Cl SK10 .....87 A1
Carnoustie Cl
Wilmslow SK9 .....60 D8
Winsford CW7 .....126 B2
Carnoustie Dr SK10 .....87 D5
Carnoustie Gr WA11 .....1 A5
Carol Dr CH60 .....41 C8
Carol St WA4 .....16 D4
Caroline Ho CH1 .....117 E6
Caroline St Irlam M44 .....11 F8
Widnes WA8 .....23 B7
Carpenter Gr WA2 .....9 A1
Carpenters Ct SK9 .....60 A1
Carr Brook Cl SK23 .....65 E5
Carr Brow SK6 .....38 A7
Carr La Alderley Edge SK9 .59 D2
Audley ST7 .....209 A1
Golborne WA3 .....4 A2
Golborne,Wash End WN7 ..4 E8
Hale L24,WA8 .....21 E4
Carr Mill Mews SK9 .....34 B1
Carr St [7] 195 F1
Carr Wood Ave SK7 .....35 E8
Carrgreen La WA13 .....19 F6
Carriage Cl L24 .....21 D1
Carriage Dr Biddulph ST8 .179 C1
Frodsham WA6 .....74 A6
Carrick Dr CH65 .....70 B2
Carrick Rd CH4 .....141 B7
Carrington Cl WA3 .....9 C4
Carrington Way CW1 ..190 B8
Carroll Dr CW2 .....205 F8
Carrs Ct SK9 .....60 B7
Carrs La CH3 .....166 F1
Carrwood
Altrincham WA15 .....32 B7
Knutsford WA16 .....57 C1
Carrwood Cl WA11 .....1 A6
Carrwood Rd SK9 .....59 F8
Carsdale Rd M22 .....33 E8
Carter Ave CW6 .....122 D4
Carter Bench Ho SK10 ..63 C1
Carter Cl CW5 .....204 D6
Carter Ct CW5 .....204 D6
Carter La SK11 .....84 B4
Carter St CH1 .....237 C3
Cartier Cl Warrington WA5 .15 C8
Warrington,Old Hall WA5 ..7 C1
Cartlake Cl CW5 .....204 C5
Cartledge Cl CW8 .....102 A3
Cartmel Ave WA2 .....8 C3
Cartmel Cl
Holmes Chapel CW4 .....130 A3
Macclesfield SK10 .....87 B2
Warrington WA5 .....7 E2
Winsford CW7 .....126 D2
Cartmel Dr CH66 .....69 F2
Cartmell Cl WA7 .....49 B6
Cartridge La WA4 .....27 E6
Cartwright Rd CW7 .....191 D5
Cartwright St
Warrington WA7 .....23 C2
Warrington WA5 .....15 C6
Carver Ave CW4 .....130 A6
Carver Cl CW7 .....127 A4
Case Rd WA11 .....1 D6
Cassia La CW2 .....206 F4
Cassia Green La CW7 ..125 D5
Cassia Rd L24 .....21 A3
Casson St CW1 .....190 B5
Castle Bank CW8 .....103 E7
Castle Cl Broughton CH5 .139 B6
Widnes WA8 .....13 F2
Pulford CH4 .....162 D2
Castle Ct Holt LL13 .....196 E8
Northwich CW8 .....103 E7
Castle Dr Chester CH1 ..237 B1
Ellesmere Port CH65 .....70 A3
Heswall CH60 .....40 F8
Castle Farm SY14 .....200 E3
Castle Gdns LL13 .....196 E8
Castle Gn WA5 .....7 B2
Castle Hall
Newton-le-W WA12 .....2 E4
Prestbury SK10 .....86 E6
Castle Hill Ct SK10 .....86 F7
Castle Hill Farm [3] CW8 .....103 E8
Castle Ho ST7 .....195 C3
Castle Inn Rd CW12 .....179 C7
Castle Mews LL13 .....196 E8
Castle Mill La WA5 .....32 B5
Castle Park Arts Ctr WA6 .....74 A8
Castle Prim Sch ST7 ..195 D6
Castle Rd Kidsgrove ST7 .195 D7
Runcorn WA7 .....23 D2
Castle Rise Prestbury SK10 .86 F6
Runcorn WA7 .....23 D2
Castle St Chester CH1 ..237 B1
Crewe CW1 .....190 C4
Holt LL13 .....196 D8
Macclesfield SK11 .....112 D8
Northwich CW8 .....103 F8
Widnes WA8 .....13 C1
Castle View Prim Sch WA7 .....49 D8

Castle Way CH4 . . . . .162 A6
Castlecroft Rd CH4 . . . . . .141 B5
Castlefields CH3 . . . . .166 C3
Castlefields Ave E WA7 . .24 A2
Castlefields Ave N WA7 . .23 F2
Castlefields Ave S WA7 . .24 A1
Castleford Dr SK10 . . . . . . .86 E6
Castlegate SK10 . . . . .86 E6
Castlegate Mews SK10 . . .86 F6
Castlehill CH4 . . . . .162 C2
Castlemead Wlk CW9 . . . .103 E4
Castlemere Cl CH4 . . . . . . .139 A3
Castlemere Dr CW1 . . . . . .190 C7
Castleton Dr SK6 . . . . .37 F6
Castletown Cl SK10 . . . . . . .87 C4
Castletown La CH3 . . . . . .197 D2
Castleview Rd ST7 . . . . . . .195 B3
Casteway WA15 . . . . .32 C7
Castnar Ave WA7 . . . . .48 E7
Catalan Cl CW7 . . . . .127 A1
Catalyst Mus* WA8 . . . . . . .23 A5
Catalyst Tade Pk WA8 . . . .23 A6
Catchpenny La SK11 . . . .108 F3
Catford Cl WA8 . . . . .12 C2
Catfoss Cl WA7 . . . . .24 F2
Cathcart Gn CH3 . . . . .119 F5
Cathedral Church of Christ &
  the Blessed Virgin Mary*
  CH1 . . . . .237 B2
Catherine Ct/Llys Catrin
  CH5 . . . . .139 B6
Catherine St
  Chester CH3 . . . . .118 B2
  Crewe CW2 . . . . .190 D2
  Macclesfield SK11 . . . . . . .112 C8
  Warrington WA5 . . . . .15 F7
  Warrington WA5 . . . . .16 A7
  Widnes WA8 . . . . .23 A7
Catherine Way WA12 . . . . .2 A4
Catholic High Sch The
  CH4 . . . . .141 D6
Catterall Ave WA2 . . . . .8 D2
Caughall Rd CH2 . . . . .95 E2
Caunce Ave Golborne WA3 . .3 A7
  Haydock WA11 . . . . .1 B6
  Newton-le-W WA12 . . . . .2 C1
Causeway Ave WA4 . . . . . .16 C3
Causeway Pk WA4 . . . . . . .16 C3
Cavalier Dr CH1 . . . . .117 E6
Cavan Dr WA11 . . . . .1 D7
Cavell Dr CH65 . . . . .70 A4
Cavendish Ave WA3 . . . . . . .9 F5
Cavendish Cl
  5 Macclesfield SK10 . . . .87 D3
  Warrington WA5 . . . . .15 D7
  Winsford CW7 . . . . .149 A8
Cavendish Cres ST7 . . . . .193 D5
Cavendish Ct WA8 . . . . .12 F1
Cavendish Farm Rd WA7 . .48 C7
Cavendish Gdns CH65 . . . .70 A4
Cavendish Mews SK9 . . . .60 A6
Cavendish Pl WA3 . . . . .9 F5
Cavendish Rd
  Chester CH4 . . . . .141 B6
  Crewe CW2 . . . . .189 C5
  Hazel Grove SK7 . . . . .36 E8
  Cavendish Sch WA7 . . . . . . .49 C5
Cavendish St 7 WA7 . . . . . .22 F2
Cavendish Way WA4 . . . . .130 A3
Caversham Cl WA4 . . . . . . .26 E6
Cawdor Dr CH3 . . . . .119 A2
Cawdor St Runcorn WA7 . . .22 F3
  Warrington WA4 . . . . .26 C8
Cawfield Ave WA8 . . . . .12 D1
Cawley Ave WA3 . . . . .4 A8
Cawley La SK10 . . . . .62 E7
Cawley St
  8 Macclesfield SK11 . . . .112 C7
  Runcorn WA7 . . . . .23 A1
Cawood Cl CH66 . . . . .69 B5
Cawthorne Ave WA4 . . . . . .17 A2
Caxton Cl
  Ellesmere Port CH66 . . . . . .69 E4
  Widnes WA8 . . . . .12 C3
Cecil Rd ST8 . . . . .179 C2
Cecil Rigby Cl 1 CW11 . .175 B6
Cecil St CH3 . . . . .119 A1
Cedab Rd CH65 . . . . .70 C6
Cedar Ave Alsager ST7 . . . .193 D3
  Connah's Quay CH5 . . . . . . .91 C1
  Connah's Quay,Garden City
  CH5 . . . . .116 A7
  Ellesmere Port CH66 . . . . . .69 D6
  Golborne WA3 . . . . .3 F7
  Kidsgrove ST7 . . . . .194 D1
  Runcorn WA7 . . . . .49 C7
  Sutton WA7 . . . . .50 B4
  Widnes WA8 . . . . .13 B2
Cedar Cl
  Connah's Quay CH5 . . . . . .116 A7
  Holmes Chapel CW4 . . . . . .130 D4
  Lostock Gralam CW9 . . . . . .80 A3
  Middlewich CW10 . . . . .151 E6
  Poynton SK12 . . . . .36 E3
  Sandbach CW11 . . . . .175 A6
Cedar Ct Audley ST7 . . . . . .209 F1
  Newton-le-W WA12 . . . . .2 D2
Cedar Ct Alsager ST7 . . . . .193 E4
  Congleton CW12 . . . . .178 F8
  Culcheth WA3 . . . . .4 F1
  Willaston CW5 . . . . .205 D6
Cedar Dr Barnton CW8 . . . .78 A4
  Chester CH2 . . . . .119 B4
Cedar Gr Chester CH2 . . . .119 B4
  Haydock WA11 . . . . .1 E7

Cedar Gr continued
  Macclesfield SK11 . . . . .112 D5
  Nantwich CW5 . . . . .205 A5
  Neston CH64 . . . . .66 F8
  Warrington WA1 . . . . .17 A7
  Warrington,Latchford WA4 . .16 D3
  Winsford CW7 . . . . .127 A1
Cedar Ho CH3 . . . . .142 B8
Cedar Lo SK7 . . . . .35 F7
Cedar Mews CH1 . . . . .117 E4
Cedar Pk CH3 . . . . .119 C2
Cedar Rd
  Newcastle-u-Lyme ST5 . . . .210 D1
  Partington M31 . . . . .11 E3
  Warrington WA5 . . . . .14 F6
  Weaverham CW8 . . . . .102 C8
Cedar St WA12 . . . . .2 C2
Cedar Way CW2 . . . . .206 B7
Cedardale Dr CH66 . . . . . . .94 F8
Cedardale Pk WA8 . . . . .13 E4
Cedarfield Rd WA13 . . . . . .19 B4
Cedars SK9 . . . . .59 F6
Cedars The Alsager ST7 . .193 D3
  Mobberley WA16 . . . . .58 E2
  8 Northwich CW9 . . . . . .103 E6
Cedarway Bollington SK10 . .88 A7
  Heswall CH60 . . . . .41 B5
  Wilmslow SK9 . . . . .59 F5
Cedarways WA4 . . . . .26 D5
Cedarwood
  Cuddington CW8 . . . . .101 D5
  Poynton SK12 . . . . .36 E3
Cedarwood Ct CW6 . . . . . .146 C3
Celandine Cl CH3 . . . . .142 A7
Celandine Way WA9 . . . . . . .6 B7
Celyn Cres CH4 . . . . .140 D5
Cement Pl CH1 . . . . .237 B3
Cemetery Rd CW2 . . . . . . .207 B5
Cemlyn Cl CH1 . . . . .117 E3
Centenary Ho WA7 . . . . . . .49 C8
Centenary Pl CW12 . . . . . .156 E3
Central Ave Alsager CW2 .192 F1
  Ellesmere Port CH65 . . . . . .70 C4
  Warrington WA2 . . . . .16 C8
  Warrington,Latchford WA4 . .16 B3
Central Dr Barnton CW8 . . .78 A3
  Haydock WA11 . . . . .1 B6
  Heald Green SK8 . . . . .34 D8
Central Expressway WA7 . .49 D6
Central Gr CW10 . . . . .104 D6
Central Rd
  Northwich CW9 . . . . .104 D7
  Partington M31 . . . . .11 F3
Central St ST7 . . . . .195 B6
Central Trad Est CH4 . . . .140 E7
Central Way WA12 . . . . .2 E2
Centre Ct ST7 . . . . .193 E4
Centre Park Sq WA1 . . . . . .16 A4
Centre Pk WA1 . . . . .16 A4
Centurion Cl WA3 . . . . .9 D4
Centurion Row WA7 . . . . . . .22 F2
Centurion Way CW10 . . . .128 D2
Century Rd ST5 . . . . .210 F2
Century Way SK10 . . . . .87 F2
Cestria Cl CW11 . . . . .174 D7
Chads Gn CW5 . . . . .206 A1
Chadwick Ave Croft WA3 . . .9 B7
  Warrington WA4 . . . . .16 E1
Chadwick Cl SK9 . . . . .34 C1
Chadwick Ct CW10 . . . . . . .151 D7
Chadwick Fields Orch
  CW10 . . . . .151 D6
Chadwick Pl WA3 . . . . .9 E5
Chadwick Rd
  Middlewich CW10 . . . . .151 C6
  Warrington WA3 . . . . .23 E3
Chadwick Terr SK10 . . . . . .87 E1
Chadwicke Cl CW5 . . . . . . .204 F4
Chaffinch Cl
  Congleton CW12 . . . . .156 E1
  Warrington WA3 . . . . .9 F3
Chaffinch Way CW7 . . . . . .149 D6
Chaigeley Sch WA4 . . . . . . .17 E4
Chailey Rise CH3 . . . . .182 D1
Chain Maker's Row CH4 .140 E7
Chalfield Ave CH66 . . . . . . .69 C5
Chalfield Cl
  1 Ellesmere Port CH66 . . .69 C5
  Wistaston CW2 . . . . .206 B7
Chalfont Cl WA4 . . . . .26 E6
Chalfont Cres CW2 . . . . . . .207 B2
Chalfont Ct WA16 . . . . .57 C3
Chalgrave Cl WA8 . . . . .13 F3
Chalkwell Dr CH60 . . . . .41 C7
Challinor St CH3 . . . . .119 A1
Chamber Brook La WA6 . . .75 D2
Chamberlain Cl CW1 . . . . .191 C4
Chamberlain Dr SK9 . . . . . .34 D1
Chambers St CW2 . . . . . . .190 D2
Chance Hall La CW12,
  ST7 . . . . .177 C3
Chancel La SK9 . . . . .60 B8
Chancellor Rd WA7 . . . . . . .24 D5
Chancery La Alsager ST7 .193 B3
  Bollington SK10 . . . . .88 B7
Chandler Way WA3 . . . . .3 E8
Chandlers Ct WA2 . . . . .22 E1
Chandlers Ct WA7 . . . . .2 C6
Change La CH64 . . . . .68 B8
Channel The CH1 . . . . .95 B4
Chantler Ave WA4 . . . . .16 E4
Chantry Ave CW8 . . . . .103 B4
Chantry Cl SK12 . . . . .38 E5
Chantry Ct Chester CH1 . .117 C2
  Crewe CW1 . . . . .190 D4
  Macclesfield SK11 . . . . .112 D5
Chantry Fold SK12 . . . . .38 E6
Chantry Rd SK12 . . . . .38 E6

Chantry The CW6 . . . . .169 E2
Chantry Wlk CH60 . . . . .41 A6
Chapel Ave WA6 . . . . .75 C2
Chapel Bank ST7 . . . . .195 D6
Chapel Cl Audlem CW3 . . .229 F3
  Cholmondeston CW7 . . . . .170 F4
  Cumberbach CW9 . . . . .78 D7
  Ellesmere Port CH65 . . . . . .70 B4
  Mount Pleasant ST7 . . . . . .195 B6
  Saughall CH1 . . . . .94 A1
  Waverton CH3 . . . . .143 A5
Chapel Cotts CH3 . . . . .143 A5
Chapel Croft SK11 . . . . .84 B3
Chapel Cross Rd WA2 . . . . .9 A2
Chapel Ct Northwich CW9 .103 F7
  Wilmslow SK9 . . . . .60 A6
Chapel Dr WA15 . . . . .32 C7
Chapel Gn CW6 . . . . .122 C5
Chapel House La CH64 . . .93 A7
Chapel La
  Acton Bridge CW8 . . . . .76 E4
  Aldford CH3 . . . . .164 D5
  Allostock WA16 . . . . .106 E3
  Altrincham WA15 . . . . .32 C7
  Appleton Thorn WA4 . . . . . .27 B4
  Burtonwood WA5 . . . . .6 F6
  Chester CH3 . . . . .119 A1
  Crewe CW1 . . . . .173 D1
  Dutton WA4 . . . . .77 B7
  Hargrave CH3 . . . . .144 A1
  Hollinfare WA3 . . . . .11 A2
  Hollins Green WA3 . . . . .10 F1
  Holt LL13 . . . . .196 D8
  Kelsall CW6 . . . . .122 E2
  Kidsgrove ST7 . . . . .195 E4
  Kingsley WA6 . . . . .75 C2
  Lulebash CH66 . . . . .68 F1
  Manley WA6,CH3 . . . . .98 F3
  Mere WA16 . . . . .30 B4
  Milton Green CH3 . . . . .165 B2
  Moulton CW9 . . . . .126 E8
  Norton in Hales TF9 . . . . . .236 C2
  Partington M31 . . . . .11 F2
  Rainow SK10 . . . . .88 E5
  Somerford Booths CW12 . .203 D2
  Rode Heath ST7 . . . . .193 F7
  Saighton CH3 . . . . .142 E1
  Threapwood SY14 . . . . .222 E8
  Warrington WA4 . . . . .6 E2
  Widnes WA8 . . . . .12 C4
  Wilmslow SK9 . . . . .60 A6
  Windyharbour SK11 . . . . . .109 D2
  Woodbank CH1 . . . . .93 E8
Chapel Lodge CH1 . . . . . .237 C3
Chapel Mews
  Alsager ST7 . . . . .193 C3
  Ellesmere Port CH65 . . . . . .70 B4
  Elton CH2 . . . . .72 B3
  1 Nantwich CW5 . . . . . . .204 E5
Chapel Mus Mow Cop*
  ST7 . . . . .195 D7
Chapel Rd
  Alderley Edge SK9 . . . . .60 A1
  Ollerton WA16 . . . . .82 F6
  Warrington WA5 . . . . .14 B3
  Whaley Bridge SK23 . . . . . . .65 F5
  Wilmslow SK9 . . . . .60 A1
  Winsford CW7 . . . . .126 F1
Chapel Rise SY14 . . . . . . .213 B3
Chapel St
  Barbridge CW5 . . . . .187 D6
  Nantwich CW5 . . . . .204 D5
Chapel St
  7 Alderley Edge SK9 . . . .60 A1
  Audley ST7 . . . . .209 E3
  Bollington SK10 . . . . .88 B8
  Chester CH3 . . . . .237 C3
  Congleton CW12 . . . . .156 D2
  Crewe CW2 . . . . .190 D3
  Haydock WA11 . . . . .1 E6
  Holt LL13 . . . . .196 D8
  Kidsgrove ST7 . . . . .194 D2
  Macclesfield SK11 . . . . .112 D6
  Moulton CW9 . . . . .126 E8
  Mount Pleasant ST7 . . . . . .195 B6
  New Mills SK22 . . . . .39 B6
  Newton-le-W WA12 . . . . .2 B3
  Northwich CW8 . . . . .103 E7
  Sandbach CW11 . . . . .175 B6
  Sandbach,Wheelock CW11 .175 A3
  Weaverham CW8 . . . . .77 C1
  Whaley Bridge SK23 . . . . . . .65 F8
  Widnes WA8 . . . . .23 A7
  Wincham CW9 . . . . .79 C3
Chapel Terr WA3 . . . . .4 B8
Chapel View
  Bebington CH62 . . . . .44 A6
  Helsby WA6 . . . . .73 B2
  3 Widnes WA8 . . . . .4 B8
Chapel Wlks
  Broomedge WA13 . . . . .19 D1
  Cheadle Hulme SK8 . . . . . . .35 B6
Chapel Yd WA2 . . . . .16 A6
Chapelfields WA6 . . . . .73 B2
Chapelmere Cl CW11 . . . .174 E7
Chapelmere Ct CW1 . . . . .190 C7
Chapman Cl WA8 . . . . .12 D4
Chapterhouse Cl CH65 . . .70 E5
Charcoal Rd WA14 . . . . .20 F3
Charity La
  Macclesfield SK11 . . . . .113 F8
  Macclesfield Forest SK11 . .114 B6
Charlcote Cres CW2 . . . . .206 C8
Charlecote Rd SK12 . . . . . .36 F4
Charles Ave
  Davenham CW9 . . . . .103 F2
  Warrington WA5 . . . . .7 A8
Charles Cres CH4 . . . . .237 C1

Charles Darwin Prim Sch
  CW8 .103 E7
Charles Forbes Ct 8
  WA1 . . . . .16 B5
Charles Price Gdns 8
  CH65 .70 C6
Charles Rd CH2 . . . . .95 C1
Charles Sq CW11 . . . . .175 F2
Charles St Chester CH1 . .237 B3
  Chester,Hoole Park CH2 . .118 F3
  Crewe CW1 . . . . .190 C4
  Irlam M44 . . . . .11 E6
  Widnes WA8 . . . . .23 A8
Charleston Cl CH66 . . . . . . .69 D3
Charlesworth Cl SK23 . . . .39 D3
Charlesworth Cres SK23 . .39 D3
Charlesworth Pl 1
  CW12 .41 C6
Charlesworth Rd SK23 . . . .39 D3
Charlock Wlk ST W1 . . . . . .190 D6
Charlock Wlk 8 M31 . . . . . .11 F3
Charlotte Cl CH7 . . . . .197 B8
Charlotte St Chester CH1 .118 B2
  Macclesfield SK11 . . . . .112 D7
Charlotte St W 1 WA8 . . . .12 C8
Charlotte Wlk 2 WA8 . . . . .23 B7
Charlton Cl WA7 . . . . .50 A7
Charlton Ct CH2 . . . . .119 A4
Charlton St
  22 Macclesfield SK11 . . .112 C8
  Warrington WA4 . . . . .16 F3
Charminster Cl WA5 . . . . . .15 B5
Charmouth Cl WA12 . . . . . . .2 B4
Charnock Ave WA12 . . . . . . .1 F3
Charnock Rd WA3 . . . . .4 F3
Charnwood ST7 . . . . .195 B1
Charnwood Cl
  Macclesfield SK10 . . . . .87 A1
  Warrington WA3 . . . . .9 D7
Charnwood Cres SK7 . . . . .36 D8
Charon Way WA5 . . . . .7 B3
Charter Ave WA5 . . . . .16 A8
Charter Cres CH66 . . . . . . .69 C3
Charter Rd SK10 . . . . .88 A7
Charter Way SK10 . . . . .87 F1
Charterhall Dr CH2 . . . . . .118 F2
Chartley Gr CW10 . . . . .128 D2
Chartwell Gr CW7 . . . . .149 C5
Chartwell Pk CW11 . . . . . .175 A4
Chase Dr CH66 . . . . .69 F2
Chase The Bebington CH63 .43 C5
  5 Heswall CH60 . . . . .41 A8
Chase Way CH66 . . . . .69 F2
Chaser Ct CH1 . . . . .117 F3
Chasewater WA7 . . . . .24 F4
Chassange Sq CW1 . . . . . .189 F7
Chatburn Ct WA3 . . . . .4 F2
Chater Dr CW5 . . . . .204 F3
Chatfield Dr WA3 . . . . .9 F4
Chatham St 8 SK11 . . . . . .112 D8
Chatham Way CW1 . . . . . . .191 C5
Chatsworth Ave
  Culcheth WA3 . . . . .4 F4
  Macclesfield SK11 . . . . .111 F6
Chatsworth Cl
  Ellesmere Port CH66 . . . . . .69 F2
  Northwich CW9 . . . . .104 A5
  Warrington WA4 . . . . .26 A7
Chatsworth Dr
  Chester CH2 . . . . .119 A5
  Congleton CW12 . . . . .155 F3
  Widnes WA8 . . . . .12 C3
Chatsworth Ho CH1 . . . . . .118 B3
Chatsworth Rd
  Hazel Grove SK7 . . . . .36 F8
  High Lane SK6 . . . . .37 F6
  Wilmslow SK9 . . . . .59 E4
Chatteris Pk WA7 . . . . .24 E2
Chatterton Dr WA7 . . . . .50 E8
Chatwell Gdns WA4 . . . . . .26 F5
Chaucer Cl CH1 . . . . .117 E6
Chaucer Gr CW1 . . . . .174 C5
Chaucer Pl WA4 . . . . .16 F4
Chaucer St WA7 . . . . .23 A1
Cheadle Hulme Coll SK8 . .35 B7
Cheadle Hulme Sch SK8 . .35 A8
Cheadle La WA16 . . . . .81 A1
Cheadle Wood SK8 . . . . . . .34 E8
Checkley Dr ST8 . . . . .179 D1
Checkley La CW3,CW5 . . . .221 E1
Checkley Rd ST5 . . . . .210 C1
Checkley Row CW5 . . . . . . .232 C8
Cheddar Gr WA5 . . . . .6 F7
Chedlee Dr SK8 . . . . .34 E8
Chedworth Dr WA8 . . . . . . .12 C4
Cheerbrook Rd CW5 . . . . .205 D4
Cheese Hill La WA6,CW8 .101 B4
Chelford Ave WA3 . . . . .4 A8
Chelford CE Prim Sch
  SK11 . . . . .84 A3
Chelford Cl Chester CH1 . .117 F1
  Warrington WA4 . . . . .26 C8
Chelford Dr CW9 . . . . .103 F5
Chelford La WA16 . . . . .83 C1
Chelford Mews 2 CH3 . . .119 B1
Chelford Rd
  Alderley Edge SK9 . . . . .59 E1
  Chelford SK10,SK11 . . . . . . .84 D1
  Chelford,Marthall WA16,
  SK11 . . . . .83 D4
  Congleton CW12 . . . . .155 E6
  Goostrey CW4 . . . . .131 B7
  Handforth SK9 . . . . .34 D5
  Macclesfield SK10,SK11 . . .111 C8
  Monks Heath SK10 . . . . .85 B1
  Nether Alderley SK9 . . . . . . .84 C7
  Ollerton WA16 . . . . .82 D7

Chelford Rd continued
  Prestbury SK10 . . . . .86 D5
  Whisterfield SK11 . . . . .109 F3
Chelford Rdbt SK11 . . . . . . .84 B1
Chelford Sta SK11 . . . . .84 A2
Chell St CW1 . . . . .190 B5
Chells Hill CW11 . . . . .172 C6
Chelsea Cl ST8 . . . . .179 C1
Chelsea Gdns WA5 . . . . . . .15 C4
Chelston Dr SK8 . . . . .34 C6
Cheltenham Cl
  2 Macclesfield SK10 . . . . .87 C4
  Warrington WA5 . . . . .15 A8
Cheltenham Cres
  Crewe CW1 . . . . .190 B7
  Runcorn WA7 . . . . .49 B6
Cheltenham Dr WA12 . . . . . .2 C5
Cheltenham Rd CH65 . . . . .70 D3
Chemical St WA12 . . . . .2 B3
Cheney Wlk CW2 . . . . .206 D8
Chepstow Cl
  Blablyn ST8 . . . . .179 C1
  Macclesfield SK10 . . . . .87 C4
  Warrington WA5 . . . . .7 E3
  1 Winsford CW7 . . . . . . .149 C7
Cherington Cl SK9 . . . . .34 F3
Cherington Cres SK11 . . . .112 B7
Cheriton Way CW2 . . . . . . .206 A8
Cherrington Rd CW5 . . . . .204 E3
Cherry Blossom Rd WA7 . .49 F4
Cherry Brow Terr CH4 . . . . .67 F8
Cherry Cl
  Newcastle-u-Lyme ST5 . . . .210 D1
  Newton-le-W WA12 . . . . .1 F4
  Willaston CH64 . . . . .67 C8
Cherry Cnr WA13 . . . . .28 A7
Cherry Cres CW7 . . . . .149 C8
Cherry Dale Rd CH4 . . . . . .139 A3
Cherry Gdns CH3 . . . . .119 A1
Cherry Gr
  Ellesmere Port CH66 . . . . . .70 A4
  Nantwich CW5 . . . . .204 D5
Cherry Grove Prim Sch
  CH3 . . . . .119 A1
Cherry Grove Rd CH3 . . . .119 A1
Cherry Tree Ave
  Barnton CW8 . . . . .78 A4
  Lawton-gate ST7 . . . . .194 A5
  Lymm WA13 . . . . .18 D2
  Poynton SK12 . . . . .36 F3
  Runcorn WA7 . . . . .49 C8
  Warrington WA5 . . . . .14 F4
Cherry Tree Cl Elton CH2 . .72 B4
  Hale L24 . . . . .21 E1
  Haydock WA11 . . . . .1 E6
  Wilmslow SK9 . . . . .60 E8
Cherry Tree Dr
  Hazel Grove SK7 . . . . .37 A8
  St Helens WA9 . . . . .1 A2
Cherry Tree Ho SK9 . . . . . . .85 C8
Cherry Tree La
  Rostherne WA14 . . . . .30 E6
  Woore CW3 . . . . .232 C2
Cherry Tree Mews 3
  CH60 .41 A8
Cherry Tree Prim Sch
  WA13 .18 C2
Cherry Tree Rd
  Audley ST7 . . . . .209 F1
  Crewe CW1 . . . . .190 E6
  Golborne WA3 . . . . .3 F8
  Newcastle-u-Lyme ST5 . . . .210 E1
Cherry Tree Way CW12 . . .156 E2
Cherry Wlk
  Cheadle Hulme SK8 . . . . . . .35 C8
  Partington M31 . . . . .11 D2
  Swan Green WA16 . . . . .106 C7
Cherryfields Rd SK11 . . . .111 F8
Cherrysutton WA8 . . . . .12 B3
Cherrysutton Mews WA8 .12 B4
Cherrywood Cres CW8 . . . .78 B4
Cherwell Cl
  Cheadle Hulme SK8 . . . . . . .35 A7
  Warrington WA2 . . . . .8 D2
Cheryl Ct CW8 . . . . .102 A4
Cheryl Dr WA8 . . . . .13 D1
Chesford Grange WA1 . . . . .17 F7
Chesham Cl SK9 . . . . .59 F4
Chesham Ct CH65 . . . . .70 D4
Chesham St CH1 . . . . .237 C3
Chesham Way 7 CW7 . . . .149 C7
Cheshire Candle
  Workshops* CH3 . . . . . . .184 C6
Cheshire Cl WA12 . . . . .2 E3
Cheshire Farm* CH3 . . . . .166 C4
Cheshire Military Mus*
  CH1 . . . . .237 A1
Cheshire Oaks Outlet Village
  CH65 .70 E2
Cheshire Oaks Way CH65 . .70 E2
Cheshire Pk WA6 . . . . .97 D5
Cheshire Rd M31 . . . . .11 D2
Cheshire Row WA16 . . . . . .108 B8
Cheshire St CW3 . . . . .229 F4
Cheshire View
  Bollington SK10 . . . . .88 B6
  Chester CH4 . . . . .141 E7
Cheshyre Dr WA7 . . . . .23 F1

Cheshyre's La WA7 ....48 E7
Chessington Cl WA4 ....26 F6
Chester Aerospace Pk
CH5 ....139 B6
Chester Ave WA3 ....3 D8
Chester Bsns Pk CH4 ...141 B3
Chester Cl Handforth SK9 .34 E2
Irlam M44 ....11 D5
Runcorn WA7 ....24 A2
Talke ST7 ....210 E7
Chester Classic The
CH1 ....237 B3
Chester Heritage Ctr*
CH1 ....237 B1
Chester High Rd
Neston CH64 ....41 E4
Willaston CH64 ....67 D7
Chester La CW7 ....125 D2
Chester New Rd WA4 ....25 F7
Chester Race Course*
CH1 ....237 A1
Chester Rd Acton CW5 ...204 A6
Audley ST7 ....209 D2
Barbridge CW5 ....187 D5
Broughton CH4 ....139 D5
Churton CH3 ....130 F6
Connah's Quay CH6 .....91 A3
Cuddington CW8 ....101 D1
Daresbury WA4 ....25 B1
Delamere CW6,CW8 ....123 C5
Dunham-on-t-H CH2,WA6 .97 D5
Ellesmere Port, Whitby
CH65,CH66 ....70 A2
Ellesmere Port,Great Sutton
CH66 ....69 D4
Frodsham WA6 ....74 A7
Gatesheath CH3 ....165 E5
Hartford CW8 ....102 E3
Hartford, Greenbank CH8 .103 C6
Helsby WA6 ....73 C4
Heswall CH60,CH64 .....41 C6
Higher Walton WA4 .....25 D5
Holmes Chapel CW4 ....130 B2
Hooton CH66 ....44 A1
Huntington CH3 ....142 A6
Kelsall CW6 ....122 D5
Macclesfield SK11 ......112 B8
Malpas SY14 ....213 B4
Mere WA16 ....56 B6
Middlewich CW10 ....128 B2
Neston CH64 ....66 E7
Over Tabley WA16 ......56 A2
Plumley WA16 ....80 E5
Poynton SK12 ....36 B4
Rostherne WA14,WA16 ...30 C5
Runcorn WA7 ....50 E5
Saltney CH4 ....140 C6
Sandycroft CH5 ....116 A2
Sutton WA7 ....50 B4
Talke ST7 ....210 D7
Warrington WA4 ....16 A2
Warrington,Grappenhall
WA4 ....17 B1
Whitchurch SY13 ....225 D2
Winsford CW7 ....125 F2
Woodford SK7 ....35 E2
Chester Ret Pk CH1 ....118 A3
Chester Row WA12 ....7 D8
Chester Sq CW1 ....190 C4
Chester St Chester CH4 .140 F7
Crewe CW1 ....190 C4
Warrington WA2 ....16 B6
Widnes WA8 ....13 B1
Chester Sta CH1 ....237 C3
Chester Toy & Doll Mus*
CH1 ....237 B2
Chester Trad Pk CH1 ....117 F2
Chester Way WA4 ....104 A8
Chester West Employment Pk
CH1 ....117 C2
Chester Zoo* CH2 ....95 E1
Chester Zoological Gdns*
CH2 ....118 D8
Chester's Croft Bk Sk8 .35 A5
Chesterbank Bsns Pk
CH4 ....140 D7
Chesterfield Cl CW7 ....125 F1
Chesterfield Rd CH62 ...43 D4
Chestergate SK10,SK11 .112 D8
Chesterton CW7 ....151 E5
Chesterton Cl CH2 .....118 D4
Chesterton Dr
Crewe CW2 ....189 F1
Winwick WA2 ....8 A5
Chesterton Gr CW11 ....174 D5
Chestnut Ave
4 Ellesmere Port CH66 ...69 F1
Irlam M44 ....11 D5
Macclesfield SK10 ......87 E2
Rode Heath ST7 ....193 F7
Shavington CW2 ....206 C5
Warrington WA5 ....14 F6
Widnes WA8 ....13 B2
Chestnut Cl Chester CH2 119 A3
Cuddington CW8 ....101 F2
Middlewich CW10 ....128 B2
Tarporley CW6 ....146 D2
Wilmslow SK9 ....60 E8
Chestnut Ct
Tarporley CW6 ....146 C2
Widnes WA8 ....12 D1
Chestnut Dr Alsager ST7 193 E2
Congleton CW12 ....156 F3
Holmes Chapel CW4 ....130 D3
Poynton SK12 ....36 F3
Chestnut Gr Barnton CW8 .78 B4
Bebington CH62 ....43 C8
Crewe CW1 ....190 E5

Chestnut Gr continued
Golborne WA3 ....3 F8
Newcastle-u-Lyme ST5 ..210 E1
Winsford CW7 ....149 C8
Chestnut Grange CH4 ..141 B7
Chestnut Ho 6 CW11 ..175 B6
Chestnut La CW3 ....73 E4
Chestnut Lodge Specl Sch
WA8 ....12 E1
Chestnut Mews WA6 ....58 E1
Chestnut Wlk M31 ......11 D2
Chetham Ct WA2 ....8 A3
Chetton Dr WA7 ....50 E7
Chetwode Mews WA4 ...52 C2
Chetwode St CW1 ......190 C5
Chetwood Dr WA8 ....12 F4
Cheveley Cl SK10 ....87 C2
Chevin Gdns SK7 ......204 E3
Cheviot Ave WA2 ....8 A3
Cheviot Cl CH66 ....69 A6
Cheviot Sq CW7 ....149 B7
Chevron Cl CH1 ....117 E4
Chevron Hey CH1 ......117 E4
Cheyne Wlk CW5 ......204 E3
Cheyney Rd CH1 ....117 B3
Chicago Ave M90 ....33 B7
Chichester Cl
Grappenhall Heys WA4 ...27 A7
Runcorn WA7 ....50 D6
Chichester Ct CH1 .....237 A3
Chichester St CH1 .....237 A3
Chidlow Cl Hough CW2 ..206 E2
Widnes WA8 ....23 A5
Child's La CW12 ....177 E6
Childer Cres CH66 .....69 B7
Childer Gdns CH66 .....69 B7
Childer Thornton Prim Sch
CH66 ....69 B8
Childwall Ct CH66 ......69 F8
Childwall Gdns CH66 ...69 F8
Childwall Rd CH66 .....69 F8
Chilham Cl CW7 ....149 C7
Chilham Pl SK11 ....111 F6
Chilington Ave WA8 ....22 D8
Chillingham Cl CW10 ..128 D2
Chiltern Ave SK11 .....112 A7
Chiltern Cl Chester CH4 .141 B5
Chorlton CW2 ....207 B1
Cuddington CW8 ....102 A2
Chiltern Cres WA2 ......8 A3
Chiltern Pl WA2 ....8 A3
Chiltern Rd Culcheth WA3 .4 E4
St Helens WA9 ....1 A3
Warrington WA2 ....8 A3
Chiltern Way CW7 .....149 B7
Chilton Dr CH66 ....69 F2
Chilwell Cl WA8 ....12 D4
Chilworth Cl CW2 .....206 C8
China La WA4 ....16 C2
Chines The CH8 ....101 D5
Chippingdall Cl WA5 ...15 C5
Chipstead Cl CW8 .....103 A4
Chirk Cl CH2 ....118 F6
Chirk Gdns CH65 ....70 D3
Chirk Pl CW7 ....126 A1
Chirton Cl WA11 ....1 D7
Chisledon Cl WA11 .....1 D7
Chislet Ct WA8 ....12 E4
Chiswick Cl WA7 ....50 D7
Chiswick Gdns WA4 ....26 F6
Chollerton Cl WA16 ....29 E2
Cholmley Dr WA12 ......2 E2
Cholmondeley Castle Gdns*
SY14 ....201 A4
Cholmondeley La SY14 .200 E7
Cholmondeley Rd
Ellesmere Port CH65 ...69 F4
Hampton Heath SY14 ..213 E2
Runcorn WA7 ....49 D4
Wrenbury CW5 ....216 C5
Cholmondeley St
Macclesfield SK11 .....112 C6
Widnes WA8 ....23 A3
Cholmondeley Rise SY14 214 B4
Chorley Bank Council Hos
CWS 201 E1
Chorley Green La CW5,
SY14 ....201 E5
Chorley St
Warrington WA3 ....9 B6
Warrington WA2 ....16 C6
Chorley Stock La CW5 ..201 E4
Chorley's La WA8 ......13 E3
Chorleywood Cl SK10 ..87 B4
Chorlton Cl WA7 ......24 D1
Chorlton La CW2 ......207 B2
Chowley Oak La CH3 ..182 F6
Chrimes Dr CW8 ......123 F6
Christ Church CE Prim Sch
CWS 70 B2
Christ Church CE Sch
CW8 ....76 B1
Christ The King RC Prim Sch
CH62 ....43 E7
Christchurch Ave CW1 .190 A1
Christie Cl CH66 ....44 A2
Christie St WA8 ....13 D1
Christleton Ave
Crewe CW2 ....189 D5
Northwich CW9 ....104 A4
Christleton Ct WA7 .....24 C4
Christleton Dr CH66 ....69 E6

Christleton High Sch
CH3 ....142 F7
Christleton Prim Sch
CH3 ....142 E8
Christleton Rd CH3 ....119 A1
Christleton Sports Ctr
CH3 ....142 F8
Christleton Way 15 SK9 .34 D5
Christopher Dr CH62 ....44 A5
Church Ave SK9 ....34 C2
Church Bank Audley ST7 209 D2
Goostrey CW4 ....107 F1
Kelsall CW6 ....122 D5
Tattenhall CH3 ....166 B2
Church Bk SK23 ....146 E8
Church Cl Handforth SK9 .34 D3
Weaverham CW8 ....77 D1
Church College Cl CH1 .118 B3
Church Coppenhall Jun Sch
CW1 ....100 B6
Church Cotts Astle SK11 .109 B8
Rainow SK10 ....88 E5
Sealand CH1 ....116 E6
Waverton CH3 ....143 C3
Church Croft CH4 .....162 A6
Church Ct
Ashton Hayes CH3 ....121 F8
Farndon CH3 ....180 E2
Church Dr
Newton-le-W WA12 ......2 C1
Warrington WA2 ....9 A1
Church End L24 ....21 D1
Church Farm Ct
Heswall CH60 ....40 F7
Willaston CH64 ....67 F8
Church Farm La WA16 ..19 B8
Church Hall Cl CH1 ....117 F4
Church Hill WA16 ......57 A2
Church La
Alderley Edge SK9 .....60 A2
Aldford CH3 ....163 F3
Backford CH1 ....95 B4
Bebington CH62 ....44 A4
Bramhall SK7 ....35 C2
Chester CH2 ....118 D7
Congleton CW12 ......134 E1
Culcheth WA3 ....4 E3
Ellesmere Port CH66 ...69 D3
Farndon CH3 ....180 E1
Golborne WA3 ....3 D7
Guilden Sutton CH3 ...119 F5
Hargrave CH3 ....144 B1
Henbury SK11 ....111 C8
Huxley CH3,CW6 ......167 C6
Lawton-gate ST7 .....194 C4
Mobberley WA16 ......58 C5
Mow Cop ST7 ....195 E7
Nantwich CWS 204 E5
Neston CH64 ....66 E7
New Mills SK22 ....39 C8
Rainow SK10 ....88 E5
Sandbach CW11 ......175 E7
Scholar Green ST7 ....194 C7
Smallwood CW11 .....176 E4
Stoak CH2 ....96 A7
Sutton Lane Ends SK11 .112 F3
Warren SK11 ....134 D8
Warrington WA4 ....17 B1
Weaverham CW8 ....77 D1
Wistaston WA8 ....205 E8
Church Lawton Prim Sch
ST7 ....194 A5
Church Mdw TF9 .....236 C2
Church Mdws
Little Leigh CW8 ....77 D5
Whitchurch SY13 .....226 A1
Church Mead CH3 .....181 A5
Church Meadow La CH60 .40 F7
Church Meadow Wlk
WA8 ....22 B5
Church Mews
Bollington SK10 ....88 B8
Higher Wincham CW9 ..79 E5
Knutsford WA16 ....57 B2
6 Macclesfield SK11 ..112 D8
Church Par 5 CH5 .....70 C6
Church Rd Alsager ST7 .193 C4
Ashton Hayes CH3 ....121 F8
Barnton CW8 ....78 B2
Broughton CH4 ....139 C4
Burwardsley CH3 .....184 A5
Cheadle Hulme SK8 ....35 B8
Dodleston CH4 ....162 B8
Eccleston CH4 ....141 E2
Frodsham WA6 ....74 C7
Hale L24 ....21 A4
Handforth SK9 ....34 D3
Haydock WA11 ....1 F7
Little Leigh CW8 ....77 D4
Lymm WA13 ....18 E2
Mouldsworth CH3 .....98 F1
New Mills SK22 ....39 C7
Northwich CW9 ....104 A8
Saughall CH1 ....94 A1
Shocklach CH3 ....197 C1
Thornton Hough CH63 ..42 B6
Tilston SY14 ....198 B2
Wilmslow SK9 ....59 E4
Worleston CWS 188 D6
Church Rise CW8 .....102 B2
Church Row CH3 ....84 E6
Church St Audley ST7 ..209 D2
Audley,Wood Lane ST7 ..210 A1
Bollington SK10 ....88 B8
Chester CH1 ....237 B4
Connah's Quay CH5 ....91 D1

Church St continued
Davenham CW9 ....104 A3
Ellesmere Port CH65 ....70 C6
Farndon LL13 ....180 E2
Frodsham WA6 ....74 B8
Great Budworth CW9 ....79 A8
Higher Wincham CW9 ...79 E5
Kelsall CW6 ....122 D4
Kidsgrove, Butt Lane ST7 .194 D1
Kidsgrove,The Rookery
ST7 ....195 C4
Macclesfield SK10,SK11 .112 D8
Malpas SY14 ....213 B3
Moulton CW9 ....126 F8
Mount Pleasant ST7 ...195 C6
Newton-le-W WA12 ......2 E4
Runcorn WA7 ....23 A3
Sandbach CW11 ......175 B6
Tarvin CH3 ....121 C2
Warrington WA1 ....16 C5
Weaverham CW8 ....77 D1
Widnes WA8 ....23 A5
Winsford CW7 ....126 E1
Church St N CW6 .....122 C5
Church View Wlk CW2 .205 E8
Church Way Alvanley WA6 .73 A1
Blacon CH1 ....117 E5
Wybunbury CW5 ......220 B8
Church Wlk
Broughton CH4 ....139 C5
Crowton CW8 ....76 C2
2 Ellesmere Port CH65 .70 C6
Holmes Chapel CW4 ...130 C3
Knutsford WA16 ....57 A2
Lower Peover WA16 ....81 E1
Malpas SY14 ....213 B3
Northwich CW9 ....104 A8
Wilmslow SK9 ....59 F6
Winwick WA2 ....8 A6
Church Wlks
Christleton CH3 ....142 E8
Norton in Hales TF9 ...236 C2
Church's Ct 15 CW5 ...204 E5
Church's Mansion*
CWS 204 F5
Churchfield Rd WA6 ...74 C8
Churchfields
Audlem CW3 ....230 A4
Barnton CW8 ....78 B3
Croft WA3 ....9 B7
Cuddington CW8 ......102 B2
Helsby WA6 ....73 C4
Knutsford WA16 ....57 A2
Widnes WA8 ....13 B5
Wybunbury CW5 ......220 B8
Churchill Ave WA3 .....5 B4
Churchill Cl CW12 ....156 A3
Churchill Dr CW6 .....146 D1
Churchill Mans 10 WA7 ..23 A3
Churchill Parkway CW7 .149 D8
Churchill Rd
Macclesfield SK11 .....112 D8
Neston CH64 ....66 E8
Churchmere Dr CW1 ...190 C7
Churchside SK10 ......112 D8
Churchside Wlk CH4 ..140 F7
Churchward Cl CH2 ...118 D4
Churchway SK10 ....86 F2
Churchway Rd L24 .....21 A2
Churchwood View WA13 .18 F2
Churchyard Side CW5 .204 E5
Churton Cl Hough CW2 .206 E3
3 Northwich CW9 .....103 E4
Churton Rd Chester CH3 .119 A2
Farndon CH3 ....180 E2
Churton St CH3 ....119 A2
Cicely Mill La WA16 ....30 D3
Cinder Cl CH3 ....119 F5
Cinder Hill CW7 ....125 F6
Cinder La Chelford SK11 ..83 E1
Guilden Sutton CH3 ...119 F5
Lostock Green CW9 ....105 A8
Nantwich CWS 188 C2
Over Peover WA16 ....108 C7
Warrington WA4 ......17 B1
Cinder Rooks Way ST7 .195 C1
Cinder-Hill La ST7 .....194 F7
Cinnamon Brow CE Prim Sch
WA2 ....8 F2
Cinnamon La WA2 ......8 F2
Cinnamon La N WA2 ....8 F2
Cinnamon Pk WA2 ......8 F2
Circle Ave CW5 ....205 E5
Circle The Crewe CW2 .190 D1
Mere WA16 ....30 C2
Circuit The
Alderley Edge SK9 .....60 B3
Cheadle Hulme SK8 ....35 A7
Wilmslow SK9 ....59 D5
City Apartments CH1 ..237 C3
City Bank CH3 ....179 C2
City Rd CH1 ....237 C3
City Walls Rd CH1 ....237 A2

Civic Way
Ellesmere Port CH65 ...70 B4
Middlewich CW10 .....128 C1
Clair Ave CH5 ....116 A3
Clamhunger La WA16 ...56 D7
Clamley Ct L24 ....21 A3
Clamley Gdns L24 .....21 E2
Clamfield Ave WA8 ....12 C3
Clap Gate Cres WA8 ...22 B5
Clap Gates Cres WA5 ..15 E7
Clap Gates Rd WA5 ....15 E7
Clare Ave Chester CH2 .119 A3
Handforth SK9 ....34 C3
Clare Dr Crewe CW2 ..189 F1
Ellesmere Port CH65 ...70 B1
Macclesfield SK10 .....87 E2
Clare Ho CH1 ....117 E6
Clare Pl CW7 ....149 C7
Clare St Kidsgrove ST7 .195 E4
Mount Pleasant ST7 ...195 C6
Claremont Ave WA8 ....13 C4
Claremont Dr WA8 ....13 B4
Claremont Rd
Cheadle Hulme SK8 ....35 A8
Crewe CW2 ....190 B2
Culcheth WA3 ....4 D4
Runcorn WA7 ....23 B2
Clarence Ave
Chester CH3 ....119 B2
Warrington WA5 ....14 D6
Widnes WA8 ....13 A4
Clarence Ct
Newton-le-W WA12 ......2 A4
Wilmslow SK9 ....60 A6
Clarence Gr CW1 .....190 B5
Clarence Mill Bsns Pk
SK10 ....63 A1
Clarence Rd
Bollington SK10 ....63 A1
Warrington WA1 ....17 B2
Clarence St
Newton-le-W WA12 ......1 F4
Runcorn WA7 ....22 F3
Warrington WA1 ....16 E7
Clarence Terr
Bollington SK10 ....63 A1
7 Runcorn WA7 ....23 A3
Clarendon Cl
Chester CH4 ....141 E6
Runcorn WA7 ....50 D7
Clarendon Cotts SK9 ..34 A3
Clarendon Ct WA2 .....7 F4
Clarendon Dr SK10 ....88 A1
Clarendon Rd M44 ....11 F7
Clares Farm Cl WA1 ...27 E7
Clarke Ave Culcheth WA3 .5 A4
Warrington WA2 ....16 D2
Clarke Gdns 3 WA8 ...23 B7
Clarke La Bollington SK10 .87 E5
Langley SK11 ....113 D3
Clarke Terr SK11 ......112 D6
Clarke's Terr WA7 .....48 D8
Clary Mdw CW8 ....78 E1
Clatterbridge Hospl
CH63 ....42 D8
Clatterbridge Rd CH63 .42 D8
Clatterwick La CW8 ....77 D7
Claude St WA1 ....16 C6
Claughton Ave CW2 ...190 C1
Claverton Cl WA7 ......49 B6
Claverton Ct CH4 .....237 C1
Clay Heyes WA7 ....84 A3
Clay La Bickerton SY14 .200 B7
Burtonwood WA5 ....6 E5
Handforth SK9 ....34 C5
Haslington CW1,CW11 ..191 D7
Over Peover WA16 ....108 B8
Sandbach CW11,CW1 .174 B2
Wilmslow SK9 ....59 C4
Winsford CW7 ....125 B4
Claydon Gdns WA3 ....10 F1
Clayhill Gn CH66 ......69 D7
Clayhill Light Ind Pk
CH64 ....41 F2
Claypit Rd CH4 ....141 B5
Claypits La CH3 ......142 F5
Clayton Ave
Congleton CW12 ......157 A5
Golborne WA3 ....3 E8
Clayton Cl CW1 ....190 A7
Clayton Cres Runcorn WA2 .22 F1
Widnes WA8 ....12 F1
Clayton Dr SY13 ......226 B1
Clayton Rd WA3 ....9 F6
Clayton's Row CW5 ...204 E7
Clayton-By-Pass CW12 .156 C3
Cleadon Way WA8 .....12 E4
Cleaver Mews SK11 ...112 C5
Cleaver Rd CH1 ....117 E4
Cledford Cres CW10 ..151 E6
Cledford Inf Sch CW10 .151 C7
Cledford Jun Sch CW10 .151 C7
Cledford La CW10 .....151 E7
Cledwen Rd/Ffordd Cledwen
CH4 ....139 D5
Cleethorpes Rd WA7 ..50 C7
Cleeve Way SK8 ....35 B6
Cleeves Cl WA1 ....16 C5
Clegge St WA2 ....16 B3
Clelland St WA4 ....16 C3
Clement Dr CW1 ......190 F3
Clemley Cl CW6 ......122 D6
Clerewood Ave SK8 ...34 B7

Clevedon Cl SK11 ....112 A7
Cleveland Dr CH66 ....69 A6
Cleveland Rd WA2 ....8 B3
Cleveland Way CW7 ....149 B7
Cleveleys Ave WA8 ....13 D2
Cleveleys Rd WA5 ....15 B4
Cleves Cl CH1 ....117 D6
Cliff La Acton Bridge CW8 ..76 C4
  Lymm WA13 ....18 F2
  Macclesfield SK10 ....88 B1
  Warrington WA4 ....17 D1
Cliff Rd Acton Bridge CW8 ..76 C4
  Wilmslow SK9 ....60 B8
Cliff Side SK9 ....60 B8
Cliff View WA6 ....74 A8
Cliffbrook Gr 2 SK9 ....34 D2
Cliffe Rd Crewe CW1 ....190 B7
  Neston CH64 ....66 F5
  Warrington WA4 ....26 C7
Cliffe St 3 WA8 ....13 C1
Clifford Dr CH4 ....140 F5
Clifford Gr CW1 ....191 C4
Clifford Pl 4 CW7 ....149 C8
Clifford Rd
  Macclesfield SK11 ....112 A8
  Poynton SK12 ....36 D3
  Warrington WA5 ....15 A4
  Wilmslow SK9 ....59 F6
Clifton Ave
  Bebington CH62 ....43 E3
  Crewe CW2 ....190 B3
  Culcheth WA3 ....4 D2
Clifton Cl WA1 ....17 C7
Clifton Cres WA6 ....49 C1
Clifton Ct WA7 ....49 B6
Clifton Dr Blacon CH1 ....117 E3
  Northwich CW9 ....104 A5
  Wilmslow SK9 ....59 E4
Clifton Gdns CH65 ....70 C3
Clifton La WA7 ....49 E3
Clifton Park Ave CH5 ....91 D1
Clifton Rd
  Runcorn,Clifton WA7 ....49 E3
  Runcorn,Heath WA7 ....49 B6
  Sandbach CW11 ....174 D7
Clifton St
  Alderley Edge SK9 ....60 A1
  Crewe CW2 ....190 B3
  Warrington WA4 ....16 C4
Cliftonmill Mdws WA3 ....2 F8
Cliftonville Rd WA1 ....17 D6
Clincton Cl WA8 ....22 A8
Clincton View WA8 ....22 A8
Clipsley Cres WA11 ....1 B7
Clipsley La WA11 ....1 C6
Clitheroe Rd CW8 ....77 E1
Clive Ave WA2 ....8 C1
Clive Back La CW7 ....150 D7
Clive La CW7 ....150 C8
Cliveden Rd CH4 ....140 F5
Clivegreen La CW10 ....150 E7
Clock Face Rd WA8 ....13 E8
Clocktower The CW4 ....130 D2
Cloister Way CH65 ....70 E5
Clones Way CW5 ....205 A4
Clonners Field CW5 ....205 A4
Close La Alsager ST7 ....192 F3
  Mow Cop ST7 ....195 D7
Close The Alsager ST7 ....193 A3
  Hartford CW8 ....103 D6
  Newton-le-W WA12 ....2 E1
  Saughall CH1 ....94 A1
  Tarporley CW6 ....146 C2
Closeburn Ave CH60 ....40 E6
Cloud The* CW12 ....158 A4
Cloud View CW12 ....157 A2
Cloudberry Wlk M31 ....11 F3
Clough Ave Handforth SK9 ..34 B2
  Warrington WA2 ....8 B2
Clough Bank SK10 ....87 F7
Clough Field Cl SK23 ....65 D8
Clough Hall Dr ST7 ....210 E6
Clough Hall Rd ST7 ....210 F8
Clough Hall Tech Sch
  ST7 ....194 F1
Clough La CW8 ....103 D6
Clough Rd CW7 ....126 E1
Clough The WA7 ....23 C1
Clough Wlk CW2 ....206 D8
Cloughside SK10 ....38 E6
Cloughwood Sch CW8 ..103 D5
Clovelly Ave WA5 ....14 E7
Clovelly Gr WA7 ....50 C5
Clover Ave WA6 ....74 D7
Clover Ct WA7 ....50 B5
Clover Dr Cw Pickmere WA16 ..79 F7
  Winsford CW7 ....126 D3
Clover La CH4 ....140 F5
Clover Pl CH4 ....140 F5
Cloverdale CW8 ....103 C7
Cloverdale Rd SK11 ....112 B5
Cloverfield Lymm WA13 ..18 F4
  Runcorn WA7 ....50 C7
Cloverfield Gdns CH66 ..69 D7
Cloverfields CW1 ....191 B4
Clowes Ave ST7 ....193 F2
Clowes St SK11 ....112 B8
Clumber Cl SK10 ....36 E3
Clumber Rd SK12 ....36 E3
Clutton CE Prim Sch
  CH3 ....182 D1
Clwyd Cl CH5 ....139 B6
Clwyd Way CH66 ....69 A6
Clyde Ave ST8 ....179 E1
Clyde Cres CW7 ....127 B1

Clyde Gr CW2 ....190 A3
Clydesdale CH65 ....70 B3
Clydesdale Ave CW2 ..190 B3
Clydesdale Rd WA4 ....26 D8
Coach Rd Broxton CH3 ..183 A3
  Edge Green SY14 ....199 D2
  Little Budworth CW6 ....147 D8
Coachway SK10 ....86 F7
Coalbrookdale Rd CH64 ..41 F2
Coalpit Hill ST7 ....210 D8
Coalpit La
  Clive Green CW10 ....150 F7
  Dunkirk CH1 ....94 E6
  Langley SK11 ....113 C5
  Mollington CH1 ....94 D4
Coalport Dr CW7 ....126 F3
Coare St SK10 ....87 D1
Coastguard La CH64 ....41 B1
Coatings By Pass Rd CH5 ..91 F2
Coatings Two CH5 ....91 E2
Cob Hall La WA6 ....98 D5
Cob Moor Rd ST7 ....195 A4
Cobal Ct WA6 ....74 B8
Cobbett's Way SK9 ....59 F4
Cobblers Cross La CW6 ..146 E2
Cobblers La / Lon Y Cryddion
  LL12 ....161 B1
Cobbles The
  Chester CH4 ....141 D7
  Cuddington CW8 ....101 D4
  Lower Peover WA16 ....81 E1
Cobblestone Ct CH2 ....119 E8
Cobbs Inf Sch The WA4 ..26 E8
Cobbs La Hough CW2 ....206 E2
Cobden St
  Newton-le-W WA12 ....2 D4
  Warrington WA2 ....16 B6
Cock Hall La SK11 ....113 D3
Cock La
  Great Budworth CW9 ....78 F8
  Sound CW5 ....217 F4
Cock Lane Ends WA8 ....22 B4
Cockhedge La WA1 ....16 C5
Cockhedge Sh Ctr WA1 ..16 B5
Cockhedge Way WA1 ..16 B5
Cockington Cl CW9 ....104 A4
Cocklade La L24 ....21 D1
Cockpit La WA8 ....102 B1
Cockshades farm CW5 ..206 C2
Cocksheadhey Rd SK10 ..63 C1
Cocksmoss La
  Congleton SK11 ....134 A3
  Marton SK11 ....133 D3
Cocoa Gdns 11 CW5 ..204 E5
Cocoa Yard The 10
  CW5 ....204 E5
Coe La WA14 ....30 C7
Cogshall La Anderton CW9 ..78 B7
  Comberbach CW9 ....78 B7
Colchester Sq CW7 ....140 F5
Coldmoss Dr CW11 ....175 C4
Coldstream Cl WA2 ....8 E3
Coldstream Dr CH66 ....68 F5
Cole Ave WA12 ....2 C4
Colebrook Cl WA3 ....10 A4
Coleclough Pl WA3 ....4 F4
Coleg Glannau
  Dyfrdwy/Deeside Coll
  CH5 ....91 B1
Colehill Bank CW12 ..156 E2
Colehill Pl CH5 ....91 D1
Colemere Cl WA1 ....17 A8
Colemere Ct CH65 ....70 C7
Coleridge Cl Blacon CH1 ..118 A5
  Sandbach CW11 ....174 C5
Coleridge Gr WA8 ....12 E1
Coleridge Way CW1 ....190 F5
Colinwood Ave CH4 ....139 B3
Coliseum Way CH65 ....70 D2
Collar House Dr SK10 ..86 E6
College Cl
  Warrington WA1 ....16 D5
  Warrington,Fearnhead WA2 ..9 B2
  Wilmslow SK9 ....59 F8
College Fields CW2 ..190 A1
College Gn CH4 ....141 D7
College View CH5 ....91 C1
Colley La CW11 ....175 D5
Colleys La CW5 ....205 B7
Collier St WA7 ....22 F3
Collier's Row WA7 ....48 E7
Colliers La CW9 ....54 E2
Colliery Green Cl CH64 ..66 E5
Colliery Green Ct CH64 ..66 E5
Colliery Green Dr CH64 ..66 E5
Collin St WA5 ....15 F5
Collinbrook Ave CW2 ..190 B1
Collingham Gn CH66 ....69 B5
Collingham Way CW7 ..126 D1
Collingtree Ave WA7 ..127 A3
Collingwood Cl
  Macclesfield SK10 ....87 B2
  Poynton SK12 ....37 A3
Collingwood Rd M22 ....33 E8
Collins Green La WA5 ....1 E1
Collins St CW2 ....190 A3
Collinson Ct 2 WA6 ....74 B8
Colne Rd WA5 ....6 F6
Colorado Cl WA5 ....15 C7
Colshaw Dr SK9 ....34 D2
Colshaw Hall Cotts WA16 ..82 F1
Colshaw La SK11 ....109 E1
Colson Ct CH2 ....237 A4

Coltsfoot Cl CH3 ....142 B5
Columbine Cl
  Huntington CH3 ....142 A6
  Widnes WA8 ....12 B4
Columbine Way WA9 ....6 B7
Columbine Wlk 8 M31 ..11 F3
Colville Ct WA2 ....8 A3
Colville Rd SK11 ....111 F8
Colwyn Cl
  Ellesmere Port CH65 ....70 D3
  Warrington WA5 ....7 F2
Colwyn Rd SK7 ....35 F8
Comber Way WA16 ....82 A8
Comberbach Dr CW5 ..205 A4
Comberbach Prim Sch
  CW9 ....78 C8
Combermere Pl CW1 ..190 B5
Comboy Dr CW9 ....104 C6
Combs Cl SK22 ....39 A8
Commercial Ave SK8 ....34 F5
Commercial Rd SK10 ..112 E8
Common Farm La SK11 ..83 E1
Common La Betley CW3 ..221 F6
  Chelford SK11 ....83 E1
  Culcheth WA3 ....4 E4
  Duddon CW6 ....145 C7
  Hapsford WA6 ....72 D1
  Kelsall CW6 ....122 C3
  Lach Dennis CW9 ....105 E5
  Norbury SY13 ....215 C5
  Stretton WA4 ....52 E8
  Warrington WA4 ....16 E2
  Waverton CH3 ....143 B4
  Winsford CW7 ....125 B5
Common St WA12 ....2 A3
Common The WA7 ....49 F8
Commongate SK10 ....112 E8
Commonhall St CH1 ..237 A2
Commons Mill CW11 ....175 B7
Commons The CW11 ....175 B6
Commonside WA6 ....73 E1
Commonwealth Cl CW7 ..149 D6
Commonwealth Ho
  WA15 ....33 B8
Commonwood Rd LL13 ..196 A8
Company's Cl WA7 ....48 E8
Compass Cl WA7 ....50 C5
Compton Cl WA11 ....1 C7
Compton Pl Chester CH4 ..141 A6
  Warrington WA7 ....50 A5
Concorde Pl WA2 ....8 D2
Concourse Way WA9 ....1 A2
Condliffe Cl CW11 ....175 C5
Conery Cl WA6 ....73 C4
Coney Gr WA7 ....50 B5
Congleton Bsns Ctr
  CW12 ....156 E3
Congleton Bsns Pk
  CW12 ....156 C4
Congleton Cl SK9 ....85 A8
Congleton Edge Rd
  CW12 ....179 B6
Congleton High Sch
  CW12 ....156 D4
Congleton La SK11 ....109 D5
Congleton Mus* CW12 ..156 D2
Congleton Rd
  Biddulph ST8 ....179 D2
  Broughton CH4 ....139 C4
  Kidsgrove ST7 ....194 D1
  Macclesfield SK11 ....112 B5
  Marton SK11 ....133 B5
  Mow Cop ST7 ....178 F1
  North Rode SK11 ....134 C6
  Sandbach CW11 ....175 B8
  Sandbach CW11 ....175 B8
  Scholar Green CW12,ST7 ..177 E3
  Siddington SK11 ....110 D8
  Smallwood CW11 ....177 A6
  Swettenham CW12 ....131 F4
  Warren SK11 ....111 E2
Congleton Rd N ST7 ..194 E6
Congleton Rd S ST7 ..194 D3
Congleton Ret Pk
  CW12 ....156 D4
Congleton Sta CW12 ..157 A1
Congleton War Meml Hospl
  CW12 ....156 F1
Conifer Cl CH66 ....95 A8
Conifer Gr Moore WA4 ..25 A7
  Warrington WA5 ....14 F7
Conifer Wlk M31 ....11 E3
Conifers The ST7 ....193 B3
Coningsby Dr CW7 ....126 E1
Coningsby Gdns 13 WA3 ..3 E8
Coniston Ave
  Bebington CH63 ....43 C4
  Congleton CW12 ....155 F2
  Warrington WA5 ....14 D4
  Winsford CW7 ....126 C2
Coniston Cl
  Alderley Edge SK9 ....84 A7
  Hooton CH66 ....44 B2
  Nantwich CW5 ....205 A6
  Runcorn WA7 ....49 D6
Coniston Dr
  Frodsham WA6 ....74 D8
  Handforth SK9 ....34 A2
  Holmes Chapel CW4 ..130 A3
Coniston Rd Chester CH2 ..118 F5
  High Lane SK6 ....37 D8
  Neston CH64 ....66 E6
  Partington M31 ....11 E4
Coniston Way SK11 ....111 F8
Connah's Quay High Sch
  CH5 ....91 C1
Connaught Ave WA1 ....16 E7

Connaught Cl SK9 ....60 C8
Connaught Dr WA12 ....2 C2
Conrad Cl CW1 ....190 E4
Conroy Way WA12 ....7 C8
Consort Cl SK10 ....87 E7
Constable Dr SK9 ....60 E8
Constables Cl WA7 ....24 A1
Constance Rd M31 ....11 F3
Constance Way WA8 ....23 A5
Convamore Rd SK7 ....35 D7
Conway Ave Irlam M44 ....11 F7
  Warrington WA5 ....7 F2
  Winsford CW7 ....149 C7
Conway Cl Crewe CW1 ..190 C8
  Knutsford WA16 ....82 A8
  Saltney CH4 ....140 D5
  Warrington WA5 ....14 F6
Conway Cres SK10 ....87 F1
Conway Ct CW5 ....70 D3
Conway Dr WA12 ....2 C2
Conwy Ct WA7 ....24 A2
Coogee Ave WA5 ....14 E7
Cook Ave WA11 ....1 F7
Cook St CH5 ....70 C6
Cooke's La CW9 ....104 F6
Cookes Cl CH64 ....41 E1
Cookes Ct CH64 ....166 B1
Cooksmere La CW11 ..175 A8
Cooks La SY13 ....225 D7
Cooksmere La CW11 ..152 F1
Coole La
  Hack Green CW5 ....218 E3
  Newhall CW3 ....229 C5
Coombe Dr WA7 ....49 A8
Coombe Park Ct 1 CH66 ..69 C6
Coombe Rd SK10 ....87 E6
Cooper Ave
  Newton-le-W WA12 ....1 F3
  Warrington WA2 ....8 B2
Cooper La WA11 ....1 C6
Cooper St
  Congleton CW12 ....156 E3
  Runcorn WA7 ....23 A3
  Widnes WA8 ....13 B1
Cooper Terr CW6 ....146 D1
Cooper's Croft CH3 ..142 A7
Cooper's Fold SK8 ....34 F6
Cooper's La CW5 ....91 D1
Cooperative St SK12 ....38 D6
Coopers Opening CW11 ..175 B7
Coopers Pl WA4 ....16 C1
Cop Mdw SK11 ....112 F2
Cope Ave CW5 ....204 D4
Copeland Gr WA7 ....49 E5
Copeland Rd WA4 ....16 B2
Copes La CW5 ....204 C4
Copeswood Cl CH4 ....139 A3
Copgrove Wlk M22 ....33 E7
Copmanford La CW2 ..190 A4
Copmanhall Heys CW7 ..190 A4
Copnall High Sch
  CW1 ....190 E5
Copnall La CW2 ....189 D4
Copper Beech Cl CH4 ..139 C3
Copper St SK11 ....112 E6
Copper Wood CW8 ....101 E5
Copperfield Cl WA3 ....9 D3
Copperfield Rd
  Cheadle Hulme SK8 ....35 B5
  Poynton SK12 ....36 D2
Copperfields
  Poynton SK12 ....36 D2
  Tarporley CW6 ....146 D2
  Wilmslow SK9 ....59 E8
Coppermill Rd CW12 ..179 B7
Coppermine La SY14 ..184 B2
Copperwood WA7 ....24 C1
Coppice Ave SK12 ....38 A8
Coppice Cl High Lane SK12 ..38 A6
  Runcorn WA7 ....49 D8
  Willaston CW5 ....205 D6
Coppice Dr Cw10 ....151 E6
Coppice Gn Elton CW2 ..72 A8
  Warrington WA5 ....7 A1
Coppice Gr WA16 ....57 A3
Coppice Ho Poynton SK12 ..36 D2
  Talke ST7 ....210 C8
Coppice La SK12 ....38 A5
Coppice Rd
  Haslington CW11 ....192 A8
  Poynton SK12 ....37 B3
  Talke ST7 ....210 C8
  Willaston CW5 ....205 D6
Coppice Rise SK11 ....112 F2
Coppice The
  Altrincham WA15 ....32 D7
  Bramhall SK7 ....35 E6
  Cuddington CW8 ....101 D5
  Nantwich CW5 ....204 F3
  Sandbach CW11 ....174 E7
  Whaley Bridge SK23 ....65 F5
  Wincham CW9 ....79 C3
Coppice Way SK9 ....34 D1
Coppicemere Dr CW1 ..191 A2
Coppins Cl Chester CH3 ..119 E4
  Helsby WA6 ....73 B4
Coppins The
  Warrington WA2 ....8 C2
  Wilmslow SK9 ....59 E4
Copse The
  Altrincham WA15 ....32 D7
  High Lane SK6 ....37 E8
  Newton-le-W WA12 ....2 B4
  Warrington WA4 ....25 F7
Copse View CW1 ....191 A2
Copthorne Cl CW12 ..156 F2
Copthorne Dr CW3 ....229 F3
Copyhold CW8 ....102 D8

Corbet Ave WA2 ....16 B8
Corbet Dr TF9 ....235 A4
Corbet St WA2 ....16 B8
Corfe Way CW7 ....149 C7
Coriander Cl CW10 ..128 C3
Corks La SK12 ....38 E5
Cormorant Cl CW1 ..190 F4
Cormorant Dr WA7 ....22 E2
Cornbrook Rd SK11 ....112 C4
Corner Croft SK9 ....60 A4
Cornerhouse La WA8 ....12 D3
Corners The CW8 ....102 E7
Cornfield Cl
  Ellesmere Port CH66 ....69 F1
  Macclesfield SK10 ....87 C3
Cornforth Way WA8 ....12 F3
Cornhill Cl ST5 ....210 D1
Cornish Cl CW12 ....33 D8
Cornishway Ind Est M22 ..33 D8
Cornishway Ind Est M22 ..33 D8
Cornubia Rd WA8 ....23 D7
Cornwall Ave WA7 ....23 A2
Cornwall Cl
  3 Congleton CW12 ..157 A1
  High Lane SK6 ....37 E7
  Macclesfield SK10 ....86 E1
  Runcorn WA7 ....50 C5
Cornwall Gr CW1 ....190 B5
Cornwall Rd Chester CH2 ..118 F7
  Heald Green SK8 ....34 B8
  Irlam M44 ....11 D5
Cornwall St
  Chester CH1 ....237 B4
  Warrington WA1 ....16 E7
Cornwell Cl SK9 ....60 D8
Coronation Ave
  Alsager ST7 ....193 A3
  Glazebury WA3 ....5 C7
  Warrington WA3 ....17 C2
  Winsford CW7 ....126 E1
Coronation Bldgs SK10 ..88 A8
Coronation Cres
  Crewe CW1 ....190 E6
  Glazebury ST7 ....194 E1
  Sandbach CW11 ....175 A5
Coronation Dr
  Frodsham WA6 ....49 D1
  Haydock WA11 ....2 A7
  Newton-le-W WA12 ....2 E1
  Widnes WA8 ....22 C8
Coronation Gr CW8 ....78 A4
Coronation Ho WA7 ....49 C8
Coronation Rd
  Broughton CH4 ....139 B3
  Congleton CW12 ....156 F3
  Ellesmere Port CH65 ....70 C4
  Middlewich CW10 ....151 D6
  Runcorn, Higher Runcorn
  WA7 ....23 B1
  Runcorn, Preston Brook
  WA7 ....50 F6
Coronation Sq 18 WA16 ..57 A2
Coronation St
  Chester CH4 ....140 F7
  Crewe CW1 ....190 D5
  Macclesfield SK11 ....112 D6
Coronation Terr CW6 ..146 D1
Coroner's La WA8 ....13 A4
Coronet Ave CW9 ....103 F3
Coronet Way WA8 ....22 B8
Correction Brow SK12 ..37 C6
Corridor Rd CH65 ....71 B6
Corwen Cl WA5 ....7 E1
Cossack Ave WA2 ....8 C1
Cote Lea Ct WA7 ....49 F6
Cotebrook Dr CH2 ....118 E7
Cotebrook Rd CW9 ....104 C8
Cotes Pl CH1 ....117 E3
Cotgreaves Cl CH4 ....141 B5
Cotswold Ave WA3 ....3 D6
Cotswold Cl Chester CH2 ..118 F6
  Cuddington CW8 ....102 A2
  Macclesfield SK10 ....86 E1
Cotswold Gr 17 CH3 ..119 A1
Cotswold Pl WA2 ....8 A3
Cotswold Rd WA2 ....8 B3
Cotswold Way CW7 ....149 B7
Cottage Cl Bebington CH63 ..43 C7
  Neston CH64 ....66 F7
  Rudheath CW9 ....104 C7
Cottage Dr E CH60 ....40 F5
Cottage Dr W CH60 ....40 F5
Cottage Gr SK9 ....59 F5
Cottage La Heswall CH60 ..40 F5
  Macclesfield SK10 ....112 F7
Cottage Lawns SK9 ....60 B2
Cottage St SK11 ....112 B8
Cottages The
  Lawton Heath End ST7 ..193 D6
  Sproston Green CW4 ..129 C2
Cottam Dr WA2 ....9 A3
Cotterdale Cl WA5 ....14 F7
Cotterill WA7 ....49 D8
Cotterill Dr WA1 ....17 E7
Cotterill St CW2 ....190 D2
Cottesmore Cl CW7 ....149 C7
Cottesmore Gdns WA15 ..32 C8
Cotton La
  Christleton CH3 ....120 D2
  Runcorn WA7 ....49 D8
  Sandbach CW11 ....175 A3
Cotton Trees CW3 ....230 A4
Cottons Bridge WA4 ....26 F5
Cottonwood Gr CW7 ....195 E4
Cottrell Rd WA15 ....32 D7

Coulton Rd WA8 ....13 F3
Council Hos Audlem CW3 .229 E2
Congleton CW12 ......156 F4
Newhall CW5 ....228 B8
Council Houses CW5 .216 B6
Countess Ave SK8 ......34 E5
Countess Cl 🔟 SK11 ...111 F7
Countess Ct 🔟 118 B5
Countess of Chester Health
Pk CH2 ....118 B6
Countess of Chester Hospl
CH2 ....118 B6
Countess Rd SK11 .....111 F7
Countess Way CW2 ...118 C5
Counting House Rd SK12 .38 E5
County Terr WA16 ......56 F1
Courier Row SK10 ......87 F7
Court 2 SK10 ....87 F1
Court Ho The 🔟 CH65 ..70 C6
Court No 4 🔟 SK10 ...112 C8
Court The CH64 ....66 F6
Courtney Gn SK9 ......34 D2
Courtney Rd CH4 ......140 E5
Courtyard The
Bostock Green CW10 ...127 D5
Congleton CW12 ......156 B3
Cuddington CW8 ......101 E2
Haughton CW6 ....186 F4
Newton-le-W WA12 ......2 F4
Smallwood CW11 ....177 A7
🔟 Warrington WA1 ....16 B5
Weaverham CW8 ......102 A8
Willaston CH64 ....67 F8
Cousens Way CH1 .....118 B8
Covell Rd SK12 ....36 D5
Coventry Ave CH66 ....94 E8
Coverdale Cl WA5 ......14 F7
Coverdale Fold CW11 .174 D5
Covert Cl CW7 ....149 B8
Covert Gdns ST7 .....210 D8
Covert Rise CH3 ......166 A2
Covington Pl SK9 ......60 B6
Cow Hey La WA7 ......49 A5
Cow La Ashley WA15 ...31 F6
Bollington SK10 ....88 B7
Hargrave CH3 ....144 A2
Macclesfield SK11 ....112 D6
Norley WA6 ....101 A5
Rainow SK10 ....88 D4
Wilmslow SK9 ....60 C7
Winsford CW7 ....149 E8
Cowanway WA8 ....12 F5
Cowbrook La SK11 ....135 B6
Cowdell St WA2 ......16 B7
Cowfields CW5 ....204 E6
Cowhey Cl CH4 ....141 B5
Cowley Way CW1 .....190 E1
Cowper Cl CW2 ....206 A8
Cowthorne Dr CH3 ....143 A4
Crab La WA2 ....9 B3
Crab Tree Cl L24 ......21 E2
Crabmill Dr CW11 ....174 E7
Crabmill La Norley WA6 .100 E6
Warmingham CW11 ....173 E7
Crabtree Ave
Altrincham WA15 ......32 D7
Disley SK12 ....38 E5
Crabtree Cl WA12 ......2 E3
Crabtree Ct SK12 ......38 D6
Crabtree Fold WA7 .....50 C8
Crabtree Gr CW1 .....190 E6
Crabtree Green Ct .101 C2
Crabtree Green Pk
CW8 ....124 C8
Crabtree La WA13 .....29 A7
Crabwall Pl CH1 ......117 F5
Crackley Bank SK15 ..210 E1
Crackley Bank Prim Sch
ST5 ....210 E1
Craddock Ct SY14 ....213 B3
Cradley WA8 ....12 C2
Cragside Way SK9 .....60 C6
Craig Cl SK11 ....112 B5
Craig Dr SK23 ....65 E6
Craig Gdns CH66 ......69 E7
Craig Rd Congleton CW12 .156 F4
Macclesfield SK11 ....112 B5
Craig Wlk ST7 ....193 F2
Craigleigh Gr CH62 ....43 F4
Craigside ST8 ....179 C1
Craithie Rd CH3 ......119 A2
Crampton Dr WA15 ....32 C8
Cranage Cl WA7 ......50 C6
Cranage Ct 🔟 CW12 ..156 F3
Cranage La CW9 ......79 D1
Cranage Rd CW7 .....190 A3
Cranage Way 🔟 SK9 ..34 D5
Cranberry Dr ST5 ....210 D1
Cranberry La Arclid ST7 .193 A3
Cranberry Jun Sch ST7 .193 A3
Cranberry La ST7 ....193 A3
Cranberry Moss La ST7 .193 A3
Cranberry Rd M31 .....11 F3
Cranbrone Ave WA4 ....16 B1
Cranborne Rd CW1 ...190 D6
Crane Ho CH1 ....118 B1
Cranebrook Cl CW1 ...190 A8
Cranfield Dr ST7 ....193 A3
Cranford Ave
Knutsford WA16 ....56 F1
Macclesfield SK11 ....112 F7
Cranford Cl CH4 ......141 A5
Warrington WA1 ....17 E8
Cranford Mews ST7 ..193 A3
Cranford Rd SK9 ......34 A1
Cranford Sq WA16 .....56 F1
Cranham Ave WA3 .....3 E7
Cranleigh Cl WA4 ......26 B7
Cranleigh Cres CH1 ..118 B4
Cranleigh Dr SK7 ......37 A8
Cranmere Cl CW9 .....104 A4
Cranshaw La WA8 .....13 B6
Cransley Sch CW9 .....53 E1
Cranswick Gn CH66 ....69 C5
Crantock Dr SK8 ......34 C8
Cranwell Ave WA3 ......4 F4
Craudford Rd CW12 ...157 A8
Craven Ave WA3 ....3 E7
Craven Ct WA2 ....7 F4
Crawford Ave WA8 ....12 B1
Crawford Pl WA7 ......49 B6
Crawford's Wlk CH2 ..118 F3
Crawley Ave WA2 ......8 A3
Crayford Ave CW12 ...157 A5
Cresanne Cl CW10 ....151 C7
Crescent Dr Helsby WA6 .73 B3
Whaley Bridge SK23 ...39 D2
Crescent Rd
Alderley Edge SK9 .....60 B2
Congleton CW12 ......156 C2
Cranage CW4 ....129 F6
Ellesmere Port CH65 ...70 D6
Rostherne WA16 ......30 B3
Crescent The
Chester CH2 ....118 C4
Congleton CW12 ......156 C2
Ellesmere Port CH65 ...70 D5
Hartford CW8 ....103 A5
Heswall,Gayton CH60 ...41 B6
Lymm WA13 ....18 F2
Macclesfield SK11 .....87 E1
Middlewich CW10 ....128 B1
Mottram St Andrew SK10 .61 A1
Nantwich CW5 ....204 F6
New Mills SK22 ....39 C8
Northwich CW9 ....103 F6
Rostherne WA16 ......30 B3
Utkinton CW6 ....146 B7
Weaverham CW8 ......77 E1
Cressbrook Rd 🔟 WA4 ..16 C1
Cressington Gdns 🔟
CH65 ....70 C6
Cresswell Ave
New Mills SK22 ....39 C8
Newcastle-u-Lyme ST5 .210 D1
Cresswell St 🔟 7 D2
Cresswell St SK22 .....39 C8
Cresswellshawe Rd ST7 .193 D4
Cresta Dr WA7 ....48 F6
Crestwood Cl CW2 ...206 B7
Crew Ave SK10 ....87 E1
Crewe Bsns Pk CW1 ..190 F2
Crewe Gates Farm Ind Est
CW1 ....190 E2
Crewe Gates Ind Est
CW1 ....207 A8
Crewe Green Ave CW1 .191 B4
Crewe Green Rd CW1 .191 A3
Crewe Hall Ent Pk CW1 .207 D8
Crewe Hill La CH3 ....197 A6
Crewe La CH3 ....180 F1
Crewe La S CH3 ......197 A7
Crewe Rd Alsager ST7 .193 B3
Alsager ST7 ....193 F4
Crewe CW1 ....190 F2
Haslington CW1,CW11 .191 D5
Hatherton CW5 ......219 F3
Nantwich CW2,CW5 ...205 D6
Sandbach CW11 ......175 A4
Shavington CW2 .....206 A4
Crewe St Chester CH1 ..237 C3
Crewe CW1 ....190 D4
Crewe Sta CW1 ......190 E2
Crewood Common Rd
CW8 ....76 A3
Crib La CW6 ....168 A8
Criccieth Ct CW7 .....70 D2
Criftin Cl CH66 ....69 C2
Crimes La CH3,CW6 ..167 D4
Crisham Ave CW5 ....218 E8
Crispin Rd M22 ....33 E8
Critchley Rd L24 .....21 A3
Croasdale Dr WA7 .....49 E5
Crocus Gdns WA9 ......6 A7
Crocus St CW8 ....78 B3
Croesmere Dr CH66 ....69 D2
Croft Cl Altrincham WA15 .32 C6
Congleton CW12 ......156 F2
Utkinton CW6 ....146 B7
Waverton CH3 ....143 A5
Croft Cotts
Dunham-on-t-H WA6 ...97 C6
Ellesmere Port CH66 ...69 A8
Croft Ct CH65 ....70 E3
Croft Gdns WA4 ......27 A7
Croft Heath Gdns WA3 ..9 A8
Croft Ho WA3 ....9 A7
Croft La Dodleston CH4 .162 A7
Knutsford WA16 ....82 B8
Croft Prim Sch WA3 ....9 A8
Croft Rd SK9 ....59 E4
Croft St Golborne WA3 ...3 A8
Widnes WA8 ....23 A6
Croft The Chester CH2 .118 D5
Norton in Hales TF9 ..236 B3
Runcorn WA7 ....23 F1
Croften Dr CH64 ......66 E5
Crofters Cl
🔟 Ellesmere Port CH66 .69 F7
Pickmere WA16 ....80 A7
Wistaston CW2 ......206 B8
Crofters Ct
Holmes Chapel CW4 ..130 C3
Newcastle-u-Lyme ST5 .210 D3
Crofters Gn SK9 ......59 F6
Crofters Heath CH66 ...69 E1
Crofters Lea CW8 ....103 D7
Crofters Pk CH5 ......116 A3
Crofters Way CH1 ....116 F8
Crofton Cl WA4 ....27 C5
Crofton Gdns WA3 ...100 B8
Crofton Gdns WA3 .....4 E3
Crofton Rd WA7 ....22 E1
Crofts The CH3 ......180 F1
Croftside WA1 ....17 F7
Croftside Way SK9 ....60 C6
Croftsway CH60 ......40 D8
Croftwood Cl 🔟 CW7 .149 A8
Crofton Way WA3 .....14 B5
Cromdale Way WA5 ....14 E6
Cromer Dr CW1 ......190 B8
Cromford Ct SK23 .....65 E6
Cromford Mews SK23 ..65 E5
Cromley Rd SK6 ....37 E6
Crompton Dr WA2 ......8 A6
Crompton Rd SK11 ...112 C7
Cromwell Ave WA5 ....15 D6
Cromwell Ave S WA5 ..15 D4
Cromwell Cl WA12 .....2 A4
Cromwell Ct Irlam M44 ..11 E7
🔟 Nantwich CW5 ....204 E5
🔟 Warrington WA1 ...16 A5
Cromwell Dr CW2 ....206 C4
Cromwell Rd
Bramhall SK7 ....35 D6
Ellesmere Port CH65 ...70 D5
Irlam M44 ....11 E7
Northwich CW8 ......103 E8
Cromwell St WA8 .....23 A6
Cronkinson Ave CW5 ..204 F4
Cronkinson Oak CW5 .204 F4
Cronton CE Prim Sch
WA8 ....12 C6
Cronton Farm Ct WA8 .12 C6
Cronton La Cronton L35 ..12 B8
Widnes WA8 ....12 F5
Cronton Park Ave WA8 .12 C6
Cronton Park Cl WA8 ..12 C6
Cronulla Dr WA5 ......14 C7
Crook La CW7 ....127 A2
Crook St CH1 ....237 A2
Crooked La CH3,CW6 ..145 C4
Crookedyard Rd SK11 .113 E7
Crookenden Cl CH2 ...95 C1
Crookenden Rd CH2 ...95 C1
Croppers Rd WA2 ......8 F3
Crosby Ave WA5 ....16 A8
Crosby Gr CH64 ......43 B1
Crosfield St WA1 .....16 B5
Cross Farm WA2 ....9 A2
Cross Gn CH2 ....118 E6
Cross Hey CH4 ......237 C1
Cross La Audley ST7 .209 E5
Church Minshull CW1,CW5 .172 C6
Congleton CW12 .....157 A1
Croft WA3 ....9 D7
Frodsham WA6 ....73 B8
Haslington CW1 .....191 F8
Middlewich CW10 ....151 D6
Neston CH64 ....66 E5
Newton-le-W WA12 .....2 B4
Sandbach CW11 ......175 D5
Smallwood CW11 .....176 F5
Swettenham CW12 ....131 A4
Warrington WA4 ....17 A3
Wilmslow SK9 ....60 F8
Cross La E M31 ....11 F3
Cross La W M31 ....11 F2
Cross Lane S WA3 .....9 E4
Cross Lanes Tarvin CH3 .121 E2
Tarvin, Old Moss CH3 ..144 C8
Cross o' th' Hill Rd
SY14 ....214 A4
Cross Rd Haslington CW1 .191 D4
Heald Green SK8 ......34 B7
Cross St Alsager ST7 .193 C3
Barnton CW8 ....78 B3
Chester CH2 ....118 F2
Congleton CW12 .....156 D3
Crewe CW1 ....190 D3
Golborne WA3 ....3 A8
Haslington CW1 .....191 D4
Holt LL13 ....196 E8
Macclesfield SK11 ....112 E6
Marston CW9 ....79 C3
Neston CH64 ....66 E8
Sandbach CW11 ......175 B6
Warrington WA2 ....16 B7
Widnes WA8 ....13 C1
Cross The Holt LL13 ..196 E8
Kingsley WA6 ....75 C2
Lymm WA13 ....18 E3
🔟 Neston CH64 ......66 E8
Cross Wood St 🔟 CW5 .204 D5
Crossall St SK11 .....112 C7
Crossdale Rd CH62 ....43 D5
Crossfield Ave
Culcheth WA3 ....4 F2
Lymm WA13 ....18 F2
Winsford CW7 ....149 D7
Crossfield Rd
Bollington SK10 ......87 E6
Handforth SK9 ....34 D4
Crossfields CH3 .....121 B2
Crossgates WA8 ....13 F3
Crossings The WA12 ....2 C1
Crosskeys Cl CW6 ....145 A6
Crossland Terr WA6 ...73 B2
Crosslands
Congleton CW12 .....157 A1
Haslington CW1 .....191 D4
Crossledge CW12 ....156 B3
Crossley Ave CH66 ....69 E6
Crossley Cres CH2 ...119 B5
Crossley Dr CH60 .....40 B8
Crossley Pk WA6 ......99 C7
Crossley St WA1 ......16 C5
Crossway Bramhall SK7 .35 E5
Crewe CW1 ....190 D6
Widnes WA8 ....22 D8
Crossway The CH63 ...42 C4
Crossways ST8 ......179 E1
Crossways Rd ST7 ...194 A4
Crosthwaite Ave CH62 .43 F4
Croston Cl
Alderley Edge SK9 .....60 C1
Sandbach CW11 ......175 C7
Crotia Ave CW2 ......207 B5
Crouch La CW12 .....157 D4
Crouchley Hall Mews
WA13 ....18 F1
Crouchley La WA13 ...18 F1
Crowan Rd 🔟 WA3 .....9 E3
Crowbrook Rd WA8 ....22 B8
Crow La E WA2 ....2 C4
Crow La W WA12 ......2 A4
Crow Wood La WA8 ....13 D2
Crow Wood Pl WA8 ...13 D2
Crow's Nest Cotts CH3 .166 C6
Crowbrook Gr 🔟 SK9 ..34 D1
Crowder's La CW9 ...105 B4
Crowe Ave WA2 ....8 B2
Crowland Gdns SK8 ...35 B6
Crowley La CW9,WA16 .28 A3
Crowmere Cl CW8 ...102 A2
Crown Ave WA8 ....22 B8
Crown Bank
🔟 Sandbach CW11 ...175 B6
Talke ST7 ....210 D6
Crown Bldgs WA6 .....73 B1
Crown Cotts CW8 ....124 A7
Crown Ct CW5 ....204 E5
Crown Ctr The 🔟 SK11 .112 D7
Crown Fields Cl WA12 ..2 B5
Crown Gate WA7 ......49 F7
Crown Gdns
Newton-le-W WA12 .....2 B4
Talke ST7 ....210 D6
Crown Gn WA13 ....19 B4
Crown La WA16 ......106 D8
Crown Mews CW3 ....229 F4
Crown Park Dr WA12 ...2 B3
Crown St
Newton-le-W WA12 .....2 A3
🔟 Northwich CW8 ...103 F8
🔟 Warrington WA1 ...16 B5
Crown St W SK11 ....112 C7
Crownest La CW9 ....179 F4
Croxton Cotts CW7 ..170 F4
Croxton Gn SY14 ....201 C6
Croxton La CW10 ....128 A4
Croxton Way CW8 ....103 A4
Croyde Cl M22 ....33 F7
Croyde Rd L24 ....21 A3
Crum Hill 🔟 CW9 ....104 A8
Cryers La Elton CW2 ...72 A2
Thornton-le-M CW2 ....96 F8
Cty High Sch Leftwich The
CW9 ....104 A4
Cuckoo Clock Mus* ..
WA16 ....80 F8
Cuckoo La Acton CW5 .203 E8
Neston CH64 ....67 C7
Cuckstoolpit Hill SK10 .112 E8
Cuddington Prim Sch
CW8 ....101 F2
Cuddington Sta CW8 .102 A4
Cuddington Way 🔟 SK9 .34 D5
Cuerdley Gn WA5 .....14 A2
Cuerdley Rd WA5 .....14 C3
Cuerdon Dr WA4 ......17 D1
Culbin Cl WA3 ....10 A6
Culcheth Hall Barns WA3 .4 F4
Culcheth Hall Dr WA3 ..4 F4
Culcheth High Sch WA3 ..5 A3
Culcheth Prim Sch WA3 ..5 A2
Culford Cl WA7 ....24 D1
Culland St CW2 ......190 C2
Cullen Cl CH63 ....43 C4
Cullen Rd WA7 ....23 C4
Cumber Cl SK9 ....59 D4
Cumber Dr SK9 ....59 D4
Cumber La SK9 ....59 D4
Cumberland Ave
Irlam M44 ....11 C5
Nantwich CW5 ....204 F6
Cumberland Cl
Crewe CW1 ....190 D5
Talke ST7 ....210 E2
Cumberland Dr
Altrincham WA14 ......31 B8
Bollington SK10 ......88 B8
Cumberland Gr CH66 ..69 C3
Cumberland Rd
Congleton CW12 .....156 A3
Partington M31 ....11 E2
Cumberland St
🔟 Macclesfield SK10 .112 D8
🔟 Warrington WA4 ...16 C3
Cumbermere Dr CW11 .174 E7
Cumberpark Dr CH64 ..67 A5
Cumbers Dr CH64 .....67 A5
Cumbers La CH64 .....67 A5
Cumbrae Dr 🔟 CH65 ..70 C1
Cumbria Cl 🔟 CH66 ..69 E1
Cou – Dal 251

Cundiff Cl SK11 ......112 E6
Cunliffe Ave WA12 ....2 B4
Cunliffe Cl WA7 ......50 A7
Cunningham Cl WA5 ..14 F5
Cunningham Dr
Bebington CH63 ......43 C7
Heald Green M22 ......34 A8
Runcorn WA7 ....22 E1
Cunningham Ho WA7 ..48 E8
Cunningham Rd WA8 ..22 D8
Cuppin St CH1 ......237 A2
Curlender Way L24 ....21 E2
Curlew Cl Golborne WA3 ..3 D8
Macclesfield SK10 .....87 C5
Winsford CW7 ....149 C5
Curlew Gr WA3 ....9 E3
Curlew Rd ST7 ......195 E1
Currans Rd WA2 ....9 E3
Curzon Ave ST7 .....193 D5
Curzon Cl CH4 ......141 B8
Curzon Dr WA4 ....27 A7
Curzon Gr CW7 .....126 F1
Curzon Mews SK9 .....60 A5
Curzon Pk N CH4 ....141 B7
Curzon Pk S CH4 ....141 B7
Curzon Rd
Heald Green SK8 ......34 B7
Poynton SK12 ....36 E2
Curzon St Chester CH4 .140 F7
🔟 Runcorn WA7 ......22 F1
Cwat Erwain CH4 .....140 E5
Cygnet Cl CH66 ....69 D4
Cygnet Ct WA1 ....16 A3
Cygnet Cl CH1 ....117 D3
Cynthia Ave WA1 .....17 B7
Cynthia Rd WA7 ......23 C5
Cypress Ave
Ellesmere Port CH66 ...69 F1
Widnes WA8 ....13 B2
Cypress Cl WA11 ......1 C2
Cypress Gr WA7 ......49 C7
Cypress Mews CW8 ..102 E7
Cypress Way SK6 .....38 A7
Cyril Bell Cl WA13 ....18 F3
Cyril St WA2 ....16 B7

D
D'Arcy Cotts CH63 ....42 B6
Daffodil Cl WA8 ....13 C4
Daffodil Gdns WA9 ....6 A7
Dagfields Craft & Antiques
Ctr* CW5 ....220 A4
Dagnall Ave WA5 ......7 F2
Dahlia Cl WA9 ....6 A7
Daintry Terr SK10 ...112 E8
Dairy Bank CW2 ....72 B4
Dairy Farm Cl WA13 ..18 F4
Dairy House La SK7,SK8 .35 B4
Dairy House Rd SK7,SK8 .35 B5
Dairy House Small Holdings
SK7 ....35 B4
Dairy House Way CW2 .189 D2
Dairy La CW5 ....188 D6
Dairybrook Gr 🔟 SK9 ..34 E1
Dairyground Rd SK7 ..35 F7
Dairylands Rd ST7 ...193 F4
Daisy Ave WA12 ....2 C2
Daisy Bank CW5 .....204 D5
Daisy Bank Cres CW5 .229 F5
Daisy Bank La CW9 ...78 C3
Daisy Bank Mill Cl WA3 .4 E3
Daisy Bank Rd
Lymm WA13 ....18 C3
Warrington WA5 ....14 F4
Daisy Cl WA16 ....79 F6
Daisy Way SK6 ....37 F7
Daisybank Dr
Congleton CW12 .....156 D4
Sandbach CW11 .....175 C6
Dakota Dr WA5 ....15 C7
Dalby Cl WA3 ....10 B5
Dalby Ct CW9 ....104 E5
Dale Ave Bebington CH62 .43 D8
Bramhall SK7 ....35 F8
Ellesmere Port CH66 ...69 C6
Dale Cl Warrington WA5 .15 B3
Widnes WA8 ....22 A8
Dale Cres CW12 .....156 F2
Dale Ct Heswall CH60 ..40 F8
Middlewich CW10 ....151 D7
Dale Dr Chester CH2 ..118 D8
Ellesmere Port CH65 ...69 F5
Dale Gdns CH65 ......70 B3
Dale Gr Congleton CW12 .156 F2
Irlam M44 ....11 E6
Dale Head Rd SK10 ...86 F4
Dale Hey CH66 ....43 E2
Dale House Fold SK12 .37 A4
Dale La WA3 ....10 A4
Dale Pl CW12 ....156 F2
Dale Rd Bebington CH62 .43 D6
Golborne WA3 ....3 A8
New Mills SK22 ....39 C7
Dale St Chester CH3 ..119 A1
Macclesfield SK10 ...112 E8
Runcorn WA7 ....23 A1
Dale The Neston CH64 ..66 E6
Tiverton CW6 ....168 C6
Warrington WA5 ......14 F5
Dale View Kidsgrove ST7 .195 C5
Newton-le-W WA12 .....2 E4
Dale's Sq CW9 ......103 F6

Dalecroft WA6 ....72 E1
Daleford Manor CW8 ...125 B8
Daleford Manor Cvn Pk CW8 ...125 A8
Dalefords La
Cuddington CW8 ....102 A1
Whitegate CW8 ....125 D7
Dales Green Rd ST7 ...195 C5
Dalesford Cl WN7 ....4 C8
Dalesford Cres SK10 ...111 E8
Daleside CH2 ....118 D8
Dalesway CH60 ....40 E8
Dalewood Cl WA2 ......16 A6
Dalewood Cres CW2 ...72 A3
Dallam Com Prim Sch WA5 ..7 A2
Dallam La WA2 ....16 A7
Dalmahoy Cl CW7 ....126 C2
Dalston Dr SK7 ....35 C5
Dalton Ave
Warrington WA5 ....15 F7
Warrington,Birchwood WA3 ..9 B4
Dalton Bank WA1 ......16 C6
Dalton Cl CH1 ....117 E3
Dalton Ct Runcorn WA7 ..23 E3
Sandbach CW11 ....174 E7
Dalton St Runcorn WA7 ..23 D2
Warrington WA3 ....9 E5
Dalton Way CW10 .....128 D1
Dalwood Cl WA7 ....50 E7
Dam Head La WA3 .....11 A5
Dam La Hollinfare WA3 ..11 A4
Mobberley WA16 ....58 C3
Warrington WA1 ....17 D7
Winwick WA3 ....8 F7
Dame Hollow SK8 ......34 D7
Damery Ct WA7 ....35 E8
Damery Rd SK7 ....35 E8
Damhead La CH64 ......67 E7
Damian Dr WA12 ....2 A5
Dams La WA16 ....106 D5
Damson La WA16 ....58 C3
Damson Wlk M31 ......11 D3
Dan's Rd WA8 ....13 E2
Danby Cl Runcorn WA7 ..49 D6
Warrington WA5 ....15 F7
Dane Bank Ave
Congleton CW12 ......156 E4
Crewe CW2 ....190 A2
Dane Bank Dr SK12 ...38 D6
Dane Bank Rd
Lymm WA13 ....18 E4
Northwich CW9 ......104 B7
Dane Bank Rd E WA13 ..18 E4
Dane Cl Alsager ST7 ..193 A3
Chester CH4 ....140 F5
Sandbach CW11 ......174 E7
Dane Dr Biddulph ST8 ..179 E1
Wilmslow SK9 ....60 D6
Dane Gdns ST7 ....195 C2
Dane Gr CH2 ....119 F8
Dane Hill Cl SK12 .....38 D5
Dane Hill Bsns Ctr CW12 ..156 C3
Dane Pl Crewe CW1 ..190 D6
Winsford CW7 ....127 B1
Dane St Congleton CW12 ..156 C3
Middlewich CW10 ....128 D2
Northwich CW9 ......103 F8
Danefield Ct SK8 ......34 D8
Danefield Rd
Holmes Chapel CW4 ..130 C4
Northwich CW9 ......104 B7
Danes Sq SK11 ....112 D5
Danescroft WA8 ....12 B3
Daneside Bsns Pk CW12 ..156 E4
Daneswell Rd L24 .....21 A2
Daniel Adamson Ave M31 ..11 D3
Daniel Cl WA3 ....10 A4
Daniel Ct M31 ....11 F4
Daniell Way CH3 .....142 A7
Danily Ct SY14 ....213 B3
Dapplehaeth Rd CW2 ..190 A1
Darby Cl CH64 ....66 E4
Darent Rd WA11 ....1 B7
Daresbury Cl
Holmes Chapel CW4 ..130 A3
Wilmslow SK9 ....60 C8
Daresbury St WA4 .....16 F1
Daresbury Expressway
Daresbury WA4 ....25 A3
Runcorn WA7 ....23 C2
Daresbury La WA4 ....25 D2
Daresbury Pk WA4 ....51 A8
Daresbury Prim Sch WA4 ..25 B2
Darian Ave M22 ....33 D8
Dario Gradi Dr CW2 ..190 D1
Dark Ark La CH3,WA6 ..99 B3
Dark La Henbury SK11 ..111 B8
Higher Whitley WA4 ...52 D6
Kingsley WA6 ....75 B1
Marston CW9 ....79 C6
Tattenhall CH3 ....183 E7
Warren SK11 ....111 C3
Whitchurch SY13 ....227 B1
Darkie Mdw CW6 .....185 E8
Darland La LL12 ....162 C1
Darley Ave Crewe CW2 ..190 A3
Warrington WA2 ....8 E3
Darley Cl WA8 ....12 B3
Darley Rd SK7 ....36 F7
Darleydale Dr CH62 ...43 F5

Darlington Ave CW1 ...189 F5
Darlington Cres CH1 ...94 A1
Darlington St 3 WA8 ..23 A7
Darlington St CW10 ..128 C1
Darnaway Cl WA3 .....10 B6
Darnhall Prim Sch CW7 ..149 D6
Darnhall School La CW7 ..149 C6
Dart Cl Alsager ST7 ..193 A4
Biddulph ST8 ....179 D1
Dart Wlk CW7 ....127 B2
Dartnall Cl SK12 ......38 A6
Darwen Gdns WA2 ......8 E1
Darwin Gr SK7 ....35 E6
Darwin Rd CH1 ....117 C4
Darwin St CW8 ....103 E7
Daryl Rd CH60 ....41 A8
Dashwood Cl WA4 ....27 A7
Daten Ave WA3 ....9 E6
Daten Pk WA3 ....9 F6
Dauncey Cl CH2 ....95 C1
Davehall Ave SK9 .....60 A7
Daven Prim Sch CW12 ..156 E2
Daven Rd CW12 ......156 F1
Davenham Ave WA1 ...16 E7
Davenham CE Prim Sch CW9 ..103 F2
Davenham Cres CW7 ..190 A3
Davenham Ct CW9 ....104 A3
Davenham Mdws CW9 ..103 E3
Davenham Rd
Davenham CW9 ......104 E3
Handforth SK9 ....34 D4
Davenham Rdbt CW9 ..103 F3
Davenham Way CW10 ..151 D5
Davenport Ave
Crewe CW2 ....206 D8
Nantwich CW5 ....204 E7
Warrington WA4 ......16 F5
Wilmslow SK9 ....59 E4
Davenport Cl CW11 ..175 D8
Davenport La
Brereton Green CW11 ..154 C2
Marton SK11 ....132 F5
Mobberley WA16 ......58 D6
Davenport Park La CW12 ..131 D2
Davenport Rd CH60 ..40 E7
Davenport Row WA7 ..49 D8
Davenport St
Congleton CW12 .....156 C2
Crewe CW1 ....190 C6
Macclesfield SK10 ...112 E8
Davey La SK9 ....60 A2
Daveylands SK9 ......60 D7
David Lewis Sch SK9 ..83 F6
David St WA8 ....18 C3
David St CW8 ....103 E7
David's Ave WA5 .....15 B5
Davidson Ave CW12 ..157 A5
Davies Ave
Heald Green SK8 .....34 B6
Newton-le-W WA12 ....2 C4
Warrington WA4 ......16 F4
Davies Cl WA8 ....23 A4
Davies St CH65 ......110 E8
Davies Way WA13 ....18 E3
Davis Cl CH7 ....193 E3
Davy Ave WA3 ....9 E2
Davy Rd WA7 ....23 E3
Dawlish Ave SK8 .....34 F7
Dawlish Cl Bramhall SK7 ..35 E7
Hollinfare WA3 ....11 B3
Dawn Cl CH64 ....67 A5
Dawn Gdns CH65 .....70 B4
Dawpool Cl CH2 .....118 D5
Dawpool Ct CH2 .....118 D5
Dawpool Dr CH62 ....43 C7
Dawson Cl 10 SK11 ...111 F7
Dawson Dr CH2 ......237 A4
Dawson Rd
Bollington SK10 ....88 A7
Heald Green SK8 .....34 D8
Macclesfield SK11 ...111 F7
Dawstone Ct CH60 ....40 F8
Dawstone Rd CH60 ...41 A7
Dawstone Rise CH60 ..40 F7
De Lacy Row WA7 ....24 A2
De Trafford Mews 9 SK9 ..34 D2
Deacon Rd WA8 ....13 B1
Deacon Trad Est WA12 ..2 A2
Deacons Cl WA3 ....9 A8
Deadman's La CW5 ..205 B2
Deakin's Rd
Winsford CW7 ....126 F4
Winsford CW7 ....127 A4
Dean Bank CH6 ......168 C3
Dean Cl Bollington SK10 ..88 A7
Handforth SK9 ....34 E4
Partington M31 ....11 F4
Sandbach CW11 .....174 E8
7 Widnes WA8 ....23 B8
Dean Cres WA2 ....8 B2
Dean Ct Bollington SK10 ..88 B8
Handforth SK9 ....3 A7
Dean Dr SK9 ....59 D2
Dean Hollow ST7 ....209 D2
Dean La SK7 ....36 E8
Dean Mdw WA12 ......2 C4
Dean Pk SY14 ....214 A5
Dean Rd Golborne WA3 ..3 A7
Handforth SK9 ....34 E3
Irlam M44 ....11 E6
Dean Row Ct 15 SK9 ..34 D1
Dean Row Jun Sch SK9 ..34 E2
Dean Row Rd SK9 ....61 A8

Dean St
Middlewich CW10 ....128 C1
Northwich CW9 ......104 C8
Widnes WA8 ....23 B8
Winsford CW7 ....126 D1
Dean Valley Com Prim Sch SK10 ..87 E8
Dean View ST7 ....209 D1
Dean's La
Barthomley CW2 .....208 C4
Newcastle-u-Lyme ST5 ..210 D2
Deane Ct CW5 ....205 B4
Deanery Cl CH2 .....118 C4
Deans Cl Chester CH2 ..118 D6
Tarvin CH3 ....121 B1
Deans La Sandbach CW11 ..174 E6
Warrington WA4 ......17 F3
Deans Rd CH65 ....70 F3
Deans Way
Higher Kinnerton CH4 ..161 A7
Tarvin CH3 ....121 B2
Deansfield Way CH2 ..72 A3
Deansgate CH65 ......70 A5
Deansgreen Ct WA13 ..29 A7
Deansway WA8 ....22 C8
Deanwater Cl WA3 .....9 D4
Deanwater Ct SK8 ....34 D7
Deanway SK9 ....34 C1
Deanway Tech Ctr SK9 ..34 D3
Deanway Trad Est SK9 ..34 D3
Dearnford Ave CH62 ..43 D6
Dearnford Cl CH62 ...43 D6
Debra Cl CH66 ....69 C4
Debra Rd CH66 ....69 C4
Decade Cl ST5 ....210 F2
Dee Banks Chester CH3 ..142 A8
Huntington CH3 .....141 F7
Dee Banks Sch CH3 ..142 A7
Dee Cl Biddulph ST8 ..179 E1
Sandbach CW11 .....174 E8
Talke ST7 ....210 E7
Dee Cres CH3 ....180 E2
Dee Fords Ave CH3 ..119 B1
Dee Hills Pk CH3 ....237 C2
Dee La Chester CH1,CH3 ..237 C2
Holt LL13 ....196 D7
Dee Mdws LL13 ......196 D7
Dee Park Cl CH60 ....41 B6
Dee Park Rd CH60 ...41 B5
Dee Pk LL13 ....196 D8
Dee Point Prim Sch CH6 ..117 D3
Dee Rd CH2 ....96 F1
Dee Side CH60 ....40 C8
Dee Sq CW7 ....127 B2
Dee View CH3 ....180 E2
Dee View Cotts CH64 ..41 D1
Dee View Rd CH64 ....66 E6
Dee View Rd
Connah's Quay CH5 ...91 E1
Heswall CH60 ....40 F8
Dee Villas LL13 ......180 E1
Dee Way CW7 ....127 A2
Deefords CH5 ....118 F1
Deep Dale WA5 ......14 F6
Deepdale WA8 ....12 C3
Deer Park Ct WA7 ....49 F6
Deerwood Cl
Ellesmere Port CH66 ..69 D7
Macclesfield SK10 ....86 F1
Deerwood Cres CH66 ..69 D7
Deeside
Ellesmere Port CH65 ..70 B2
Holt LL13 ....196 E8
Deeside Cl CH65 ......70 B2
Deeside Coll/Coleg Glannau Dyfrdwy CH5 ..91 B1
Deeside Cres CH1 ...116 E5
Deeside Ct Chester CH3 ..237 C2
Neston CH64 ....41 B1
Deeside Ind Pk/Parc Ddiwydiannol Glannau Dyfrdwy CH5 ..92 C2
Deeside La CH1 ......116 D4
Deirdre Ave WA8 .....13 A1
Delafield Cl WA2 ....8 F3
Delaisy Way CW7 ....127 A1
Delamere Ave
Bebington CH63 ......43 E4
Ellesmere Port CH66 ..69 E5
Widnes WA8 ....12 C1
Delamere CE Prim Sch CW6 ..123 C5
Delamere Cl Barnton WA8 ..78 A3
Bebington CH62 ......43 E4
Sandbach CW11 .....174 E8
Delamere Ct Alsager ST7 ..192 F4
Bebington CH62 ......43 E4
Delamere Forest Sch WA6 ..100 C4
Delamere Forest Trail* WA6 ..100 A4
Delamere Forest Visitor Ctr* WA6 ..100 C4
Delamere Gr CW8 ....69 E5
Delamere Gr CW8 ...123 D7
Delamere La CH3 .....99 B2
Delamere Park Way E CW8 ..101 D5
Delamere Park Way W CW8 ..101 D5
Delamere Rd
Congleton CW12 .....155 F3
Handforth SK9 ....34 E4

Delamere Rd continued
Nantwich CW5 ....204 F3
Norley WA6 ....100 B6
Delamere Rise CW7 ..126 B1
Delamere St
Chester CH1 ....237 A3
Crewe CW1 ....190 C4
Warrington WA5 ......15 E5
Winsford CW7 ....126 B1
Delamere Sta CW8 ..100 D1
Delamere's Acre CH64 ..68 A8
Delavor Cl CH60 ......40 E8
Delavor Rd CH60 .....40 E8
Delenty Dr WA3 ....9 E4
Delery Dr WA1 ....16 E8
Delfur Rd SK7 ....35 F7
Delhi Rd M44 ....11 F8
Dell Cl CH63 ....43 B6
Dell Dr WA2 ....9 A2
Dell La CH60 ....41 B7
Dell The Ashley WA14 ..31 E8
Cuddington CW8 ....101 D5
Guilden Sutton CH3 ..119 F5
Kelsall CW6 ....122 D5
Whaley Bridge SK23 ..65 F5
Delmar Rd WA16 .....57 C1
Delph La Daresbury WA4 ..25 A2
Warrington,Houghton Gn WA2 ..8 E6
Winwick WA2 ....8 A5
Delphfields Rd WA4 ..26 C7
Delphield WA7 ....50 D8
Delphside ST7 ....209 F2
Delta Cres WA5 ....7 C2
Delta Ct CH4 ....140 B6
Delves Ave WA5 ......15 F7
Delves Broughton Ct CW1 ..191 D5
Delves Cl CW2 ....206 B4
Delves Wlk CH3 .....142 B7
Delvine Dr CH2 ......118 D6
Demage Dr CH66 .....69 D3
Demage La Backford CH1 ..94 F4
Chester CH2 ....118 C8
Demage La S CH2 ..118 D7
Den La CW3,CW5 ....221 D4
Denbigh Cl
Hazel Grove SK7 ......36 C8
Helsby WA6 ....73 A1
Denbigh Cres CW10 ..151 C7
Denbigh Ct CH65 .....70 D3
Denbigh Dr CW7 ....149 B7
Denbigh Gdns CH65 ..79 C3
Denbigh St CH1 ......118 B3
Denbury Ave WA4 ....16 F2
Dene Ave WA12 ....1 F4
Dene Dr CW7 ....149 D8
Denehurst Cl WA5 ...14 F4
Denehurst Park Way CW8 ..101 D5
Denesgate 1 CW7 ..149 D8
Deneside Ave CW1 ..190 C6
Deneway Bramhall SK7 ..35 D7
High Lane SK6 ....37 F8
Denewood Ct 3 SK9 ..60 A6
Denford Cl CH4 ....139 C4
Denford Pl ST7 ......193 D6
Denhall Cl CH2 ......118 E5
Denhall La CH64 ......67 A3
Denham Ave WA5 ....15 B5
Denham Dr SK7 ....35 D7
Denise Ave WA5 ......14 E5
Denison Rd SK7 ......36 E8
Dennett Cl WA1 ....17 E6
Dennis Dr CH4 ......141 B5
Dennis Rd WA8 ....23 C7
Dennison Rd SK8 .....35 B8
Densham Ave WA2 ....8 B2
Denston Cl CW2 ....190 B1
Denstone Dr CH4 ...141 A4
Dentdale Wlk M22 ...33 C8
Dentith Dr CH1 ......117 E5
Denton Cl CW7 ......126 C1
Denton Dr CW9 ....79 C1
Denton Drive Ind Est CW9 ..79 C2
Denton St WA8 ....13 C1
Denver Ave CW2 ....190 B3
Denver Rd WA4 ....17 A3
Denwall Ho 5 CH64 ..66 E8
Depenbech Cl SY14 ..213 B4
Depmore La WA6 .....75 A2
Derby Cl Irlam M44 ..11 C5
Newton-le-W WA12 ....2 B3
Derby Dr WA1 ....16 F7
Derby Knoll SK23 ....39 F1
Derbyshire Rd
Partington M31 ....11 E2
Poynton SK12 ....37 D5
Dereham Way WA7 ...24 D3
Derek Ave WA2 ....8 E1
Derfel Cotts 4 WA6 ..74 B8
Derrington Ave CW2 ..190 C3
Derwent Ave CW7 ...127 B2
Derwent Cl Alsager ST7 ..193 A4
Culcheth WA3 ....5 A2

Derwent Cl continued
Holmes Chapel CW4 ..130 A3
Macclesfield SK11 ...112 A6
Partington M31 ....11 F4
Willaston CW5 ....205 D6
Derwent Cres ST7 ....23 C5
Derwent Dr Biddulph ST8 ..179 E1
Bramhall SK7 ....35 C5
Congleton CW12 ....156 F1
Handforth SK9 ....34 C5
Hooton CH66 ....43 D1
Derwent Rd Chester CH2 ..119 A5
High Lane SK6 ....37 E8
Warrington WA4 ......16 B2
Widnes WA8 ....12 C1
Derwent Way
Neston CH64 ....66 F7
Alderley Edge SK9 ....83 F7
Desoto Rd WA8 ....22 E5
Desoto Rd E WA8 .....22 E5
Desoto Rd W WA8 ....22 F6
Deva CH64 ....140 D6
Deva Bsns Pk CH5 ...116 A8
Deva Cl SK12 ....36 B4
Deva Ct CH2 ....118 F2
Deva Hts CH3 ....141 F7
Deva La CH2 ....118 C6
Deva Link CH1 ....118 A3
Deva Ret Pk CH1 ....189 A4
Deva Roman Experience Mus* CH1 ..237 B2
Deva Stad (Chester City FC) CH1 ..117 E1
Deva Terr CH3 ....237 C2
Devon Cl
Macclesfield SK10 ....86 F2
Middlewich CW10 ...128 D2
Devon Gr ST8 ....179 C1
Devon Pl
Congleton CW12 ....156 E4
Widnes WA8 ....13 B3
Devon Rd Chester CH2 ..118 F3
Irlam M44 ....11 D5
Partington M31 ....11 E2
Devon St CW9 ....60 B2
Devonshire Gdns WA12 ..2 C2
Devonshire Pl CH4 ..141 E7
Devonshire Rd
Broughton CH4 ......139 C4
Hazel Grove SK7 ......36 F8
Warrington WA1 ......16 F8
Dewar Ct WA7 ....23 E3
Dewa St WA5 ....9 E5
Dewes St CW1 ....190 B5
Dewhurst Rd WA3 .....9 D2
Dexter Way CW10 ...128 D2
Dial Cotts CH64 ......67 A5
Dial La CW12,SK11 ..158 B1
Dial Rd WA15 ....32 C8
Dial St WA1 ....16 C5
Diamond Ave 3 ST7 ..195 B2
Dibbins Gn CH63 .....43 A3
Dibbinsdale Rd CH63 ..43 B7
Dickens Cl
Cheadle Hulme SK8 ..35 B5
Sandbach CW11 .....174 D6
Dickens La SK12 ......36 E2
Dickenson St WA1 ...16 C7
Dickinson Cl WA11 ...1 A6
Dickinson Way ST7 ..193 A3
Dicklow Cob SK11 ...132 A8
Dickson Cl WA8 ......23 B8
Dickson St Widnes WA8 ..23 A8
2 Widnes WA8 ....23 A8
Dierden St CW7 ......126 C1
Dierden Terr CW10 ..128 C1
Dig La Acton CW5 ...203 E4
Frodsham WA6 ....74 A7
Shavington CW5 ....206 B2
Warrington WA2 ....9 B3
Diglake Cl ST7 ......210 C6
Diglake Cotts ST7 ..204 E2
Diglake St ST7 ......209 F3
Diglee Rd SK23 ....39 D3
Dillors Croft CW1 ...173 A1
Dimelow Ct SY14 ....213 A2
Dinas Cl CH1 ....117 D3
Dingle Ave
Newton-le-W WA12 ....1 F2
Row-of-trees SK9 .....59 D3
Dingle Bank
Chester CH4 ....141 C7
Sandbach CW11 .....175 C6
Dingle Bank Cl WA13 ..18 E3
Dingle Cl SK10 ....87 B3
Dingle La
Bridgemere CW5 ....231 F6
Kelsall CW6 ....122 C6
Sandbach CW11 .....175 C6
Warrington WA4 ....26 E1
Winsford CW7 ....126 E1
Dingle Prim Sch The CW1 ..191 D6
Dingle The Barnton CW8 ..78 B3
Haslington CW1 .....191 D5
Dingle Way CW8 ....101 E5
Dingle Wlk 4 CW7 ..126 D1
Dinglebrook Gr 5 SK9 ..34 E1
Dingleway WA4 ....26 D1
Dinnington St WA8 ...12 E3
Diploma Dr CW10 ...128 C2
Dipping Brook Ave WA4 ..26 E6
Disley Prim Sch SK12 ..38 D6
Disley Sta SK12 ......38 C6

Distaff Rd SK12 .36 B4
District CE Prim Sch The WA12 .2 A4
Ditchfield La WA16 .29 D3
Ditchfield Pl WA8 .22 B8
Ditchfield Rd
Warrington WA5 .14 E3
Widnes WA8 .22 B8
Ditton CE Prim Sch WA8 .12 A1
Ditton Prim Sch WA8 .12 E1
Ditton Rd WA8 .22 D6
Dixon Ave WA12 .2 C5
Dixon Cl WA11 .2 A8
Dixon Dr SK11 .84 B3
Dixon Rd CW12 .157 A5
Dixon St Irlam M44 .11 F8
Warrington WA1 .16 A5
Dixon's Hos CH3 .142 E8
Dobb Hedge Cl WA15 .32 C6
Dobell's Rd CW9 .103 F6
Dobers La WA6 .74 C4
Dobson Ct SY14 .213 B3
Dock Rd Northwich CW9 .103 F7
Widnes WA8 .22 F5
Dock Road Edwardian Pumping Station The* CW9 .103 F7
Dock St
Ellesmere Port CH65 .70 C7
Widnes WA8 .23 A5
Dock Yard Rd CH65 .70 E6
Dodd's Green La CW5, SY13 .228 C4
Dodd's La SY13,SY14 .224 E7
Doddington Dr CW11 .175 C8
Doddington Rd CW2 .190 A3
Doddlespool Barns CW3 .221 F7
Dodds La CW12 .178 C6
Doddswood Dr 2 CW12 .156 F4
Dodgsley Dr WA6 .75 C1
Dodleston CE Prim Sch CH4 .162 A7
Dodleston La CH4 .162 C3
Doe's Meadow Rd CH63 .43 B7
Doeford Cl WA3 .4 E5
Dog La
Brereton Green CW4, CW11 .153 E7
Kelsall CW6 .122 B5
Nantwich CW5 .204 E6
Tattenhall CH3 .182 D4
Threapwood SY14 .223 C7
Dogmore La CW6 .147 C4
Dolly La SK23 .39 F3
Dolmans La 10 WA1 .16 B5
Dolphin Cres CH66 .69 E2
Dolphin Ct CH4 .141 A7
Dombey Rd SK12 .36 D2
Domestic App M90 .33 C6
Domville Cl WA13 .18 E3
Don Wlk CH65 .70 A7
Donagh Cl SK10 .86 F2
Donkey La SK9 .60 A5
Donne Pl CH1 .117 F6
Donnington Way CH4 .140 F7
Dood's La WA4 .27 A5
Dooley's Grig SK11 .108 F1
Dooley's La SK9 .33 C2
Dorac Ave SK8 .34 C7
Dorchester Cl
Kidsgrove ST7 .195 A3
Wilmslow SK9 .60 D8
Dorchester Pk WA7 .24 E3
Dorchester Rd
Chester CH4 .140 F5
Warrington WA5 .15 C5
Dorchester Way
Burtonwood WA5 .6 F6
Macclesfield SK10 .87 C4
Doreen Ave CW12 .179 B8
Dorfold Cl CW11 .175 C7
Dorfold Dr CW5 .204 D5
Dorfold Hall* CW5 .204 B5
Dorfold St CW1 .190 C4
Dorfold Way CH2 .118 E6
Doric Ave WA6 .74 D7
Dorin Park Sch CH2 .118 D6
Dormer Cl CH3 .143 A5
Dorney Cl WA4 .26 E6
Dornoch Ct CW4 .130 B2
Dorothea St WA2 .16 C7
Dorric Way CW1 .190 C7
Dorrington Cl WA7 .50 E8
Dorrit Cl SK12 .36 E2
Dorset Cl CW12 .156 E4
Dorset Ct WA7 .50 A6
Dorset Dr ST8 .179 C1
Dorset Pl Chester CH2 .119 A5
Kidsgrove ST7 .195 A2
Dorset Rd Chester CH2 .118 F7
Irlam M44 .11 D5
Dorset Way WA1 .17 B8
Dorset Wlk SK10 .86 F2
Douglas Ave WA9 .6 B6
Douglas Cl
Northwich CW8 .103 C5
Widnes WA8 .13 F3
Douglas La CW7 .171 A6
Douglas Pl CH4 .140 E6
Doulton Cl CW7 .126 F3
Doune Ct CH65 .70 D3
Dounrey Cl WA2 .9 A2
Dove Bank Prim Sch ST7 .195 A2
Dove Cl
Ellesmere Port CH66 .70 A8
Elton CH2 .72 C4
Dove Cl *continued*
Helsby WA6 .73 C5
Sandbach CW11 .175 A8
Warrington WA3 .9 F4
Dove Gr ST8 .179 D1
Dove Ho ST7 .195 C3
Dove Pl CW7 .127 B2
Dovecote Cl CW2 .206 B8
Dovecote Dr WA11 .1 C7
Dovecote Gn WA5 .7 A1
Dovedale Ave CH62 .43 E5
Dovedale Cl
Congleton CW12 .157 A4
High Lane SK6 .37 E7
Warrington WA2 .8 E3
Dovedale Ct WA8 .12 B3
Dover Cl WA7 .50 E6
Dover Ct CH65 .70 D2
Dover Dr
Ellesmere Port CH65 .70 D2
Winsford CW7 .149 B6
Dover Rd Chester CH4 .141 A6
Macclesfield SK10 .87 F2
Warrington WA4 .17 A3
Dover St WA7 .23 B3
Dovesmead Rd CH60 .41 C7
Doward St WA8 .13 C2
Downes Cl SK10 .87 A1
Downesway SK9 .59 F1
Downham Ave WA3 .4 F2
Downham Ct 1 CH60 .41 A8
Downham Dr CH60 .41 A8
Downham Pl CH1 .117 E4
Downham Road S CH60 .41 A8
Downing Cl SK11 .112 F3
Downs End WA16 .57 C1
Downs Rd WA7 .23 A1
Downs The CW8 .101 D5
Downsfield Rd CH4 .141 A6
Downside WA8 .12 B3
Downswood Ct CH2 .118 C4
Downswood Dr CH2 .118 C4
Downway La WA9 .1 A1
Dragon Yd WA8 .13 B4
Dragon's La
Middlewich CW11 .151 F1
Sandbach CW11 .152 B1
Dragons Wharf CW11 .152 C1
Drake Ave M44 .11 E6
Drake Cl WA5 .7 D1
Drake La CW5 .203 F4
Drake Rd CH64 .41 E1
Drakelow La CW10 .128 F8
Drakes Way SY14 .213 B5
Draxford Ct SK9 .60 B6
Draycott Dr ST5 .210 D2
Drayton Cl Runcorn WA7 .22 F1
13 Handforth SK9 .34 D1
Drayton Cres CW1 .190 F5
Drayton Dr SK8 .34 B7
Drenfell Rd ST7 .194 F7
Drill Field Rd CW9 .103 F8
Drillfield Ct 20 CW9 .103 F8
Drillfield Rd CW9 .104 A8
Drive A CH5 .93 A2
Drive B CH5 .93 A2
Drive C CH5 .93 A2
Drive D CH5 .93 A1
Drive The
Altrincham WA15 .32 D8
Bollington SK10 .87 F7
Broomedge WA13 .19 D1
Holmes Chapel CW4 .130 C2
Drome Rd CH5 .93 A2
Drovers Way CW11 .175 A5
Drumber La ST7 .195 B8
Drumber The CW7 .126 D1
Drumble Field SK11 .84 A3
Drummond Ave CH66 .69 C4
Drummond Ct WA8 .13 D2
Drummond Way SK10 .86 E1
Druridge Dr WA5 .14 F4
Drury Cl CW1 .190 F5
Drury La Knutsford WA16 .57 A2
Warmingham CW1 .173 D4
Dryden Cl CW2 .190 A1
Dryden Pl WA2 .8 C2
Dryersfield 5 CH3 .142 A8
Dryhurst Dr SK12 .38 D6
Dryhurst La SK12 .38 D6
Dublin Croft CH66 .69 E1
Duchess Pl CH2 .237 A4
Duchy Rd CW1 .207 A8
Duck La CH3 .121 F7
Duckworth Gr WA2 .9 A1
Duddon Cl Duddon CW6 .145 B6
3 Northwich CW9 .103 F4
Duddon Hook La CW6 .144 F6
Duddon Rd CW6 .145 B5
Duddon St Peter's CE Prim Sch CW6 .145 B6
Dudleston Rd CH66 .69 B6
Dudley Ave WA7 .23 D2
Dudley Cres CH65 .44 B3
Dudley Rd
Ellesmere Port CH65 .70 B5
Irlam M44 .11 D4
Dudley St WA2 .16 B7
Dudley Wlk 2 SK11 .111 F7
Dudlow Green Rd WA4 .26 E5
Dufton Wlk M22 .33 E8
Duke Ave
Cheadle Hulme SK8 .34 F6
Glazebury WA3 .5 C7
Duke Cl WA7 .22 F2
Duke St Alderley Edge SK9 .60 B2
Chester CH1 .237 B1
Congleton CW12 .156 D2
Duke St *continued*
Crewe CW2 .190 C3
Macclesfield SK11 .112 D7
Newton-le-W WA12 .2 B3
Duke's Cres CW11 .175 A7
Duke's Ct CH1 .237 B1
Dukes Ct 2 SK11 .112 D7
Dukes Way CW9 .103 E5
Dukes Wharf WA7 .50 E6
Dukesway CH2 .118 E7
Dulas Ct CH2 .118 E8
Dulverton Ave CH3 .119 C2
Dumbah La SK10 .87 D6
Dumbers SK11 .136 A2
Dumbill Ho ST7 .210 C8
Dunbar Cl
Connah's Quay CH5 .91 D1
Ellesmere Port CH66 .69 C5
Holmes Chapel CW4 .130 C2
Dunbar Ct CH66 .69 C5
Duncan Ave
Newton-le-W WA12 .2 C5
Runcorn WA7 .23 C1
Duncan St WA2 .16 C7
Duncansby Cres WA5 .14 E6
Duncansby Dr CH63 .43 C4
Dundalk Rd WA8 .22 E8
Dundee Cl WA2 .8 F4
Dundee Ct CH65 .70 E3
Dundonald Ave 5 WA4 .16 C1
Dundonald Rd SK8 .35 A7
Dundrennan Cl SK12 .36 D5
Dunge Valley Gdns* SK23 .89 F8
Dunham Cl Alsager ST7 .193 C3
Bebington CH62 .43 F3
Sandbach CW11 .175 C6
Dunham Cres CW2 .206 B8
Dunham Ct WA6 .97 E6
Dunham Hill Prim Sch WA6 .97 E6
Dunham Ho WA14 .20 F3
Dunham Massey Hall* WA14 .20 D3
Dunham Pk* WA14 .20 D3
Dunham Rd
Altrincham,Bowgreen WA14 .20 F1
Handforth SK9 .34 D5
Mossbrow WA13 .19 E7
Northwich CW9 .104 A4
Dunham Way CH2 .118 F6
Dunkirk ST7 .210 A6
Dunkirk Ave CW7 .149 D8
Dunkirk Dr CH65 .70 B1
Dunkirk La
Capenhurst CH1 .94 C7
Ellesmere Port CH65 .70 A1
Dunkirk Trad Est CH1 .94 D6
Dunley Cl WA3 .10 A5
Dunlin Ave WA12 .2 C4
Dunlin Cl Poynton SK12 .36 A4
Runcorn WA7 .49 F5
Warrington WA2 .8 E3
Dunlin Rise SK10 .87 B5
Dunlop St WA4 .16 B3
Dunmore Cl CW10 .151 C7
Dunmore Cres CH66 .69 B6
Dunmore Rd CH66 .69 B6
Dunmow Rd WA4 .17 C3
Dunn's Cotts CW1 .192 C1
Dunn's La CH3 .121 F7
Dunnillow Field CW5 .205 A4
Dunnock Cl WA2 .8 E3
Dunnock Gr WA3 .9 E4
Dunnocksfold Rd ST7 .193 A4
Dunnockswood ST7 .193 A4
Dunoon Cl CW4 .130 B2
Dunraven Rd CH64 .67 A7
Dunscar Cl WA3 .9 D5
Dunsford WA8 .12 B3
Dunsmore Cl WA11 .1 C7
Dunstan La CH64 .67 E3
Dunster Cl CW9 .104 A4
Dunster Gr CH60 .41 B7
Dunster Rd SK10 .87 F1
Dunwood Dr ST7 .193 D6
Dunwoody Way CW1, CW2 .190 B4
Durban Ave CH3 .142 D7
Durber Cl ST7 .209 D1
Durham Cl
Macclesfield SK10 .86 F2
Warrington WA1 .17 E7
Durham Ct CH65 .70 E3
Durham Dr CW7 .149 C6
Durham Gr M44 .11 C6
Durham Rd Blacon CH1 .117 F5
Widnes WA8 .13 B3
Durlston Cl WA8 .12 C2
Durrell Way WA3 .3 E8
Dutton Gn CH2 .70 F3
Dutton Hall Ct WA4 .76 E8
Dutton La CW8,WA6 .101 B6
Dutton Way Crewe CW1 .190 B6
Nantwich CW5 .204 E3
Dutton's La CW6 .122 C5
Duttons Bsns Ctr CW9 .103 F7
Duxford Ct WA2 .8 E1
Dyar Terr CW8 .78 D1
Dye House La SK22 .39 C8
Dyers Cl WA13 .19 A4
Dyers Ct SK10 .88 B8
Dyers La WA13 .19 A4
Dykin Cl WA8 .13 E3
Dykin Rd WA8 .13 E3
Dysart Bldgs CW5 .204 E5
Dyserth Rd CH1 .117 D3
Dystelegh Rd SK12 .38 D6

E

Eadie Gr CW1 .190 A7
Eaglais Way SK10 .86 F2
Eagland Pl CW12 .156 E4
Eagle Brow WA13 .18 D3
Eagle La CH66 .69 D7
Eagle Mount WA4 .16 C2
Eagle Park Dr WA2 .8 A1
Eagles Way WA7 .49 E6
Eaglesfield CW8 .103 C4
Ealing Cl WA7 .24 D1
Ealing Rd WA5 .15 B5
Eanleywood La WA7 .50 C7
Eardley Cres CW12 .156 E4
Eardley Ct CW1 .190 B5
Eardleyend Rd ST7 .209 E7
Eardswick Cl CH2 .237 B4
Eardswick La CW1 .172 D5
Eardswick Rd CW10 .151 C6
Earl Rd SK8,SK9 .34 E5
Earl St WA2 .16 B7
Earl's Port CH1 .118 B2
Earl's Villas CH1 .237 C3
Earle Cl WA12 .1 F3
Earle Cres CH64 .41 D1
Earle Dr CH64 .41 D1
Earle Rd WA8 .23 C7
Earle St Crewe CW1 .190 D4
Newton-le-W WA12 .2 A3
Earle's La CW6 .122 C5
Earles La CW9 .79 E6
Earlestown Sta WA12 .2 B3
Earls Gdns CH65 .70 B5
Earls Oak CH2 .118 D7
Earls Rd CW2 .206 B4
Earls Way
Northwich CW9 .103 E4
Runcorn WA7 .49 E6
Earlston Ct CH3 .237 C2
Earlsway Chester CH4 .141 A8
Macclesfield SK11 .111 F7
Earlswood Mews CW9 .103 F3
Easby Cl
Cheadle Hulme SK8 .35 B6
Poynton SK12 .36 D4
Runcorn WA7 .23 C2
Easenhall Cl WA8 .13 C5
East Ave Bollington SK10 .87 F7
Heald Green SK8 .34 D8
Northwich CW9 .104 D6
Warrington WA2 .16 C8
Warrington, Stockton Heath WA4 .16 D1
Warrington,Great Sankey WA5 .15 A4
Weston CW2 .207 C5
East Ct ST7 .193 E4
East Dam Wood Rd L24 .21 A2
East Dudley St CW7 .126 F1
East Gn CH5 .116 A6
East La Cuddington CW8 .102 A3
Runcorn WA7 .49 F7
East Lancashire Rd WA11, WA12,WA3 .2 C7
East Mains L24 .21 A3
East Millwood Rd L24 .21 A4
East Park Rd SK11 .112 B5
East Rd Halewood L24,L26 .21 A5
Middlewich CW10 .128 B1
Woodhouse Park M90 .33 C7
East St WA8 .13 D1
East Terr WA16 .56 F1
East View
10 Nantwich CW5 .204 E6
Warrington WA4 .17 B2
Eastbury Cl WA8 .13 C5
Eastcott Cl CW12 .155 F4
Eastdale WA15 .31 F8
Eastdale Rd WA1 .17 A7
Easter Ct WA5 .7 B2
Eastern Pathway CH4 .237 C1
Eastern Rd CW5 .205 F5
Eastfields Gr CH1 .117 A8
Eastford Rd WA4 .16 A1
Eastgate SK10 .112 E8
Eastgate Rd
Holmes Chapel CW4 .130 D3
Runcorn WA7 .24 E5
Eastgate Row N CH1 .237 B2
Eastgate Row S CH1 .237 B2
Eastgate St CH1 .237 B2
Eastgate Way WA7 .24 D4
Eastham Ctry Pk* CH62 .44 A8
Eastham Ho CH62 .44 A4
Eastham Mews CH62 .44 A4
Eastham Rake CH62,CH64 .43 D3
Eastham Rake Sta CH63 .43 D3
Eastham Village Rd CH62 .44 A5
Eastham Way 11 SK9 .34 D5
Eastward Ave SK9 .59 F6
Eastway
Ellesmere Port CH66 .69 D7
Widnes WA8 .12 D1
Eastwood WA7 .24 C2
Eastwood Ave WA12 .2 F3
Eastwood Ct CH5 .139 B7
Eastwood Rd WA5 .6 F7
Eaton Ave CH4 .141 D7
Eaton Bank CW12 .156 F4
Eaton Bank Ind Est CW12 .156 F4
Eaton Bank Sch CW12 .156 F5
Eaton Cl Broughton CH4 .139 C4
Poynton SK12 .37 A3
Sandbach CW11 .175 C7
Eaton Cres CW9 .103 E2
Eaton Ct
1 Northwich CW9 .103 E5
Wilmslow SK9 .60 A6
Eaton Dr Alderley Edge SK9 .59 F2
Middlewich CW10 .151 B8
Eaton Gr CH4 .140 E6
Eaton La Davenham CW9 .103 E2
Eaton CW6 .147 A5
Goostrey CW4 .107 C1
Macclesfield SK11 .112 D5
Tarporley CW6 .168 E8
Eaton Mews CH4 .141 D7
Eaton Pl CW8 .102 F4
Eaton Prim Sch CW6 .147 B3
Eaton Rd Alsager ST7 .193 D4
Chester CH4 .141 E4
Tarporley CW6 .146 D1
Wettenhall CW7 .170 B8
Eaton St Crewe CW2 .190 C4
14 Runcorn WA7 .23 A2
Eaton View CW9 .126 E8
Eaton Way CW3 .230 A4
Eaves Brow Rd WA3 .9 B7
Eaves Knoll Rd SK22 .39 B8
Ebnal La SY14 .213 E4
Ebury Pl CH4 .141 D7
Eccles Cl SK23 .65 D8
Eccles Rd SK23 .65 F5
Eccleston Ave
Chester CH4 .141 D6
Ellesmere Port CH66 .69 E5
Eccleston CE Prim Sch CH4 .141 E2
Eccleston Cl WA3 .9 C5
Eccleston Ct 5 CW9 .103 E5
Eccleston Dr WA7 .23 C1
Eccleston Rd CH4 .161 A7
Eccleston Way 3 SK9 .34 D4
Ecclestone Ave CH62 .43 C8
Eccups La SK9 .59 C8
Echo Cl CH4 .140 E5
Ecton Ave SK10 .113 A7
Ecton Cl CW7 .127 A4
Edale Cl Bebington CH62 .43 E5
Heald Green SK8 .34 D7
Edale Dr CW6 .122 D5
Edburton Ct WA3 .3 A8
Eddisbury Cl SK11 .112 F7
Eddisbury Dr ST5 .210 D2
Eddisbury Hill CW6,CW8 .123 D7
Eddisbury Hill Pk CW8 .123 D7
Eddisbury Rd CH66 .69 F1
Eddisbury Sq WA6 .74 B8
Eddisbury Terr SK11 .112 F7
Eddisbury Way CW9 .103 E3
Eddisford Dr WA3 .4 D4
Edelsten St WA5 .15 F5
Eden Ave
Fowley Common WA3 .5 C4
High Lane SK6 .37 E7
Winsford CW7 .126 F2
Eden Cl Biddulph ST8 .179 E1
5 Ellesmere Port CH66 .69 C5
Kidsgrove ST7 .195 B2
Wilmslow SK9 .59 E5
Eden Dr SK10 .87 F1
Eden Park Rd SK8 .34 E8
Edenbridge Cl CW2 .207 B2
Edenbridge Gdns WA4 .26 E3
Edendale WA8 .12 B2
Edenfield Cl WA16 .58 A3
Edenfield Rd WA16 .58 A4
Edenhall Cl CW4 .130 A3
Edgar Ct Chester CH4 .237 B1
25 Macclesfield SK11 .112 C8
Edgar Pl CH4 .237 B1
Edgars Dr WA2 .9 A2
Edge Gr CH2 .118 F2
Edge La SY14 .199 C1
Edge View La SK9 .59 B2
Edgecroft CH3 .166 A1
Edgehill Chase SK9 .60 E7
Edgerley La CH3 .181 B6
Edgerton Rd WA3 .3 F8
Edgeview Rd CW12 .179 B7
Edgeway Henbury SK11 .111 C8
Wilmslow SK9 .60 B5
Edgewell La CW6 .147 A3
Edgewood 3 CH3 .142 A8
Edgewood Dr
Bebington CH62 .43 D5
Wistaston CW2 .206 A7
Edgworth St WA2 .16 A6
Edinburgh Ct CH65 .70 D3
Edinburgh Dr SK10 .87 A1
Edinburgh Pl CW12 .156 F2
Edinburgh Rd
Congleton CW12 .156 F2
Widnes WA8 .22 A8
Wistaston CW2 .205 E8
Edinburgh Way CH4 .237 C1
Edison Rd WA7 .23 D3
Edith St WA7 .22 F3
Edleston Hall La CW5 .203 F2
Edleston Prim Sch CW2 .190 C3
Edleston Rd CW2 .190 D3
Edlestone Gr 2 SK9 .34 E1
Edmund Wright Way CW5 .204 C5
Edna St CH2 .118 F3
Edward Gdns WA1 .17 F6
Edward Rd WA5 .14 D6
Edward St Audley ST7 .209 F3
Crewe CW2 .190 D2

Edward Ct *continued*
Ellesmere Port CH65 . . . . . .70 C7
Haydock WA11 . . . . .1 A6
Macclesfield SK11 . . . . . . .112 B7
Northwich CW9 . . . . .104 C8
Widnes WA8 . . . . .13 D1
Edwards Ave CW2 . . . . . .206 C5
Edwards CI CW2 . . . . . . .206 C5
Edwards Ct SK7 . . . . .36 F8
Edwards Rd CH4 . . . . . . .141 A6
Edwards Way
Alsager ST7 . . . . .193 E4
Widnes WA8 . . . . .22 C8
Edwin St WA8 . . . . .13 C1
Egdon CI WA8 . . . . .13 E2
Egerton WA16 . . . . .29 C5
Egerton Ave
Handforth CW8 . . . . .103 A4
Partington WA13 . . . . .19 C8
Warrington WA1 . . . . .16 F7
Egerton Ct CW6 . . . . . . .122 B5
Egerton Dr CH2 . . . . .118 D5
Egerton Mews ⓵ WA4 . . .16 C1
Egerton Moss WA15 . . . . .31 E5
Egerton Rd Blacon CH1 . . .117 E5
Handforth SK9 . . . . .34 B1
Lymm WA13 . . . . .18 D2
Egerton Sq ⓺ WA16 . . . . . .57 A2
Egerton St Chester CH1 . . .237 C3
Congleton CW12 . . . . .156 C2
Ellesmere Port CH65 . . . . . .70 C6
Runcorn WA7 . . . . .22 F3
Warrington, Stockton Heath
WA4 . . . . .16 C1
Egerton Terr CW9 . . . . . .105 D4
Egerton Wlk CH4 . . . . . . .162 A7
Eggbridge La CH3 . . . . . .143 A5
Egypt St
⓹ Warrington WA1 . . . . . . .16 A5
Widnes WA8 . . . . .22 F7
Eilison Ct CH1 . . . . .237 B3
Eisenhower CI WA5 . . . . . .15 B5
Elaine CI
Ellesmere Port CH66 . . . . . .69 C4
Widnes WA8 . . . . .13 C1
Elaine Price Ct ⓶ WA7 . . .22 F1
Elaine St WA1 . . . . .16 D7
Elanor Rd CW11 . . . . .174 D7
Elcombe Ave WA3 . . . . .3 E7
Elder Dr CH4 . . . . .140 E5
Elderberry Way SK9 . . . . . .60 E8
Elderberry Wlk M31 . . . . . .11 E3
Eldon Rd SK10 . . . . .111 F8
Eldon St WA1 . . . . .16 C5
Eldon Terr CH64 . . . . .66 E7
Eleanor Cl CW1 . . . . .189 F5
Eleanor St
Ellesmere Port CH65 . . . . . .70 C6
⓹ Widnes WA8 . . . . .23 A7
Electra Way CW1 . . . . . . .191 A2
Electricity St CW2 . . . . . .190 C3
Elgar Ave CH62 . . . . .43 E5
Elgar Cl CH65 . . . . .69 F3
Elgin Ave
Holmes Chapel CW4 . . . . . .130 B2
Macclesfield SK10 . . . . .87 A2
Warrington WA4 . . . . .17 B5
Elgin Cl CH3 . . . . .119 B3
Eliot Cl CW1 . . . . .191 A4
Elizabeth Ave SK12 . . . . . .38 D5
Elizabeth Cl Kelsall CW6 . .122 D5
Sandbach CW11 . . . . .174 D7
Elizabeth Cres CH4 . . . . .237 C1
Elizabeth Ct Talke ST7 . . .210 C6
Widnes WA8 . . . . .23 B7
Elizabeth Dr WA1 . . . . .17 A8
Elizabeth Gaskell Ct
WA16 . . . . .56 F2
Elizabeth Ho ⓯ SK11 . . . .112 E7
Elizabeth Rd Haydock WA11 . .1 F7
Partington M31 . . . . .11 F4
Elizabeth St
Congleton CW12 . . . . .156 C2
Crewe CW1 . . . . .190 B5
Macclesfield SK11 . . . . . . .112 D7
Elizabeth Terr WA8 . . . . . .12 D1
Elizabethan Way CW9 . . .108 E6
Elk View SY14 . . . . .222 F5
Elkan Cl WA8 . . . . .13 E6
Elkan Rd WA8 . . . . .13 E6
Ella Gr WA16 . . . . .57 B2
Elland Dr CH66 . . . . .69 F4
Ellen Brook Rd M22 . . . . . .33 D8
Ellen St WA5 . . . . .15 F2
Ellerby Cl WA7 . . . . .50 E7
Ellerton Ave CH66 . . . . . . .69 C5
Ellerton Cl WA8 . . . . .12 D3
Ellesmere Ave
Broughton CH4 . . . . .139 D4
Chester CH2 . . . . .118 D5
Ellesmere Cl CW1 . . . . . . .174 F8
Ellesmere Pl CW1 . . . . . . .190 B5
Ellesmere Port Hospl
CH65 . . . . .70 A2
Ellesmere Port RC High Sch
CH65 . . . . .70 A2
Ellesmere Port Sta CH65 .70 C5
Ellesmere Port Stadium The
CH65 . . . . .70 E4
Ellesmere Rd Culcheth WA3 . .4 E3
Northwich CW9 . . . . .104 A4
Warrington WA4 . . . . .16 B1

Ellesmere St
Runcorn WA7 . . . . .23 B2
Warrington WA1 . . . . .16 C5
Ellesworth Cl WA5 . . . . . . .15 C8
Ellingham Way CW9 . . . . .103 E3
Elliot Ho CH1 . . . . .118 A5
Elliot St ⓽ WA8 . . . . .23 B8
Elliott Ave WA1 . . . . .16 E7
Ellis La WA6 . . . . .49 D1
Ellis St Crewe CW1 . . . . . .190 B6
Widnes WA8 . . . . .22 F7
Ellison St
Warrington, Howley WA1 . . .16 C5
Warrington, Stockton Heath
WA4 . . . . .16 D1
Elloway Rd L24 . . . . .21 A3
Ellwood Cl L24 . . . . .21 E2
Ellwood Gn CW2 . . . . .206 E3
Elm Ave Newton-le-W WA12 . .2 C2
⓶ Partington M31 . . . . .11 F3
Poynton SK12 . . . . .36 F3
Tarporley CW6 . . . . .146 D2
Elm Cres SK9 . . . . .60 B3
Elm Ct CW1 . . . . .190 D6
Elm Dr Crewe CW1 . . . . . .190 E6
Holmes Chapel CW4 . . . . . .130 D4
Macclesfield SK10 . . . . .87 E2
Elm Gn CH64 . . . . .67 A8
Elm Gr Alderley Edge SK9 . . .60 B2
Alsager ST7 . . . . .193 E4
Ellesmere Port CH66 . . . . . .70 A1
Handforth SK9 . . . . .34 C3
Saltney CH4 . . . . .140 E5
Warrington WA1 . . . . .16 F7
Widnes WA8 . . . . .13 B1
Winsford CW7 . . . . .127 A1
Elm Ho ⓻ CW11 . . . . .175 B6
Elm Rd Congleton CW12 . . .156 B3
Haydock WA11 . . . . .1 E7
High Lane SK6 . . . . .37 F7
Hollinfare WA3 . . . . .11 A2
Middlewich CW10 . . . . .151 D7
Runcorn WA7 . . . . .49 C8
Warrington WA5 . . . . .14 F4
Warrington, Winwick Quay
WA2 . . . . .8 B4
Weaverham CW8 . . . . .102 D7
Willaston CH64 . . . . .67 F8
Elm Ridge Dr WA15 . . . . . .32 C8
Elm Rise Frodsham WA6 . . .74 C7
Prestbury SK10 . . . . .86 E6
Elm Sq CH4 . . . . .140 F6
Elm St Ellesmere Port CH65 .70 C7
Northwich CW9 . . . . .79 B1
Elm Terr CW1 . . . . .190 E6
Elm Tree Ave Lymm WA13 . .18 D2
Warrington WA1 . . . . .16 F8
Elm Tree Cotts CH3 . . . . .166 A7
Elm Tree Ct CW6 . . . . .147 A3
Elm Tree Dr SK7 . . . . .209 F1
Elm Tree La CW11 . . . . . . .174 D8
Elm Tree Rd Golborne WA3 . .3 F8
Lymm WA13 . . . . .18 D2
Elmfield Cl SK9 . . . . .60 B2
Elmfield Rd SK9 . . . . .60 B2
Elmore Cl
Holmes Chapel CW4 . . . . . .130 B3
Runcorn WA7 . . . . .24 D1
Elmridge Ct WA3 . . . . .3 F8
Elmridge Prim Sch
WA15 . . . . .32 C8
Elmridge Way CW8 . . . . . . .78 D1
Elms The Golborne WA3 . . . . .3 F8
Mobberley WA16 . . . . .58 E2
⓻ Northwich CW9 . . . . . . .103 E6
Runcorn WA7 . . . . .22 F1
Tallarn Green/Tallwrn Green
SY14 . . . . .222 F5
Elmsett Cl WA5 . . . . .14 E5
Elmstead Cres CW1 . . . . .189 F8
Elmstead Rd SK11 . . . . . . .84 A3
Elmsway Altrincham WA15 . .32 B8
Bollington SK10 . . . . .88 A8
Bramhall SK7 . . . . .35 C7
High Lane SK6 . . . . .37 E6
Elmuir CH1 . . . . .117 E3
Elmwood WA7 . . . . .24 C1
Elmwood Ave
Chester CH4 . . . . .118 F4
Warrington WA1 . . . . .16 E7
Elmwood Cl ST7 . . . . .194 A4
Elmwood Gr CW7 . . . . . . .149 F8
Elmwood Rd CH4 . . . . .78 B4
Elnor Ave SK23 . . . . .65 E5
Elnor La SK23 . . . . .65 F4
Elsby Rd ST7 . . . . .193 F2
Elsham Dr WA12 . . . . .2 C5
Elstree Ave CH3 . . . . .119 B3
Elswick Ave SK7 . . . . .35 E7
Eltham Cl WA8 . . . . .13 E3
Eltham Wlk WA8 . . . . .13 E3
Elton Cl Bebington CH62 . . .43 E3
Golborne WA3 . . . . .2 F7
Handforth SK9 . . . . .34 E1
Warrington WA3 . . . . .9 C4
Elton Crossings Rd
CW11 . . . . .174 D6
Elton Dr SK7 . . . . .36 D8
Elton La Elton CH2 . . . . . . .72 E4
Haslington CW11,CW1 . . . .174 D1
Winterley CW11 . . . . .191 F8
Elton Lordship La WA6 . . . .73 B7
Elton Prim Sch CH2 . . . . . .72 C4
Elton Rd CW11 . . . . .174 D5

Elvington Cl
Congleton CW12 . . . . .156 E2
Runcorn WA7 . . . . .49 F4
Elwood Way CW5 . . . . . . .205 B4
Elworth Ave WA8 . . . . .13 A5
Elworth CE Prim Sch
CW11 . . . . .174 E7
Elworth Ct
⓯ Congleton CW12 . . . . . .156 F3
Sandbach CW11 . . . . .174 E8
Elworth Hall Prim Sch
CW11 . . . . .174 E7
Elworth Rd CW11 . . . . . . .174 E6
Elworth St CW11 . . . . .175 A7
Elworth Way ⓺ SK9 . . . . . .34 D4
Elwyn Dr L26 . . . . .21 A8
Ely Cl CH66 . . . . .94 E8
Ely Pk WA7 . . . . .24 E2
Embassy Ct CH1 . . . . .117 C4
Emberton Pl CW3 . . . . . . .230 A5
Embleton Ct WA7 . . . . .49 D5
Embridge Cswy SK10,
SK17 . . . . .90 B5
Emerald Dr CW11 . . . . . . .175 C8
Emerald Rd M22 . . . . .33 F7
Emily St ⓻ WA8 . . . . .23 A7
Emmett St CW8 . . . . .78 A3
Empire Ct WA1 . . . . .16 A4
Empress Dr CW2 . . . . .190 B3
Emral Ct SY14 . . . . .211 A1
Emslie Ct CH64 . . . . .66 C7
Enderby Rd CH1 . . . . .237 A3
Endon Ave SK10 . . . . .88 A7
Endon Hall Mews SK10 . . .88 B5
Endsleigh Cl CH2 . . . . . . .118 E8
Endsleigh Gdns CH2 . . . . .118 E8
Enfield Cl CW2 . . . . .206 B3
Enfield Park Rd WA2 . . . . . .9 A3
Enfield Rd CH65 . . . . .70 B5
Englesea Brook La CW2 . .208 A3
Engineer Pk CH5 . . . . .116 A4
Englefield Ave CH4 . . . . . .140 D6
Englefield Cl CW1 . . . . . . .190 A8
Englesea Brook Mus of
Primitive Methodism*
CW2 . . . . .208 A3
Englesea Gr CW2 . . . . . . .190 B1
Ennerdale Chester CH2 . . .118 F5
Macclesfield SK11 . . . . . . .111 F5
Ennerdale Ave
Bebington CH62 . . . . .43 F4
Warrington WA2 . . . . .8 B3
Ennerdale Cl
Alderley Edge SK9 . . . . .83 F7
Winsford CW7 . . . . .126 D3
Ennerdale Dr
Congleton CW12 . . . . .156 B2
Frodsham WA6 . . . . .74 C8
Ennerdale Rd
Crewe CW2 . . . . .189 D3
Partington M31 . . . . .11 E3
Ennis Cl L24 . . . . .21 D2
Ensor Way SK22 . . . . .39 C7
Enterprise Ctr The
CW12 . . . . .156 E3
Enterprise Way WA3 . . . . . .4 A7
Enticott Rd M44 . . . . .11 C5
Enville St WA4 . . . . .16 C4
Epping Dr WA3 . . . . .4 F7
Epsom Ave SK8,SK9 . . . . . .34 E4
Epsom Ct CH1 . . . . .118 B2
Epsom Gdns WA4 . . . . .26 E7
Epworth Cl WA5 . . . . .6 F7
ERF Way CW10 . . . . .151 E8
Eric Ave WA11 . . . . .16 E8
Eric Fountain Rd CH65 . . .44 D3
Eric St WA8 . . . . .13 C2
Erindale Cres WA8 . . . . . . .74 A6
Ermine Rd CH2 . . . . .237 C4
Ernest St CW2 . . . . .190 C1
Ernley Cl CW5 . . . . .204 D6
Errington Ave CH65 . . . . . .70 C6
Errwood Forest Walks*
SK17 . . . . .90 E2
Erskine Rd M41 . . . . .11 F3
Erwood St WA2 . . . . .16 B6
Esk Dale Cl CW7 . . . . .126 C2
Esk La WA7 . . . . .127 A2
Eskdale CH65 . . . . .70 B3
Eskdale Ave
Bebington CH62 . . . . .43 E5
Bramhall SK7 . . . . .35 C5
Warrington WA2 . . . . .8 B3
Eskdale Cl WA7 . . . . .49 D5
Essex Cl WA12 . . . . .156 E5
Essex Dr Biddulph ST8 . . .179 D2
Kidsgrove ST7 . . . . .194 F2
Essex Gdns M44 . . . . .11 C4
Essex Rd CH2 . . . . .119 A5
Essex Wlk SK10 . . . . .86 F1
Esthers La CW8 . . . . .102 D8
Etchells Prim Sch SK8 . . . .34 C8
Ethelda Dr CH2 . . . . .119 A5
Etherow Cl CW11 . . . . . . .174 E7
Eton Dr CH63 . . . . .41 F6
Eton Rd CH65 . . . . .70 D4
Ettiley Ave CW11 . . . . .174 C5
Ettrick Pk CH3 . . . . .119 A2
Euclid Ave WA4 . . . . .17 B2
Europa Bvd WA5 . . . . .7 D3
Europa Way CH65 . . . . .70 C6
Eustace St WA2 . . . . .16 A6
Eva St CW11 . . . . .174 D8
Evans Cl WA11 . . . . .1 F7
Evans Pl WA4 . . . . .16 D3
Evans St SK11 . . . . .112 E7
Evans St CW1 . . . . .190 C6
Evansleigh Dr CH5 . . . . . .116 A3

Evelyn St WA5 . . . . .15 D4
Evelyn Street Prim Sch
WA5 . . . . .15 E4
Evenwood CI WA7 . . . . . . .24 E4
Everdon CI CW7 . . . . .126 F4
Everest CI CH66 . . . . .69 F3
Everest Rd ST7 . . . . .195 C3
Everglade CI SK11 . . . . . . .112 B5
Evergreen Way WA9 . . . . . . .6 A7
Everite Rd WA8 . . . . .22 B7
Eversley WA8 . . . . .12 B2
Eversley CI Frodsham WA6 .74 C6
Warrington WA4 . . . . .26 F5
Eversley Ct CH2 . . . . .118 C4
Eversley Pk CH2 . . . . .118 C4
Evesham Cl
Macclesfield SK10 . . . . .87 E4
Warrington WA4 . . . . .26 C8
Evesham Dr SK9 . . . . .34 C2
Evington Ho ⓶ SK11 . . . . .112 B6
Ewart St CW6 . . . . .140 B7
Ewloe Ct CH65 . . . . .70 D2
Ewrin La SK10 . . . . .89 D5
Excalibur Ind Est CH4 . . . .193 E3
Excalibur Prim Sch ST7 . .193 E2
Excalibur Way WA4 . . . . . .11 F7
Exchange Cl ⓮ SK11 . . . .112 D8
Exchange St SK11 . . . . . . .112 D8
Exeter Cl SK8 . . . . .34 F8
Exeter Dr CH1 . . . . .117 F5
Exeter Rd CH65 . . . . .70 C5
Exeter Wlk SK7 . . . . .35 F7
Exit Rd W M90 . . . . .33 B7
Exmouth Cres WA7 . . . . . .50 E6
Exmouth Way WA5 . . . . .6 E6
Express Ind Est WA8 . . . . .22 A7
Exton Pk CH1 . . . . .237 A4
Eyam Rd SK7 . . . . .36 E8
Eyebrook Rd WA14 . . . . . . .20 F1
Eyre Pl CH65 . . . . .70 B6
Eyston CI CW9 . . . . .103 E5

F

Facit Glen Ind Est CH4 . . .140 F7
Factory La
Warrington WA1,WA5 . . . . . .15 F4
Widnes WA8 . . . . .13 B2
Factory Rd CH5 . . . . .116 A3
Fair Haven's Ct WA8 . . . . . .23 B8
Fair Isle Cl CH65 . . . . .70 C1
Fair Mead WA16 . . . . .57 A4
Fair Oak Rd ST5 . . . . .210 D1
Fair View Cl CW8 . . . . .77 F3
Fairacre Dr CW10 . . . . . . .151 E6
Fairacres Rd SK6 . . . . .37 E8
Fairbourne Ave
Alderley Edge SK9 . . . . .60 B3
Wilmslow SK9 . . . . .59 F4
Fairbourne Cl
Warrington WA5 . . . . .7 E3
Wilmslow SK9 . . . . .59 F4
Fairbourne Dr SK9 . . . . . . .59 F4
Fairbrook CW2 . . . . .189 E2
Fairbrother Cres WA2 . . . . .8 D2
Fairburn Ave CW2 . . . . . . .189 F4
Fairburn Cl WA8 . . . . .13 E3
Fairclough Ave WA1 . . . . . .16 C4
Fairclough Cres WA11 . . . . .1 A6
Fairclough St
Burtonwood WA5 . . . . .6 E6
Newton-le-W WA12 . . . . . . .2 B3
Fairfax Dr Nantwich CW5 . .204 D6
Runcorn WA7 . . . . .23 D2
Wilmslow SK9 . . . . .59 F4
Fairfield Ave
Bollington SK10 . . . . .88 A8
Ellesmere Port CH65 . . . . . .70 A2
Sandbach CW11 . . . . .175 B5
Fairfield Gdns WA4 . . . . . . .16 E2
Fairfield High Sch WA8 . . .13 B3
Fairfield Inf Sch WA8 . . . . .13 B2
Fairfield Jun Sch WA8 . . . .13 B2
Fairfield Rd
Broughton CH4 . . . . .139 B4
Chester CH2 . . . . .119 A4
Irlam M44 . . . . .11 C5
Lymm WA13 . . . . .18 F3
Northwich CW9 . . . . .104 A4
Warrington WA4 . . . . .16 E2
Fairfield St WA1 . . . . .16 D6
Fairfields Audley ST7 . . . . .209 F2
Whitchurch SY13 . . . . .225 F1
Fairford Cl CW5 . . . . .15 B6
Fairford Rd CH4 . . . . .140 F6
Fairhaven CW2 . . . . .207 B1
Fairhaven Cl Bramhall SK7 .35 F8
Macclesfield SK10 . . . . .87 B4
Warrington WA5 . . . . .15 B4
Fairhaven Dr CH63 . . . . . . .43 C5
Fairhaven Rd WA8 . . . . . . .13 C2
Fairhills Ind Est M44 . . . . .11 F8
Fairhills Rd M44 . . . . .11 F8
Fairholme Ave CH64 . . . . . .41 D1
Fairholme Cl CW8 . . . . .78 A3
Fairholme Pl ⓶ CH3 . . . . .119 A1
Fairholme Rd CW9 . . . . . .127 A8
Fairlawn Cl CH63 . . . . .43 A6
Fairmeadow CH4 . . . . .162 D2
Fairoak Cl ⓮ CW7 . . . . . . .149 A8
Fairoak Ct WA8 . . . . .50 F3
Fairoak La WA7 . . . . .50 F3
Fairview LL13 . . . . .196 E8
Fairview Ave
Alsager ST7 . . . . .193 D4

Fairview *continued*
Weston CW2 . . . . .207 B5
Fairview Rd
Ellesmere Port CH65 . . . . . .70 A2
Macclesfield SK11 . . . . . . .112 A6
Fairway Bramhall SK7 . . . . .35 D6
Sandycroft CH5 . . . . .116 A2
Fairway The ST7 . . . . .193 C4
Fairways Frodsham WA6 . . .74 D7
Warrington WA4 . . . . .26 D5
Fairways Dr
Ellesmere Port CH66 . . . . . .69 D7
Whitchurch SY13 . . . . .226 A1
Fairways The
Macclesfield SK10 . . . . .87 B4
Winsford CW7 . . . . .126 A2
Fairywell Cl SK9 . . . . .34 D1
Falcon Cl
Middlewich CW10 . . . . .151 D5
New Mills SK22 . . . . .39 D8
Winsford CW7 . . . . .149 D6
Falcon Dr CW1 . . . . .190 B8
Falcon Rd CH66 . . . . .69 F3
Falcondale Rd WA2 . . . . . . .8 B6
Falconers Gn WA5 . . . . .7 B2
Falcons Way WA7 . . . . .49 E6
Falkirk Ave WA8 . . . . .12 F3
Fallibroome Cl SK10 . . . . .111 E8
Fallibroome High Sch
SK10 . . . . .86 E2
Fallibroome Rd SK10 . . . . .111 E8
Fallon Ct CW10 . . . . .151 C7
Fallowfield WA7 . . . . .23 D1
Fallowfield Cl CW7 . . . . . . .125 F1
Fallowfield Ct CW1 . . . . . .190 A6
Fallowfield Gr WA2 . . . . .9 B1
Falmouth Cl SK10 . . . . . . .111 E8
Falmouth Dr WA5 . . . . .14 E3
Falmouth Pl WA7 . . . . .50 E6
Falmouth Rd
Congleton CW12 . . . . .178 E8
Crewe CW1 . . . . .190 A6
Falstone Cl WA3 . . . . .10 B6
Falstone Dr WA7 . . . . .50 E7
Fanner's La WA16 . . . . .28 D5
Fanny's Croft ST7 . . . . . . .193 D2
Fanshawe La ST7 . . . . .33 D5
Fanshawe Wlk CW2 . . . . . .206 C8
Faraday Dr
Ellesmere Port CH65 . . . . . .70 A4
Runcorn WA7 . . . . .23 D3
Faraday St WA3 . . . . .9 E5
Farams Rd ST7 . . . . .193 E7
Farbailey Cl CH4 . . . . .141 B5
Farfields Cl SK11 . . . . .111 E1
Farley Cl CW10 . . . . .151 B8
Farm Cl CW8 . . . . .77 D1
Farm Dr CH5 . . . . .91 C1
Farm Hollow ST7 . . . . .210 A3
Farm La High Lane SK12 . . .38 A6
Warrington WA4 . . . . .26 C6
Withington Green SK11 . . .108 E1
Farm Rd Northwich CW9 . .104 E7
Oakmere CW8 . . . . .124 A8
Weaverham CW8 . . . . .77 D1
Farm Way WA12 . . . . .2 E1
Farm Wlk WA14 . . . . .20 E1
Farmdale Dr CH2 . . . . .72 A3
Farmer Cl CW2 . . . . .190 A4
Farmer's La WA5 . . . . .7 A6
Farmers Heath CH66 . . . . . .69 D2
Farmfield Dr SK10 . . . . . . .87 C3
Farmfields Rise CW3 . . . . .232 C1
Farmfold SK9 . . . . .33 F3
Farmleigh Dr CW1 . . . . . . .189 F8
Farmleigh Gdns WA5 . . . . .15 C6
Farmside Cl WA5 . . . . .15 E1
Farmstead Way CH66 . . . . .69 E1
Farndale WA8 . . . . .13 A5
Farndale Cl
Warrington WA5 . . . . .14 F7
Wistaston CW2 . . . . .206 A6
Farndale Wlk SK11 . . . . . .112 D6
Farndon Cl
Broughton CH4 . . . . .139 C4
Cuddington CW8 . . . . .102 A3
Farndon Prim Sch CH3 . .180 E2
Farndon Rd CH66 . . . . .69 E6
Farne Cl CH65 . . . . .95 C8
Farnham Ave SK11 . . . . . .112 A6
Farnham Cl
Cheadle Hulme SK8 . . . . . . .35 A7
Warrington WA4 . . . . .26 E7
Farnhill Cl WA7 . . . . .50 D8
Farnley St WA7 . . . . .24 D1
Farnworth CE Prim Sch
WA8 . . . . .13 A4
Farnworth Cl WA8 . . . . . . .13 A4
Farnworth Rd WA5 . . . . . . .14 C4
Farnworth St WA8 . . . . . . .13 A4
Farr Hall Dr CH60 . . . . .40 E7
Farr Hall Rd CH60 . . . . . . .40 F8
Farrant St WA8 . . . . .23 B8
Farrell Rd WA4 . . . . .16 C8
Farrell St WA1 . . . . .16 C6
Farriers Way CW7 . . . . . . .126 A1
Farrington Rd WA3 . . . . .8 B6
Farthing La CW9 . . . . .78 F8
Farthings The WA13 . . . . . .18 D4
Farwood Cl SK10 . . . . .86 F2
Faulkner Dr CW10 . . . . . . .151 E6
Faulkner St CH2 . . . . .118 F3
Faulkner's La WA16 . . . . . .58 E2
Faulkners Cl CH4 . . . . .161 A7
Faulkners La CH3 . . . . . . .142 D8
Fawns Keep SK9 . . . . .60 D7
Fawns Leap CW8 . . . . .101 E5
Fearndown Way SK10 . . . . .87 C4

Fearnhead Cross WA2 ....8 F2
Fearnhead La WA2 ....9 A2
Fearnley Way WA12 ....2 C1
Feather La CH60 ....40 F8
Feather's La CH1 ....237 B2
Feilden Ct CH1 ....94 F1
Felix Rd CW8 ....103 E8
Felskirk Rd M22 ....33 C8
Fence Ct SK10 ....112 E8
Fence Ave Ind Est SK10 .112 E8
Fence Ct SK10 ....112 E8
Fence La CW12 ....178 D4
Fenham Dr WA5 ....14 F4
Fennel St WA1 ....16 C5
Fenton Cl
  Congleton CW12 ....157 A1
  Widnes WA8 ....12 C3
Fenwick La WA7 ....49 D6
Fenwick Rd CH66 ....69 E2
Ferguson Ave CH66 ....69 E6
Ferguson Dr WA2 ....8 D1
Ferma La CH3 ....120 D6
Fern Ave WA12 ....2 D2
Fern Cl
  Mount Pleasant ST7 ...195 C6
  Warrington WA3 ....9 D4
Fern Cres CW12 ....157 A3
Fern Ct CW1 ....190 E3
Fern Lea Dr SK11 ....112 A8
Fern Rd CH65 ....70 B2
Fern Way CW8 ....77 C1
Fernbank Cl Crewe CW1 .190 F3
  Warrington WA3 ....9 E4
  Winsford CW7 ....127 B1
Fernbank Rise SK10 ....88 B8
Ferndale SK9 ....34 D3
Ferndale Ave CH2 ....72 A3
Ferndale Cl
  Bold Heath WA8 ....13 E7
  Sandbach CW11 ....175 C5
  Warrington WA1 ....17 C7
  Weston CW2 ....207 B5
Ferndale Cres SK11 ....111 E7
Ferndale Gdns ST7 ....195 E3
Fernhill Rd CH1 ....117 E6
Fernhurst WA7 ....49 D8
Fernlee Cott SK23 ....65 E1
Fernlea Ct CH1 ....116 F8
Fernlea Rd Heswall CH60 .41 A8
  Marston CW9 ....79 B6
Fernleaf Cl ST7 ....193 F8
Fernleigh CW8 ....103 C7
Fernleigh Cl
  Middlewich CW10 ....151 E6
  Whitchurch WA7 ....126 A1
Fernway CW7 ....127 B1
Fernwood WA7 ....127 B1
Fernwood Gr SK9 ....60 C8
Fernyess La CH64 ....67 E7
Ferrous Way M44 ....11 F6
Ferry Cl CH5 ....116 A6
Ferry La Sealand CH1 ....117 C1
  Warrington WA4 ....17 E14
Ferry Rd CH62 ....44 A6
Festival Ave
  Buerton CW3 ....230 E3
  Warrington WA2 ....8 D2
Festival Cres WA2 ....8 D2
Festival Dr SK10 ....85 F6
Festival Hill CW12 ....156 F2
Festival Rd CH65 ....69 F5
Festival Way WA7 ....49 C8
Ffordd Cledwen/Cledwen Rd
  CH4 ....139 D5
Ffordd Smithfield/Smithfield
  Dr LL13 ....196 D8
Fiddler's Ferry Rd WA8 .13 D1
Fiddlers Ferry Rd WA8 ..23 C8
Fiddlers La CH1 ....94 C1
Field Ave CW2 ....189 F1
Field Cl Bollington SK10 .87 F7
  Bramhall SK7 ....35 D4
  Northwich CW8 ....103 C7
  Tarvin CH3 ....121 B2
Field Hey La CH64 ....43 B1
Field La Crewe CW1 ....189 E2
  Tarvin CH3 ....121 B2
  Tattenhall CH3 ....166 B1
  Warrington WA4 ....26 C6
Field Side Cl WA16 ....58 A4
Field View ST8 ....179 D1
Field View Dr SK11 ....112 E5
Field Way ST7 ....193 E4
Field Wlk M31 ....11 E3
Fieldbank Rd CW11 ....112 B8
Fieldfare CW7 ....150 A8
Fieldfare Cl Golborne WA3 .3 D8
  Warrington WA3 ....9 F4
Fieldgate WA8 ....22 B6
Fieldhead Mews SK9 ....60 E8
Fieldhead Rd SK9 ....60 E8
Fieldhouse Row WA7 ....49 D7
Fielding Ave SK12 ....36 E3
Fields Cl ST7 ....193 E4
Fields Dr CW11 ....175 A5
Fields Rd Alsager ST7 ..193 E3
  Congleton CW12 ....178 F8
  Haslington CW1 ....191 D4
Fields The CW5 ....205 D5
Fields View CW3 ....228 D1
Fields View Cl CW5 ....220 B8
Fieldsend Dr WN7 ....4 C8
Fieldside CW6 ....145 B6
Fieldside Cl CW4 ....107 E1
Fieldside Ct CH4 ....139 B4
Fieldsway WA7 ....49 A6
Fieldview Dr WA2 ....8 C1
Fieldway Chester CH2 ..118 E4

Fieldway continued
  Ellesmere Port CH66 ....69 B7
  Frodsham WA6 ....74 C7
  Saughall CH1 ....94 A2
  Weaverham CW8 ....77 C1
  Widnes WA8 ....13 E2
Fieldways WA13 ....18 C4
Fife Rd WA1 ....16 F7
Fifth Ave Kidsgrove ST7 .194 E1
  [2] Runcorn WA7 ....49 F7
Fildes Cl WA5 ....15 C5
Filkin's La CH3 ....119 A1
Finch La L26 ....21 B7
Finchdale Gdns WA3 ....4 B8
Finchett Ct CH1 ....118 B3
Finchett Dr CH1 ....118 B3
Findlay Cl WA12 ....2 C1
Finger Post La WA6 ....101 A4
Finlan Rd WA8 ....22 F7
Finlay Ave WA5 ....14 E3
Finlow Hill La SK10 ....85 E6
Finney Cl SK9 ....34 C2
Finney Dr SK9 ....34 C2
Finney Gr WA11 ....1 E6
Finney La SK8 ....34 B8
Finney's La CW10 ....128 B2
Finningley Cl WA2 ....8 E1
Finsbury Cl WA5 ....15 C4
Finsbury Pk WA8 ....13 C5
Finsbury Way SK9 ....34 E2
Finsbury Wlk CW7 ....149 A8
Fir Ave Bramhall SK7 ....35 E8
  Halewood L26 ....21 A8
Fir Cl Halewood L26 ....21 A8
  Poynton SK12 ....36 F3
  Tarporley CW6 ....146 D2
Fir Ct SK10 ....86 F3
Fir Gr Macclesfield SK11 .112 D5
  Warrington WA1 ....16 F7
  Weaverham CW8 ....102 E8
Fir La CW8 ....102 A2
Fir Rd SK7 ....35 E8
Fir St Irlam M44 ....11 D6
  Widnes WA8 ....13 C2
Fir Tree Ave Chester CH4 .141 B5
  Golborne WA3 ....3 F8
  Knutsford WA16 ....82 C8
Fir Tree Cl WA4 ....26 D1
Fir Tree Cotts CW2 ....208 C5
Fir Tree La
  Burtonwood WA5 ....7 A7
  Chester CH3 ....119 E2
  Faddiley CW5 ....202 B3
Fir Tree Wlk WA3 ....4 B8
Fir Trees Holiday Pk
  CH1 ....117 C2
Fir Way CH60 ....41 B5
Firbank CW2 ....72 C3
Firbank Cl WA7 ....24 D1
Firbeck Cl
  Broughton CH4 ....139 B3
  Congleton CW12 ....155 F3
Firbeck Gdns CW12 ....189 D4
Firdale Rd CW8 ....103 D7
Firecrest Ct WA1 ....16 A3
Firemans Sq CH1 ....237 A3
Firman Cl WA5 ....15 B8
Firs La WA4 ....26 B6
Firs Pottery The* CW5 .217 C1
Firs Sch CH2 ....118 C2
Firs The SK9 ....60 A5
Firs View WA6 ....73 D4
First Ave
  Connah's Quay CH5 ....93 A2
  Crewe CW1 ....190 F2
  Kidsgrove ST7 ....194 E1
  Poynton SK12 ....36 D1
  Sandbach CW11 ....175 A5
First Dig La CW5 ....219 C8
First Wood St CW5 ....204 D5
Firth Fields CW9 ....103 F7
Firthfields Cl CW9 ....103 F2
Firtree Ave WA1 ....17 A8
Firtree Cl Barnton CW8 ..78 B4
  Winsford CW7 ....127 B1
Firtree Gr CH66 ....95 A8
Firwood Rd ST8 ....179 E1
Firwood Wlk CW2 ....190 C1
Fisher Ave WA2 ....8 B2
Fisher Rd CH1 ....117 E4
Fisher St WA7 ....23 B2
Fisherfield Dr WA3 ....10 A6
Fishermans Cl CW11 ....191 F7
Fishers Gn CW6 ....146 B5
Fishers La CW5 ....203 C8
Fishpool Rd CW8 ....123 F3
Fishwicks Ind Est WA11 ...1 F8
Fistral Ave SK8 ....34 C8
Fitton St CW9 ....80 A2
Fitton's Cl CW5 ....217 F5
Fitz Cl SK10 ....87 D3
Fitz Crcs SK10 ....87 D3
Fitzherbert St WA2 ....16 C7
Fitzwalter Rd WA1 ....17 D7
Fitzwilliam Ave SK11 ..112 A7
Fitzwilliam Wlk WA7 ....24 A2
Five Ashes Rd CH4 ....141 B5
Five Ways CH64 ....41 F3
Fiveashes Cotts SK10 ....88 B5
Fivelanes End WA6 ....74 C6
Fiveways Par SK7 ....35 E8
Fiveways Pk CH64 ....41 F3
Flacca Ct CH3 ....166 B1
Flag La Crewe CW1,CW2 .190 C4
  Neston CH64 ....66 F7
Flag La N CH2 ....118 E4
Flag La S CH2 ....118 E4
Flander Cl WA8 ....12 C2

Flash La Antrobus CW9 ...53 F5
  Bollington SK10 ....87 D7
Flashes La CH64 ....67 B5
Flat La Kelsall CW6 ....122 C4
  Sandbach CW11 ....175 B6
Flatt La CH65 ....70 B5
Flatts La SK23 ....64 F4
Flavian Cl CW10 ....128 C2
Flavian Ct WA7 ....23 E2
Flaxley Cl WA3 ....10 A5
Flaxmere Dr CH3 ....142 B8
Flaxyards CW6 ....146 F2
Fleet La WA9 ....1 A2
Fleet St CH65 ....70 A5
Fleetwood Cl WA5 ....15 B4
Fleetwood Dr WA12 ....2 B4
Fleetwood Wlk WA7 ....50 C6
Fleming Dr WA2 ....8 A6
Fleming St CH65 ....70 C6
Flers Ave WA4 ....16 C3
Fletcher Ct WA16 ....56 F1
Fletcher St SK10 ....37 F6
Fletcher Cl CW9 ....104 C6
Fletcher St Crewe CW1 ..190 B5
  Warrington WA4 ....16 B3
Fletcher's Bldgs
  Chester CH1 ....237 B2
  [6] Runcorn WA7 ....23 F1
Fletcher's Row [5] WA7 .23 F1
Fletchers La WA13 ....18 F4
Fletsand Rd SK9 ....60 D6
Flexible House Havannah
  Bsns Ctr [6] CW12 ....156 F4
Flint Cl CH64 ....66 E6
Flint Ct CH65 ....70 D2
Flint Dr CH64 ....66 E6
Flint Gr M44 ....11 E6
Flint Mdw CH64 ....66 E7
Flint St SK10 ....112 E8
Flittogate La WA16 ....80 E8
Flixton Dr CW2 ....190 A2
Florence St WA4 ....16 D3
Florida Cl WA5 ....15 C7
Flour Mill Way CW1 ....191 A3
Flowcrete Bsns Pk
  CW11 ....152 C1
Flower St CW8 ....103 E7
Flowers La CW1 ....172 E1
Flowerscroft CW5 ....205 A4
Fluin La WA6 ....74 C8
Flying Fields Dr SK11 ..112 A5
Foden Ave ST7 ....194 A3
Foden La
  Alderley Edge SK9 ....59 C1
  Bramhall SK7 ....35 D3
Foden St SK10 ....87 D1
Foden Wlk [7] SK9 ....34 D2
Fodens Terr CW11 ....175 A6
Fog Cotts CW3 ....221 E4
Fogg's La CW9,WA4 ....53 A6
Fol Hollow CW12 ....155 E7
Fold La Biddulph ST8 ..179 E4
  Bosley SK11 ....135 D2
Fold The SK10 ....87 A8
Folds La SK23 ....65 F3
Folds The CH63 ....42 A6
Foley Wlk M22 ....33 E8
Folkestone Cl SK10 ....87 B2
Folkestone Way WA7 ....50 C7
Folly La WA5 ....14 E5
Forbes Cl SK10 ....9 E3
Forbes Pk SK7 ....35 D7
Ford Cl CW1 ....190 B5
Ford Ct CW7 ....149 C6
Ford La Crewe CW1 ....190 B6
  Tattenhall CH3 ....166 F4
Ford St WA1 ....16 D6
Ford's La SK7 ....35 D6
Fordington Rd WA5 ....15 B5
Fords La ST7 ....194 C1
Fordsham Manor House Prim
  Sch WA6 ....49 C2
Fordsham Weaver Vale Prim
  Sch WA6 ....49 C2
Fordton Leisure Ctr WA2 .8 A3
Foregate St CH1 ....237 B2
Foreland Cl WA5 ....14 C7
Forest Ave CW4 ....107 C1
Forest Cl
  Cuddington CW8 ....101 F2
  Rainow SK10 ....88 E5
Forest Dr Broughton CH4 .139 C3
  Langley SK11 ....113 C5
Forest Gate Com Prim Sch
  M31 ....11 D3
Forest Gate La CW6 ....122 E7
Forest Gdns M31 ....11 D3
Forest Ho SK10 ....87 A8
Forest La CH3 ....100 C6
Forest Rd [3] CW9 ....79 A1
Forest Rd
  Cuddington CW8 ....101 F2
  Delamere CW6 ....123 C6
  Ellesmere Port CH66 ....69 E7
  Heswall CH60 ....41 A8
  Macclesfield SK11 ....113 C6
  Tarporley CW6 ....146 D3
  Winsford CW7 ....149 C8
Forest Road Pk CW6 ..122 F7
Forest St Congleton CW12 .156 F3
  Weaverham CW8 ....102 C8
Forest Wlk [5] WA7 ....50 C7
Forester Ave WA4 ....57 C2
Foresters Cl WA6 ....101 A6
Forge Cl Cronton WA8 ....12 C5
  Warren SK11 ....111 D2
Forge Fields CW11 ....174 F3
Forge La Congleton CW12 .156 B3

Forge La continued
  Norton in Hales TF9 ....236 C1
Forge Mill La CW10 ....151 C1
Forge Rd
  Ellesmere Port CH66 ....69 C6
  Warrington WA5 ....14 F5
  Whaley Bridge SK23 ....65 E7
Forge Sh Ctr The WA4 ..16 C1
Forge St CW1 ....190 D4
Forge Way CH4 ....140 F4
Formby Cl WA5 ....14 F4
Formby Dr SK8 ....34 B8
Forrest Way WA5 ....15 D3
Forshaw St WA2 ....6 E7
Forshaw's La WA5 ....6 E8
Forster Ave CW8 ....102 E8
Forster St WA2 ....16 B7
Forsythia Wlk [2] M31 ...11 E2
Forty Acre La CW4,
  CW12 ....131 D6
Forum The CH1 ....237 A2
Forwood Rd CH62 ....43 D8
Fossa Cl CW10 ....128 C2
Foster Rd CW12 ....157 A5
Foster St WA8 ....13 B1
Fothergill Grange SK8 ...35 A8
Fothergill St WA1 ....16 D7
Fotheringay Ct [3] CH65 .70 D2
Foulkes Ave CW1 ....189 F6
Foundry Bank CW12 ....156 E3
Foundry Ct SK22 ....39 C7
Foundry La
  Sandbach CW11 ....174 D7
  Scholar Green ST7 ....194 F7
  Widnes WA8 ....22 C5
Foundry St
  Bollington SK10 ....88 B8
  Newton-le-W WA12 ....2 B3
  Warrington WA2 ....16 B6
Fountain Cl SK12 ....36 D4
Fountain Ct
  Biddulph ST8 ....179 D1
  Davenham CW9 ....103 F2
  [2] Winsford CW7 ....126 D1
Fountain Ho SK10 ....112 E8
Fountain La
  Davenham CW9 ....103 F2
  Fenton WA6 ....74 A8
  Fountain Pl SK12 ....36 D4
Fountain Sq SK12 ....38 C6
Fountain St
  Congleton CW12 ....156 D2
  Macclesfield SK10 ....112 E8
Fountains Ave WA11 ....1 F7
Fountains Cl
  Middlewich CW10 ....128 B1
  Runcorn WA7 ....50 C5
Fountains Rd SK7,SK8 ...35 C6
Fountains Wlk WA3 ....4 B8
Four Lane Ends
  Alvanley WA6 ....74 B1
  Warrington WA3 ....9 D3
Four Lanes Ct [2] CW7 .149 B8
Four Lanes End
  Betley CW2 ....207 F2
  Thornton Hough CH63 ..42 D5
Fourlanes End CW11 ....176 E4
Fourseasons Cl CW2 ....206 B8
Fourth Ave
  Connah's Quay CH5 ....92 E2
  Crewe CW1 ....190 F1
  Kidsgrove ST7 ....194 F1
  [1] Runcorn WA7 ....49 F7
Fourways CW2 ....207 B5
Fourways Tech Pk
  CW11 ....176 E4
Fowey Cl SK10 ....86 D1
Fowler Rd CH1 ....117 D4
Fowler St SK10 ....87 D1
Fowlers Bench La CH3 ..184 C5
Fowley Common La WA3 ..5 C5
Fox Bank Cl WA8 ....12 F4
Fox Bench Cl SK7 ....35 C6
Fox Cover CH3 ....119 F5
Fox Cover Rd CH60 ....41 D7
Fox Covert WA7 ....50 C7
Fox Covert La
  Hoole Bank CH2 ....119 B8
  Picton CH2 ....96 A1
Fox Covert Way CW1 ..173 A1
Fox Gdns Lymm WA13 ...18 C4
  Talke ST7 ....210 D8
Fox Gr SK10 ....57 C1
Fox Hill CW6 ....122 D4
Fox La Clutton CH3 ....182 D1
  Waverton CH3 ....143 B5
Fox Lea CH1 ....117 A8
Fox St Congleton CW12 ..156 F3
  Runcorn WA7 ....23 A1
Fox Wood Sch WA3 ....9 E3
Fox's Dr CH5 ....116 A6
Foxall Way CH66 ....69 D2
Foxcote CH1 ....117 D5
Foxcovert La WA16 ....106 E7
Foxdale Ct WA4 ....26 C7
Foxendale Cl CW8 ....103 D7
Foxes Covert CW11 ....152 B8
Foxes Fold CW3 ....237 C2
Foxes Hey CW8 ....101 D5
Foxes Hollow CW1 ....190 E7
Foxes La CH3 ....142 A4
Foxfield Cl WA2 ....9 C2
Foxfield La CW7 ....126 A1
Foxglove Cl
  Bollington SK10 ....88 C8
  [2] Golborne WA3 ....3 D8

Foxglove Cl continued
  Huntington CH3 ....142 A6
  Wistaston CW2 ....206 B7
Foxglove Ct WA6 ....74 C8
Foxglove Dell WA6 ....73 D2
Foxglove Way CH64 ....66 E5
Foxglove Wlk M31 ....11 F2
Foxhill Ct CW6 ....146 E1
Foxhill Gr WA6 ....73 D4
Foxhills Cl WA4 ....26 D3
Foxhunter Cl CH3 ....121 F7
Foxlea CW9 ....78 C7
Foxley Cl WA13 ....19 A2
Foxley Hall Mews WA13 .19 A1
Foxley Heath WA8 ....22 E8
Foxwist Cl CH2 ....237 B4
Foxwist Gn CW8 ....125 E6
Foxwood Dr WA16 ....108 A8
Frances St Crewe CW2 ..190 D2
  Irlam M44 ....11 E5
  Macclesfield SK11 ....112 B8
Francesca Ct CH1 ....237 B2
Francis Cl WA8 ....22 C8
Francis Ct CH1 ....237 C3
Francis La Holt LL13 ....196 B6
  Holt LL13 ....196 B6
Francis Rd Frodsham WA6 .49 C1
  Irlam M44 ....11 F8
  Warrington WA4 ....16 B1
Francis St CH1 ....237 C3
Frank Bott Ave CW1 ....190 A7
Frank Perkins Way WA4 .11 F7
Frank St WA8 ....13 C1
Frank Webb Ave CW1 ..190 A6
Franklin Cl
  Macclesfield SK11 ....112 B5
  Warrington WA5 ....15 C8
Franklyn Ave CW2 ....190 B3
Fraser Ct CH4 ....141 D7
Fraser Rd WA5 ....14 D6
Frawley Ave WA12 ....2 C5
Freckleton Cl WA5 ....15 B4
Frederick St
  Warrington WA4 ....16 E3
  Widnes WA8 ....23 B8
Frederick Terr WA8 ....22 A4
Fredric Pl WA7 ....23 B3
Free Green La WA16 ....107 A8
Freedom Dr ST7 ....195 E3
Freen's Ct WA5 ....218 C5
French Lane End CW5 ..218 E5
French St WA8 ....13 D1
Freshfield SK8 ....34 B8
Freshfield Dr SK10 ....87 C3
Freshfields
  Comberbach CW9 ....78 C7
  Knutsford WA16 ....56 E3
  Wistaston CW2 ....206 A7
Freshfields Dr WA2 ....9 C1
Freshmeadow La WA6 ...73 B2
Freshwater Ct WA5 ....14 D7
Freshwater Dr CW2 ....221 C8
Friar's Cl SK9 ....59 E8
Friars Ave WA5 ....14 E5
Friars Cl Rainow SK10 ...88 D5
  Wistaston CW2 ....205 F8
Friars Ct [3] WA1 ....16 B5
Friars Gate Chester CH1 .237 B2
  Warrington WA1 ....16 B4
Friars La WA1 ....16 B4
Friars Way SK10 ....86 F2
Frida Cres CW9 ....103 E6
Friends La WA5 ....14 D3
Friesian Gdns ST5 ....210 C2
Frith Ave CW8 ....123 D8
Frith La CW5 ....216 C4
Frith Terr SK11 ....112 D4
Frobisher Ct WA5 ....15 D8
Frobisher Rd CH64 ....66 E8
Froda Ave WA6 ....74 B7
Frodsham CE Prim Sch
  WA6 ....74 C7
Frodsham Rd WA6 ....73 D1
Frodsham Sch WA6 ....74 B8
Frodsham Sq CH1 ....237 B3
Frodsham St
  Chester CH1 ....237 B3
  Helsby WA6 ....73 B4
Frodsham Way SK9 ....34 E1
Frog La Holt LL13 ....196 D8
  Milton Green CH3 ....165 E2
  Pickmere WA16 ....55 B1
  Worthenbury SY14 ....211 B1
Froghall La
  High Legh WA16 ....29 D7
  High Legh WA16 ....29 E6
  Warrington WA5 ....15 F5
Frome Ct CH65 ....70 B7
Front St LL11 ....175 C6
Frosts Mews CH65 ....70 B6
Fryer Rd CW9 ....80 A3
Fryer St [16] WA7 ....23 A3
Fuchsia Cl CH66 ....69 F1
Fulbeck WA8 ....12 C2
Fulbeck Ct CW1 ....206 B8
Fulbrook Dr SK8 ....35 A6
Fuller Dr CW2 ....206 B7
Fullerton Rd CW8 ....103 A4
Fulmar Cl SK12 ....36 A4
Fulmards Cl SK9 ....60 C7
Fulshaw Ave SK9 ....60 A6
Fulshaw Ct SK9 ....60 A5
Fulshaw Pk SK9 ....60 A5

Fulshaw Pk S SK9 . . . . .60 A4
Fulton Gr CW9 . . . . .103 F2
Fulwood Gdns CH66 . . . . . . .69 C6
Fulwood Mews CH66 . . . . . .69 C6
Fulwood Rd
  Ellesmere Port CH66 . . . . . . .69 C5
  Golborne WA3 . . . . .3 E7
Furber St CW1 . . . . .190 C5
Furne Rd CH1 . . . . .117 E4
Furness Cl
  Holmes Chapel CW4 . . . . . .130 A3
  Poynton SK12 . . . . .36 D4
  Winsford CW7 . . . . .149 B8
Furness Ct WA7 . . . . .24 F4
Furness Lodge Cl SK23 . . .39 D4
Furness Rd SK8 . . . . .35 C6
Furness Vale Bsns Ctr
  SK23 . . . . .39 D4
Furness Vale Prim Sch
  SK23 . . . . .39 D3
Furness Vale Sta SK23 . . .39 D4
Furnival St CW2 . . . . .190 C2
Furnivall St CW11 . . . . . . .175 B7
Furrocks Cl CH64 . . . . .66 F5
Furrocks La CH64 . . . . .66 F5
Furrocks Way CH64 . . . . . . .66 F5
Furrows The CH66 . . . . .94 F8
Fylde Ave SK8 . . . . .34 C8
Fytton Cl SK11 . . . . .111 D1

G

Gable Ave SK9 . . . . .60 A7
Gable Ct S CW5 . . . . .204 E6
Gable St WA12 . . . . .2 B3
Gables Cl WA2 . . . . .8 F3
Gables The ST7 . . . . .193 C3
Gabriel Bank CW8 . . . . .76 A1
Gadbrook Bsns Ctr
  CW9 . . . . .104 D5
Gadbrook Pk CW9 . . . . . . .104 D5
Gadbrook Rd CW9 . . . . . . .104 D6
Gail Cl SK9 . . . . .60 D8
Gainford Cl WA8 . . . . .12 C3
Gainsborough Cl SK9 . . . .60 D8
Gainsborough Cl WA8 . . .12 B1
Gainsborough Inf Sch
  CW2 . . . . .190 B3
Gainsborough Jun Sch
  CW2 . . . . .190 B2
Gainsborough Rd
  Crewe CW2 . . . . .190 B3
  Warrington WA4 . . . . .16 B2
Gairloch Cl WA2 . . . . .8 F4
Gaisgill Ct WA8 . . . . .12 C1
Gala Cl CH4 . . . . .139 C3
Galbraith Cl CW12 . . . . . .156 C2
Gale Ave WA5 . . . . .7 F1
Galion Way WA8 . . . . .12 F3
Galleys Bank ST7 . . . . . . .195 B3
Gallimore Ho ST7 . . . . . . .210 D8
Galloway Cl
  Holmes Chapel CW4 . . . . . .130 C2
  Middlewich CW10 . . . . .128 E2
Gallowsclough La WA6 . .100 F4
Galway Ave WA8 . . . . .12 E3
Galway Gr CW2 . . . . .206 B4
Game St CW11 . . . . .175 A3
Gamul Pl CH1 . . . . .237 B1
Ganton Cl WA8 . . . . .13 B4
Garden Cl SK10 . . . . .87 E1
Garden Ct CH2 . . . . .42 A3
Garden La Chester CH1 . . . .237 A3
  Harthill CH3 . . . . .183 E3
Garden Rd WA16 . . . . .56 F3
Garden St Bollington SK10 . .87 F8
  Congleton CW12 . . . . .156 C3
  Macclesfield SK10 . . . . .87 E1
Garden Terr
  Chester CH1 . . . . .237 A3
  Chester,Boughton CH2 . . . .118 F2
Garden Villas SK8 . . . . . . .34 B7
Garden Wlk M31 . . . . .11 E1
Gardens The Holt LL13 . . .180 E1
  Sandbach CW11 . . . . .175 B6
Gardiner Ave WA11 . . . . . . .1 C6
Garfit St CW10 . . . . .128 C2
Garner St WA2 . . . . .16 C7
Garnett Ave WA4 . . . . .17 A4
Garnett Cl CW5 . . . . .204 F4
Garnetts La WA8 . . . . .222 A3
Garrett Field WA3 . . . . .9 D5
Garrigill Cl WA8 . . . . .13 C5
Garsdale Cl WA8 . . . . .13 C5
Garside Ave WA3 . . . . .3 D7
Garth Dr CH2 . . . . .118 C5
Garth Hts SK9 . . . . .60 C7
Garth Rd CH65 . . . . .71 A5
Garton Dr WA3 . . . . .3 E8
Garven Pl WA1 . . . . .16 A5
Gas Rd SK11 . . . . .112 D8
Gas Works Ind Est ST7 . .196 E2
Gaskell Ave
  Knutsford WA16 . . . . .56 F2
  Warrington WA4 . . . . .17 A3
Gaskell St WA4 . . . . .16 C1
Gatcombe Mews S SK9 . .60 A6
Gate Warth St WA5 . . . . . . .15 D4
Gatesacre Ct CH66 . . . . . . .69 F8
Gatefield St CW1 . . . . .190 C4
Gateley Cl WA4 . . . . .17 E3
Gatesheath Dr CH2 . . . . . .118 E7
Gatesheath La CH3 . . . . . .165 F5

Gatewarth Ind Est WA5 . . .15 D3
Gateway Crewe CW1 . . . .190 F2
  Newcastle-u-Lyme ST5 . . .210 D2
Gathurst Ct WA8 . . . . .22 D8
Gauntley Bird of Prey Ctr*
  SK10 . . . . .85 B2
Gauntons Bank SY13 . . . .215 E3
Gaunts Way WA7 . . . . .49 E6
Gavin Rd WA8 . . . . .22 B7
Gaw End La SK11 . . . . . . .112 C2
Gawer Pk CH2 . . . . .118 C4
Gawsworth Ave CW2 . . . .189 F3
Gawsworth Cl
  Alsager ST7 . . . . .193 C3
  Bramhall SK7 . . . . .35 E6
  Holmes Chapel CW4 . . . . . .130 B3
  Northwich CW8 . . . . .104 A4
  Poynton SK12 . . . . .36 F2
Gawsworth Dr CW11 . . . .175 C7
Gawsworth Hall* SK11 . . .134 E8
Gawsworth Prim Sch
  SK11 . . . . .111 D2
Gawsworth Rd
  Ellesmere Port CH66 . . . . . . .69 E5
  Macclesfield SK11 . . . . .111 D5
Gawsworth Way SK9 . . . .34 E4
Gayhurst Ave WA3 . . . . .2 E8
Gaymoore Cl CH2 . . . . . . .237 A4
Gaynor Ave WA11 . . . . .1 F7
Gayton Cl CH2 . . . . .118 E5
Gayton Farm Rd CH60 . . .41 A5
Gayton La CH60 . . . . .41 B6
Gayton Mill Cl CH60 . . . . .41 B7
Gayton Parkway CH60 . . .41 C5
Gayton Prim Sch CH60 . . .41 A6
Gayton Rd CH60 . . . . .41 A6
Gemini Bsns Pk WA5 . . . . .7 E3
Gemmull Cl WA3 . . . . .229 F4
General St WA1 . . . . .16 C5
Genesis Ctr The WA3 . . . . .9 E5
Geneva Rd CW7 . . . . .126 C1
Geo Hampson's Bldgs
  WA3 .5 C8
George Bates Cl ST7 . . . .193 C3
George Ho CW5 . . . . .204 E7
George Kenyon Mews
  CH4 . . . . .140 E6
George Rd WA5 . . . . .15 C4
George St
  Alderley Edge SK9 . . . . .60 A1
  Audley ST7 . . . . .209 D1
  Barnton CW8 . . . . .78 B3
  Chester CH1 . . . . .237 A3
  Ellesmere Port CH65 . . . . . . .70 C7
  Knutsford WA16 . . . . .57 A2
  Macclesfield SK11 . . . . .112 D7
  Newton-le-W WA12 . . . . .2 A4
  Sandbach CW11 . . . . .174 E8
  Whaley Bridge SK23 . . . . . . .65 E7
  Winsford CW7 . . . . .126 E1
George St W SK11 . . . . . .112 C8
George VI Ave CW10 . . . .151 D6
George VI Ave CW10 . . . .151 D6
George's Cl SK12 . . . . .36 E3
George's La CW9 . . . . .54 D1
George's Prec WA5 . . . . . .14 D6
George's Rd E SK12 . . . . . .36 E3
George's Rd W SK12 . . . . .36 E3
George's Wlk CW11 . . . . .175 B6
Georges Cres WA4 . . . . . .17 B2
Georges Ct S SK10 . . . . .112 C8
Georges Way ST7 . . . . . . .209 F2
Georgia Pl WA5 . . . . .15 C7
Gerard Dr CW5 . . . . .204 C4
Gerosa Ave WA2 . . . . .8 B8
Gerrard Ave
  Ellesmere Port CH66 . . . . . . .69 C4
  Warrington WA5 . . . . .15 F7
Gerrard Dr CW8 . . . . .77 D1
Gerrard Rd WA3 . . . . .9 A7
Gerrard St WA8 . . . . .23 B8
Gerrards Ave CH3 . . . . . . .119 A1
Giantswood La
  Congleton CW12 . . . . .156 C6
  Marton CW12 . . . . .132 F1
Gibb Hill CW9 . . . . .53 D1
Gibbon Dr CW9 . . . . .80 B3
Gibson Cl CW5 . . . . .204 D6
Gibson Cres CW11 . . . . . .174 D6
Gibson Cl Trad Est CH5 .70 C8
Gibson St
  Warrington, Howley WA1 . . .16 C5
  Warrington, Stockton Heath
  WA4 .16 D1
Gig La WA1 . . . . .17 E8
Gigg La Moore WA4 . . . . . .25 B5
  Warrington WA4 . . . . .17 E3
Gilbert Cl S ST7 . . . . . . .195 A2
Gilbert Ct WA1 . . . . .4 F3
Gilchrist Ave SK11 . . . . . .111 E7
Gilchrist Rd M44 . . . . .11 F6
Gilderdale Cl WA3 . . . . .10 B6
Gillan Cl WA7 . . . . .50 C5
Gillbent Rd SK8 . . . . .35 A7
Gillow Cl CW1 . . . . .190 A8
Gillthrook Cl WA8 . . . . .13 B3
Gilwell Ct WA4 . . . . .26 D8
Gingerbread La CW5 . . . .205 A5
Gipsy Cnr SY13 . . . . .224 E2
Girton Cl CH65 . . . . .70 D4
Girton Rd CH65 . . . . .70 D4
Girvin Dr CH64 . . . . .66 F6
Gladewood Cl SK9 . . . . . . .59 D5
Gladstone Ave Cl SK9 . .60 E8
Gladstone Ave CH4 . . . . .118 B2
Gladstone Rd
  Broughton CH4 . . . . .139 C4
  Chester CH1 . . . . .118 B3

Gladstone Rd continued
  Neston CH64 . . . . .66 E8
Gladstone St Crewe CW1 .190 C4
  Northwich CW8 . . . . .103 E7
  Warrington WA2 . . . . .16 A6
  S Widnes WA8 . . . . .23 B8
  Willaston CW5 . . . . .205 D6
  Winsford CW7 . . . . .149 D8
Gladstone Way WA12 . . . . .2 A4
Glaisdale Cl CW2 . . . . . . .206 A6
Glamis Cl Chester CH3 . . .119 A2
  Wistaston CW2 . . . . .205 E8
Glan Aber Dr CH4 . . . . . . .140 F7
Glan Aber Pk CH4 . . . . . . .141 A7
Glanaber Ct CH4 . . . . .141 A7
Glandon Dr SK8 . . . . .35 C8
Glastonbury Ave
  Cheadle Hulme SK8 . . . . . . .35 C6
  Chester CH2 . . . . .118 F7
Glastonbury Cl WA7 . . . . .24 F3
Glastonbury Dr
  Middlewich CW10 . . . . .128 B1
  Poynton SK12 . . . . .36 D5
Glastonbury Mews WA4 . .26 C2
Glazebrook La WA3 . . . . . .11 B5
Glazebrook St WA3 . . . . . .16 B6
Glazebrook Sta WA3 . . . . .11 B5
Glazebury CE Prim Sch
  WA3 .5 C7
Glaziers La WA3 . . . . .4 D2
Gleadmere WA8 . . . . .12 C2
Gleaner Cl WA7 . . . . .22 F3
Gleave Ave SK10 . . . . .88 B8
Gleave Rd Burtonwood WA5 . .6 F6
  Weaverham CW8 . . . . .77 D1
Glebe Ave WA4 . . . . .17 C1
Glebe Cl CW5 . . . . .220 A8
Glebe Farm Mews CH2 . . .71 E2
Glebe Green Dr WA7 . . . .149 C6
Glebe La WA8 . . . . .13 B5
Glebe Mdws CH2 . . . . .96 F1
Glebe Rd CW8 . . . . .102 A4
Glebe St ST7 . . . . .194 D2
Glebe The WA7 . . . . .23 E1
Glebecroft Ave CH2 . . . . . .72 A3
Glebeland WA3 . . . . .4 E2
Glebelands Rd WA16 . . . .57 A1
Glebeway Rd CH65 . . . . . . .70 F5
Glegg St SK11 . . . . .112 E7
Gleggs Cl CH3 . . . . .142 B7
Glen Cl WA3 . . . . .11 B2
Glen Rd CH66 . . . . .69 C4
Glen The Blacon CH1 . . . .117 E5
  Runcorn WA7 . . . . .49 F5
Glenathol Rd CH66 . . . . . .69 C4
Glenbourne Pk SK7 . . . . . .35 D5
Glenburn Ave CH62 . . . . . .43 E4
Glencoe Cl CH4 . . . . .130 C2
Glencoe Rd CH66 . . . . .69 C4
Glencourse Rd WA8 . . . . . .13 A5
Glendale Ave Elton CH2 . . .72 A3
  Sandycroft CH5 . . . . .116 A3
Glendale Bsns Pk CH5 . .116 A3
Glendale Cl Buerton CW3 .230 F4
  Crewe CW2 . . . . .189 D3
Glendale Pk CH5 . . . . .116 A3
Glendene Ave SK7 . . . . . . .35 D6
Glendyke Rd CH66 . . . . . . .69 C4
Gleneagles Cl
  Bramhall SK7 . . . . .36 A7
  Chester CH3 . . . . .119 B3
  Golborne WA3 . . . . .3 E7
  Wilmslow SK9 . . . . .60 D8
Gleneagles Dr
  Haydock WA11 . . . . .1 A5
  Holmes Chapel CW4 . . . . . .130 B2
  Macclesfield SK10 . . . . .87 C4
  Warrington WA1 . . . . .17 D7
Gleneagles Rd
  Heald Green SK8 . . . . .34 C7
  Kidsgrove ST7 . . . . .195 A3
  Knutsford WA16 . . . . .81 F8
  Poynton SK12 . . . . .36 D4
Glenesk Rd CH66 . . . . .69 C4
Glenfield Dr SK12 . . . . .36 D3
Glenholme Rd SK7 . . . . . . .35 D7
Glenmaye Rd CH66 . . . . . .69 C4
Glenn Pl WA8 . . . . .12 E1
Glenorchy Cl CW4 . . . . . .130 C2
Glenside Cl CH1 . . . . .117 D5
Glenside Dr SK9 . . . . .60 C6
Glenton Pk CH64 . . . . .66 F6
Glenville Cl WA7 . . . . .50 D7
Glenwood CH1 . . . . .117 D4
Glenwood Cl S WA7 . . . . . .50 D7
Glenwood Gdns CH66 . . . .69 C6
Glenwood Rd CH66 . . . . . . .69 C6
Gleyve WA16 . . . . .29 C5
Gloucester Ave WA3 . . . . . .3 B8
Gloucester Cl
  Ellesmere Port CH66 . . . . . . .94 E8
  Macclesfield SK10 . . . . .87 E4
  Warrington WA1 . . . . .17 D7
Gloucester Rd
  Heald Green SK8 . . . . .34 C7
  Kidsgrove ST7 . . . . .195 A3
  Knutsford WA16 . . . . .81 F8
  Poynton SK12 . . . . .36 D4

Godfrey St WA2 . . . . .16 D7
Godscroft La WA6 . . . . .73 E6
Godshill Cl WA5 . . . . .14 D7
Godstall La CH1 . . . . .237 B2
Godstow WA7 . . . . .24 A4
Godward Rd SK22 . . . . .39 B8
Golborne Dale Rd WA3,
  WA12 . . . . .3 A5
Golborne Jun & Inf Sch
  WA3 .3 A8
Golborne Rd Golborne WA3 . .28 F3
  Golborne Rd Golborne WA3 . .3 C8
  Winwick WA12,WA2 . . . . .8 A7
Gold Triangle Complex
  WA8 . . . . .22 C5
Goldcliffe Cl WA5 . . . . .7 D3
Goldcrest Cl Runcorn WA7 . .49 F5
  Winsford CW7 . . . . .149 C5
Golden Sq WA1 . . . . .16 B5
Goldfinch Cl CW12 . . . . . .156 E1
Goldfinch Dr ST7 . . . . . . .193 B3
Goldfinch La WA3 . . . . .9 E4
Goldfinch Rd ST7 . . . . . . .195 F1
Goldford La CW3 . . . . .199 F6
Goldsmith Dr CW11 . . . . .174 D6
Golftyn Dr CH5 . . . . .91 C1
Golftyn La CH5 . . . . .91 C1
Gongar La
  Ashton Hayes CH3 . . . . . . .121 E8
  Mouldsworth CH3 . . . . .98 E1
Gonsley Cl CH2 . . . . .237 B4
Gonville Ave SK11 . . . . . .112 F3
Gooch Dr WA12 . . . . .2 D2
Goodall St SK11 . . . . .112 E7
Goodall's Cnr CW2 . . . . . .206 C3
Goodrington Rd SK9 . . . . .34 E3
Goodwin Cres CW2 . . . . .206 C4
Goodwood Cl
  Barnton CW8 . . . . .78 B3
  Chester CH1 . . . . .118 B2
Goodwood Gr CH66 . . . . . .69 D3
Goodwood Rise CW10 . .128 A2
Goose La WA4 . . . . .26 A2
Gooseberry La
  Kelsall CW6 . . . . .122 E3
  Runcorn WA7 . . . . .24 D1
Goosebrook Cl CW9 . . . . .78 D8
Goosebrook La WA4,CW9 .52 F2
Goosetrey Com Prim Sch
  CW4 . . . . .130 F8
Goostrey Com Prim Sch (The
  Annexe) CW4 . . . . .107 F1
Goostrey Ct S CW12 . . . .156 F3
Goostrey La
  Goostrey CW4 . . . . .130 B8
  Holmes Chapel CW4 . . . . . .131 A6
  Station CW4 . . . . .131 A8
Gordale
  Congleton CW12 . . . . .157 A5
  Northwich CW8 . . . . .103 D8
  Warrington WA5 . . . . .14 F7
  Winnington CW8 . . . . .78 D1
Gordon Ave
  Bebington CH62 . . . . .43 E7
  Haydock WA11 . . . . .1 F7
  Warrington WA1 . . . . .17 B7
  Widnes WA8 . . . . .13 D1
Gordon La CH1 . . . . .95 B5
Gore La SK9 . . . . .59 C3
Gorran Haven WA7 . . . . . .50 C5
Gorse Bank Rd WA15 . . . .32 C7
Gorse Cl WA6 . . . . .101 A6
Gorse Covert CW9 . . . . . . .79 C3
Gorse Covert Prim Sch
  WA3 . . . . .10 B5
Gorse Covert Rd WA3 . . . .10 B6
Gorse La CW12 . . . . .178 D5
Gorse Sq M31 . . . . .11 D3
Gorse Stacks CH1 . . . . . .237 B3
Gorse The WA14 . . . . .31 B8
Gorse Way CH3 . . . . .142 A5
Gorsefield Ave CH62 . . . . .43 D5
Gorsefield Cl CH62 . . . . . .43 D5
Gorsefield Hey SK9 . . . . . .60 E8
Gorselands SK8 . . . . .35 B5
Gorsewood Prim Sch
  WA7 . . . . .50 D7
Gorsewood Rd WA7 . . . . . .50 D6
Gorsey Bank Cres CW5 .220 A8
Gorsey Bank Prim Sch
  SK9 .59 F7
Gorsey La
  Partington WA13 . . . . .19 C7
  St Helens WA5,WA9 . . . . . . .6 E5
  Warrington WA1,WA2 . . . . . .16 D7
  Widnes WA8 . . . . .13 E1
Gorsey Rd SK9 . . . . .59 F8
Gorseywell La WA7 . . . . . .50 F6
Gorstage La CW8 . . . . .102 C7
Gorsthills Com Prim Sch
  CH66 . . . . .69 C3
Gorston Wlk M22 . . . . .33 C8
Gorstons La CH64 . . . . .67 A6
Gorsty Hill Cl CW2 . . . . . .207 F2
Gorstyrihole La CW12 . . .158 A2
Gosforth Ct WA7 . . . . .49 E7
Gosforth Pl CH2 . . . . .118 F3
Gosforth Rd CW2 . . . . .189 F2
Gosling Rd WA3 . . . . .9 C2
Gosling Way WA3 . . . . . . .156 A3
Gosport Cl WA2 . . . . .8 F1
Goss St CH1 . . . . .237 A2

Gough Ave WA2 . . . . .8 B2
Gough's La WA16 . . . . .82 C7
Goulden St Crewe CW1 . .190 A5
Goulden St Warrington WA1 . .15 E6
Goulders Ct WA7 . . . . .50 B5
Goulders Ct WA7 . . . . .50 B5
Gowy Cl Alsager ST7 . . . .192 F3
  Handforth SK9 . . . . .34 E1
  Sandbach CW11 . . . . .174 E8
Gowy Cres CH3 . . . . .121 B2
Gowy Ct Alpraham CW6 . .169 E2
  Ellesmere Port CH66 . . . . . . .69 E8
Gowy Rd CH2 . . . . .96 F1
Gowy Wlk CW7 . . . . .127 A3
Goyt St SK23 . . . . .65 E7
Goyt Rd Disley SK12 . . . . .38 D5
  New Mills SK22 . . . . .39 C6
  Whaley Bridge SK23 . . . . . . .65 E6
Goyt Valley Ind Est SK23 . .39 D4
Goyt View SK22 . . . . .39 B6
Goyt's La SK17 . . . . .90 F2
Grace Ave WA2 . . . . .16 B8
Grace Cl CW1 . . . . .191 C4
Grace Rd CH65 . . . . .70 C7
Gradbach Mill* SK17 . . . .138 A1
Grafton Mews CH2 . . . . . .237 B4
Grafton Rd CH65 . . . . .70 C7
Grafton St
  Newton-le-W WA12 . . . . .2 B3
  Warrington WA5 . . . . .15 E6
Graham Ave CH66 . . . . . . .69 D5
Graham Cl WA8 . . . . .12 C1
Graham Cres M44 . . . . . . .11 C3
Graham Dr Disley SK12 . . .38 C6
Halewood L26 . . . . .21 A8
Graham Rd Blacon CH1 . .117 F3
  Widnes WA8 . . . . .22 C8
Grainger's Rd CW9 . . . . .103 F5
Grammar School Ct WA4 .16 F3
Grammar School Rd
  Lymm WA13 . . . . .18 F2
  Warrington WA4 . . . . .16 F3
Grampian Way
  Bebington CH62 . . . . .43 E4
  Neston CH64 . . . . .66 E5
  Winsford CW7 . . . . .149 A7
Granary Mill WA7 . . . . . . .50 F6
Granby Cl WA7 . . . . .50 C5
Granby Rd
  Cheadle Hulme SK8 . . . . . . .35 B8
  Warrington WA4 . . . . .16 E4
Grand Junction Ret Pk
  CW1 . . . . .190 D3
Grandford La CW5 . . . . . .217 D2
Grange Ave Barnton CW8 . .78 A3
  Warrington WA4 . . . . .16 E4
Grange Cl Crewe CW1 . . .190 E3
  Golborne WA3 . . . . .3 C6
  Sandbach CW11 . . . . .174 F7
Grange Com Prim Sch
  CW7 . . . . .126 B1
Grange Comp Sch WA7 . .23 C1
Grange Cres CH66 . . . . . . .44 A1
Grange Ct Biddulph ST8 . .179 D2
  S Knutsford WA16 . . . . .57 A2
  Winsford CW7 . . . . .126 B2
Grange Dr Hartford CW8 . .103 A6
  Thornton Hough CH63 . . . . . .42 A7
  Warrington WA5 . . . . .15 C5
  Widnes WA8 . . . . .12 D1
Grange Farm Cl WA5 . . . .15 D6
Grange Green Manor
  WA4 . . . . .25 E7
Grange Inf Sch The WA7 .23 C1
Grange Jun Sch The
  Runcorn WA7 . . . . .23 C1
Grange La Tilston SY14 . .198 E3
  Weaverham CW8 . . . . .102 A7
  Whitegate CW8 . . . . .125 F7
Grange Lea CW10 . . . . . .128 B1
Grange Park Ave
  Runcorn WA7 . . . . .23 C2
  Wilmslow SK9 . . . . .60 A8
Grange Park Dr ST8 . . . . .179 E3
Grange Pl M44 . . . . .11 E5
Grange Rd Barnton CW8 . .78 A3
  Biddulph ST8 . . . . .179 E3
  Chester CH2 . . . . .118 D4
  Ellesmere Port CH66 . . . . . . .70 C4
  Chester,Vicars Cross CH3 .119 C2
  Cuddington CW8 . . . . .101 F3
  Ellesmere Port CH65 . . . . . . .70 C4
  Haydock WA11,WA12 . . . . . . .1 F7
  Macclesfield SK11 . . . . .112 C6
  Mouldsworth CH3 . . . . .99 B1
  Northwich,Rudheath CW9 .104 D6
  Runcorn WA7 . . . . .23 C2
Grange Rd N WA7 . . . . . . .23 C2
Grange Rd W CH3 . . . . . . .119 C2
Grange Terr The CW8 . . .103 B6
Grange The
  Hartford CW8 . . . . .103 B5
  Macclesfield SK11 . . . . .112 A6
Grange Valley WA11 . . . . .1 D6
Grange Valley Prim Sch
  WA11 . . . . .1 D6
Grange Villas CH3 . . . . . .142 F6
Grange Way WA7 . . . . .50 F6
Grange Pk S CH66 . . . . . .69 D3
Grangebrook Dr CW7 . . .126 C3
Grangelands SK10 . . . . . . .86 F2
Grangemoor WA7 . . . . .49 D8
Grangeside CH2 . . . . .118 D7
Grangeway Handforth SK9 . .34 D4
  Runcorn WA7 . . . . .49 C8
Grangeway Ct WA7 . . . . . .49 C8
Grangewood Dr SK11 . . . .83 F3
Granston Cl WA5 . . . . .7 E2

Grant Cl WA5 ....7 D1
Grant Rd WA5 ....15 B6
Grantham Ave
  Warrington WA4 ....26 B8
  Warrington,Bruche WA1 ...16 E7
Grantham Cl CW9 ....104 C7
Granville Dr CH66 ....69 B7
Granville Rd
  Chester CH1 ....118 B3
  Northwich CW9 ....104 A5
  Wilmslow SK9 ....59 F5
Granville Sq CW7 ....149 E8
Granville St
  15 Runcorn WA7 ....23 A3
  Warrington WA1 ....16 D6
  Winsford CW7 ....149 E8
Grapes St 9 SK11 ....112 D7
Grappenhall Hall Sch
  WA4 ....17 B1
Grappenhall Heys Com Prim
  Sch WA4 ....27 A7
Grappenhall La WA4 ...27 E6
Grappenhall Rd
  Ellesmere Port CH65 ....69 F3
  Warrington WA4 ....16 D1
Grappenhall St Wilfrid's CE
  Prim Sch WA4 ....17 B1
Grasmere SK11 ....112 A6
Grasmere Ave
  Congleton CW12 ....155 F2
  Crewe CW2 ....189 F5
  Warrington WA2 ....8 C7
Grasmere Cl CW7 ....126 D2
Grasmere Cres
  Bramhall SK7 ....35 E8
  High Lane SK6 ....37 E8
Grasmere Dr
  Holmes Chapel CW4 ...130 A3
  Runcorn WA7 ....49 D5
Grasmere Rd
  Alderley Edge SK9 ....60 A1
  Chester CH2 ....118 F5
  Ellesmere Port CH65 ....70 C2
  Frodsham WA6 ....74 C8
  Lymm WA13 ....18 F4
  Neston CH64 ....66 E6
  Partington M31 ....11 E3
Grason Ave WA3 ....34 C1
Grassfield Way WA16 ...82 A8
Grassmoor Cl CH62 ....43 D8
Grassy Green La ST7 ...209 E1
Gratrix Rd CH62 ....43 D8
Gravel La SK9 ....59 E5
Gravenhunger La CW3 .232 D1
Graveyard La WA16 ....58 F5
Gray Ave WA11 ....1 D6
Gray's Cl ST7 ....195 B7
Graylag Cl WA7 ....50 B6
Graymarsh Dr SK12 ....36 E2
Greasby Dr CH66 ....69 E4
Great Ashfield WA8 ....12 D3
Great Budworth CE Prim Sch
  CW9 ....79 B8
Great Delph WA11 ....1 D7
Great King St SK11 ....112 C7
Great Oak Rd ST7 ....209 F4
Great Queen St SK11 ...112 C8
Great Riding WA7 ....50 C7
Great Sankey High Sch
  WA5 ....14 E7
Great Sankey Prim Sch
  WA5 ....15 A5
Greater Grace Sch CH1 ...95 B4
Greaves La E SY14 ....222 E6
Greaves La E SY14 ....222 E7
Greaves Rd SK9 ....59 E7
Grebe Cl Knutsford WA16 ...57 B3
  Poynton SK12 ....36 B4
Greeba Ave WA4 ....16 B3
Greek St WA7 ....22 F3
Green Acre Cl WA16 ...82 B8
Green Ave
  Alpraham CW6 ....169 D4
  Barnton CW8 ....78 A3
  Davenham CW9 ....103 F3
Green Bank
  Adderley TF9 ....235 A5
  Chester CH4 ....141 E6
Green Bridge Cl WA7 ...24 A2
Green Coppice WA7 ....50 C8
Green Dr Alsager ST7 ...193 D4
  Handforth SK9 ....34 D2
Green Farm CH4 ....163 B2
Green Hall Mews SK9 ...60 B6
Green La Acton CW5 ...204 B3
  Alderley Edge SK9 ....60 A1
  Audlem CW3 ....229 F2
  Barbridge CW5 ....187 A7
  Bollington SK10 ....63 B1
  Burtonwood WA5 ....6 E7
  Chester CH4 ....140 E4
  Chester,Vicars Cross CH3 .119 B3
  Davenham CW9 ....103 F3
  Disley SK12 ....38 D4
  Ellesmere Port CH65 ....70 C4
  Ellesmere Port,Great Sutton
    CH66 ....69 C4
  Higher Kinnerton CH4 ...161 B6
  Higher Wincham CW9 ...79 F4
  Irlam M44 ....11 E5
  Kelsall CW6 ....122 D4
  Knutsford WA16 ....56 D4
  Lindow End SK9 ....84 F8
  Over Peover WA16 ....83 D1
  Picton CH2 ....96 C3
  Plumley WA16 ....80 E6
  Poynton SK12 ....37 C4

Green La continued
  Sandbach CW11 ....173 F7
  Saughall CH1 ....117 C7
  Shocklach SY14 ....211 C7
  Tattenhall CH3 ....182 F5
  Tilston SY14 ....212 B8
  Warrington,Dudlow's Green
    WA4 ....26 F5
  Warrington,Paddington
    WA1 ....17 A8
  Widnes WA8 ....12 E1
  Willaston CW5 ....205 E5
  Wilmslow SK9 ....60 B7
  Winwick WA2 ....8 A7
Green Lake La CH3 ...163 F3
Green Lane CH4 ....17 B8
Green Lane Com Spcl Sch
  WA1 ....17 B8
Green Lane E
  Connah's Quay CH5 ....93 C1
  Sealand CH5 ....116 D7
Green Lane Est
  Connah's Quay CH5 ....93 C1
  Sealand CH5 ....116 C8
Green Lane W CH5 ....93 B3
Green Lawns Dr CH66 ...94 F8
Green Mdws Golborne WA3 .3 E5
  Macclesfield SK11 ....111 A8
Green Oaks Path WA8 ...23 C8
Green Oaks Way WA8 ...23 C8
Green Pk CW8 ....102 E7
Green Rd M31 ....11 E3
Green St
  9 Alderley Edge SK9 ....60 A1
  Holt LL13 ....180 E1
  Knutsford WA16 ....57 A2
  Macclesfield SK10 ....112 C7
  Sandbach CW11 ....175 B6
  Warrington WA5 ....15 E5
  Warrington WA5 ....15 F5
Green The
  Cheadle Hulme SK8 ....34 F8
  Congleton CW12 ....156 C2
  Ellesmere Port CH65 ....70 B2
  Hale L24 ....21 D1
  Handforth SK9 ....34 E3
  Harthill CH3 ....183 E3
  Higher Kinnerton CH4 ...161 B7
  Lawton-gate ST7 ....194 A4
  Middlewich CW10 ....151 D6
  Nantwich CW5 ....204 D8
  Neston CH64 ....66 E6
  Neston, Little Neston CH64 .66 F6
  Partington M31 ....11 F4
  4 Runcorn WA7 ....23 F1
  Tarvin CH3 ....121 F2
  Thornton Hough CH63 ...42 C4
  Wrenbury CW5 ....216 E4
Green View WA16 ....59 E4
Green Villa Pk SK9 ....59 E4
Green Wlk
  Cuddington CW8 ....102 B4
  Partington M31 ....11 E3
Greenacre Dr CH63 ....43 C7
Greenacre Rd CH4 ...140 F4
Greenacres Crewe CW1 .190 C6
  Duddon CW6 ....145 A6
  Frodsham WA6 ....74 C6
  Sandbach CW11 ....175 A7
Greenacres Cl WA3 ....4 B8
Greenacres Ct CH2 ....95 F1
Greenacres Rd CW12 ...155 F2
Greenacres The WA13 ...19 A4
Greenall Ave WA5 ....16 C2
Greenall Rd CW9 ....104 B8
Greenall's Ave WA4 ....16 C2
Greenbank CH4 ....141 E6
Greenbank Ave CH66 ...69 F7
Greenbank Cl CW5 ....205 D6
Greenbank Dr SK10 ....88 A8
Greenbank Gdns WA4 ...16 F2
Greenbank La CH4 ....103 D6
Greenbank Pk CW11 ...175 A2
Greenbank Rd
  Chester CH2 ....119 A4
  Warrington WA4 ....16 F2
Greenbank Residential Sch
  CW8 ....103 D6
Greenbank Sta CW8 ...103 D6
Greenbridge Rd WA7 ...24 B2
Greencourts Bsns Pk
  M22 ....34 A8
Greendale Dr
  Middlewich CW10 ....151 B7
  Newcastle-u-Lyme ST5 .210 D1
Greendale Gdns CW5 ...190 E5
Greendale La SK10 ....86 D8
Greenfield Ave CH4 ...161 A7
Greenfield Cl SK22 ....39 A3
Greenfield Cres
  Chester CH2 ....119 B5
  Waverton CH3 ....143 B6
Greenfield Farm Ind Est
  CW12 ....156 B3
Greenfield Gdns CH2 ...72 B3
Greenfield La
  Chester CH2 ....119 C5
  Frodsham WA6 ....49 B1
Greenfield Rd
  Bollington SK10 ....88 A4
  Broughton CH4 ....139 C4
  Congleton CW12 ....156 B3
  Ellesmere Port CH66 ....69 B7
  Waverton CH3 ....143 B6
Greenfield Way CW8 ...102 A4

Greenfields Chester CH2 ...95 F1
  Winsford CW7 ....127 B1
Greenfields Ave
  Bebington CH62 ....43 C7
  Shavington CW2 ....206 B4
  Warrington WA4 ....26 D8
Greenfields Cl
  Neston CH64 ....66 F5
  Newton-le-W WA12 ....2 C4
  Warrington WA4 ....17 C7
Greenfields Cres CH62 ...43 C7
Greenfields Croft CH64 ...66 E5
Greenfields Dr
  Alsager ST7 ....193 E3
  Neston CH64 ....66 F5
Greenfields La
  Malpas SY14 ....213 B4
  Rowton CH3 ....142 F5
Greenfields Lodge CH3 .120 D6
Greenfields Prim Sch
  CW7 ....126 A1
Greengate WA15 ....32 D7
Greengate Rd ST7 ....195 B4
Greengates Cres CH64 ...66 E5
Greenhaven Ct CW5 ...219 E5
Greenhill La WA4 ....52 A5
Greenhill Wlk SK12 ....38 D6
Greenhills Cl SK11 ....112 E7
Greenhouse Farm Rd
  WA7 ....50 B6
Greenhythe Rd SK8 ....34 C6
Greenlake Rd L24 ....21 D1
Greenlands CH1 ....166 B3
Greenlands Cl 3 SK8 ...34 E8
Greenlaw Cl CW9 ....104 A5
Greenlea Cl CH65 ....70 B2
Greenoaks Ctr WA8 ...23 B8
Greenoaks Farm Ind Est
  WA8 ....23 C8
Greenoak Mews WA8 ...12 C3
Greenore Dr L24 ....21 D2
Greens The WA15 ....32 D7
Greenshall La SK12 ....38 F5
Greenshank Cl WA12 ....2 C4
Greenside Ave WA6 ....74 D7
Greenside Ct CW9 ....105 D5
Greenside Dr CW9 ....105 A8
Greenway CH4 ....141 A7
Greenway Alsager ST7 ...193 B5
  Bramhall SK7 ....35 D6
  Congleton CW12 ....156 B3
  Crewe CW1 ....190 D7
  Farndon CH3 ....180 F1
  Neston CH64 ....41 B2
  Saughall CH1 ....94 A1
  Tilston SY14 ....198 C3
  Warrington WA4 ....26 D7
  Warrington,Great Sankey
    WA5 ....14 E7
  Warrington,Paddington
    WA1 ....16 F7
  Wilmslow SK9 ....60 B6
Greenway Cl Helsby WA6 .73 B3
  Rode Heath ST7 ....193 F8
Greenway Dr CW9 ....104 C7
Greenway Rd
  Biddulph ST8 ....179 E2
  Heald Green SK8 ....34 C6
  Runcorn WA7 ....23 A1
  Speke L24 ....21 A3
  Widnes WA8 ....22 B5
Greenway St CH4 ....237 B1
Greenway Wlk CW9 ...104 C7
Greenways ST7 ....209 F2
Greenways Ct CH62 ...43 C6
Greenwell Rd WA11 ....1 C6
Greenwich Ave WA8 ...13 D4
Greenwood Ave
  Chester CH4 ....141 D7
  Congleton CW12 ....156 F3
Greenwood Cl CW8 ....77 D1
Greenwood Cres WA2 ...8 E2
Greenwood Dr
  Newton-le-W WA12 ....2 C4
  Runcorn WA7 ....24 F4
  Wilmslow SK9 ....60 B7
Greenwood Rd WA13 ...18 F2
Greenwood Terr WA16 ...58 A4
Greenwood The CW6 ...168 D8
Greg Ave SK10 ....87 E8
Greg Mews SK9 ....34 E3
Gregory Cl WA5 ....15 C7
Gregorys Row WA3 ....4 A8
Gregson Rd WA8 ....13 C1
Grenfell Cl CH64 ....41 C1
Grenfell Cl CH64 ....66 E5
Grenfell Pk CH64 ....41 C1
Grenfell St 11 WA8 ....23 A7
Grenville Cl CW1 ....191 C5
Grenville Cres CH63 ...43 C7
Grenville Rd CH64 ....41 F1
Gresford Ave CH2 ....237 C4
Gresley Ave CW1 ....190 B8
Gresley Way ST7 ....209 F2
Gresty Bldgs 3 CW5 ...204 E6
Gresty Green Rd CW2 .206 D7
Gresty La CW2 ....204 F4
Gresty Rd CW2 ....190 D1
Gresty Road Football Gd (
  Crewe Alexandra FC)
  CW2 ....190 D2
Gresty Terr CW1 ....190 E4
Greta Ave SK8 ....34 C6
Greville Dr CW7 ....127 A1
Grey Friars CH1 ....237 A2
Grey St WA1 ....16 C6
Greyfriars Cl WA4 ....9 A3

Greyfriars Rd WA2 ....9 A3
Greyhound Park Rd
  CH1 ....118 A3
Greyhound Pk CH1 ..118 A3
Greyhound Rd SK10 ...86 B5
Greymist Ave WA1 ....17 C7
Greys Ct WA1 ....9 C1
Greystoke Dr SK9 ....60 A2
Greystoke Rd SK10 ....87 F2
Greystone Pk CW1 ...190 D4
Greystone Rd WA5 ....14 F4
Greystones CH66 ....69 D4
Greystones Rd CH3 ...119 C1
Grice St WA4 ....16 C1
Griffin Cl Blacon CH1 ...117 F6
  New Mills SK22 ....39 D6
  Norton in Hales TF9 ...236 C2
Griffin La SK8 ....34 D7
Griffin Mews WA8 ....13 B3
Griffith Ave WA3 ....9 E5
Griffiths Dr CW9 ....104 D6
Griffiths Rd
  Lostock Gralam CW9 ....79 F1
  Northwich CW9 ....104 E8
Griffiths St WA4 ....16 F4
Grig Pl ST7 ....193 C5
Grimsditch La WA4 ....52 B5
Grimshaw Ave SK10 ...88 A7
Grimshaw La SK10 ....88 A7
Grindley Bank CH2 ...119 F8
Grindley Gdns CH65 ...70 C2
Grindley Gn SY13 ...228 B3
Grisedale Ave WA2 ....8 B3
Grisedale Cl WA7 ....49 E5
Grisedale Rd CH62 ...43 F8
Grisedale Way SK11 ...112 A5
Gritstone Dr SK10 ....112 A8
Grizedale WA8 ....12 B2
Grizedale Cl CW2 ....189 D2
Groarke Dr WA5 ....14 D5
Groby Rd CW1 ....190 E8
Grocotts Row 12 CW5 ...204 E5
Grosvenor Ave
  Alsager ST7 ....193 D5
  3 Golborne WA3 ....3 D8
  Hartford CW8 ....103 A4
  Warrington WA3 ....16 F7
Grosvenor Cl
  Warrington WA5 ....15 C5
  Wilmslow SK9 ....60 A4
Grosvenor Cotts CH4 ...141 D7
Grosvenor Ct
  Chester CH1 ....237 C2
  Winsford CW7 ....149 C7
  Grosvenor Ctr SK11 ...112 D7
Grosvenor Dr SK12 ....36 D3
Grosvenor Gdns WA12 ...2 C2
Grosvenor Grange WA1 ...9 B1
Grosvenor Mus* CH1 ...237 A1
Grosvenor Nuffield Hospl
  CH4 ....141 C6
Grosvenor Pk Rd CH1 ...237 C2
Grosvenor Pk Terr CH1,
  CH3 ....237 C2
Grosvenor Pl CH1 ....237 B1
Grosvenor Rd
  Chester CH1 ....141 C7
  Congleton CW12 ....156 A3
  Haydock WA11 ....1 B7
  Tarvin CH3 ....121 A2
  Widnes WA8 ....23 A3
Grosvenor Sh Ctr The
  CH1 ....237 B2
Grosvenor St
  Chester CH1 ....237 A2
  Crewe CW1 ....190 B5
  Runcorn WA7 ....22 F3
  Winsford CW7 ....149 E8
Grotsworth La SY14 ...214 E8
Grotto La WA16 ....108 B7
Grounds St WA2 ....16 B7
  Kidsgrove ST7 ....194 E1
  Lawton-gate ST7 ....194 A4
  Lostock Gralam CW9 ....80 A3
  Wilmslow SK9 ....60 B7
Grove Ct Alsager ST7 ...193 E4
  Lymm WA13 ....18 C3
Grove Gdns CH3 ....119 E2
Grove La SK8 ....35 A5
Grove La SK8 ....35 A6
Grove Pk WA16 ....57 A1
Grove Rd CH1 ....94 E4
Grove Rise New Mills SK22 ...39 B7
  Runcorn WA7 ....22 F3
Grove St Chester CH4 ...141 D7
  Lymm WA13 ....18 C3
Grove Terr WA4 ....73 C4
Grove The
  Cheadle Hulme SK8 ....35 A6
  Knutsford WA16 ....57 A1
  Lawton-gate ST7 ....194 A4
  Tarporley CW6 ....146 C2
  Warrington WA1 ....14 F4
  Whitchurch SY13 ....225 F1
Grove Way SK9 ....60 B7
Grovemount CW9 ....103 F2
Groves The Chester CH1 .237 B2
  Ellesmere Port CH66 ....69 D3
Grovewood Mews SK11 .112 C6

Grub La CW6 ....122 C5
Grundy Cl WA8 ....12 F3
Grundy St WA3 ....3 A7
Guardian St WA5 ....15 F6
Guardian Street Ind Est
  WA5 ....15 F6
Guernsey Cl
  Congleton CW12 ....157 A2
  Middlewich CW10 ....128 D2
  Warrington WA4 ....26 D8
Guernsey Dr CH65 ....70 C2
Guernsey Ho CW2 ....119 B5
Guernsey Rd WA8 ....13 E3
Guest St WA8 ....22 A2
Guests Slack WA6 ....100 B8
Guilden Gn CH3 ....119 E4
Guilden Sutton CE Prim Sch
  CH3 ....119 D5
Guilden Sutton La CH3 ...119 D5
Guildford Ave SK8 ....35 A6
Guildford Cl
  1 Chester CH4 ....140 F6
  Warrington WA2 ....9 A1
Guillemot Cl CW1 ....190 F5
Gull Cl SK12 ....36 B3
Gullane Cl SK10 ....87 B4
Gullet The CW5 ....204 E5
Gullivers World Theme Pk*
  WA5 ....7 E1
Gulls Way CH60 ....40 E7
Gunco La
  Macclesfield SK11 ....112 C6
  Prestbury SK10 ....87 C8
Gunn Gr CH64 ....66 F8
Gutterscroft CW1 ...191 D5
Gutticar Rd WA8 ....12 B1
Guy La CH3 ....143 D5
Gwyneth Morley Ct SK9 ...34 D3
Gypsy La CH1 ....94 C3

H

Hack Green Secret Nuclear
  Bunker* CW5 ....218 D4
Hacked Way La SK11 ...113 F6
Haddon Cl
  Alderley Edge SK9 ....59 F2
  High Lane SK6 ....37 E6
  Holmes Chapel CW4 ...130 B3
  Macclesfield SK11 ....112 A8
  Wistaston CW2 ....206 B7
Haddon Dr WA8 ....12 C3
Haddon Ho 4 CH64 ....66 E8
Haddon La CH64 ....67 C4
Haddon Rd Burton CH64 ...67 D2
  Heald Green SK8 ....34 C7
Hadfield Cl WA8 ....79 B1
Hadfield St WA7 ....23 A2
Hadleigh Cl WA5 ....14 E5
Hadley Ave CH62 ....43 C8
Hadlow La CH64 ....67 F4
Hadlow Rd CH64 ....67 F6
Hadlow Terr CH64 ....67 F7
Hadrian Dr CH1 ....117 C6
Hadrian Way
  Cuddington CW8 ....102 B2
  Middlewich CW10 ....128 C2
  Connah's Quay CH5 ....91 C1
Hadyn Jones Dr CW5 ...204 F4
Hafod Cl Blacon CH1 ...117 D3
Hag Bank La SK12 ....38 D7
Hague Bar Prim Sch
  SK22 ....38 E8
Hague Bar Rd Disley SK22 ...38 F8
  New Mills SK22 ....39 A7
Hague Fold Rd SK22 ...38 F8
Haig Ave Irlam M44 ....11 C4
Haig Rd Knutsford WA16 ...57 C4
  Widnes WA8 ....13 A1
Hale Ave SK12 ....36 E4
Hale Bank Terr WA8 ....22 A4
Hale CE Prim Sch L24 ...21 E1
Hale Gate Rd Hale WA8 ...21 F3
  Widnes WA8 ....22 A3
Hale Gr WA5 ....15 A6
Hale View Altrincham WA15 ...32 D8
  Widnes,Ditton WA8 ....22 C2
Hale Road Ind Est WA8 ...22 B4
Haley Rd N WA5 ....6 E6
Haley Rd S WA5 ....6 E5
Half St SK11 ....112 D6
Halfacre La WA4 ....17 F2
Halghton La LL13 ....227 A2
Halifax Cl WA2 ....8 D2
Halkett Cl CH4 ....140 E5
Halkyn Rd CH2 ....237 C4
Hall Acres La SK8 ....34 E8
Hall Ave WA8 ....12 A1
Hall Bank WA16 ....58 C4
Hall Bank N WA16 ....58 C4
Hall Bank S WA16 ....58 C4

Hall Cl SK10 ....87 D4
Hall Dr Alsager ST7 ...193 C3
Marston CW9 ....79 B6
Warrington WA4 ....26 D6
Willaston CW5 ....205 C6
Hall Farm CH62 ....44 A4
Hall Farm Cl SK23 ....65 D8
Hall Gr SK10 ....87 D3
Hall Hill SK10 ....87 E7
Hall La
 Appleton Thorn WA4 ....27 B8
 Audlem CW3 ....230 C7
 Brown Knowl CH3 .....199 C7
 Cronton L35 ....12 C7
 Daresbury WA4 ....25 D2
 Haughton CW6 ....186 D5
 Kelsall CW6 ....122 D6
 Little Leigh CW9 ....77 F8
 Lostock Gralam CW9 ..79 F5
 Mobberley WA16 ......58 D4
 Newton-le-W WA5 .....7 B8
 Ollerton WA16 ....83 B5
 Partington M31 ......11 F4
 Pickmere WA16 ....55 B1
 Sandbach CW11 ....174 B5
 Shotwick CH1 ....93 B5
 St Helens WA9 ....6 A4
 Stretton WA4 ....52 D8
 Sutton Lane Ends SK11 .112 F3
 Utkinton CW6 ....146 C6
 Winsford CW7 ....149 B3
Hall La The CW6 ......147 D2
Hall Moss La SK7 .....35 C4
Hall Nook WA5 ....14 F3
Hall O'shaw St CW1 ...190 E4
Hall Rd Handforth SK9 .34 E3
 Haydock WA11 ....17 C7
 Warrington WA1 ......17 C7
 Wilmslow SK9 ....60 A7
Hall St Audley ST7 ...209 D2
 Macclesfield SK10 ...112 C8
 New Mills SK22 ......39 B8
 Warrington WA1 ......16 C5
Hall Terr WA5 ....6 E7
Hall View CH3 ....166 B1
Hall View Cl CW8 .....102 A7
Hall Wood Ave WA11 ...1 E8
Halla-Way WA4 ....16 E3
Hallams Dr CW5 ....205 B4
Hallastone Rd WA6 ....73 C4
Hallcroft M31 ....11 F4
Hallcroft Pl WA4 .....17 A2
Hallefield Cres 5 SK11 .112 E7
Hallefield Dr 4 SK11 .112 E7
Hallefield Rd SK10,SK11 .112 E7
Hallfield Dr CH2 .....9 E3
Hallfield Pk CH66 ....69 D4
Hallfields Rd Tarvin CH3 .121 C2
 Warrington WA2 ......8 D1
Hallgreen La CW12 ....155 D8
Halliday Cl WA3 ......9 E1
Halliwel Jones Stad
 (Warrington Wolves RLFC)
 The WA2 ....16 A6
Halliwell's Brow WA16 .29 B3
Hallows Ave WA2 ......16 D8
Hallows Cl CW6 ....122 C4
Hallows Dr CW6 ....122 C4
Hallowsgate Cl CW6 ..122 C4
Halls Rd Biddulph ST8 .179 C1
 Mow Cop ST7 ....195 C7
Hallsgreen La CH2 ....96 F7
Hallshaw Ave CW1 ....190 E5
Hallside Pk WA16 ....57 C1
Hallwood Cl WA7 .....49 D6
Hallwood Dr CH66 ....68 D4
Hallwood Link Rd WA7 .49 F6
Hallwood Park Ave WA7 .49 E6
Hallwood Park Prim Sch
 WA7 ....49 E6
Hallwood Rd SK9 .....34 D2
Hallsall Ave WA2 ....16 D8
Hallsall Cl WA7 .....49 E3
Hallsall's Cotts WA8 .21 E5
Halstone Ave SK9 ....59 E4
Halton Brook Ave WA7 .23 D1
Halton Brow WA7 .....23 E1
Halton Castle* WA7 ..23 F1
Halton Coll WA8 .....23 D6
Halton Coll Runcorn Campus
 WA7 ....22 E3
Halton Cres CH66 ....69 E2
Halton Ct WA7 ....23 D2
Halton Dr CW2 ....189 D5
Halton General Hospl
 WA7 ....49 E6
Halton High Sch WA7 .50 C6
Halton Lea S Ctr WA7 .49 E8
Halton Link Rd WA7 ..49 E8
Halton Lodge Ave WA7 .49 D7
Halton Lodge Prim Sch
 WA7 ....49 D8
Halton Rd Chester CH2 .118 F6
 Ellesmere Port CH66 .69 E2
 Runcorn WA7 ....23 D2
 Warrington WA5 .....14 F6
Halton St WA11 ......1 A6
Halton Station Rd WA7 .49 F3
Halton View Rd WA8 ..13 C1
Halton Way CH66 .....69 E1
Hamble Dr WA5 ....14 F3
Hamble Way SK10 .....86 E1
Hambleton Cl CH66 ...69 A6
Hambleton Cl WA13 ...12 C3
Hambleton Rd SK8 ....34 C8

Hambleton Way CW7 ...149 A7
Hambletts Hollow WA6 .100 F6
Hamilton Ave Irlam M44 .11 D4
 Sandycroft CH5 ......116 A3
Hamilton Cl
 Haslington CW1 ......191 C4
 Macclesfield SK10 ...113 A8
 Neston CH64 ....41 B2
Hamilton Ct CH64 ....66 F8
Hamilton Pl CH1 .....237 A2
Hamilton Rd CH5 .....91 D1
Hamilton St CH2 .....118 F3
Hamlin Cl WA7 ....49 A6
Hammond Sch CH2 ....119 B7
Hammond St CW2 ......190 C3
Hamnett Ct WA3 ......9 E2
Hampshire Cl CW12 ...156 D4
Hampshire Rd M31 ....11 D2
Hampshire Wlk SK10 ..86 F2
Hampson Ave WA3 .....4 F3
Hampson Cres SK9 ....34 C4
Hampstead Ct 7 CW7 .149 A8
Hampton Cl Neston CH64 .66 E6
 Widnes WA8 ....13 E3
Hampton Cres
 Neston CH64 ....66 E6
 No Man's Heath SY14 .214 A5
Hampton Ct WA7 ......24 C4
Hampton Dr Cronton WA8 .12 C5
 Warrington WA5 .....15 C4
Hampton Gdns CH65 ...70 A5
Hampton Heath Ind Est
 SY14 ....213 D7
Hampton Rd
 Chester CH4 ....140 F6
 Irlam M44 ....11 D4
Hamson Dr SK10 ......63 B1
Hamsterley Cl WA3 ...10 B6
Hanbury Cl CW2 ......206 B7
Hancock Ct WA4 ......16 C4
Hancock Rd CW12 .....156 F4
Hand St SK11 ....112 B8
Handa Dr CH65 ....95 B8
Handbridge CH4 ......237 B1
Handford Ave CH62 ...43 F5
Handford Rd CH2 .....118 F6
Handforth Cl WA4 ....17 C3
Handforth La WA7 ....49 D6
Handforth Rd
 Crewe CW2 ....189 E3
 Wilmslow SK9 ....34 E1
Handforth Sta SK9 ...34 D3
Handley Hill CW7 ....149 C8
Handley Hill Prim Sch
 CW7 ....149 C8
Handley St WA7 ......22 F3
Hangman's La CW9 ...105 C7
Hankelow Cl
 Chester CH2 ....237 B4
 Middlewich CW10 ....151 C6
Hankey St 2 WA7 ....22 F2
Hankins Heys La CW3 .231 A1
Hankinson Cl M31 ....11 E2
Hanley Cl Disley SK12 .38 D5
 Widnes WA8 ....12 C1
Hanley Rd WA8 ....12 C1
Hannah's Wlk 2 CW10 .151 C8
Hanns Hall Farm CH64 .67 D8
Hanns Hall Rd CH64 ..67 D8
Hanover Ct WA7 ......50 A6
Hanover Dr 2 CW7 ...149 A8
Hanover Ho CH66 .....103 C5
Hanover St WA1 ......16 A4
Hapsdale View WA6 ...72 E1
Hapsford Cl WA3 .....9 C4
Hapsford La
 Dunham-on-t-H WA6 ..97 E8
 Elton CH2 ....72 C4
Hapsford Mews WA6 ..72 E4
Harbarrow Cl CH2 ....118 E7
Harbord St WA1 ......16 C4
Harbour Cl WA7 ......50 D6
Harbour La SK11 .....111 C1
Harburn Wlk M22 .....33 E8
Harcourt Cl WA3 .....9 E3
Harden Pk SK9 ....60 A3
Harding Ave
 Tattenhall CH3 .....166 C2
 Warrington WA2 .....8 E1
Harding Rd Chester CH2 .118 B8
 Nantwich CW5 ....204 C4
Hardings Mdw ST7 ...194 F2
Hardings Row ST7 ....195 D7
Hardingswood Rd ST7 .194 F2
Hardknott Rd CH66 ...43 E8
Hardwick Cl SK6 .....37 F6
Hardwick Dr SK11 ....112 B5
Hardwick Grange WA1 .17 E8
Hardwicke Ct CW1 ...190 E4
Hardwicke Rd SK12 ..36 F4
Hardy Cl
 Ellesmere Port CH66 .69 F3
 Wistaston CW2 ......205 F8
Hardy Dr SK7 ....35 D7
Hardy Rd WA13 ......18 C2
Hardy St WA2 ....16 B6
Hare Hill Gdn* SK10 ..86 B6
Hare La CH3 ....119 D3
Hare's La WA6 ....73 F7
Harebell Cl CH3 .....142 A6
Harebell St CW1 .....191 F1
Harecastle Ave ST7 ..194 E1
Harecastle Ct 7 SK10 .210 E6
Harefield Dr SK9 ....60 B5
Harefield Rd SK9 ....34 E4
Harewood Ave CH66 ..69 C4

Harewood Cl
 Northwich CW9 ......103 F4
 Winsford CW7 ....126 A1
Harewood Way SK11 ..112 B5
Harfield Gdns CH66 ..69 C5
Harford Cl WA5 ......14 F4
Hargrave Ave CW2 ...189 F3
Hargrave Dr CH66 ....69 E5
Hargrave La
 Bebington CH64 .....43 A4
 Thornton Hough CH63,CH64 .42 F5
Hargreave Ho 7 CH64 .66 E8
Hargreaves Ct WA8 ...13 D1
Hargreaves Ho 5 WA8 .13 D1
Hargreaves Rd CW9 ..104 C8
Harington Cl CH2 ...118 C8
Harlech Cl WA5 ......7 E2
Harlech Ct CH65 .....70 D3
Harlech Gr 3 WA7 ...23 F1
Harlech Way CH65 ....70 D3
Harlow Cl WA4 ....17 C3
Harlyn Ave SK7 ......35 F7
Harlyn Gdns WA5 .....14 D3
Harn The CH66 ....69 C3
Harold Rd WA11 ......1 F7
Haroldgate SY13 .....225 F1
Harper Cl CH66 ......69 D4
Harper Gr CW12 .....156 E4
Harpers Rd WA2 ......9 B2
Harpur Cl SK11 .....112 D6
Harpur Cres ST7 ....193 B5
Harrier Rd WA2 ......8 E2
Harriet St WA4 ......11 E5
Harrington Dr SK11 ..111 D1
Harris Cl CW1 ....173 B1
Harris Rd CW9 ....80 A2
Harris St WA8 ....13 C1
Harrisehead La ST7 ..195 D4
Harrison Dr
 Goostrey CW4 ....107 B1
 Haydock WA11 ....1 A6
Harrison Gr CH5 ....116 A3
Harrison Sq WA5 .....7 F1
Harrison St WA8 .....22 B6
Harrison Way WA12 ..2 C4
Harrisons Pl 4 CW8 ..103 E8
Harrisons Terr CH66 .69 C6
Harrogate Cl
 Bebington CH62 .....43 D4
 Warrington WA5 .....7 A1
Harrogate Rd CH62 ..43 D4
Harrop La SK10 ......62 E5
Harrop Rd Bollington SK10 .88 C8
 Runcorn WA7 ....23 B1
Harrow Cl Crewe CW2 .190 A1
 Haydock WA11 ....1 A6
Harrow Gr WA5 ......23 E2
Harrow Gr CH64 .....66 E8
Harrow Rd CH65 .....70 D4
Harrow Way WA9 ....103 E3
Hartford Ave SK9 ...59 F5
Hartford Bsns Ctr CW8 .102 F4
Hartford Cl CW11 ...175 C7
Hartford Dr CH65 ...69 F4
Hartford High Sch CW8 .103 C5
Hartford Manor Com Prim
 Sch CW8 ....103 C5
Hartford Mews 3 CH3 .119 B1
Hartford Prim Sch CW8 .103 B4
Hartford Rd CW9 ....103 D3
Hartford St 4 CW9 ..103 A4
Hartford Way CH1 ...118 A2
Harthill Cl CW9 .....103 E5
Harthill La CH3 .....183 E4
Harthill Rd Blacon CH1 .117 E6
 Burwardsley CH3 ....183 A6
Hartington Dr SK7 ...36 E8
Hartington Rd
 Bramhall SK7 ....35 E6
 Newton-le-W WA12 ..2 D3
 High Lane SK12,SK6 .37 F7
Hartington St CH4 ..141 E7
Hartland Cl Poynton SK12 .36 D5
 Widnes WA8 ....13 A5
Hartley Cl 1 CH3 ...18 F3
Hartley Gn SK10 ....87 F8
Harton Cl WA8 ......12 E3
Hartswood Cl WA4 ...26 E8
Hartwell Gr CW7 ....126 F4
Harty Rd WA11 ......1 A5
Harvard Cl WA7 .....24 D2
Harvard Ct WA2 .....8 A3
Harvest Cl CW9 .....126 F8
Harvest Rd SK10 ....87 C2
Harvey Ave
 Nantwich CW5 ......205 A6
 Newton-le-W WA12 ..1 F3
Harvey Ct WA3 ......8 B3
Harvey Rd CW12 ....156 D2
Harwood Gdns WA4 ..17 A2
Harwood St WA8 ....13 D3
Haseley Cl SK12 ....36 E5
Haslemere Ave WA15 .32 C6
Haslemere Dr WA5 ..14 D4
Haslemere Way CW1 .190 D6
Haslin Cres CH3 ....142 D7
Haslington Cl ST5 ..210 D1
Haslington Gr L26 ..21 A6
Haslington Prim Sch
 CW1 ....191 D4
Hassall Rd Alsager ST7 .193 B5
 Haslington CW11 ....192 B7
 Sandbach CW11 .....175 A4
 Winterley CW11 .....191 F8
Hassall Way 7 SK9 ..34 E5
Hassals La CH2 .....96 F3

Hastings Ave WA2 ....8 B4
Hastings Rd CW5 ....204 F5
Hasty La Altrincham WA15 .32 E8
 Woodhouse Park WA15 .32 F8
Hatch Mere* WA6 ....100 C4
Hatchery Cl WA4 ....27 B4
Hatchings The WA13 .18 E2
Hatchmere Cl
 Sandbach CW11 .....174 F7
 Warrington WA5 ....15 E5
Hatchmere Dr CH3 ...142 B8
Hatchmere Pk WA6 ...100 C5
Hatfield Cl CW4 ....130 B3
Hatfield Gdns WA4 ..26 E4
Hathaway Cl SK8 ....34 B7
Hathaway Dr SK11 ..112 C5
Hatherton Cl
 Newcastle-u-Lyme ST5 .210 D2
 5 Northwich CW9 ...103 F4
Hatherton Gr L26 ...21 A6
Hatherton Way CH2 .237 B4
Hatley La WA6 ......73 F7
Hatter St CW12 .....156 E3
Hatton Ave CH62 ....43 E3
Hatton Bldgs CH2 ..237 C4
Hatton Brow Terr SK11 .112 F4
Hatton La Hartford CW8 .103 D6
 Stretton WA4 ....52 E1
Hatton Rd CH1 ......117 E6
Hatton St SK11 .....112 C7
Haughton Cl SK10 ...86 F1
Haven La
 Congleton CW12 ....156 F6
 St Helens WA9 .....1 B3
Havannah Prim Sch
 CW12 ....157 A6
Havannah St CW12 ..156 F4
Haven The Crewe CW1 .190 D7
 Sandbach CW11 ....174 E7
Havergal St 3 WA7 ..22 F1
Haverhill Cl CW2 ...207 C3
Haverty Prec WA12 ..2 B1
Havisham Cl WA3 ....9 D5
Hawarde Cl WA12 ....2 A4
Hawarden Airport CH4,
 CH5 ....139 B8
Hawarden Gdns CH65 .70 D2
Hawarden Ind Est WA11 .1 B8
Hawarden Pk CH5 ...139 B6
Haweswater Ave
 Crewe CW1 ....173 B1
 Haydock WA11 ......1 A6
Haweswater Cl WA7 .50 A5
Haweswater Dr CW7 .126 D2
Hawick Cl CH66 .....69 A5
Hawk Rd SK22 ....39 D8
Hawk St CW11 ....175 B6
Hawker Cl CH4 ......139 C4
Hawkins Cl SK10 ....88 D4
Hawkins Rd CH64 ....41 F1
Hawkins View CH3 ..120 E6
Hawks Cl WA7 ......49 E6
Hawks Way CH60 ....40 E8
Hawkshaw Cl WA3 ...9 C4
Hawkshead Cl WA7 ..50 A4
Hawkshead Way CW7 .126 D2
Hawkstone Gr WA6 ..73 C4
Hawley La WA15 ....32 B8
Hawley's Cl WA5 ....7 F1
Hawley's La WA2,WA5 .8 A1
Hawley's Lane Trad Pk
 WA2 ....8 A1
Haworth Ave CW12 ..157 A5
Haworth Cl SK11 ...112 B5
Haworth Rd
 3 Nantwich CW5 ....204 F5
 Newton-le-W WA12 ..2 D3
 Runcorn WA7 ....23 A1
 1 Widnes WA8 ......13 A2
 Wilmslow SK9 ......60 A7
Hawthorn Bank SK22 .39 B6
Hawthorn Cl
 Holmes Chapel CW4 .130 D3
 Winsford CW7 ......126 D3
Hawthorn Cotts CH60 .40 F8
Hawthorn Dr M44 ...11 D5
Hawthorn Gdns ST7 .210 D8
Hawthorn Gn 2 SK9 ..60 A7
Hawthorn Gr
 Bramhall SK7 ....35 C6
 Crewe CW1 ....190 D7
 Warrington WA4 ....16 D1
 Wilmslow SK9 ......60 A7
Hawthorn Pk 1 SK9 ..60 A7
Hawthorn Rd
 Bollington SK10 ....87 F8
 Chester CH4 ....141 A6
 Christleton CH3 ....142 E7
 Ellesmere Port CH66 .69 D6
 Lymm WA13 ....18 D3
 Neston CH64 ....41 C1
 Newcastle-u-Lyme ST5 .210 E1
 Plumley WA16 ......80 D7
 Weaverham CW8 ....102 C8
Hawthorn View
 Connah's Quay CH5 .116 A7
 Lindow End WA16 ..59 B2
 Wilmslow SK9 ......60 A7

Hawthorn Villas CW4 ...130 C3
Hawthorn Way SK10 ...87 E2
Hawthorn Wlk
 3 Partington M31 ...11 E3
 Wilmslow SK9 ....60 A7
 Wincham CW9 ....79 C3
Hawthorne Ave
 Audley ST7 ....209 F1
 Fowley Common WA3 ..5 C5
 Newton-le-W WA5 ...15 A6
 Warrington,Woolston WA1 .17 B7
Hawthorne Bsns Pk WA5 .16 A8
Hawthorne Cl
 Congleton CW12 ....156 A4
 Haydock WA11 ......1 A5
Hawthorne Ct ST7 ...193 E4
Hawthorne Dr
 Sandbach CW11 ....175 D6
 Willaston CH64 .....43 B1
Hawthorne Gr
 Barnton CW8 ....77 F4
 Poynton SK12 ....37 C4
 Warrington WA4 ....16 D3
 Warrington,Bruche WA1 .16 F7
 Widnes WA8 ....77 C4
Hawthorne La CH62 ..43 D8
Hawthorne Rd
 Frodsham WA6 ......49 B1
 Warrington WA4 ....26 C8
Hawthorne St WA5 ..16 A8
Hawthorns The
 Bunbury CW6 ....185 E8
 Ellesmere Port CH66 .69 F7
 Haslington CW1 ....191 D5
 Northwich CW8 ....103 C7
 Tarporley CW6 .....146 D1
Haycroft SK8 ....34 E8
Haycroft Cl CH66 ...69 D2
Haydan Mews WA6 ...73 E6
Haydn Jones Dr CW5 .204 F3
Haydock Cl Chester CH1 .118 B2
 Macclesfield SK10 ..87 C3
Haydock English Martyrs' RC
 Prim Sch WA11 .....1 E7
Haydock High Sch WA11 .1 C6
Haydock La WA11 ...1 C7
Haydock La Ind Est WA11 .1 E8
Haydock Park Racecourse
 WA11 ....2 E8
Haydock St
 Newton-le-W WA12 ..2 A3
 Warrington WA2 ....16 B6
Haye's Rd M44 ......11 E5
Hayes Cl CW5 ....204 E7
Hayes Cres WA6 .....49 C1
Hayes Dr CW8 ....78 C3
Hayes Pk CH1 ....237 A4
Hayfield Cl SK10 ...87 B3
Hayfield Rd
 New Mills SK22 .....39 D8
 Warrington WA1 ....17 C7
Hayfields Hill WA6 ..57 C3
Hayfields Gr CW3 ...229 F3
Hayhead Cl ST7 .....195 B2
Hayhurst Ave CW10 .151 C8
Hayhurst Cl CW9 ...103 F8
Hayle Cl SK10 ......86 D1
Hayling Cl WA1 .....190 B8
Haymakers Cl CH4 ..140 F4
Haymakers Way CH1 .117 A8
Haymoor Green Rd
 CW5 ....205 E3
Hayscastle Cl WA5 ..7 E1
Hayside Wlk SY14 ..213 A3
Hayton St WA16 ....56 F1
Haywood Cres WA7 .24 D2
Hazel Ave
 Macclesfield SK11 ..112 A5
 Runcorn WA7 ....48 E8
Hazel Cl
 1 Ellesmere Port CH66 .69 F1
 Kidsgrove ST7 .....195 B3
Hazel Dr Heald Green M22 .34 A8
 Lymm WA13 ....18 F2
 Poynton SK12 ......36 F3
Hazel Gr Alsager ST7 .194 A3
 Crewe CW1 ....190 C7
 Golborne WA3 ......3 B8
 Warrington WA1 ....17 A8
Hazel Grove High Sch
 SK7 ....36 C8
Hazel Rd CH4 ....140 F6
Hazel St WA1 ....16 D7
Hazel Wlk M31 .....11 E3
Hazelbadge Cl SK12 .36 C4
Hazelbadge Rd SK12 .36 C4
Hazelbank CH65 .....70 D4
Hazelborough Cl WA3 .10 B5
Hazelcroft SK9 .....85 A8
Hazelcroft Gdns SK9 .85 A8
Hazeldean Ct 17 SK9 .34 E1
Hazelhurst Dr SK10 .88 A8
Hazelmere Cl CW8 ..103 C5
Hazelshaw La CW11 .154 B8
Hazelwood Cl WA8 ..22 A8
Hazelwood Mews WA7 .17 C1
Hazelwood Rd
 Barnton CW8 ....78 B4
 Wilmslow SK9 ......60 B8
Hazlehurst Rd WA6 ..74 D6
Hazlemere Ave SK11 .112 A6
Headland Cl WA3 ....3 E6
Headlands The CH1,CH3 .237 C2
Headworth Cl CW7 ..103 F4
Heald Ct SK9 ....60 A7
Heald Green Ho M22 .34 A8

Heald Green Sta M22 . . . . . .34 A8
Heald St WA12 . . . . .1 F3
Healey Cl CW1 . . . . .190 A8
Heapy St SK11 . . . . .112 E6
Hearn's La CW5 . . . . .202 E5

Heath Ave
Ellesmere Port CH65 . . . . . .70 A1
Rode Heath ST7 . . . . .193 F7
Sandbach CW11 . . . . .175 E6
Heath Bank CH3 . . . . .119 D5

Heath Bsns & Technical Pk
The WA7 . . . . .49 A7
Heath Cl Chester CH3 . . . .142 B8
Sandbach CW11 . . . . .175 D6
Tarvin CH3 . . . . .121 B1
Heath Ct Alsager ST7 . . . .193 F6
Ellesmere Port CH66 . . . . .69 B6
Heath Dr Knutsford WA16 . .56 F2
Runcorn WA7 . . . . .49 A7
Tarvin CH3 . . . . .121 B1
Heath End Rd ST7 . . . . . .193 B5
Heath Gn CW6 . . . . .146 C4
Heath Gr CH66 . . . . .69 B7
Heath La Chester CH3 . . . .142 A8
Culcheth WA3 . . . . .4 A1
Ellesmere Port,Little Sutton
CH66 . . . . .69 B7
Golborne WA3 . . . . .3 D6
Golborne,Kenyon WA3 . . . . .3 E6
Great Barrow CH3 . . . . . . .120 E6
Great Budworth CW9 . . . . .54 A1
High Legh WA16 . . . . .28 D5
Little Leigh WA4,CW8 . . . . .77 B7
Marbury SY13 . . . . .226 E6
Stoak CH2 . . . . .95 E7
Stoak CH2 . . . . .95 E7
Swan Green WA16 . . . . . . .106 F6
Willaston CH64,CH66 . . . . .68 D7
Heath Park Rd WA7 . . . . . .48 F8
Heath Rd Bollington SK10 . .87 E6
Chester CH2 . . . . .118 E7
Congleton CW12 . . . . .156 A2
Runcorn WA7 . . . . .23 B2
Sandbach CW11 . . . . .175 D6
Warrington WA5 . . . . .14 F5
Weaverham CW8 . . . . .77 E1
Widnes WA8 . . . . .12 D2
Heath Rd S WA7 . . . . .48 F6
Heath Sch The WA7 . . . . . .49 B7
Heath St Crewe CW1 . . . . .190 D4
Golborne WA3 . . . . .3 A8
Warrington WA4 . . . . .16 E5
Heath Terr Chester CH2 . .118 E8
Smallwood CW11 . . . . .154 B1
Heath View WA5 . . . . .154 E4
Weston CW2 . . . . .207 B5
Heath Way CW6 . . . . .168 D8
Heathbank Rd SK8 . . . . . . .34 F8
Heathbrook CW9 . . . . .104 D7
Heathcote Cl CH2 . . . . . . .118 C4
Heathcote Gdns CW9 . . . .104 D7
Heathcote St CW7 . . . . . . .195 A2
Heather Ave WA4 . . . . .11 D6
Heather Brae WA12 . . . . . . .2 A4

Heather Cl
Ellesmere Port CH66 . . . . .69 E3
Macclesfield SK11 . . . . . . .112 C3
Runcorn WA7 . . . . .9 D5
Warrington WA3 . . . . .9 D5
Heather Ct CH3 . . . . .142 A8
Heather Falls SK22 . . . . . .39 B8
Heather Wlk M31 . . . . .11 E3
Heatherfield Ct SK9 . . . . . .60 E8
Heathergate Pl CW2 . . . . .206 B8
Heatherside ST7 . . . . .195 C6
Heatherways CW6 . . . . . . .146 C3
Heathfield SK9 . . . . .60 A5
Heathfield Ave CW1 . . . . .190 C4

Heathfield Cl
Congleton CW12 . . . . .155 F3
Nantwich CW5 . . . . .204 F6

Heathfield Ct
Ellesmere Port CH65 . . . . .70 B5
Ellesmere Port CH66 . . . . .95 A8
Northwich Dr ST5 . . . . . . .210 D1

Heathfield Pk
Warrington WA4 . . . . .17 A2
Widnes WA8 . . . . .12 D3

Heathfield Rd
Audlem CW3 . . . . .230 A5
Ellesmere Port CH65 . . . . .70 B5
Heathfield Sq WA16 . . . . . .56 F2
Heathfields Cl CH2 . . . . . .237 B4
Heathgate Ave CH4 . . . . . .21 A2
Heathlands Ho WA16 . . . . .56 F2
Heathlands Rd CH66 . . . . .69 B7
Heathmoor Ave WA3 . . . . . .3 D6
Heaths La CW6 . . . . .123 D2
Heathside CW5 . . . . .204 F6
Heathview CW1 . . . . .191 D3
Heathview Ct WA8 . . . . . . .22 A5
Heathview Rd WA8 . . . . . . .22 A5
Heathway CH60 . . . . .41 B7
Heathwood Dr ST7 . . . . . .193 B5
Heathwood Gr WA1 . . . . . .17 B7
Heatley Cl WA13 . . . . .19 A4
Heatley Ave CH3 . . . . .217 F3
Heatley Way ⁵ SK9 . . . . . .34 D4
Heaton Cl CW10 . . . . .151 C6
Heaton Ct WA3 . . . . .9 F6
Heaton Sq CW7 . . . . .149 C8
Heaward Cl CW2 . . . . .206 B4
Hebden Ave WA3 . . . . .5 B5

Hebden Green Com Sch
CW7 . . . . .149 A7

Hebden Green Specl Sch
Grounds CW7 . . . . .149 A7
Heber Wlk CW9 . . . . .104 A8
Heber's Cl SY14 . . . . .213 C5
Hedge Hey WA7 . . . . .24 A1
Hedge Row SK10 . . . . .63 E1
Hedgerow Dr CW9 . . . . . . .79 C3
Hedgerows The WA11 . . . . .1 F7
Hedingham Cl ⁷ SK10 . . .111 F8

Hefferston Grange Dr
CW8 . . . . .102 A7
Hefferston Rise CW8 . . . .102 A7
Heights The WA6 . . . . .73 C4
Helena Cl WA16 . . . . .57 C2
Hellath Wen CW5 . . . . . . .204 E2
Hellyar-Brook Rd ST7 . . .193 B4
Helmdon Cl CW7 . . . . . . .127 A3
Helmsdale Cl CW1 . . . . . .190 B6
Helmsdale La WA5 . . . . . . .15 C6
Helmsley Cl WA5 . . . . .15 E7
Helsby Ave CH62 . . . . .43 F3
Helsby High Sch WA6 . . . . .73 D5
Helsby Hillside Prim Sch
WA6 . . . . .73 D4
Helsby Pk WA6 . . . . .73 E5
Helsby Rd WA6 . . . . .73 C1
Helsby St WA1 . . . . .16 D6
Helsby Way ⁴ SK9 . . . . . . .34 D4
Helston Cl Bramhall SK7 . . .35 F7
Runcorn WA7 . . . . .50 B5
Warrington WA5 . . . . .14 E5
Helston Gr SK8 . . . . .34 C8
Helton Cl CW4 . . . . .130 A3
Hemingford Cl CW8 . . . . . .103 E7
Hemleigh Vale WA6 . . . . . .73 B2
Hemming St CW8 . . . . .78 D1
Hemmingshaw La CW11 .176 B8
Hemswell Cl CW7 . . . . . . .149 E8
Hemsworth Ave CH66 . . . .69 C5
Henbury Cl CW10 . . . . . . .151 C7
Henbury Gdns WA4 . . . . . .26 E3
Henbury High Sch SK10 .111 E8
Henbury La SK8 . . . . .34 F6
Henbury Pl WA7 . . . . .49 B6
Henbury Rd SK9 . . . . .34 D4
Henbury Rise SK11 . . . . . .111 C8
Henderson Cl WA5 . . . . . . .14 D4

Henderson Rd
⁴ Widnes WA8 . . . . .13 A1
Widnes,Lower House WA8 . .22 F8
Henderson St SK11 . . . . . .112 C7
Hendon Cl CW1 . . . . .190 F5
Henley Ave WA4 . . . . .16 F4

Henley Cl
Macclesfield SK10 . . . . .87 B4
Neston CH64 . . . . .66 E6
Warrington WA4 . . . . .26 E6
Henley Ct WA7 . . . . .23 D2
Henley Dr CW7 . . . . .126 F1
Henley Rd Chester CH4 . .140 F6
Chorlton CW2 . . . . .207 B1
Neston CH64 . . . . .66 E6
Henrietta St CW12 . . . . . .156 C3
Henry Pl CH1 . . . . .237 B3
Henry St Crewe CW1 . . . .190 D5
Haslington CW1 . . . . .191 D4
⁵ Lymm WA13 . . . . .18 E3
Tarporley CW6 . . . . .146 C2
Warrington WA1 . . . . .16 A5
⁴ Widnes WA8 . . . . .13 C1
Henry Wood Ct CH4 . . . .140 E6
Henshall Ave WA4 . . . . . . .16 F4
Henshall Dr CW11 . . . . . .175 D8
Henshall Hall Dr CW12 . .157 B1
Henshall La WA14 . . . . .20 C6
Henshall Rd SK10 . . . . . . .87 F7
Henshall St CW11 . . . . . . .237 A4
Henshaw La SK11 . . . . . . .110 E2
Hepherd St WA5 . . . . .15 F6
Hepley Rd SK12 . . . . .37 A3
Herald Dr CW1 . . . . .190 E3
Herald Pk CW1 . . . . .190 E3
Heralds Cl WA8 . . . . .22 C8
Heralds Gn WA5 . . . . .7 A2
Herbert St Burtonwood WA5 .6 E1
Congleton CW12 . . . . .156 C3
Crewe CW1 . . . . .191 A5
Lostock Gralam CW9 . . . . .80 A2

Herbert Swindells Cl
CW2 . . . . .190 D1
Herberts La CH60 . . . . .40 F8
Herdman St CW2 . . . . . . .190 D2

Hereford Ave
Ellesmere Port CH66 . . . . .94 E8
Golborne WA3 . . . . .3 B8

Hereford Cl
Macclesfield SK10 . . . . .86 F1
Warrington WA1 . . . . .17 D7
Hereford Dr SK9 . . . . .34 E3
Hereford Pl CW1 . . . . .111 D4
Hereford Way CW10 . . . . .128 E2
Hereward Rd CH3 . . . . . . .119 B1
Heritage Ct CH1 . . . . .237 B2

Hermitage Ct
Holmes Chapel CW4 . . . . .130 D3
Saughall CH1 . . . . .94 A1
Hermitage Dr CW4 . . . . . .130 D3
Hermitage Green La WA2,
WA12 . . . . .8 A8
Hermitage La CW4 . . . . . .130 C7
Hermitage Prim Sch
CW4 . . . . .130 D4
Hermitage Rd CH1 . . . . . .130 D4
Hermitage The CH60 . . . . .40 F7
Heron Cl Broughton CH4 . .139 C4
Farndon CH3 . . . . .180 F1
Knutsford WA16 . . . . .57 B3

Heron Cl continued
Runcorn WA7 . . . . .50 D8
Winsford CW7 . . . . .149 D5
Heron Cres CW1 . . . . .190 F5
Heron Ct Neston CH64 . . . .66 C7
Northwich CW9 . . . . .79 C2
Heron Dr SK12 . . . . .36 A3
Heron Pl CH2 . . . . .237 B4
Herons Way Chester CH4 .141 B2
Runcorn WA7 . . . . .24 F4
Herrick Cl CW2 . . . . .206 A8

Hertford Apartments WA2 . .9 A3
Hertford Cl
Congleton CW12 . . . . .156 E4
Warrington WA1 . . . . .17 E7
Hertford Gr M44 . . . . .11 C6
Hesketh Cl WA5 . . . . .14 F4
Hesketh Croft CW1 . . . . . .190 A8
Hesketh Dr CW9 . . . . .80 A3
Hesketh Grange Cotts
CH63 . . . . .42 A7
Hesketh Meadow La WA3 . . .3 B8
Hesketh Rd L24 . . . . .21 E2
Hesketh St N WA5 . . . . . . .15 D4
Hesketh St W WA5 . . . . . . .15 D4
Hesnall Cl WA3 . . . . .5 C8
Hessle Dr CH60 . . . . .40 F7
Heswall Ave WA3 . . . . .4 F3
Heswall Rd CH66 . . . . .69 D4
Heswall Sta CH60 . . . . .40 E8
Hetherson Green La
SY14 . . . . .214 D8
Hewetson Cres SK11 . . . .111 E7
Hewitt Dr CW7 . . . . .150 D8
Hewitt Gr CW9 . . . . .79 F5
Hewitt St Chester CH2 . . .118 F3
Crewe CW2 . . . . .190 D2
Northwich CW9 . . . . .79 D2
Warrington WA4 . . . . .16 C3
Hexham Ct CH1 . . . . .118 B2
Hexham Way ⁶ SK10 . . . . .87 C4
Hey Lock Cl WA12 . . . . .7 C8
Hey Shoot La WA3 . . . . .5 C5
Hey Wood Cl WA12 . . . . . . .7 C8
Heybridge La SK10 . . . . . . .87 B6
Heybrook Cl CW12 . . . . . .156 C3
Heyes Ave WA11 . . . . .1 D5
Heyes Dr WA13 . . . . .18 C2
Heyes Farm Rd SK11 . . . .111 E8
Heyes Ho SK11 . . . . .111 E8

Heyes La
Alderley Edge SK9 . . . . . . .60 B3
Warrington WA4 . . . . .26 E8
Heyes Pk CW8 . . . . .102 F4
Heyes Rd WA8 . . . . .22 C8
Heyeswood La CW8 . . . . .103 A4
Heyfield Park Rd CH66 . . .69 B7
Heygarth Prim Sch CH62 . .43 E5
Heygarth Rd CH62 . . . . . . .43 E5
Heys Ave CH62 . . . . .43 E8
Heys The Bebington CH62 . .43 F5
Runcorn WA7 . . . . .24 F4
Heysbank Rd SK12 . . . . . . .38 D5
Heysham Rd L30 . . . . .21 A8
Heysoms Ave CW8 . . . . . .103 D7
Heysoms Cl CW8 . . . . . . .103 D7
Heythrop Dr CH60 . . . . . . .41 D8
Heywood Cl SK9 . . . . .60 B2
Heywood Gn CW2 . . . . . . .206 C8
Heywood La CW3,SY13 . . .234 C7

Heywood Rd
Alderley Edge SK9 . . . . . . .60 B2
Ellesmere Port CH65 . . . . .69 D5
Heywood St CW12 . . . . . .156 D4
Heywoods Ridge CW3 . . .229 E3
Heywoods The CH2 . . . . . .118 E5
Hibbert St New Mills SK22 . .39 B6
⁶ Widnes WA8 . . . . .23 B8
Hibel Rd SK10 . . . . .87 D1
Hickhurst La CW6 . . . . . . .147 D3
Hickmore Heys CH3 . . . .119 F5
Hickory Cl WA1 . . . . .17 E7
Hickson St CW8 . . . . .78 B3
Hidcote Cl CW2 . . . . .206 B8
Hield Brow CW9 . . . . .79 C8
Hield Gr CW9 . . . . .79 C8
Hield La CW9 . . . . .79 C8
Higginbotham Gn SK11 .112 E6
Higginson Cl CW12 . . . . . .179 C8
High Bank CW4 . . . . .130 C3
High Bent Ave SK8 . . . . . . .35 A6
High Carr Bsns Pk ST5 . .210 F2
High Carr Network Ctr
ST5 . . . . .210 F2
High Cross La CH3 . . . . . .182 D1
High Ct SK10 . . . . .88 B8
High Elm Dr WA15 . . . . . . .32 C8
High Elm Rd WA15 . . . . . . .32 C8
High Elms WA8 . . . . .13 D3
High Field WA14 . . . . .20 B2
High Gates Cl WA5 . . . . . . .15 E5
High Gates Lodge WA5 . . .15 E7
High Hill Rd SK22 . . . . .39 C7
High Lane Prim Sch SK6 . .37 F8
High Legh Prim Sch
WA16 . . . . .29 C5
High Legh Rd WA13 . . . . . .29 C8
High Lowe Ave CW12 . . . .157 A4
High Mdw ⁸ SK8 . . . . .34 C8
High Mount CH60 . . . . .40 F8
High St Audley ST7 . . . . . .210 A1
Bollington SK10 . . . . .88 B8
Congleton CW12 . . . . .156 D2
Crewe CW2 . . . . .190 D2
Duddon CW6 . . . . .145 C5

High St continued
Farndon CH3 . . . . .180 E2
Frodsham WA6 . . . . .49 B1
Golborne WA3 . . . . .3 A8
Great Budworth CW9 . . . . .79 A7
Hale L24 . . . . .21 D1
Kidsgrove, Harriseahead
ST7 . . . . .195 E5
Kidsgrove, Newchapel ST7 .195 E2
Kidsgrove, The Rookery
ST7 . . . . .195 C4
Macclesfield SK11 . . . . . . .112 D6
Malpas SY14 . . . . .213 B3
Mow Cop ST7 . . . . .195 D7
Nantwich CW5 . . . . .204 E5
Neston CH64 . . . . .66 E7
New Mills SK22 . . . . .39 C8
Newton-le-W WA12 . . . . . . .2 D4
Norley WA6 . . . . .100 F5
Northwich CW9 . . . . .103 F8
Runcorn WA7 . . . . .23 A2
Saltney CH4 . . . . .140 E7
Sandbach CW11 . . . . .175 B6
Talke ST7 . . . . .210 D6
Tarporley CW6 . . . . .146 C2
Tarvin CH3 . . . . .121 B1
Tattenhall CH3 . . . . .166 B1
Warrington WA1 . . . . .16 C5
Weaverham CW8 . . . . .77 C1
Winsford CW7 . . . . .126 D1
High View Helsby WA6 . . . .73 C4
Mount Pleasant ST7 . . . . .195 B5
High Warren Cl WA4 . . . . .26 C5
Higham Ave WA5 . . . . .7 F1
Highbank Cl CW8 . . . . .78 B3

Highbank Rd
Kingsley WA6 . . . . .75 C2
Northwich CW8 . . . . .103 D7
Highcliffe Ave CH1 . . . . . .118 B4
Highcroft Ave CW12 . . . . .156 F2
Higher Ash Rd ST7 . . . . . .210 D8
Higher Ashton WA8 . . . . . .12 E4
Higher Carden La SY14 . .198 D6
Higher Downs WA16 . . . . .57 C2
Higher Fence Rd SK10 . . . .87 F1
Higher Ferry CH1 . . . . . . .140 B8
Higher Heyes Dr WA6 . . . .75 C1
Higher Knutsford Rd
WA4 . . . . .16 F2
Higher La Bollington SK10 . .88 B6
Disley SK12 . . . . .38 E1
Dutton WA4 . . . . .51 D4
Kettleshulme SK23 . . . . . . .64 E6
Lymm WA13 . . . . .19 B1
Higher Rd L26,WA8 . . . . . .21 C5

Higher Works Cotts
SK11 . . . . .158 C6
Higher Ct ⁶ ST7 . . . . .195 A2
Highfield Elton CH2 . . . . . .72 B4
Prestbury SK10 . . . . .87 A5

Highfield Ave
Audlem CW3 . . . . .230 A4
Golborne WA3 . . . . .2 F8
Warrington ST7 . . . . .195 B2
Lostock Gralam CW9 . . . . .80 A3
Warrington WA5 . . . . .14 F6
Warrington,Dudlow's Green
WA4 . . . . .26 D4
Highfield Cl CH4 . . . . .66 E8
Highfield Cres
Handforth SK9 . . . . .34 C1
Runcorn WA7 . . . . .24 A4
Highfield Dr Lymm WA13 . .18 C2
Macclesfield SK10 . . . . .87 A1
Nantwich CW5 . . . . .205 A6
Highfield La WA4 . . . .
Highfield Est SK9 . . . . .34 C1

Highfield La
Coddington CH3 . . . . .181 E4
Golborne WA3 . . . . .8 C7
Winwick WA2 . . . . .8 B3
Highfield Parkway SK7 . . .35 D4
Highfield Pl ⁵ CW8 . . . . .103 E8
Highfield Rd Blacon CH1 . .117 D5
Bollington SK10 . . . . .88 A8
Cheadle Hulme SK8 . . . . . .34 F8
Congleton CW12 . . . . .156 E2
Ellesmere Port CH65 . . . . .70 D3
Ellesmere Port,Little Sutton
CH66 . . . . .69 B6
Lymm WA13 . . . . .18 C2
Macclesfield SK11 . . . . . . .112 C7
Neston CH64 . . . . .66 E6
Northwich CW9 . . . . .103 D7
Poynton SK12 . . . . .36 A4
Widnes WA8 . . . . .22 F5
Highfield Sch CW5 . . . . . .204 E6
Highfield Terr SK22 . . . . . .39 D8
Highfields SY13 . . . . .224 A2

Highfields Com Prim Sch
CW5 . . . . .204 F6
Highgate Cl Crewe CW1 . .190 A8
Runcorn WA7 . . . . .50 D7
Highgrove Mews ⁵ SK9 . . .60 A6
Highland Way WA16 . . . . . .82 A7
Highlands Rd WA7 . . . . . . .48 F8
Highlands The CW6 . . . . .185 E8
Highmarsh Cres WA12 . . . .2 A4
Hightown Crewe CW1 . . . .190 C4
Middlewich CW10 . . . . . . .128 C1
Sandbach CW11 . . . . .175 C6
Hilary Ave SK8 . . . . .35 A8
Hilary Cl Chester CH3 . . . .119 B1

Hilary Cl continued
Warrington WA5 . . . . .14 D6
Widnes WA8 . . . . .13 E3
Hilbre Ave CH60 . . . . .40 E8
Hilbre Bank CW6 . . . . .169 D4
Hilbre Dr CH65 . . . . .70 C1
Hilden Pl WA2 . . . . .16 D8
Hilden Rd WA2 . . . . .8 E1
Hill Cl CH64 . . . . .67 B5
Hill Cliffe Rd WA4 . . . . .26 B8
Hill Cotts CH3 . . . . .164 A4
Hill Croft CW11 . . . . .191 F8
Hill Ct CH64 . . . . .67 B5
Hill Dr Handforth SK9 . . . . .34 E2
Whaley Bridge SK23 . . . . . .65 D8
Hill Fields Cl CW12 . . . . . .156 A2
Hill La Brown Knowl CH3 . .199 C8
Peckforton CW6 . . . . .184 E6
Hill Rd CH4 . . . . .141 E2
Hill Rd N WA6 . . . . .73 D3
Hill Rd S WA6 . . . . .73 C3
Hill Side Cl SK12 . . . . .38 E6
Hill St Crewe CW1 . . . . . . .190 D4
Macclesfield SK11 . . . . . . .112 D6
Runcorn WA7 . . . . .23 A2
Sandbach CW11 . . . . .174 D7
Warrington WA1 . . . . .16 A5
Winsford CW7 . . . . .126 F1
Hill Terr ST7 . . . . .209 D2
Hill The Knutsford WA16 . . .57 A8
Sandbach CW11 . . . . .175 D5
Hill Top Altrincham WA15 . .32 A8
Barnton CW8 . . . . .78 B2

Hill Top Ave
Cheadle Hulme SK8 . . . . . .35 B8
Wilmslow SK9 . . . . .60 B8
Winsford CW7 . . . . .126 C1
Hill Top La Heswall CH60 . .41 B8
Neston CH64 . . . . .67 B5

Hill Top Rd
Acton Bridge CW8 . . . . . . .76 F2
Dutton WA4 . . . . .51 C1
Runcorn WA7 . . . . .50 F6
Warrington, Stockton Heath
WA4 . . . . .16 F2
Warrington,Woolston WA1 . .17 C7
Hill Top Rise SK23 . . . . . . .65 D8
Hill View Bollington SK10 . .87 F7
Whaley Bridge SK23 . . . . . .65 C8
Widnes WA8 . . . . .12 F5
Hill View Ave WA6 . . . . . . .73 A1
Hill View Prim Sch WA7 . . .49 E4

Hillary Ave CW12 . . . . . .157 A2
Hillary Cl WA3 . . . . .3 D3
Hillary Rd Bebington CH62 . .43 E5
Kidsgrove ST7 . . . . .195 B3
Hillberry Cres WA4 . . . . . .16 B3
Hillbre Way ⁴ SK9 . . . . . . .34 D4
Hillbrook Rd SK7 . . . . .35 D6
Hillcourt Rd SK6 . . . . .37 F7
Hillcrest WA7 . . . . .23 D1
Hillcrest Ave CW4 . . . . . . .130 B3
Hillcrest Dr CH66 . . . . .69 A6

Hillcrest Rd
Bollington SK10 . . . . .87 F7
Ellesmere Port CH66 . . . . .69 B6
Kelsall CH3 . . . . .122 E6
Warren SK11 . . . . .112 A4
Hillesden Rise CW12 . . . .156 F2
Hillfield Frodsham WA6 . . . .74 B7
Runcorn WA7 . . . . .50 D8
Hillfield Gdns CW5 . . . . . .204 E4
Hillfield Pl CW5 . . . . .204 E4
Hillfield Rd CH66 . . . . .69 D7
Hillfield View CW5 . . . . . .204 E4

Hillfields
Congleton CW12 . . . . .156 D3
Congleton CW12 . . . . .156 D4
Hillfoot Cres WA4 . . . . .26 B7
Hillfoot La WA6 . . . . .74 E3
Hilliards Ct CH4 . . . . .141 B3
Hillingden Ave L26 . . . . . . .21 A7
Hillock La WA1 . . . . .17 C8
Hillsboro Ave CH66 . . . . . .74 C7
Hillsdown Way CH66 . . . . .69 C2
Hillside Broomedge WA13 . .19 E1
Runcorn WA7 . . . . .103 C7
Hillside Ave
Newton-le-W WA12 . . . . . . .1 F2
Hillside Cl Bramhall SK7 . . .36 A7
Hillside La WA6 . . . . .73 D4
Helsby WA6 . . . . .73 D4
Kidsgrove ST7 . . . . .195 A8
Hillside Dr SK10 . . . . .88 A1
Hillside Dr Crewe CW1 . . .190 E5
Ellesmere Port CH66 . . . . .69 E7
Macclesfield SK10 . . . . .88 A1
Hillside Gr WA5 . . . . .14 F4
Hillside La CW9 . . . . .126 E7
Hillside Rd Blacon CH1 . . .117 C7
Frodsham WA6 . . . . .49 C2
Heswall CH60 . . . . .41 A7
Kelsall CH3 . . . . .122 D4
Hillside View SK22 . . . . . . .39 A4
Hilltop WA7 . . . . .50 C7
Hilltop Com Prim Sch
ST7 . . . . .210 D2
Hilltop Pk WA16 . . . . .79 F7

Hilltop Rd
Guilden Sutton CH3 . . . . .119 F5
Lymm WA13 . . . . .18 C2
Hillview Cl WA6 . . . . .74 C7

Hilary Cl continued

Hillview Rise CW8 ....78 E1
Hilton Ave WA5 ....15 B5
Hilton Cl
9 Macclesfield SK11 .....111 F7
Middlewich CW10 ....151 B8
Hilton Dr M44 ....11 C5
Hilton Gr SK12 ....36 D4
Hilton Rd Disley SK12 .....38 B7
Poynton SK12 ....37 C5
Hinchley Cl CW8 ....103 A5
Hinckley Ct CW12 ....156 A3
Hind Heath La CW11 ....174 F4
Hind Heath Rd CW11 ....174 E4
Hinde St CW5 ....204 D4
Hinderton Dr CH60 ....40 F6
Hinderton Gn CH64 ......66 F8
Hinderton La CH64 ....67 A8
Hinderton Rd CH64 ....66 F8
Hinderton Sch CH65 ......69 F3
Hindle Ave WA5 ....7 F1
Hindley Cres CW8 ....78 A3
Hinton Cres WA4 ....26 E8
Hinton Rd Crewe CW2 ...206 D8
Runcorn WA7 ....23 A1
Hirsch Cl CW5 ....205 A4
Hitch Lowes SK11 ....84 A3
Hitchen's Cl WA7 ....50 D7
Hitchens La SY14 ....184 D1
Hob Hey La WA3 ....4 D3
Hob La Churton CH3 .....180 F5
Dunham-on-t-H WA6 ....97 C6
Hobart Cl SK7 ....35 F4
Hobart Way CH1 ....117 D4
Hobb La WA4 ....25 C5
Hobbs Cl CW1 ....191 D4
Hobbs Hill La WA16 ......28 E1
Hobby Ct WA7 ....49 E6
Hobcroft La WA16 ....58 A7
Hobson St SK11 ....112 D6
Hockenhull Ave CH3 .....121 B2
Hockenhull Cres CH3 ...121 B2
Hockenhull La
Tarvin CH3 ....121 B1
Tarvin CH3 ....121 B2
Hocker La
Adder's Moss SK10 ....85 F4
Nether Alderley SK10 ......85 C4
Hockerley Ave SK23 ......65 D8
Hockerley Cl SK23 ....65 D8
Hockerley La SK23 ....65 D8
Hockerley New Rd SK23 ..65 D8
Hockley Cl SK12 ....37 A3
Hockley Paddock SK12 ...36 F3
Hockley Rd SK12 ....37 A3
Hodge La Hartford CW8 ..103 A6
Weaverham CW8 ....102 D5
Hodgehill La SK11 ......132 E5
Hodgkin Cl CW5 ....204 F4
Hodgkinson Ave WA5 ......7 F1
Hoghton Rd L24 ....21 E2
Hogshead La CW8 ......124 C7
Holbeck WA7 ....50 C7
Holbein Cl CH4 ....141 E6
Holborn Ct WA8 ....12 F3
Holbrook Cl WA5 ....14 E5
Holbury Cl CW1 ....190 B8
Holcombe Ave WA3 ....3 C8
Holcombe Dr SK10 ....87 B3
Holcot Ct CW7 ....127 A4
Holcroft La WA3 ....5 D2
Holdings La CW3 ....232 F4
Hole House La CW8 ......77 E4
Holehouse La
Langley SK11 ....113 C4
Scholar Green ST7 ....194 D8
Whiteley Green SK10 ......62 D2
Holes La WA1 ....17 B7
Holford Ave
Lostock Gralam CW9 ....80 A3
Warrington WA5 ....15 F8
Holford Cres WA16 ....57 B1
Holford Moss WA7 ....24 D3
Holford St CW12 ....156 D3
Holford Way WA12 ....2 F3
Holgrave Cl WA16 ....29 C4
Holkam Cl CW9 ....103 F5
Holker Cl SK12 ....36 F4
Holkham Cl WA8 ....12 F1
Holkham The CH3 ....119 B1
Holland Cl CW11 ....175 C5
Holland Ct SK12 ....36 E3
Holland Rd SK7 ....35 E7
Holland St Crewe CW1 ..190 B6
5 Macclesfield SK11 .....112 C7
Hollands La CW6 ....122 C5
Hollands Pl SK11 ....112 F7
Hollands Rd CW9 ....103 F7
Hollies La SK9 ....60 F7
Hollies The Moulton CW9 .126 E8
1 Northwich CW9 ....103 E6
Runcorn WA7 ....49 D8
Shavington CW2 ....206 B4
Hollin Green La CW5 ....202 E6
Hollin La Langley SK11 ...113 A1
Newhall CW5 ....228 D8
Styal SK9 ....33 F5
Sutton Lane Ends SK11 ....136 C6
Hollin Rd SK10 ....88 A7
Hollingford Pl WA16 ......82 A8
Hollingreen La CW5 ....229 B7
Hollinhey Prim Sch
SK11 ....112 F3
Hollins Cres ST7 ....194 E1
Hollins Dr WA2 ....8 A6
Hollins Grange ST7 .....210 D8
Hollins Green St Helens CE
Prim Sch WA3 ....11 B2
Hollins Hill CW6 ....146 F8
Hollins La Antrobus CW9 ...53 F4
Marbury SY13 ....226 E7
Winwick WA2 ....7 E6
Hollins Park Hospl WA2 ...7 F6
Hollins Rd SK11 ....112 F6
Hollins Terr SK11 ....112 F6
Hollins Way WA8 ....22 B5
Hollinshead Cl ST7 .....194 F7
Hollinwood Cl ST7 ......210 E8
Hollinwood Rd
Disley SK12 ....38 D6
Talke ST7 ....210 E8
Hollow Dr WA4 ....16 E1
Hollow La Kingsley WA6 ...75 B3
Knutsford WA16 ....57 B1
Hollow Oak La CW8 .....101 D4
Hollow The ST7 ....195 B5
Holloway WA7 ....22 F1
Hollowmoor Heath CH3 .121 A6
Hollowood Rd SY14 .....213 B5
Holly Ave WA12 ....2 D3
Holly Bank Frodsham WA6 .74 C8
Helsby WA6 ....73 D2
Lymm WA13 ....18 D2
Holly Bank Rd SK9 ....34 B1
Holly Bush La WA3 ....10 C2
Holly Cl
Connah's Quay CH5 ....91 C1
Hale L24 ....21 D2
Mickle Trafford CH2 ......119 F8
Holly Cotts Marton CW12 .132 C1
Wilmslow SK9 ....59 E8
Holly Croft CW12 ....154 F6
Holly Ct Helsby WA6 ......73 C5
Middlewich CW10 ....128 B2
Holly Dr CW7 ....149 D8
Holly Farm Ct WA8 ....12 E4
Holly Gr Over Tabley WA16 .56 A3
Warrington WA1 ....17 A7
Holly Heath Cl CW11 ....175 C5
Holly Hedge La WA4 .....25 D6
Holly House Est CW10 ..129 C6
Holly La Alsager ST7 .....193 E3
Kidsgrove ST7 ....195 F5
Styal SK9 ....33 E5
Holly Mount CW2 ....206 E5
Holly Rd Bramhall SK7 ....35 E5
Chester CH4 ....140 F5
Ellesmere Port CH65 ....70 C5
Golborne WA3 ....3 C8
Haydock WA11 ....1 A6
High Lane SK6 ....37 F7
Lymm WA13 ....19 B5
Macclesfield SK11 ....112 B7
Newcastle-u-Lyme ST5 ....210 D1
Poynton SK12 ....36 E3
Warrington WA5 ....14 E5
Weaverham CW8 ....102 C8
Holly Rd N SK9 ....60 B6
Holly Rd S SK9 ....60 B5
Holly Terr Tilston SY14 ...198 C3
Warrington WA5 ....14 F5
Holly Tree Dr
Biddulph ST8 ....179 C2
Swan Green WA16 ....106 D7
Holly Wlk Northwich CW8 .103 C7
Partington M31 ....11 D3
Hollybank Audlem CW3 ...229 E3
Moore WA4 ....25 B5
Hollybank Cl CW8 ....78 D1
Hollybank Ct WA8 ....12 F1
Hollybank Rd WA7 ....49 F8
Hollybush Cres CW5 ....205 D5
Hollyfield Rd CH65 ......70 B5
Hollyfields CW11 ....191 F8
Hollyhurst Rd SY13 .....227 B7
Hollythorn Ave SK8 ......35 C7
Hollytree Rd WA16 ....80 F3
Holm Dr CH2 ....72 C3
Holm Oak Way CH66 .....94 F8
Holme St CH3 ....120 F2
Holmefield Dr SK8 ....35 B8
Holmes Chapel Bsns Pk
CW4 ....130 D3
Holmes Chapel Comp Sch
CW4 ....130 A2
Holmes Chapel Prim Sch
CW4 ....130 B3
Holmes Chapel Rd
Allostock WA16 ....106 B3
Brereton Green CW4,
CW12 ....154 D8
Congleton CW12 ....155 C4
Knutsford WA16 ....82 C3
Lach Dennis CW9 ....105 E4
Middlewich CW10 ....128 E2
Sandbach CW11 ....153 E1
Sproston Green CW4,
CW10 ....129 B2
Withington Green SK11 ...109 A7
Holmes Chapel Sta
CW4 ....130 D2
Holmes Ct WA3 ....9 C4
Holmesville Ave CW12 ..156 B3
Holmeswood Cl SK9 .....60 C8
Holmfield Ave WA7 ......23 C2
Holmfield Dr CH66 ....69 D3
Holmlea Dr CW1 ....190 F3
Holmlee Way SK10 ....86 D6
Holmsfield Rd WA1 ......16 D5
Holmshaw La CW1 ......192 B3
Holmwood Dr CH65 ......70 B2
Holt Hey CH64 ....67 A5
Holt La WA7 ....49 F8
Holt St CW1 ....190 B4
Holt's Com Prim Sch
LL13 ....196 D8
Holt's La SK9 ....33 F3
Holtridge La SY13 ......215 E6
Holy Family RC Prim Sch
WA8 ....12 D5
Holy Spirit RC Prim Sch
WA9 ....1 A3
Holy Spirit RC Prim Sch The
WA7 ....49 D7
Holyhead Cl WA5 ....7 D3
Holyrood Ave WA8 ....13 A4
Holyrood Dr CW2 ....205 E8
Holyrood Way CH3 .....119 B2
Holywell Cl CH64 ....41 B1
Holywell La CH3 ....182 D2
Home Cl CH3 ....142 E7
Home Farm Ave SK10 ....86 F1
Home Farm Pk CW5 ....172 A8
Home Pk CH1 ....94 F1
Homecrofts CH64 ....66 E5
Homedee Ho CH1 ....237 A3
Homeshire Ho ST7 ......193 D3
Homestead Ave WA11 .....1 E6
Homestead Ct CW9 .....104 D7
Homestead Rd SK12 .....38 C6
Homesteads The CW5 ..172 A6
Homeway WA6 ....73 B2
Homewood Cres CW8 ...103 B5
Honey Fields CW6 ......146 C1
Honey Suckle Cl CH66 ....94 F8
Honeysuckle Cl
Broughton CH4 ....139 C3
Widnes WA8 ....13 B4
Honford Ct SK9 ....34 D3
Hong Kong Ave M90 ......33 A8
Honister Ave WA2 ....8 C2
Honister Gr WA7 ....49 E5
Honiton Way
Middlewich CW10 ....128 D2
Warrington WA5 ....14 E4
Hoo Green La WA16 ......29 E1
Hood La WA5 ....15 C4
Hood La N WA5 ....15 C6
Hood Rd WA8 ....12 F1
Hoofield La CH3 ....145 A1
Hook La CW6 ....145 A6
Hooker St CW8 ....103 E7
Hookstone Dr CH66 ......69 C6
Hoole CE Prim Sch CH2 .119 A3
Hoole Gdns CH2 ....119 B3
Hoole Ho CH2 ....119 B4
Hoole La CH2 ....119 A3
Hoole Pk CH2 ....118 F2
Hoole Rd CH2 ....118 F3
Hoole Way CH1 ....237 B3
Hooleyhey La SK10,SK11 ..89 D4
Hoolpool La WA6 ....72 F5
Hooton Gn CH66 ....44 B2
Hooton La CH66 ....44 B1
Hooton Rd CH64,CH66 ....43 D1
Hooton Sta CH66 ....43 D1
Hooton Way
14 Handforth SK9 ....34 D5
Hooton CH66 ....44 A2
Hope Ave SK9 ....34 C3
Hope Croft CH66 ....69 F2
Hope Farm Prec CH66 ....69 F2
Hope Farm Rd CH66 .....69 E2
Hope Green Way SK10 ...36 D2
Hope La Midway SK10 ....36 D1
Wardsend SK10 ....36 E1
Hope Rd CH4 ....139 B3
Hope St Audley ST7 .....209 F3
Chester CH4 ....140 F7
Crewe CW2 ....190 D2
Macclesfield SK10 ....112 E8
Newton-le-W WA12 ....2 B3
Northwich CW8 ....103 E7
Sandbach CW11 ....175 B6
Hope St W SK10 ....112 C8
Hopefield Rd WA13 ......19 B4
Hopkins Cl CW12 ....156 B3
Hopkinson Ct CH1 ......118 B1
Hopwood Cl 5 WA3 ......3 F8
Hopwood St WA1 ....16 C6
Horace Black Gdns CH65 .70 C6
Horace Lawton Ct 2
CW12 ....156 D3
Horbury Gdns CH66 ......69 C5
Horn's Mill Prim Sch
WA6 ....73 A1
Hornbeam Ave CH66 .....69 F1
Hornbeam Cl
Chester CH2 ....119 B3
Runcorn WA7 ....24 C1
Hornbeam Dr CW8 ......102 E4
Hornbeam Rd L26 ....21 A7
Hornby Dr
Congleton CW12 ....156 A3
Nantwich CW5 ....205 A5
Hornby La WA2 ....8 A6
Horncastle Cl 4 WA3 ......3 F8
Horridge Ave WA12 ....2 C5
Horrocks La WA1 ....16 B5
Horrocks Rd CH2 ....118 E5
Horsemarket St WA1 .....16 B5
Horseshoe Cl WA6 ....75 B2
Horseshoe Cres WA2 ......8 E3
Horseshoe Dr SK11 .....112 B7
Horseshoe La SK9 ....60 A2
Horsley La CW6 ....167 E1
Horstone Cres CH66 .....69 F2
Horstone Gdns CH66 ....70 A2
Horstone Rd CH66 ....69 F2
Horton Way CW5 ....205 A4
Horwood Ho SK9 ....60 B2
Hoscar Ct WA8 ....22 D7
Hospital La CW5 ....203 E2
Hospital of St John
Almhouses CH1 ....237 A3
Hospital St Crewe CW1 ..190 D6
Nantwich CW5 ....204 E5
Hospital Way WA7 ....49 F7
Hotel Rd M90 ....33 C7
Hotel St WA12 ....2 B3
Hothershall Cl CW1 .....173 B1
Hough Cl SK10 ....88 D5
Hough Cotts CW2 ....206 E3
Hough Gn Ashley WA15 ...31 E5
Chester CH4 ....141 B7
Hough Green Rd WA8 ....12 B3
Hough Green Sta WA8 ...12 A2
Hough La
Alderley Edge SK9 ....60 D3
Barnton CW8,CW9 ....78 B4
Comberbach CW9 ....78 A7
Norley WA6 ....100 F5
Hough's La WA4 ....26 A6
Hougher Wall Rd ST7 ...209 D1
Houghley Cl SK10 ....87 C2
Houghton Cl
Chester CH2 ....118 F3
Newton-le-W WA12 ....2 B3
9 Northwich CW9 ....103 F4
Widnes WA8 ....13 D2
Houghton Croft WA8 .....12 C5
Houghton St
Newton-le-W WA12 ....2 B3
Warrington WA2 ....16 B6
Widnes WA8 ....13 D2
Houndings La CW11 ....175 B4
Hourd Way CH66 ....94 E8
Housesteads Dr CH2 ....118 F3
Housman Cl CH1 ....118 A5
Hove Cl CW1 ....190 B8
Hove The WA7 ....50 D6
Hovis Mill SK11 ....112 E7
Howard Ave
Bebington CH62 ....43 D8
Lymm WA13 ....19 B4
Howard Ct Neston CH64 ...41 F1
Runcorn WA7 ....24 C4
Howard Rd Culcheth WA3 ...5 A2
Saltney CH4 ....140 D6
Howard St CW1 ....191 A5
Howards Way CH64 ......67 A6
Howarth Ct 4 WA7 ....23 B2
Howbeck Cres CW5 .....220 A8
Howbeck Wlk CW2 .....206 D8
Howe Rd CH4 ....141 B7
Howe St SK10 ....87 F1
Howells Ave CH66 ....69 D3
Howey Hill CW12 ....156 D1
Howey La
Congleton CW12 ....156 D2
Frodsham WA6 ....74 B7
Howey Rise WA6 ....74 B7
Howgill Cl CH66 ....68 F6
Howley La WA1 ....16 E5
Howley Quay Ind Est
WA1 ....16 D5
Howson Rd WA2 ....8 C3
Howty Cl SK9 ....34 D1
Hoylake Cl WA7 ....50 C6
Hoyle St WA5 ....15 F7
Hubert Dr CW10 ....151 C8
Hubert Worthington Ho 8
SK9 ....60 A1
Hudson Cl WA5 ....15 D8
Hudson Gr 9 WA3 ....3 E8
Hugh St CH4 ....141 D7
Hughes Ave WA2 ....8 D2
Hughes Dr CW2 ....189 F4
Hughes Pl WA2 ....8 D2
Hughes St WA4 ....16 C3
Hulley Pl SK10 ....87 F1
Hulley Rd SK10 ....87 F2
Hullock's Pool Rd ST7 ..209 E5
Hulme Hall Ave SK8 ......35 B8
Hulme Hall Cres SK8 .....35 A8
Hulme hall Gram Sch
SK8 ....35 A8
Hulme Hall La WA16 ....106 B4
Hulme Hall Rd SK8 ....35 A8
Hulme La WA16 ....106 C7
Hulme Sq SK11 ....112 D5
Hulme St CW1 ....189 F5
Hulse La CW9 ....105 D6
Hulseheath La WA16 ......30 A3
Hulton Cl CW12 ....157 B1
Humber Cl WA8 ....13 F3
Humber Dr ST8 ....179 E1
Humber Rd
Ellesmere Port CH66 ....69 F2
Warrington WA2 ....8 E2
Humble Bee Bank Cotts
CW5 ....187 C8
Hume St WA1 ....16 D6
Humphrey's Cl WA7 ......50 D7
Hungerford Ave CW1 ...190 E4
Hungerford Pl
Barthomley CW2 ....208 D5
Sandbach CW11 ....175 A5
Hungerford Prim Sch
CW1 ....190 E5
Hungerford Rd CW1 ....190 F4
Hungerford Terr CW1 ..190 F4
Hungerford Villas CW1 ..190 F4
Hunsterson Rd
Bridgemere CW5 ....231 D8
Hatherton CW5 ....220 B3
Hunt Cl WA5 ....15 B8
Hunt Rd WA11 ....1 E6
Hunter Ave
Shavington CW2 ....206 D7
Hunter Ave *continued*
Warrington WA2 ....8 B3
Hunter St CH1 ....237 A3
Hunter's Cres CH3 .....121 C1
Hunter's Dr CH3 ....121 C1
Hunter's View SK9 ....34 C3
Hunters Cl SK9 ....34 F1
Hunters Ct Helsby WA6 ....73 D4
Runcorn WA7 ....49 E6
Hunters Field CW8 .....103 D7
Hunters Hill Kingsley WA6 .75 C1
Weaverham CW8 ....77 C1
Hunters Lodge SK9 ....34 F1
Hunters Mews SK9 ....60 C7
Hunters Pointe CW12 ...155 C6
Hunters Pool La SK10 ....86 C8
Hunters Rise CW7 ......126 C1
Hunters Way Neston CH64 .66 C8
Talke ST7 ....210 D8
Hunters Wlk CH1 ....237 A2
Huntersfield CW2 ....206 B3
Hunting Lodge Mews
CW8 ....102 A4
Huntington Com Prim Sch
CH3 ....142 A5
Huntley St WA5 ....15 C4
Huntly Chase SK9 ....60 C7
Hunts Cl CH3 ....119 B1
Hunts Field Cl WA13 .....18 D2
Hunts La WA4 ....16 F2
Huntsbank Bsns Pk
CW2 ....205 E7
Huntsbank Dr ST5 ......210 D1
Huntsman Dr M44 ....11 F7
Hurdsfield Cl CW10 .....151 C7
Hurdsfield Com Prim Sch
SK10 ....87 F2
Hurdsfield Gn SK10 ......87 E2
Hurdsfield Ind Est SK10 ..87 E3
Hurdsfield Rd SK10 ......87 E1
Hurford Ave CH65 ....69 F3
Hurlbote Cl SK9 ....34 D5
Hurleston Bldgs CW5 ...204 E6
Hurlestone Cl CH2 ....96 F1
Hurley Cl WA5 ....15 C5
Hurn Cl CW1 ....190 B8
Hurst Ave SK8 ....35 C6
Hurst Cl ST7 ....210 D6
Hurst Ct CW6 ....185 E8
Hurst La Bollington SK10 ..88 A8
Glazebury WA3 ....5 C7
Hurst Lea Ct SK9 ....60 A2
Hurst Lea Rd SK22 ....39 C7
Hurst Mews WA6 ....75 C2
Hurst Mill La WA3 ....5 C8
Hurst Rd ST8 ....179 F4
Hurst St WA8 ....23 A4
Hurst The WA6 ....75 C2
Hursthead Inf Sch SK8 ...35 C6
Hursthead Jun Sch SK8 ..35 C7
Hursthead Rd SK8 ....35 B7
Hurstwood CH3 ....143 A4
Hush Ho CH1 ....237 A2
Huskisson Way WA12 ......2 B4
Hutchins' Cl CW10 ......151 E6
Hutchinson St WA8 ......22 F6
Huttfield Rd L24 ....21 A4
Hutton Cl WA3 ....4 E5
Hutton Dr CW12 ....157 A2
Huxley CE Prim Sch
CH3 ....167 A7
Huxley Cl Bramhall SK7 ...35 E7
Macclesfield SK10 ....87 B2
Huxley Ct CH66 ....69 F8
Huxley Dr SK7 ....35 E7
Huxley La CW6 ....168 B6
Huxley St CW8 ....103 E7
Hyacinth Cl WA11 ....1 F6
Hyacinth Wlk 9 M31 .....11 E2
Hyde Bank Ct SK22 ......39 C7
Hyde Bank Rd SK22 .....39 C8
Hyde Cl
Ellesmere Port CH65 ....69 F4
Runcorn WA7 ....49 D6
Hydrangea Way WA9 ......6 A7
Hylton Ct CH65 ....70 E2
Hylton Dr SK8 ....35 C8
Hythe Ave CW1 ....190 B8

I

Ian Rd ST7 ....195 D3
Iberis Gdns WA9 ....6 A7
Ibis Ct WA1 ....16 A3
Ikey La CW5 ....202 F6
Ikins Dr ST7 ....209 F2
Ilex Ave WA2 ....8 B7
Imperial Ave CH1 ......117 C4
Imperial Mews
Crewe CW2 ....190 D3
Ellesmere Port CH65 ....70 B6
Ince & Elton Sta CH2 ....72 B4
Ince Ave CH62 ....43 E3
Ince Dr CH3 ....180 F1
Ince La Elton CH2 ....72 B3
Wimbolds Trafford CH2 .....96 F5
Ince Orchards CH2 ....72 B4
Indigo Rd CH65 ....70 F6
Ingersley Ct SK10 ....88 B8
Ingersley Rd SK10 ....88 C8
Ingersley Vale SK10 .....88 B8
Ingham Ave WA12 ....2 C1
Ingham Cl CH3 ....119 A1
Ingham Rd WA8 ....12 F4
Inglegreen CH60 ....41 B8
Inglenook Rd WA5 ....14 F4

Ingleton Cl
Holmes Chapel CW4 ......130 A3
Newton-le-W WA12 ....2 B4
Ingleton Gr WA7 ....49 D5
Inglewood Ave CW10 ...151 D5
Inglewood Cl
Partington M31 ....11 F4
Warrington WA3 ....10 B6
Inglewood Cvn Pk M31 ...11 F4
Inman Ave WA9 ....1 B2
Inner Gosling Cl WA4 ....25 F1
Innisfree Cl 4 CH66 ......69 C5
Innovation Ho CW7 .....149 A7
Insall Rd WA2 ....8 F2
Int Peace Ctr WA5 ....15 D5
Intack La WA16 ....28 B3
Intake Cl CH64 ....68 A8
International App M90 ...33 C7
Inveresk Rd SY14 ....198 C3
Inward Way CH65 ....70 B7
Ion Path CW7 ....127 C1
Irby Cl CH66 ....69 E4
Ireland Blackburne Ho
WA1 ....16 E7
Ireland Rd Hale L24 ....21 E1
Haydock WA11 ....1 C6
Ireland St Warrington WA2 .16 B8
Widnes WA8 ....13 D2
Iris Cl WA8 ....12 C2
Iris Wlk 7 M31 ....11 E2
Irlam & Cadishead Com High
Sch M44 ....11 E7
Irlam Ind Est M44 ....11 E7
Irlam Sta M44 ....11 E7
Ironbridge Dr CW4 .....130 C2
Irons La CH3 ....120 F7
Irvin Dr M22 ....34 A8
Irving's Cres CH4 ....140 E6
Irwell La WA7 ....23 B3
Irwell Rd WA4 ....16 B2
Irwell Rise SK10 ....87 F7
Irwell St WA8 ....23 A4
Irwin Dr SK9 ....34 C5
Isabella Ct CH4 ....140 E6
Isherwood Cl WA2 ....8 F3
Isis Cl CW12 ....156 F1
Islay Cl CH65 ....70 C1
Iveagh Cl WA7 ....50 A7
Iver Cl Chester CH2 ......118 E7
Cronton WA8 ....12 C6
Iver Rd CH2 ....118 E7
Ivy Ave WA12 ....2 C2
Ivy Bank Prim Sch SK11 .112 A5
Ivy Cotts SY13 ....225 A8
Ivy Ct CH4 ....162 D2
Ivy Dr CW8 ....102 A2
Ivy Farm Ct L24 ....21 D1
Ivy Farm Dr CH64 ....66 F6
Ivy Farm Gdns WA3 ....4 D4
Ivy Farm La CH3 ....183 C1
Ivy Gdns CW12 ....156 C2
Ivy Ho Macclesfield SK11 ..112 A7
Nether Alderley SK9 ....84 C7
Ivy House Rd ST8 ....179 C2
Ivy La Alsager ST7 ....193 E2
Macclesfield SK11 ....112 A6
Ivy Meade Cl 10 SK11 ....111 F7
Ivy Meade Rd SK11 ......111 F6
Ivy Mews CH2 ....119 A5
Ivy Rd Golborne WA3 ....3 B8
Macclesfield SK11 ....112 A7
Poynton SK12 ....36 E3
Warrington WA1 ....17 E7
Ivy St WA7 ....23 A1
Ivy Wlk M31 ....11 D3
Ivychurch Mews WA7 ....23 D2

J

Jack La
Moulton CW9,CW10 ......127 A7
Weston CW2 ....207 D6
Jackie Stewart Bsns Ctr
CW6 ....147 D6
Jackson Ave Culcheth WA3 ..4 E3
Nantwich CW5 ....204 F5
Warrington WA1 ....16 F6
Jackson Ct CH5 ....139 B7
Jackson Ho CW12 ......156 D2
Jackson La SK10 ....88 B7
Jackson Rd CW12 ....156 E5
Jackson St
Burtonwood WA5 ....6 E6
Haydock WA11 ....1 A7
Macclesfield SK11 ....112 D6
Jackson's La SK7 ....36 C8
Jacksons Cl SK10 ....88 B7
Jacksons Edge Rd SK12 ..38 B6
Jacobs Way WA16 ....79 F7
Jamage Rd ST7 ....210 D5
James Atkinson Way
CW1 ....189 F7
James Ave CH66 ....69 C3
James Cl WA8 ....23 A4
James Hall St CW5 .....204 E6
James Pl CH2 ....118 F2
James Rd WA11 ....1 F7
James St Chester CH1 ....237 B3
Macclesfield SK11 ....112 D6
Northwich CW9 ....104 C8
6 Warrington WA1 ....16 B5
Jamieson Cl Alsager ST7 .193 E4
Chester CH3 ....119 A2
Jan Palach Ave CW5 ....204 F4
Jane Maddock Cotts
ST7 ....193 B3
Jankyns Croft SK12 ......38 E5
Japonica Gdns WA9 ....6 A7
Jarman SK11 ....112 F4
Jasmin Way ST7 ....195 F2
Jasmine Cres ST7 ......195 D2
Jasmine Gdns WA9 ....6 A7
Jasmine Gr WA8 ....22 D8
Jasmine Wlk M31 ....11 F2
Jay Cl WA3 ....10 A4
Jays Cl WA7 ....50 E7
Jedburgh Ave CH66 ......69 A6
Jellicoe Ave M44 ....11 E6
Jennet's La WA3 ....5 C8
Jenny La SK7 ....35 E4
Jensen Ct WA7 ....23 C3
Jersey Ave CH65 ....70 C1
Jersey Cl CW12 ....157 A2
Jersey Way CW10 ....128 D2
Jervis Cl WA2 ....9 A3
Jesmond Cres CW2 .....190 B2
Jesmond Gr SK8 ....35 B8
Jesmond Rd CH1 ....118 B2
Jessop Way CW1 ....191 C4
JH Godwin Prim Sch
CH1 ....117 D4
Jockey St WA2 ....16 B7
Jodrell Bank Obsy*
CW4 ....108 C3
Jodrell Bank Visitor Ctr*
SK11 ....108 D3
Jodrell Cl
Holmes Chapel CW4 ......130 A3
Macclesfield SK11 ....112 E7
Jodrell Mdw SK23 ....65 E8
Jodrell Rd SK23 ....65 D8
Jodrell St
Macclesfield SK11 ....112 E7
New Mills SK22 ....39 B7
John Brunner Cres
CW9 ....103 E6
John Fryer Ave CW9 .....80 A5
John Gresty Dr CW5 ....205 D6
John Lloyd Ct M44 ....11 F8
John May Ct SK10 ....87 B2
John Middleton Cl L24 ...21 E2
John Morris Ho 1 WA1 ..16 C5
John Nicholas Cres
CH65 ....70 C6
John Rd WA13 ....18 C3
John St Bollington SK10 ....88 B8
Congleton CW12 ....156 C2
Crewe CW1 ....190 C5
Ellesmere Port CH65 ....70 B6
Golborne WA3 ....3 A8
Irlam M44 ....11 E5
Macclesfield SK11 ....112 D6
1 Northwich CW9 ....104 A8
Utkinton CW6 ....146 B7
Warrington WA2 ....16 B6
Winsford CW7 ....126 C1
John Street Com Prim Sch
CH65 ....70 B6
Johns Ave Haydock WA11 ...1 E7
Runcorn WA7 ....48 F8
Johns Cl SK10 ....88 D5
Johnson Ave WA12 ....2 B5
Johnson Cl CW12 ....157 B1
Johnson St SK23 ....65 E8
Johnson's La WA8 ....13 E1
Johnsons Cl CH4 ....141 B5
Jonathan's Way CH1 .....117 E5
Jones's La CW10 ....152 D6
Jonson Rd CH64 ....66 E8
Jordangate SK10 ....112 D8
Joseph Cres ST7 ....193 F2
Joseph Groome Twrs 10
CH65 ....70 C6
Joseph St WA8 ....13 C2
Joy La WA5 ....6 E4
Joyce Ave CW7 ....126 C2
Jubilee Almshouses
CW5 ....204 E6
Jubilee Ave Crewe CW2 ..190 B3
Warrington WA5 ....14 E4
Warrington,Padgate WA1 ...16 F8
Jubilee Cres WA11 ....1 F7
Jubilee Ct
2 Handforth SK9 ....34 E5
Holmes Chapel CW4 ......130 A3
Jubilee Gdns
Nantwich CW5 ....204 E4
New Mills SK22 ....39 C7
Jubilee Gn CH65 ....70 C4
Jubilee Gr WA13 ....18 C4
Jubilee Rd CW12 ....156 E2
Jubilee St SK22 ....39 C7
Jubilee Terr CW5 ....204 E4
Jubilee Villas CW11 .....175 C2
Jubilee Way Widnes WA8 ..12 E1
5 Winsford CW7 ....126 D1
Jubits La WA8 ....13 A8
Juddfield St WA11 ....1 A7
Julian Way WA8 ....12 F4
July Cotts CH4 ....141 E2
Jumper La SK10 ....88 F7
Junction Eight Bsns Ctr
CH65 ....70 A7
Junction La WA12 ....2 B3
June Ave CH62 ....43 E8
Juniper Cl ST5 ....210 E1
Juniper Ct CH2 ....119 B4
Juniper Dr CH66 ....69 E1
Juniper Gr CH66 ....69 F1
Juniper La WA3 ....18 A7
Juniper Rise SK10 ....86 E1
Jupiter Dr CH1 ....117 E2
Jurby Ct WA2 ....8 F1
Justice St SK10 ....87 D1

K

Kansas Pl WA5 ....15 B7
Karen Cl WA5 ....7 A6
Karen Way CH66 ....69 D3
Kay La WA13 ....29 B8
Kaye Ave WA3 ....4 F3
Keats Cl
Ellesmere Port CH66 ....94 E8
Widnes WA8 ....22 F8
Keats Dr Macclesfield SK10 .86 F1
Rode Heath ST7 ....193 E8
Wistaston CW2 ....206 A8
Keats Gr WA2 ....8 C2
Keats La CW9 ....80 A5
Keats Terr CH1 ....118 A5
Keble St WA8 ....23 B7
Keckwick La WA4 ....25 A3
Keel Hey CH64 ....43 B1
Keele Cres SK11 ....112 B6
Keeper's La CW8 ....102 E8
Keeper's Rd WA4 ....27 A7
Keepers Cl WA16 ....57 D3
Keepers La CW9 ....53 D4
Keepers Wlk WA7 ....23 F2
Keith Ave WA5 ....14 E6
Keith Dr CH63 ....43 D5
Kelburn Ct WA3 ....9 F6
Kelmscott Cl CH66 ....69 D2
Kelsall Ave CH62 ....43 F3
Kelsall Cl Bebington CH62 ..43 E3
Warrington WA3 ....9 C3
Widnes WA8 ....12 D1
Kelsall Com Prim Sch
CW6 ....122 C4
Kelsall Rd CH3 ....121 C4
Kelsall St CW12 ....156 E3
Kelsall Way Audley ST7 ..209 D1
6 Handforth SK9 ....34 D5
Kelsborrow Cl CW9 .....103 E3
Kelsborrow Way CW6 ...122 D4
Kelso Way SK10 ....87 C4
Kelstern Cl 2 CW9 ......104 B8
Kelsterton Ct CH5 ....91 C1
Kelsterton La CH6 ....91 B1
Kelsterton Rd
Connah's Quay CH5,CH6 ....91 C2
Flint/Y Fflint CH6 ....91 A3
Kelvin Cl WA3 ....9 D6
Kelvin Gr CH2 ....118 E4
Kelvin St WA3 ....9 F5
Kemberton Dr WA8 ....13 A5
Kemble Cl CW2 ....206 B8
Kemmel Ave WA4 ....16 C3
Kempsell Way L26 ....21 A7
Kempsell Wlk L26 ....21 A7
Kempton Ave CW1 ......190 C7
Kempton Cl Chester CH1 .118 B2
Newton-le-W WA12 ....2 D5
Runcorn WA7 ....49 C6
Kempton Way SK10 ....87 C4
Kendal Ave WA2 ....8 C2
Kendal Cl Chester CH2 ...119 A6
Ellesmere Port CH66 ....69 D2
Macclesfield SK11 ....111 E6
Kendal Ct CW12 ....156 A2
Kendal Dr Bramhall SK7 ...35 C5
Ellesmere Port CH66 ....69 E2
Kendal Rd
Macclesfield SK11 ....111 F6
Widnes WA8 ....12 C1
Kendal Rise WA7 ....49 D5
Kendal Way CW2 ....207 C1
Kendrick Cl CW8 ....77 D1
Kendrick St WA1 ....16 A5
Kenilworth Ave
Handforth SK9 ....34 D3
Knutsford WA16 ....57 C2
Runcorn WA7 ....49 B8
Kenilworth Cl
Macclesfield SK11 ....111 F6
Wistaston CW2 ....206 A7
Kenilworth Ct CH65 ......70 E2
Kenilworth Dr
Hazel Grove SK7 ....36 D8
Warrington WA1 ....16 F8
Kenilworth Gdns WA12 ....2 C1
Kenilworth Gn SK11 .....111 F6
Kenilworth Ho CH1 .....237 C3
Kenilworth Rd
Golborne WA3 ....3 E7
Macclesfield SK11 ....111 F6
Neston CH64 ....66 E5
Kenley Ave WA8 ....12 D5
Kenmare Bank CW9 .....104 A5
Kenmore Gr M44 ....11 D6
Kennedy Ave SK10 ....86 F2
Kennedy Cl CH2 ....119 A5
Kennel La
Cuddington CW8 ....102 A1
Little Budworth CW8 ......124 E7
Kennelwood Rd CW9 .....78 C7
Kennerley Ct 3 SK9 ......60 A7
Kennerley's La SK9 ....60 A7
Kennet Cl SK9 ....34 D2
Kennet Dr CW12 ....156 F1
Kennet Rd WA11 ....1 C6
Kennet Way 10 SK11 ....111 F8
Kenneth Rd WA8 ....22 C8
Kennington Pk WA8 ......12 E4
Kenrick Cl CW3 ....232 C1
Kensington Ave WA4 .....17 C2
Kensington Cl
Chester CH4 ....141 A6
Widnes WA8 ....13 D4
Kensington Ct
Alsager ST7 ....192 F3
Kensington Ct *continued*
Wilmslow SK9 ....60 A6
Winsford CW7 ....149 C7
Kensington Dr
Congleton CW12 ....156 F4
Willaston CW5 ....205 D4
Kensington Gn CH4 .....140 F6
Kensington Pl 9 CW5 ...204 E6
Kensington Rd
Chester CH4 ....141 A6
Ellesmere Port CH65 ....70 A5
Kensington Way CW9 ...103 E3
Kent Ave SK10 ....87 E6
Kent Cl CH63 ....43 B8
Kent Dr CW12 ....156 D4
Kent Gdns CH2 ....118 F5
Kent Gr WA7 ....23 B1
Kent Ho ST7 ....210 D6
Kent Rd Chester CH2 .....118 F5
Irlam M44 ....11 C5
Partington M31 ....11 E2
Warrington WA5 ....15 C4
Kent St Warrington WA4 ...16 C4
Widnes WA8 ....13 B1
Kent Way WA12 ....2 C1
Kent Wlk SK10 ....86 F1
Kent's Green La CW1,
CW11 ....191 E7
Kent's La CW1 ....173 C1
Kentmere Ave CW7 .....126 D2
Kentmere Pl WA2 ....8 A3
Kenton Rd L26 ....21 A7
Kentridge Dr CH66 ....69 D3
Kentwell Dr SK10 ....87 C3
Kenview Cl WA8 ....22 A4
Kenwick Cl CH66 ....69 C3
Kenwood Ave SK7 ....35 D5
Kenyon Ave WA5 ....14 E5
Kenyon Ct WA8 ....23 A6
Kenyon La Culcheth WA3 ....4 A4
Golborne WA3 ....3 F5
Golborne,Kenyon WA3 ....3 F3
Kenyon's La S WA11 ....1 F7
Kenyons La N WA11 ....1 F8
Kerfoot Bsns Pk WA2 ....16 A8
Kerfoot St WA2 ....16 A7
Keristal Ave CH3 ....142 A7
Kerridge Cl CW10 ....151 B8
Kerridge Rd SK10 ....88 B3
Kerry Croft CH66 ....69 E1
Kershaw Gr SK11 ....112 B8
Kershaw St WA8 ....12 D1
Kershaw Way WA12 ......2 C5
Kestrel Ave WA16 ....57 B3
Kestrel Cl
Congleton CW12 ....156 E1
Middlewich CW10 ....151 D6
Winsford CW7 ....149 D5
Kestrel Dr CW1 ....190 B8
Kestrel La WA3 ....9 E4
Kestrel Rd Heswall CH60 ..41 C7
Northwich CW8 ....103 C7
Kestrels Way WA7 ....49 F6
Keswick Ave
Bebington CH63 ....43 C4
Macclesfield SK11 ....111 F5
Warrington WA2 ....8 C2
Keswick Cl Chester CH2 ..119 A5
Crewe CW2 ....189 E3
Irlam M44 ....11 D4
Macclesfield SK11 ....111 F6
Widnes WA8 ....12 C1
Winsford CW7 ....126 D2
Keswick Cres WA2 ....8 C2
Keswick Ct CW12 ....156 A2
Keswick Dr Bramhall SK7 ..35 C5
Frodsham WA6 ....74 D8
Keswick Gdns CH63 ......43 C5
Keswick Rd SK6 ....37 E8
Ketlan Ct CH4 ....140 E7
Kettell Ave CW1 ....190 A6
Kettle La CW3 ....230 C2
Kettleshulme St James CE
Prim Sch SK23 ....64 F4
Kettleshulme Way SK12 ..37 A3
Kettleshulme Wlk 4 SK9 .34 E1
Kew Gardens Cl WA8 ....13 D4
Keyes Cl WA3 ....9 F4
Keyes Gdn WA3 ....9 F4
Keysbrook CH3 ....166 C2
Keysbrook Ave CH3 .....166 C2
Kidderton Cl CW5 ......202 E7
Kidderton La CW5 ......202 F7
Kidsgrove Sta ST7 ....194 F1
Kidston Dr CW1 ....189 F7
Kilbuck La WA11 ....2 A8
Kilburn Ave CH62 ....43 E6
Kilburn Cl SK8 ....34 B7
Kildare Cl L24 ....21 D2
Kildonan Rd WA4 ....17 A2
Kilford Cl WA5 ....7 E2
Killingworth La WA3 .....10 B5
Kilmorey Park Rd CH2 ...118 F3
Kilmorey Pk CH2 ....118 F4
Kilmorey Pk Ave CH2 ...237 C4
Kiln Croft La SK9 ....34 E4
Kiln La CW5 ....220 B8
Kilncroft WA7 ....50 B5
Kilsby Dr WA8 ....13 E2
Kilshaw Rd WA5 ....6 F6
Kilsyth Cl WA2 ....8 F4
Kimberley Dr WA4 ....16 C1
Kimberley St WA5 ....15 E5
Kimberley Terr CH2 .....118 F2
Kinder Dr CW2 ....189 D3
Kinder View SK22 ....39 C7
Kinderton Cl WA16 ....29 C4
Kinderton Mobile Home Pk
CW10 ....152 A7
Kinderton St CW10 .....128 D1
King Arthur's Wlk WA7 ...24 A1
King Charles Ct CH1 ....237 A3
King Edward Bldgs 4
CH3 ....119 A1
King Edward Cl CW9 ....103 F5
King Edward Rd
Knutsford WA16 ....57 A2
3 Macclesfield SK10 .....112 D8
King Edward St
Macclesfield SK10 ....112 D8
Middlewich CW10 ....128 C1
Warrington WA1 ....16 E7
King George Ave CW9 ...104 B8
King George Cres WA1 ...16 E7
King George Rd WA11 .....2 A7
King Ho ST7 ....210 D5
King James Ct WA7 ......49 E6
King Pl CW5 ....204 E6
King St Audley ST7 ......209 D1
Chester CH1 ....237 A3
Congleton CW12 ....156 F4
Ellesmere Port CH65 ....70 C6
Hartford CW8 ....103 B5
Kidsgrove ST7 ....195 A2
Knutsford WA16 ....57 A2
Macclesfield SK10 ....112 E8
Middlewich CW10 ....128 B5
Newton-le-W WA12 ....2 B3
Northwich CW9 ....104 F6
Runcorn WA7 ....23 A3
Sandbach CW11 ....174 E8
Talke ST7 ....210 D5
King Street Trad Est
CW10 ....128 C2
King's Ave WA3 ....3 F7
King's Bldgs CH1 ....237 A3
King's Cres CW10 ....128 C2
King's Cres E CH3 ....119 A1
King's Cres W CH3 ......119 A1
King's Ct CH1 ....237 A3
King's Gate CW8 ....102 A2
King's La
Allostock CW10,WA16 ....106 C1
Nantwich CW5 ....204 D5
King's Rd SK9 ....59 E8
King's Sch The
Chester CH4 ....141 B4
Macclesfield SK10 ....112 E8
Macclesfield SK10 ....87 C1
Kingfisher Cl
Congleton CW12 ....156 E1
Farndon CH3 ....180 F1
Nantwich CW5 ....204 E8
Runcorn WA7 ....49 F5
Warrington WA3 ....9 F4
Kingfisher Ct
Chester CH2 ....237 A4
Northwich CW9 ....79 C2
Kingfisher Dr 5 CW7 ...149 D6
Kingfisher Gr CW9 ....79 F5
Kingham Cl 3 WA8 ....13 D1
Kings Cl Chester CH4 ....140 F5
Wilmslow SK9 ....60 A6
Kings Croft CH5 ....91 D1
Kings Ct Nantwich CW5 ..204 D5
Runcorn WA7 ....24 D4
Kings Dr Helsby WA6 .....73 B3
Wistaston CW2 ....205 E8
Kings Grove Sch CW2 ...190 A3
Kings La CW6 ....147 D4
Kings Lea Ho CH3 ....142 A8
Kings Mdw Hough CW2 ..206 E2
Runcorn WA7 ....50 C8
Kings Mews CH66 ....69 C7
Kings Rd
Connah's Quay CH5 ....91 D1
Ellesmere Port CH66 ....69 C7
Golborne WA3 ....3 A7
Irlam M44 ....11 E6
Warrington WA2 ....9 A2
Kings Wood Wlk CW6 ...122 D5
Kingsbury Cl WA4 ....26 D3
Kingsbury Dr 15 SK9 .....34 D1
Kingsbury Rd WA8 ....13 D4
Kingsdale Rd WA5 ....14 F7
Kingsdown Cl CW2 .....207 C1
Kingsfield Ct CH4 ....141 C3
Kingshead Cl WA7 ....24 A2
Kingsland Grange WA1 ....9 D1
Kingslawn Cl CW9 ......103 F5
Kingsley Ave
Bebington CH62 ....43 E3
Handforth SK9 ....34 C2
Kingsley Cl
Northwich CW8 ....103 C5
Talke ST7 ....210 D6
Kingsley Com Prim Sch
WA6 ....74 F2
Kingsley Cres WA7 ....23 A1
Kingsley Ct CW11 ......174 D8
Kingsley Dr
Northwich CW9 ....104 A6
Warrington WA4 ....26 C7
Kingsley Gdns CH3 .....142 B8
Kingsley Gn WA6 ....74 E5
Kingsley Rd Chester CH3 .142 B8
Congleton CW12 ....157 A3
Crowton CW8 ....76 B1
Ellesmere Port CH65 ....70 C5
Frodsham WA6 ....74 E4
Haslington CW1 ....191 C4
Runcorn WA7 ....23 A1

Kingsley Rd continued
Talke ST7 ....210 D6
Kingsley Wlk CW7 ....126 B2
Kingsmead Chester CH2 ..118 C8
Northwich CW9 ....103 F5
Kingsmead Crossroads 10
CW9 ....103 F4
Kingsmead Ct WA3 ....9 A8
Kingsmead Prim Sch
CW9 ....103 E5
Kingsmead Sq CW9 ....103 E4
Kingston Ave
Macclesfield SK11 .....112 F7
Warrington WA5 ....14 E6
Kingston Cl WA7 ....23 E2
Kingston Ct
10 Handforth SK9 ......34 E1
Saughall CH1 ....94 B2
Kingston Pl ST8 ......179 E2
Kingston Rd SK9 ....34 D5
Kingstreet SK7 ....35 B1
Kingsway Bollington SK10 ..87 E7
Chester CH2 ....118 F5
Crewe CW2 ....190 B2
Frodsham WA6 ....74 B8
Heswall CH60 ....41 C6
Newton-le-W WA12 ....2 C2
Northwich CW9 ....104 B8
Widnes WA8 ....133 A6
Winsford CW7 ....126 F1
Kingsway High Sch CH2 .118 F5
Kingsway Ho WA4 ....16 F4
Kingsway N WA1 ....16 F6
Kingsway S WA1,WA4 ....16 F4
Kingsway W CH2 ....118 E4
Kingswood ST7 ....195 B1
Kingswood Ave
Chorlton CW2 ....207 B3
Saughall CH1 ....94 C1
Kingswood Cres CW10 .151 E5
Kingswood Ct 7 SK9 ...60 B7
Kingswood La CH1 ......94 C1
Kinloch Cl Crewe CW1 .190 B6
Halewood L26 ....21 A7
Kinnerley Rd CH65 .....70 A3
Kinnersley Ave ST7 ...210 F8
Kinnersley St 1 ST1 ..195 A2
Kinnerton Cl CH4 .....140 E5
Kinnerton Hts CH4 ....161 A7
Kinnerton La CH4 .....161 A8
Kinnerton Rd CH4 .....162 A7
Kinnington Way CH1 ....94 F7
Kinnock Pk WA5 ....6 E6
Kinross Cl WA2 ....8 F4
Kinsale Dr WA3 ....9 C4
Kinsey Rd CH65 ....70 D1
Kinsey St CW12 ....156 E2
Kinsey's La CH2 ....71 F6
Kintore Cl Bebington CH63 .43 C4
Winsford CW7 ....127 A3
Kintore Dr WA5 ....14 D6
Kintyre Cl CH65 ....70 C1
Kipling Ave WA2 ....8 C1
Kipling Cres WA8 ......22 F8
Kipling Rd CH1 ....117 F5
Kipling Way CW1 ......190 F4
Kirby Cl CH2 ....118 C5
Kirkacre Ave WA12 ......7 C8
Kirkby Rd WA3 ....3 E5
Kirkcaldy Ave WA5 ....14 D6
Kirkfell Dr SK6 ....37 E8
Kirkham Ave WA3 ....3 E6
Kirkham Cl WA5 ....15 A4
Kirkham Rd
Heald Green SK8 ....34 C8
Widnes WA8 ....13 C2
Kirkstall Cl
Macclesfield SK10 ......87 B2
Poynton SK12 ....36 D4
Kirkstead Rd SK8 ......35 C6
Kirkstead Way WA3 ......3 A8
Kirkstone Ave WA2 ......8 C2
Kirkstone Cres WA7 ....50 A4
Kirkstone Ct CW12 ....156 A1
Kirkwall Dr WA5 ....15 A3
Kirkwood Cl CH3 ......119 A2
Kishfield La SK23 ......65 A6
Kitchen St CH1 ....118 B1
Kitchener Ave M44 .....11 C4
Kite Gr ST7 ....195 D3
Kitfield Ave CW10 ....151 D7
Kitt's Moss La SK7 ....35 D6
Knap The CH60 ....41 A6
Knebworth Ct CW12 ...179 B8
Knight Rd WA5 ....6 F6
Knight St SK11 ....112 E7
Knight's Cl SK11 .....112 E7
Knight's Grange (Sports
Complex) CW7 ....126 B3
Knights La CW6 ....123 E1
Knights Mdw CW7 ......126 C3
Knights Way CW2 ......206 B3
Knightsbridge Ave
4 Northwich CW9 .....103 E3
Warrington WA4 ....17 C2
Knightsbridge Cl
1 Handforth SK9 ......34 D1
Widnes WA8 ....13 D4
Knightsbridge Ct
Chester CH4 ....237 C2
Warrington WA1 ....16 A5
Knightwake Rd SK22 ....39 A8
Knole Ave SK12 ....36 F4
Knoll St SK22 ....39 B8

Knoll The WA7 ....49 F7
Knott's Hos WN7 ....4 B8
Knottingley Dr CH66 ...69 C5
Knotty La CW12 ....179 F8
Knowe The CH64 ....68 A8
Knowl Hey Rd L26 ......21 A6
Knowl La CH3 ....180 E5
Knowl The CH3 ....180 F5
Knowle Cl CH66 ....69 E3
Knowle Gn SK9 ....34 C3
Knowle Pk SK9 ....34 C3
Knowles Ind Est SK23 ..39 D3
Knowles St 2 WA8 .....13 C2
Knowsley Ave WA3 ......3 B8
Knowsley Ct CH2 .....118 F4
Knowsley Expressway
L35,WA8 ....21 F8
Knowsley La ST7 .....194 F4
Knowsley Rd
Chester CH2 ....118 F4
Hazel Grove SK7 ....36 F8
Macclesfield SK11 ....112 C5
Knutsford & Dist Hospl
WA16 ....56 F1
Knutsford High Sch (Lower
Sch) WA16 ....56 E1
Knutsford High Sch (Upper
Sch) WA16 ....56 F1
Knutsford Old Rd WA4 .17 A2
Knutsford Rd
Alsager ST7 ....193 F6
Antrobus CW9 ....53 D4
Chelford SK11 ....84 A2
Grappenhall WA4 ....17 C1
Great Budworth CW9 ....54 A2
Holmes Chapel CW4 ...130 B5
Mobberley WA16 ....57 E4
Row-of-trees SK9,WA16 .59 D3
Warrington WA4 ....16 D3
Knutsford Road Wlk 12
SK11 ....112 E7
Knutsford Sta WA16 ....57 A1
Knutsford View WA15 ..32 C8
Knutsford Way CH1 ...117 F2
Kohima Cres CH3 .....142 B5
Kronsbec Ave CH66 ....69 D6
KUS Ind Est SK11 ....139 A6
Kynaston Dr CH4 .....140 C7

L

Laburnam Cl ST7 .....210 E8
Laburnum Ave
2 Crewe CW2 ....189 F2
3 Nantwich CW5 ......204 F5
Warrington WA1 ....17 C7
Laburnum Cl CW12 ....156 A4
Laburnum Cres CW8 ....78 B3
Laburnum Ct WA13 ......19 B4
Laburnum Farm Cl CH64 .67 A5
Laburnum Gr
Crewe CW1 ....190 D6
Ellesmere Port CH66 ...95 A8
Runcorn WA7 ....49 C7
Saltney CH4 ....140 E6
Weaverham CW8 ....102 D8
Laburnum La
Altrincham WA15 ....31 E8
Warrington WA5 ....14 C5
Laburnum Pl ST5 .....210 D1
Laburnum Rd
Davenham CW9 ....103 F3
Golborne WA3 ....3 F7
Irlam M44 ....11 D5
Macclesfield SK11 ....112 E5
Northwich CW9 ....104 C6
Laburnum Way LL13 ...180 D1
Lacey Ave SK9 ....34 E3
Lacey Ct SK9 ....34 B1
Lacey Ct Handforth SK9 .34 B1
Widnes WA8 ....23 B7
Lacey Gn SK9 ....34 B1
Lacey Green Prim Sch
SK9 ....34 B1
Lacey St 3 WA8 ....23 A7
Lache Hall Cres CH4 ..140 F4
Lache La
Chester,Roughill CH4 ..140 E3
Chester,Westminster Park
CH4 ....141 B5
Roughhill CH4 ....140 D1
Lache Park Ave CH4 ..141 A6
Lache Prim Sch CH4 ..141 A5
Ladies Mile WA16 ......56 F2
Ladies Wlk CH64 ....66 E8
Lady Acre Cl WA13 .....18 D2
Lady Helen Wlk CW5 ..204 E6
Lady La Croft WA3 ......9 C8
Culcheth WA3 ....4 C1
Mobberley WA16 ....58 C7
Lady Richeld Cl WA7 ...50 D8
Ladybarn Ave WA3 ......3 A8
Ladybarn Cres SK7 .....35 F6
Ladybarn Manor SK7 ...35 F6
Ladybrook Gr 6 SK9 ...34 D2
Ladybrook Prim Sch SK7 .35 F7
Ladycroft Cl WA1 ......17 C7
Ladyfield St WA9 ....60 B7
Ladyfield Terr SK9 .....60 C7
Ladypit Rd SK23 ....39 E4
Ladypool L24 ....21 E1
Ladys Cl SK12 ....36 E4
Ladythorn Cres SK7 ....35 F6
Ladythorn Gr SK7 ......35 F6
Ladythorn Rd SK7 ......35 E6

Ladywood Rd WA5 ....7 D1
Lagos Gr CW7 ....126 E2
Laidon Ave CW2 ......206 A7
Laira Ct WA2 ....16 C7
Laira St WA2 ....16 C7
Lake House Cl CW8 .....77 D1
Lake La WA4 ....52 F5
Lake View Alsager ST7 .193 C2
Congleton CW12 ....156 B2
Whaley Bridge SK23 ....39 D4
Lakelands Cl SK10 ....112 F7
Lakemore Ctry Pk*
CW1 ....174 C1
Lakeside Bosley SK11 .158 D8
Chester CH4 ....141 B2
Lakeside Cl Chester CH2 .118 F7
Widnes WA8 ....22 A8
Lakeside Cvn Pk CW7 .149 F7
Lakeside Dr Poynton SK12 .36 E5
Warrington WA1 ....16 A3
Lakeside Rd WA13 .....18 D2
Lakeside View
Moulton CW7 ....126 F7
Nantwich CW5 ....204 E3
Lakewood CH4 ....141 B2
Laleston Cl WA8 ....22 E8
Lamb Cottage Cvn Pk
CW8 ....125 C7
Lamb La WA14 ....31 D2
Lamb St ST7 ....195 A2
Lambert Cres CW5 ....204 C6
Lambert Way CW8 .....103 A4
Lambert's La CW12 ...156 E1
Lambourn Ave WA8 .....12 C5
Lambourn Cl SK12 .....36 D4
Lambourn Dr CW1 .....173 B1
Lambourne Cl
Middlewich CW10 .....128 C1
St Helens WA9 ....1 A4
Lambs House Sch CW12 .156 F4
Lambs La Warrington WA1 .17 A7
Warrington,Padgate WA1 .17 A8
Lambsickle Cl WA7 .....49 A6
Lambsickle La WA7 .....49 A6
Lamerton Cl WA5 ......14 D4
Lamerton Way SK9 .....34 E2
Lampeter Cl WA5 ....7 E2
Lampits La CH3 ......120 E6
Lamport Cl WA8 ....13 E3
Lanark Gdns WA8 ......12 E3
Lanark Rd SK10 ....86 F2
Lancashire Rd M31 ....11 E2
Lancaster Ave
Golborne WA3 ....3 C8
Runcorn WA7 ....48 E8
Widnes WA8 ....12 A2
Lancaster Cl
Hazel Grove SK7 ....36 D8
Newton-le-W WA12 ......1 F4
Warrington WA2 ....8 F2
Winsford CW7 ....149 D6
Lancaster Ct 3 WA4 ...16 E1
Lancaster Dr CH3 ....119 B2
Lancaster Fields CW1 .191 A2
Lancaster Gdns CH65 ..70 D3
Lancaster Pk CH4 ....139 A3
Lancaster Rd
Handforth SK9 ....34 E1
Irlam M44 ....11 D5
Widnes WA8 ....13 B3
Lanceley Ct SY14 .....213 B3
Lancelyn Dr SK9 ....60 D8
Lancer Ct WA7 ....23 E3
Lancers Croft CH66 ....69 E1
Lancing Ave WA3 ....9 D3
Lancing Rd CH65 ......70 D4
Land Cut La WA3 ....9 D3
Land La SK9 ....60 C6
Lander Cl WA5 ....15 D7
Landor Cl WA3 ....3 E8
Landscape Dene WA6 ...73 D4
Landseer Ave
Neston CH64 ....66 F7
Warrington WA4 ....16 B2
Landsdown Cl SK10 ....111 E8
Landswood Pk CW8 ...103 B4
Lane Ends WA8 ....21 D5
Lane Head Ave WA3 .....3 F8
Lane The SY13,SY14 ..223 C3
Lanehead Rd SK23 .....65 E5
Laneside Rd SK22 .....39 E7
Langcliffe Cl WA3 ......4 E3
Langdale Ave WA13 ....18 F4
Langdale Cl High Lane SK6 .37 E8
Macclesfield SK11 ....111 F5
Warrington WA2 ....8 E2
Widnes WA8 ....22 C8
Winsford CW7 ....126 D2
Langdale Ct CW12 ....156 A1
Langdale Gr CH66 .....69 F2
Langdale Rd Bramhall SK7 .35 C5
Crewe CW2 ....189 D2
Partington M31 ....11 E3
Runcorn WA7 ....23 B1
Langdale Way WA6 .....49 C1
Langden Cl WA3 ....4 F3
Langdon Ho CH4 .....141 A7
Langfield WA3 ....9 C7
Langford St 31 SK11 ..112 C8
Langford Way WA4 .....7 D4
Langland Cl WA5 ....7 E2

Langley Ave WA12 ......2 C1
Langley Cl
Newcastle-u-Lyme ST5 .210 D2
Sandbach CW11 ....175 C8
Langley Ct CH65 ....70 E3
Langley Dr Chester CW2 .190 A2
Handforth SK9 ....34 E3
Langley Hall Cl SK11 .113 B4
Langley Hall Cotts SK11 .113 B4
Langley Rd Langley SK11 .113 B3
Northwich CW9 ....104 A6
Langport Dr CH3 .....119 C2
Langton Cl
Newton-le-W WA12 ......2 A4
Widnes WA8 ....12 B3
Langton Gn WA1 ....17 D7
Langwell Cl WA3 ....10 A5
Lanreath Cl SK10 ......86 D1
Lansbrook Ct WA7 .....23 C2
Lansdown Cl SK8 ......35 C7
Lansdown Rd CH4 ....139 B4
Lansdowne Culcheth WA3 .4 E2
Frodsham WA6 ....74 D6
Lansdowne Gr CH4 ...141 A7
Lansdowne Rd
Connah's Quay CH5 ....91 D1
Crewe CW1 ....190 F5
Great Barrow CH3 ....120 D3
Lansdowne St SK10 ....87 E1
Lapwing Cl Golborne WA3 .3 D8
Newton-le-W WA12 ......2 C3
Packmoor ST7 ....195 E1
Winsford CW7 ....149 C5
Lapwing Gr WA7 ....50 A6
Lapwing La Moore WA4 ..25 A8
Whisterfield SK11 ....109 C4
Whisterfield SK11 ....109 C6
Lapwing Rd ST7 ......195 D3
Lapwing Rise CH60 ....40 F6
Larch Ave Hough CW2 .206 F5
Macclesfield SK11 ....112 A5
Newton-le-W WA12 ......2 C2
Warrington WA5 ....14 E5
Widnes WA8 ....13 B2
Larch Cl Golborne WA3 ..3 F6
Poynton SK12 ....36 F3
Runcorn WA7 ....49 C7
Weaverham CW8 ....102 D7
Larch Rd Crewe CW2 ..189 E2
Haydock WA11 ....1 E1
Partington M31 ....11 E3
Runcorn WA7 ....49 C7
Larch Rise SK10 ....86 D6
Larch Way CH4 ....140 E6
Larchdale Cl CH66 .....94 F8
Larches The WA16 .....58 E2
Larchfields CH1 ......117 A8
Larchtree Cl CW8 ......78 B4
Larchway Bramhall SK7 ..35 C7
High Lane SK6 ....37 F7
Larchways WA4 ....26 D8
Larchwood Dr SK9 .....60 E8
Lark Ave ST7 ....195 D3
Lark Hall Cl SK10 ....113 A7
Lark Hall Cres SK10 .113 A8
Lark Hall Rd SK10 ...113 A7
Lark Hill Cotts SK22 ..39 A8
Larkfield ST7 ....195 B1
Larkfield Ave WA1 .....17 A7
Larkspur Cl Chester CH4 .140 F4
Nantwich CW5 ....204 E8
Runcorn WA7 ....49 F4
Larkstoke Cl WA4 .....26 C6
Larkway CH60 ....41 B8
Larkwood Way SK10 ...87 E5
Larne Ct WA8 ....12 E2
Larne Dr CH4 ....139 D4
Laskey La WA4 ....17 E8
Laskey Lane Farm WA4 .17 E4
Latchford CE Prim Sch
WA4 ....16 B4
Latchford Rd CH60 ....41 B6
Latchford St WA4 .....17 A3
Latham Ave Helsby WA6 .73 B1
Newton-le-W WA12 ......2 B4
Latham Ho WA12 ....2 B4
Latham Rd CW11 ......175 A5
Latham St CW7 ....126 C1
Lathom Ave WA2 ....16 B8
Lathom Rd M44 ....11 F8
Lathom Way SK10 ......87 F2
Latimer Dr CW2 ......190 A4
Launceston Cl
Runcorn WA7 ....50 C6
Winsford CW7 ....149 B7
Launceston Dr
Bramhall SK7 ....35 F7
Warrington WA5 ....14 E3
Laura St CW7 ....190 D1
Laurel Ave
Newton-le-W WA12 ......2 D3
Warrington WA5 ....14 E6
Laurel Bank
Widnes WA8 ....13 A3
Winsford CW7 ....149 D8
Laurel Cl Barnton CW8 ..78 A4
Middlewich CW10 .....128 D2
Sandbach CW11 ....175 C5
Laurel Dr Crewe CW2 .189 F2
Ellesmere Port CH65 ...70 B2
Kidsgrove ST7 ....195 C4
Laurel Gr Chester CH2 .119 A3
Golborne WA3 ....3 C8
Laurel Pk CW6 ....145 A6
Laurel Way SK8 ....35 C8

Laurel Wlk M31 ....11 E2
Laurels Farm Ct CH2 ...72 B3
Laurels The SK6 ....37 F8
Laurelwood Dr 4 CH66 .69 E1
Laureston Ave CW1 ...190 F4
Laurion Cl WA7 ....23 C1
Lavender Dr CW9 .....104 E7
Lavender Gdns WA9 .....6 A7
Lavender Wlk M31 .....11 E2
Lavenham Cl
Hazel Grove SK10 ......87 C2
Macclesfield SK10 .....87 C2
Lavister Cl CW9 ......103 F4
Lavister Wlk LL12 ....162 C1
Law St CW2 ....118 F3
Lawford Cl CW1 ......189 F8
Lawford Dr CH60 ......41 C8
Lawn Ave WA1 ....16 F8
Lawn Dr CH2 ....118 D7
Lawns Ave CH63 ....43 B6
Lawns The SK9 ....59 E4
Lawnside CW8 ....101 D5
Lawnswood Gr CH2 ....72 B3
Lawrence Ave
Middlewich CW10 .....128 C1
Moulton CW9 ....126 E8
Lawrence Ave E CW10 .128 C1
Lawrence Cl
Cranage CW4 ....130 A5
3 Sandbach CW11 ....174 D6
Lawrence Ho SK12 .....36 D2
Lawrence Pl SK12 .....36 D2
Lawrence St Crewe CW1 .190 C4
Sandycroft CH5 ....116 A3
Laws Gdns CH3 ....142 A8
Lawson Cl WA1 ....17 E7
Lawton Ave Bramhall SK7 .35 E8
Lawton Coppice ST7 ..194 E4
Lawton Hall ST7 .....194 C4
Lawton Heath Rd ST7 .193 F5
Lawton Rd ST7 ....193 E4
Lawton St
Congleton CW12 .....156 E2
Crewe CW2 ....190 C3
Kidsgrove ST7 ....195 C4
Lawton Way CW11 .....174 E7
Lawtongate Est ST7 ..194 A5
Laxey Ave WA1 ....17 D6
Laxton Cl CH66 ....94 F8
Laxton Way CW10 ....128 C2
Layland Ave WA3 ....4 E4
Layton Cl WA3 ....9 E3
Lea Ave Crewe CW1 ...190 F4
Goostrey CW4 ....107 C1
Lea Bank Cl SK11 ....112 A8
Lea Cl CW11 ....175 C5
Lea Cross Gr WA8 .....12 C2
Lea Dr Nantwich CW5 .204 C4
Wimboldsley CW10 ...151 A4
Lea Hall Pk CH1 ....95 A3
Lea Homes CW5 ....217 B7
Lea La CH3 ....164 C3
Lea St WA22 ....39 B8
Lea Way ST7 ....193 D3
Lea's Pas CW10 ....128 B1
Leacroft Rd WA3 ......10 A7
Leadbeaters Cl SK11 .112 F7
Leadbeaters Rd SK11 .112 F7
Leadgate La CH3 .....144 F2
Leadsmithy St CW10 .128 C1
Leadworks La CH1 ...237 C2
Leaf Gr CW7 ....126 B1
Leaf La CW7 ....127 A2
Leaf Lane Inf Sch CW7 .127 A2
Leafield Dr SK8 ....34 E6
Leafield Rd SK12 ......36 F6
Leafy Way CW8 ....102 D7
Leahurst Cl CW2 .....118 F4
Leamington Ave WA12 ..2 C1
Leamington Cl
Neston CH64 ....66 E6
Warrington WA5 ....15 A8
Leamington Rd
Congleton CW12 .....155 F3
Macclesfield SK10 .....86 F1
Lear Dr CW2 ....205 F8
Leas Cl 3 CH66 ....69 C5
Leaside WA2 ....23 D1
Leaside Rd CH1 ......117 E6
Leaside Way SK9 ......60 C6
Leather's La WA3 ......9 E3
Leathers La L26 ....21 A7
Leawood Cl CW8 ......103 A6
Ledbury Dr CW2 ......206 A6
Ledge Ley SK8 ....34 E8
Ledger Rd WA11 ....1 A5
Ledley St SK10 ....87 F7
Ledsham Cl WA3 ....10 A3
Ledsham Hall La CH66 ..68 E4
Ledsham La CH66 ......68 F3
Ledsham Park Dr CH66 .69 A6
Ledsham Rd CH66 .....69 B6
Ledsham Village CH66 .68 F2
Ledston Cl WA7 ....24 D1
Ledward St CW7 ......127 A1
Ledyard Cl WA5 ....15 D7
Lee Cl ST7 ....195 C6
Lee Ct Runcorn WA7 ...23 D2
Warrington WA2 ....8 C2
Lee Dr CW8 ....103 A4
Lee Green La CW5 ....150 A1
Lee Rd WA5 ....15 B6
Lee St CH1 ....237 C3
Leech Rd SY14 ....213 B3
Leek Old Rd SK11 .....112 E2
Leek Rd CW12 ....179 A8

Leen La CH1 . . . . 237 B2
Lees La
Ellesmere Port CH65 . . . . . 70 E4
Mottram St Andrew SK10 . . . 61 B7
Neston CH64 . . . . 67 A7
Lees Mill SK22 . . . . 39 C7
Lees Rd SK7 . . . . 35 D5
Leftwich Com Prim Sch
CW9 . . . . 104 A4
Leftwich Warehouse
CW9 . . . . 103 F7
Legh Cl SK12 . . . . 36 E4
Legh Ct Golborne WA3 . . . . . 3 A8
Knutsford WA16 . . . . 57 D4
Legh Gdns WA16 . . . . 57 B1
Legh Ho **2** WA16 . . . . 57 B1
Legh Rd Adlington SK10 . . . 62 C5
Haydock WA11 . . . . 36 A6
High Lane SK12 . . . . 38 A6
Knutsford WA16 . . . . 82 B8
Prestbury SK10 . . . . 87 A8
Legh St Golborne WA3 . . . . 3 A8
3 Lymm WA13 . . . . 18 E3
Newton-le-W WA12 . . . . 2 A3
Warrington WA1 . . . . 16 A5
Legh Vale Prim Sch WA11 . 1 B6
Leicester Ave ST7 . . . . . . 193 D5
Leicester St
Northwich CW9 . . . . 79 A1
Warrington WA5 . . . . 15 C7
Leigh Ave Knutsford WA16 . 57 C3
Widnes WA8 . . . . 13 A1
Leigh Green Cl **4** WA8 . . 22 C8
Leigh La CW8 . . . . 77 C5
Leigh Rd Congleton CW12 . 157 B5
Wilmslow SK9 . . . . 59 D5
Leigh St SK11 . . . . 112 E7
Leigh Way CW8 . . . . 77 C1
Leigh's Brow CW8 . . . . 77 C5
Leighstone Ct CH2 . . . . . . 237 A4
Leighton Chase CH64 . . . . 41 D1
Leighton Ct CH64 . . . . 66 D8
Leighton Dr WN7 . . . . 4 B8
Leighton Hospl CW1 . . . . 172 E1
Leighton Pk CH64 . . . . 66 D8
Leighton Prim Sch CW1 . 189 F8
Leighton Rd CH64 . . . . 41 D2
Leighton St CW1 . . . . 190 B5
Leighton View WA1 . . . . . 190 A8
Leightons The CH64 . . . . . 66 D8
Leinster Gdns WA7 . . . . 22 F3
Leinster St WA7 . . . . 22 F3
Leiria Way WA7 . . . . 23 B2
Lenham Wlk M22 . . . . 33 D8
Lenthall Ave CW12 . . . . . 178 E8
Leon Cl WA5 . . . . 14 D7
Leonard St Chester CH1 . 118 B3
Runcorn WA7 . . . . 48 D7
Warrington, Stockton Heath
WA4 . . . . 16 C1
Leslie Rd CW7 . . . . 149 A7
Lessingham Rd WA8 . . . . . 12 F3
Lester Cl ST7 . . . . 193 D4
Leven Ave CW7 . . . . 126 F2
Leven Wlk CH66 . . . . 40 C2
Levens Way **6** WA8 . . . . . 22 C8
Leveret Rd L24 . . . . 21 A3
Levisham Gdns WA5 . . . . . 15 E7
Lewin St CW10 . . . . 128 C1
Lewis Ave WA5 . . . . 7 D4
Lewis Cl
Ellesmere Port CH65 . . . . . 95 C8
Nantwich CW5 . . . . 205 A5
Lewis Cres WA3 . . . . 23 A7
Lewis Gr WA8 . . . . 12 D1
Lewis St CW1 . . . . 190 C3
Lexden St WA5 . . . . 15 C6
Lexington Wlk WA5 . . . . . . 15 C7
Leycester Cl WA16 . . . . . . 82 C8
Leycester Dr WA16 . . . . . 57 F7
Leycester Rd WA16 . . . . . 82 B8
Leyfield Cl CH4 . . . . 140 F5
Leygate View SK22 . . . . . 39 B8
Leyland Dr CH4 . . . . 140 C6
Leyland Gr
Haslington CW1 . . . . 191 C4
Haydock WA11 . . . . 1 B6
Leyland Wlk CW7 . . . . 149 C6
Leyton Cl WA7 . . . . 49 B6
Libris Ct **3** WA16 . . . . 57 A1
Libris Ho **1** WA16 . . . . . 57 A1
Libris Pl **3** WA16 . . . . . 57 A1
Libson Cl WA2 . . . . 9 A3
Lichfield Ave
Golborne WA3 . . . . 3 D4
Grappenhall Heys WA4 . . . 27 A7
Lichfield Cl WA16 . . . . 57 D2
Lichfield Ct CW7 . . . . 149 D7
Lichfield Dr CH66 . . . . 94 E8
Lichfield Rd Blacon CH1 . 117 F5
Talke ST7 . . . . 210 D7
Lichfield St CW10 . . . . 128 D2
Lidgetts La SK10 . . . . 88 C3
Liebig St WA8 . . . . 23 B8
Lift La CW9 . . . . 79 B2
Light Alders La SK12 . . . . 38 A6
Light Oaks Rd WA3 . . . . 5 C6
Lightburn St **5** WA7 . . . 22 F1
Lightfoot Cl CH60 . . . . 41 B7
Lightfoot La Eaton CW6 . 147 A4
Heswall CH60 . . . . 41 A7
Lightfoot St CH2 . . . . 118 F2
Lightley Cl CW11 . . . . 175 A4
Lightwood Green Ave
CW3 . . . . 229 A2
Lightwood Rd ST5 . . . . . . 210 D1

Lilac Ave Knutsford WA16 . 56 E1
Warrington WA5 . . . . 15 A5
Widnes WA8 . . . . 13 B2
Lilac Cl Kelsall CW6 . . . . . 122 E2
Newcastle-u-Lyme ST5 . . 210 D1
Lilac Cres WA7 . . . . 49 C8
Lilac Ct CW12 . . . . 156 E2
Lilac Dr CW8 . . . . 103 D6
Lilac Gr
Ellesmere Port CH66 . . . . . 95 A8
Warrington WA1 . . . . 16 E1
Lilac Wlk M31 . . . . 11 E3
Lilford Ave WA5 . . . . 15 F8
Lilford Dr WA5 . . . . 14 F6
Lilford Sq SK11 . . . . 112 D5
Lilford St WA5 . . . . 15 F7
Lilyfield CH60 . . . . 40 F6
Lily Ave WA12 . . . . 2 D2
Lily La CW10 . . . . 129 B6
Lilybrook Dr WA16 . . . . . 57 B1
Limbrick Rd ST7 . . . . . . 209 A1
Lime Ave Frodsham WA6 . . 74 C8
Northwich CW9 . . . . 103 F5
Weaverham CW8 . . . . 102 D8
3 Widnes WA8 . . . . 13 B2
Lime Cl Hollinfare WA3 . . . 11 A2
Middlewich CW10 . . . . 128 B1
Sandbach CW11 . . . . 175 A7
Tarporley CW6 . . . . 146 D2
Lime Ct CW9 . . . . 103 F5
Lime Gr Alsager ST7 . . . . 193 E2
Chester CH2 . . . . 119 A3
Elton CH2 . . . . 72 A3
Golborne WA3 . . . . 3 E6
Macclesfield SK10 . . . . . 112 E8
Runcorn WA7 . . . . 49 C8
Saltney CH4 . . . . 140 D6
Shavington CW2 . . . . . . 206 C4
Winsford CW7 . . . . 127 A1
Lime Kiln La ST7 . . . . 194 E2
Lime St Congleton CW12 . 156 D2
Crewe CW1 . . . . 190 C6
Ellesmere Port CH65 . . . . . 70 C7
Lime Tree Ave
Congleton CW12 . . . . 156 B3
Crewe CW1 . . . . 190 E6
Lime Tree Cl CH66 . . . . . 95 A8
Lime Tree Dr CH3 . . . . . . 180 F1
Lime Tree Gr CH60 . . . . . 41 C8
Lime Tree La WA16 . . . . . 29 D6
Lime Wlk
6 Handforth SK9 . . . . 34 D1
Partington M31 . . . . 11 D3
Limefield Ave WA13 . . . . . 18 F2
Limehurst Gr CH62 . . . . . 43 D6
Limekiln La WA5 . . . . 6 E3
Limekiln Row WA7 . . . . 50 A8
Limerick Cl WA8 . . . . 12 E3
Limes Cl CW1 . . . . 191 C4
Limes La WA4 . . . . 52 D6
Limes The Culcheth WA3 . . 4 D4
Golborne WA3 . . . . 3 D6
Middlewich CW10 . . . . 128 B1
Limetree Ave
Warrington, Stockton Heath
WA4 . . . . 17 A8
Limewood Cres CW8 . . . . . 78 B4
Limewood Gr CW8 . . . . 78 B4
Linacre La WA8 . . . . 12 E5
Lincoln Ave
Heald Green SK8 . . . . 34 B7
Irlam M44 . . . . 11 C4
Lincoln Cl Golborne WN7 . . 4 C8
Macclesfield SK10 . . . . 87 B2
Rainow SK10 . . . . 88 E5
Runcorn WA7 . . . . 49 C6
Warrington WA1 . . . . 17 E6
Lincoln Ct WA6 . . . . 73 B3
Lincoln Dr CH2 . . . . 119 A5
Lincoln Pl SK10 . . . . 86 F2
Lincoln Rd Blacon CH1 . 117 F5
Ellesmere Port CH66 . . . . . 69 E7
Handforth SK9 . . . . 34 E1
Kidsgrove ST7 . . . . 194 F2
Lincoln Sq WA8 . . . . 12 E5
Lincoln St WA5 . . . . 190 B5
Lincoln Wlk SK10 . . . . 86 F2
Lincombe Hey SK10 . . . . . 87 C8
Lincombe Rd M22 . . . . 33 D8
Lindale Cl CW12 . . . . 157 A5
Linden Cl
Congleton CW12 . . . . 179 A8
Ellesmere Port CH66 . . . . . 94 F8
Lymm WA13 . . . . 19 A4
Warrington WA1 . . . . 17 D7
Linden Ct
Macclesfield SK10 . . . . 87 B2
Sandbach CW11 . . . . 174 F3
Widnes WA8 . . . . 12 E5
Linden Dr Biddulph ST8 . 179 C1
Crewe CW1 . . . . 190 B8
Helsby WA6 . . . . 73 B1
Mickle Trafford CH2 . . . . . 96 F1
Linden Gr Biddulph ST8 . 179 C1
Bramhall SK7 . . . . 35 E8
Chester CH2 . . . . 119 A4
Saltney CH4 . . . . 140 D6
Linden Way High Lane SK6 . 38 A7
Widnes WA8 . . . . 12 F4
Lindens The CW10 . . . . 128 B1
Lindfield Cl WA8 . . . . 25 A5
Lindfield Est N SK9 . . . . . 60 C8
Lindfield Est S SK9 . . . . . 59 F6
Lindfields CH4 . . . . 140 F6
Lindi Ave WA4 . . . . 17 C2

Lindisfarne Ave
Ellesmere Port CH65 . . . . . 70 C2
Golborne WA3 . . . . 4 C8
Lindisfarne Cl CW10 . . . . 128 B1
Lindisfarne Ct WA8 . . . . . 12 F6
Lindisfarne Dr SK12 . . . . . 36 D4
Lindley Ave WA4 . . . . 16 F4
Lindop Cl WA16 . . . . 57 C2
Lindow Com Prim Sch
SK9 . . . . 59 D3
Lindow Court Pk WA16 . 59 B5
Lindow Ct SK9 . . . . 59 E8
Lindow Fold Dr SK9 . . . . . 59 D5
Lindow La SK9 . . . . 59 E6
Lindow Par SK9 . . . . 59 F6
Lindrick Cl SK10 . . . . 87 C4
Lindrum Ave SK11 . . . . . . 112 D2
Lindsay Way ST7 . . . . 193 A4
Lindsay Wlk CW8 . . . . 102 A4
Lindsworth Cl WA5 . . . . . 15 C6
Linear View WA12 . . . . 2 C1
Linen Hall Pl CH1 . . . . . . 237 A2
Lines Rd M44 . . . . 11 F8
Lingdale Wlk SK11 . . . . . 112 D5
Lingfield Cl SK10 . . . . 87 C4
Lingfield Dr CW1 . . . . . . 190 F2
Lingfield Rd WA7 . . . . 48 E8
Lingfield Rd WA7 . . . . 50 A1
Lingley Green Ave WA5 . . 14 D8
Lingley Mere Bsns Pk
WA5 . . . . 14 D8
Lingley Rd WA5 . . . . 14 C8
Linglongs Ave SK23 . . . . . 65 C5
Linglongs Rd SK23 . . . . . 65 C5
Lingmell Gdns CW4 . . . . 129 F3
Lingwell Ave WA8 . . . . 22 D7
Lingwood Rd WA5 . . . . 14 F6
Link The SK9 . . . . 34 D3
Link Wlk M31 . . . . 11 D2
Links Ave CH66 . . . . 69 C7
Links Cl CH63 . . . . 43 B6
Links Rd SK9 . . . . 59 E4
Links Way CH66 . . . . 69 C7
Linkside Ave WA2 . . . . 8 B6
Linkside Way CH66 . . . . . 94 F8
Linksway Chester CH2 . . 118 C2
Congleton CW12 . . . . 178 E8
Linksway Cl CW12 . . . . . 178 F8
Linley Gr ST7 . . . . 193 F3
Linley La ST7 . . . . 194 A2
Linley Rd Alsager ST7 . . 193 F2
Cheadle Hulme SK8 . . . . 35 B8
Talke ST7 . . . . 210 C8
Linley Trad Est ST7 . . . 194 C1
Linnards La CW9,WA16 . . 80 B5
Linnet Cl Crewe CW1 . . . 190 A7
Newton-le-W WA12 . . . . 2 C3
Winsford CW7 . . . . 150 B8
Linnet Gr
Macclesfield SK10 . . . . 87 A1
Warrington WA3 . . . . 9 E4
Linnets Pk WA7 . . . . 23 C3
Linnets Way CH60 . . . . 40 E8
Linnett Gr ST7 . . . . 195 E1
Linton Ct CW7 . . . . 149 A8
Linum Gdns WA9 . . . . 6 B7
Linwood CW7 . . . . 150 B8
Linwood Cl WA7 . . . . 50 C5
Lion Salt Works Mus*
CW9 . . . . 79 C3
Liskeard Cl WA7 . . . . 50 D6
Liskeard Dr SK7 . . . . 35 F7
Lismore Wlk M22 . . . . 33 E8
Lister Cl CW10 . . . . 151 D6
Lister Rd WA7 . . . . 23 C3
Little Abbey Gateway
CH1 . . . . 237 A3
Little Aston Cl SK10 . . . . 87 C4
Little Bollington CE Prim Sch
WA14 . . . . 20 B2
Little Budworth Ctry Pk*
CW6 . . . . 147 C8
Little Delph WA11 . . . . 1 C7
Little Gn CH66 . . . . 69 D3
Little Heath Cl CW3 . . . 230 A5
Little Heath La WA14 . . . 20 D5
Little Heath Rd
Chester CH3 . . . . 119 E1
Christleton CH3 . . . . 142 E8
Little La CH64 . . . . 41 C1
Little Leigh Prim Sch
CW8 . . . . 77 D5
Little Meadow Cl SK10 . . 86 E6
Little Moreton Hall*
CW12 . . . . 177 E2
Little Moss Cl ST7 . . . . . 194 E5
Little Moss La ST7 . . . . . 194 E5
Little Roodee CH5 . . . . . . 139 B7
Little St Congleton CW12 . 156 D2
Little Stanney La CH2 . . . 95 F8
Little Sutton CE Prim Sch
CH66 . . . . 69 C6
Little Sutton Sta CH66 . . 69 C6
Little Wissage CH66 . . . . . 69 F2
Littlebourne WA7 . . . . 50 E7
Littlecote Gdns WA4 . . . . 26 E7
Littledale Rd WA5 . . . . 14 F7
Littler Ct CW7 . . . . 125 F1
Littler La CW7 . . . . 125 F1
Littler Rd WA11 . . . . 1 A5

Littlestone Cl WA8 . . . . 13 A4
Littleton Cl
1 Northwich CW9 . . . . . 103 F4
Warrington WA5 . . . . 15 D4
Littleton La CH3 . . . . 119 E2
Littondale Cl CW12 . . . . 157 A5
Liverpool Pl WA8 . . . . 12 C1
Liverpool Rd
Backford CH1,CH2 . . . . 95 B4
Chester CH2 . . . . 118 C6
Haydock WA11 . . . . 1 B8
Irlam,Cadishead M44 . . . . . 11 D4
Kidsgrove ST7 . . . . 195 A1
Neston CH64 . . . . 41 F1
Newcastle-u-Lyme ST5 . . 210 D2
Warrington WA5,WA1 . . . . 15 F5
Warrington,Great Sankey
WA5 . . . . 14 E6
Warrington,Penketh WA5 . . 15 B4
Widnes WA8 . . . . 12 C1
Liverpool Rd E ST7 . . . . 194 E2
Liverpool Rd W ST7 . . . 194 B4
Liverpool Row WA12 . . . . . 7 D8
Liverpool St CW9 . . . . . . 104 C8
Livingstone Cl
Macclesfield SK10 . . . . . . 111 F8
Warrington WA5 . . . . 15 D7
Livingstone Rd CH65 . . . . 70 C7
Livingstone Way CW10 . 151 D6
Liz Kaye Ho SK11 . . . . . . 112 E7
Llandaff Cl CH66 . . . . 69 E1
Llandovery Cl CW7 . . . . . 149 B7
Lloyd Cl CH3 . . . . 180 E2
Lloyd Cres WA12 . . . . 1 F3
Lloyd Dr CW2 . . . . 206 B8
Lloyd Pl CH1 . . . . 117 E4
Llyndir La LL12 . . . . 162 B1
Llys Cadnant/Cadnant Ct
CH4 . . . . 139 D5
Llys Caer CH4 . . . . 139 A3
Llys Catrin/Catherine Ct
CH5 . . . . 139 B6
Llys Derwen CW4 . . . . 161 A8
Llys Maes Y Ffynnon /
Springfield Ct CH4 . . . . 161 A8
Llys Rhuddlan/Rhuddlan Ct
CH4 . . . . 140 F6
Llys Sant Iago/St James Ct
CH5 . . . . 91 D1
Loachbrook Ave CW12 . . 156 A2
Lobelia Gr WA7 . . . . 49 F4
Lobelia Wlk **6** M31 . . . . 11 E2
Loch St **5** Runcorn WA7 . 23 A2
Lochinvar Ave CH66 . . . . . 68 F6
Lochleven Rd CW2 . . . . . 206 A1
Lochmaben Cl CW4 . . . . . 130 B2
Lock La M31 . . . . 11 E3
Lock Rd Bebington CH62 . . 44 A8
Warrington WA1 . . . . 16 F6
Locker Ave WA2 . . . . 8 B2
Lockerbie Cl
Holmes Chapel CW4 . . . . 130 C2
Warrington WA2 . . . . 8 E3
Lockett Rd WA8 . . . . 13 B3
Lockett St WA4 . . . . 16 F3
Lockgate E WA7 . . . . 24 C2
Lockgate W WA7 . . . . 24 C2
Locking Stumps Com Prim
Sch WA3 . . . . 9 D4
Locking Stumps La WA3 . . 9 B4
Lockitt St CW2 . . . . 190 D3
Locks The WA4 . . . . 17 B3
Lockton La WA5 . . . . 15 E7
Lodge Brow SK10 . . . . 63 A1
Lodge Cl WA13 . . . . 19 B8
Lodge Dr Culcheth WA3 . . 4 F3
Lodge Gdns CH2 . . . . 118 D6
Lodge Hollow WA6 . . . . 73 B4
Lodge La Antrobus CW9 . . 54 A6
Dutton WA4 . . . . 51 E7
Hartford CW8 . . . . 103 B4
Hatherton CW5 . . . . 220 A4
Haydock WA11,WA12,WN4 . . 2 B8
Lostock Gralam CW9 . . . . . 80 A2
Middlewich CW10 . . . . 128 E2
Runcorn WA7 . . . . 49 F8
Warrington WA5 . . . . 14 B8
Widnes WA8 . . . . 12 B4
Lodge Rd Alsager ST7 . . 193 C4
Knutsford WA16 . . . . 57 C3
Sandbach CW11 . . . . 174 E5
Talke ST7 . . . . 210 D6
Widnes WA8 . . . . 12 B4
Lodgefields Com Prim Sch
CW2 . . . . 189 E4
Lodgefields Dr CW2 . . . . 189 E4
Lodmore La SK13 . . . . . . 233 C6
Lofthouse Gate WA8 . . . . 12 F4
Lomas Sq SK11 . . . . 112 D5
Lomax Rd CW5 . . . . 205 D6
Lombard Ave CH4 . . . . . . 140 D6
Lombardy Cl WA7 . . . . 50 A8
Lon Y Cryddion / Cobblers La
LL12 . . . . 161 B1
Lon yr Orsaf / Station App
CH1 . . . . 116 F7
Lon yr Ywen / Yew Tree Ave
CH1 . . . . 116 F7
Londean Ct SK10 . . . . 62 C5
Alderley Edge SK9 . . . . 60 B2
Allostock WA16 . . . . 106 F3
Bridgemere CW5,CW3 . . . 232 A5
Davenham CW9 . . . . 104 A1

London Rd continued
Frodsham WA6 . . . . 74 B8
Hatherton CW5 . . . . 220 D4
Holmes Chapel CW4 . . . . 130 C2
Macclesfield SK11 . . . . . . 112 D3
Midway SK10,SK12 . . . . . . 36 C1
Nantwich CW5 . . . . 204 F5
Northwich CW9 . . . . 103 F7
Northwich CW9 . . . . 104 A5
Sandbach CW11 . . . . 174 D8
Stapeley CW5 . . . . 205 B3
Warrington WA4 . . . . 26 D5
Woore CW3 . . . . 232 C1
London Rd N SK12 . . . . 36 E5
London Rd S SK12 . . . . 36 E4
London Road Terr SK11 . 112 D5
London Row WA12 . . . . 7 D8
Long Acre St SK11 . . . . . 112 C7
Long Acre
Cuddington CW8 . . . . 101 D4
Weaverham CW8 . . . . 77 C1
Long Acres Rd CH64 . . . . . 41 E2
Long Barn La
Warrington WA1 . . . . 9 B2
Warrington,Woolston WA1 . 17 D8
Long Croft La SK8 . . . . 34 E8
Long Gn CH3 . . . . 97 E1
Long Hill SK23 . . . . 65 F2
Long La Alpraham CW6 . 169 E4
Bickerton SY14 . . . . 199 F4
Bollington SK10 . . . . 63 B2
Burland CW5 . . . . 203 A8
Chester CH2 . . . . 118 F7
Hargrave CH3 . . . . 143 D2
Haughton CW6 . . . . 186 D4
Huxley CH3 . . . . 166 C8
Kidsgrove ST7 . . . . 195 E4
Middlewich CW10 . . . . 151 C7
Saughall CH1 . . . . 94 B2
Swan Green WA16 . . . . . . 107 D7
Swettenham CW12 . . . . . 131 F5
Tilston SY14 . . . . 198 B3
Warrington WA2 . . . . 8 B1
Long Lane Com Prim Sch
WA2 . . . . 8 B1
Long Looms CW3 . . . . 120 D6
Long Marl Dr SK9 . . . . 34 F4
Long Mdw CH60 . . . . 40 F6
Long Row ST7 . . . . 195 A1
Long Shoot CW4 . . . . 130 D8
Long Shoot Rd SK11 . . . 108 E1
Long Spinney WA7 . . . . 50 C8
Long Valley Rd ST8 . . . . 179 C1
Long Wlk M31 . . . . 11 D3
Longacre St SK10 . . . . 112 C8
Longacres Rd WA15 . . . . . 32 D7
Longbarn Bvd WA2 . . . . 9 C2
Longbarn Com Prim Sch
WA2 . . . . 9 B1
Longbenton Way WA7 . . . 24 B4
Longburgh Cl CH2 . . . . 118 C4
Longbutt La WA13 . . . . 19 A2
Longclough La SK11 . . . . 111 E2
Longcliffe La SK11 . . . . . 111 E2
Longdale Dr CH1 . . . . 117 C5
Longden Ct SK7 . . . . 35 E5
Longden La SK11 . . . . 113 A6
Longden St SK10 . . . . 112 E8
Longdin Wlk WA12 . . . . 1 C3
Longdown Rd CW12 . . . . 155 F4
Longfield Ave
Chester CH2 . . . . 118 E7
Heald Green SK8 . . . . 34 C7
Longfield Gdns M44 . . . . . 11 D4
Longfield Rd WA3 . . . . 8 C1
Longford Dr WA8 . . . . 12 E2
Longford St
8 Crewe CW2 . . . . 190 D2
Warrington WA2 . . . . 16 B7
Longhill La CW3 . . . . 230 E5
Longhorn Cl CW10 . . . . . 128 D2
Longlands Dr SK22 . . . . . 39 B8
Longlands Rd SK22 . . . . . 39 B8
Longley Ave CW6 . . . . 122 D6
Longleat Gdns SK9 . . . . . 60 C6
Longmeadow
Cheadle Hulme SK8 . . . . . 35 C7
Heswall CH60 . . . . 41 A8
Longmoss Cl CW10 . . . . . 151 B8
Longmynd Rise CW7 . . . 149 B8
Longnor Rd
Hazel Grove SK7 . . . . 36 E7
Longridge WA16 . . . . 57 D3
Longsdon Cl ST5 . . . . 210 C1
Longshaw St
Warrington,Bewsey WA5 . . 15 F8
Warrington,Dallam WA5 . . . 7 F1
Longsides Rd WA15 . . . . . 32 C7
Longsight La SK8 . . . . 34 F6
Longster Cl WA6 . . . . 73 B2
Longstone La CW6 . . . . . 124 E3
Longton Ave WA3 . . . . 3 C7
Longwood Cl CW10 . . . . 151 C7
Longwood Rd WA4 . . . . . 26 E5
Lonsdale Cl
Warrington WA5 . . . . 14 F8
3 Widnes WA8 . . . . 22 C8

Lonsdale Ct CH4 ....140 F4
Looe Cl WA8 ....12 E2
Looms The CH64 ....41 B2
Loont The CW7 ....149 C7
Lord Nelson St WA1 ...16 C5
Lord St Bollington SK10 ..88 B8
  Chester CH3 ....118 F2
  Crewe CW2 ....190 D3
  Croft WA3 ....9 A8
  Macclesfield SK11 ....112 D6
  Macclesfield SK11 ....112 D7
  Newton-le-W WA12 ....2 A3
  Runcorn WA7 ....22 F3
  Warrington WA4 ......16 B4
Lord's St M44 ....11 C5
Lords La WA3 ....9 C4
Lords Mill Rd CW2 ....206 B4
Lordship La WA6 ....73 B7
Lordshire Pl ST7 .....195 F2
Lorne St CH1 ....237 A3
Lorraine St ST7 ......195 F1
Lostock Ave Poynton SK12 ..36 B4
  Warrington WA5 ......15 F8
Lostock Cl **2** CW9 ...103 E5
Lostock Ct SK9 ....34 D4
Lostock Gn CW9 ....80 A1
Lostock Gralam CE Prim Sch
  CW9 ....80 A2
Lostock Gralam Sta CW9 ..80 A2
Lostock Hall Prim Sch
  SK12 ....36 B3
Lostock Hall Rd SK12 ..36 B3
Lostock Hollow CW9 ....80 A2
Lostock Rd SK12 ....36 D2
Lostock Way SK9 ....34 D4
Lotus Gdns WA9 ....6 A7
Louise St CH1 ....237 A3
Loushers La WA4 ......16 D2
Lovat Dr WA16 ....82 B7
Lovatt Ct WA13 ....19 B4
Love La
  Hassall Green CW11 ...176 C3
  Nantwich CW5 ....204 E5
Love Lane (Overton Heath
  Lane) SY14 ....213 A4
Love St CH1 ....237 B2
Lovel Terr WA8 ....22 B5
Lovell Ct CW4 ....130 C3
Lovely La WA5 ....15 E6
Low Hill WA6 ....97 D5
Low Leighton Rd SK22 ..39 D8
Low Mdw SK23 ....65 D8
Low St ST7 ....193 E8
Lowcross La SY14 .....198 D3
Lowe Ave
  Congleton CW12 ......156 E2
  Warrington WA4 ......16 F4
Lowe Cres CW9 ....53 C4
Lowe Dr WA16 ....57 B2
Lowe St Golborne WA3 ...3 A8
  Macclesfield SK11 ....112 D7
Lower Appleton Rd WA8 ..13 B1
Lower Ash Rd ST7 .....22 A2
Lower Bank St **10** SK11 ..112 E7
Lower Beech Cotts SK10 ..87 D2
Lower Bridge St CH1 ..237 B1
Lower Brook St CH5 ...91 D1
Lower Church St WA8 ..25 A3
Lower Cl L26 ....21 A8
Lower Darwin St CW9 ..103 E6
Lower Exchange St
  SK11 ....112 D8
Lower Farm Mews CW6 ..147 B3
Lower Greenshall La
  SK12 ....38 F6
Lower Hague ST7 ......38 E8
Lower Haigh St **8** CW7 ..149 C8
Lower Hall La CH3 ....182 D2
Lower Hall Mews CH3 ..182 C2
Lower Hall Rd SY13 ...215 D4
Lower Heath CW12 .....156 E4
Lower Heath Ave CW12 ..156 E4
Lower Heath Terr CW12 ..156 E4
Lower High St ST7 ....195 D7
Lower House La WA8 ....22 F8
Lower La Aldford CH3 ..164 A2
  Eaton CW6 ....147 A3
Lower Macclesfield Rd
  SK23 ....65 E6
Lower Meadow Dr
  CW12 ....156 C3
Lower Meadow Rd SK9 ..34 E4
Lower Mersey St CH65 ..70 C7
Lower Park Cres SK12 ..36 C6
Lower Park Prim Sch
  SK12 ....36 C4
Lower Park Rd
  Chester CH4 ....237 C2
  Poynton SK12 ....36 B5
Lower Park St CW12 ...156 E3
Lower Peover CE Prim Sch
  WA16 ....81 C1
Lower Rake La WA6 ....73 B4
Lower Rd L26 ....21 C7
Lower Robin Hood La
  WA6 ....73 B3
Lower Rock St SK22 ...39 C7
Lower Sandy La CH3 ...199 C7
Lower Wash La WA4 ....16 E3
Lowerfield Rd
  Chester CH4 ....141 A5
  Macclesfield SK10 ....87 E1
Lowerhouse SK10 ......97 E8
Lowerlea WA3 ....38 C6

Lowes La SK11 ....111 F2
Loweswater Cl WA2 ....8 B3
Loweswater Cres WA11 ..1 A6
Lowfield Gdns WA3 ....5 C7
Lowfields Ave CH62 ...43 E3
Lowfields Cl CH62 ....43 E3
Lowland Way WA16 .....82 A8
Lowlands Rd **6** WA7 ..22 F2
Lownorth Rd M22 ......33 E8
Lowood SK9 ....60 B2
Lowry Cl WA5 ....15 D6
Lowther Ave WA3 ......4 F4
Lowther St SK10 ......88 C8
Lowton Bsns Pk WA3 ...4 A7
Lowton Com Sports Coll
  WA3 ....4 B8
Lowton Gdns WA3 .....3 B5
Lowton Jun & Inf Sch
  WA3 ....4 A7
Lowton Rd WA3 ....3 C8
Lowton St Mary's CE Prim
  Sch WA3 ....4 A8
Lowton West Prim Sch
  WA3 ....3 D8
Loxdale Dr CH65 ......69 F4
Loxley Cl
  Macclesfield SK11 ....112 B7
  Warrington WA5 ......15 A8
Loyola Hey L35 ....12 E8
Lucerne Cl CH3 ....142 B6
Ludford Cl ST5 ....210 D2
Ludford St CW1 ....190 C5
Ludlow Ave CW1 ....190 F3
Ludlow Cl
  Macclesfield SK10 ....87 E2
  Warrington,Paddington
  WA1 ....17 B8
  Winsford CW7 ....149 B7
Ludlow Cres WA7 .....49 B8
Ludlow Dr CH65 ......70 E3
Ludlow Rd CH1 ....118 A5
Ludwell Cl CH4 ......141 B6
Lugsdale Rd WA8 .....23 B7
Lulworth Cl CW7 .....149 B7
Lumb Brook Mews **5**
  WA4 ....16 E1
Lumb Brook Rd
  Appleton Thorn WA4 ...27 A5
  Warrington WA4 ......26 F8
Lumb Cl SK7 ....35 E6
Lumb Ho SK7 ....35 E6
Lumb La SK7 ....35 E6
Lumber La WA5 ....6 F8
Lumley Pl CH1 ....237 B2
Lumley Rd Chester CH2 ..118 C4
  Macclesfield SK11 ....111 F7
Lumley Wlk L24 ......21 E1
Lumpy St CW12 ....156 C3
Lundy Dr CH65 ....95 C8
Lune Cl **1** CW1 .....157 A1
Lune Way WA8 ....12 C1
Lunehurst **12** WA3 ...3 E8
Lunt Ave CW2 ....190 C2
Lunt's Heath Rd WA8 ..13 B5
Lunts Heath Prim Sch
  WA8 ....13 B5
Lunts Moss ST7 ......194 C6
Luntswood Gr WA12 ...2 A4
Lupin Dr Haydock WA11 ..1 F6
  Huntington CH3 ......142 B6
Lupus Way CH66 ......69 F3
Luscombe Cl L26 .....21 A8
Luther Gr WA9 ....1 A2
Luton Rd CH65 ....70 A5
Luton St WA9 ....23 A7
Lutyens Cl SK10 .....111 F8
Lyceum Cl CW1 ....190 A8
Lyceum Way CW1 ......190 A8
Lychgate WA4 ....25 F7
Lycroft Cl WA7 ......49 B6
Lydbury Cl WA5 ......7 D2
Lydden Rd CH65 ......70 B7
Lydgate Cl CW2 ......205 F8
Lydiat La SK9 ....60 A1
Lydiate La Runcorn WA7 ..48 D7
  Willaston CH64 ....42 E1
Lydiate The CH60 ....40 F7
Lydney Ave SK8 ......34 C7
Lydyett Cl WA5 ......7 C2
Lydyett La CW8 ......78 B3
LyMCote Dr CW8 ......103 A4
Lyme Ave Handforth SK9 ..34 B1
  Macclesfield SK11 ....112 D8
Lyme Com Prim Sch WA12 ..1 F4
Lyme Gr WA13 ....18 C2
Lyme Green Bsns Pk
  SK11 ....112 C1
Lyme Green Settlement
  SK11 ....112 D2
Lyme Lea Cl SK8 .....35 B8
Lyme Park Ctry Pk*
  SK12 ....38 B2
Lyme Pk* SK12 ....38 B2
Lyme Rd High Lane SK12 ..38 A6
  Poynton SK12 ....37 C3
Lyme St Haydock WA11 ..1 F6
  Newton-le-W WA12 ....1 F4
Lyme View SK11 ......112 D2
Lymewood Dr Disley SK12 ..38 C6
  Wilmslow SK9 ....60 E8
Lymm Brook **1** WA13 ..18 E3
Lymm Hall WA13 ......18 E3
Lymm High Sch WA13 ..19 B3
Lymm Rd
  Little Bollington WA14 ..20 B1
  Warrington WA4 ......17 F4
Lymmhay La WA13 ....18 E4
Lymmington Ave WA13 ..18 C3

Lynalls Cl CW12 .....155 F3
Lynbrook Rd CW1 .....190 F4
Lyncastle Rd WA4 ....27 D4
Lyncastle Way WA4 ...27 D4
Lyncombe Cl SK8 .....35 B6
Lyncroft Cl CW1 .....190 F3
Lyndale Ave
  Bebington CH62 ......43 E4
  Warrington WA2 ......16 D8
  Warrington, Fearnhead WA2 ..8 F2
Lyndale Ct CW7 ......127 A3
Lyndale Sch The CH62 ..43 F5
Lyndhurst Cl SK9 ....59 D5
Lyndon Gr WA7 ......49 B8
Lyneal Ave CH66 .....69 C3
Lyngard Cl SK9 ......34 E1
Lynham Ave WA5 .....15 B5
Lynn Ave ST7 ....210 C8
Lynn Cl WA7 ....49 C7
Lynn Gr SK11 ....112 C6
Lynndene CH66 ....69 D7
Lynside Wlk M22 ....33 E8
Lynthorpe Ave M44 ..11 D6
Lynton Ave M44 .....11 E6
Lynton Cl Chester CH4 ..140 F6
  Heswall CH60 ....41 B6
  Knutsford WA16 .....57 C1
  Warrington WA5 ......14 E4
Lynton Cres WA8 ....12 E2
Lynton Dr SK6 ....37 E8
Lynton Gdns WA4 ....26 D4
Lynton Gr CW1 ......191 D5
Lynton Mews SK9 ....60 A2
Lynton Park Rd SK8 ..34 F8
Lynton Pl Alsager ST7 ..193 D4
  Broughton CH4 ......139 B4
Lynton Way CW2 .....206 A8
Lynwood Altrincham WA15 ..32 A8
  Wilmslow SK9 ....60 A6
Lynwood Ave
  Golborne WA3 ....3 E6
  Warrington WA4 ......26 C7
Lynwood Rd CH1 .....117 F5
Lyon Ct WA4 ....16 F3
Lyon St Chester CH1 ..237 B3
  Crewe CW1 ....190 D4
  Macclesfield SK11 ....112 C7
  Warrington WA4 ......16 E6
Lyon's La WA4 ....26 E6
Lyons Rd WA5 ....15 A4
Lyster Cl WA3 ....9 F3
Lytham Cl WA5 ......15 B3
Lytham Dr Bramhall SK7 ..36 A7
  Winsford CW7 ....126 C2
Lytham Rd WA3 ......13 C2
Lytherton Ave M44 ..11 D4
Lythgoes La WA2 ....16 B6

M

Mabledon Cl SK8 .....34 D8
Mablins La CW1 ......190 B8
Mablins Lane Com Prim Sch
  CW1 ....190 B8
Macarthur Rd WA5 ...15 B6
Macbeth Ho ST7 .....210 C8
Macclesfield Coll SK11 ..112 B6
Macclesfield District General
  Hospl SK10 ....112 A7
Macclesfield Forest Walks*
  SK11 ....114 A1
Macclesfield Heritage Ctr*
  SK11 ....112 D7
Macclesfield Prep Sch
  SK11 ....112 B8
Macclesfield Rd
  Alderley Edge SK9 ....85 D7
  Congleton CW12 ......156 F6
  Eaton CW12 ....134 B2
  Hazel Grove SK7 .....36 F8
  Holmes Chapel CW4 ..130 E4
  Kettleshulme SK23,SK10 ..64 D3
  Prestbury SK10 ......86 F4
  Rainow SK10 ....89 B7
  Whaley Bridge SK23 ..65 D6
  Wilmslow SK9 ....60 D6
  Macclesfield Sta SK11 ..112 D8
Macclesfield Rd W SK10 ..88 A5
Macdonald Rd M44 ...11 E8
Macdonald Rd M44 ...11 E8
Macon Ct CW1 ....190 E3
Macon Ind Pk CW1 ...190 E3
Macon Way CW1 ......190 E3
Maddock St ST7 .....209 D1
Maddocks Hill WA6 ..100 F5
Madeley Cl
  Altrincham WA14 ....31 E8
  Broughton CH4 ......139 C4
Madeley St CW2 .....190 C1
Madeline McKenna Ct
  WA8 ....12 C3
Madron Ave SK10 ....86 D1
Maelor Cl CH63 .....43 C6
Magda Rd SK10 ......88 A8
Mag La WA13,WA16 ..28 F6
Magdala Pl CW9 .....104 C8
Magecroft CW1 ......173 B1
Magenta Ave M44 ...11 E6
Maggoty La SK11 ....111 D1
Magnolia Cl
  Ellesmere Port CH66 ..69 F1
  Partington M31 .....11 E2
Magnolia Dr WA7 ....49 F4
Magnolia Rise SK10 ..86 E6
Magpie Cres **9** ST7 ..195 B2

Maiden Est CW5 .....228 C8
Maiden Gdns CH65 ...70 D3
Maidenhills CW10 ...128 D1
Maidstone Cl WA8 ...87 B2
Maidwell Cl CW7 ....127 A4
Main Cl WA11 ....1 A6
Main La WA3 ....3 F3
Main Rd Betley CW2,CW3 ..221 F8
  Broughton CH4 ......139 B4
  Goostrey CW4 ....107 E1
  Higher Kinnerton CH4 ..161 A8
  Langley SK11 ....113 C4
  Moulton CW9 ....126 F8
  Norton in Hales TF9 ..236 C1
  Shavington CW2 .....206 B4
  Weston CW2 ....207 C6
  Worleston CW5 ......188 F5
  Wybunbury CW5 ......220 B8
Main St Frodsham WA6 ..74 B8
  Great Barrow CH3 ....120 C5
  Runcorn WA7 ....49 F4
Maintree Cres L24 ...21 A4
Mainwaring Cl CW5 ..205 A4
Mainwaring Dr
  Saltney CH4 ....140 C7
  Wilmslow SK9 ....60 D8
Mainwaring Rd
  Bebington CH62 ......43 D8
  Over Peover WA16 ...108 A8
Mairesfield Ave WA4 ..17 B2
Maisterson Ct **7** CW5 ..204 E5
Maitland Way CH1 ....117 E8
Maitland-Wood Cl CW9 ..104 D7
Major Cross St **9** WA8 ..23 A7
Makepeace Cl CH3 ...119 C3
Makerfield Dr WA12 ..2 A5
Malaga Ave M90 .....33 B7
Malahide Cl WA8 ....12 E2
Malam Dr CW9 ....104 D6
Malbank CW5 ....204 E6
Malbank Rd CW2 .....189 E4
Malbank Sch CW5 ....204 C6
Malcolm Ave WA2 ....8 D1
Malcolm Cres CH63 ..43 C6
Malcolm St WA7 .....23 B2
Malham Cl WA5 .....14 F3
Malhamdale Rd CW12 ..157 A5
Malin Cl L24 ....21 D2
Maliston Rd WA5 ....15 B5
Mallaig Cl CW4 .....130 C2
Mallard Cl Knutsford WA16 ..57 B3
  Runcorn WA7 ....49 F5
  Warrington WA2 ......9 F3
Mallard Cres SK12 ..36 A4
Mallard Ct Chester CH2 ..118 F7
  Crewe CW1 ....191 A2
  Great Barrow SK8 ....34 B8
Mallard La WA3 .....9 F3
Mallard Way Crewe CW1 ..191 A2
  Winsford CW7 ....149 D6
Mallory Ct
  Congleton CW12 ......155 F3
Mobberley WA16 .....58 A4
Mallory Rd CH65 ....70 A4
Mallory Wlk CH4 ....162 A7
Mallow Cl CW3 ......142 A6
Mallow Wlk M31 ....11 F2
Mallowdale Cl CH62 ..43 F5
Malmesbury Cl
  Middlewich CW10 ....128 B1
  Poynton SK12 ....36 D4
Malmesbury Pk WA7 ..24 E2
Malmesbury Rd SK8 ..35 B6
Malory Cl CW1 ......190 F5
Malpas Alport Prim Sch
  SY14 ....213 B4
Malpas Cl Handforth SK9 ..34 E1
  Northwich CW9 ......104 B7
Malpas Dr WA5 ......15 C4
Malpas Rd
  Ellesmere Port CH65 ..69 F4
  Northwich CW9 ......104 C7
  Runcorn WA7 ....49 C7
Malpas Way WA5 ....15 C4
Malt Kiln Rd WA16 ..80 F4
Malt St WA16 ....57 A2
Malta Rd CH2 ....95 B1
Maltmans Rd WA13 ..18 D3
Malton Ave WA3 .....3 E7
Malton Cl WA8 ......12 C5
Malton Dr SK7 ......36 D7
Malvern Ave CH65 ...70 D3
Malvern Cl
  Congleton CW12 ......155 F3
  Shavington CW2 .....206 B4
  Warrington WA5 ......15 E6
Malvern Dr SK10 ....87 E4
Malvern Rd Blacon CH1 ..118 A5
  Haydock WA9 ....1 A2
  Knutsford WA16 .....81 F8
Malvern Way CW7 ...149 B7

Manchester Rd
  Congleton CW12 ......156 E5
  Handforth SK9 ....34 C2
  Hollinfare WA3 ......11 A2
  Hollinfare,Hollins Green
  WA3 ....11 B3
  Knutsford WA16 .....56 E4
  Macclesfield SK10 ....87 D4
  Partington WA13 .....11 F4
  Warrington WA3 .....18 D7
  Warrington,Bruche WA1 ..16 F7
  Warrington,Woolston WA1 ..17 C7
  Wincham CW9 ....79 D1
Manchester Row WA12 ..7 D8
Mancroft Cl WA1 ....17 E7
Mandarin Ct WA1 ....16 A3
Manifold Cl CW11 ...174 E8
Manifold Dr SK6 ....37 F6
Manley Cl Antrobus CW9 ..53 C4
  Holmes Chapel CW4 ..130 A3
Manley Gdns WA5 ...15 F5
Manley Gr SK7 .....35 E6
Manley La
  Dunham-on-t-H WA6 ..97 F5
  Manley WA6 ....98 C4
Manley Mere* WA6 ...98 B5
Manley Rd Frodsham WA6 ..74 B3
  Manley WA6 ....98 E7
  Warren SK11 ....112 A5
Manley View CH2 ....72 C3
Manley Village Sch WA6 ..99 A5
Manna Dr CH2 ....72 C3
Manners La CH60 ....40 E6
Manning St CW2 .....190 D1
Mannings La CH2 ...119 B6
Mannings La S CH2 ..119 A5
Manor Ave Crewe CW2 ..190 A1
  Golborne WA3 ....3 C8
  Goostrey CW4 ....107 F1
  Marston CW9 ....79 B6
  Newton-le-W WA12 ....1 F4
Manor Bsns Pk CW4 ..130 D3
Manor Cl Broughton CH5 ..139 C7
  Cheadle Hulme SK8 ...35 C8
  Congleton CW12 ......157 A1
  Great Barrow CH3 ....120 E6
  Lymm WA13 ....18 E2
  Neston CH64 ....66 C7
  Warrington WA1 ......17 D7
  Wilmslow SK9 ....59 F8
Manor Cres
  Broughton CH4 ......139 C8
  Knutsford WA16 .....57 B2
  Macclesfield SK10 ....87 D3
  Middlewich CW10 ....151 C7
Manor Ct Crewe CW2 ..190 B1
  Golborne WA3 ....3 C8
  Knutsford WA16 .....57 B1
  2 Nantwich CW5 ...204 E6
  Ravensmoor CW5 ....204 B4
Manor Dr Barnton CW8 ..78 B2
  Chester CH3 ....119 C1
  Northwich,Rudheath CW9 ..104 E6
Manor Farm Barns WA7 ..24 D4
Manor Farm Cl CW2 ..119 F8
Manor Farm Cres CH1 ..94 B8
Manor Farm Ct
  Broughton CH5 ......139 B7
  3 Frodsham WA6 ...49 C1
Manor Farm Rd WA7 ..24 D4
Manor Fell WA7 .....50 B7
Manor Fields CW7 ...151 C7
Manor Gdns
  Nantwich CW5 ......204 E6
  Wilmslow SK9 ....60 D7
Manor Gr CW8 ......103 C6
Manor Ho Bebington CH62 ..43 D8
  Ellesmere Port CH66 ..69 D2
  Row-of-trees SK9 ....59 D3
  Manor Ind Est WA4 ..16 F4
Manor La Broughton CH5 ..139 B7
  Davenham CW9 ....22 D2
  Ellesmere Port CH66 ..69 D3
  Holmes Chapel CW4 ..130 D3
  3 Middlewich CW10 ..151 C8
  Ollerton WA16 ......82 E6
Manor Park Ave WA7 ..24 C4
Manor Park Dr CH66 ..69 D3
Manor Park N WA5 ...57 C2
Manor Park Prim Sch
  WA16 ....57 C2
Manor Park Rd CW12 ..134 D2
Manor Park S WA5 ..57 C1
Manor Pk Broughton CH5 ..139 B7
  Great Barrow CH3 ....120 E6
Manor Pl WA8 ....12 B1
Manor Rd Bebington CH62 ..43 E6
  Chester CH4 ....141 B5
  Cuddington CW8 .....101 F2
  Frodsham WA6 ......49 C1
  Haydock WA11 ......1 F7
  Heswall CH60 ....40 E8
  Knutsford WA16 .....57 B2
  Mow Cop ST7 ....195 D7
  Nantwich CW5 ......204 E6
  Runcorn WA7 ....23 D2
  Sandbach CW11 ......175 D6
  Sealand CH5 ....116 A6
  Thornton Hough CH63 ..42 A7
  Whaley Bridge SK23 ..65 E5
  Wilmslow SK9 ....53 C8
Manor Rd N CW5 ....204 E7
Manor Sq CW7 ......149 B8
Manor St CW8 ....103 D6
Manor Terr SK11 ...113 B3
Manor Way Crewe CW2 ..190 C1

Manor Way continued
Sandbach CW11 . . . . .175 E6
Manora Rd CW9 . . . . .104 A8
Manorfield Cl CH1 . . . . . . .69 A1
Manorial Rd CH64 . . . . . . .66 C8
Manorial Rd S CH64 . . . . . .66 C7
Manse Field Rd WA6 . . . . .75 B1
Manse Gdns WA12 . . . . . . .2 D4
Mansell Cl WA8 . . . . .13 C5
Mansfield Apartments
WA2 . . . . .9 A3
Mansfield Cl WA3 . . . . . . .10 A4
Mansfield Prim Sch
CH65 . . . . .69 F3
Mansfield Rd CH65 . . . . . .70 A2
Mansion Ct B CW5 . . . . .204 F5
Mansion Dr WA16 . . . . . . .57 B2
Manston Rd WA5 . . . . .14 F3
Manuel Perez Rd WA5 . . .15 B6
Manx Rd WA4 . . . . .16 B3
Maori Dr WA6 . . . . .74 A8
Maple Ave Alsager ST7 . .193 E2
Disley SK12 . . . . .39 A6
Ellesmere Port CH66 . . . . .69 D6
Golborne WA3 . . . . .3 F7
Haydock WA11 . . . . .1 A4
Macclesfield SK11 . . . . . .112 D5
Newcastle-u-Lyme ST5 . .210 E1
Newton-le-W WA12 . . . . . . .2 D2
Poynton SK12 . . . . .36 F3
Runcorn WA7 . . . . .49 C8
Sutton WA7 . . . . .50 A4
Talke ST7 . . . . .210 D8
B Widnes WA8 . . . . .13 B1
Maple Cl
Brereton Green CW11 . . . .153 F5
Congleton CW12 . . . . . . .155 F4
Holmes Chapel CW4 . . . . .130 D4
Sandbach CW11 . . . . .175 C6
Maple Cres WA5 . . . . .14 F3
Maple Ct CW7 . . . . .127 A3
Maple Gr Barnton CW8 . . . .78 B4
Bebington CH62 . . . . .43 C8
Chester CH2 . . . . .119 B4
Crewe CW1 . . . . .190 E6
Ellesmere Port CH66 . . . . .95 A8
Northwich, Greenbank
CW8 . . . . .103 C7
Saltney CH4 . . . . .140 D5
Warrington WA4 . . . . .16 D3
Winsford CW7 . . . . .127 A1
Maple La CW8 . . . . .101 F2
Maple Pl ST7 . . . . .193 F7
Maple Rd
Alderley Edge SK9 . . . . . . .60 B3
Bramhall SK7 . . . . .35 E6
Partington M31 . . . . .11 E3
Warrington WA1 . . . . .17 E7
Winwick WA2 . . . . .8 B6
Maples SK9 . . . . .59 F6
Maples The
Mobberley WA16 . . . . .58 E1
Winsford CW7 . . . . .127 A3
Mapleton Dr WA7 . . . . .49 F3
Maplewood SK11 . . . . . . .112 D5
Maplewood Cl WA8 . . . . . .22 A7
Maplewood Gr CH1 . . . . .117 B8
Maplewood Rd SK9 . . . . . .60 E8
Mapplewell Cres WA5 . . . .15 A6
Marble Arch D WA16 . . . .57 A2
Marbury Gdns CH65 . . . . .69 F6
Marbury House Farm
WA4 . . . . .52 E5
Marbury La CW9 . . . . .78 E5
Marbury Park Ctry Pk*
CW9 . . . . .78 E5
Marbury Rd Chester CH3 .119 C2
Comberbach CW9 . . . . .78 D6
Handforth SK9 . . . . .34 B1
Norbury SY13 . . . . .215 B3
Marbury St WA4 . . . . .16 C3
March St CW1 . . . . .190 E4
Marchwiel Rd CH65 . . . . . .70 D4
Marcien Way WA8 . . . . . . .12 F3
Marcliff Gr WA16 . . . . .57 A1
Marcross Cl WA5 . . . . .7 E1
Mardale Ave WA2 . . . . . . .216 F4
Mardale Cl CW12 . . . . . . .157 B5
Mardale Cres WA13 . . . . . .18 F3
Mardale Ct CW4 . . . . .130 A2
Mardon Cl WA16 . . . . .57 D3
Marfields Prim Sch
CW12 . . . . .156 C2
Marford Cl CW9 . . . . .103 E5
Marfords Ave CH63 . . . . . .43 C7
Margaret Ave WA1 . . . . . . .17 B7
Margaret Ct WA8 . . . . .23 B7
Margaret's La CH66 . . . . . .69 A7
Margery Ave ST7 . . . . . . .194 E7
Marian Ave WA12 . . . . .1 F3
Marian Dr CH3 . . . . .142 B8
Marian Rd WA11 . . . . .1 E7
Marie Cl CW5 . . . . .216 F4
Marie Dr WA4 . . . . .17 D2
Marigold Cl SK11 . . . . . . .111 F8
Marigold Way WA9 . . . . . . .6 A7
Marina Ave WA5 . . . . .15 C4
Marina Cl WA3 . . . . .34 D5
Marina Dr Chester CH2 . .118 E7
Ellesmere Port CH65 . . . . .70 B5
Warrington WA2 . . . . .9 C1
Marina Flats CH3 . . . . . . .142 E7
Marina Gr WA7 . . . . .23 B1
Marina La WA7 . . . . .50 E7
Marina Village WA7 . . . . . .50 E7
Marina Wlk CH65 . . . . .70 B5
Marine App CW8 . . . . .103 F8
Marine Ave M31 . . . . .11 D3

Marine Dr CH60 . . . . .40 D6
Mariner Cl WA7 . . . . .50 D6
Marion Dr WA7 . . . . .48 F6
Maritime Cl WA12 . . . . .2 C5
Mark Ave CH66 . . . . .69 C4
Mark Cl CH2 . . . . .118 F2
Market Cl CW1 . . . . .190 D5
Market Ct CW6 . . . . .146 C2
Market Ctr CW1 . . . . .190 D4
Market Gate WA1 . . . . .16 B5
Market Pl Bollington SK10 . .88 B8
Hampton Heath SY14 . . . .213 D7
Macclesfield SK10,SK11 . .112 D8
Winsford CW7 . . . . .126 F1
Market Sq Chester CH1 . .237 A2
Congleton CW12 . . . . . . .156 D2
Crewe CW1 . . . . .190 D4
D Sandbach CW11 . . . . .175 B6
Market St
Congleton CW12 . . . . . . .156 D3
Crewe CW1 . . . . .190 D4
Crewe CW1 . . . . .190 D5
Disley SK12 . . . . .38 D6
Kidsgrove ST7 . . . . .195 A1
Nantwich CW5 . . . . .204 E5
New Mills SK22 . . . . .39 B8
Newton-le-W WA12 . . . . . . .2 A3
Whaley Bridge SK23 . . . . . .65 E7
Widnes WA8 . . . . .23 A7
Market Way D CW9 . . . . .103 F8
Markham Cl WA8 . . . . .22 A4
Marl Cl CW8 . . . . .122 A7
Marl Croft CH3 . . . . .142 B7
Marl Edge SK10 . . . . .87 A5
Marl Heys CH2 . . . . .118 E7
Marlborough Ave
Alderley Edge SK9 . . . . . . .60 B2
Winsford CW7 . . . . .126 C3
Marlborough Cl
Knutsford WA16 . . . . .57 C4
Macclesfield SK10 . . . . . . .87 E4
Wistaston CW2 . . . . .205 E8
Marlborough Cres
Warrington WA4 . . . . .16 F2
Widnes WA8 . . . . .13 A5
Marlborough Ct
D Chester CH3 . . . . .119 B2
D Macclesfield SK11 . . . .112 D7
Marlborough Dr
Helsby WA6 . . . . .73 B2
Macclesfield SK10 . . . . . . .87 D4
Marlborough Ho D
SK11 . . . . .111 F8
Marlborough Prim Sch The
SK10 . . . . .87 D4
Marlborough Rd CH65 . . . .70 D3
Marlborough Way WA11 . . .1 E8
Marlborough Wlk CH65 . . .70 C3
Marleston Ct WA4 . . . . . .140 E1
Marley Ave CW1 . . . . .190 B7
Marley Gn SY13 . . . . .227 C8
Marley Rd SK12 . . . . .36 E2
Marley Way CH4 . . . . .140 E7
Marlfield Rd
Altrincham WA15 . . . . .32 D7
Warrington WA4 . . . . .17 A2
Marline Ave CH64 . . . . . . .43 C6
Marling Cl WA6 . . . . .74 D6
Marlow Ave CH2 . . . . .118 F7
Marlow Cl
Sandbach CW11 . . . . .174 D5
Warrington WA3 . . . . .9 C5
Marlow Dr
Altrincham WA14 . . . . .20 F2
Handforth SK9 . . . . .34 C5
Marlowe Cl Blacon CH1 . .118 A5
Widnes WA8 . . . . .12 F1
Marlowe Ct SK11 . . . . . . .112 C5
Marlowe Dr CW5 . . . . . . .204 F3
Marlowe Rd
D Neston CH64 . . . . .66 E8
Northwich CW9 . . . . .104 C6
Marlston Ave CH4 . . . . . .141 A6
Marlston Pl WA7 . . . . .49 B6
Marlwood Pl CH4 . . . . . . .139 A3
Maroon Rd M22 . . . . .33 F7
Marple Cres CW2 . . . . . . .189 E2
Marple Rd CH66 . . . . .69 F3
Marquis Dr SK8 . . . . .34 D7
Marriott Rd CW11 . . . . . . .174 F3
Marron Ave WA2 . . . . .8 B2
Marryat Cl WA2 . . . . .8 A7
Marsden Ave WA4 . . . . . . .17 A4
Marsden Ct WA8 . . . . .12 E4
Marsden Terr D SK11 . . .112 C7
Marsh Ave ST7 . . . . .195 E2
Marsh Cl ST7 . . . . .193 A3
Marsh Gr ST8 . . . . .179 C3
Marsh Green Cl ST8 . . . . .179 D2
Marsh Green Rd CW11 . . .174 E8
Marsh Hall Pad WA8 . . . . .13 B4
Marsh House La WA1,
WA2 . . . . .16 C7
Marsh La Alsager ST7 . . . .193 A3
Ashley WA16 . . . . .31 A4
Barton CH3,SY14 . . . . . . .181 E3
Churton CH3 . . . . .181 B5
Dutton WA4 . . . . .51 B8
Elton CH2 . . . . .72 B4
Frodsham WA6 . . . . .74 A8
Holmes Chapel CW4 . . . . .130 B3
Ince CH2 . . . . .72 D6
Mere WA16 . . . . .30 E1
Nantwich CW5 . . . . .204 C5
New Mills SK22,SK23 . . . . .39 D6
Norley CW8,WA6 . . . . . . .101 B7

Marsh La continued
Ravensmoor CW5 . . . . . . .203 F2
Runcorn WA7 . . . . .23 F3
Warrington WA4 . . . . .16 E3
Warrington,Penketh WA5 . .14 C2
Marsh Lane Trad Est
SK22 . . . . .39 D7
Marsh Rd WA4 . . . . .27 B4
Marsh St Warrington WA1 . .16 D7
Widnes WA8 . . . . .23 A6
Marshall Ave WA5 . . . . .7 F2
Marshall Gr CW12 . . . . . .179 B8
Marshall La CW8 . . . . . . .103 D6
Marshall Rd WA1 . . . . .17 C7
Marshalls Ct D CW8 . . . .103 C5
Marshfield Ave CW2 . . . . .189 D4
Marshfield Bank CW2 . . .189 D4
Marshfield La ST8 . . . . . .179 C2
Marshgate WA8 . . . . .22 B6
Marshgate Pl WA6 . . . . . . .49 D2
Marshgreen Rd ST8 . . . . .179 D3
Marshlands Rd CH64 . . . . .66 E5
Marshway Dr WA12 . . . . . .2 B5
Marson St WA2 . . . . .16 A6
Marston Cl CH62 . . . . .43 E3
Marston Gdns CH65 . . . . . .69 F6
Marston La CW9 . . . . .79 C6
Marten Ave CH63 . . . . .43 C7
Martens Rd M44 . . . . .11 E5
Marthall La WA16 . . . . .83 B7
Marthall Way D SK9 . . . . .34 E5
Martham Cl WA4 . . . . .17 A3
Martin Ave
Newton-le-W WA12 . . . . . . .2 C5
Warrington WA2 . . . . .8 E1
Martin Cl Chester CH2 . . .118 C8
Runcorn WA7 . . . . .50 A7
Martin Rd Chester CH2 . .118 C8
Frodsham WA6 . . . . .74 B8
Martin's La CH3 . . . . .143 F3
Martindale Gr WA7 . . . . . .49 D5
Martins Mill CW12 . . . . . .139 D3
Martinscroft Gn WA1 . . . . .17 F7
Martinsfields CW8 . . . . . . .77 A5
Martland Ave WA3 . . . . .3 E7
Martlet Ave SK12 . . . . .38 C6
Marton & District CE Prim
Sch SK11 . . . . .133 C5
Marton Cl
Congleton CW12 . . . . . . .156 E5
Culcheth WA3 . . . . .4 E4
Hough CW2 . . . . .206 E3
Macclesfield SK10 . . . . . . .86 F1
Marton Hall La SK11 . . . .133 D7
Marton La Marton SK11 . .133 D7
Warren SK11 . . . . .111 B1
Marton Rd CH4 . . . . .139 C3
Marton Way D SK9 . . . . . .34 E5
Martree Ct CW1 . . . . .174 D8
Mary St Crewe CW1 . . . . .190 E5
Widnes WA8 . . . . .23 D7
Maryfield Cl WA3 . . . . .3 A7
Maryhill Cl ST7 . . . . .195 A3
Maryhill High Sch ST7 . . .195 A3
Maryhill Prim Sch ST7 . . .195 A3
Maryhill Rd WA7 . . . . .49 A8
Maryland Cl WA5 . . . . .15 C7
Marys Gate CW2 . . . . .205 E8
Maryville Cl D CH65 . . . . .70 C6
Masefield Ave WA8 . . . . . .22 F8
Masefield Dr Blacon CH1 .117 E6
Crewe CW1 . . . . .190 F4
Winwick WA2 . . . . .8 A5
Masefield Way CW11 . . . .174 D5
Maskery Pl CW12 . . . . . . .156 E4
Mason Ave
Warrington WA1 . . . . .16 B3
Widnes WA8 . . . . .13 B4
Mason Cl SK9 . . . . .60 D2
Mason St Chester CH2 . . .237 A3
Runcorn WA7 . . . . .23 C3
Warrington WA1 . . . . .16 C3
Mason's Row CW5 . . . . . .169 E2
Masons La SK10 . . . . .87 F1
Massey Ave
Hartford CW8 . . . . .103 A4
Warrington WA3 . . . . .18 B2
Winsford CW7 . . . . .7 F2
Winsford CW7 . . . . .126 F1
Massey Brook La WA13 . . .18 B2
Massey Cl CW5 . . . . .205 A4
Massey Hall Sch WA4 . . . .17 F7
Massey St D SK9 . . . . . . .60 A1
Masters Ct WA16 . . . . .56 F1
Mastiff La SY14 . . . . .213 B1
Mates La SY14 . . . . .213 B6
Mather Ave Golborne WA3 . .3 E6
Runcorn WA7 . . . . .48 D7
Mather Cl CW7 . . . . .151 C8
Mather Dr
Comberbach CW9 . . . . .78 C8
Northwich CW9 . . . . .104 D7
Mathers Cl WA2 . . . . .8 E1
Mathieson Rd WA8 . . . . . .22 E5
Matlock Cl WA5 . . . . .14 E4
Matlock Dr SK7 . . . . .36 E8
Matlock Rd SK8 . . . . .34 C7
Matterdale Cl WA6 . . . . . . .74 D7
Matthew Cl CH2 . . . . .118 F2
Matthews Pl CW12 . . . . . .157 A2
Matthews St WA1 . . . . . . .16 D7
Matty's La WA6 . . . . .74 B8
Mavor Ct CW1 . . . . .190 B4
Maw Green Cl CW1 . . . . .190 C7
Maw Green Rd CW1 . . . . .190 C7
Maw La CW1 . . . . .191 A8
Mawdsley Ave WA1 . . . . . .17 E7

Mawdsley Cl ST7 . . . . . . .193 A3
Mawson Cl WA5 . . . . .15 D8
Maxfield Cl SK11 . . . . . . .111 F8
Maxwell Cl CH65 . . . . .70 A2
Maxwell Rd CW12 . . . . . .179 A8
Maxwell St Crewe CW2 . .190 C3
Warrington WA3 . . . . .9 C5
May Ave SK6 . . . . .38 D6
May Rd Cheadle Hulme SK8 . .35 B6
Heswall CH60 . . . . .41 A8
May Wlk D M31 . . . . .11 E3
Mayberry Gr WA2 . . . . .9 A1
Maybrook Pl WA4 . . . . . . .16 F3
Maydor Ave CH4 . . . . .140 C7
Mayfair Cl Poynton SK12 . .36 E4
Warrington WA5 . . . . .14 D7
Mayfair Ct CH4 . . . . .162 E5
Mayfair Dr CW9 . . . . .103 F3
Mayfair Gr WA8 . . . . .12 D1
Mayfield Ave
Macclesfield SK11 . . . . . .112 C5
Widnes WA8 . . . . .12 B1
Mayfield Cl CW1 . . . . .130 D3
Mayfield Ct WA8 . . . . .13 A2
Mayfield Dr
Bebington CH62 . . . . .44 B6
Cuddington CW8 . . . . . . .102 A4
Golborne WN7 . . . . .4 C8
Winsford CW7 . . . . .127 A3
Mayfield Gdns CH64 . . . .41 E1
Mayfield Gr
Cuddington CW8 . . . . . . .102 A4
Wilmslow SK9 . . . . .59 E5
Mayfield Mews CW1 . . . .189 F6
Mayfield Rd Blacon CH1 . .117 D5
Bramhall SK7 . . . . .35 E4
Mobberley WA16 . . . . .57 F4
Northwich CW9 . . . . .104 C8
Warrington WA4 . . . . .17 A2
Mayfield Terr SK11 . . . . . .112 C5
Mayfield View WA13 . . . . .18 F2
Mayflower Rd CW5 . . . . . .204 E3
Mayrick Cl WA12 . . . . .2 A3
Maythorn Ave WA3 . . . . . . .9 A7
Maytree Ave CH3 . . . . . . .119 B2
Maywood SK9 . . . . .59 E4
Mc Clellan Pl WA8 . . . . . .13 B1
McCarthy Cl WA3 . . . . .10 A3
McGarva Way CH65 . . . . . .70 C4
McGowan Ho ST7 . . . . . .210 D8
McKee Ave WA2 . . . . .8 B2
Mckellin Cl ST7 . . . . .209 E2
Mckinley Way WA8 . . . . . .12 F3
McLaren St CW1 . . . . .190 C7
McMinnis Ave WA9 . . . . . . .1 B2
McNeill Ave CW5 . . . . . . .190 A5
Mead Ave ST7 . . . . .194 E7
Mead Cl WA16 . . . . .56 F1
Mead Rd WA1 . . . . .17 A8
Meade The SK9 . . . . .60 C8
Meadow Ave
Congleton CW12 . . . . . . .156 C1
Goostrey CW4 . . . . .107 C1
Warrington WA4 . . . . .16 B2
Weston CW2 . . . . .207 B5
Meadow Bank
Adderley TF9 . . . . .235 A4
Kelsall CW6 . . . . .122 C4
Meadow Bank Cvn Pk
WA4 . . . . .25 C6
Meadow Brow SK9 . . . . . . .60 A2
Meadow Cl
Cuddington CW8 . . . . . . .102 A4
Farndon CH3 . . . . .180 F1
Goostrey CW4 . . . . .107 C1
Helsby WA6 . . . . .73 B3
High Lane SK6 . . . . .37 F8
Neston CH64 . . . . .66 E6
Newton-le-W WA12 . . . . . . .1 F3
Shavington CW2 . . . . .206 D5
Tarvin CH3 . . . . .121 B2
Whaley Bridge SK23 . . . . . .65 D8
Widnes WA8 . . . . .22 F8
Willaston CH64 . . . . .67 F8
Wilmslow SK9 . . . . .59 E4
Winsford CW7 . . . . .126 C3
Meadow Cotts B CW12 .156 D3
Willaston CH64 . . . . .67 F8
Meadow Ct
Frodsham WA6 . . . . .49 C1
Mollington CH1 . . . . .94 F1
Nr Man's Heath SY14 . . . .214 A5
Packmoor ST7 . . . . .195 E2
Meadow Dr Barnton CW8 . .78 A3
Knutsford WA16 . . . . .81 F8
Prestbury SK10 . . . . .87 B7
Wistaston CW2 . . . . .205 F7
Meadow Gate CW9 . . . . . .79 F5
Meadow Gr
Northwich CW9 . . . . .104 B5
Winsford CW7 . . . . .126 E5
Meadow Home Pk CW7 .126 D6
Meadow House Pk
CW6 . . . . .185 D5
Meadow La
Comberbach CW9 . . . . .78 C7
Disley SK12 . . . . .38 D6
Ellesmere Port CH65 . . . . .70 C6
Huntington CH3 . . . . .142 A5
Moulton CW9 . . . . .126 F8
Partington WA14 . . . . .20 D4
Warrington WA2 . . . . .9 A2
Willaston CH64 . . . . .67 F8

Meadow Prim Sch CH66 . .69 E2
Meadow Rd
Broughton CH4 . . . . .139 B4
Weaverham CW8 . . . . .102 E7
Meadow Rise
Clutton CH3 . . . . .182 D2
Winsford CW7 . . . . .126 A1
Meadow Row WA7 . . . . . . .24 A1
Meadow St
New Mills SK22 . . . . .39 B8
B Northwich CW9 . . . . . .104 A8
Meadow The CW4 . . . . . .130 D8
Meadow View
Chester CH3 . . . . .118 F1
Elton CH2 . . . . .72 A3
Lymm WA13 . . . . .18 D4
Middlewich CW10 . . . . . . .128 B2
Sealand CH5 . . . . .116 A6
Meadow View Dr WA6 . . . .74 A7
Meadow Way
Lawton-gate ST7 . . . . .194 A5
Macclesfield SK10 . . . . . . .87 E2
Wilmslow SK9 . . . . .59 E4
Meadow Wlk
Partington M31 . . . . .11 E3
B Runcorn WA7 . . . . .49 F7
Meadowbank Gdns WA3 . .5 C7
Meadowcroft
Higher Kinnerton CH4 . . . .161 A7
Saughall CH1 . . . . .94 B1
Meadowfield
Tarporley CW6 . . . . .146 C1
Whaley Bridge SK23 . . . . . .65 D8
Meadowfield Rd CH4 . . . .141 A5
Meadowgate Cl CW11 . . .174 D5
Meadowgate Farm WA7 . .49 F2
Meadows La
Chester CH4 . . . . .237 C1
Saughall CH1 . . . . .117 A8
Tilston SY14 . . . . .212 B6
Meadows PI CH4 . . . . . .141 E7
Meadows Rd
Cheadle Hulme SK8 . . . . . .34 F8
Warrington WA4 . . . . .17 A1
Meadows The
Ashton Hayes CH3 . . . . . .121 E7
Congleton CW12 . . . . . . .156 E3
Irlam M44 . . . . .11 E6
Neston CH64 . . . . .66 F6
Meadowside Disley SK12 . .39 A6
Fourlane-ends SK10 . . . . . .63 B8
Northwich CW9 . . . . .103 D7
Whaley Bridge SK23 . . . . . .65 D8
Meadowside Ave ST7 . . .209 D2
Meadowside La ST7 . . . .195 B7
Meadowside Mews CH1 . .118 B4
Meadowside Rd CH62 . . . .43 D8
Meadowsway CH2 . . . . . .118 D8
Meadowsweet Rd WA16 . .57 F3
Meadowvale Cl CW5 . . . .204 E7
Meads Rd ST7 . . . . .193 D4
Meadscroft Dr SK9 . . . . . .59 F1
Meadway Bramhall SK7 . . .35 E5
Ellesmere Port CH66 . . . . .69 B7
Golborne WA3 . . . . .3 D8
Heswall CH60 . . . . .40 F6
High Lane SK6 . . . . .37 F8
Poynton SK12 . . . . .36 B4
Prestbury SK10 . . . . .87 A5
Runcorn WA7 . . . . .49 E8
Widnes WA8 . . . . .12 A1
Meakin Cl CW12 . . . . .157 B1
Meal St SK22 . . . . .39 C8
Mealors New Cotts CH64 .67 A4
Mealors Weint CH64 . . . . .41 B1
Meddings Cl SK9 . . . . .85 A8
Medina Ave CW7 . . . . . . .126 F2
Medina Way ST7 . . . . .195 B2
Medlar Cl CH4 . . . . .140 F5
Medway Cl Golborne WN7 . .4 C8
Handforth SK9 . . . . .34 D2
Warrington WA2 . . . . .8 E2
Medway Dr ST8 . . . . .179 C1
Medway Rd WA3 . . . . .5 A2
Mee St SK11 . . . . .112 E5
Meeanee Dr CW5 . . . . . . .204 D4
Meeting House La WA6 . . .74 F2
Meg La Langley SK11 . . . .113 D1
Macclesfield SK10 . . . . . . .111 E8
Megacre ST7 . . . . .210 A1
Megs La CW9 . . . . .53 B4
Meir Rd ST7 . . . . .193 C3
Melbourne Ave M90 . . . . . .33 A8
Melbourne Gr CW1 . . . . . .191 C5
Melbourne Rd
Blacon CH1 . . . . .117 D4
Bramhall SK7 . . . . .35 F5
Melbury Ct WA3 . . . . .9 B8
Melbury Rd SK9 . . . . .35 B6
Melchett Cres CW9 . . . . .104 D7
Melford Cl CW12 . . . . . . .206 C8
Melford Ct Lymm WA13 . . .18 E3
Warrington WA1 . . . . .17 D8
Melford Dr
Macclesfield SK10 . . . . . . .87 C2
Runcorn WA7 . . . . .23 C1
Meliden Gr WA6 . . . . .73 B1
Melkridge Cl CH2 . . . . . . .119 A3
Melksham Cl SK11 . . . . . .112 A7
Mellard St ST7 . . . . .209 D1
Mellock Cl CH64 . . . . .66 F6
Mellock La CH64 . . . . .66 F7
Mellor Cl WA7 . . . . .50 C6
Mellor Cres WA16 . . . . . . .56 E1

Mellor St Crewe CW1 ....190 D5
Packmoor ST7 ....195 F2
Mellors Bank ST7 ....195 D6
Melrose Ave
  Burtonwood WA5 ....6 F7
  Chester CH3 ....119 B2
  Warrington WA4 ....26 D8
Melrose Cres SK12 ......37 D5
Melrose Ct 15 SK9 ......34 E1
Melrose Dr Crewe CW1 ..190 B8
  Ellesmere Port CH66 ......94 F8
Melton Ave WA4 ....26 B8
Melton Cl CW12 ....155 F3
Melton Dr CW12 ....155 F3
Melton Rd WA7 ....49 C7
Melverly Dr CH1 ....117 C4
Melville Cl
  Warrington WA2 ....16 B7
  2 Widnes WA8 ....13 D1
Melville Rd WA4 ....11 C5
Mendell Cl CH62 ....43 E8
Mendell Prim Sch CH62 ..43 E8
Mendip Ave WA2 ....8 B3
Mendip Cl
  Ellesmere Port CH66 ......69 E3
  Heald Green SK8 ....34 B7
  Winsford CW7 ....149 B8
Menin Ave WA4 ....16 C3
Menlow Cl WA4 ....17 C1
Mentmore Gdns WA4 ....26 F5
Meols Cl
  Ellesmere Port CH66 ......69 E4
  Hale L24 ....21 E2
Mercer Cl SY14 ....213 B3
Mercer Rd WA11 ....1 D6
Mercer St Burtonwood WA5 ..6 E6
  Newton-le-W WA12 ....2 C3
Mercer Way Chester CH4 ..140 F6
  Nantwich CW5 ....204 E7
Mercer Wlk CH65 ....70 C4
Merchants Ct CW1 ......190 C7
Mercian Cl CW2 ....206 B4
Mercury Ct CH1 ....117 E2
Mere Ave CH63 ....43 B6
Mere Bank CW9 ....127 A8
Mere Brook Wlk CW2 ..190 C1
Mere Cl
  Ellesmere Port CH66 ......69 D2
  Haslington CW1 ....191 D4
  Pickmere WA16 ....80 A7
Mere Cres CW8 ....123 F6
Mere Ct Alsager ST7 ..193 D4
  Chelford SK11 ....83 F3
  5 Knutsford WA16 ......57 A2
  Weston CW2 ....207 B5
Mere Hall WA16 ....56 A8
Mere Home Farm WA16 ..56 B8
Mere La Cuddington CW8 ..102 A2
  Pickmere WA16 ....79 F7
Mere Rd Marston CW9 ....79 B6
  Newton-le-W WA12 ....2 F4
  Warrington WA2 ....9 A2
  Weston CW2 ....207 B5
Mere St CW1 ....191 D4
Mere View Gdns WA4 ....26 E5
Merebank Rd CW2 ......190 B1
Merebrook Rd SK11 ....111 F8
Merecroft 1 CH3 ......119 A1
Meredith Ave WA4 ......17 B2
Meredith St CW1 ......190 C5
Merehaven Cl WA16 ....80 A7
Merehaeth La WA16 ....56 E5
Mereheath Pk WA16 ....56 F3
Merelake Rd ST7 ......210 B8
Meremore Dr ST5 ......210 D2
Mereside Ave CW12 ....156 B3
Mereside Cl SK22 ....39 A8
Mereside Gdns SK23 ....65 D6
Mereside Rd WA16 ......30 C2
Merevale Cl WA7 ....49 E6
Merewood Cl WA2 ....8 D3
Mereworth Dr CW9 ....103 F5
Meridian Ho CW7 ......127 B3
Meriton Rd SK9 ....34 C1
Merlin Ave WA16 ....57 B3
Merlin Cl Runcorn WA7 ..24 A1
  Winsford CW7 ....150 A8
Merlin Way Crewe CW1 ..190 A8
  Kidsgrove ST7 ....195 D3
Merrick Cl WA2 ....8 E3
Merridale The WA15 ....32 A8
Merriden Rd SK10 ....87 B2
Merrill's Ave CW7 ......189 E5
Merriman Ave WA16 ....57 C3
Merrivale Rd CW2 ......206 B8
Merrydale Cl SK10 ......86 F1
Merryman's La SK9 ......84 B7
Mersey Cl CW7 ....127 B1
Mersey Rd Runcorn WA7 ..23 A3
  Widnes WA8 ....16 B5
Mersey St St Helens WA9 ..1 A3
  Warrington WA1 ....16 B5
Mersey View WA7 ....48 D7
Mersey View Rd WA8 ....22 B4
Merseyton Rd CH65 ....70 B8
Merseyton Road Workshops
  CH65 ....70 C7
Mersham Ct WA8 ....13 E3
Merton Ave SK7 ....36 F8
Merton Cl CH64 ....66 E5
Merton House Sch CH2 ..118 C4
Merton Rd Bebington CH65 ..44 B3
  Ellesmere Port CH66 ......69 F3

Merton Rd *continued*
  Poynton SK12 ....36 B4
Mertoun Rd WA4 ....16 B1
Mervyn Rd CW8 ....77 E1
Merwood Ave SK8 ....34 D8
Messuage La CW12 ......132 E4
Meteor Cres WA2 ....8 D2
Mevagissey Rd WA7 ......50 C5
Mevril Rd SK23 ....65 E5
Mevril Springs Way SK23 ..65 E5
Mews The Barnton CW8 ..78 B2
  Burtonwood WA5 ....6 E6
  Holmes Chapel CW4 ......130 C3
  New Mills SK22 ....39 D8
  Styal SK9 ....33 D4
  Tarporley CW6 ....168 C8
  Willaston CH64 ....68 A8
Meynell Cl CW2 ....190 A1
Meynell Pl CH1 ....118 A5
Micawber Rd SK12 ......36 E2
Mickle Trafford Village Sch
  CH2 ....119 E8
Micklegate
  Mickle Trafford CH2 ......119 E8
  Runcorn WA7 ....50 D7
Micklewright Ave CW1 ..190 D5
Mickley Hall La CW5 ....218 A4
Mid Cheshire Coll (London
  Road Studios) CW9 ....103 F6
Mid Cheshire Coll (Verdin
  Ctr) CW7 ....126 D1
Mid-Cheshire Coll (Hartford
  Campus) CW8 ....103 C6
Middle La Aldford CH3 ..163 F3
  Congleton CW12 ....157 D4
  Kingsley WA6 ....74 F2
Middle Wlk
  Frodsham WA6 ....74 B7
  Knutsford WA16 ....57 B2
Middlecroft CH3 ....119 E5
Middlehills SK11 ....113 A6
Middlehurst Ave WA8 ..102 E8
Middlehurst Rd WA4 ....17 A2
Middlewich High Sch
  CW10 ....151 C8
Middlewich Prim Sch
  CW10 ....151 B8
Middleworth Rd
  Allostock WA16 ....106 D5
  Church Minshull CW1,
  CW10 ....172 E5
  Cranage CW4,CW10 ......129 E6
  Crewe CW5 ....189 B6
  Crewe CW5 ....189 B1
  Delamere CW6,CW8 ......123 D5
  Holmes Chapel CW4 ......130 B3
  Knutsford WA16 ....82 A3
  Lower Peover WA16 ......81 F2
  Nantwich CW5 ....204 F7
  Northwich CW9 ....104 D7
  Sandbach CW11 ....174 E7
  Winsford CW7,CW10 ....127 E1
Middlewich Road Ind Est
  CW10 ....129 A6
Middlewich St CW1 ......190 D6
Middlewood WA3 ....3 E8
Middlewood Rd
  Hazel Grove SK7,SK12 ....37 C7
  High Lane SK6 ....37 D7
  Poynton SK12 ....37 B4
  Middlewood Sta SK12 ....37 D6
  Middlewood View SK6 ....37 D7
Midfield Cl ST8 ....179 C2
Midhurst Cl SK8 ....34 F8
Midland St WA8 ....13 B1
Midland Terr SK22 ....39 C7
Midland Way WA1,WA5 ..16 B5
Midlothian Ho CH1 ......237 C3
Midpoint 18 Motorway Ind
  Est CW10 ....128 E1
Midway SK8 ....35 B5
Milborne Cl CH2 ....118 E5
Mildenhall Cl WA5 ......15 B6
Mile Bank Rd SY13 ......226 D3
Miles Cl WA3 ....9 F3
Milford Gdns WA4 ......26 D4
Milk St CW12 ....156 D3
Mill Ave WA5 ....14 E7
Mill Bank CH64 ....67 A5
Mill Bridge Cl CW1 ....190 F3
Mill Brow WA8 ....13 C1
Mill Cl Chester CH2 ....118 D6
  Knutsford WA16 ....57 D4
  Warrington WA2 ....8 E4
Mill Cotts Bollington SK10 ..88 B8
  Christleton CH3 ....142 D8
  Willaston CH64 ....42 F1
Mill Cross CH3 ....143 B5
Mill Ct CH65 ....69 F6
Mill Farm Cl WA16 ......57 D4
Mill Farm Est CW5 ......217 A3
Mill Field Cl CH3 ......180 F2
Mill Gn Congleton CW12 ..156 D3
  Willaston CH64 ....67 F8
Mill Gr Bulkeley SY14 ..184 E2
  Kidsgrove ST7 ....194 D1
Mill Green Cl CW11 ....174 C6
Mill Green La WA12 ......2 E7
Mill Hill Ave SK12 ......36 D7
Mill Hill Dr CW11 ......175 A5
Mill Hill Hollow SK10 ..90 C7
Mill Hill La CW11 ......175 A4
Mill Ho CW5 ....204 D5
Mill La Adlington SK10 ..62 B6
  Alsager CW11 ....192 E8
  Altrincham WA15 ....32 E4
  Audlem, Little Heath CW3 ..230 A4
  Audlem, Swanbach CW3 ..229 E2

Mill La *continued*
  Barthomley CW2 ....208 C7
  Blakenhall CW5 ....221 B4
  Bold Heath WA8 ....13 D6
  Bollington SK10 ....88 C8
  Brereton Green CW4 ......153 E8
  Bulkeley SY14 ....184 E2
  Burton CH64 ....67 C1
  Chester CH2 ....118 D6
  Christleton CH3 ....120 D2
  Congleton CW12 ....179 C8
  Cronton WA8 ....12 D6
  Cuddington CW8 ....101 F4
  Duddon CW6 ....145 A7
  Eaton CW6 ....147 B2
  Ellesmere Port CH66 ......69 E5
  Frodsham WA6 ....49 E2
  Goostrey CW4 ....107 E2
  Great Barrow CH3 ....120 E5
  Hazel Grove SK7 ....36 F8
  Heswall CH60 ....41 B8
  Higher Walton WA4 ....25 E7
  Holmes Chapel CW4 ......154 A8
  Huxley CH3 ....144 C2
  Kelsall CW6 ....122 C1
  Kingsley WA6 ....75 E3
  Lindow End SK9 ....84 A7
  Little Budworth CW6 ....148 A8
  Lymm WA13 ....19 C4
  Macclesfield SK11 ....112 D7
  Marton CW12 ....132 F2
  Middlewich CW10 ....128 D1
  Middlewich,Stud Green
  CW11 ....152 C1
  Mobberley WA16 ....58 B4
  Mottram St Andrew SK10 ..61 C5
  Neston CH64 ....67 C5
  Newton-le-W WA12 ....2 E3
  Over Peover WA16,SK11 ..108 D8
  Prestbury SK10 ....61 A6
  Sandbach CW11 ....174 C8
  Sandbach,Wheelock CW11 ..175 B2
  Siddington SK11 ....109 F6
  Smallwood CW11 ....176 D7
  Tarvin CH3 ....121 C4
  The Bank ST7 ....195 A7
  Warrington WA2 ....7 F4
  Warrington,Houghton Gn
  WA2 ....8 E4
  Warrington,Stockton Heath
  WA4 ....16 E1
  Weston CW2 ....207 B6
  Whitegate CW7,CW8 ......126 B6
  Willaston CH64 ....42 F1
Mill Lane Cotts CH3 ....220 F5
Mill Mdw WA12 ....2 E3
Mill Park Dr CH62 ......43 E3
Mill Pool La CW5 ......187 C6
Mill Rd Macclesfield SK11 ..112 D6
  Wilmslow SK9 ....60 B7
Mill Rise ST7 ....195 A1
Mill Row CW11 ....175 C6
Mill St Chester CH4 ....237 B1
  Congleton CW12 ....156 D3
  Congleton, Buglawton
  CW12 ....156 F4
  Crewe CW2 ....190 D3
  Golborne WA3 ....3 A8
  Macclesfield SK11 ......112 D7
  Nantwich CW5 ....204 E5
  Neston CH64 ....66 D8
  Wilmslow SK9 ....60 B7
Mill Stream Cl CW7 ....107 E1
Mill The ST7 ....195 C5
Mill View Cl SY14 ......184 E2
Mill View Prim Sch CH2 ..118 E6
Mill Way CW5 ....204 F2
Mill Wharf CH3 ....143 B5
Millar Cres WA8 ....23 A7
Millbank WA13 ....18 E3
Millbank Cl SK11 ....84 A3
Millbank Cotts CH3 ....166 C2
Millbank Dr SK10 ....86 F1
Millbank La WA16 ......74 A8
Millbeck Cl CW2 ....207 B5
Millbridge Gdns WA12 ....2 E3
Millbrook Cl
  Fowley Common WA3 ......5 C5
  Winsford CW7 ....148 F8
Millbrook Ct CW10 ....128 D1
Millbrook End CH3 ....166 A2
Millbrook Fold SK7 ......36 F8
Millbrook Gr 1 SK9 ....34 D1
Millbuck Way CW11 ....174 C6
Millcroft Neston CH64 ....41 E1
  Sandbach,Wheelock CW11 ..174 F8
Milldale Rd WN7 ....4 B8
Millend La ST7 ....209 C5
Millenium Ct CH64 ......41 E2
Millenium Way ST5 ....210 F2
Miller St WA4 ....16 C4
Millers Cl CH3 ....143 A4
Millers Croft 1 SK10 ..112 C8
Millers Ct 1 SK10 ......112 C8
Millers La WA13 ....19 B5
Millers Mdw SK10 ....88 C5
Millers View ST7 ......195 A1
Millers Wharf ST7 ......193 E7
Millersdale Cl CH62 ....43 F5
Millersdale Gr WA7 ....49 D6
Millfield La WA16 ......60 D1
Millfield CH64 ....41 C1
Millfield Bsns Ctr WA1 ..1 F6
Millfield La Haydock WA11 ..1 B8
  Saighton CH3 ....142 F1
  Tarporley CW6 ....146 C2
Millfield Rd WA8 ....13 C2
Millfield Terr CW7 ......69 C7

Millfields CW5 ....204 D4
Millfields Prim Sch
  Bebington CH62 ....43 E4
  Nantwich CW5 ....204 C5
Millgate CW8 ....101 F4
Millhouse Ave WA4 ......16 D1
Millhouse La WA3 ....9 A6
Millingford The CW4 ..130 C2
Millingford Ind Est WA3 ..3 A8
Millington Cl
  Runcorn WA7 ....49 F4
  Widnes WA8 ....22 F8
Millington Hall La WA14 ..30 B5
Millington La
  Rostherne WA14 ....30 B6
  Weaverham CW8 ....102 B6
Millmead ST7 ....193 F7
Millport Cl WA2 ....9 A2
Millrace Dr CW2 ....206 B8
Mills Way CW1 ....173 B1
Millstone Ave ST7 ......194 E1
Millstone Cl SK12 ....36 F5
Millstone La CW5 ......204 F5
Millstone Pas SK11 ....112 E6
Millway Altrincham WA15 ..32 C7
  Waverton CH3 ....143 B5
Millway Rd L24 ....21 A4
Millwood WA7 ....24 C1
Millwood Dr CW11 ....174 A4
Millwood Ct 4 SK8 ......34 E8
Millwood Ct L24 ....21 A4
Millyard The CH4 ......162 C1
Milne Cl CW2 ....190 C1
Milner Cop CH60 ....41 A8
Milner Rd Heswall CH60 ..41 A8
  Northwich CW8 ....103 C6
Milner St WA5 ....15 F5
Milnthorpe Rd WA5 ......6 E6
Milton Ave Irlam M44 ....11 E6
  Newton-le-W WA12 ....2 B3
  Widnes WA8 ....22 F8
Milton Cl
  Higher Wincham CW9 ......80 A5
  Middlewich CW10 ....151 D5
Milton Cres ST7 ....210 C8
Milton Dr Poynton SK12 ..36 D4
  Wistaston CW2 ....206 A8
Milton Gr Helsby WA6 ....73 A1
  Warrington WA4 ....16 D3
Milton Rd Blacon CH1 ..117 F6
  Ellesmere Port CH65 ......70 D4
  Golborne WA3 ....3 D7
  Widnes WA8 ....23 A8
Milton Rough CW8 ......76 E2
Milton St Chester CH1 ..237 B3
  Widnes WA8 ....23 A5
Milton Way CW1 ....174 D6
Milvain Dr WA2 ....8 C1
Milverton Dr SK7 ....35 B5
Mimosa Cl CH2 ....72 C4
Mine Way WA11 ....1 F7
Miners Way Speke L24 ..21 A3
  Widnes WA8 ....13 D5
Minerva Ave CH1 ......117 E2
Minerva Cl WA7 ....24 D2
Minerva Ct CH1 ....117 E2
Minn-End-La SK11 ......159 B6
Minor Ave SK11 ....112 D3
Minshull La CW5,CW7 ..171 D4
Minshull New Rd CW1 ..189 F7
Minshull St WA16 ......57 A3
Minster Ct Runcorn WA7 ..48 E8
  Wistaston CW2 ....205 E8
Minster Dr WA14 ....31 A8
Minton Cl CW12 ....157 B1
Minton Way WA8 ....13 B5
Mirfield Cl WA3 ....3 D7
Mirion St CW1 ....190 C4
Mission Mews CH2 ......118 F2
Misty Cl WA8 ....12 C2
Mitchell Ave
  Burtonwood WA5 ....6 E5
  Kidsgrove ST7 ....194 D1
Mitchell Dr ST7 ....194 D1
Mitchell Fold SK10 ......63 D8
Mitchell St Golborne WA3 ..3 A8
  Warrington WA4 ....26 C8
Mithril Cl WA8 ....13 E3
Mitton Cl WA3 ....4 E5
Moat Ho 18 CW8 ......103 F8
Moat La Audley ST7 ....209 B3
  Hollins Green WA3 ....11 D1
Mobberley CE Prim Sch
  WA16 ....58 C5
Mobberley Rd
  Ashley WA14,WA15,WA16 ..31 E3
  Knutsford WA16 ....57 B3
  Wilmslow SK9 ....33 D1
  Mobberley Sta WA16 ....57 F7
Modgyn CH2 ....118 C4
Moelfre Dr SK8 ....35 C7
Moggie La SK10 ....36 F1
Mold Rd CH4 ....161 A8
Mold St CH4 ....78 B3
Mollington Ct CH1 ......94 F2
Mollington Rd M22 ......33 E8
Molly Pitcher Way WA5 ..15 B5
Molly Potts Cl WA16 ....82 B8
Molyneux Ave WA5 ......15 B6
Mona St CH1 ....237 B3
  Iriam M44 ....11 E6
Monarch Dr CW9 ......103 E5
Monck Dr CW5 ....204 D6
Mond Rd WA8 ....23 B8
Mond St CW8 ....78 B3
Monica Dr WA8 ....13 A5

Monk St CW1 ....190 A5
Monk's Heath Crossroads
  SK10 ....85 A1
Monk's La CW3 ....230 C5
Monks Coppenhall Prim Sch
  CW1 ....190 E7
Monks Gr CH65 ....70 B6
Monks Heath Hall Wrkshps
  SK10 ....85 B1
Monks La Acton CW5 ....203 F7
  Crewe CW1 ....189 F5
  Nantwich CW5 ....204 E5
Monks Orch CW5 ....204 F5
Monks St WA5 ....15 E6
Monks Way WA8 ....103 B4
Monkswood Cl WA5 ......7 E2
Monmouth Cl WA1 ......17 E7
Monroe Cl WA1 ....17 B8
Monsall Cl SK11 ....112 F7
Monsall Dr SK11 ....112 F7
Montana Cl WA5 ....15 C7
Montclare Cres WA4 ....16 F7
Montcliffe Cl WA3 ....9 C5
Montgomery Cl WA16 ..57 C4
Montgomery Rd WA8 ....22 D8
Montgomery Way CW7 ..149 B7
Montmorency Rd WA16 ..57 D3
Montpelier Ave WA7 ....48 F6
Montrose Cl
  Macclesfield SK10 ....87 A1
  Shavington CW2 ....206 B3
  Warrington WA2 ....8 F3
Montrose Ct Chester CH4 ..140 F7
  Holmes Chapel CW4 ....130 B2
Monument Rd ST7 ......210 D6
Monument View ST7 ..209 F2
Moody St CW12 ....156 D2
Moor Cl ST8 ....179 E1
Moor Cres CH4 ....139 D1
Moor Ho WA6 ....74 B8
Moor La Bramhall SK7 ....35 E3
  Elton WA6 ....72 E1
  Frodsham WA6 ....74 B8
  Heswall CH60 ....40 F8
  Higher Kinnerton CH4 ..161 D8
  Lower Kinnerton CH4 ....161 C6
  Sandycroft CH5 ....116 A2
  Waverton CH3 ....143 A5
  Widnes WA8 ....22 F7
Moor La S WA8 ....23 A7
Moor Lane Bsns Ctr WA8 ..23 A7
Moor St CW12 ....156 E2
Moor-Park Way CW9 ..103 F4
Moorcroft WA16 ....80 F3
Moorcroft Cres CH3 ....119 B1
Moorcroft Cres CH4 ....140 D6
Moordale Rd WA16 ......57 B2
Moorditch La
  Frodsham WA6 ....48 F1
  Frodsham WA6 ....48 F1
Moore Ave St Helens WA9 ..1 B3
  Warrington WA4 ....17 D3
  Widnes WA8 ....13 D2
Moore Cl WA8 ....13 D6
Moore Dr WA11 ....1 F6
Moore Gr WA13 ....19 B5
Moore La WA4 ....25 A5
Moore Prim Sch WA4 ....25 A5
Moorfield Cres WA3 ......4 A7
Moorfield Dr Neston CH64 ..41 C1
  Wilmslow SK9 ....59 E5
Moorfield Prim Sch WA8 ..13 D3
Moorfield Rd WA8 ....13 D3
Moorfields CW5 ....205 E6
Moorhead La CW11 ....154 D3
Moorhill Rd SK11 ......112 C4
Moorhouse Ave WA4 ..193 E4
Moorhouse Cl CH2 ......118 D5
Mooring Cl WA7 ....50 D6
Moorings Cl CH64 ......156 E1
Moorings The
  Christleton CH3 ....142 E7
  Disley SK12 ....38 E6
  Heswall CH60 ....40 C8
  Middlewich CW10 ....128 C1
  Moorland CH60 ....41 A7
Moorland Dr
  Cheadle Hulme SK8 ....34 F8
  Runcorn WA7 ....50 C7
Moorland Pk CH60 ......41 A7
Moorland Rd
  Biddulph ST8 ....179 D1
  Crewe CW2 ....190 A3
  Kidsgrove ST7 ....195 D7
Moorlands Ave CW8 ..102 A4
Moorlands Cl CW8 ......57 C3
Moorlands Dr CW5 ....206 A1
Moorlands Pk CW8 ....102 A4
Moors La CW7 ....149 D5
Moorsbrook Gr 9 SK9 ..34 E1
Moorsfield Ave CW3 ..229 F3
Moorside Ave CH64 ......66 C8
Moorside Cl WA8 ....22 F7
Moorside La Neston CH64 ..66 D8
  Pott Shrigley SK10 ....63 E4
Moorson Ave ST7 ......194 F8
Moorview Gdns ST7 ..195 E6
Moran Cl WA3 ....9 E3
Moran Cres SK11 ......112 A7
Moran Dr WA5 ....1 A1
Moran Rd SK11 ....112 B7
Morcott La L24 ....21 D2
Moresby Cl WA7 ....50 E7

Moreton Ave SK7 ....35 E5
Moreton Cl CW11 ....175 C7
Moreton Dr Alsager ST7 .193 C3
Handforth SK9 ....34 E3
Holmes Chapel CW4 ....130 B3
Poynton SK12 ....36 F4
Moreton Pl ST7 ....194 E6
Moreton Rd CW2 ....189 F3
Moreton St CW8 ....78 D1
Moreton Terr WA6 ....74 A8
Moreville Cl CW9 ....103 E3
Morgan Ave WA2 ....8 C2
Morgan Cl Blacon CH1 ..117 F6
Crewe CW2 ....190 A4
Morgans Way WA3 ......4 A8
Morland Ave
Bebington CH62 ....43 D6
Neston CH64 ....66 F7
Morley Cl CH2 ....119 F8
Morley Dr CW12 ....157 A1
Morley Green Rd SK9 ...33 C1
Morley Rd Runcorn WA7 .23 A1
Warrington WA4 ....16 A1
Morley St WA1 ....16 D6
Mornant Ave CW8 ......103 A3
Mornington Ave CH65 ..79 C7
Mornington Cl CW11 ...174 D7
Morphany La WA4 ......51 E6
Morreys La CW6 ....122 F7
Morris Ave WA4 ....16 F4
Morris Cl WA11 ....1 A5
Morris Dr CW8 ....77 D1
Morris Pk CW8 ....103 B4
Morrison Cl WA5 ....15 A5
Mort Ave WA4 ....17 A5
Mortimer Ave WA2 .....16 B8
Mortimer Dr CW11 .....175 C5
Mortlake Cl WA8 ....12 C3
Mortlake Cres CH3 .....119 A1
Morton Ave WA6 ....73 B8
Morton Cl WA5 ....15 C8
Morton Dr SK11 ....112 F3
Morton Gdns CH1 ......117 E4
Morton Rd Blacon CH1 ..117 E4
Runcorn WA7 ....50 D8
Morval Cres WA7 ......23 D1
Morven Cl WA2 ....8 E3
Mosedale Gr WA7 ......49 E5
Moseley Ave WA4 ......17 A3
Moses Ct CH1 ....237 C3
Moss Bank Bramhall SK7 .35 C5
Chester CH2 ....118 C4
Winsford CW7 ....126 C1
Moss Bank Rd WA8 ....23 D7
Moss Bower Rd SK11 ...112 C4
Moss Brow SK10 ....87 E7
Moss Brow La WA16 ...28 D4
Moss Cl Warrington WA4 .16 E2
Willaston CH64 ....68 A8
Moss Croft CW1 ....190 A8
Moss Dr Manley WA6 ...98 F4
Middlewich CW10 ......151 D6
Moss End La CW11 .....176 E8
Moss Farm Barns CW8 .102 D4
Moss Farm Recn Ctr
CW8 ....103 D8
Moss Fields Alsager ST7 .193 A3
Crewe CW1 ....173 A1
Moss Gate WA3 ....10 A5
Moss Gr Lymm WA13 ...19 B4
Newcastle-u-Lyme ST5 .210 D3
Saltney CH4 ....140 D6
Moss Green Way WA9 ..1 A1
Moss Hall La CW6 .....147 C4
Moss Hey Prim Sch SK7 .35 C5
Moss La Alderley Edge SK9 .60 B1
Bollington SK10 ....87 E8
Bramhall SK7 ....35 D5
Brereton Green CW12 ..154 F5
Byley CW10 ....129 B7
Congleton CW12 ....156 E6
Crewe CW1 ....173 A2
Cuddington CW8 ......102 A3
Fowley Common WA3 ..5 D5
Golborne WA3 ....3 C7
Harthill CH3,SY14 ....183 F1
High Legh WA16 ......29 E6
High Legh, Sink Moss WA16 .28 D4
Hollins Green WA3 ....10 E5
Irlam M44 ....11 D5
Lawton-gate ST7 ......194 F4
Lostock Green CW9 ...105 D8
Macclesfield SK11 ....112 C4
Manley WA6 ....79 A4
Mere WA16 ....56 C5
Mobberley WA16 ......58 F4
Moore WA4 ....25 A6
Mottram St Andrew SK10 .61 A2
Norbury SY13 ....215 C5
Norley WA6 ....101 B5
Northwich CW8 ......103 D7
Over Peover WA16 ...83 C3
Partington M31 ......11 F3
Partington WA13 .....11 B1
Partington WA13 .....20 B8
Sandbach CW11 .....174 C7
Siddington SK11 .....109 E2
St Helens,Moss Nook WA9 .1 A1
Styal SK9 ....33 E6
Tarporley CW6 ....146 B2
Warmingham CW11 ..173 C3
Wilmslow SK9 ....59 F7
Moss Lane Bsns Ctr
CW11 ....174 D6
Moss Lane Ind Est
CW11 ....174 D7
Moss Mere CW11 ....176 F7
Moss Pl ST7 ....195 B3

Moss Rd Alderley Edge SK9 .60 C2
Congleton CW12 ....178 F7
Irlam M44 ....11 C7
Northwich CW8 ....103 D8
Warrington WA4 ......17 A3
Moss Rose SK9 ....60 B2
Moss Rose Football Gnd
SK11 ....112 D4
Moss Side La
Antrobus CW9 ....53 D7
Hollinfare WA3 ....11 A2
Hollins Green WA3 ...10 F3
Moore WA4 ....24 F7
Moss Side Rd M44 ....11 E6
Moss Sq Crewe CW1 ..190 C4
Macclesfield SK11 ....112 D4
Moss St Weaverham CW8 .77 D1
Widnes WA8 ....23 D7
Moss Terr Warren SK11 .112 A1
Wilmslow SK9 ....60 F8
Winnington CW8 .....78 D1
Moss The CW9 ....78 D7
Moss View Rd SK11 ..112 A4
Moss Way ST7 ....193 A3
Mossdale Cl Crewe CW2 .189 E4
Warrington WA5 .....15 A7
Mossfield Cres 4 ST7 .195 B2
Mossford Ave CW1 ...190 B7
Mosshall La WA4 .....26 F1
Mosslands Cl CH66 ...69 E2
Mossley Ave CH62 ...43 D8
Mossley CE Prim Sch
CW12 ....179 B8
Mossley Ct CW12 ....178 F8
Mossley Garth Cl 4
CW12 ....157 A1
Mossvale CH66 ......69 D8
Mossways Pk SK9 ....59 C7
Mosswood Rd SK9 ...34 E1
Moston Ct 5 CW12 ..156 F3
Moston Gr WA13 ....18 D3
Moston Rd Chester CH2 .118 D8
Sandbach CW11 .....174 D6
Moston Way CW9 ...45 F8
Mostyn Ave CH60 ...40 C8
Mostyn Gdns CH64 ..41 B1
Mostyn House Sch CH64 .66 C8
Mostyn Pl CH1 ......117 E6
Mostyn Sq CH64 ....41 B1
Mote Hill Ct WA1 ...16 D6
Motherwell Cl WA8 ..12 E3
Mottershead 1 WA8 .23 A8
Mottershead Rd WA8 .23 A8
Mottram Cl
Middlewich CW10 ...151 B7
Warrington WA4 ....17 B3
Mottram Dr CW5 ...205 A4
Mottram Rd SK10 ...60 D1
Mottram St Andrew Prim Sch
SK10 ....61 B1
Mottram Way SK10 ..87 C2
Moughland La WA7 ..49 A8
Moulders La WA1 ...16 B4
Mouldsworth Cl 2 CW9 .103 E4
Mouldsworth Motor Mus*
CH3 ....98 E1
Mouldsworth Sta CH3 .99 A2
Moulton Cl
Knutsford WA16 ....57 C1
Northwich CW9 .....103 E4
Runcorn WA7 ....49 F4
Moulton Sch CW9 ...126 F8
Mount Ave CH60 ....40 F8
Mount Barns CH2 ...95 C6
Mount Ct CW5 ......204 F6
Mount Ct 3 CH60 ...40 F8
Mount Dr CW5 ......204 F6
Mount Farm Way CH66 .69 C2
Mount Mews CH60 ..40 F8
Mount Pl CW2 ......118 F2
Mount Pleasant
Audlem CW3 ....230 B4
Congleton CW12 ....156 C2
Crewe CW1 ....190 B6
Elton CH2 ....72 A4
Haslington CW1 ....191 D4
Kidsgrove ST7 .....195 A1
Macclesfield SK10 ..87 B1
Rainow SK10 ....88 D3
Widnes WA8 ....13 A1
Wilmslow SK9 .....60 B8
Mount Pleasant Ave WA9 .1 B3
Mount Pleasant Dr
CW7 ....149 A7
Mount Pleasant Rd
Davenham CW9 ....103 F2
The Bank ST7 ......195 B7
Mount Pleasant Residential
Pk CW4 ....130 D8
Mount Pleasent CH4 .140 F7
Mount Rd Kidsgrove ST7 .195 B2
Runcorn WA7 ......49 F8
Mount St WA8 .....13 A1
Mount Terr SK11 ...112 F7
Mount The
Altrincham,Hale WA15 .32 C8
Chester CH3 ....118 F1
Congleton CW12 ...156 A2
Great Budworth CW9 .79 A7
Heswall CH60 ......41 A8
Kidsgrove ST7 .....195 A1
Mount Way CH3 ...143 A4
Mountain View
Helsby WA6 ....73 B3
Saltney CH4 ....140 E6
Mountbatten Ct CW2 .190 A3

Mountbatten Way
CW12 ....156 E3
Mountfield Rd SK7 ...35 E5
Mourne Cl CH66 ......69 A6
Mow Cop Rd ST7 .....195 D6
Mow La
Mount Pleasant ST7 ..195 A5
Mow Cop ST7 ....179 B2
Mowcroft La WA5 ....14 B3
Mowpen Brow WA16 ..29 B6
Moxon Ave WA4 .....16 F5
Moyles Cl WA8 ......12 D2
Mudhouse La CH64 ..67 F2
Mudhurst La SK12 ...38 E3
Muir Rd CH1 ....117 E3
Muirfield Cl
Northwich CW9 ....104 A5
Warrington WA2 ...9 A3
Wilmslow SK9 .....60 D8
Muirfield Dr
Macclesfield SK10 ..87 D4
Winsford CW7 ......126 C2
Muirfield Mews CW7 .126 C2
Mulberry Ave WA3 ...3 F7
Mulberry Cl Elton CH2 .72 C3
Heald Green SK8 ...34 C7
Warrington WA1 ....17 E7
Mulberry Ct
Macclesfield SK11 ..112 D4
Warrington WA4 ...16 D1
Mulberry Dr SK10 ..87 E1
Mulberry Rd CW2 ..189 E2
Mulberry Rise CW8 .103 C7
Mulcaster Ct CW1 ..191 D5
Mull Cl CH65 ....70 C1
Mullein Cl WA3 ....3 D8
Mullen Cl WA5 .....7 F1
Mullins Ave WA12 ..2 C5
Mullion Cl Runcorn WA7 .50 A6
Mullion Gr WA2 ....9 A3
Mulsford Cl LL13 ..222 A8
Mulsford La LL13,SY14 ..222 B8
Murdishaw Ave WA7 .50 D6
Murdishaw West Com Prim
Sch WA7 ....50 D6
Muriel Cl WA5 .....24 A6
Murray Cl SK10 ...87 A1
Murrayfield Rd WA5 .87 A5
Murrayfield Dr CW5 .205 D5
Museum St WA1 ...16 A4
Music Hall Pass CH1 .237 B2
Mustard La WA3 ...4 B1
Myddleton La WA2 ..8 C6
Myrica Gr CH2 ....119 B3
Myrtle Ave Haydock WA11 .1 B7
Higher Kinnerton CH4 .161 A7
Newton-le-W WA12 ..2 C2
Myrtle Gr Warrington WA4 .16 D3
Widnes WA8 ....13 B1
Myrtle Rd M31 .....11 D3
Myrtle St Crewe CW2 .190 C3
Ellesmere Port CH65 .70 C7
Mythorne Ave WA4 .11 C3
Mytton Dr CW5 .....204 D6

N

Nab Cl SK10 ....63 C1
Nab La SK10 ....63 C1
Nabbs Cl ST7 ......195 B2
Nabbswood Rd ST7 .195 B2
Nairn Ave CW4 ....130 B2
Nairn Cl Bebington CH63 .43 D4
Warrington WA2 ...9 B3
Nancy View SK10 ..88 B8
Nansen Cl WA5 ...15 D7
Nansmoss La SK9 .33 D1
Nant Peris CH1 ...117 D3
Nantwich Mus * CW5 .204 E5
Nantwich Rd Audley ST7 .209 B1
Barbridge CW5 ....187 B8
Betley ST7 ....208 E1
Broxton CH3 ......183 C1
Crewe CW2 ....190 C2
Ellesmere Port CH66 .69 F3
Middlewich CW10 ..161 A7
Sound CW5 ....217 B5
Tarporley CW6 ....168 D7
Wimboldsley CW10 .150 F5
Wistaston CW2,CW5 .189 C2
Woore CW3 ....232 B1
Wrenbury CW5 ...201 E2
Nantwich Sta CW5 .204 F4
Nantwich Way SK9 .34 E5
Naomi Cl CH1 ....117 D5
Napier Gdns 3 ST7 .195 A2
Napier Rd CH2 ...118 C8
Napier St WA1 ....16 C5
Napley Dr ST7 ...236 C2
Napley Rd TF9 ...236 D1
Nares Cl WA5 ....7 C1
Narrow La
Crewe Green CW1 .191 C3
Wardsend SK10 ...37 A1
Naseby Rd CW12 .156 A3
Nat La CW7 ......126 D1
Nat Lane Ret Pk CW7 .126 F2
Nathan Dr WA11 .1 B7
Nathans Mdw CW12 .179 C7
Naughton Lea WA8 .12 D3
Naughton Rd 8 WA8 .23 A8
Navan Ct CW1 ...190 B5
Navigation Cl WA7 .50 A8
Navigation Ho 17 CW8 .103 F8
Navigation Rd CW8 .103 F7
Navigation St WA8 .16 D5

Naylor Ave WA3 ....3 B8
Naylor Cres
Ellesmere Port CH66 ..69 F8
Nantwich CW5 .....205 A4
Naylor Ct
Ellesmere Port CH66 ..69 E6
12 Northwich CW9 ...103 F8
Naylor Rd WA8 ....13 D1
Naylor St WA1 ....16 B5
Neal Ave SK8 .....34 A8
Neath Cl SK12 ....36 D5
Needham Cl WA7 ..23 D2
Needham Dr
Cranage CW4 ....130 A5
Hartford CW8 .....103 A4
Needhams Bank CW11 .174 C6
Needhams Wharf Cl
SK10 ....88 A1
Neil St WA8 .....13 C2
Neills Rd WA5 ...6 B6
Nelson Ave SK12 ..37 A3
Nelson Cl SK12 ..37 A3
Nelson Dr M44 ...11 E6
Nelson Gr ST7 ...193 F2
Nelson Ind Est ST7 .194 C1
Nelson Rd
Ellesmere Port CH65 .70 C7
Warrington,Birchwood WA3 .9 D4
Nelson St Chester CH1 .237 C3
Congleton CW12 ..156 C2
Crewe CW2 ......190 C2
Macclesfield SK11 .112 D7
Newton-le-W WA12 .2 A3
6 Runcorn WA7 ..23 A2
Widnes WA8 ....23 A6
Nemos Cl WA6 ..73 C2
Neptune Cl WA7 ..50 D7
Nesfield Cl CW11 .191 F7
Nesfield Dr CW11 .191 F7
Ness Acre La CH64 .67 E8
Ness Botanic Gdns*
CH64 ....67 A3
Ness Ho CH64 ..66 D8
Nessina Gr CW2 .205 F8
Neston Dr CH2 ...118 E5
Neston Gn CH66 .69 D4
Neston High Sch CH64 .41 F1
Neston Prim Sch CH64 .66 E7
Neston Rd
Heswall CH63,CH64 .41 F5
Neston CH64 ....67 B3
Willaston CH64 ..67 B3
Neston Road Cotts CH63 .42 A6
Neston St M11 ..11 E6
Neston Way SK9 .34 D3
Nether Alderley Mill*
SK10 ....85 A5
Nether Alderley Prim Sch
SK10 ....85 A6
Nether Fold SK10 ..87 A8
Nether Lea CW4 ...130 C8
Netherfield WA8 ..22 E8
Netherfields SK9 ..85 A8
Netherley Rd WA8 ..12 A2
Netherpool Rd CH66 .69 F8
Netherton Dr WA6 ..74 A7
Netherton Farm Cotts
WA6 ....74 A7
Neumann St CW9 ..104 B8
Nevada Cl WA5 ...15 C8
Neville Ave St Helens WA9 .1 B7
Warrington WA2 .8 D1
Neville Cres WA5 .15 A3
Neville Dr CH3 ..119 B1
Neville Rd Bebington CH62 .43 E8
Chester CH3 ....119 B1
Neville St Crewe CW2 .190 D1
Newton-le-W WA12 .2 D3
Nevin Cl SK0 ...36 A7
Nevin Rd CH1 ..117 D3
Nevis Dr CW2 ..189 D3
New Albert Terr WA7 .23 B3
New Bank Pl WA8 .12 B1
New Bank Rd WA8 .12 B1
New Barnet WA8 .12 F4
New Bridge Rd CH65,CH2 .70 F3
New Chester Rd
Bebington,Eastham CH62 .43 E7
Hooton CH62,CH66 .44 A2
New Cotts
Hampton Heath SY14 .213 C7
Manley WA6 .....99 C7
New Crane Bank CH1 .118 B1
New Crane St CH1 .118 B1
New Cut La WA4 ..17 B7
New Cut La WA1 ..17 B7
New Farm Cotts M44 .11 A7
New Farm Ct
Great Barrow CH3 .120 E5
Malpas SY14 ...213 A5
New Grosvenor Rd CH65 .70 C7
New Hall Ave WA5 .14 D3
New Hall La Culcheth WA3 .5 A2
Culcheth,Wigshaw WA3 .4 E1
New Hall St SK10 ..87 D1
New Hampshire Cl WA5 .15 B7
New Hey La CH64 ..68 A6
New Heyes CH64 ..41 E1
New Home Farm Cotts
CH64 ....67 A7
New Horwich Rd SK23 .65 E7
New Hos CW5 ...187 D6
New Houses CH3 .143 B7
New Inn Cotts WA11 .108 C8
New Inn La WA16 ..108 C8
New King St Audley ST7 .209 C1
Middlewich CW10 .128 C2

New La
Appleton Thorn WA4 ...27 B5
Churton CH3 ......180 F6
Croft WA3 ....9 B7
Harthill CH3 ......183 F3
Winsford CW7 ....149 F4
New Lane End WA3 ..4 A2
New Manchester Rd
WA1 ....17 A7
New Manor Rd WA4 ..51 B6
New Market Wlk 11 WA1 .16 B5
New Mills Central Sta
SK22 ....39 B7
New Mills Newtown Sta
SK22 ....39 B6
New Mills Prim Sch SK22 .39 B8
New Mills Sch & Sixth Form
Ctr SK22 ....39 C8
New Moss Rd M44 ..11 D6
New Pale Rd WA6 ..99 C6
New Park Ct SK22 ..39 D7
New Platt La CW4 ..107 B1
New Rd Anderton CW9 ..78 D4
Antrobus CW9 ....27 D1
Astbury CW12 ....178 B4
Audley ST7 ....209 E3
Duddon CW6 .....145 B6
Ellesmere Port CH66 ..69 E7
Lymm WA13 .....18 E3
Marton CW12 ....132 D1
Mere WA16 ......30 E3
Mossend CW11 ..154 F2
Prestbury SK10 ..87 A7
Warrington WA4 ..16 C4
Whaley Bridge SK23 ..65 E6
SK23 ....39 F1
Winsford CW7 ....126 E2
Wrenbury CW5 ..216 E5
New Russia Hall Craft Ctr*
CH3 ....165 E5
New School La CH66 ..44 B1
New St Congleton CW12 .156 E2
Haslington CW1 ..191 D4
Nantwich CW5 ...66 E5
New Mills SK22 ..39 D7
10 Runcorn WA7 .23 A2
Sandbach CW11 ..174 D7
Widnes WA8 .....23 B8
Wilmslow SK9 ...59 E5
New Street Cotts CW12 .157 A6
New Warrington Rd CW9 .79 C3
New York Cotts WA16 ..29 F2
Newall Ave CW1 ..175 A5
Newall Cl CH3 ...166 B1
Newall Cres CW7 ..127 A1
Newbiggin Way 10
SK10 ....112 C8
Newbold Ct 9 CW12 .156 F3
Newbold Way CW5 .204 E3
Newborough Cl WA5 ..7 E2
Newbridge Cl
Runcorn WA7 ....50 C6
Warrington WA5 ..7 D2
Newbridge Rd CH65 .70 F4
Newburgh Cl WA7 ..24 D1
Newbury Ave
Crewe CW1 ......190 C7
8 Winsford CW7 .149 A8
Newbury Cl
Cheadle Hulme SK8 ..35 A6
Widnes WA8 .....13 A3
Newbury Ct SK9 ..60 A6
Newbury Rd Chester CH4 .140 F6
Heald Green SK8 .34 C7
Newbury Way WA16 .57 C1
Newcastle Rd
Astbury CW12 ....178 A7
Brereton Green CW11 .153 F4
Congleton CW12 ..156 A2
Hassall Green CW11 .176 A3
Nantwich CW5 ...205 B4
Shavington CW2,CW5 .206 C3
Smallwood CW11 ..176 A3
Talke ST7 ....210 E7
Willaston CW5 ...205 E4
Woore CW3 ......232 E1
Newcastle Rd N CW11 .153 E5
Newcastle Rd S CW11 .153 E5
Newcastle Road Cvn Pk
WA3 ....4 E2
Newchurch Com Prim Sch
WA3 ....4 F2
Newcombe Ave WA2 ..16 E8
Newcroft CH1 ....94 B2
Newdigate St
Crewe CW1 ......190 C4
Crewe CW1 ......190 C4
Newfield Ct WA13 ..19 A5
Newfield Dr CW1 ..190 E6
Newfield Rd WA13 ..18 D3
Newfield St CW11 ..175 B7
Newfield Terr WA6 ..73 B2
Newgate CW5 ....204 F5
Newgate Rd SK9 ..59 D7
Newgate St CH1 ..237 B2
Newgate Wlk CH1 ..237 B2
Newhall Ct CH2 ..118 E6
Newhall La CW5 ..216 F6
Newhall St SK11 ..112 F3
Newhaven Rd WA2 ..8 B4

Newland Cl WA8 . . . . .12 C3
Newland Mews WA3 . . . . . .4 E5
Newland Way CW5 . . . . .205 B4
Newlands Ave
 Bramhall SK7 . . . . .35 F8
 Cheadle Hulme SK8 . . . . . .35 A7
Newlands Cl
 Cheadle Hulme SK8 . . . . . . .35 A7
 Frodsham WA6 . . . . .74 C6
Newlands Dr Golborne WA3 .3 D8
 Wilmslow SK9 . . . . .59 E5
Newlands Rd
 Macclesfield SK10 . . . . . . .111 E7
 Warrington WA4 . . . . .16 F2
Newlyn Ave
 Congleton CW12 . . . . .178 F8
 Macclesfield SK10 . . . . .86 D1
Newlyn Cl WA7 . . . . .50 B6
Newlyn Gdns WA5 . . . . . . .14 D3
Newman Cl CW12 . . . . . .156 B3
Newman St WA4 . . . . .16 F3
Newman's La CW5 . . . . . .219 D8
Newmarket Cl ⬛ SK10 . . .87 C4
Newmoore La WA7 . . . . . .24 F4
Newnham Dr CH65 . . . . . .70 C4
Newport Gr ST5 . . . . .210 E2
Newquay Cl WA7 . . . . .50 B6
Newquay Ct CW12 . . . . . .178 E8
Newquay Dr Bramhall SK7 .35 F7
 Macclesfield SK10 . . . . . . .111 D8
Newry Ct CH2 . . . . .118 D4
Newry Pk CH2 . . . . .118 D4
Newry Pk E CH2 . . . . .118 D4
Newsham Cl WA8 . . . . .12 B4
Newsholme Cl WA3 . . . . . . .4 F3
Newspaper Ho WA5 . . . . . .14 D3
Newstead Cl SK12 . . . . . . .36 D5
Newstead Rd WA8 . . . . . . .21 F6
Newtech Sq CH5 . . . . .92 F2
Newton Ave WA3 . . . . .9 E5
Newton Bank
 Middlewich CW10 . . . . . . .128 B1
 Preston on t H WA4 . . . . . . .51 B8
Newton Bank Sch WA12 . .2 E4
Newton Comm Hospl
 WA12 . . . . .2 B2
Newton Cotts CH3 . . . . . .166 C4
Newton Gr WA2 . . . . .8 F3
Newton Hall CH2 . . . . . . .118 F5
Newton Hall Ct CH2 . . . .118 F5
Newton Hall Dr CH2 . . . . .118 F5
Newton Hall La WA16 . . . .58 E5
Newton Hall Mews ⬛
 CW10 . . . . .151 C8
Newton Heath CW10 . . . .128 B1
Newton Ho CH2 . . . . .118 F5
Newton Hollow WA6 . . . . .74 D1
Newton La Chester CH2 . .118 A4
 Daresbury WA4 . . . . .51 C8
 Daresbury WA4 . . . . .51 E7
 Golborne WA12 . . . . .22 E6
 Tattenhall CH3 . . . . .166 D4
Newton Park Dr WA12 . . .2 F3
Newton Park View CH2 . .118 D4
Newton Pl CW12 . . . . .156 F2
Newton Prim Sch CH2 . .118 E4
Newton Rd
 Ellesmere Port CH65 . . . . . .70 C5
 Golborne,Lowton Common
 WA3,WN7 . . . . .4 A8
 Golborne,Town of Lowton
 WA12,WA3 . . . . .3 D5
 Handforth SK9 . . . . .34 A1
 St Helens WA9 . . . . .1 A3
 Winwick WA2 . . . . .8 A5
Newton St Crewe CW1 . . .190 D5
 Macclesfield SK11 . . . . . . .112 C7
**Newton-le-Willows Com
 High Sch** WA12 . . . . .2 D3
Newton-le-Willows Prim Sch
 WA12 . . . . .2 D3
Newton-le-Willows Sta
 WA12 . . . . .2 E3
Newtons Cres CW11 . . . .191 F7
Newtons Gr CW11 . . . . . .191 E7
Newtons La CW11 . . . . . .191 E7
Newtown Kidsgrove ST7 . .195 F2
 Neston CH64 . . . . .66 F7
Newtown Cl CH1 . . . . .237 B3
Newtown Prim Sch SK22 .39 B6
Nicholas Ave CW9 . . . . . .104 C6
Nicholas Ct CH1 . . . . .237 A2
Nicholas Rd
 Weaverham CW8 . . . . .77 D1
 Widnes WA8 . . . . .22 C8
Nicholas St CH1 . . . . .237 A2
Nicholas St Mews CH1 . .237 A2
Nicholls St WA4 . . . . .17 B2
Nicholson Ave SK10 . . . . .87 E1
Nicholson Cl SK10 . . . . . .87 E1
Nicholson St WA1 . . . . . . .15 F5
Nicklety Rd SK12 . . . . . . .36 E3
Nickleford Hall Dr WA8 . .12 F6
Nickolson Cl CH2 . . . . . . .119 F8
Nicol Ave WA1 . . . . .17 F8
Nidderdale Cl CW12 . . . .157 A5
Niddries Ct CW9 . . . . .126 F7
Niddries La CW9 . . . . . . .126 F7
Nield Ct CH2 . . . . .118 D7
Nigel Gresley Cl CW1 . . .191 A4
Nigel Rd CH60 . . . . .41 C8
Nigel Wlk WA7 . . . . .24 A2
Nightingale Cl
 Farndon CH3 . . . . .180 F1
 Handforth SK9 . . . . .34 B1

Nightingale Cl continued
 Middlewich CW10 . . . . . . .151 D6
 Runcorn WA7 . . . . .49 F5
 Warrington WA3 . . . . .9 F4
Nightingale Ct 4 CW7 . .149 D6
Nightingale Way ST7 . . .193 B3
Nile St CW2 . . . . .190 C2
Nine Hos The CH3 . . . . . .166 B1
Nixon Dr CW7 . . . . .126 B2
Nixon Rd CW8 . . . . .101 F3
Nixon St Crewe CW1 . . . .189 F5
 Macclesfield SK11 . . . . . . .112 B8
Nixon's Row CW5 . . . . . .204 C5
No 1 Road N CW2 . . . . . .192 F1
No 1 Road S CW2 . . . . . . .192 F1
No 156 CH1 . . . . .237 C2
No 2 Road N CW2 . . . . . .192 F1
No 2 Road S CW2 . . . . . . .192 F1
Noahs Ark La WA16 . . . . .58 F1
Noble Cl WA3 . . . . .9 E3
Nook La Antrobus CW9 . . .53 E6
 Golborne WA3 . . . . .3 B8
 Warrington WA4 . . . . .17 A3
 Warrington, Fearnhead WA2 .9 B2
Nook The Backford CH1 . . .95 B4
 Bramhall SK7 . . . . .35 D5
 Chester CH2 . . . . .118 E4
 Guilden Sutton CH3 . . . . . .119 C4
 Saltney CH4 . . . . .140 E6
Noon Cl WA12 . . . . .2 B1
Noonsun Farm WA16 . . . .58 E1
Nora St WA1 . . . . .16 C5
Norbreck Ave CW2 . . . . .190 B2
Norbreck Cl WA5 . . . . .15 A4
Norbury Ave WA2 . . . . . . .16 D8
Norbury Cl Hough CW2 . .206 E3
 Knutsford WA16 . . . . .57 C3
 Widnes WA8 . . . . .13 E1
Norbury Dr
 Congleton CW12 . . . . .156 E4
 Macclesfield SK10 . . . . . . .151 B8
Norbury Hollow Rd SK7 . .37 B8
Norbury St
 Macclesfield SK11 . . . . . . .112 C7
 Northwich CW9 . . . . .104 B8
Norbury Town La SY13 . .215 C3
Norbury Way ⑨ SK9 . . . .34 D5
Norcott Ave WA4 . . . . .16 D2
Norcott Dr WA5 . . . . .6 F6
Norden Cl WA3 . . . . .9 C5
Norfolk Cl M44 . . . . .11 C5
Norfolk Dr WA5 . . . . .14 E6
Norfolk Gr ST8 . . . . .179 C1
Norfolk Ho ST7 . . . . .210 D6
Norfolk House Prep Sch
 CW11 . . . . .175 B7
Norfolk Pl WA8 . . . . .22 C8
Norfolk Rd Chester CH2 .118 F4
 Congleton CW12 . . . . .156 E4
 Ellesmere Port CH65 . . . . . .70 C5
 Kidsgrove ST7 . . . . .194 F2
Norfolk St WA7 . . . . .23 B3
Norfolk Wlk SK10 . . . . . . .86 F2
Norgrove Cl WA7 . . . . .50 E8
Norland St WA8 . . . . .13 D1
Norland's La L35,WA8 . . .22 F7
Norlands Pk WA8 . . . . . . .12 F6
Norleane Cres WA7 . . . . . .49 B8
Norley Ave
 Bebington CH62 . . . . .43 E3
 Ellesmere Port CH65 . . . . . .69 F6
Norley CE Prim Sch
 WA6 . . . . .100 F5
Norley Cl WA5 . . . . .15 E6
Norley Dr CH3 . . . . .119 C1
Norley La CW8 . . . . .101 A8
Norley Pl CW9 . . . . .103 E5
Norley Rd
 Cuddington CW8,WA6 . . . .101 E4
 Kingsley WA6 . . . . .75 A1
 Norley WA6 . . . . .100 D7
Norman Ave Haydock WA11 .1 F7
 Newton-le-W WA12 . . . . .2 E3
Norman Cl CH66 . . . . .94 F8
Norman Dr CW7 . . . . .149 C6
Norman Ho ⑧ CW8 . . . .103 C5
Norman Rd WA7 . . . . .23 A1
Norman St WA2 . . . . .16 B6
Norman Way CH1 . . . . . . .117 B5
Norman's La WA4 . . . . . . .52 F4
Normanby Cl WA5 . . . . . . .15 E7
Normandy Ave ⑦ CW7 . .149 D8
Normandy Rd CW2 . . . . . .95 C1
Normans Cotts ⬛ CH4 . .66 F7
Norreys Ave WA5 . . . . . . .15 F8
Norris Rd CH1 . . . . .117 E5
Norris St WA2 . . . . .16 D6
North Ave WA2 . . . . .16 B8
North Brook Rd CW6 . . . .146 B7
North Cheshire Hospl
 WA4 . . . . .26 D2
North Crofts CW5 . . . . . . .204 E5
North Downs WA16 . . . . . .57 D2
North Dr Heswall CH60 . . .41 A7
 High Legh WA16 . . . . .29 C4
 Northwich CW9 . . . . .104 E7
North Florida Rd WA11 . . .1 D8
North Gn CH5 . . . . .116 A6
North Par CH64 . . . . .41 B2
North Park Brook Rd WA5 .7 E3
North Rd Altrincham WA15 .32 A8
 Ellesmere Port CH65 . . . . . .44 E3
 Connah's Quay CH5 . . . . . .91 E2
 Ellesmere Port CH65 . . . . . .70 B8
 Halewood L26 . . . . .21 A5
North St Chester CH3 . . . .119 A1
 Congleton CW12 . . . . .156 D3
 Crewe CW1 . . . . .190 C7

North St continued
 Haydock WA11 . . . . .1 E6
 Mount Pleasant ST7 . . . . . .195 B6
 Newton-le-W WA12 . . . . . . .1 F4
 Saltney CH4 . . . . .140 B7
 Sandycroft CH5 . . . . .116 A3
North Stafford St CW1 . .190 D4
North View Crewe CW1 . .190 A6
 Ellesmere Port CH66 . . . . . .69 C7
 Middlewich CW10 . . . . . . .128 B2
 Warrington WA5 . . . . .14 E7
North Way
 Holmes Chapel CW4 . . . . . .130 C3
 Shavington CW2 . . . . .206 D5
Northbank Ind Pk M44 . . .11 F6
Northbank Wlk CW2 . . . .206 C8
Northbury Rd CH66 . . . . . .69 E1
Northcote Rd SK7 . . . . . . .35 F7
Northdale Rd WA1 . . . . . . .17 A8
Northern La WA8 . . . . .12 A3
Northern Pathway CH4 .237 C1
Northern Rise CH66 . . . . . .69 E4
Northfield Dr
 Biddulph ST8 . . . . .179 E2
 Wilmslow SK9 . . . . .60 B8
Northfield Pl CW2 . . . . . .206 C5
Northfields WA16 . . . . .57 C3
Northgate CW6 . . . . .146 B7
Northgate Ave
 Chester CH2 . . . . .237 B4
 Macclesfield SK10 . . . . .87 C1
Northgate Row CH1 . . . .237 B2
Northgate St CH1 . . . . . . .237 A3
Northlands CW3 . . . . .232 C1
Northolt Ct WA2 . . . . .8 E1
Northumberland Rd M31 .11 E2
Northward Rd SK9 . . . . . . .59 F6
Northway Chester CH4 . . .141 A7
 Lymm WA13 . . . . .18 D4
 Runcorn WA7 . . . . .49 F8
 Warrington WA2 . . . . .8 B2
 Widnes WA8 . . . . .12 D1
 Winnington CW8 . . . . .78 D1
Northwich Rd
 Allostock CW4,WA16 . . . . .106 E1
 Antrobus CW9 . . . . .53 B2
 Dutton WA4 . . . . .51 B2
 Great Budworth CW9 . . . . . .78 F8
 Knutsford WA16 . . . . .56 D1
 Runcorn, Brookvale WA7 . . .50 C5
 Weaverham CW8 . . . . .102 E7
Northwich Ret Pk CW9 . .79 C1
Northwich Sta CW9 . . . . .104 B8
Northwood Ave
 Middlewich CW10 . . . . . . .151 C5
 Newton-le-W WA12 . . . . . . .2 F3
Northwood La WA16 . . . . .28 F1
Northwood Rd WA7 . . . . . .23 E2
Norton Ave Saltney CH4 .140 D6
 Warrington WA5 . . . . .14 E5
Norton Cotts WA7 . . . . . . .50 E7
Norton Gate WA7 . . . . .50 C8
Norton Hill WA7 . . . . .24 C2
Norton La Runcorn WA7 . .50 B8
 Runcorn, Norton WA7 . . . . .24 D1
 Runcorn, Town Park WA7 . . .50 A8
Norton Priory Mus*
 WA7 . . . . .24 E8
Norton Priory Walled Gdn*
 WA7 . . . . .24 B3
Norton Rd CH3 . . . . .119 C2
Norton St SK10 . . . . .112 E8
Norton Station Rd WA7 . .50 D8
Norton View WA7 . . . . .50 A8
Norton Village WA7 . . . . . .24 D1
Norton Way CW11 . . . . . .174 D7
Norton's La CH3 . . . . .98 B2
Norton-in-Hales CE Prim Sch
 TF9 . . . . .236 C2
Nortons La CW6 . . . . .122 E7
Nortonwood La WA7 . . . . .24 C1
Norville CH66 . . . . .69 D7
Norwich Ave WA3 . . . . .3 D8
Norwich Dr CH66 . . . . .94 E8
Norwood Ave
 Bramhall SK7 . . . . .35 D5
 Golborne WA3 . . . . .3 F7
 Warrington WA5 . . . . .14 E6
Norwood Dr CH4 . . . . . . .141 B6
Nottingham Cl WA1 . . . . . .17 E6
Nun House Cl CW7 . . . . . .127 B2
Nun House Dr CW7 . . . . .127 B2
Nuns Rd CH1 . . . . .237 A1
Nunsmere Cl CW7 . . . . . .127 B1
Nursery Ave WA15 . . . . . .31 E8
Nursery Cl St Crewe CW2 .190 A2
 Kidsgrove ST7 . . . . .194 D1
 Shavington CW2 . . . . .206 C3
 Widnes WA8 . . . . .13 D3
Nursery Dr Biddulph ST8 .179 C2
 Poynton SK12 . . . . .36 D4
Nursery Gr M31 . . . . .11 F4
Nursery La
 Congleton CW12 . . . . .156 E2
 Nether Alderley SK10 . . . . .84 D5
 Siddington SK11 . . . . .110 A3
 Wilmslow SK9 . . . . .59 F5
Nursery Pk WA6 . . . . .100 B7
Nursery Rd Barnton CW8 . .78 B3
 Wilmslow SK9 . . . . .59 F5
Nursery The CW8 . . . . . . .103 C6
Nutfield Ave CW1 . . . . . . .190 B7
Nuthurst Gdns 4 CW5 . .204 F5
Nuttall Ct WA3 . . . . .9 C4
Nuttall St M44 . . . . .11 E6

O

O'Connell Cl WA11 . . . . . .1 C6
O'leary St WA2 . . . . .16 C7
Oak Ave Alsager ST7 . . . .193 E2
 Disley SK12 . . . . .39 A6
 Golborne WA3 . . . . .3 B8
 Haydock WA11 . . . . .1 E7
 Irlam M44 . . . . .11 D5
 Macclesfield SK11 . . . . . . .112 A5
 Newton-le-W WA12 . . . . .2 D3
 Wilmslow SK9 . . . . .59 F5
 Winsford CW7 . . . . .149 D7
Oak Bank SK12 . . . . .39 A6
Oak Bank Cl CW5 . . . . . .205 E4
Oak Bank Dr SK10 . . . . . .63 B1
Oak Bank La CH2 . . . . . . .119 C6
Oak Brow Cotts SK9 . . . . .33 E4
Oak Cl SK9 . . . . .59 F6
Oak Cotts Styal SK9 . . . . . .33 E4
 Wrenbury CW5 . . . . .216 F4
Oak Dr Cheadle Hulme SK7 .35 C7
 Higher Kinnerton CH4 . . . .161 A7
 Middlewich CW10 . . . . . . .151 D7
 Runcorn WA7 . . . . .49 C7
 Scholar Green ST7 . . . . . . .194 E6
Oak Farm CW6 . . . . .186 C5
Oak Gr
 Ellesmere Port CH65 . . . . . .70 A3
 Nantwich CW5 . . . . .204 E3
 Poynton SK12 . . . . .36 D4
 Oak Grove Sch SK8 . . . . . .34 C7
Oak Ho 7 CW11 . . . . . . .175 B6
Oak House La CW7 . . . . .149 B8
Oak La Astbury CW12 . . . .178 B4
 Cuddington CW8 . . . . .101 F2
 Kerridge SK10 . . . . .88 A6
 Marton SK11 . . . . .133 C5
 Wilmslow SK9 . . . . .59 F6
Oak Lea Ave WA16 . . . . . .60 A5
Oak Lo SK7 . . . . .35 F7
Oak Mdw CW8 . . . . .102 F7
Oak Mews SK9 . . . . .34 C1
Oak Rd Chelford SK11 . . . .84 A3
 Chester CH4 . . . . .140 F5
 Hooton CH66 . . . . .43 E1
 Lymm WA13 . . . . .18 C3
 Morley Green WA16 . . . . . .59 B5
 Mottram St Andrew SK10 . .86 B7
 Partington M31 . . . . .11 D2
 Warrington WA5 . . . . .14 F3
Oak St Crewe CW2 . . . . . .190 D3
 Croft WA3 . . . . .9 A8
 Ellesmere Port CH65 . . . . . .70 C7
 Northwich CW9 . . . . .79 A1
 Rode Heath ST7 . . . . .193 E8
 Sandbach CW11 . . . . .174 D8
Oak Tree Cl CW1 . . . . . . .190 F5
Oak Tree Ct CW6 . . . . . . .122 E2
Oak Tree Dr CW1 . . . . . . .190 F5
Oak Tree Gate CW3 . . . . .229 F3
Oak Tree La CW10 . . . . . .129 E7
Oak View Knutsford WA16 . .57 C1
 Marton SK11 . . . . .133 C5
 Sandbach CW11 . . . . .21 A3
Oak Villas CW5 . . . . .216 F4
Oak Wood Rd WA16 . . . . . .29 F2
Oakdale Ave
 Frodsham WA6 . . . . .74 D6
 Warrington WA4 . . . . .16 D1
Oakdale Cl
 Broughton CH4 . . . . .139 B3
 Chorlton CW2 . . . . .207 B3
Oakdene Ave
 Ellesmere Port CH66 . . . . . .69 C5
 Heald Green SK8 . . . . .34 B8
 Warrington WA1 . . . . .17 C7
Oakdene Cl CH62 . . . . .43 D5
Oakdene Way CW6 . . . . .168 D8
Oakenbank La SK10 . . . . . .88 D7
Oakenclough Cl SK9 . . . . .34 D2
Oakenclough Prim Sch
 SK9 . . . . .34 D1
Oakes Cnr CW5 . . . . .219 E3
Oakfield Ave
 Chester CH2 . . . . .118 E8
 Knutsford WA16 . . . . .57 C3
 Wrenbury CW5 . . . . .216 F3
Oakfield Cl
 Alderley Edge SK9 . . . . .60 B3
 Bramhall SK7 . . . . .35 E4
 Wrenbury CW5 . . . . .216 F3
Oakfield Com Prim Sch
 WA8 . . . . .22 B8
Oakfield Dr Chester CH2 .118 E8
 Widnes WA8 . . . . .22 A8
Oakfield Rd
 Alderley Edge SK9 . . . . .60 B2
 Bebington CH62 . . . . .43 C8
 Blacon CH1 . . . . .117 D4
 Ellesmere Port CH66 . . . . . .68 E8
 Plumley WA16 . . . . .80 F3
 Poynton SK12 . . . . .36 F4
Oakfield Rise CW4 . . . . . .130 B3
Oakfield Terr CH66 . . . . . .68 E8
Oakfold SK10 . . . . .88 A6
Oakhill Cl SK10 . . . . .87 B4
Oakhurst Chase SK9 . . . . .60 A2
Oakhurst Dr CW2 . . . . . . .206 B3
Oakland Ave CW1 . . . . . .191 C4
Oakland Ct SK12 . . . . .36 D4
Oakland St
 Warrington WA1 . . . . .16 C7
 Widnes WA8 . . . . .23 A4
Oaklands CH3 . . . . .119 F4
Oaklands Ave CH3 . . . . . .166 B2
Oaklands Cl SK9 . . . . .34 E1

Oaklands Com Inf Sch
 SK9 . . . . .34 E1
Oaklands Cres CH3 . . . . .166 B2
Oaklands Dr WA13 . . . . . .18 D2
Oaklands Rd Golborne WA3 . .3 F7
 Ollerton WA16 . . . . .82 F6
Oaklands Sch CW7 . . . . .149 B7
Oaklea Ave CH2 . . . . .118 F4
Oakleaf Lodge SK11 . . . .112 D5
Oakleigh WA16 . . . . .82 C7
Oakleigh Ct CW12 . . . . . .155 F3
Oakleigh Ho SK10 . . . . . . .88 B8
Oakleigh Rd SK8 . . . . .34 E8
Oakleigh Rise CW8 . . . . . .78 E1
Oakley Cl CW11 . . . . .175 A8
Oakley Ct CH65 . . . . .70 C4
Oakley St CW1 . . . . .190 C5
Oakmere Barns CW8 . . . .124 A7
Oakmere Cl CW11 . . . . . .174 F7
Oakmere Dr Chester CH3 .142 B8
 Ellesmere Port CH66 . . . . . .69 F1
 Warrington WA5 . . . . .14 F3
Oakmere Hall CW8 . . . . . .101 C1
Oakmere Pl CW11 . . . . . .190 B5
Oakmere Rd
 Handforth SK9 . . . . .34 D5
 Winsford CW7 . . . . .149 B8
Oakmere St 8 WA7 . . . . .23 A2
Oakmoore WA7 . . . . .24 F4
Oaks Com Prim Sch The
 CH65 . . . . .70 D3
Oaks Dr The CH2 . . . . . . .118 D7
Oaks Pk WA8 . . . . .23 A7
Oaks The
 Alderley Edge SK9 . . . . .60 A2
 Bebington CH62 . . . . .43 C8
 Goostrey CW4 . . . . .130 D8
 Mobberley WA16 . . . . .58 E1
 5 Northwich CW9 . . . . . . .103 E6
Oaksway CH60 . . . . .41 C6
Oakthorn Gr WA11 . . . . . . .1 C6
Oaktree Cl Barnton CW8 . .78 B4
 Tarporley CW6 . . . . .146 D2
Oaktree Ct CH2 . . . . .119 A3
Oaktree La ST7 . . . . .210 D5
Oakways WA4 . . . . .26 D4
Oakwood Ave
 Warrington WA1 . . . . .16 E7
 Wilmslow SK9 . . . . .59 E6
Oakwood Avenue Com Prim
 Sch WA1 . . . . .16 D7
Oakwood Cl CH66 . . . . . . .69 D1
Oakwood Cres
 Crewe CW2 . . . . .189 E4
 Sandbach CW11 . . . . .175 E6
Oakwood Ct WA14 . . . . . . .31 B8
Oakwood Dr SK10 . . . . . . .87 C6
Oakwood Gate WA3 . . . . . .3 F7
Oakwood Ho
 Alderley Edge SK9 . . . . .85 B8
 Barnton CW8 . . . . .78 A2
Oakwood La
 Altrincham WA14 . . . . .31 B8
 Barnton CW8 . . . . .78 A2
 Sandbach CW11 . . . . .174 B8
Oakwood Pk CH62 . . . . . . .43 E8
Oakwood Rd Disley SK12 .38 D6
 Rode Heath ST7 . . . . .193 F8
Oakworth Cl CW12 . . . . . .156 A3
Oat Market 3 CW5 . . . . .204 E5
Oathills Cl CH6 . . . . .146 D1
Oathills Dr CW6 . . . . .146 D1
Oathills Lea CW6 . . . . . . .146 D1
Oatlands SK9 . . . . .34 D2
Oban Dr CH60 . . . . .41 A8
Oban Gr WA2 . . . . .9 A3
Obelisk Way CW12 . . . . . .156 C3
Oddfellows Pas CW10 . . .128 B1
Odeon Bldg CH1 . . . . .237 A3
Off Leys CW10 . . . . .128 C2
Offal Pit La WA6 . . . . .100 B5
Offley Inf Sch CW11 . . . .175 B7
Offley Jun Sch CW11 . . . .175 B7
Offley Rd CW11 . . . . .175 B7
Ogden Rd SK7 . . . . .35 D5
Oglet La L24 . . . . .46 E8
Oil Sites Rd CH65 . . . . .71 C5
Okell St WA7 . . . . .23 A2
Old Alder La WA2,WA5 . . . .7 F6
Old Applecroft CW11 . . . .174 C5
Old Boston WA11 . . . . .2 A7
Old Boston Trad Est WA11 .2 B8
Old Brickworks Ind Est
 SK10 . . . . .63 E4
Old Butt La ST7 . . . . .194 D2
Old Cherry La WA13 . . . . .28 A7
Old Chester Ct CW5 . . . .187 D6
Old Chester Rd
 Barbridge CW5 . . . . .187 D6
 Ellesmere Port CH66 . . . . . .69 D4
 Helsby WA6 . . . . .73 C4
 Higher Walton WA4 . . . . . . .25 F7
Old Church Cl CH65 . . . . . .70 C7
Old Coach Rd
 Brown Knowl SY14,CH3 . . .199 B6
 Kelsall CW6 . . . . .122 D5
 Runcorn WA7 . . . . .22 F3
Old Constabulary The ⬛
 CW5 . . . . .204 D5
Old Court Ho The ⑨
 WA16 . . . . .57 A2
Old Creamery The CW5 .217 A3
Old Farm Cl
 Macclesfield SK10 . . . . .87 A2
 Willaston CH64 . . . . .68 A8
Old Farm Cotts CH1 . . . .116 A3
Old Farm Mews SK8 . . . . .35 C7

Old Foundary Est WA8 . . . . .23 B7
Old Gate CI CW10 . . . . . . .151 B7
Old Gorse CI CW2 . . . . . . .189 E3
Old Hall CI WA4 . . . . .26 A8
Old Hall Cres SK9 . . . . .34 E3
Old Hall Ct
 Ashton Hayes CH3 . . . . . .121 F7
 Malpas SY14 . . . . .213 B3
Old Hall Dr
 Ellesmere Port CH65 . . . . . .70 B4
 Whaley Bridge SK23 . . . . . .65 E4
Old Hall Gdns CH2 . . . . . .237 C4
Old Hall La Elton CH2 . . . . . .72 B3
 Over Tabley WA16 . . . . .55 E4
 Woodford SK7 . . . . .35 D1
Old Hall Pk CH3 . . . . .119 F5
Old Hall PI CH1 . . . . .237 A2
Old Hall Rd
 Northwich CW9 . . . . .104 A5
 Warrington WA5 . . . . .15 D7
Old Hall St SK10 . . . . .87 D1
Old Hey Wlk WA12 . . . . .2 C1
Old Higher Rd WA8 . . . . . . .21 D5
Old Hutte La L26 . . . . .21 A6
Old Knutsford Rd ST7 . . .194 A6
Old La Acton Bridge CW8 . . .76 F3
 Antrobus CW9 . . . . .53 C3
 Davenham CW9 . . . . .104 D2
 Heswall CH60 . . . . .41 D8
 Pulford CH4 . . . . .162 E2
Old Liverpool Rd WA5 . . . .15 E4
Old Man of Mow* ST7 . . . .195 D8
Old Market PI 7 WA16 . . .57 A2
Old Marsh Farm Ho
 CH5 . . . . .116 A8
Old Mill CI Heswall CH60 . .41 B7
 Lymm WA13 . . . . .19 C6
Old Mill Ct CH2 . . . . .118 D6
Old Mill Dr
 Hazel Grove SK7 . . . . .37 A8
 Higher Whitley WA4 . . . . . .52 F3
 Macclesfield SK11 . . . . . . .112 E6
Old Mill PI CH3 . . . . .166 B1
Old Mill Rd CW11 . . . . . . .175 C6
Old Mill The CH66 . . . . .69 C7
Old Moss La
 Fowley Common WA3 . . . . . .5 E6
 Tarvin CH3 . . . . .144 D7
Old Newcastle Rd CW5 . . .205 D4
Old Orch SK9 . . . . .60 A7
Old Orchard The
 Antrobus CW9 . . . . .53 C4
 Cuddington CW8 . . . . . . .101 F4
Old Paddock The CW4 . . .130 F8
Old Pale Cotts CW8 . . . . .123 C7
Old Park Rd CW1 . . . . .207 D8
Old Pearl La CH3 . . . . . . .119 B1
Old Pewterspear La WA4 . .24 E4
Old Pump Ho The CH66 . . .68 E8
Old Quay CI CH64 . . . . .66 C7
Old Quay La CH64 . . . . .66 D7
Old Quay St WA7 . . . . .23 B3
Old Rd Anderton CW9 . . . . .78 D3
 Audley ST7 . . . . .209 E3
 Handforth SK9 . . . . .34 D3
 Warrington WA4 . . . . .16 B4
 Whaley Bridge SK23 . . . . . .65 F3
 Whaley Bridge, New Horwich
 SK23 . . . . .65 E6
 Whaley Bridge,Furness Vale
 SK23 . . . . .39 D4
 Wilmslow SK9 . . . . .60 B8
Old School CI
 Barnton CW8 . . . . .78 B2
 Farndon CH3 . . . . .180 E2
 Kidsgrove ST7 . . . . .195 A1
 Neston CH64 . . . . .66 F5
Old School Ho The
 CW1 . . . . .190 A5
Old School House La WA2 . .8 A7
Old School La SK8 . . . . . . .35 A8
Old Smithy La WA13 . . . . . .18 C2
Old Stack Yd CH3 . . . . . . .120 E6
Old Tannery CW5 . . . . . . .204 F6
Old Upton La WA8 . . . . .12 E4
Old Vicarage Gdn CW3 . . .230 A3
Old Vicarage La CW8 . . . .103 C5
Old Vicarage Rd CH64 . . . .68 A8
Old Wargrave Rd WA12 . . . .2 C3
Old Warrington Rd CW9 . . .79 A2
Old Whint Rd WA11 . . . . . . .1 A6
Old Woman's La CH3 . . . . .142 D7
Old Wrexham Rd CH4 . . . .141 C7
Oldcastle La SY14 . . . . . . .222 E8
Olde George The CH1 . . . .237 B3
Oldfield Brow Prim Sch
 WA14 . . . . .20 F5
Oldfield Cres CH4 . . . . . . .140 F5
Oldfield Dr Chester CH3 . . .119 C2
 Mobberley WA16 . . . . .58 A4
Oldfield La WA14 . . . . .20 F4
Oldfield Prim Sch CH3 . . .119 C3
Oldfield Rd
 Ellesmere Port CH65 . . . . . .70 B5
 Lymm WA13 . . . . .18 C4
 Sandbach CW11 . . . . .174 F3
Oldgate WA8 . . . . .22 D7
Oldhall St SY14 . . . . .213 B3
Oldham St Bollington SK10 . .88 A7
 Warrington WA4 . . . . .16 D3
Oldham's Rise SK10 . . . . . .87 D3
Oldhams Hill CW8 . . . . .78 F1
Oldhill CI ST7 . . . . .210 C8
Olive Dr CH64 . . . . .66 E8
Olive Gr ST5 . . . . .210 D1
Olive Rd CH64 . . . . .66 E8
Oliver CI SK10 . . . . .87 F7

Oliver Ho CH66 . . . . .69 D4
Oliver La CH66 . . . . .69 D4
Oliver St WA2 . . . . .16 B6
Ollersett Ave SK22 . . . . . . .39 D8
Ollersett Dr SK22 . . . . .39 D8
Ollersett Ho SK22 . . . . . . .39 D8
Ollershaw La CW9 . . . . . . .79 C4
Ollerton CI WA4 . . . . .17 B3
Ollerton Pk WA5 . . . . .6 E7
Ollerton Rd SK9 . . . . .34 E5
Ollier St 8 WA8 . . . . .23 A7
Omega Bvd WA5 . . . . .6 D1
On The Air', The
 Broadcasting Mus & Vintage
 Sound Shop* CH1 . . . . .237 B2
One Oak La SK9 . . . . .60 F7
Onslow Rd CH1 . . . . .117 D4
Onston La CW8 . . . . .101 E8
Openshaw La M44 . . . . .11 E6
Orange Gr WA2 . . . . .8 E2
Orchard Ave
 Bebington CH62 . . . . .43 E7
 Wilmslow SK9 . . . . .60 D6
Orchard Brow WA3 . . . . . . .11 A2
Orchard CI Barnton CW8 . . .78 B3
 Bunbury CW6 . . . . .185 F8
 Cheadle Hulme SK8 . . . . . .35 C7
 Chester CH2 . . . . .118 D5
Ellesmere Port CH66 . . . . . .69 F1
 Frodsham WA6 . . . . .74 A6
 Goostrey CW4 . . . . .107 E1
 Higher Wincham CW9 . . . . .80 A6
 Macclesfield SK11 . . . . . . .112 B6
 Middlewich CW10 . . . . . . .151 D7
 Poynton SK12 . . . . .36 E3
 Weaverham CW8 . . . . .77 D1
 Wilmslow SK9 . . . . .59 F5
 Winsford CW7 . . . . .149 D7
Orchard Cotts CW6 . . . . . .146 D1
Orchard Cres
 Kidsgrove ST7 . . . . .194 D1
 Nantwich CW5 . . . . .204 E3
 Nether Alderley SK10 . . . . .84 F6
Orchard Croft CH3 . . . . . . .119 A1
Orchard Ct Alsager ST7 . . .193 E4
 3 Chester CH3 . . . . .119 A1
 Frodsham WA6 . . . . .74 A8
 Haslington CW1 . . . . .191 D4
Orchard Dene CW8 . . . . . .101 D5
Orchard Dr Handforth SK9 . .34 E2
 Little Leigh CW8 . . . . .77 D5
 Neston CH64 . . . . .66 E5
Orchard Gdns
 Congleton CW12 . . . . . . .156 A3
 Tarporley CW6 . . . . .168 D8
 Weaverham CW8 . . . . .77 B1
Orchard Gn SK9 . . . . .60 B1
Orchard Gr CH3 . . . . .180 F1
Orchard Haven CH66 . . . . .69 E1
Orchard Ho SK10 . . . . .86 B3
Orchard La CH66 . . . . .69 A8
Orchard Park La CH2 . . . . .72 B4
Orchard Pk 8 Helsby WA6 . .73 C4
 Poynton SK12 . . . . .36 D4
Orchard Rd
 Ellesmere Port CH65 . . . . . .70 D2
 Lymm WA13 . . . . .19 B5
 Whaley Bridge SK23 . . . . . .65 D7
Orchard Rise CW9 . . . . . . .126 E8
Orchard St Chester CH1 . . .237 A3
 Crewe CW1 . . . . .190 C5
 Northwich CW9 . . . . .104 B8
 Warrington WA1 . . . . .16 C5
 Warrington, Fearnhead WA2 . .9 A2
 Warrington,Stockton Heath
 WA4 . . . . .26 C8
 Willaston CW5 . . . . .205 D6
Orchard The
 Alderley Edge SK9 . . . . . . .85 B8
 Chester CH3 . . . . .142 A8
 Disley SK12 . . . . .38 D6
 Helsby WA6 . . . . .73 B2
 8 Runcorn WA7 . . . . .49 F7
Orchards The Holt LL13 . . . .196 E8
 Pickmere WA16 . . . . .79 F7
 Saltney CH4 . . . . .140 D6
 Shavington CW2 . . . . .206 C4
Orchid CI Huntington CH3 . .142 A6
 Irlam M44 . . . . .11 E8
Orchid Way WA3 . . . . .6 B7
Orchil CI CH66 . . . . .69 A6
Ordnance Ave
 Warrington WA3 . . . . .9 F4
Ordsall CI CW11 . . . . .174 F3
Orford CI Golborne WA3 . . . .3 A7
 Warrington WA2 . . . . .16 D8
Orford CI Golborne WA3 . . . .3 A7
 Hale L24 . . . . .21 E2
 High Lane SK6 . . . . .37 E7
Orford Gn WA2 . . . . .8 D1
Orford La WA2 . . . . .16 B7
Orford Rd WA2 . . . . .16 E8
Orford St WA1 . . . . .16 B5
Organsdale Cotts CW6 . . .123 B5
Oriel Ho CH2 . . . . .118 C4
Orion Bvd WA5 . . . . .6 B1
Orkney CI
 3 Ellesmere Port CH65 . . . .70 C1
 Widnes WA8 . . . . .13 E3

Orme CI Macclesfield SK10 . .87 D3
 Prestbury SK10 . . . . .87 A8
Orme Cres SK10 . . . . .87 D3
Orme St SK9 . . . . .60 A1
Ormerod CI CW11 . . . . . . .175 C5
Ormesby Gr CH63 . . . . .43 B6
Ormond CI WA8 . . . . .12 C2
Ormonde Rd CH2 . . . . . . .118 C4
Ormonde St CH1 . . . . .237 C3
Orrell CI WA5 . . . . .15 A6
Orton CI CW7 . . . . .127 A4
Orwell CI SK9 . . . . .34 D2
Osborne Ave WA2 . . . . .8 D1
Osborne CI CW11 . . . . . . .174 D5
Osborne CI CW2 . . . . .206 C5
Osborne Ho SK9 . . . . .60 A6
Osborne Rd Golborne WA3 . .3 A7
 Warrington WA4 . . . . .16 B1
Osbourne CI
 Bebington CH62 . . . . .43 E7
 Wilmslow SK9 . . . . .60 D6
Osier CI CH2 . . . . .72 C3
Osmere CI SY13 . . . . .226 B1
Osnath Wks WA2 . . . . .16 B6
Osprey Ave CW7 . . . . .149 D5
Osprey CI
 Middlewich CW10 . . . . . . .151 D5
 Runcorn WA7 . . . . .49 F5
 Warrington WA2 . . . . .8 E3
Osprey Ct CW2 . . . . .237 A4
Osprey Dr SK9 . . . . .60 C8
Osprey View ST7 . . . . .195 D3
Ossett CI WA7 . . . . .50 D8
Ostler's La CW11 . . . . .174 F8
Osters La WA5 . . . . .58 E7
Oteley Ave CH62 . . . . .43 D8
Otters Bank 2 CW7 . . . . . .126 A1
Ottersbank Mews CW8 . . .123 F3
Oughtrington Com Prim Sch
 WA13 . . . . .19 B4
Oughtrington Cres WA13 . .19 B4
Oughtrington La WA13 . . . .19 A2
Oughtrington View WA13 . .19 B4
Oulton Ave CH2 . . . . .118 E7
Oulton CI WA4 . . . . .17 B2
Oulton Dr CW12 . . . . .155 F3
Oulton Mill La CW6 . . . . . .147 B7
Oulton PI CH1 . . . . .237 B3
Paddock The
 Chester CH4 . . . . .141 B7
 Ellesmere Port CH66 . . . . . .69 D3
 Elton CH2 . . . . .72 A3
 Handforth SK9 . . . . .34 D4
 Hartford CW8 . . . . .103 C3
 Hassall Green CW11 . . . . .175 F2
 Helsby WA6 . . . . .73 C2
 Heswall CH60 . . . . .41 C8
 Lymm WA13 . . . . .18 F5
 Sandbach CW11 . . . . .175 B7
 Tarporley CW6 . . . . .146 D1
 Whaley Bridge SK23 . . . . . .65 F6
 Willaston CW5 . . . . .205 D4
Paddock View CW10 . . . . .128 C2
Paddock Way CH4 . . . . . . .161 A4
Paddock Wlk CW8 . . . . . . .101 D5
Paddockhall La WA16 . . . . .59 A3
Paddocks Gn CW12 . . . . . .178 F8
Paddocks The
 Prestbury SK10 . . . . .87 A5
 Whitegate CW8 . . . . .125 F7
Padgate Bsns Ctr WA1 . . . .17 B8
Padgate CE Prim Sch
 WA2 . . . . .9 A1
Padgate Com High Sch
 WA2 . . . . .8 F1
Padgate La
 Warrington WA1 . . . . .16 D7
 Warrington,Padgate WA1 . . .16 F8
Padgate Sta WA1 . . . . .9 A1
Padge La CH3 . . . . .183 C2
Padmore CI CW1 . . . . .190 A7
Padston Dr ST7 . . . . .193 B3
Padstow CI Crewe CW1 . . .190 C8
 Macclesfield SK10 . . . . . . .111 E8
 Warrington WA5 . . . . .14 C3
Padstow Dr SK8 . . . . .34 F7
Padworth PI CW1 . . . . .173 B1
Page Gr CW2 . . . . .206 B2
Page La WA8 . . . . .13 C1
Paignton CI WA5 . . . . .14 E4
Painswick Rd CH66 . . . . . .69 E2
Paisley Ave CH62 . . . . .43 E4
Palace Fields Ave WA7 . . . .50 A6
Palace Fields Local Ctr
 WA7 . . . . .50 A6
Palace Hey CH64 . . . . .67 A5
Palacefields Prim Sch
 WA7 . . . . .50 A6
Palatine Ind Est WA4 . . . . .16 C3
Palgrave CI CH1 . . . . .118 A5
Palin Dr WA5 . . . . .14 F6
Pall Mall CW5 . . . . .204 E5
Palm CI CW8 . . . . .77 E1
Palm Gr CH66 . . . . .70 A1
Palma Ave M90 . . . . .33 B8
Palmer CI CW9 . . . . .103 F5
Palmer Cres WA5 . . . . .15 B7
Palmer Rd WA1 . . . . .175 C4
Palmerston CI CW1 . . . . . .190 B8
Palmerston Rd SK10 . . . . .112 A7
Palmerston St CW12 . . . . .156 D3
Palmerston Way SK10 . . . .111 F8
Palmerstone CI CH1 . . . . .118 A5
Palmyra Sq N WA1 . . . . . . .16 A5
Palmyra Sq S WA1 . . . . . . .16 A5

Owley Wood Rd CW8 . . . . . .77 E1
Owlhurst The SK10 . . . . . . .88 B8
Owlsfield WA12 . . . . .2 E3
Ox-Hey Cres ST8 . . . . .179 D1
Ox-Hey Dr ST8 . . . . .179 D1
Oxborough CI WA8 . . . . . . .12 F4
Oxenham Rd WA2 . . . . .8 A3
Oxford CI CH66 . . . . .94 E8
Oxford Ct WA4 . . . . .16 C6
Oxford Dr Halewood L26 . . .21 A8
 Heswall CH63 . . . . .41 F6
Oxford Gr WA4 . . . . .11 C6
Oxford Rd Chester CH4 . . .140 F6
 Macclesfield SK11 . . . . . . .112 B7
 Runcorn WA7 . . . . .49 A8
Oxford St Crewe CW1 . . . .190 B5
 Newton-le-W WA12 . . . . . . .2 B3
 Warrington WA4 . . . . .16 C4
 Widnes WA8 . . . . .23 B7
Oxhey Fst Sch ST8 . . . . . .179 E1
Oxheys WA7 . . . . .50 C8
Oxmead CI WA7 . . . . .9 B1
Oxmoor CI WA7 . . . . .50 A5
Oxney CI SK11 . . . . .111 F8
Oxton CI WA8 . . . . .12 C4
Oxton Gn CH66 . . . . .69 D4

P

Packmoor Prim Sch
 ST7 . . . . .195 F1
Packsaddle Pk SK10 . . . . . .86 E5
Padarn CI CH4 . . . . .140 D5
Paddington Bank WA1 . . . .16 F6
Paddock Brow SK10 . . . . . .87 A5
Paddock Chase SK12 . . . . .36 F4
Paddock CI SK23 . . . . .64 F4
Paddock Dr CH64 . . . . .41 D2
Paddock La Audlem CW3 . .230 B2
 Kettleshulme SK23 . . . . . . .64 F4
 Lymm WA13 . . . . .19 C7
 Partington WA14 . . . . .20 B5
 Whaley Bridge SK23 . . . . . .65 F5
Paddock Rd CH4 . . . . .141 B7
Paddock Rise WA7 . . . . . . .49 E4
Paddock Row CH1 . . . . . . .237 B2

Pangbourne CI WA4 . . . . . .26 E6
Panton PI CH2 . . . . .118 F3
Panton Rd CH2 . . . . .118 F3
Parade Rd M90 . . . . .33 C7
Parade The
 1 Alderley Edge SK9 . . . . . .60 A1
 Blacon CH1 . . . . .117 E5
 Culcheth WA3 . . . . .4 E3
 Neston CH64 . . . . .41 B1
Paradise CH4 . . . . .237 B1
Paradise La CW5 . . . . .171 E7
Paradise Mill & Silk Mus*
 SK11 . . . . .112 D7
Paradise St SK11 . . . . .112 D7
Paragon CI WA8 . . . . .13 B5
Parbold Ct WA8 . . . . .22 D8
Parc Ddiwydiannol Glannau
 Dyfrdwy/Deeside Ind Pk
 CH5 . . . . .92 E2
Parc Ddiwydiannol Y
 Ffin/Borders Ind Pk The
 CH4 . . . . .140 C7
Parchments The WA12 . . . . .2 B4
Parish CI ST7 . . . . .193 B4
Park Ave Bramhall SK7 . . . .35 D5
 Haydock WA11 . . . . .1 A6
 Poynton SK12 . . . . .36 E4
 Saltney CH4 . . . . .140 E6
 Saughall CH1 . . . . .94 A2
 Talke ST7 . . . . .210 D8
 Tattenhall CH3 . . . . .166 B2
 Warrington WA4 . . . . .16 D3
 Weaverham CW8 . . . . .77 D1
 Whaley Bridge SK23 . . . . . .39 D3
 Widnes WA8 . . . . .13 B1
 Wilmslow SK9 . . . . .60 C8
 Winsford CW7 . . . . .127 A3
Park Bank WA7 . . . . .2 C2
Park Ave S WA12 . . . . .2 C2
Park Bank CW12 . . . . .156 F2
Park Brook Rd SK11 . . . . .112 A8
Park Bvd WA1 . . . . .16 B4
Park CI CH3 . . . . .121 B2
Park Cres
 Cuddington CW8 . . . . . . .101 F4
 Handforth SK9 . . . . .34 B1
 Warrington WA4 . . . . .26 D6
 Whaley Bridge SK23 . . . . . .39 D3
Park Ct Chester CH1 . . . . .237 C2
 Frodsham WA6 . . . . .74 A8
 Runcorn WA7 . . . . .49 A8
 1 Warrington WA1 . . . . . . .16 A5
Park Dr Chester CH2 . . . . .119 A4
 Ellesmere Port CH65 . . . . . .70 B3
 Wistaston CW2 . . . . .205 F8
Park Dr S CW2 . . . . .119 A4
Park East CW7 . . . . .206 D5
Park Gn SK11 . . . . .112 D7
Park Gr SK11 . . . . .112 C6
Park House Dr
 Prestbury SK10 . . . . .87 A8
 Sandbach CW11 . . . . .175 C8
Park House La SK10 . . . . . .87 A8
Park House Mews
 CW11 . . . . .175 C8
Park La Audley ST7 . . . . . .209 B4
 Congleton CW12 . . . . . . .156 F2
 Frodsham WA6 . . . . .74 B8
 Hargrave CH3 . . . . .144 E3
 Hartford CW8 . . . . .103 A7
 Hatherton CW5 . . . . .219 E4
 Higher Walton WA4 . . . . . . .25 F5
 Little Bollington WA14 . . . . .20 B2
 Littleton CH3 . . . . .119 F3
 Macclesfield SK11 . . . . . . .112 C6
 Moulton CW9 . . . . .126 F7
 Pickmere CW9,WA16 . . . . .79 C8
 Poynton SK12 . . . . .36 F3
 Pulford CH4 . . . . .162 E5
 Sandbach CW11 . . . . .174 F6
 Park Lane Sch SK11 . . . . .112 B6
Park Mills CI CW5 . . . . . . .205 D5
Park Mount CI SK11 . . . . .112 A6
Park Mount Dr SK11 . . . . .112 A6
Park Prim Sch The WA7 . . .24 A1
Park Rd
 Bebington,Eastham CH62 . . .43 F6
 Congleton CW12 . . . . . . .156 F3
 Congleton, North Rode
 CW12 . . . . .134 F2
 Ellesmere Port CH65 . . . . . .70 C4
 Golborne WA3 . . . . .3 A7
 Haslington CW1 . . . . .191 D5
 Heswall CH60 . . . . .41 B8
 High Lane SK12 . . . . .37 F6
 Little Budworth CW6 . . . . .124 F1
 Lymm WA13 . . . . .29 D8
 Middlewich CW10 . . . . . . .128 C1
 Nantwich CW5 . . . . .204 E3
 New Mills SK22 . . . . .39 C7
 Partington,Warburton
 WA3 . . . . .19 C8
 Runcorn WA7 . . . . .23 A3
 Sandbach CW11 . . . . .174 D8
 Tarporley CW6 . . . . .146 D2
 Thornton-le-M CH2 . . . . . .71 E1
 Warrington WA5 . . . . .14 C6
 Warrington, Orford WA2 . . . .8 D2
 Whaley Bridge SK23 . . . . . .65 D6
 Widnes WA8 . . . . .13 B1
 Willaston CH64 . . . . .68 B8
 Willaston(nr Nantwich)
 CW5 . . . . .205 C5

Park Rd continued
Wilmslow SK9 ....59 F7
Winnington CW8 ....78 D1
Park Rd N WA12 ....2 E4
Park Rd S WA12 ....2 D2
Park Rd W CH4 ....141 A7
Park Road Com Prim Sch
WA5 ....14 E6
Park St Bollington SK10 ...88 B8
Chester CH1 ....237 B2
Congleton CW12 ....156 E2
Haydock WA11 ....1 A6
Macclesfield SK11 ....112 D7
Neston CH64 ....66 E8
Northwich CW8 ....103 E7
Park The Christleton CH3 .142 E8
Warrington WA5 ....14 D3
Park Vale Rd SK11 ....112 C6
Park View Audlem CW3 .230 C8
Bebington CH62 ....43 C8
Congleton CW12 ....156 E3
Hazel Grove SK7 ....37 B8
Little Bollington WA14 ...20 B2
Nantwich CW5 ....204 F6
Newton-le-W WA12 ....2 E3
Warrington WA2 ....8 E3
Park View Ct SK12 ......36 E4
Park View Rd ST7 ....195 B3
Park W CH60 ....40 E7
Park Way CH1 ....94 A2
Park Wlk CH2 ....118 E4
Parkdale Ind Est WA1 ....16 C6
Parkdale Rd WA1 ....17 A7
Parker Ave CW8 ....103 A6
Parker Dr CH3 ....180 E1
Parker Dr S CH3 ....180 F1
Parker St
Macclesfield SK11 ....112 E7
Runcorn WA7 ....23 B3
Warrington WA1 ....16 A5
Parker Way CW12 ....156 A3
Parker's Bldgs CH1 .....237 C3
Parker's Rd CW1 ....190 A8
Parker's Row CH3 ......180 F6
Parkers Ct WA7 ....49 E6
Parkett Heyes Rd SK11 .111 E7
Parkfield CW1 ....173 A1
Parkfield Ave WA4 ......17 A4
Parkfield Dr
Ellesmere Port CH65 .....70 A3
Helsby WA6 ....73 B3
Nantwich CW5 ....204 E4
Parkfield Rd
Broughton CH4 ....139 C3
Knutsford WA16 ....82 B8
Northwich CW9 ....104 C8
Parkfields La WA2 ....8 F2
Parkgate WA16 ....57 C3
Parkgate Ave WA16 .....108 B8
Parkgate Ct CH1 ....118 B4
Parkgate Ho CH64 ......41 B2
Parkgate La Heswall CH64 .41 F5
Knutsford WA16 ....57 C3
Parkgate Prim Sch CH64 .41 C1
Parkgate Rd Blacon CH1 .118 A6
Macclesfield SK11 ....112 C4
Neston CH64 ....66 D8
Puddington CH66 ....68 C2
Saughall CH1 ....94 C3
Warrington WA4 ....16 D1
Woodbank CH1 ....93 E7
Parkgate Trad Est WA16 .57 C4
Parkgate Way
7 Handforth SK9 ....34 D4
Runcorn WA7 ....50 D7
Parkhill Ct WA16 ....57 B1
Parkhouse Ind Est ST5 ..210 F1
Parkhouse Rd E ST5 ...210 F1
Parkhouse Rd W ST5 ...210 E1
Parkland Cl WA4 ....27 B4
Parkland Dr CH2 ....72 B3
Parklands
Ellesmere Port CH66 .....69 D6
Kidsgrove ST7 ....195 B1
Widnes WA8 ....12 C3
Parklands Com Prim Sch
CH66 ....69 D5
Parklands Dr CH60 ......41 C6
Parklands Gdns CH66 ...69 D6
Parklands The CW12 ...157 A2
Parklands Way SK12 ....36 E4
Parklea CH66 ....69 D6
Parkleigh CW12 ....156 E2
Parkroyal Com Sch
SK11 ....112 C7
Parkside Bsns Pk WA3 ...3 A8
Parkside Ct High Lane SK6 .37 D8
Neston CH64 ....66 D8
Parkside Ct WA8 ....13 A2
Parkside Rd WA12,WA2 ...3 B2
Parkstone Dr CW1 ......190 B8
Parksway WA1 ....17 D7
Parkview Ct CH60 ....40 F8
Parkview Pk
Broomedge WA13 ....19 D1
Lymm WA13 ....29 D8
Parkway
Connah's Quay CH5 ......92 E1
Holmes Chapel CW4 .....130 C3
Wilmslow SK9 ....60 B6
Parkway Bsns Ctr CH5 ...92 E1
Parkwood Cl
Bebington CH62 ....43 E8
Lymm WA13 ....18 D2

Parliament St 4 CW8 ...103 E7
Parliament Way CH66 ...94 F8
Parlington Cl WA8 ....22 C7
Parnell Sq CW12 ....157 A2
Parr Gr WA11 ....1 A6
Parr St Macclesfield SK11 .112 C8
Warrington WA1 ....16 C4
1 Widnes WA8 ....13 C1
Parrs Wood View WA4 .17 A1
Parry Dr WA4 ....17 E3
Parson St CW1 ....190 D3
Parsonage Gn Hale L24 ...21 E1
9 Wilmslow SK9 ....60 B7
Parsonage Rd WA8 .....23 A4
Parsonage St SK11 ....112 D7
Parsonage Way WA5 .....15 A5
Parsons La CH2 ....118 B7
Partington Prim Sch
M31 ....11 F3
Partington Sh Ctr M31 ...11 F3
Partridge Cl
Congleton CW12 ....156 E1
Warrington WA3 ....9 E4
Winsford CW7 ....149 D5
Partridge Way CW9 ....79 F5
Parvey La SK11 ....112 E2
Pasture Cl Kelsall CW6 .122 C4
Macclesfield SK11 ....87 C3
Pasture Dr WA3 ....9 B7
Pasture La WA2 ....9 B1
Pastures The WA9 ......6 A7
Patch La SK7 ....35 D5
Patmos La WA16 ....105 F8
Patrivale Cl WA1 ....16 F6
Patten La WA1 ....6 B6
Patterdale Ave WA2 ....8 C2
Patterdale Cl CW2 .....189 D3
Patterdale Rd M31 .....11 E3
Patterson Cl WA3 ......3 D7
Patterson St WA12 .....2 B3
Patton Dr WA5 ....15 B6
Paul Cl WA5 ....14 D6
Paul St WA2 ....16 A6
Paulden Rd CW9 ....80 A2
Pavement La WA16 .....57 F3
Pavilion Way
Congleton CW12 ....156 C3
Macclesfield SK10 ....86 F1
Pavilions The
Chester CH4 ....141 B3
Davenham CW9 ....103 E2
Paxford Pl SK9 ....60 A5
Payne Cl WA5 ....15 D6
Paythorne Cl WA3 ......4 F3
Peace Dr WA5 ....15 D5
Peach Field CH3 ....142 B7
Peach Gr WA11 ....1 E7
Peach La CW5 ....189 A1
Peach Tree Cl L24 ......21 E2
Peacock Ave
Warrington WA1 ....16 E6
Winsford CW7 ....149 C5
Peacock Dr SK8 ....34 B6
Peacock La WA16 ......29 E6
Peacock St 5 SK9 ....34 D5
Peak Rd SK22 ....39 D8
Pear Tree Ave
Crewe CW1 ....190 B7
Runcorn WA7 ....49 C7
Pear Tree Cl
Frodsham WA6 ....49 D1
Hale L24 ....21 E1
Weaverham CW8 ....77 C1
Winsford CW7 ....149 D7
Pear Tree Dr CW7 ......80 A6
Pear Tree Farm Cotts
CW9 ....104 F4
Pear Tree Field CW5 ...205 A4
Pear Tree La
Acton Bridge CW8 ....76 E4
Whitchurch SY13 ....225 D1
Pear Tree Prim Sch
CW5 ....205 A4
Pear Tree Rd ST7 ......209 F1
Pear Tree Way
Chester CH2 ....118 F6
5 Ellesmere Port CH66 ..69 E1
Pearl La Chester CH3 ..119 C1
Littleton CH3 ....119 D1
Pearl St SK10 ....87 A7
Pearle St SK10 ....87 D1
Pearlings The CH3 .....119 B1
Pearson Ave 9 SK11 ..112 E7
Peartree Cl CW11 ......175 E6
Peartree La SY14 ....222 D1
Peartree Pl WA4 ....16 C4
Pearwood Cl CW6 ......146 D1
Peasley Cl WA2 ....9 B1
Pebble Brook Prim Sch
CW2 ....190 C1
Peck Mill La WA6 ......98 A7
Peckfield Cl WA7 ....50 A5
Peckforton Cl CW11 ...174 E7
Peckforton Dr
Ellesmere Port CH66 .....69 E3
Runcorn WA7 ....49 F4
Peckforton Hall Farm
CW6 ....185 A6
Peckforton Hall La CW6 .185 B6
Peckforton Way
Chester CH2 ....118 F6
2 Northwich CW8 ......103 E7
Peckforton Wlk 11 SK9 .34 E1
Peckmill Cl SK9 ....34 E2
Peckmill Rdbt CW9 ....127 B8

Pedley Hill
Booth Green SK10 ....62 F7
Rainow SK10 ....88 E4
Pedley House La WA16 ..58 E1
Pedley La Chelford WA16 ..83 D8
Congleton CW12 ....157 F4
Pedley St CW2 ....190 D2
Peebles Cl
Ellesmere Port CH66 .....68 F6
Holmes Chapel CW4 .....130 B2
Peel Cl WA1 ....17 D6
Peel Cres CH3 ....121 E7
Peel Ct 4 ST7 ....195 A2
Peel Dr CW12 ....178 B7
Peel Hall La CH3 ....121 E7
Peel Hollow ST7 ......209 A2
Peel House La WA8 .....13 B2
Peel La CW12 ....178 D7
Peel Sq CW1 ....190 B5
Peel St Crewe CW1 ....190 B5
Macclesfield SK11 ....112 D6
Newton-le-W WA12 ....2 A3
Runcorn WA7 ....22 F3
Peel Terr CH1 ....237 C3
Peerswood Ct CH64 ....66 E5
Peewit Cl CW7 ....149 D5
Peggie's La SK10 ....62 D2
Pelham Cl WA1 ....191 C5
Pelham Rd WA4 ....17 C3
Pelican Cl CW1 ....191 A5
Pemberton Cl CH64 ....68 A8
Pemberton Rd CH1 ....237 A3
Pembridge Ct CH65 ....70 E3
Pembridge Gdns CH65 ..70 E3
Pembroke Apartments
WA2 ....9 A3
Pembroke Cl CH4 ......141 E6
Pembroke Ct WA7 ......24 D5
Pembroke Dr CH65 .....70 A3
Pembroke Gdns WA4 ...26 D4
Pembroke Gr WA4 .....11 C6
Pembroke Rd SK11 ....111 F7
Pembroke Way CW7 ...149 B7
Penare WA7 ....50 C6
Penbrook Cl CW2 .....189 D3
Penda Way CW11 .....175 B6
Pendine Cl WA5 ....7 C2
Pendle Cl Crewe CW1 ..191 A5
Ellesmere Port CH66 .....68 F6
Pendle Gdns WA3 ......4 E2
Pendlebury St WA4 ....17 A2
Penfold Cl CH1 ....94 B8
Penfold Hey CH2 ......118 D7
Penfold Way CH4 ......162 A7
Penfolds WA7 ....23 D1
Penhale Mews SK7 .....35 F7
Peninsula Ho WA2 .....16 C7
Penistone Dr CH66 .....69 B5
Penketh Ave WA5 ......15 F8
Penketh Bsns Pk WA5 ....15 B4
Penketh South Com Prim Sch
WA5 ....14 D4
Penketh Ct
1 Runcorn WA7 ....23 B2
Warrington WA5 ....14 D6
Penketh High Sch WA5 ..15 A5
Penketh Rd WA5 ....15 D5
Penketh South Com Prim Sch
WA5 ....14 E3
Penketh's La 19 WA7 ..23 A3
Penkford La WA5 ....1 D2
Penkford St WA12 ......1 E3
Penkford Tech Sppcl Sch
WA12 ....1 A2
Penkmans La WA6 .....74 C6
Penlington Cl CW5 ....204 F6
Penmann Cres L26 ....21 A7
Penmark Cl WA5 ....7 C2
Penmon Cl CH1 ....117 D3
Penn Bridge SK11 .....158 E6
Penn Gdns CH65 ......70 B5
Penn House Cl SK7 .....35 E8
Penn La WA4 ....27 F1
Pennant Cl WA3 ....10 A3
Pennine Cl SK10 ....87 E2
Cronton L35,WA8 ....12 B6
Rainow SK10 ....88 D3
Pennine Way
Biddulph ST8 ....179 E1
Winsford CW7 ....149 B8
Pennine Wlk CH66 .....69 B6
Pennington Cl WA6 .....74 E4
Pennington Dr WA12 ...2 E3
Pennington Gn CH66 ...69 C3
Pennington La WA5,WA9 ..1 D2
Penningtons La SK11 ..111 F5
Pennsylvania La CH3 ..184 C6
Penny Bank Cl CH4 ...139 A3
Penny La Collins Green WA5 .1 D1
Cronton L35,WA8 ....12 B6
Rainow SK10 ....88 D3
Penny's La
Northwich CW9 ....104 F7
Rudheath CW9 ....105 B5
Pennyfields Rd ST7 ...195 D2
Pennygate Dr CW10 ...128 D2
Pennypleck La CW9 ....28 A2
Penrhyn Cres
Hazel Grove SK7 ....36 C8
Runcorn WA7 ....49 B7
Penrhyn Rd CW8 ......103 E8
Penrith Ave
Macclesfield SK11 ....111 F5
Warrington WA2 ....8 C2
Penrith Cl Frodsham WA6 .49 D1
Partington M31 ....11 E3
Penrith Ct CW12 ......156 A2
Penrose Gdns WA5 .....14 D3

Penry Ave M44 ....11 E6
Penryn Cl WA5 ....14 E3
Pensarn Gdns WA5 .....7 D2
Pensby Ave CH2 ......118 D5
Pensby Dr CH66 ....69 D4
Pensby Rd CH60 ....40 F8
Penshaw Ct WA7 ....49 E7
Pentland Ave WA2 .....8 B3
Pentland Cl Chester CH3 .119 A2
Winsford CW7 ....149 B8
Pentland Pl WA2 ....8 B3
Pentre Cl CH3 ....121 F7
Pentre La CH3 ....121 F7
Penzance Cl SK10 .....111 E8
Peony Gdns WA9 ....6 B7
Peover Hall & Gdns*
WA16 ....107 E8
Peover La Chelford SK11 .108 F8
Congleton CW12 ....157 F6
Peover Prim Sch WA16 ..108 B8
Peover Rd SK9 ....34 E5
Pepper Ct SK9 ....60 A6
Pepper St
Appleton Thorn WA4 .....27 B3
Ashley WA16 ....31 F1
Chelford SK11 ....83 E2
Chester CH4 ....237 B2
Christleton CH3 ....142 D8
Hale L24 ....21 D1
Henbury SK11 ....111 B8
Lymm WA13 ....18 F3
Middlewich CW10 ....128 C1
Nantwich CW5 ....204 E5
Peppers The WA13 .....18 F3
Percival Cl CH2 ....118 C8
Percival La WA7 ....22 E2
Percival Rd Chester CH2 .118 C8
Ellesmere Port CH65 .....70 B6
Percival St WA1 ....16 C5
Percivals La WA16 .....83 B3
Percy James Cl ST7 ...193 E4
Percy Rd CH4 ....141 D7
Percy St Nantwich CW9 .104 A8
Warrington WA5 ....16 B5
Percyvale St SK10 .....112 E8
Peregrine Cl CW7 .....149 D5
Perimeter Rd CW7 .....72 D5
Perrin Ave WA7 ....48 E8
Perrins Rd WA5 ....6 F6
Perry Fields CW1 .....173 B1
Perry Rd WA7 ....22 D3
Perth Cl Bramhall SK7 ..35 F5
Holmes Chapel CW4 .....130 B2
Warrington WA2 ....8 F4
Peter Destapleigh Way
CW5 ....205 A3
Peter Ellson Cl CW2 ...190 D1
Peter House Rd SK11 ..112 F3
Peter Rd CH65 ....70 D4
Peter St Golborne WA3 ...3 A8
Macclesfield SK11 ....112 C7
Northwich CW9 ....79 B1
Peter St W 1 SK11 ....112 C7
Peterborough Cl
Ellesmere Port CH66 .....94 F7
Macclesfield SK10 ....87 A2
Peters Cl SK10 ....87 A7
Petersfield Gdns WA3 ...4 A4
Petersgate WA7 ....50 D7
Petersham Dr WA4 .....26 E5
Peterstone Cl WA5 .....7 D2
Petham Ct WA8 ....12 E4
Petrel Ave SK12 ....36 B4
Petrel Cl CW1 ....149 D5
Petunia Cl
Macclesfield SK11 ....112 B5
St Helens WA9 ....6 A7
Petworth Ave WA9 .....8 B3
Petworth Cl CW2 ......206 B8
Pevensey Dr WA16 .....82 A8
Peveril Cl WA4 ....26 D8
Peveril Dr SK7 ....36 E8
Peveril Gdns SK12 .....39 A6
Peveril Mews SK12 .....39 A6
Peveril Wlk 3 SK11 ...111 F7
Pewit La CW5 ....231 C7
Pewithall Prim Sch WA7 .49 B7
Pewterspear Green Rd
WA4 ....26 E3
Pewterspear La WA4 ...26 E4
Pex Hill Ct WA8 ....12 E5
Pexall Rd SK11 ....134 C3
Pexhill Dr SK10 ....111 E7
Pexhill Rd SK11 ....111 C5
Pheasant Cl WA3 ....9 F4
Pheasant Dr CW9 ....79 F5
Pheasant Field L24 ....21 C2
Pheasant Wlk 18 SK9 ..34 D5
Pheasant Wlk WA16 ...29 C4
Philip Rd WA8 ....22 B8
Philip St CH5 ....116 A2
Philips Dr WA5 ....15 D11
Philips La CH66 ....69 C4
Phillip St CH5 ....116 A3
Phillips Rd CH1 ....117 D3
Phillips St CW2 ....190 D2
Phipps' La WA5 ....6 F7
Phoenix Ave WA5 ......7 F2
Phoenix Cl ST7 ....195 C2
Phoenix St CH5 ....116 A3
Phythian Cres WA5 ....14 D4
Pichael Nook WA4 ....17 A4
Pickenham Cl SK11 ...111 E7
Pickering Cres WA4 ...17 D3
Pickering Way CW5 ...204 F6

**Pickering's Pasture (Nature
Reserve)*** WA8 ....22 B3
Pickerings Cl WA7 .....49 C6
Pickerings Lock Cvn PK
CW8 ....76 A5
Pickerings O The Boat
CW8 ....76 A5
Pickerings Rd WA8 .....22 B5
Pickford St SK11 ......112 D7
Pickmere Cl CW11 ....174 F7
Pickmere Ct Crewe CW1 .190 D5
1 Handforth SK9 ....34 D5
Pickmere Dr
Bebington CH62 ....43 F3
Bebington CH62 ....43 F4
Chester CH3 ....142 B8
Runcorn WA7 ....50 C5
Pickmere La
Higher Wincham CW9 ....79 F6
Pickmere WA16 ....55 D2
Pickmere Rd SK9 ......34 D5
Pickmere St WA5 ......15 E5
Pickwick Cl CW11 .....175 C8
Pickwick Pl ST7 ......194 D2
Pickwick Rd SK12 .....36 D3
Picow Farm Rd WA7 ...22 E1
Picow St 1 WA7 ....22 E1
Picton Ave
Ellesmere Port CH65 .....70 C5
Runcorn WA7 ....23 B2
Picton Cl Bebington CH62 .43 E3
2 Northwich CW9 ......103 F4
Warrington WA3 ....9 C4
Picton Dr Handforth SK9 ..34 E2
Winsford CW7 ....126 B2
Picton Gorse La CH2 ..119 B7
Picton La CH2 ....119 A6
Picton Sq CW4 ....130 C3
Piele Rd WA11 ....1 A8
Pierce St SK11 ....112 C8
Pierpoint La CH1 ......237 B2
Pierpoint St WA5 ......15 F7
Pigot Pl WA4 ....16 F5
Pike La WA6 ....75 A3
Pike Rd SK10 ....89 B6
Pike St WA4 ....16 F6
Pike The CW5 ....204 E3
Pikemere Prim Sch ST7 .193 B5
Pikemere Rd ST7 .....193 B5
Pikenall La CW8 ....76 D3
Pilgrim Cl WA2 ....8 A6
Pilgrims Way WA7 .....24 D2
Pillar Box La CW11 ...153 B3
Pillmoss La WA4 ....52 B8
Pillory St CW5 ....204 E5
Pimblett Rd WA11 ......1 E7
Pimblett St WA3 ....3 A7
Pimlico Rd WA7 ....22 E2
Pine Ave
Newton-le-W WA12 ....2 D7
4 Widnes WA8 ....13 B2
Pine Cl Haydock WA11 ....1 C6
Macclesfield SK10 ....87 F1
Talke ST7 ....210 D7
Pine Ct ST7 ....193 E4
Pine Gdns CH2 ....118 C6
Pine Gr Chester CH2 ...119 B4
Ellesmere Port CH66 .....70 A1
Golborne WA3 ....3 C8
Sandbach CW11 ....175 C6
Warrington WA1 ....17 A7
Winsford CW7 ....127 A1
Pine Lo SK7 ....35 F7
Pine Lodge SK12 ....36 D3
Pine Rd Bramhall SK7 ...35 F8
Heswall CH60 ....41 C8
Macclesfield SK10 ....87 F1
Poynton SK12 ....36 E3
Runcorn WA7 ....49 C8
Pine Tree Cl CH4 ......139 C3
Pine Trees WA16 ......57 F8
Pine Wlk Nantwich CW5 ..204 F4
8 Partington M31 .....11 E3
Pineapple Pk CW7 ......127 B2
Pinedale Cl CH66 ......95 A8
Pinehey CH64 ....41 D1
Pinehurst SK10 ....86 E6
Pinellas WA7 ....23 B3
Pines The
Mobberley WA16 ....58 E1
6 Northwich CW9 ......103 E6
Pinetree Cl Barnton CW8 ..78 B4
Winsford CW7 ....127 A1
Pineways WA4 ....26 D5
Pinewood Ave WA1 ....16 E7
Pinewood Cl CW7 .....127 A2
Pinewood Dr CW2 .....206 B7
Pinewood Rd CH66 .....95 B8
Pinewood St WA5 .....210 E1
Pinewood
Burtonwood WA5 ....6 F7
Wilmslow SK9 ....60 E8
Winsford CW7 ....127 B2
Pinfold Cl WA15 ....32 D7
Pinfold Craft Ctr* CW5 .188 B3
Pinfold Ct CH4 ....141 E6
Pinfold La
Alpraham CW6 ....169 D5
Chelford SK11 ....83 D6
Chester CH4 ....141 E7
Little Budworth CW6 ....147 D8
Middlewich CW10 ....128 B1
Plumley WA16 ....61 A8
Woodhouse Park M90,
WA15 ....32 F6
Pinfold Rd SK11 ....55 D3
Pinfold St 18 SK10 ....112 C8
Pinfold The LL13 ......196 D8

Pinfold Way CW8 . . . . .77 D1
Pingard's La CW8 . . . . . .101 C6
Pingate Dr SK8 . . . . .35 A6
Pingate La SK8 . . . . .35 A6
Pingate La S SK8 . . . . .35 A6
Pingot Croft CH3 . . . . . . .142 B7
Pingot La WA6 . . . . .99 A5
Pingot Rd SK22 . . . . .39 D8
Pinmill Brow WA6 . . . . . . .74 B7
Pinmill Cl WA6 . . . . .74 C7
Pinners Brow WA2 . . . . . . .16 B6
Pinners Brow Ret Pk
WA2 . . . . .16 B6
Pinners Fold WA7 . . . . . . .24 B1
Pinsley Green Rd CW5 .216 E2
Pinsley View CW5 . . . . . .216 E4
Pintail Pl CW7 . . . . .149 D6
Pinwood Ct 18 SK9 . . . . . .34 F1
Piper's Cl CH60 . . . . .40 D8
Piper's End CH60 . . . . .40 D8
Piper's La CH60 . . . . .40 D8
Pipers Ash CW7 . . . . .126 A1
Pipers Ct CW7 . . . . .119 B4
Pipers La Chester CH2 . .119 B4
Puddington CH64 . . . . . . .93 A8
Pipers The Golborne WA3 . .3 F8
Heswall CH60 . . . . .40 D8
Pipit Ave WA12 . . . . .2 C3
Pipit La WA3 . . . . .9 E3
Pippin Cl CW10 . . . . .151 C7
Pippits Row WA7 . . . . .49 E4
Pirie Cl CW12 . . . . .157 A4
Pirie Rd CW12 . . . . .157 A4
Pit La Hough CW2 . . . . . .206 E2
Talke ST7 . . . . .210 C6
Widnes WA8 . . . . .13 A4
Pitcher La CW11 . . . . .177 A8
Pitt La SK11 . . . . .132 B8
Pitt St Macclesfield SK11 . .112 D6
Warrington WA5 . . . . .15 F7
Widnes WA8 . . . . .23 A5
Pitts Cl CH3 . . . . .121 C2
Pitts Heath La WA7 . . . . . .24 E3
Pitville Terr WA8 . . . . .22 C7
Plaistow Ct WA7 . . . . .49 E7
Plane Gr ST5 . . . . .210 E7
Plane Tree Dr CW1 . . . . .190 E6
Plane Tree Gr WA11 . . . . . . .2 A7
Plane Tree Rd M31 . . . . . .11 D3
Plant La CW11 . . . . .174 B7
Plant St CW11 . . . . .175 A7
Plantagenet Cl 3 CW7 .179 D6
Plantation Cl WA7 . . . . . . .24 A1
Plantation Dr CH66 . . . . . .69 E7
Plas Dinas CH1 . . . . .117 D3
Plas Newton La CH2 . . . .118 F5
Plas Newydd CH4 . . . . . .161 B6
Platt Ave CW11 . . . . .175 A7
Platt's La CH3 . . . . .164 E5
Platts La Christleton CH3 .143 D8
Duddon CH3,CW6 . . . . . .144 E7
Tarvin CH3 . . . . .121 B2
Tarvin, Broom Bank CH3 . .144 B8
Tattenhall CH3 . . . . .183 F7
Platts St WA11 . . . . .1 A6
Pleasance Way WA12 . . . . .2 D4
Pleasant St
Macclesfield SK10 . . . . . . .87 F1
Northwich CW8 . . . . .103 E7
Pleasant View SK10 . . . .111 C8
Pleasant Way SK8 . . . . . . .35 C6
Pleck Rd CH65 . . . . .70 A2
Plemstall Cl CH2 . . . . . . .119 F8
Plemstall La CH2 . . . . .97 A1
Plemstall Way CH2 . . . . . .96 F1
Plemstation Ct CH66 . . . . .69 F8
Plex The ST7 . . . . .193 D4
Plinston Ave WA4 . . . . . . .16 F4
Plough Croft ST7 . . . . . . .193 A3
Plough Inn Pk The CW8 .125 E5
Plough La CH3 . . . . .143 B7
Ploughmans Cl CH66 . . . .94 E8
Ploughmans Way
Ellesmere Port CH66 . . . . .94 E8
Macclesfield SK10 . . . . . . .87 B3
Plover Ave CW7 . . . . .149 D5
Plover Cl Farndon CH3 . .180 F1
Newton-le-W WA12 . . . . . . .2 C3
Plover Dr WA7 . . . . .50 D8
Plover Way WA3 . . . . .3 E8
Plovers La WA6 . . . . .75 C3
Plum Terr CH1 . . . . .237 A3
Plumbs Fold CW8 . . . . . . .78 A2
Plumley Cl Chester CH3 .119 C1
18 Macclesfield SK11 . . . .112 E7
Plumley Gdns WA8 . . . . . .12 A1
Plumley Moor Rd WA16 . .81 C2
Plumley Rd SK9 . . . . .34 D5
Plumley Sta WA16 . . . . . .81 A3
Plumpstons La WA4 . . . . .26 C8
Plumpton Cross 6 WA6 . .13 B2
Plumtre Ave WA5 . . . . .15 F8
Plymouth Cl WA7 . . . . .50 E6
Plymouth Dr SK7 . . . . .35 F7
Plymyard Ave CH62 . . . . . .43 D5
Plymyard Cl CH62 . . . . . . .43 D5
Poachers' La WA4 . . . . . . .26 B4
Pochard Ave CW7 . . . . . .149 D6
Pochard Dr SK12 . . . . .36 A4
Pochard Rise WA7 . . . . . . .50 D8
Pochin Way CW10 . . . . . .128 E1
Pocket Nook La WA3 . . . . . .4 B7
Pocklington Ct WA7 . . . . . .8 F1
Polden Cl CH66 . . . . .69 A6
Pole La CW9 . . . . .53 E2
Pole Lane Ends CW9 . . . .53 C4
Poleacre Dr WA8 . . . . .12 D2
Pollard Ave WA6 . . . . .74 D7

Pollard Dr CW5 . . . . .205 B4
Polperro Cl
Macclesfield SK10 . . . . . . .86 D1
Warrington WA5 . . . . .14 E3
Pond Cotts CH2 . . . . .72 A3
Pond St WA3 . . . . .4 A8
Pond View Cl CH60 . . . . . .41 C8
Pond Wlk WA9 . . . . .1 A1
Pool Bank Bsns Pk CH3 .121 C3
Pool Bank Cotts CH3 . . . .121 C3
Pool End Cl SK10 . . . . .87 D4
Pool End Rd SK10 . . . . . . .87 D4
Pool Hall Ind Est CH65,
CH66 . . . . .70 A8
Pool House Rd SK12 . . . . .37 D5
Pool La Cuddington CW8 .102 B2
Haslington CW11 . . . . . . .192 A7
Ince CH2 . . . . .71 F4
Lymm WA13 . . . . .18 B4
Runcorn WA7 . . . . .23 B3
Tarvin CH3 . . . . .121 C4
Warrington WA4 . . . . .16 A1
Pool Meadows Rd CW1 .191 B4
Pool Rd WA3 . . . . .11 A3
Pool Side ST7 . . . . .194 A8
Pool St Macclesfield SK11 .112 E6
Widnes WA8 . . . . .23 B7
Pool View CW11 . . . . .191 F7
Poole Ave WA2 . . . . .8 B2
Poole Cres WA2 . . . . .8 B2
Poole Hall La CH66 . . . . . .69 E8
Poole Hall Rd CH66 . . . . .69 F8
Poole Hill Rd CW5 . . . . . .188 A2
Poole La CH2 . . . . .71 E2
Poole Old Hall La CW5 .188 D4
Poolford La CW4 . . . . . . .129 E2
Pools La CW11 . . . . .177 A6
Pools Platt La CW9 . . . . . .53 E6
Poolside Ct ST7 . . . . .193 E4
Poolside Rd WA7 . . . . .23 B1
Pooltown Rd CH65 . . . . . .69 F5
Poplar Ave Culcheth WA3 . .4 F3
Moulton CW9 . . . . .126 F8
Newton-le-W WA12 . . . . . . .2 D3
Runcorn WA7 . . . . .49 C7
Warrington WA5 . . . . .14 C3
Wilmslow SK9 . . . . .59 F5
Poplar Cl
Congleton CW12 . . . . . . .156 A4
Cuddington CW8 . . . . . . .102 A3
Ellesmere Port CH65 . . . . .70 B4
Runcorn WA7 . . . . .49 C7
Winsford CW7 . . . . .149 B8
Poplar Dr Alsager ST7 . .193 E2
Kidsgrove ST7 . . . . .195 A1
Middlewich CW10 . . . . . .151 D7
Poplar Gr Bollington SK10 . .88 A8
Crewe CW1 . . . . .190 E5
Elton CH2 . . . . .72 A3
Haydock WA11 . . . . .1 C6
Irlam M44 . . . . .11 D6
Poplar La CW9 . . . . .236 F5
Poplar Rd Chester CH4 .140 F5
Haydock WA11 . . . . .1 C6
Macclesfield SK11 . . . . . .112 D6
Weaverham CW8 . . . . . . .102 D8
Poplar View WA8 . . . . .28 A7
Poplar Way SK6 . . . . .38 A7
Poplar Weint 2 CH64 . . . .66 E8
Poplar Wlk M31 . . . . .11 D3
Poplars Ave
Warrington,Hulme WA2 . . . .8 C3
Warrington,Winwick Quay
WA2 . . . . .8 A4
Poplars Pl WA2 . . . . .8 D2
Poplars The
Golborne,Wash End WN7 . .4 C8
Lymm WA13 . . . . .18 D4
Wistaston CW2 . . . . .205 F7
Poppyfields ST7 . . . . .193 B3
Porlock Cl Heswall CH60 . .41 B6
Warrington WA5 . . . . .14 E4
Port Arcs The CH65 . . . . . .70 C5
Porter Ave WA12 . . . . .2 A4
Porter Dr CW9 . . . . .104 C6
Porter St WA7 . . . . .23 C2
Porter Way CW9 . . . . .104 C6
Porters Croft CH3 . . . . . .119 F5
Portford Cl SK10 . . . . .86 F1
Porthcawl Cl WA8 . . . . . . .12 C3
Porthleven Rd WA7 . . . . . .50 E7
Portland Dr
Biddulph ST8 . . . . .179 D2
Scholar Green ST7 . . . . . .194 E6
Portland Gr CW1 . . . . . . .191 D5
Portland Pl WA6 . . . . .73 C4
Portland St
Newton-le-W WA12 . . . . . . .1 F4
Runcorn WA7 . . . . .22 F3
Portland Wlk 4 SK11 . . .111 F7
Portloe Rd SK8 . . . . .34 B7
Portman Pl 3 CW7 . . . . .149 A8
Portmarnock Cl SK10 . . . .87 B3
Portola Cl WA7 . . . . .17 C2
Portree Ave CH63 . . . . . . .43 D5
Portree Dr CW4 . . . . .130 B2
Portrush Cl
Macclesfield SK10 . . . . . . .87 C4
Widnes WA8 . . . . .12 E3
Portside WA7 . . . . .50 E7
Portside Bsns Pk CH65 . .70 B8
Portsmouth Pl WA7 . . . . . .50 E6
Portway M22 . . . . .33 D8
Post Office La
Betley CW3 . . . . .207 F1
Hampton Heath SY14 . . .213 D7
Norley WA6 . . . . .100 E5
Runcorn WA7 . . . . .48 D7

Post Office Pl 1 CW9 . . . .79 A1
Postles Pl CW9 . . . . .103 F6
Pott Shrigley Church Sch
SK10 . . . . .63 C3
Potter Cl CW5 . . . . .205 D4
Potters Barn The*
CW11 . . . . .176 A1
Potters End ST8 . . . . .179 C1
Potters La WA8 . . . . .21 F5
Poulton Cres WA1 . . . . . . .17 D8
Poulton Dr WA8 . . . . .22 D8
Poulton Hall Rd CH63 . . . .43 A7
Poulton Rd CH63 . . . . .43 A8
Pound Rd CH66 . . . . .69 C7
Povey Rd WA2 . . . . .8 D1
Powell Ave WA3 . . . . .9 E4
Powell St WA4 . . . . .16 F3
Powell's Orch CH4 . . . . .141 C7
Powey La CH1 . . . . .94 B5
Pownall Ave WA7 . . . . .35 F7
Pownall Rd SK9 . . . . .59 F8
Pownall Sq SK11 . . . . . . .112 C8
Pownall St SK10 . . . . .87 D1
Powy Dr ST7 . . . . .195 B2
Powys Ct CW1 . . . . .237 A3
Powys St WA5 . . . . .15 F5
Pownall Green Prim Sch
SK7 . . . . .35 E7
Pownall Hall Sch SK9 . . . .59 F8
Poynton CE Prim Sch
SK10 . . . . .86 F7
Poynton High Sch SK12 . .36 F2
Poynton Cl WA4 . . . . .17 B3
Poynton St 18 SK11 . . . .112 C8
Poynton Sta SK12 . . . . . . .36 C4
Pratchitts Row CW5 . . . .204 E5
Precinct The CW2 . . . . . .189 F2
Preece Cl WA7 . . . . .12 D4
Preece Ct CW1 . . . . .190 B5
Preesall Ave SK8 . . . . .34 B8
Prenton Pl CH4 . . . . .141 E7
Prescot Cl WA8 . . . . .12 D2
Prescot Dr CW2 . . . . .118 F3
Prescott Rd SK9 . . . . .34 E1
Prescott St WA4 . . . . .16 E3
Prestbury CE Prim Sch
SK10 . . . . .86 F7
Prestbury Cl
8 Northwich CW9 . . . . . .103 F4
Widnes WA8 . . . . .22 E8
Prestbury Ct SK10 . . . . . . .86 F6
Prestbury Dr WA4 . . . . . . .17 D4
Prestbury La SK10 . . . . . . .87 B7
Prestbury Pk SK10 . . . . . . .86 E6
Prestbury Rd
Adder's Moss SK10 . . . . . .85 F6
Macclesfield SK10 . . . . . . .87 B1
Nether Alderley SK10 . . . . .86 A5
Prestbury Sta SK10 . . . . . .87 A7
Preston Ave M44 . . . . .11 F7
Preston St W SK11 . . . . .112 B6
Prestwich Ave WA3 . . . . . . .4 E3
Prestwick Cl
Macclesfield SK10 . . . . . . .87 C5
Widnes WA8 . . . . .12 E3
Winsford CW7 . . . . .126 C2
Prestwood Cl WA3 . . . . . . .10 A7
Pretoria St CH4 . . . . .141 D7
Price Ave CW11 . . . . .175 A5
Price Dr CW11 . . . . .175 A5
Price Gr WA9 . . . . .1 A2
Pride Cl WA12 . . . . .2 E2
Priest La SK10 . . . . .61 B1
Priestfield Rd CH65 . . . . . .70 C5
Priestley Bsns Ctr WA5 . .15 F5
Priestley Coll WA5 . . . . . .16 C3
Priestley St WA5 . . . . .15 F5
Priestly 18 CW5 . . . . .204 E5
Priestner Dr WA6 . . . . .73 B4
Priestway La CH64 . . . . . . .67 E1
Priesty Ct CW12 . . . . .156 D2
Priesty Fields CW12 . . . .156 D2
Primary Cl M44 . . . . .11 D5
Primitive St ST7 . . . . .195 C7
Primrose Ave
Haslington CW1 . . . . .191 C5
Macclesfield SK11 . . . . . .112 B5
Primrose Chase CW4 . . .130 B8
Primrose Cl
Huntington CH3 . . . . .142 A6
Runcorn WA7 . . . . .50 A8
Warrington WA3 . . . . .9 D2
Widnes WA8 . . . . .12 E1
Primrose Gr WA11 . . . . . . .1 E7
Primrose Hill
Crewe CW2 . . . . .189 E5
Cuddington CW8 . . . . . . .101 F4
Kelsall CW6 . . . . .122 E6
Primrose La WA6 . . . . .73 B1
Primula Cl WA9 . . . . .6 A7
Primula Dr WA3 . . . . .3 D8
Prince Albert St CW1 . . .190 D4
Prince Edward St CW5 . .204 E6
Prince Henry Sq 4 WA1 . .16 B5
Prince Rd SK12 . . . . .37 C5
Prince William Ave CH5 .116 B3
Prince's St WA12 . . . . .23 A8
Princes Ave
Bebington CH62 . . . . .43 D7
Chester CH1 . . . . .237 C3
Northwich CW9 . . . . .103 F7
Princes Cl WA7 . . . . .23 C1
Princes Ct CW5 . . . . .205 A4
Princes Pk CW9 . . . . .78 A2
Princes Rd WA4 . . . . .16 F3
Princes Rd CH65 . . . . .70 B6
Princes St WA12 . . . . .2 B3

Princes Way SK11 . . . . . .111 E7
Princess Ave Audley ST7 .209 D1
Haydock WA11 . . . . .2 A7
Warrington,Bruche WA1 . .16 F6
Warrington,Great Sankey
WA5 . . . . .14 E7
Warrington,Padgate WA1 . .17 A8
Princess Cl CW2 . . . . . . .205 F8
Princess Cres
Middlewich CW10 . . . . . .151 D6
Warrington WA1 . . . . .16 F6
Princess Ct ST7 . . . . .210 D5
Princess Dr
Bollington SK10 . . . . .87 E7
Nantwich CW5 . . . . .205 A6
Sandbach CW11 . . . . . . .175 A7
Wistaston CW2 . . . . .205 F8
Princess Gr CW2 . . . . . . .205 F8
Princess Rd
Allostock WA16 . . . . .106 E3
Lymm WA13 . . . . .18 C3
Wilmslow SK9 . . . . .59 F5
Princess St
Bollington SK10 . . . . .87 E7
Chester CH1 . . . . .237 A2
Congleton CW12 . . . . . . .156 D3
Crewe CW1 . . . . .190 C3
Knutsford WA16 . . . . .57 A2
Northwich CW9 . . . . .79 E2
Runcorn WA7 . . . . .23 A3
Warrington WA5 . . . . .15 D4
Winsford CW7 . . . . .127 A2
Warrington WA1 . . . . .16 F6
Princess Wlk SK7 . . . . . . .36 A7
Princeway WA6 . . . . .74 B8
Priors Cl CW2 . . . . .207 E3
Priory Ave CW9 . . . . .103 F4
Priory Cl Chester CH2 . . .118 C4
Congleton CW12 . . . . . . .179 B7
Crewe CW1 . . . . .190 A8
Runcorn WA7 . . . . .24 A1
Winsford CW7 . . . . .126 C3
Priory Cl SK10 . . . . .86 F1
Priory Dr SK10 . . . . .86 E2
Priory La SK10 . . . . .86 E2
Priory Pl Chester CH1 . . .237 B2
Blisgrove ST7 . . . . .195 B3
Priory Rd Altrincham WA14 .31 D8
Runcorn WA7 . . . . .24 C2
Wilmslow SK9 . . . . .59 E8
Priory St Altrincham WA14 .31 C8
Northwich CW9 . . . . .104 A8
Warrington WA4 . . . . .16 E3
Priory The Neston CH64 . .41 E1
Winwick WA2 . . . . .8 A7
Priory Way CW8 . . . . .103 B4
Priscilla St CW1 . . . . .190 E4
Pritchard Dr CW9 . . . . . .103 E2
Private Wlk CH3 . . . . .142 A8
Probert Cl CW2 . . . . .190 A4
Proctors Cl WA8 . . . . .13 D2
Proctors La CW11 . . . . . .174 E5
Proffits La WA6 . . . . .73 E4
Promenade Cvn Pk WA4 . .25 B7
Promised Land La CH2 .142 E5
Prospect Ave M44 . . . . . . .11 E6
Prospect Dr
Altrincham WA15 . . . . .32 D8
Davenham CW9 . . . . .103 E2
Prospect La WA3 . . . . .10 D3
Prospect Rd M44 . . . . .11 E6
Prospect Row WA7 . . . . . .48 F7
Prospect St CW12 . . . . . .156 C2
Prosperity Way CW10 . . .128 D1
Prospect St WA7 . . . . .23 C2
Protector Way M44 . . . . . .11 F8
Provan Way CH1 . . . . . . .117 D5
Provident St WA9 . . . . .1 A3
Prunus Rd CW1 . . . . .190 E6
Pryors The CH3 . . . . .121 C3
Ptarmigan Pl CW7 . . . . . .149 D5
Public Hall St 18 WA7 . . . .23 A3
Pudding La CW6 . . . . .168 A8
Puddington La CH64 . . . . .92 E8
Puddle Bank La CW12 . .178 F5
Puffin Ave SK12 . . . . .36 A4
Puffin Cl CH65 . . . . .95 C8
Pulford Cl
Northwich CW9 . . . . .103 E4
Runcorn WA7 . . . . .49 E6
Pulford Ct CH4 . . . . .162 D2
Pulford La CH4 . . . . .162 C5
Pulford Rd Blacon CH1 . .117 E5
Ellesmere Port CH65 . . . . .69 F4
Winsford CW7 . . . . .126 C1
Pullman Cl CH60 . . . . .41 D8
Pullman Dr CW9 . . . . .104 C8
Pump St ST7 . . . . .209 E2
Pump La Churton CH3 . . .181 A5
Runcorn WA7 . . . . .49 A6
Tattenhall CH3 . . . . .182 C6
Pumptree Mews SK11 . . .111 E7
Purdy Cl WA5 . . . . .7 C8
Puritan Bldgs WA7 . . . . . .23 C2
Purley Dr M44 . . . . .11 E6
Purser La SY14 . . . . .222 E3
Purton Cl WA7 . . . . .49 D6
Putney Ct WA7 . . . . .49 F7
Pye Cl WA11 . . . . .2 B8
Pye Rd CH60 . . . . .41 A8
Pyecroft Cl WA5 . . . . .14 D6
Pyecroft St CH4 . . . . .141 D7
Pym's La CW1 . . . . .190 A7
Pyrus Ave CW1 . . . . .190 E6
Pyrus Gr WA6 . . . . .73 C4
Pytcheley Hollow WA6 . .100 F6

Quad The CH1 . . . . .117 E2
Quadrant Cl WA7 . . . . .50 D6
Quadrant The
Chester CH1 . . . . .117 E2
Warrington WA3 . . . . .9 F5
Quail Cl WA2 . . . . .8 D3
Quaintways CW8 . . . . . . .103 C4
Quakers Coppice CW1 . .191 A2
Quakers Way LL13 . . . . .180 E1
Quantock Cl
Ellesmere Port CH66 . . . . .69 A6
Winsford CW7 . . . . .149 A7
Quarry Ave CH3 . . . . .180 F1
Quarry Bank CW6 . . . . . .146 D8
Quarry Bank Cotts CW6 .184 F5
Quarry Bank Mill* SK9 . .33 F2
Quarry Bank Rd SK9 . . . . .33 F3
Quarry Bank Rise CW7 . .149 B8
Quarry Cl Chester CH4 . .141 C7
Ellesmere Port CH66 . . . . .69 A6
Quarry Ct Farndon CH3 .180 F1
Widnes WA8 . . . . .12 C1
Quarry Hill CH3 . . . . .180 F1
Quarry La
Christleton CH3 . . . . .142 E7
Kelsall CW6 . . . . .122 D5
Newhall CW5 . . . . .26 C6
Quarry Rd Neston CH64 . .42 C1
New Mills SK22 . . . . .39 D7
Quarry Terr ST7 . . . . .195 A1
Quarrybank CW6 . . . . . . .184 F6
Quay Fold WA5 . . . . .15 F4
Quay Pl WA7 . . . . .50 C7
Quay Side WA6 . . . . .49 D1
Quay The WA6 . . . . .49 D2
Quayle Cl WA11 . . . . .1 C6
Quayside
Congleton CW12 . . . . . . .156 E1
Neston CH64 . . . . .66 E5
Quayside Mews WA13 . . .18 F3
Quayside Way SK11 . . . .112 E7
Queastybirch La WA4 . . . .26 A1
Quebec Rd WA2 . . . . .16 D7
Queen Anne Cl SK9 . . . . .60 C6
Queen Annes Ct 5
SK11 . . . . .112 B6
Queen Elizabeth Ho 79 A1
Queen St Audley ST7 . . .209 C1
Bollington SK10 . . . . .88 B8
Bunbury CW6 . . . . .185 E8
Chester CH1 . . . . .237 B2
Congleton CW12 . . . . . . .156 C2
CW12 . . . . .156 F4
Crewe CW1 . . . . .190 E5
Ellesmere Port CH65 . . . . .70 C7
Golborne WA3 . . . . .3 B8
Kidsgrove ST7 . . . . .195 A2
Knutsford WA16 . . . . .56 F2
Macclesfield SK10 . . . . . .112 D8
Middlewich CW10 . . . . . .128 C1
Nantwich CW5 . . . . .204 E5
Northwich CW9 . . . . .103 F7
Queen's Cl
Macclesfield SK10 . . . . . . .87 E2
Runcorn WA7 . . . . .22 F1
Queen's Cres CW1 . . . . .172 E2
Queen's Dr Chester CH4 .237 C1
Middlewich CW10 . . . . . .151 D7
Nantwich CW5 . . . . .204 D4
Sandbach CH5 . . . . .116 A3
Widnes WA8 . . . . .22 B8
Queen's Par
Crewe CW1 . . . . .126 D1
Queen's Dr CW1 . . . . . . .189 F3
Queen's Park Gdns
CW2 . . . . .189 E4
Queen's Park Ho CH4 . . .237 B1
Queen's Park View 237 B1
CH4 . . . . .237 B1
Queen's Rd Chester CH1 .237 C3
Runcorn WA7 . . . . .22 F1
Wilmslow SK9 . . . . .60 A6
Queen's Sch (Lower)
CH2 . . . . .118 C4
Queen's Sch The CH1 . . .237 A2
Queen's Way CW12 . . . . .139 B4
Queens Ave
Ellesmere Port CH65 . . . . .70 A3
Macclesfield SK10 . . . . . . .87 E2
Newton-le-W WA12 . . . . . . .2 C5
Queens Cl SK10 . . . . .87 E2
Queens Cres
Chester CH2 . . . . .118 E7
Warrington WA1 . . . . .17 A3
Queens Dr Golborne WA3 . .3 C8
Helsby WA6 . . . . .73 B2
Heswall CH60 . . . . .40 E8
Newton-le-W WA12 . . . . . . .2 C5
Warrington WA4 . . . . .17 A2

Queens Gdns
Ellesmere Port CH65 . . . . .70 B5
Talke ST7 . . . . .210 D5
Queens Park High Sch
CH4 .237 B1
Queens Pl CH1 . . . . .237 B3
Queens Rd Chester CH3 . . . .119 B3
Ellesmere Port CH66 . . . . .69 C7
Haydock WA11 . . . . .2 A7
Queens Terr SK9 . . . . .34 D3
Queensbury Cl
16 Handforth SK9 . . . . .34 D1
Wilmslow SK9 . . . . .60 D8
Queensbury Way WA8 . . . . .12 E3
Queensgate Bramhall SK7 . .35 E5
Northwich CW8 . . . . .103 E8
Queensgate Prim Sch
SK7 . . . . .2 C8
Queensway Alsager ST7 . .193 B5
Chester CH2 . . . . .118 F5
Crewe CW1 . . . . .190 C4
Frodsham WA6 . . . . .49 B2
Heald Green SK8 . . . . .34 C8
Heswall CH60 . . . . .41 C6
Knutsford WA16 . . . . .56 E3
Partington M31 . . . . .11 F4
Poynton SK12 . . . . .36 D3
Runcorn WA7 . . . . .22 F3
Winsford CW7 . . . . .149 D8
Queensway Trad Est
WA8 .23 A5
Quill Ct M44 . . . . .11 E6
Quillet The CH64 . . . . .66 F7
Quinn St WA8 . . . . .23 B7
Quinta Prim Sch The
CW12 . . . . .156 A2
Quinta Rd CW12 . . . . .156 A3

R

Raby Ave CH63 . . . . .43 B6
Raby Cl Bebington CH63 . . . .43 A7
Heswall CH60 . . . . .40 F7
Widnes WA8 . . . . .13 E2
Raby Ct CH65 . . . . .70 D3
Raby Dr CH63 . . . . .43 A6
Raby Gdns CH64 . . . . .66 E8
Raby Hall Rd CH63 . . . . .43 A6
Raby Mere Rd CH63 . . . . . . .42 D5
Raby Park Cl CH64 . . . . .66 E8
Raby Park Rd CH64 . . . . . . .66 F8
Raby Rd Neston CH64 . . . . . .66 E8
Thornton Hough CH63 . . . . . .42 B5
Race The SK9 . . . . .34 D2
Racecourse La CW6 . . . . . .124 A1
Racecourse Pk SK9 . . . . . . .59 F6
Racecourse Rd SK9 . . . . . . .59 E6
Racefield Cl WA13 . . . . .18 F3
Racefield Rd WA14 . . . . .56 F2
Radbroke Cl CW11 . . . . .175 C6
Radcliffe Ave WA3 . . . . .4 E3
Radcliffe Cl CH3 . . . . .121 C3
Radcliffe Rd
Sandbach CW11 . . . . .174 F3
Sutton Lane Ends SK11 . . . .135 D7
Raddel La WA4 . . . . .52 C5
Raddle Wharf CH65 . . . . . . .70 C7
Raddon Pl WA4 . . . . .16 E3
Radford Cl WA8 . . . . .22 C7
Radlett Cl WA5 . . . . .14 E3
Radley Dr CH63 . . . . .41 F6
Radley La WA2 . . . . .8 E4
Radnor Cl
Congleton CW12 . . . . .156 B3
Sandbach CW11 . . . . .174 E7
Radnor Dr Chester CH4 . . . .141 A4
Widnes WA8 . . . . .12 D2
Radnor Park Ind Ctr
CW12 . . . . .156 A4
Radnor Park Trad Est
CW12 . . . . .156 B4
Radnor St WA5 . . . . .15 E6
Radway Gn CH66 . . . . .69 E5
Radway Green Bsns & Tech
Ctr CW2 . . . . .192 F1
Radway Green Rd
Alsager CW2 . . . . .208 E8
Barthomley CW2 . . . . .208 D6
Raeburn Ave
Bebington CH62 . . . . .43 E6
Neston CH64 . . . . .66 E7
Raglan Prim Sch CH62 . .43 D6
Raglan Ct WA3 . . . . .9 F6
Raglan Rd SK10 . . . . .87 F2
Ragley Cl SK12 . . . . .36 F4
Railbrook Ct CW2 . . . . .190 D2
Railton Ave CW1 . . . . .190 A7
Railway Age Mus The*
CW1 . . . . .190 D3
Railway Cotts
Congleton CW12 . . . . .157 A1
Hollinfare WA3 . . . . .11 B5
Hooton CH66 . . . . .43 D1
Wimboldsley CW10 . . . . .150 F1
Railway St Crewe CW2 . . . .190 D2
Newton-le-W WA12 . . . . .2 B3
Railway View WA5 . . . . .1 D1
Railway View WA3 . . . . .12 C3
Rainbow St CW1 . . . . .190 D4
Rainford Cl ST7 . . . . .195 F1
Rainow Cl CW10 . . . . .151 B7

Rainow Dr SK12 . . . . .37 A2
Rainow Prim Sch SK10 . . . .88 D4
Rainow Rd SK10 . . . . .88 B2
Rainow View SK10 . . . . .63 C1
Rainow Way 10 SK9 . . . . . . .34 E1
Rajar Cotts WA16 . . . . .57 F4
Rake House Mews WA6 . . .73 B4
Rake La Backford CH2 . . . . . .95 D6
Broughton CH5 . . . . .139 A8
Christleton CH3 . . . . .143 A7
Dunham-on-t-H WA6 . . . . . . .97 B7
Dunham-on-t-H WA6 . . . . . . .97 E7
Eccleston CH4 . . . . .141 C1
Helsby WA6 . . . . .73 C4
Helsby, Helsby Marsh WA6 . .73 A5
Rake The Bebington CH62 . .43 C8
Burton CH64 . . . . .67 D1
Rake Way CH1 . . . . .4 A1
Raleigh Cl WA5 . . . . .7 D1
Raleigh Rd CH64 . . . . .41 F1
Ramp Rd E M90 . . . . .33 C7
Ramp Rd S M90 . . . . .33 C7
Ramp Rd W M90 . . . . .33 B7
Rampit Cl WA11 . . . . .1 F7
Ramsay Cl WA3 . . . . .9 E3
Ramsbottom St CW1 . . . . .190 B5
Ramsbrook La L24,WA8 . . .21 C3
Ramsdale Rd SK7 . . . . .35 E8
Ramsden Ct CH4 . . . . .140 F4
Ramsey Cl WA8 . . . . .13 E3
Ramsey Rd CH65 . . . . .70 C1
Ramsfield Rd L24 . . . . .21 A4
Randal Cres SK23 . . . . .65 E5
Randall Cl WA12 . . . . .2 B4
Randle Bennett Cl
CW11 . . . . .174 E7
Randle Mdw CH66 . . . . .69 F7
Randle Meadow Ct CH66 . .69 F7
Randle's View CW12 . . . . . .179 C8
Range Ct SK10 . . . . .87 E1
Rangemoor Cl WA3 . . . . . . .10 A6
Rannoch Cl CH66 . . . . .69 F3
Ranulph Ct WA6 . . . . .74 C7
Ranworth Ct CH22 . . . . .237 B4
Ranworth Dr WA3 . . . . .3 E7
Ranworth Rd WA5 . . . . .14 E6
Rappax Rd WA15 . . . . .32 A8
Raquets Ct The CW10 . . . .127 D5
Rathbone Pk CW6 . . . . .146 D2
Rathlin Cl WA8 . . . . .13 E3
Rathmell Cl WA3 . . . . .4 E3
Rathvale Dr M22 . . . . .33 C8
Raven Cl CW11 . . . . .175 A8
Raven Cotts TF9 . . . . .235 A5
Raven's La ST7 . . . . .209 F3
Ravenbank Com Prim Sch
WA13 . . . . .18 F3
Ravendale Cl CW7 . . . . . . .149 E8
Ravenfield Dr WA8 . . . . . . .12 C3
Ravenho La SK10 . . . . .88 D4
Ravenhurst Ct WA3 . . . . .9 F5
Ravenoak Park Rd SK8 . . .35 B8
Ravenoak Rd SK8 . . . . .35 B8
Ravens Cl WA3 . . . . .9 F6
Ravens Cnr CW5 . . . . .203 E5
Ravens La CW5 . . . . .203 E5
Ravenscar Cres M22 . . . . . .33 D8
Ravenscliffe Rd ST7 . . . . . .195 A1
Ravenscroft CW4 . . . . .130 A3
Ravenscroft Cl CW11 . . . . .175 C7
Ravenscroft Rd CW2 . . . . .189 E3
Ravensdale Cl WA2 . . . . .8 D3
Ravensfield CW8 . . . . .101 D4
Ravensholme Cl CH3 . . . . .166 A2
Ravensholme La CH3 . . . . .166 A2
Ravensmead Com Prim Sch
ST7 .209 E3
Ravenswood CW8 . . . . .103 B4
Ravenswood Dr SK8 . . . . . .35 B8
Ravenswood Rd SK9 . . . . . .59 E4
Ravenwood Dr WA15 . . . . . .32 D7
Rawcliffe Cl WA8 . . . . .12 F4
Rawdon Cl WA7 . . . . .50 A7
Rawlings Cl WA3 . . . . .9 F3
Rawlinson Cres L26 . . . . . . .21 B8
Rawson Rd CH1 . . . . .117 E3
Ray Ave CW5 . . . . .204 F7
Rayleigh Ave CW9 . . . . . . .127 A8
Rayleigh Way SK10 . . . . . . .86 E1
Raymond Ave WA4 . . . . . . .16 D2
Raymond St CH1 . . . . .237 A3
Raymond Way CH64 . . . . . . .67 A7
Rays Brow CW8 . . . . .78 B2
Reade's La CW12 . . . . .179 D8
Readesdale Ave CW2 . . . . .189 F2
Reading Room La SY14,
CH3 . . . . .199 D8
Rean Mdw CH3 . . . . .166 B2
Reaper Cl WA5 . . . . .15 D6
Reaseheath Coll CW5 . . . .188 D1
Reay St WA8 . . . . .13 C2
Record Bsns Pk WA2 . . . . . .16 A8
Rectory Ave WA3 . . . . .3 D8
Rectory Cl Farndon CH3 . . .180 E1
Holt LL13 . . . . .60 F7
8 Nantwich CW5 . . . . .204 E5
Winwick WA2 . . . . .8 A6
Wistaston CW2 . . . . .205 E8
Rectory Gdns Lymm WA13 .18 E3
Talke ST7 . . . . .210 D6
Rectory La Adderley TF9 . . .235 B5
Capenhurst CH1 . . . . .94 A8
Heswall CH60 . . . . .40 F7
Lymm WA13 . . . . .18 E3
Lymm WA13 . . . . .18 E3
Rectory View ST7 . . . . .210 D6
Red Bank Ave WA12 . . . . . . .2 F1
Red Brow La WA7,WA4 . . . .50 F8

Red Cow Yd 10 WA16 . . . . .57 A2
Red Gables WA4 . . . . .27 B3
Red Ho SK10 . . . . .87 E1
Red House La WA14 . . . . . . .20 C8
Red La Disley SK12 . . . . .38 C5
Frodsham WA6 . . . . .74 C7
Huxley CH3 . . . . .166 D6
Lower Whitley WA4 . . . . .52 C1
Sandbach CW11 . . . . .174 C6
Warrington WA4 . . . . .26 C7
Red Lion Cl ST7 . . . . .210 D7
Red Lion La
Ellesmere Port CH66 . . . . . . .69 C7
Nantwich CW5 . . . . .204 D5
Red Lodge SK12 . . . . .38 A6
Red Pike CH66 . . . . .69 D8
Red Row SK7 . . . . .37 B8
Red Stone Hill WA6 . . . . . . .73 C4
Redacre SK12 . . . . .36 F6
Redacre Cl WA4 . . . . .51 A3
Redbourne Dr
Chorlton CW2 . . . . .207 D1
Widnes WA8 . . . . .12 B4
Redbrook Cl CH62 . . . . .43 D6
Redbrook Gr 7 SK9 . . . . . .34 D1
Redbrook Rd M31 . . . . .11 E2
Redbrook Way SK10 . . . . . .62 C5
Redcar Dr CH62 . . . . .43 D5
Reddish Ave SK23 . . . . .65 D6
Reddish Cres WA13 . . . . . . .18 F4
Reddish La Lymm WA13 . . . .19 A5
Reddish Rd SK23 . . . . .65 D6
Reddy La
Little Bollington WA14 . . . . . .20 B1
Rostherne WA14 . . . . .30 B8
Redesdale Cl WA7 . . . . .8 E2
Redesmere Cl
Macclesfield SK10 . . . . .87 A1
Northwich CW9 . . . . .104 A5
Sandbach CW11 . . . . .174 F7
Redesmere Dr SK9 . . . . .60 A1
Redesmere La SK11 . . . . . .110 B3
Redesmere Rd SK9 . . . . . . .34 D5
Redfern Ave CW12 . . . . . . .156 F4
Redgate CW8 . . . . .103 D7
Redhill Mews CH65 . . . . . . .70 B6
Redhill Rd Chester CH4 . . .140 F6
Kelsall CW6 . . . . .122 C5
Redhouse La WA8 . . . . .38 E7
Redhouses SK11 . . . . .113 D3
Redland Cl CH4 . . . . .141 A7
Redland Ho CH4 . . . . .141 B7
Redmain Gr WA3 . . . . .3 E8
Redmayne Cl WA12 . . . . .2 B5
Redmere Dr CH60 . . . . .41 D8
Redmoor La Disley SK12 . . .39 A4
New Mills SK22 . . . . .39 B6
Redpoll La WA3 . . . . .9 E4
Redrock Cres ST7 . . . . .195 C1
Redruth Ave SK10 . . . . .86 E1
Redruth Cl WA7 . . . . .50 C6
Redshank Ave CW7 . . . . . .149 C5
Redshank Cl WA12 . . . . .2 C4
Redshank Dr SK10 . . . . .87 C5
Redshank La WA3 . . . . .9 F4
Redshaw Cl CW10 . . . . .151 C6
Redstart Cl 7 WA3 . . . . . . .3 E8
Redstone Dr 3 CW7 . . . . .126 A1
Redtail Cl WA7 . . . . .22 F3
Redvales Ct WA3 . . . . .9 C4
Redvers Ave CH66 . . . . .44 A2
Redway La SK10 . . . . .88 B7
Redwing Cl ST7 . . . . .195 F1
Redwood Cl Barnton CW8 . .78 B4
Holt LL13 . . . . .196 D8
Saltney CH4 . . . . .140 E6
Warrington WA1 . . . . .17 E7
Redwood Ct SK10 . . . . .87 E5
Redwood Dr Crewe CW1 . .189 F7
Ellesmere Port CH66 . . . . . . .94 E8
Elton CH2 . . . . .72 C4
Reece Cl CH2 . . . . .119 E8
Reed La CW9 . . . . .53 C6
Reedgate La CW9 . . . . .27 F1
Reedsmere Cl WA4 . . . . . . .16 E2
Reedsmere Wlk CW9 . . . . . .78 D8
Reeman St SK9 . . . . .34 B2
Rees Cres CW4 . . . . .130 C3
Reeve St WA3 . . . . .4 B8
Reeves Rd CH3 . . . . .142 B8
Regal Cl
Ellesmere Port CH66 . . . . . . .69 E3
Northwich CW9 . . . . .103 E4
Regal Cres WA8 . . . . .22 B8
Regency Cl ST7 . . . . .210 D5
Regency Ct Chester CH2 . .119 E8
Winsford CW7 . . . . .149 C7
Regency Gdns SK8 . . . . . . .34 E8
Regency Hospl SK11 . . . . .112 B8
Regency Pk SK9 . . . . .59 F5
Regency Way CW9 . . . . . . .103 E4
Regent & Foundry Ct 19
SK11 . . . . .112 C8
Regent Ave Haydock WA11 . .1 B7
Macclesfield SK11 . . . . .112 B6
Warrington WA8 . . . . .13 C1
Regent Bank SK9 . . . . .59 F5
Regent Cl Bramhall SK7 . . . .35 D4
Shavington CW2 . . . . .206 B3
Wilmslow SK9 . . . . .59 F5
Regent Ct WA15 . . . . .32 C8
Regent Rd CW5 . . . . .13 B1
Regent St
Ellesmere Port CH65 . . . . . . .70 A5
Moulton CW9 . . . . .126 F8
Newton-le-W WA12 . . . . .2 A3
Ridge Pk SK7 . . . . .35 D6

Regent St continued
Warrington WA1 . . . . .16 A5
Regents Cl CH3 . . . . .119 B2
Regents Gate CW5 . . . . . . .205 A5
Regents The SK9 . . . . .60 C8
Regents Theological Coll
CW5 . . . . .205 A5
Regents Way 4 CW7 . . . . .149 A8
Reginald Mitchell Prim Sch
The ST7 . . . . .194 D1
Registry Cl CW9 . . . . .103 E4
Reid Ave WA5 . . . . .15 F8
Reid Cl CH66 . . . . .69 C7
Reid St CW1 . . . . .190 C6
Reins Croft CH64 . . . . .41 E1
Rembury Pl WA4 . . . . .51 A3
Remer St CW1 . . . . .190 D7
Renaissance Ct CW1 . . . . .191 A4
Renaissance Way CW1 . . .191 A3
Rendel Cl WA12 . . . . .2 D2
Rendlesham Cl WA3 . . . . . . .10 B6
Renfrew Ave CH62 . . . . .43 E5
Renfrew Cl SK10 . . . . .86 F2
Renown Cl WA3 . . . . .9 D4
Renshaw Rd CW9 . . . . .79 D2
Rensherds Pl WA16 . . . . . . .29 C5
Renton Ave WA7 . . . . .23 D2
Repton Cl WA16 . . . . .29 C4
Repton Dr CW1 . . . . .191 D5
Repton Rd CH65 . . . . .70 D4
Reservoir Rd SK23 . . . . .65 D7
Reservoir Terr CH2 . . . . . . .118 F2
Retreat The CW1 . . . . .190 C6
Revesby Cl WA8 . . . . .12 D2
Rex Bldgs SK9 . . . . .60 B6
Reynold's La CW11 . . . . . . .175 F6
Reynolds Ave
St Helens WA9 . . . . .1 B2
Warrington WA3 . . . . .9 E5
Reynolds Mews SK9 . . . . . . .60 E8
Reynolds St WA4 . . . . .16 F3
Rhoden St CW1 . . . . .191 A6
Rhodes Cl CW1 . . . . .191 D4
Rhodes St WA2 . . . . .16 C7
Rhodesway CH60 . . . . .41 B7
Rhona Cl CH63 . . . . .43 C4
Rhona Dr WA5 . . . . .14 E6
Rhone Ct CH3 . . . . .142 A8
Rhuddlan Ct CH65 . . . . .70 D2
Rhuddlan Ct/Llys Rhuddlan
8 CH4 . . . . .140 F6
Rhuddlan Rd CH1 . . . . .117 D3
Rhum Cl CH65 . . . . .70 C2
Rhyl St WA8 . . . . .22 F7
Ribble Ave CW7 . . . . .127 B1
Ribble Cl Culcheth WA3 . . . . .4 F2
Ribble Dr ST8 . . . . .179 E1
Ribble Pl CW7 . . . . .127 B1
Ribblesdale CH65 . . . . .70 B3
Ribblesdale Ave CW12 . . .157 A5
Ribblesdale Cl CH62 . . . . . .43 F5
Ribchester Gdns WA3 . . . . . .5 A3
Richard Cl WA7 . . . . .24 A2
Richard Evans Com Prim Sch
WA11 .1 A6
Richard Moon St CW1 . . . .190 B8
Richard Reynolds St M44 .11 E6
Richard St Crewe CW1 . . . .190 B5
Northwich CW9 . . . . .104 C7
Richards Croft CH3 . . . . . . .142 A7
Richards Gr CW12 . . . . .156 A3
Richardson Cl
4 Sandbach CW11 . . . . . . .174 D6
Shavington CW2 . . . . .206 D5
Richardson St WA2 . . . . . . .16 C8
Richbell Cl M44 . . . . .11 F7
Richmond Ave
Handforth SK9 . . . . .34 D4
Haydock WA11 . . . . .1 B7
Runcorn WA7 . . . . .23 E2
Warrington WA4 . . . . .17 A4
Richmond Cl
Chorlton CW2 . . . . .207 D1
Culcheth WA3 . . . . .19 B4
Lymm WA13 . . . . .19 B4
Sandbach CW11 . . . . .174 E7
Richmond Cres CH3 . . . . . .119 C2
Richmond Ct
Chester CH3 . . . . .118 F2
Ellesmere Port CH65 . . . . . . .70 D3
Richmond Dr Lymm WA13 . .19 B4
Northwich CW9 . . . . .104 A4
Richmond Gdns WA12 . . . . .2 C2
Richmond Gn SK7 . . . . .35 F6
Richmond Hill
8 Knutsford WA16 . . . . . . .57 B1
Macclesfield SK11 . . . . .112 C6
Richmond Mews CH2 . . . . .118 F2
Richmond Pl SK11 . . . . .112 C6
Richmond Rd CW1 . . . . . . .190 E5
Richmond St
Widnes WA8 . . . . .13 C1
Richmond Village CW5 . . .205 A5
Rickaby Cl CH63 . . . . .43 C8
Ridding La WA7 . . . . .50 B6
Riddings Ct CW8 . . . . .103 B4
Riddings La
Hartford CW8 . . . . .103 B4
Wybunbury CH5 . . . . .220 A8
Riddings The CH65 . . . . .70 B4
Ridge Ave WA15 . . . . .32 C6
Ridge Hill Langley SK11 . . .113 B2
Utkinton CW6 . . . . .146 B5
Ridge Pk SK7 . . . . .35 D6

Ridge The CW8 . . . . .123 D7
Ridge View SK11 . . . . .112 C5
Ridgeborne Cl WA5 . . . . .7 D2
Ridgeway Golborne WA3 . . . .3 E7
Wilmslow SK9 . . . . .60 F7
Ridgeway Cl CH66 . . . . .69 C2
Ridgeway Ho CH3 . . . . .121 C3
Ridgeway The
Alvanley WA6 . . . . .74 A1
Cronton WA8 . . . . .12 C6
Heswall CH60 . . . . .41 B7
Runcorn WA7 . . . . .50 D6
Tarvin CH3 . . . . .121 C3
Ridgewell Ave 4 WA3 . . . . .3 D8
Ridgmont Rd SK7 . . . . .35 E5
Ridgway Gdns WA13 . . . . . .18 D3
Ridgway St Crewe CW1 . . .190 D5
Warrington WA3 . . . . .9 F8
Ridgway The SK12 . . . . .38 C6
Ridings Com Inf Sch The
CH1 . . . . .94 A1
Ridings The
Saughall CH1 . . . . .117 B8
Wilmslow SK9 . . . . .59 D4
Ridley Cl CW7 . . . . .206 E2
Ridley Dr WA5 . . . . .15 C4
Ridley Hill Farm CW6 . . . .185 C3
Ridley Rd SK10 . . . . .87 E8
Ridley Wood Rd LL13 . . . .196 A3
Ridsdale 2 WA8 . . . . .22 C8
Rigby Ave CW1 . . . . .190 A7
Rigby Rd ST7 . . . . .195 B3
Rigby St WA3 . . . . .3 A8
Riley Bank Mews WA6 . . . .74 B1
Riley Cl CW11 . . . . .174 E5
Riley Dr WA7 . . . . .49 A8
Rileys Way ST7 . . . . .209 F2
Rilshaw La CW7 . . . . .150 B8
Rilston Ave WA3 . . . . .4 D3
Rimington Cl WA3 . . . . .4 E3
Rimsdale Cl CW2 . . . . .206 A7
Ring Rd Chester CH2,CH3 . .119 C2
Connah's Quay CH5 . . . . .91 E2
Ring-o-Bells La SK12 . . . . . .38 D6
Ringsfield Rd L24 . . . . .21 A2
Ringstead Cl SK9 . . . . .34 D1
Ringstead Dr 9 SK9 . . . . . .34 D1
Ringway Shavington Way SK23 . . .65 D8
Ringway
Ellesmere Port CH66 . . . . . . .69 E4
Neston CH64 . . . . .41 E1
Waverton CH3 . . . . .143 B5
Ringway Cl SK10 . . . . .87 B4
Ringway Rd Runcorn WA7 . .23 D2
Woodhouse Park M22,M90 . .33 D7
Ringway St 3 WA3 . . . . .9 F8
Ringwood Cl WA3 . . . . .10 B5
Ripley Ave SK8 . . . . .35 B5
Ripley Cl SK7 . . . . .36 D7
Ripley St WA5 . . . . .15 E6
Ripon Ave
Ellesmere Port CH66 . . . . . . .69 C5
Ripon Cl Macclesfield SK10 .87 C3
Newton-le-W WA12 . . . . .2 C5
Ripon Dr CW2 . . . . .206 A7
Ripon Row WA7 . . . . .49 D6
Rise The SK23 . . . . .65 C6
Riseley St SK10 . . . . .112 C8
Rising Sun Cl SK11 . . . . . . .112 A5
Rising Sun Rd SK11 . . . . . .112 A4
Risley Moss Local Nature
Reserve Visitor Ctr*
WA3 .10 B4
Risley Rd WA3 . . . . .9 F6
Rivacre Brow CH66 . . . . . . .69 E8
Rivacre Bsns Ctr CH66 . . . .69 E7
Rivacre Rd CH62,CH65,
CH66 . . . . .44 C2
Rivacre Valley Ctry Pk*
CH66 . . . . .69 D8
Rivacre Valley Prim Sch
CH66 . . . . .69 E7
River La Chester CH4 . . . . . .141 C7
Farndon CH3 . . . . .180 E2
Partington M31 . . . . .11 F4
Saltney CH4 . . . . .140 E7
River Rd
Connah's Quay CH5 . . . . .91 F1
Warrington WA4 . . . . .16 B3
Warrington WA4 . . . . .16 C3
River St Congleton CW12 . .156 D3
Macclesfield SK11 . . . . .112 E6
Wilmslow SK9 . . . . .60 B8
Wilmslow SK9 . . . . .60 C7
River Wlk 3 WA7 . . . . .49 F7
Riverbank Cl
Bollington SK10 . . . . .87 F8
Heswall CH60 . . . . .40 F6
Nantwich CW5 . . . . .204 E8
Riverbank Rd CH60 . . . . . . .40 E6
Riverdane Rd CW12 . . . . . .156 F4
Riverpark Rd WA15 . . . . . . .32 C7
Riversdale Frodsham WA6 . .49 C1
Warrington WA1 . . . . .17 F8
Riversdale Rd WA7 . . . . .49 E8
Rivershill Gdns WA15 . . . . .32 B8
Riverside Nantwich CW5 . . .204 D5
Northwich CW9 . . . . .103 F8
Riverside Bsns Pk SK9 . . . .60 B7
Riverside Cres CW4 . . . . . .130 C4
Riverside Ct
Huntington CH3 . . . . .141 F7
Langley SK11 . . . . .113 C4

Riverside Dr SK10 ....87 A5
Riverside Gr CW7 ....189 D3
Riverside Pk CW9 ....103 E6
Riverside Ret Pk WA1 ...16 C4
Riverside Trad Est
  Northwich CW9 ....103 F7
  Warrington WA5 ....14 D1
Riverside Wlk CH64 ......66 D5
Riversmead CH3 ....142 A6
Riverview Rd CH64 ......66 F5
Rivington Cl WA1 ....17 E8
Rivington Gr M44 ....11 D6
Rivington Rd
  Ellesmere Port CH65 ....70 C5
  Runcorn WA7 ....50 F3
Rixton Ave WA5 ....15 F8
Rixton Clay Pits Nature
  Reserve* WA3 ....10 E2
Rixton Park Homes WA3 .10 F2
Roaches The SK11 ....112 B5
Road Beta CW10 ....151 D8
Road Five CW7 ....127 C2
Road Four CW7 ....127 B2
Road One Weston CW1 ..207 D8
  Winsford CW7 ....127 B3
Road Three CW7 ....127 C2
Road Two Weston CW1 ..207 C8
  Winsford CW7 ....127 B2
Roadside Ct WA3 ....3 C8
Roan Ct SK11 ....112 F7
Roan House Way SK11 ..112 F7
Roan Mews SK11 ....112 F7
Roan Way SK9 ....85 B8
Rob La WA1 ....2 C1
Robert Moffat WA16 ....29 C5
Robert St Northwich CW9 .103 E6
  Runcorn WA7 ....23 C2
  Warrington WA5 ....15 F6
  Widnes WA8 ....13 B1
Robert's Terr CH1 ....118 B1
Roberts Ave WA11 ....1 A5
Roberts Ct WA7 ....49 F6
Roberts Dr CW9 ....100 D8
Roberts Fold WA3 ....9 D4
Roberts Rd CW9 ....80 A2
Robin Cl Chelford SK11 ..84 A2
  Rainow WA7 ....88 E5
  Runcorn WA7 ....50 D7
  Sandbach CW11 ....175 A8
Robin Cres SK11 ....112 D2
Robin Hood Ave SK11 ..112 D5
Robin Hood La WA6 ....73 B2
Robin La Chelford SK11 ..84 A3
  Sutton Lane Ends SK11 ..112 D2
Robin's La SK7 ....35 D7
Robins Cl SK7 ....35 E7
Robins Croft CH66 ......69 F2
Robins La WA3 ....4 D2
Robins Way SK10 ....88 A7
Robinsbay Rd M22 ......33 E8
Robinsons Croft CH3 ...142 B7
Robson St WA1 ....16 D6
Robson Way ⊠ WA3 ....3 F8
Roby Gr WA5 ....15 A6
Roche Gdns SK8 ....35 B6
Rochester Cl Golborne WA3 .3 A8
  Warrington WA5 ....15 C5
Rochester Cres CW1 ....190 F6
Rochester Dr CH65 ......70 D3
Rochester Ho SK10 ......86 F1
Rock Bank SK23 ....65 E6
Rock Dr WA6 ....49 C1
Rock Farm Cl CH64 ......67 A6
Rock Farm Dr CH64 .....67 A6
Rock Farm Gr CH64 .....67 A6
Rock La Burwardsley CH3 .184 C6
  Chester CH2 ....237 A4
  Widnes WA8 ....12 F4
Rock Mill La SK22 ....39 B7
Rock Rd
  Connah's Quay CH5 .....91 E1
  Warrington WA4 ....16 E4
Rock St SK22 ....39 C7
Rock The WA6 ....73 C2
Rock Villas LL13 ....180 E1
Rockfield Cl WA8 ....12 D2
Rockfield Dr WA6 ....73 C2
Rockfield Mews WA4 ....16 F2
Rockford Lodge WA16 ..57 C1
Rockhouse La ST7 ......210 C7
Rockingham Cl WA3 ....10 C6
Rocklands La CH63 ......42 C8
Rocklee Gdns CH64 .....67 A6
Rockliffe La CH6 ....91 A3
Rocksavage Expressway
  WA7 ....49 D5
Rockside ST7 ....195 C6
Rockwood Ave CW2 .....190 A3
Rockwood Cl CW2 ....190 A3
Rocky La Heswall CH60 ..40 F8
  Tattenhall CH3 ....182 F7
Rocky La S CH60 ....41 A8
Roddy La WA6 ....75 E2
Rode Ct [7] CW12 ......156 F3
Rode Hall* ST7 ....194 B7
Rode Heath Prim Sch
  ST7 ....193 F7
Rode St CW6 ....146 A3
Rode The ST7 ....193 D4
Rodeheath Cl SK9 ......60 D7
Rodehouse Cl ST7 ......193 F7
Rodepool Cl WA3 ....9 C4
Rodney St WA16 ....56 F1
Rodney St SK11 ....112 D7
Roe Pk CW12 ....178 E1
Roe St Congleton CW12 .156 E2
  Macclesfield SK11 ......112 D7

Roebourne Rise CH1 ...117 D4
Roebuck St CW1 ....190 C5
Reburn Way WA5 ....14 D3
Roedean Wlk CW10 .....190 D6
Roehampton Dr WA7 ....49 E7
Roehurst La CW7 ....126 D2
Roemarsh Ct WA7 ......49 E6
Roewood La
  Higher Hurdsfield SK10 ..88 A1
  Macclesfield SK10 ......113 B8
Roften Ind Est CH66 ....43 D1
Rokeby Ct WA7 ....24 D5
Rokeden WA12 ....2 D4
Roland Ave WA7 ....22 F1
Rolands Wlk WA7 ....23 F2
Rolleston St WA2 ....16 A6
Rolls Ave CW1 ....190 A6
Rolt Cres CW1 ....151 C7
Roman Cl
  Newton-le-W WA12 .....2 C2
  Runcorn WA7 ....23 E2
Roman Ct CH64 ....66 F7
Roman Dr CH1 ....117 D6
Roman Way CW11 ......174 F7
Romanes St CW8 ......103 E7
Romiley Rd CH66 ......69 E6
Romney Cl Neston CH64 .66 E7
  Widnes WA8 ....13 E2
Romney Croft CH64 .....66 F7
Romney Way CH64 .....66 F7
Romsey Dr SK8 ....35 C6
Rona Ave CH65 ....70 C3
Ronald Dr WA2 ....9 B2
Ronaldshay WA8 ....13 E2
Ronaldsway Halewood L26 .21 A8
  Heswall CH60 ....40 F6
Ronan Rd WA8 ....22 E5
Rood Hill CW12 ....156 D3
Rood La CW12 ....156 E4
Rook St CW2 ....190 C2
Rookery Cl
  [8] Nantwich CW5 .....204 F5
  Sandbach CW11 ......174 C5
Rookery Ct CW11 ......174 C5
Rookery Dr
  Nantwich CW5 ....204 E4
  Tattenhall CH3 ....182 F7
Rookery Farm Rd CW6 .169 A6
Rookery Gdns CW9 ....103 E3
Rookery Rd
  Kidsgrove ST7 ....195 C3
  Tilston SY14 ....198 B3
Rookery Rise WA7 .....150 A8
Rookery The
  Broughton CH4 ....139 B3
  Saughall CH1 ....117 A8
Rookerypool Cl SK9 ....34 D2
Rooks Way CH60 ....40 E8
Rope Bank Ave CW2 ...206 A4
Rope La Shavington CW2 .206 A5
  Wistaston CW2 ....205 F7
Rope Wlk CW7 ....156 D3
Ropewalk The CH64 ....66 C8
Ropeworks The CH1 ...118 B2
Rosam Ct WA7 ....49 E6
Roscoe Ave
  Newton-le-W WA12 ....2 C2
  Warrington WA1 ....16 D8
Roscoe Cres WA7 ......48 E7
Roscoes Yd [3] WA16 ..57 A2
Roscommon Way WA8 .12 E3
Roscote Cl CH60 ....40 F7
Roscote The CH60 .....40 F7
Rose Ave WA11 ....1 E6
Rose Bank Bollington SK10 .87 F7
  Lymm WA13 ....18 E3
Rose Cl WA7 ....50 D5
Rose Cnr CW5 ....166 A1
Rose Cotts CW12 ......154 E6
Rose Cres WA8 ....22 F7
Rose Farm CW6 ....146 B7
Rose Farm Ct CW9 .....79 E4
Rose Farm Mews WA6 .73 B4
Rose Gdns CH64 ....66 F6
Rose Lea Cl WA8 ....13 A4
Rose St CW8 ....22 F7
Rose Terr CW1 ....190 C5
Rose View Ave WA8 ....13 A2
Rose Wlk [4] M31 ......11 E3
Rosebank Cl CW7 ......149 F8
Rosebank Mews CW10 .129 E5
Rosebank Rd WA11 ....1 C4
Rosebank Sch CW8 ....78 A3
Rosebank Wlk CW8 ....78 A4
Rosebery Way CW1 ....191 C4
Rosecroft CH62 ....43 C6
Rosedale Ave
  Golborne WA3 ....3 C7
  Warrington WA1 ....17 C7
Rosedene Cl CW2 ......218 E8
Roseheath Dr L26 ......21 A6
Rosehill Rd CW7 ......190 B1
Roselands Ct LL12 .....162 C1
Rosemary Ave
  Runcorn WA7 ....49 F4
  Warrington WA4 ....16 C1
Rosemary Cl
  Broughton CH4 ....139 C3
  Warrington WA5 ....15 C6
Rosemary La WA3 ......2 F1
Rosemary La LL12 .....161 D1
Rosemary Row CH3 ...166 A1
Rosemary Wlk M31 .....11 F2
Rosemere Dr CH1 ......94 F7

Rosemoor Gdns WA4 ....26 F5
Rosemount CW10 ......128 C1
Rosemount Cotts WA2 ...8 B8
Rosetree Mdw CW7 ....80 A2
Rosevale Rd ST5 ......210 F1
Roseville Dr CW12 .....179 B8
Roseway SK11 ....112 D5
Rosewood Ave
  Chester CH2 ....118 D5
  Frodsham WA6 ....74 D7
  Warrington WA1 ....16 E7
Rosewood Cl CW1 .....190 E6
Rosewood Dr CW7 ....126 A1
Rosewood Gr
  Saughall CH1 ....117 B8
  Widnes WA8 ....22 B8
Rosewood Ho CW12 ...156 A3
Ross Cl WA5 ....15 D7
Ross Dr CH66 ....69 F5
Ross Rd CH65 ....70 A6
Ross St WA8 ....13 B1
Rossall Cl L24 ....21 E2
Rossall Ct SK7 ....35 E6
Rossall Dr SK7 ....35 E6
Rossall Gr CH66 ......69 F6
Rossall Rd
  Warrington WA5 ....15 B4
  Widnes WA8 ....13 D2
Rossbank Rd CH65 ....70 A7
Rosscliffe Rd CH65 ....70 A7
Rossenclough Rd SK9 ..34 D1
Rossendale Dr WA3 ....9 D4
Rossendale Rd SK8 ....34 C8
Rossett Ave M22 ......33 D8
Rossett Bsns Village
  LL12 ....162 B1
Rossett Cl
  Northwich CW9 ....103 E4
  Warrington WA5 ....7 F2
Rossett Pk LL12 ......162 C1
Rossett Rd L24 ....180 A1
Rossfield Rd CH65 .....70 A6
Rossfield Rd N CH65 ...70 B7
Rosslyn Cl CH5 ....116 A2
Rosslyn La CW8 ....102 A3
Rosslyn Rd CH3 ......119 B3
Rossmill La WA15 ......32 B7
Rossmore Bsns Pk CH65 .70 B7
Rossmore Gdns CH66 ..65 D6
Rossmore Ind Est CH65 .70 A6
Rossmore Rd E CH66 ..69 F7
Rossmore Rd W CH66 ..69 D7
Rossmore Terraced Factories
  CH65 ....70 A6
Rossmount Rd CH65 ...70 A6
Rosswood Rd CH65 ....70 A6
Rostherne Ave
  Ellesmere Port CH65 ...69 E4
  Golborne WA3 ....3 D8
  High Lane SK6 ....37 E8
Rostherne Cl WA5 .....15 D4
Rostherne Cres WA8 ...12 D2
Rostherne La WA16 ....30 E4
Rostherne Rd SK9 .....59 F4
Rostherne Way CW11 ..174 F7
Rosyth Cl WA7 ....49 F3
Rothay Dr WA5 ....14 D3
Rothbury Cl WA7 ......24 F1
Rother Cl CH65 ....70 A7
Rother Dr Bsns Ctr CH65 .70 A7
Rotherhead Dr SK11 ..112 B5
Rotherwood Rd SK9 ...59 D6
Rothesay Cl WA7 ......23 F2
Rothesay Dr CH62 ....43 E4
Rothesay Rd CH4 .....141 A7
Rough Bank CW12 ....179 E8
Rough Heys La SK11 ..111 A8
Roughlea Ave WA3 ....4 D4
Roughlyn Cres CH4 ...140 E1
Roughwood La
  Alsager CW11,ST7 ....193 B7
  Hassall Green CW11 ...176 A1
Round Gdns SK10 ......88 A8
Round Hill Mdw CH3 ..142 B7
Round Mdw SK10 .....88 E5
Round Thorn WA3 ......9 A8
Roundabout The WA8 ..12 D6
Roundhey SK8 ....34 C8
Roundway SK7 ....35 C6
Roundy La SK10 ....62 F6
Routledge St WA8 .....13 B1
Row The
  [3] Winsford CW7 ....126 D1
  Wrenbury CH5 ....217 B5
Rowan Ave WA3 ....3 F7
Rowan Cl Alsager ST7 ..193 D3
  Delamere CW8 ....123 D7
  Lawton Heath End ST7 .193 D6
  Middlewich CW10 .....151 E6
  Runcorn WA7 ....49 C7
  Sandbach CW11 ......174 F7
  Winsford CW7 ....126 D3
Rowan Ct CW8 ....30 A4
Rowan Dr SK8 ....35 C8
Rowan Gr CH5 ....91 C1
Rowan Lo SK7 ....35 C6
Rowan Pk CH3 ....142 E7
Rowan Pl CW2 ....119 B4
Rowan Rd CW8 ....102 D8
Rowan Rise WA8 ....78 A3
Rowan Tree Rd WA16 ..56 F5
Rowan Way SK10 ......87 E1
Rowan Wlk M31 ....11 E2

Rowans The
  Broughton CH4 ....139 B3
  [4] Northwich CW9 ...103 E6
Rowanside SK10 ....86 E6
Rowanside Dr SK10 ....60 E8
Rowcliffe Ave CH4 ....141 A4
Rowden Cl WA7 ....50 C5
Rowena Ct CH2 ....118 F3
Rowland Cl WA2 ....9 A3
Rowlands View CW6 ...146 B7
Rowley Bank La WA16 ..29 F1
Rowley Rd SK7 ....36 E8
Rowley Way WA16 .....82 B7
Rowson Dr M44 ....11 D6
Rowswood Farm WA4 ..25 C5
Rowthorn Cl WA8 ......22 E8
Rowton Bridge Rd CH3 .142 E7
Rowton Ct CW7 ....149 A8
Rowton La CH3 ....142 F6
Rowton Rd CW2 ....189 D4
Roxborough Cl WA5 ....7 A5
Roxburgh Cl SK10 .....87 A1
Roxburgh Rd CH66 ....68 F6
Roxby Way WA16 ......82 A7
Roxholme Wlk M22 ....33 C8
Royal Arc [3] CW1 ....190 C4
Royal Ave WA8 ....12 A1
Royal Gdns
  Altrincham WA14 ......20 F2
  Northwich CW9 ....103 E3
Royal La CW5 ....147 A3
Royal Mdws SK10 .....87 A1
Royal Mews CW9 .....104 D5
Royal Mews SK8 ......34 C8
Royal Pl WA8 ....12 A1
Royal Rd SK12 ....38 D5
Royal Schools for The Deaf &
  Communication Disorders
  SK8 ....34 D6
Royal Sh Arc The [9]
  CH64 ....66 E8
Royce Cl CW1 ....190 A7
Royce Ct WA5 ....15 B8
Rubin Dr CW1 ....189 F7
Rudd Ave WA9 ....1 B2
Rudheath Cl CW2 .....189 D5
Rudheath Com High Sch
  CW9 ....104 D6
Rudheath Com Prim Sch
  CW9 ....104 D6
Rudheath La WA7 ......24 D3
Rudheath Way CW9 ...104 E5
Rudloe Ct WA2 ....8 F3
Rudstone Cl CH66 .....69 B5
Rudyard Cl SK11 ......112 B6
Rue De Bohars CW6 ..168 D8
Rufford Cl Widnes WA8 .12 C2
  Wistaston CW2 ....206 B8
Rufford Ct WA1 ....17 E8
Rufus Ct CH1 ....237 A3
Rugby Cl SK10 ....87 E4
Rugby Dr SK10 ....87 E4
Rugby Ho SK10 ....87 D3
Rugby Rd CH65 ....70 D3
Rugby Wlk CH65 ......70 D3
Ruislip Ct WA2 ....8 F2
Runcorn All Saints CE Prim
  Sch WA7 ....23 A3
Runcorn Docks Rd WA7 .22 D2
Runcorn East Sta WA7 ..50 D7
Runcorn Rd Barnton CW8 .78 B2
  Higher Walton WA4 ...25 E8
  Little Leigh CW8 ......77 D5
Runcorn Spur Rd WA7 ..23 B1
Runcorn Sta WA7 ......22 F2
Runger La M90,WA15 ..32 F8
Runnell The CH64 ......41 D4
Runnymede WA1 ......16 D7
Runnymede Ct [2] WA8 .13 C1
Runnymede Dr WA11 ..1 C7
Runnymede Gdns [5]
  WA8 ....13 C1
Runymede Wlk [3] WA8 .13 C2
Rupert Row WA7 ......50 A8
Ruscoe Ave CW11 .....174 E6
Ruscolm Cl WA5 ......14 D7
Rush Gdns WA13 ......19 A4
Rushes Mdw WA13 ....19 B5
Rushey Cl WA15 ......32 D7
Rushfield Cres WA7 ...50 B5
Rushfield Rd
  Cheadle Hulme SK8 ....35 A6
  Chester CH4 ....141 B5
Rushgreen Rd WA13 ..19 A4
Rushmere Cl SK10 ....62 F2
Rushmere La CH3 ....163 F3
Rushmore Gr WA1 ....17 A7
Rusholme Cl L26 ......21 A6
Rushside Rd SK8 ......35 A6
Rushton Ave WA12 ....2 A4
Rushton CE Prim Sch
  SK11 ....159 B2
Rushton Cl
  Burtonwood WA5 ......6 F7

Rushton Cl *continued*
  Northwich CW9 ....104 C7
  Widnes WA8 ....12 F3
Rushton Dr Chester CH2 .118 E7
  Hough CW2 ....206 E2
  Middlewich CW10 .....151 C7
Rushton Fold SK10 ......61 A2
Rushton La CW6 ....147 D6
Rushton Rd SK8 ....35 A6
Rushy View WA12 ......2 A4
Ruskin Ave
  Newton-le-W WA12 ....2 C4
  Warrington WA2 ....8 C2
Ruskin Cl WA16 ....57 A2
Ruskin Dr CH65 ....70 D3
Ruskin Rd
  Congleton CW12 ......156 C2
  Crewe CW2 ....190 C2
Ruskin Sports Coll & Com
  High Sch CW2 ....190 C2
Ruskin Way WA16 ......57 A3
Russel Cl WA8 ....13 B4
Russell Ave Alsager ST7 .193 D5
  High Lane SK6 ....37 E7
Russell Cl CW12 ......179 A8
Russell Dr CW1 ....191 C5
Russell Rd Runcorn WA7 ..48 E8
  Winsford CW7 ....149 C8
Russell St CH1,L3 ....237 C3
Russet Cl CW10 ....128 B2
Russet Rd CW8 ....102 D8
Russett Sch & Cheshire MSI
  Unit The CW8 ....102 E8
Rutherford Dr WA16 ...82 C7
Ruthin Cl WA5 ....7 E3
Ruthin Ct CH65 ....70 D3
Ruthin Wlk WA6 ....73 A1
Rutland Ave Golborne WA3 .3 D7
  Halewood L26 ....21 A8
  Warrington WA4 ....26 B8
Rutland Cl
  Congleton CW12 ......156 E4
  Sandbach CW11 ......174 C5
Rutland Dr
  Middlewich CW10 .....151 C7
  Weaverham CW8 ......77 C1
Rutland Pl CH2 ....119 A5
Rutland Rd
  Hazel Grove SK7 ......36 E8
  Irlam M44 ....11 D5
  Kidsgrove ST7 ....195 A2
  Macclesfield SK11 ....112 D4
  Partington M31 ....11 E2
Rutland St [1] WA7 ....22 F2
Rutter Ave WA5 ....7 F2
Ryburn Cl CW2 ....207 B3
Ryburn Rd SK11 ......112 B6
Rydal Ave High Lane SK6 .37 E8
  Warrington WA4 ....16 A2
Rydal Cl
  Ellesmere Port CH65 ...70 C2
  Holmes Chapel CW4 ..130 B2
  Neston CH64 ....66 F6
  Winsford CW7 ....126 D3
Rydal Ct CW12 ....156 A2
Rydal Dr WA15 ....32 D8
Rydal Gr Chester CH4 ..141 A6
  Helsby WA6 ....73 B1
  Runcorn WA7 ....49 B8
Rydal Mount SK9 ......34 E1
Rydal Pl SK11 ....112 A6
Rydal St CW12 ....2 C3
Rydal Way Alsager ST7 .193 C5
  Widnes WA8 ....12 C1
Ryde Cl CW1 ....190 B8
Ryder Rd Warrington WA1 .17 C7
  Widnes WA8 ....13 B4
Ryders St CW8 ....103 E8
Rye Cl ST7 ....193 B3
Ryebank Ave CW1 .....190 B7
Ryebank Rd SK10 .....87 C3
Ryecroft CH2 ....72 B3
Ryecroft Ct CW10 ....151 B7
Ryecroft La
  Duddon CH3,CW6 .....144 C6
  Mobberley WA16 ......57 E4
Ryecroft Rd CH60 .....41 C7
Ryedale Way CW12 ...179 C8
Ryehills ST7 ....209 E1
Rylands Cl SY14 ......213 B4
Rylands St
  Warrington WA1 ......16 B5
  [3] Widnes WA8 ......23 B8
Ryle Cl CW1 ....112 D6
Ryle St SK11 ....112 C6
Ryle's Park Rd SK11 ...112 C6
Ryles Cres SK11 ......112 C6
Ryles Ho SK11 ....112 C5
Ryleys Farm SK9 ......59 F1
Ryleys La SK9 ....59 F1
Ryleys Sch The SK9 ...59 F1

S

Sabre Cl WA7 ....50 D7
Sack La CW9 ....54 F6
Sacred Heart RC Prim Sch
  WAS 15 E5
Saddleback Dr SK10 ...86 F7
Saddlers Rise WA7 ....50 C8
Sade Ct CW7 ....190 B5
Sadler Cl CW7 ....126 D1
Sadler Rd CW7 ....126 D1

Sadler St WA8 13 C1
Sadler's Cl CW4 130 B3
Sadlers La CW6 124 A1
Sadlers Wells CW6 185 E8
Saffron Cl Golborne WA3 3 E8
Warrington WA2 9 B1
Saffron Wlk M31 11 F2
Sagars Rd Handforth SK9 34 C3
Styal SK9 34 B4
Sage Cl WA2 9 C2
Saighton CE Prim Sch CH3 142 E1
Saighton La CH3 142 F2
SS Peter & Paul RC High Sch WA8 12 F2
St Aelred's RC Tech Coll WA12 2 D4
St Aidans Dr WA8 12 F6
St Alban Rd WA5 14 E5
St Alban's RC Prim Sch
Macclesfield SK10 86 F1
Warrington WA5 15 F6
St Albans Cl WA11 2 A7
St Albans Dr CW5 204 F3
St Albans Pl SK22 39 C7
St Albans St SK22 39 C8
St Ambrose Coll WA15 32 B8
St Ambrose RC Prim Sch L24 21 A2
St Ambrose Rd WA8 13 C1
St Andrew's Ave CW2 190 C1
St Andrew's CE Prim Sch WA2 8 C3
St Andrew's Gdns ST7 193 E2
St Andrew's Rd
Ellesmere Port CH65 70 E3
Macclesfield SK11 112 B7
St Andrews Cl
Northwich CW9 104 E7
Warrington WA2 9 A4
St Andrews Ct
Crewe CW2 190 C1
Ellesmere Port CH65 70 E2
Macclesfield SK11 112 B7
St Andrews Dr
Holmes Chapel CW4 130 B2
Kidsgrove ST7 195 C3
St Andrews Wlk
Mickle Trafford CH2 96 F1
New Mills SK22 39 D8
St Ann's Rd CW10 151 C8
St Ann's Rd S SK8 34 C8
St Ann's Sq SK8 34 C8
St Anne St CH1 237 B3
St Anne's Ave CW10 151 D8
St Anne's Fulshaw CE Prim Sch SK9 59 F6
St Anne's La CW5 204 D5
St Anne's RC Prim Sch CW5 204 E3
St Anne's Rd WA8 13 B2
St Annes CH1 237 B3
St Annes Ave WA4 17 B2
St Annes Ave E WA4 17 B2
St Anthony Pl WA2 8 B6
St Anthony's RC Prim Sch CH4 140 E6
St Asaph Dr WA5 7 E3
St Asaph Rd CH66 94 E8
St Augustine's Ave WA4 16 F4
St Augustine's RC Prim Sch
Runcorn WA7 24 A2
Warrington WA4 16 F4
St Austell Ave SK10 86 E1
St Austell Cl
Macclesfield SK10 86 E1
Runcorn WA7 50 B6
Warrington WA5 14 E3
St Austell Dr SK8 34 B8
St Austins La WA1 16 B4
St Barnabas CE Prim Sch
Macclesfield SK11 112 D6
Warrington WA5 15 F5
St Barnabas Ct SK11 112 D6
St Barnabas Pl WA5 15 E6
St Bartholomews Ct CH5 116 E6
St Basil's RC Prim Sch WA8 12 A2
St Bede's Ave CW8 77 D1
St Bede's RC Inf Sch WA8 13 A1
St Bede's RC Jun Sch WA8 13 A1
St Bede's RC Prim Sch CW8 102 F7
St Benedict's RC Prim Sch
Handforth SK9 34 E3
Warrington WA2 16 D7
St Benedicts Cl WA2 16 B7
St Bernard's RC Prim Sch CH65 70 D3
St Berteline's CE Prim Sch WA7 50 C8
St Brannocks Rd SK8 35 B7
St Brides Cl WA5 14 E3
St Bridget's RC Prim Sch WA2 8 E3
St Bridgets Cl WA2 8 F3
St Bridgets Ct CH4 141 B6
St Catherine Dr CW8 103 A4
St Catherine's RC Prim Sch WA3 3 E7
St Chad's CE Prim Sch
Newcastle-u-Lyme ST5 210 D2
St Chad's CE Prim Sch *continued*
Winsford CW7 149 E8
St Chad's Fields CW7 149 C5
St Chad's RC High Sch WA7 49 D7
St Chad's Rd CH1 117 F4
St Chads Cl CW5 220 A8
St Chads Way TF9 236 C2
St Christophers Cl CH2 118 D8
St Clair St CW2 190 D1
St Clare's RC Prim Sch CH4 141 A5
St Clement's RC Prim Sch WA7 49 A8
St David Rd CH62 44 A6
St David's High Sch CH4 140 C6
St David's Terr CH4 140 C6
St Davids Dr
Ellesmere Port CH66 94 F8
Warrington WA5 7 E2
St Davids' Ret Pk CH4 140 D7
St Edward's RC Prim Sch
Macclesfield SK11 112 C5
Runcorn WA7 23 B3
St Edwards Cl SK11 112 D6
St Elmo Pk SK12 37 C4
St Elphin's (Fairfield) CE Prim Sch WA1 16 D6
St Elphins Cl WA1 16 C5
St Gabriel's RC Prim Sch ST7 193 C3
St Gabriels Ct ST7 193 C3
St George's CE Prim Sch SK22 39 C8
St George's Cl WA16 82 C8
St George's Cres
Chester CH4 237 C1
Waverton CH3 143 A5
St George's Ct WA8 22 D8
St George's Pl 11 SK11 112 D7
St George's Rd CW7 149 C8
St George's St SK11 112 D6
St George's Way
Northwich CW9 103 F5
Thornton Hough CH63 42 A7
St Georges Ave CH66 94 F8
St Georges Cl WA4 26 E3
St Georges Rd SK22 39 C8
St Gerard's RC Prim Sch WA8 23 B7
St Gregory's RC High Sch WA5 15 D5
St Gregory's RC Prim Sch SK10 87 F8
St Helens Cl WA3 11 B3
St Helens Coll Newton Campus WA12 2 B4
St Helens Rd Golborne WN7 4 B8
5 Northwich CW9 104 A8
St Hilda's Dr WA6 49 C1
St Ives Cl SK10 86 E1
St Ives Pk CH5 116 A3
St Ives Way CH5 116 A3
St James Ave
Chester CH2 118 F7
Congleton CW12 156 C2
Warren SK11 111 E2
St James Cl Audlem CW3 230 A4
1 Frodsham WA6 49 C1
St James Ct Audley ST7 209 D2
Cheadle Hulme SK8 34 F6
Chester CH2 118 F3
St James Ct/Llys Sant Iago CH5 91 D1
St James St CH1 237 B3
St James Terr 9 CW7 149 A8
St James Wlk 1 CW8 103 E7
St James' CE Prim Sch WA11 1 E6
St James' Ct
Biddulph ST8 179 E3
Warrington WA4 16 B3
St James' Dr SK9 60 A6
St James' RC High Sch SK8 34 F6
St James' Sq SK22 39 C8
St James' Way SK8 34 F6
St John Ave WA4 16 B2
St John Fisher RC Prim Sch WA8 13 D1
St John St Chester CH1 237 B2
Newton-le-W WA12 2 A3
St John The Evangelist CE Prim Sch SK11 112 A7
St John The Evangelist RC Prim Sch (Annexe) ST7 194 F1
St John's Ave
Knutsford WA16 56 F1
Lostock Gralam CW9 79 F3
St John's Brow WA7 23 B3
St John's CE Prim Sch
Bollington SK10 88 A7
Kingsley WA6 75 C2
Sandbach CW11 175 E6
St John's Cl CW9 104 E8
St John's Ct
Knutsford WA16 57 C2
Warrington WA1 16 F7
St John's Rd
Bebington CH62 44 A5
Chester CH4 237 C1
Congleton CW12 157 A5
Knutsford WA16 57 A1
7 Macclesfield SK11 112 C7
Wilmslow SK9 59 E3
St John's Rear Rd CH4 237 C1
St John's St WA7 23 B3
St John's Way
Cuddington CW8 102 B2
Sandbach CW11 175 E6
St John's Wood ST7 194 F1
St John's Wood Com Sch WA16 57 D2
St Johns Ct Chester CH1 237 B2
Winsford CW7 126 B1
St Johns Dr CW7 149 A8
St Joseph's Cl WA5 14 E5
St Joseph's RC Prim Sch
Warrington WA5 14 E5
Winsford CW7 149 B8
St Josephs Way CW5 205 A5
St Katherines Way WA1 16 D5
St Kilda Cl CH65 70 C1
St Lawrence Ct CW5 204 F6
St Lawrence Rd WA6 74 B8
St Leonard's Way CW3 232 C1
St Lewis RC Prim Sch WA3 4 B1
St Luke's Ave WA3 3 D8
St Luke's CE Prim Sch WA3 3 E7
St Luke's Cres WA8 13 B4
St Luke's Ho 3 SK10 111 F8
St Luke's RC Prim Sch WA6 74 C8
St Luke's Way WA6 49 B1
St Lukes Cl CW4 130 D3
St Margaret's Ave WA2 8 D1
St Margaret's CE Prim Sch WA2 8 C1
St Mark's CE Prim Sch CW9 53 C4
St Mark's RC Prim Sch L26 21 A8
St Mark's St WA11 1 A6
St Marks Cres CH66 94 F8
St Marks Rd CH4 140 F6
St Martin's Rd ST7 210 E6
St Martin's Way CH1 237 A3
St Martins Dr CH66 69 D2
St Martins La WA7 50 D7
St Martins RC Prim Sch WA7 50 D7
St Mary of the Angels RC Prim Sch CH66 69 D6
St Mary's Ave CW8 77 D1
St Mary's CE Inf Sch CH2 118 E7
St Mary's CE Prim Sch
Bebington CH62 44 A5
Bosley SK11 158 D8
Irlam M44 11 C5
Runcorn WA7 50 A8
St Mary's Cl Alsager ST7 193 C5
Hale L24 21 E2
Warrington WA4 26 C6
St Mary's Ct CW12 156 A2
St Mary's Ct WA3 4 B8
St Mary's Dr CW8 126 A8
St Mary's Hill CH1 237 B1
St Mary's RC Inf Sch WA12 2 C4
St Mary's RC Jun Sch WA12 2 B3
St Mary's RC Prim Sch
Congleton CW12 156 D3
Crewe CW2 190 A1
Middlewich CW10 151 C8
New Mills SK22 39 B8
St Mary's Rd Disley SK12 38 D5
Dodleston CH4 162 A7
Nantwich CW5 204 E7
New Mills SK22 39 B7
Runcorn WA8 23 F1
Warrington WA5 14 F5
Widnes WA8 23 A4
St Mary's St Crewe CW1 190 C4
Warrington WA4 16 D3
St Mary's Way CH4 139 C5
St Marys Ct CW5 204 A7
St Matthews CE Prim Sch WA4 26 E2
St Matthews Cl
Haslington CW1 191 D4
Warrington WA4 26 D7
St Mawes Cl WA8 12 E2
St Mawes Ct SK10 86 E1
St Mawgan Ct WA2 8 F2
St Michael's Ave SK7 35 E8
St Michael's Cl
Little Leigh CW8 77 D5
Widnes WA8 22 C7
St Michael's Cotts CW12 156 B7
St Michael's Ind Est WA8 22 C7
St Michael's RC Prim Sch WA8 22 C7
St Michael's Rd WA8 22 C7
St Michael's Sq CH1 237 B2
St Michael's View CW1 190 B5
St Michael's Way CW10 128 C1
St Michaels Terr 10 SK11 112 D8
St Monica's RC Prim Sch WA4 26 D7
St Monicas Cl WA4 26 D7
St Nicholas Ct CW5 204 F5
St Nicholas RC High Sch CW8 103 D6
St Nicholas Rd WA3 4 A8
St Olave St CH1 237 B1
St Oswald's CE Prim Sch CH1 94 F2
St Oswald's Cres CW11 153 F5
St Oswald's RC Prim Sch WA1 16 F8
St Oswald's Worleston CE Prim Sch CW5 188 E6
St Oswalds CH1 237 B3
St Oswalds Cl
Malpas SY14 213 B3
Winwick WA2 8 B6
St Oswalds Way CH1, CH2 237 B3
St Paul of the Cross RC Prim Sch WA5 6 E6
St Paul's Cl CW1 190 C4
St Paul's Ct
2 Macclesfield SK11 112 E7
Warrington WA2 16 A6
St Paul's Inf Sch CH3 237 C3
St Paul's Pl 2 CW9 79 A1
St Paul's RC Prim Sch SK12 36 E2
St Paul's Rd
3 Macclesfield SK11 112 E7
Widnes WA8 23 A7
St Paul's St CW1 190 C4
St Pauls Gdns CH66 69 B7
St Peter's Ave WA16 56 F1
St Peter's CE Prim Sch WA12 2 E4
St Peter's Cl Heswall CH60 40 F7
Lymm WA13 19 A4
St Peter's Ct WA2 16 C6
St Peter's Dr CW6 147 F7
St Peter's Ho SK11 112 E6
St Peter's RC Prim Sch WA1 17 C7
St Peter's Rise CW11 174 E7
St Peter's Way WA2 16 B6
St Peters Rd CW12 156 E1
St Peters Way CH2 119 F8
St Philip (Westbrook) CE Prim Sch WA5 7 B1
St Saviour's CE Prim Sch ST7 194 D1
St Saviour's RC Inf Sch CH66 69 E3
St Saviour's RC Jun Sch CH66 69 E3
St Saviour's St ST7 194 D1
St Stephen Rd WA5 14 F5
St Stephen's Ave WA2 8 B3
St Stephen's RC Prim Sch WA2 8 B3
St Stephens Cl CH60 41 C6
St Stephens Ct
11 Congleton CW12 156 F3
Sandbach CW11 174 D7
St Teresa's RC Prim Sch M44 11 E8
St Theresa's RC Prim Sch CH1 117 F5
St Thomas CE Prim Sch ST7 195 A1
St Thomas Ct WA8 12 E1
St Thomas More RC High Sch CW2 190 A2
St Thomas of Canterbury Blue Coat CE Jun Sch CH1 237 A4
St Thomas St ST7 195 E7
St Thomas' View CH65 70 B4
St Thomas's CE Prim Sch WA4 16 D1
St Thomas's Pathway CH1 237 B2
St Vincent Dr CW8 102 F3
St Vincent Rd WA5 14 F5
St Vincent's RC Prim Sch
Knutsford WA16 57 C1
Warrington WA5 14 F3
St Wenefredes Gn SY13 214 F6
St Werburgh St CH1 237 B2
St Werburgh's & St Columba's RC Prim Sch CH2 118 F2
St Wilfrid's Dr WA4 17 C1
St Wilfrid's RC Prim Sch CW8 103 D5
St Wilfrids Cl CW9 104 A3
St Winefride's RC Prim Sch CH64 66 F7
Salander Cres CW2 206 A7
Salerno Rd CH2 95 B1
Salesbrook La CW5 228 C7
Salford CW3 230 A4
Salford Pl CW12 156 E3
Salisbury Ave
Crewe CW2 190 C1
Saltney CH4 140 E6
Salisbury Cl Crewe CW2 190 C1
Ellesmere Port CH66 94 F8
Salisbury Pl SK10 87 E4
Salisbury Rd WA11 1 E8
Salisbury St Chester CH1 118 B3
Golborne WA3 3 A8
Runcorn WA7 23 A1
Warrington WA1 16 D6
4 Widnes WA8 23 B8
Salkeld St 8 CW9 104 B8
Salop Pl ST7 195 A3
Salop Wlk SK10 86 F2
Salt Line Way CW11 174 D6
Salt Mdws CW5 204 C5
Salt Mus The* CW9 103 F7
Saltash Cl WA7 50 B6
Salter's La
Bickerton SY14 199 F8
Broxton CH3,SY14 183 E1
Salter's La *continued*
Hoole Bank CH2 119 C8
Salters Ford CW8 77 F3
Salters La
Lower Withington SK11 132 B8
Windyharbour SK11 109 D1
Saltersbrook Gr 12 SK9 34 E1
Saltersford Cnr CW4 130 E3
Saltersgate CH66 69 F2
Saltney Bsns Ctr CH4 140 F7
Saltney Ferry Prim Sch CH4 140 B6
Saltney Ferry Rd CH4 140 B7
Saltney Terr CH4 140 B7
Salton Gdns WA5 15 E7
Saltwood Dr WA7 50 C5
Saltworks Cl WA6 49 D2
Samian Cl CW10 128 C2
Samphire Gdns WA9 6 B7
Samuel St Chester CH1 237 C3
Crewe CW1 190 B5
Macclesfield SK11 112 D7
Packmoor ST7 195 F1
Warrington WA5 15 E4
Sanbec Gdns WA8 12 D5
Sand La SK10 84 F5
Sandalwood WA7 24 C1
Sandalwood Cl WA2 8 D2
Sandbach Com Prim Sch CW11 175 A6
Sandbach Crosses* CW11 175 B6
Sandbach Dr CW9 103 E6
Sandbach High Sch & Sixth Form Coll CW11 175 A7
Sandbach Rd
Congleton CW12 156 A3
Rode Heath ST7 193 E7
Sandbach Rd N ST7 193 C4
Sandbach Rd S ST7 193 D3
Sandbach Sch CW11 175 A6
Sandbach Sta CW11 174 D8
Sanderling Rd WA12 2 C4
Sanders Hey Cl WA7 50 B5
Sanders Sq SK11 112 D5
Sanderson Cl
Crewe CW2 206 C8
Warrington WA5 14 D6
Sandfield Ave CW5 216 F3
Sandfield Cl 3 WA3 3 E8
Sandfield Cres WA3 5 C7
Sandfield Ct
3 Frodsham WA6 74 B8
Wrenbury CW5 216 F4
Sandfield Hall WA3 3 A4
Sandfield La
Acton Bridge CW8 76 E1
Hartford CW8 103 C4
Sandfield Pk CH60 40 D8
Sandfield Terr CW8 76 F1
Sandfields WA6 74 B8
Sandford Cres CW2 207 D2
Sandford Rd CW5 204 F7
Sandgate Rd SK10 87 F2
Sandham Gr CH60 41 D7
Sandham Rd L24 21 A4
Sandheys CH64 41 C1
Sandhill Terr WA4 16 E3
Sandhole Cotts 1 CW7 149 B8
Sandhole La
Chelford WA16 83 D4
Crowton CW8 101 B7
Sandhurst Ave CW2 190 A1
Sandhurst Dr 2 SK9 60 C8
Sandhurst Rd L26 21 A6
Sandhurst St WA4 16 F3
Sandicroft Cl WA3 9 C5
Sandiford Rd CW4 130 C3
Sandiford Sq CW9 104 A8
Sandileigh Ave WA16 56 F2
Sandington Dr CW8 101 F2
Sandiway Bebington CH63 43 C6
Knutsford WA16 57 B2
Sandiway Ave WA8 12 A1
Sandiway Cl CW8 102 A2
Sandiway La CW9 53 A2
Sandiway Pk CW8 102 E4
Sandiway Prim Sch CW8 102 B3
Sandiway Rd
Crewe CW1 190 A7
Handforth SK9 34 D5
Sandle Bridge La WA16, SK9 83 E5
Sandle Bridge Rise WA16 83 F6
Sandon Cres CH64 66 E5
Sandon Park Gdns CW2 189 D4
Sandon Pl WA8 13 D1
Sandon Rd CH2 118 E4
Sandon St CW1 190 D4
Sandown Cl Culcheth WA3 4 F4
Middlewich CW10 151 C8
Runcorn WA7 49 C6
Wilmslow SK9 60 D8
Sandown Cres CW8 102 A3
Sandown Dr WA15 32 D6
Sandown Pl SK11 111 F7
Sandown Rd CW1 190 C7
Sandown Terr CH3 118 F1
Sandpiper Cl WA12 2 C4
Sandpiper Ct
Chester CH4 141 B2
Kidsgrove ST7 195 C2
Sandpiper Way CH4 141 B3
Sandra Dr WA12 2 E3
Sandringham Ave
Chester CH3 119 A2
Helsby WA6 73 B4

Sandringham Cl
Altrincham WA14 ....20 F1
Northwich CW9 ....103 E4
Winsford CW7 ....126 C3
Sandringham Ct
Golborne WA3 ....3 E7
5 Wilmslow SK9 ....60 A6
Sandringham Dr
Poynton SK12 ....36 D3
Warrington WA5 ....15 C4
Wistaston CW2 ....205 E8
Sandringham Gdns 2
CH65 ....70 D2
Sandringham Rd
Congleton CW12 ....156 F4
Macclesfield SK10 ....87 F1
Widnes WA8 ....13 A4
Sandringham Way 4
SK9 ....60 A6
Sandrock Rd CH3 ....142 E7
Sands Rd ST7 ....195 E6
Sandsdown Cl ST8 ....179 C1
Sandside Rd ST7 ....193 B3
Sandstone Mews WA8 ....12 E4
Sandstone Wlk CH60 ....41 A7
Sandwich Dr SK10 ....87 C4
Sandwood Ave CW4 ....139 B3
Sandy Brow La WA3 ....3 E2
Sandy Cl SK10 ....87 F7
Sandy La Allostock CW4 ....106 E1
Astbury CW12 ....177 E6
Aston CW5 ....217 C2
Bold Heath WA8 ....14 B6
Brown Knowl CH3 ....199 C7
Bulkeley SY14 ....184 C1
Chester CH3 ....119 A1
Congleton CW12 ....155 D3
Congleton, Astbury Marsh
CW12 ....156 B2
Croft WA3 ....9 A8
Cronton WA8 ....12 D5
Culcheth WA3 ....4 A1
Golborne WA3 ....2 F8
Golborne,Lowton Common
WA3 ....4 A8
Goostrey CW4 ....107 D1
Haslington CW11 ....192 B7
Hatherton CW5 ....219 F5
Helsby WA6 ....73 B2
Higher Kinnerton CH4 ....161 A6
Huntington CH3 ....141 F8
Knutsford WA16 ....82 D3
Lymm WA13 ....19 B4
Macclesfield SK10 ....86 C2
Neston CH64 ....67 A7
Runcorn WA7 ....48 E7
Runcorn, Preston Brook
WA7 ....50 F6
Saighton CH3 ....142 C3
Saltney CH4 ....140 D6
Sandbach CW11 ....174 D5
Swan Green WA16 ....106 E6
Swettenham CW12 ....131 F3
Tarvin CH3 ....121 C4
Threapwood SY14 ....222 E8
Warrington, Longford WA2 ....8 C2
Warrington,Penketh WA5 ....15 A4
Warrington,Stockton Heath
WA4 ....26 D8
Weaverham CW8 ....77 C2
Whitegate CW8 ....125 D6
Wilmslow SK9 ....59 E8
Sandy La W WA2 ....8 B3
Sandy Moor La WA7 ....24 D3
Sandy Rd ST9 ....179 C2
Sandy Way CW7 ....149 B8
Sandybank CW8 ....78 D1
Sandyfield Ct ST8 ....179 C1
Sandyhill Pl 1 CW7 ....149 D6
Sandyhill Rd CW7 ....149 D6
Sandylands Cres ST7 ....193 F5
Sandylands Pk WA6 ....22 D5
Sandylane Mews CW12 ....156 C5
Sandymere Ct CW7 ....126 B1
Sandymoor La WA7 ....24 D3
Sankey Bridges Ind Est
WA5 ....15 C4
Sankey For Penketh Sta
WA5 ....14 F6
Sankey St Golborne WA3 ....3 A8
Newton-le-W WA12 ....2 A3
Warrington WA1 ....16 A5
Widnes WA8 ....23 A6
Sankey Valley Ind Est
WA12 ....2 A2
Sankey Valley Pk*
Newton-le-W WA5 ....1 E3
Newton-le-W WA5 ....15 D5
Sankey Valley St James CE
Prim Sch WA5 ....15 C6
Sankey Way WA5 ....15 D5
Sanky La WA4 ....25 F1
Santon Dr WA3 ....3 E8
Sapling La CW6 ....146 F3
Sark Ave CH65 ....95 B8
Sark Ho CH2 ....119 B4
Sarl Williams Ct CH1 ....237 A3
Sarn Bank Rd SY14 ....222 E6
Sarn Rd SY14 ....222 D8
Sarra La CH3 ....184 B5
Sarsfield Ave 1 WA3 ....3 D8
Sarus Ct WA7 ....24 B4
Saughall Cl CW9 ....103 E4
Saughall Hey CH1 ....94 A1
Saughall Rd Blacon CH1 ....117 E5
Blacon,Abbot's Meads
CH1 ....118 A4
Saunders St CW1 ....190 B4

Saundersfoot La WA5 ....7 E2
Saunderton Cl WA11 ....1 C7
Saville Ave WA5 ....15 F7
Saville St SK11 ....112 E7
Savoy Rd CW1 ....207 A8
Sawley Cl Culcheth WA3 ....5 A2
Runcorn WA7 ....50 E7
Sawley Dr SK8 ....35 C6
Sawpit St WA13,WA14 ....20 A6
Sawyer Dr ST8 ....179 C1
Saxon Cl WA4 ....26 B5
Saxon Crossway CW7 ....126 B1
Saxon Rd WA7 ....23 C2
Saxon Terr 4 WA8 ....13 B1
Saxon Way Blacon CH1 ....117 E6
Ellesmere Port CH66 ....94 F8
Sandbach CW11 ....175 C6
Saxons La Hartford CW9 ....103 E6
Northwich CW8 ....103 D7
Sayce St WA8 ....13 B1
Scafell Ave WA2 ....8 C3
Scafell Cl Bebington CH62 ....43 D3
High Lane SK6 ....37 E8
Scaife Rd CW5 ....204 F5
Scaliot Cl SK22 ....39 B8
Scar La SY14 ....198 F1
Sceptre Cl WA12 ....2 A3
Scholar Green Prim Sch
ST7 ....194 E6
Scholar's Ct 3 CH64 ....66 E8
Scholars Cl
Macclesfield SK10 ....111 D8
Saltney CH4 ....140 E6
Scholars Green La WA13 ....18 F2
School Ave CH64 ....66 F6
School Bank Norley WA6 ....101 A6
Wybunbury CW5 ....220 B8
School Brow WA1 ....16 C6
School Cl Audley ST7 ....210 A1
Knutsford WA16 ....56 E1
Marbury SY13 ....226 E8
Poynton SK12 ....36 F3
School Cotts
Bradwall Green CW11 ....153 B4
Wimboldsley CW10 ....150 F4
School Cres CW1 ....190 E4
School Dr CW8 ....78 A3
School Field Ct CW3 ....230 F4
School Gn CH3 ....182 C1
School Hill CH60 ....40 F7
School Hos SK11 ....109 A1
School House Cotts
CH66 ....69 B6
School La Aldford CH3 ....163 F2
Antrobus CW9 ....53 C3
Astbury CW12 ....178 B8
Audlem CW3 ....230 A4
Bold Heath WA8 ....13 E7
Brereton Green CW11 ....153 F5
Bunbury CW6 ....168 E1
Burwardsley CH3 ....184 B6
Cuddington CW8 ....102 A2
Eaton (nr Congleton)
CW12 ....156 E8
Ellesmere Port CH66 ....69 A8
Elton CH2 ....72 B3
Frodsham WA6 ....74 C7
Great Budworth CW9 ....79 B8
Guilden Sutton CH3 ....119 E5
Hartford CW8 ....103 C4
Henbury SK11 ....113 B1
Higher Whitley WA4 ....52 E6
Hollinfare WA3 ....11 A3
Hoofon CH66 ....43 F1
Irlam M44 ....11 D5
Lostock Gralam CW9 ....80 A2
Manley WA6 ....99 A5
Marton SK11 ....133 C5
Mickle Trafford CH2 ....119 E8
Moulton CW9 ....126 F8
4 Nantwich CW5 ....204 E6
Neston CH64 ....42 B2
Neston, Little Neston CH64 ....66 F6
Neston,Parkgate CH64 ....41 B1
Nether Alderley SK10 ....86 A6
Norbury SY13 ....215 E2
Norley WA6 ....100 D5
Ollerton WA16 ....83 B4
Onneley CW3 ....232 B8
Parthington WA14 ....20 D5
Poynton SK12 ....36 F4
Runcorn WA7 ....49 F8
Sandbach CW11 ....174 D7
Sandbach Heath CW11 ....175 E6
Smallwood CW11 ....176 F5
Warmingham CW11 ....173 E7
Warrington WA3 ....18 C5
School Mews SK7 ....35 E7
School Rd
Ellesmere Port CH65 ....70 B5
Handforth SK9 ....34 D4
Northwich,Higher Shurlach
CW9 ....104 D6
Warrington WA2 ....8 C1
Winsford,Meadowbank
CW7 ....126 E5
Warrington WA2 ....8 C1
School Rd N CW9 ....104 E6
School Rd S CW9 ....104 E6
School St Chester CH2 ....118 F3
Golborne WA3 ....3 A8
Haslington CW11 ....191 D5
Newton-le-W WA12 ....2 B3
Warrington WA1 ....16 B5
School Terr WA3 ....3 A8
School Way
Northwich CW9 ....104 A8
Widnes WA8 ....13 D3

Schoolfold La SK10 ....63 A7
Schooner Cl WA7 ....50 D6
Scilly Cl CH65 ....70 C1
Scope Ho CW1 ....190 E1
Scotch Hall La CW9 ....53 A3
Scotia Wlk 1 WA3 ....3 F8
Scotland Rd WA1 ....16 B5
Scott Ave Crewe CW1 ....190 F4
Widnes WA8 ....22 F8
Scott Cl
Macclesfield SK10 ....113 A7
Rode Heath ST7 ....193 E8
2 Sandbach CW11 ....174 D6
Scott Rd SK10 ....87 A7
Scott St WA2 ....16 C6
Scott Wlk WA12 ....2 C1
Scotthope Cl SK11 ....111 F6
Scotton Ave CH66 ....69 B5
Scroggins La M31 ....11 F4
Sea Bank CW10 ....128 D1
Sea La WA7 ....23 D2
Sea View CH64 ....66 E4
Seabank Rd CH60 ....40 E6
Seabury St WA4 ....17 A3
Seacombe Dr CH66 ....69 F3
Seafield Ave CH60 ....40 E6
Seaford Cl WA2 ....24 D1
Seaford Pl WA2 ....8 A4
Seagrave Cl CW9 ....103 F5
Seagull Cl CW1 ....190 F5
Seahill Rd CH1 ....116 F8
Seal Rd SK7 ....36 A7
Sealand Ave 2 WA12 ....2 B1
Sealand Ind Est CH1 ....117 F2
Sealand Rd Blacon CH1 ....117 C3
Chester CH1 ....118 A2
Sealand CH1,CH5 ....117 A4
Sealand Trad Pk CH1 ....117 F2
Sealand Way 2 SK9 ....34 D4
Seathwaite Cl WA7 ....49 E5
Seaton Cl CW1 ....190 B8
Seaton Pk WA7 ....24 E3
Seaton St CW7 ....127 D1
Seaview Ave CH62 ....44 A5
Seaville St CH3 ....237 C3
Secker Ave WA4 ....16 D2
Secker Cl WA4 ....16 D2
Second Ave
Connah's Quay CH5 ....92 F3
Crewe CW1 ....190 F2
Kidsgrove ST7 ....194 E1
Poynton SK12 ....36 D1
Runcorn WA7 ....49 F8
Sandbach CW11 ....175 A5
Second Dig La CW5 ....219 C8
Second Wood St CW5 ....204 D5
Sedbergh Cl CW4 ....130 A3
Sedbergh Gr WA7 ....49 E5
Seddon St CW10 ....128 C2
Sedgefield Cl 3 SK10 ....87 C4
Sedgefield Rd CH1 ....118 B2
Sedgeford Cl WA3 ....3 A8
Sedgemere Ave CW1 ....190 A8
Sedgewick Cres WA5 ....6 E6
Sedum Cl CH3 ....142 A6
Sefton Ave
Congleton CW12 ....157 A1
Widnes WA8 ....13 A3
Sefton Dr SK9 ....34 C2
Sefton Rd CH2 ....119 A4
Sefton St WA12 ....1 F3
Selby Cl Poynton SK12 ....36 D5
Runcorn WA7 ....50 E7
Selby Gdns SK8 ....35 C6
Selby Gn CH66 ....69 E5
Selby St WA5 ....15 E5
Selkirk Ave
Bebington CH62 ....43 E4
Warrington WA4 ....17 A3
Selkirk Cl
Ellesmere Port CH66 ....68 F5
Macclesfield SK10 ....86 F2
Selkirk Dr Chester CH4 ....141 A7
Holmes Chapel CW4 ....130 B2
Selkirk Rd CH4 ....141 A7
Seller St CH1 ....237 C3
Selsdon Ct CH4 ....141 A5
Selsey Cl CW1 ....190 B8
Selwyn Cl
Newton-le-W WA12 ....2 B5
Widnes WA8 ....13 F3
Selwyn Dr
Cheadle Hulme SK8 ....35 C7
Sutton Lane Ends SK11 ....112 F3
Semper Cl CW12 ....157 A4
Seneschal Ct WA7 ....49 E6
Senna La CW9 ....78 C8
Sennen Cl WA7 ....50 C5
Sens Cl CH1 ....237 A2
Sephton Ave WA3 ....4 F3
Serin Cl WA12 ....2 C3
Serpentine The CH4 ....141 B7
Servite Cl CH65 ....69 F6
Servite Pl CH64 ....67 A6
Sett Cl SK22 ....39 B8
Seven Row CH64 ....66 E5
Seven Sisters La WA16 ....82 E5
Sevenoaks Cl SK10 ....87 B2
Severn Cl Biddulph ST8 ....179 F1
Congleton CW12 ....156 F1
Macclesfield SK10 ....86 F1
Warrington WA8 ....13 B7
Widnes WA8 ....13 B7
Severn Dr SK7 ....35 C6
Severn Rd WA3 ....4 F2

Severn Wlk CW7 ....127 A2
Severnvale CH65 ....70 B3
Sewell St 7 WA7 ....23 B2
Sextant Cl WA7 ....50 D6
Sexton Ave WA9 ....1 B2
Seymour Chase WA16 ....82 A8
Seymour Ct WA7 ....24 C4
Seymour Dr
Ellesmere Port CH66 ....69 E6
Warrington WA1 ....17 A8
Seymour Ho 10 SK9 ....34 E1
Seymour Rd SK8 ....35 A8
Sgt York Loop WA5 ....15 B6
Shackleton Cl WA5 ....15 D8
Shade Terr SK6 ....37 F7
Shadowood Cres WA4 ....17 B2
Shadowood Rd SK11 ....112 A6
Shadowmoss Rd M22 ....33 E8
Shady Brook La CW8 ....77 C1
Shady Gr ST7 ....193 D4
Shaftesbury Ave
Chester CH3 ....119 C2
Warrington WA5 ....14 E2
Shaftesbury Way WA5 ....6 F7
Shaftway Cl WA11 ....1 E7
Shakerley Ave CW12 ....156 F3
Shakespeare Cl CW9 ....104 C7
Shakespeare Dr CW1 ....191 A4
Shakespeare Gr WA2 ....8 C2
Shakespeare Rd
Neston CH64 ....41 E1
Widnes WA8 ....13 A1
Shalcombe Cl CH26 ....21 A7
Shallacres CH65 ....69 F7
Shallcross Ave SK23 ....65 F4
Shallcross Cres SK23 ....65 E4
Shallcross Mill Cotts
SK23 ....65 E5
Shallcross Mill Rd SK23 ....65 E5
Shallcross Rd SK23 ....65 E4
Shambles The WA16 ....57 B1
Shanklin Cl WA5 ....14 C6
Shannon Cl Chester CH4 ....140 E5
Willaston CW5 ....205 D6
Shannon Gr WA8 ....12 E2
Shargate Cl SK9 ....34 C1
Sharnbrook Dr CW2 ....189 D4
Sharon Park Cl WA4 ....17 C1
Sharp St Warrington WA2 ....16 C6
Widnes WA8 ....23 A8
Sharpley St 11 SK10 ....112 C8
Sharston Cres WA16 ....57 B1
Shavington Ave CH2 ....118 F4
Shavington High Sch
CW2 ....206 A5
Shavington Home Farm
TF9 ....234 B3
Shavington Prim Sch
CW2 ....206 C4
Shavington Way CW9 ....103 F4
Shaw Cl
Ellesmere Port CH66 ....69 E4
Ellesmere Port,Great Sutton
CH66 ....69 C4
Shaw Dr WA16 ....57 C3
Shaw Entry L35,WA8 ....12 C7
Shaw Heath View WA16 ....57 C3
Shaw St Culcheth WA3 ....5 B7
Haydock WA11 ....1 E6
Macclesfield SK11 ....112 C8
Runcorn WA7 ....22 F2
Shaw's Ave WA2 ....16 C8
Shaw's Row 4 WA4 ....17 A8
Shawell Cl WA4 ....13 E2
Shaws Fold SK9 ....33 F3
Shaws La Winsford CW7 ....126 F4
Winsford CW7 ....127 A3
Shay La
Ashton Hayes CH3 ....121 F7
Hampton Heath SY14 ....200 A1
Tarvin CH3 ....121 E3
Shay's La CW6 ....124 E4
Sheaf Cl CH3 ....121 C2
Shearbrook La CW4 ....107 E1
Sheardhall Ave SK12 ....38 E5
Sheath St CW9 ....104 A8
Shed La CH3 ....119 B2
Sheepfield Cl CH66 ....69 C7
Sheerwater Cl WA1 ....16 F7
Sheffield Cl WA5 ....15 C5
Sheffield Row WA12 ....7 D8
Sheilings The WA3 ....3 F8
Shelagh Ave WA8 ....13 A1
Shelbourne Mews 2
SK10 ....111 F8
Shelburne Dr CW1 ....191 C5
Sheldon Ave
Chester CH3 ....119 B2
Congleton CW12 ....157 A1
Sheldon Cl M31 ....11 F3
Sheldon Rd SK10 ....88 B8
Sheldon Rd
Hazel Grove SK7 ....36 E8
Poynton SK12 ....37 C2
Poynton SK12 ....37 C2
Shell Green Est WA8 ....23 E8
Shellbrook Gr 3 SK9 ....34 D1
Shelley Ave CW9 ....80 A5
Shelley Cl Crewe CW1 ....190 F4
Widnes WA8 ....13 A1
Shelley Dr Crewe CW1 ....190 F4
Widnes WA8 ....13 A1
Shelley Gr WA4 ....16 F4
Shelley Rd Blacon CH1 ....117 F5
Widnes WA8 ....13 A1
Shellow La CW12,SK11 ....134 C5
Shellway Rd CH2 ....71 A3

Shelton Cl WA8 ....13 F3
Shenhurst Cl SK9 ....59 E4
Shepcroft La WA4 ....26 C3
Shepherd's La CH2 ....118 D5
Shepherds Fold Dr
CW7 ....126 C3
Shepherds Row WA7 ....23 F2
Shepherds View WA8 ....78 B2
Shepley Cl SK7 ....36 D8
Sheppard Cl CW1 ....190 D5
Sheppenhall Gr CW5 ....217 C1
Sheppenhall La CW5,
SY13 ....228 D5
Shepperton Cl WA4 ....26 C6
Shepsides Cl CH66 ....69 C3
Shepton Rd CH66 ....69 E2
Sheraton Rd CH3 ....143 B5
Sherborne Cl WA7 ....24 F3
Sherborne Rd CW1 ....190 D6
Sherbourne Ave CH4 ....141 B5
Sherbourne Cl SK8 ....35 B6
Sherbourne Rd
Ellesmere Port CH65 ....70 D3
Macclesfield SK11 ....111 F7
Sherbourne Way WA5 ....6 F6
Sherbrook Rise SK9 ....60 C6
Sherbrooke Rd SK12 ....38 D6
Sheri Dr WA12 ....2 E2
Sheridan Ave WA3 ....3 D7
Sheridan Cl CW1 ....173 B1
Sheridan Pl WA2 ....8 A5
Sheridan Way WA7 ....24 D2
Sheringham Cl CH4 ....140 E5
Sheringham Dr CW1 ....190 B8
Sheringham Rd WA5 ....14 E6
Sherlock Ave WA11 ....1 E7
Sherratt Cl
Congleton CW12 ....156 E2
Nantwich CW5 ....204 F4
Sherrington's La CH3 ....199 D8
Sherwin St CW2 ....190 C1
Sherwood Cl WA3 ....12 C1
Sherwood Cres WA5 ....6 E6
Sherwood Gr WA6 ....73 A3
Sherwood Rd
Ellesmere Port CH66 ....70 D3
Macclesfield SK11 ....112 D5
Shetland Cl
Warrington WA2 ....8 E4
Widnes WA8 ....13 E3
Shetland Dr
Bebington CH62 ....43 E8
Ellesmere Port CH65 ....70 C1
Warrington WA2 ....8 E3
Shevington Wlk WA8 ....13 E3
Shiggins Cl WA5 ....15 D6
Shillingford Cl WA4 ....26 E5
Shilton Cl CW10 ....151 E5
Ship St WA6 ....49 C1
Shipbrook Rd
Chester CH2 ....118 F6
Davenham CW9 ....104 C2
Northwich CW9 ....104 C6
Shipgate St CH1 ....237 B1
Shipgate The CH1 ....237 B1
Shipton Cl
Warrington WA5 ....15 B8
Widnes WA8 ....12 D3
Shirley Ave SK8 ....34 C6
Shirley Cl WA4 ....17 A2
Shirleys Cl SK10 ....87 A6
Shirleys Dr SK10 ....87 A6
Shocklach Oviatt CE Prim
Sch SY14 ....211 C7
Shocklach Rd CH2 ....118 F6
Shones Croft CH64 ....67 A5
Shop La Congleton CW12 ....156 E1
Little Budworth CW6 ....124 F2
Shopping Precinct The
CH2 ....72 B3
Shoreham Dr WA5 ....15 A3
Shores Green Dr CW9 ....79 F5
Shores La CW5 ....203 D2
Short Cl WA12 ....1 E3
Short St Haydock WA11 ....1 E6
Newton-le-W WA12 ....112 D8
Widnes WA8 ....23 A5
Shorthorn Cl CW10 ....128 D2
Shorwell Cl WA5 ....14 C7
Shotwick La CH1 ....93 D6
Shotwick Rd CH5 ....92 F3
Shrewbridge Cres WA5 ....204 E4
Shrewbridge Rd CW5 ....204 D4
Shrewsbury Dr ST5 ....210 E2
Shrewsbury Rd 4 CH65 ....70 C5
Shrewsbury St WA4 ....16 D3
Shrewsbury Way CH4 ....140 F6
Shrigley Cl SK9 ....34 D1
Shrigley Rd
Pott Shrigley SK10 ....63 B5
Poynton SK10,SK12 ....37 C2
Shrigley Rd N SK12 ....37 C3
Shrigley Rd S SK10 ....63 C1
Shropshire Cl
Middlewich CW10 ....151 C8
Warrington WA1 ....17 E6
Shropshire Cl SY13 ....227 E2
Shropshire Rd CH2 ....119 A3
Shropshire St CW3 ....229 F4
Shuldham Cl WA16 ....29 C5
Shurlach Rd CW9 ....104 C6
Shutley La CW8 ....77 D6
Shutlingsloe Way SK10 ....112 A8

Sibbersfield La CH3 .....180 F4
Sibell St CH1 ....237 C3
Siddall St 7 CW9 ....104 B8
Siddals Ct CW5 ....204 C5
Siddeley Cl CH4 ....139 C4
Siddeley Dr WA12 ....1 F4
Siddington Ave CW9 ....104 A4
Siddington Rd
Handforth SK9 ....34 D5
Poynton SK12 ....36 F2
Siddorn St CW7 ....126 E1
Side End La SK23 ....64 F3
Side La CW6 ....144 E6
Sidings The SK23 ....65 E8
Sidlaw Cl CH66 ....69 A6
Sidmouth Cl WA5 ....14 E4
Sidmouth Gr SK8 ....34 F7
Sidney Rd CH64 ....41 F1
Siemens Rd M44 ....11 E5
Sienna Cl M44 ....11 E6
Signal Ct CH2 ....118 F2
Silk Hill SK23 ....65 F8
Silk Mill
Macclesfield SK11 ....112 D6
Poynton SK12 ....36 C4
Silk Mill St WA16 ....57 A2
Silk Rd The
Bollington SK10 ....87 E4
Macclesfield SK10 ....112 E8
Silk St CW12 ....156 C2
Silkstone Cres WA7 ......50 B7
Silsden Ave WA3 ....4 B8
Silvan Ct SK10 ....87 B1
Silver Ave WA11 ....1 A5
Silver La Croft WA3 ....9 F7
Warrington WA3 ....10 C6
Warrington,Risley WA3 ......9 F7
Silver St Bollington SK10 ...88 B8
Congleton CW12 ....156 E2
Warrington WA2 ....16 B6
Silver Terr CW11 ....175 D6
Silverbirch Croft CH4 ...139 B3
Silverbirch Way CH66 ....94 F8
Silverdale CW8 ....103 D7
Silverdale Cl
Chorlton CW2 ....207 C2
Frodsham WA6 ....74 C7
High Lane SK6 ....37 E8
Silverdale Dr SK9 ....60 A4
Silverdale Rd
Newton-le-W WA12 ....2 B4
Warrington WA4 ....16 B2
Silvergate Ct CW12 .....178 E8
Silvermine Cl 8 ST7 ....195 B2
Silvermuir CH1 ....117 E3
Silverne Dr CH65 ....70 A2
Silverwood ST7 ....195 B1
Simkin Ave WA4 ....16 F4
Simmonds Cl CW9 ......103 E3
Simms Cross Prim Sch
WA8 ....23 A8
Simons La WA6 ....74 B5
Simonside WA8 ....12 C2
Simonstone Rd CH4 ....139 D4
Simonswood Cl CW10 ...151 B8
Simpson Cl CH2 ....95 C1
Simpson Ct CW1 ....173 B1
Simpson La SK10 ....63 D7
Simpson Rd CH2 ....95 C1
Simpson St SK9 ....59 F6
Simpson's Ct 17 SK11 ...112 C8
Simpsons Way CH4 ......139 B3
Sinclair Ave Alsager ST7 .193 B3
Warrington WA2 ....8 B2
Widnes WA8 ....23 A8
Sinderland La
Partington WA13 ....20 B8
Partington WA14 ....20 E8
Singapore Ave M90 ......33 A8
Singleton Ave CW1 ......190 C6
Singleton Rd CH65 ....69 F4
Sir John Deane's Coll
CW9 ....103 F6
Sir Thomas Boteler CE High
Sch WA4 ....16 E3
Siskin Cl WA12 ....2 C3
Six Acre Gdns WA4 ....25 A5
Six Acre La WA4 ....25 A5
Sixth Ave CH5 ....92 E1
Skeath Cl CW11 ....175 E6
Skellern St ST7 ....194 D2
Skellorn Green La
Skellorn Green SK10 ....62 F8
Wardsend SK10 ....36 F1
Skiddaw Cl WA7 ....50 A4
Skip's La CH3 ....142 F7
Skipton Cl
Hazel Grove SK7 ....36 C8
2 Runcorn WA7 ....23 F1
Skipton Dr CH66 ....69 C5
Skye Cl
Ellesmere Port CH65 ....70 C1
Widnes WA8 ....13 E3
Skylark Cl CW1 ....189 F7
Slack St SK11 ....112 E6
Slacken La ST7 ....194 D2
Slade La Mobberley WA16 ..58 A7
Nether Alderley SK10 ....85 E5
Slade St 5 CW9 ....104 B8
Slag La Golborne WA3 ......3 D8
Haydock WA11 ....1 B7
Slater St
Macclesfield SK11 ....112 C6
Warrington WA4 ....16 D3
Slicks Bsns Ctr CW8 .....78 C2
Slindon Cl ST5 ....210 D1
Slutchers La WA1 ....16 A3
Small Ave WA2 ....8 C2
Small Cres WA2 ....8 C2
Small La WA16 ....58 A8
Smallbrook Wlk CW2 ...206 C8
Smallman Rd CW2 ......190 C1
Smallwood CE Prim Sch
CW11 ....176 F5
Smallwood Cl
4 Middlewich CW10 .....151 C8
Newcastle-u-Lyme ST5 ....210 D1
Smallwood Ct 1 CW12 ...156 F3
Smallwood Forge
CW11 ....176 D5
Smethwick La CW11,
CW12 ....154 E4
Smith Cl ST7 ....193 B4
Smith Cres WA2 ....16 D8
Smith Dr WA2 ....16 D8
Smith Gr CW1 ....190 A6
Smith La Ashley WA16 .....31 E1
Mobberley WA16 ....57 F6
Rainow SK10 ....89 A5
Smith Rd WA8 ....22 F7
Smith St
Macclesfield SK11 ....112 D6
Warrington WA1 ....16 B5
Smith's La CW8 ....77 C1
Smith's Terr SK11 ....112 E6
Smithfield Dr/Ffordd Smithfield LL13 ....196 D8
Smithfield Gn LL13 ......196 D8
Smithfield La CW11 .....175 C6
Smithfield St LL13 ......196 D8
Smithfields CH3 ....166 C2
Smithills Cl WA3 ....9 D5
Smiths Lawn SK9 ....60 A5
Smithy Bank Acton CW5 .204 A6
Winsford CW7 ....149 A3
Smithy Brow
Bollington SK10 ....88 C8
Winwick WA3 ....8 F7
Smithy Cl Cronton WA8 ....12 C5
Neston CH64 ....67 A4
Saughall CH1 ....94 A1
Smithy Cotts SY14 ......213 A2
Smithy Ct
Christleton CH3 ....142 E7
5 Ellesmere Port CH66 .....69 C6
Smithy Gn
Cheadle Hulme SK8 ....35 A8
Gatesheath CH3 ....165 E5
Smithy Gr CW11 ....176 A2
Smithy Hill CH63 ....42 A6
Smithy La Alsager CW2 ..208 D7
Altrincham WA14 ....20 D3
Barthomley CW2 ....208 C6
Biddulph ST8 ....179 D2
Bosley SK11 ....158 E6
Broxton CH3 ....183 D1
Congleton CW12 ....156 C7
Crewe CW1 ....189 E8
Croft WA3 ....9 A7
Cronton WA8 ....12 C5
Cuddington CW8 ....102 A5
Ellesmere Port CH66 ....69 C6
Great Budworth CW9 ....79 A8
Helsby WA6 ....73 C5
Kingsley WA6 ....75 B2
Little Leigh CW8 ....77 B6
Lostock Gralam CW9 ....80 A2
Malpas SY14 ....213 A2
Mottram St Andrew SK10 ....61 C2
Mouldsworth CH3 ....98 F2
Partington M31 ....11 F3
Rainow SK10 ....88 E5
Utkinton CW6 ....146 C6
Weston CW2 ....207 C5
Willaston CH64 ....68 A7
Smithy Pathway CH4 ....140 F4
Smithy The CH2 ....118 E8
Smithy Wlk CW11 ....174 F3
Smokehall La CW7,CW9 ..126 F6
Smokehall Lane Ind Est
CW7 ....127 A5
Smokey La SY13 ....224 A1
Smokies Way ST8 ....179 C1
Smyth Rd WA8 ....13 D2
Snab La Neston CH64 .....66 F4
Norbury SY13 ....215 B5
Snabwood Cl CH64 ....66 E5
Snaefell Rise WA4 ....26 C7
Snape Hollow CW2 .....207 F4
Snape La CW2 ....207 E4
Snape Rd Crewe CW2 ....206 D8
Macclesfield SK10 ....87 E2
Snapebrook Gr 6 SK9 ....34 E1
Snelson La Chelford SK11 .108 E7
Chelford,Marthall WA16,
SK9 ....83 D3
Snipe Cl SK12 ....36 A4
Snow Hill SK11 ....112 E6
Snowberry Cl WA8 ....13 E4
Snowberry Wlk M31 ......11 E3
Snowdon Cl
Ellesmere Port CH66 ....69 A6
Warrington WA5 ....14 E6
Snowdon Cres CH4 ......141 A5
Snowdon Dr CW2 ....189 D3
Snowdon St CW8 ....77 F3
Snowdonia Way CW7 ....149 B7
Snowdrop Cl WA7 ....49 F4
Solly Cres CW12 ....156 A2
Solvay Rd CW8 ....78 D1
Solway Cl WA2 ....8 F4
Solway Ct CW1 ....191 A2
Solway Gr WA7 ....49 D5
Somerford Ave CW2 ....190 A3
Somerford Cl CW11 .....175 C8
Somerford Ct 2 CW12 ..156 F3
Somerford Rd CH4 ......139 C4
Somerford Way 3 SK9 ....34 E5
Somerford Wlk WA8 .....13 E3
Somerley Cl CW1 ....190 B8
Somerset Ave ST7 ......194 F2
Somerset Cl
Congleton CW12 ....156 D4
Irlam M44 ....11 D6
Somerset Rd CH2 ....118 F5
Somerset St CH1 ....237 B4
Somerset Way WA1 ......17 B8
Somerton Cl 5 SK11 ....111 F7
Somerton Rd SK11 ......111 F7
Somerville Cl
Bebington CH63 ....43 B6
High Legh WA16 ....29 C4
Neston CH64 ....66 E5
Somerville Cres CH65 ....70 C4
Somerville Rd WA8 ....22 D8
Somerville St CW2 ......190 B2
Soot Hill CW8,CW9 ....78 C3
Sorbus Cl CH2 ....72 C3
Sorbus Dr CW1 ....190 E6
Sorby Rd M44 ....11 F7
Sorrel Cl Huntington CH3 .142 A6
Warrington WA2 ....9 C2
Soss Moss Hospl (Mary Dendy Unit) SK10 ....84 C6
Sossmoss La SK10 ....84 D6
Sound & District Prim Sch
CW5 ....217 F5
Sound La
Ravensmoor CW5 ....203 E1
Sound CW5 ....217 D7
Souter's La CH1 ....237 B2
South Acre Dr
Handforth SK9 ....34 D3
Macclesfield SK11 ....113 A7
South Ave Chester CH2 ...237 C4
Haslington CW1 ....191 D4
Warrington WA2 ....16 B8
Warrington, Stockton Heath
WA4 ....16 C1
South Bank CH2 ....118 C4
South Bank Cl SK9 ....60 B2
South Bank Gr CW12 ....156 F2
South Bank Terr WA7 .....22 F3
South Cheshire Coll
CW2 ....190 B2
South Cheshire Private Hospl
CW1 ....172 E1
South Cl Tarporley CW6 ..146 C2
Wilmslow SK9 ....59 F6
South Crescent Rd CH4 .237 C1
South Croft CW6 ....185 D6
South Crofts CW5 ......204 F5
South Dale WA5 ....14 F5
South Downs WA16 ......57 C1
South Downs Dr WA14 ....31 D8
South Dr Heswall CH60 ....41 A7
Northwich CW9 ....104 D6
Plumley WA16 ....80 F3
Wilmslow SK9 ....60 B6
South Gn CH5 ....116 A6
South Gr 9 SK9 ....60 A1
South La
Warrington WA5,WA8 ......14 E5
Widnes WA8 ....13 F4
South Lane Entry WA8 ...13 F5
South Lodge CW6 ......168 D8
South Mead SK12 ....36 B5
South Meadway SK6 ......37 F7
South Oak La SK9 ....59 F5
South Par WA7 ....48 D7
South Park Dr SK12 ......36 E5
South Park Rd SK11 ....112 C7
South Pier Rd CH65 ......70 D7
South Rd
Altrincham,Ashley Heath
WA14 ....31 E8
Ellesmere Port CH65 ....70 C3
Halewood L24 ....21 A4
Runcorn WA7 ....48 D7
Stanlow CH65 ....70 F4
South St Alderley Edge SK9 .60 A1
Chester CH3 ....119 A1
Congleton CW12 ....156 D3
Crewe CW2 ....190 D2
Mount Pleasant ST7 ......195 B6
3 Widnes WA8 ....23 B8
South Terr 12 SK9 ....60 A1
South View Chester CH4 ..141 D7
Christleton CH3 ....142 F7
Lower Withington SK11 ...132 A8
New Mills SK22 ....39 B8
South View Ave SK11 ...111 D2
South View Cotts ST7 ...193 F4
South View La CW7 .....170 F2
South View Rd CH1 .....118 B2
South Way CH1 ....117 F4
South West Ave SK10 ....87 F6
South Wirral High Sch
CH62 ....43 D4
Southampton Way WA7 ..50 E6
Southbank CW9 ....79 A7
Southbank Ave CW2 ....206 C5
Southdale Rd WA1 ....17 A7
Southdown Cl SK10 ......87 D4
Southdown Cres SK8 .....34 F8
Southern St WA4 ....16 C1
Southey Cl
8 Sandbach CW11 ....174 D6
Widnes WA8 ....22 F8
Southfield SK10 ....87 A4
Southfield Cl SK9 ....34 C3
Southfield Rd CH66 ......69 C7
Southfields WA16 ....57 C3
Southfields Ave WA5 .....14 F6
Southfields Cl CW5 .....220 A8
Southlands CW4 ....130 C2
Southlands Ave WA5 .....14 F3
Southlands Ct WA7 ......48 F8
Southlands Mews 7
WA7 ....22 F1
Southlands Rd CW12 ....157 A1
Southlands View CW4 ...107 E1
Southlawn SK9 ....60 A5
Southport St WA9 ....1 A3
Southward Rd WA11 ....2 A7
Southwark Pl CW7 ......149 A8
Southway
Middlewich CW10 ....128 C1
Runcorn WA7 ....49 F7
Widnes WA8 ....22 D8
Southway Ave WA4 ....26 D7
Southwell Cl WA3 ....3 C8
Southwold Cres WA5 .....14 E5
Southwood Ave WA7 .....24 C2
Southworth Ave WA5 .....15 F8
Southworth La WA2,WA3 ..8 E5
Southworth Rd WA12 ......2 F4
Sovereign Cl Golborne WA3 .3 E7
Northwich CW9 ....104 F6
Runcorn WA7 ....50 D7
Sovereign Ct WA3 ....9 C4
Sovereign Way CH1 .....117 E2
Sowcar Way SK10 ....88 C8
Spark Hall Cl WA4 ....26 E1
Spark La Runcorn WA7 ....23 F1
Smallwood CW11 ....154 C2
Sparks Cl CH3 ....142 B7
Sparrow La WA16 ....57 B1
Sparrowbutts Gr ST7 ...195 C2
Sparrowhawk Cl WA7 ....50 A7
Spath La SK8 ....34 F5
Spath La E SK8 ....35 B5
Spath Wlk SK8 ....35 B5
Spawell Cl WA3 ....3 E8
Speakman Ave WA12 ......2 C5
Speakman St WA7 ....22 F3
Speed's Way CH3 ....180 E2
Speedwell Cl
11 Golborne WA3 ....3 E8
Heswall CH60 ....41 C8
Huntington CH3 ....142 A5
Speedwell Dr CH60 ......41 C8
Speedwell Rd ST5 ......210 F1
Speke Bvd L24,L26,WA8 ...21 B5
Speke Ho L24 ....21 A2
Speke Rd WA8 ....22 C6
Spencer Brook SK10 ......86 F6
Spencer Cl Alsager ST7 ..192 F4
Wistaston CW2 ....206 A8
Spencer Mews SK10 ......87 D6
Spencer St Barnton CW8 ..78 B3
Northwich CW8 ....103 E7
Spenlow Cl SK12 ....36 E1
Spennymoor Ct WA7 .....49 E7
Spenser Cl WA8 ....12 F1
Spenser Rd CH64 ....41 E1
Spey Cl Middlewich CW10 .128 D3
Winsford CW7 ....126 F2
Spey Dr ST7 ....195 C2
Spike Island (Nature Reserve)* WA8 ....23 A5
Spindle St CW12 ....156 E2
Spink La WA16 ....80 A6
Spinnaker Cl WA7 ....50 D5
Spinner Cres CW9 ....78 D7
Spinners La SK12 ....36 C4
Spinners Way SK10 ....87 F7
Spinney Ave
Goostrey CW4 ....107 F1
Widnes WA8 ....12 A1
Spinney Cl Handforth SK9 ..34 C3
Winsford CW7 ....150 A8
Spinney Dr
Ellesmere Port CH66 ....69 D2
Weston CW2 ....207 B5
Spinney End CH3 ....166 A1
Spinney Gdns WA4 ....27 B4
Spinney La WA16 ....56 E3
Spinney Mead SK10 ......87 E2
Spinney The
Cuddington CW8 ....101 D5
Heswall CH60 ....41 C5
Lawton-gate ST7 ....194 E4
Neston CH64 ....41 D1
Norley WA6 ....100 E5
Sandbach CW11 ....175 C6
Willaston CW5 ....205 D6
Spinney Wlk WA7 ....24 A1
Spires Gdns WA2 ....8 A7
Spital Wlk CH2 ....118 F2
Spodegreen La WA14 ....30 C8
Spout La WA16 ....58 B4
Spragg St CW12 ....156 E3
Spring Ave 2 CH66 ....69 C6
Spring Bank ST7 ....195 A7
Spring Bank Rd SK22 ....39 C8
Spring Cl ST7 ....193 E8
Spring Ct 2 WA7 ....23 B2
Spring Gdns Crewe CW1 .190 E5
Ellesmere Port CH66 ....69 C6
Macclesfield SK10 ....87 D1
Mobberley WA16 ....58 D5
Nantwich CW5 ....204 F5
Spring Hill CW6 ....168 C8
Spring La
Coddington CH3 ....181 E6
Croft WA3 ....9 B6
Lymm WA13 ....19 F3
Spring Mdw CW8 ....78 E1
Spring Mount SK22 ....39 C8
Spring Rd SK12 ....36 F2
Spring St
Congleton CW12 ....156 E2
Widnes WA8 ....23 A6
Wilmslow SK9 ....60 A7
Springbank SK10 ....87 F7
Springbank Cl WA7 ......49 B6
Springbank Cres CW7 ...149 C8
Springbank Gdns WA13 ..19 B5
Springbourne WA6 ....74 D6
Springburn Gdns WA1 ....17 F7
Springcroft CH64 ....41 C1
Springe La CW5 ....203 B5
Springfield Ave
Golborne WA3 ....2 F8
Helsby WA6 ....73 B3
Lymm WA13 ....19 B5
Malpas SY14 ....213 C3
Warrington, Grappenhall
WA4 ....17 B3
Warrington,Padgate WA1 ...17 A8
Springfield Cl CH4 ......161 A7
Springfield Cres CW8 ....77 F3
Springfield Ct / Llys Maes Y Ffynnon CH4 ....161 A8
Springfield Dr Talke ST7 .210 E8
Wilmslow SK9 ....59 D5
Wistaston CW2 ....205 F7
Springfield Ho 5 SK9 ....60 A7
Springfield Pk WA11 ......1 C7
Springfield Rd
Macclesfield SK11 ....111 F8
Malpas SY14 ....213 B3
Mobberley WA16 ....57 F4
Widnes WA8 ....22 A8
Springfield Sch CW1 ....191 A3
Springfield St WA1 ......16 A5
Springfields
Cuddington CW8 ....101 D4
Helsby WA6 ....73 B3
Knutsford WA16 ....57 C3
Mickle Trafford CH2 ......119 E8
Prestbury SK10 ....87 A7
Springfields Dr CW12 ...156 D3
Springhead Cl ST7 ......210 D6
Springhead Prim Sch
ST7 ....210 D6
Springhill SK10 ....88 A1
Springhill Ave CH62 ......43 D6
Springholm Dr WA4 ....26 D3
Springmount WA3 ....3 E7
Springvale Ind Est
CW11 ....174 D6
Springwell Cl CW2 ......206 C8
Springwood Ave WA16 ...57 C3
Springwood Cl
Blacon CH1 ....117 C4
Macclesfield SK10 ....87 D5
Springwood Way SK10 ....87 D5
Sprink La CW12 ....157 D5
Sproston Way CW9 .....103 E4
Spruce Ave CW8 ....102 B3
Spruce Cl Golborne WA3 ....3 F7
Warrington WA1 ....17 E7
Spruce Gr ST7 ....193 F7
Spuley La SK10 ....63 D2
Spunhill Ave CH66 ....69 D2
Spurling Rd WA5 ....6 F6
Spurston Cl WA16 ....29 C4
Spurstow Mews SK8 ......35 B8
Square St SK11 ....112 E6
Square The
Altrincham WA15 ....32 C8
Audlem CW3 ....229 F4
Christleton CH3 ....142 E8
Holmes Chapel CW4 ......130 C3
Ince CH2 ....71 F5
6 Lymm WA13 ....18 E3
Woore CW3 ....232 C1
Squires Ave WA8 ....23 A8
Squires Cl WA11 ....1 B6
Squirrel Cl CW8 ....103 C7
Squirrel's Jump SK9 ......60 C1
Squirrels Chase SK10 ....86 F5
St Michael's Row CH1 ..237 B2
Stable La
Mouldsworth CH3 ....99 A3
Utkinton CW6 ....123 F1
Stables The
Bostock Green CW10 .....127 D5
Guilden Sutton CH3 ......119 F5
Stablings The SK9 ....60 A5
Stadium Way CH1 ....118 B3
Stadmorslow La ST7 ....195 F4
Staffin Ave CH65 ....95 B8
Stafford Cl SK10 ....86 F2
Stafford Gdns CH65 ......70 B5
Stafford Rd WA4 ....16 C2
Stafford St Audlem CW3 ..230 A4
Crewe CW1 ....190 C5
Stafford Wlk SK10 ....86 F2
Stage La WA13 ....19 C4
Stainer Cl WA12 ....2 B5
Staines Cl WA4 ....26 E5
Stainforth Cl WA3 ....4 D4
Stainmore Cl WA3 ....10 B6
Staithes Rd M22 ....33 D8
Stalbridge Rd CW2 .....190 C2
Stallard Way CW10 .....151 C8
Stalmine Ave SK8 ....34 B8
Stamford Ave CW2 ......190 C3
Stamford Cl SK11 ....112 C4
Stamford Ct Chester CH3 .119 C2
Lymm WA13 ....18 F3
Macclesfield SK11 ....112 C5
Stamford La CH3 ....120 A1
Stamford Pl SK9 ....60 B7

Stamford Rd
Alderley Edge SK9 60 B1
Blacon CH1 117 E6
Handforth SK9 34 A1
Little Bollington WA14 20 B2
Macclesfield SK11 112 C4
Stamford St CH65 70 A5
Stamp Ave CW1 190 D6
Stamp Cl CW1 190 D6
Standford Dr CW9 104 A5
Standish Ct WA8 22 D8
Stanford Cl CW9 103 F5
Stanhope Ave CW1 190 E3
Stanhope Cl SK9 60 D8
Stanier Cl CW1 191 A4
Stanlaw Rd CH65 70 C4
Stanley & Brocklehurst Ct 5 SK10 112 C8
Stanley Ave
Warrington WA5 14 D7
Warrington, Stockton Heath WA4 16 F2
Stanley Bank Rd WA11 1 A7
Stanley Cl Hartford CW8 103 A4
Widnes WA8 13 C2
Stanley Ct ST7 193 C4
Stanley Dr
Heald Green SK9 34 D6
Newcastle-u-Lyme ST5 210 C1
Stanley Gr CW9 79 E2
Stanley Green Ind Est SK8 34 E5
Stanley Green Ret Pk SK8 34 F6
Stanley Hall La SK12 38 C6
Stanley La CH62 43 F4
Stanley Park Ct CH4 140 E5
Stanley Park Dr CH4 140 E5
Stanley Pl Chester CH1 237 A2
Warrington WA4 16 F2
Stanley Place Mews CH1 237 A2
Stanley Rd Biddulph ST8 179 C2
Ellesmere Port CH65 70 C7
Handforth SK8,SK9 34 E6
Knutsford WA16 56 F2
Stanley Rd Ind Est WA16 57 A1
Stanley St Chester CH1 237 A2
1 Crewe CW1 190 C4
7 Macclesfield SK11 112 D8
Newton-le-W WA12 2 A3
Northwich CW9 104 C8
Runcorn WA7 23 B3
Warrington WA1 16 B4
Stanley Villas 6 WA7 22 F1
Stanlow & Thornton Sta CH2 71 D5
Stanlow Abbey Bsns Ctr CH65 70 D2
Stanmore Rd WA7 23 D2
Stannage La CH3 180 F5
Stanner Cl WA5 7 D2
Stannerhouse La CW11 175 E4
Stanney Cl
Bebington CH62 43 E3
Neston CH64 66 E7
Stanney Grange Sports Complex The CH65 70 E3
Stanney High Sch CH65 70 C2
Stanney La
Ellesmere Port CH65 70 C3
Stoak CH2 70 E1
Stanney Mill Ind Est CH2 70 F3
Stanney Mill La CH2 70 F2
Stanney Mill Rd CH2 70 F2
Stanney Ten Ind Est CH2 70 F1
Stanney Woods Ave CH65 70 C1
Stanney Woods Ctry Pk* CH65 70 B1
Stanneybrook Cl CW6 101 A6
Stanneylands Cl SK9 34 C2
Stanneylands Dr SK9 34 B2
Stanneylands Rd SK9 34 B2
Stansfield Ave WA1 16 F6
Stansfield Dr WA4 27 A7
Stanstead Ave WA5 14 F3
Stanthorne Ave CW2 190 A3
Stanton Cl WA11 1 C6
Stanton Ct CH64 66 E8
Stanton Dr CH2 118 D5
Stanton Rd WA4 17 D3
Stanyer Ct CW5 205 A4
Stapeley Broad Lane CE Prim Sch CW5 205 A1
Stapeley Cl CW9 103 E4
Stapeley Ct CW1 190 B5
Stapeley Gdns L26 21 A6
Stapeley Terr CW5 205 A4
Stapeley Water Gdns* CW5 205 A3
Stapleford Ct CH66 69 F8
Stapleton Ave WA2 16 D8
Stapleton Ct WA6 74 C8
Stapleton Rd SK10 87 B2
Stapleton Way WA8 22 B5
Stapley Cl WA7 22 F1
Star La Lymm WA13 18 C4
Macclesfield SK11 112 D4
Starbeck Dr CH66 69 B5
Starkey Gr WA4 16 F4
Starling Cl Farndon CH3 180 F1
Kidsgrove ST7 195 D3
Runcorn WA7 50 D7
Start La SK23 65 B7
Statham Ave Lymm WA13 18 D3
Warrington WA2 8 C2
Statham Cl WA13 18 D3
Statham Com Prim Sch WA13 18 C4
Statham Dr WA13 18 D3
Statham La WA13 18 B5
Statham St SK11 112 D7
Station App / Lon yr Orsaf CH1 116 F7
Station Ave
Ellesmere Port CH66 69 C7
Helsby WA6 73 B4
Station Cl CH64 66 F7
Station Cotts CH1 116 F7
Station Gn CH66 69 C7
Station Hill CW8 76 F2
Station La
Dunham-on-t-H CH3 97 D3
Guilden Sutton CH2,CH3 119 F7
Rushton Spencer SK11 159 B2
Station Rd Adderley TF9 235 A5
Alpraham CW6 169 E2
Alsager ST7 193 D3
Astbury ST7,CW12 178 B1
Backford CH1 95 A3
Biddulph ST8 179 C1
Bosley CW12 135 A2
Burton CH64 67 B1
Chelford SK11 84 A2
Chester CH1 237 C4
Crowton CW8 76 D2
Delamere CW8 123 D8
Ellesmere Port CH65 70 C6
Ellesmere Port,Little Sutton CH66 69 C6
Elton CH2 72 A5
Goostrey CW4 131 A8
Handforth SK9 34 D3
Haydock WA11 1 C6
Heswall CH60 40 F6
Holmes Chapel CW4 130 D2
Irlam M44 11 E7
Kidsgrove ST7 194 F1
Kidsgrove, Newchapel ST7 195 E2
Lostock Gralam CW9 80 A2
Mobberley WA16 57 F7
Mouldsworth CH3 99 A2
Mow Cop ST7 195 C8
Nantwich CW5 204 E5
Neston CH64 66 F7
Neston, Parkgate CH64 66 C8
New Mills SK22 39 B7
Northwich CW9 79 B1
Partington WA14 20 B5
Runcorn WA7 22 F2
Sandbach CW11 174 D7
Sandycroft CH5 116 A2
Scholar Green ST7 194 F7
Styal SK9 34 A4
Sutton WA7 50 B4
Warrington WA4 16 E2
Warrington, Fearnhead WA2 9 A2
Warrington,Great Sankey WA5 14 F6
Warrington,Penketh WA5 14 E3
Weaverham CW8 77 A1
Whaley Bridge SK23 39 D4
Wilmslow SK9 60 B7
Winsford CW7 127 A1
Worleston CW5 188 E6
Wrenbury CW5 216 F3
Station Rd N WA2 9 A1
Station Rd S WA2 9 A1
Station St SK10 87 D1
Station Terr WA7 50 B4
Station View
Chester CH2 118 F2
Hampton Heath SY14 213 D7
Nantwich CW5 204 E4
Sandbach CW11 174 D8
Station Yard Trad Est CW4 130 D3
Staveley Dr CW7 126 D2
Steadings Rise WA16 56 D6
Steadings The CH3 120 A4
Steam Mill St CH1,CH3 237 C3
Stearns Cl CH1 118 A5
Stearns Ho CH1 118 A5
Steel St WA1 16 D7
Steele Rd CW10 151 D5
Steele St CH1 237 B2
Steeple Ct CH64 66 E7
Steeple St SK10 87 E1
Stein Ave WA3 3 E8
Stenhills Cres WA7 23 C2
Stephen St WA1 16 D6
Stephen's Gr WA6 73 B2
Stephens Gdns CH66 69 B6
Stephens Terr CH66 69 B6
Stephens Way ST7 209 F2
Stephenson Dr CW1 191 A4
Stephenson Rd WA12 2 D2
Stephenson Wlk CW7 149 A8
Sterling Cl
Congleton CW12 156 C3
Northwich CW9 103 F5
Sterne Cl CW11 174 D6
Stetchworth Rd WA4 16 B1
Steven Ct CH3 237 C3
Stevenage Cl SK11 112 B7
Stevenage Dr SK11 112 B7
Stevens Rd CH60 41 C7
Stevens St SK9 60 A1
Steventon WA7 24 E4
Steward's Ave WA8 22 F8
Stewart St CW2 190 A3
Stile End CH2 119 F8
Stiles The CW8 101 D5
Stiperstones Cl CH66 69 A6
Stirling Cl Chester CH3 119 A2
Stirling Cl *continued*
Macclesfield SK10 86 F2
Warrington WA1 17 E7
Winsford CW7 127 A3
Stirling Ct
Ellesmere Port CH65 70 D3
Holmes Chapel CW4 130 B2
Stirrup Cl WA2 9 A3
Stoak Lodge CH65 70 C4
Stock La CW2,CW5 206 B2
Stockdale Dr WA5 14 E7
Stockham Cl WA7 50 A8
Stockham La WA7 50 B7
Stockley Farm* CW9 54 E7
Stockley La WA4 52 F7
Stockport Rd WA4 17 E3
Stocks Ave 5 CH3 119 A1
Stocks Hill CW7 149 F7
Stocks La Chester CH3 119 A1
Ollerton WA16 82 E1
Rainow SK10 88 E5
Warrington WA5 14 D5
Stockswell Rd WA8 12 A3
Stockton Heath Prim Sch WA4 16 C1
Stockton La WA4 16 F1
Stockton Rd SK9 59 F4
Stockton View WA4 16 B2
Stockwell Farm Ct WA8 12 E4
Stoke Abbot Cl SK7 35 E7
Stoke Cl CH62 43 E3
Stoke Gdns CH65 70 C4
Stoke Hall La CW5 187 E6
Stoke Wlk CH65 70 C4
Stokes St WA3 9 E5
Stokesay Ct CH65 70 E3
Stone Bank Rd ST7 195 B1
Stone Barn La WA7 49 F6
Stone Chair La ST7 194 E7
Stone Cotts CW12 157 E2
Stone Croft CH3 142 B7
Stone Cross Dr WA8 12 E5
Stone Cross La N WA3 3 C7
Stone Cross La S WA3 3 C6
Stone Cross Pk WA3 3 B7
Stone Heyes La CW8,CW9 77 F5
Stone House La CW6 184 E4
Stone Mead Ave WA15 32 C7
Stone Pit La WA3 3 F2
Stone Pl CH2 118 F3
Stoneacre Gdns WA4 26 E4
Stonebank Dr CH64 67 A6
Stonebridge Rd CW5 204 E3
Stonechat Cl
10 Golborne WA3 3 E8
Runcorn WA7 49 E5
Stonecrop Cl
Runcorn WA7 49 F4
Warrington WA3 9 C4
Stonehaven Dr WA2 9 A3
Stoneheads SK23 65 D8
Stoneheads Rise SK23 65 D8
Stonehill Cl WA4 26 D4
Stonehills Ct WA7 23 C2
Stonehills La WA7 23 C2
Stonehouse Gn 6 CW12 156 D3
Stonelea WA7 24 B2
Stoneleigh Cl SK10 87 C2
Stoneleigh Ct WA4 17 D1
Stoneleigh Gdns WA4 17 D1
Stoneley Ave CW1 190 D7
Stoneley Rd CW1 190 D8
Stones Manor La CW8 103 C5
Stoneway Ct 1 CH60 40 F8
Stoney Holt WA7 50 C8
Stoney La Delamere CW6 123 C6
Wilmslow SK9 59 F5
Stoneyfold La SK11 113 A6
Stoneyford La CW8 101 C2
Stoneyland Dr SK22 39 B8
Stony La CW12 156 C1
Stonyhurst Cres WA3 4 D5
Stopsley Cl CW12 155 F4
Store St SK10 88 B8
Stores Rd M90 33 A6
Stour Ct CH65 70 B7
Stradbroke Cl WA3 4 A7
Straight Length WA6 73 E7
Straight Mile CH4 162 F5
Straker Ave CH65 69 F6
Stratford Gdns CH1 117 E4
Stratford Rd Blacon CH1 117 E4
Neston CH64 66 D6
Stratford Sq SK8 34 C7
Stratford Way SK11 112 C5
Strathaven Ave CW2 205 E8
Strathearn Rd CH60 40 F7
Strathmore Cl CW4 130 B2
Stratton Cl WA7 50 B6
Stratton Pk WA8 12 F5
Stratton Rd WA5 15 B5
Strawberry Cl WA3 9 C4
Strawberry Dr CH66 95 A8
Strawberry Fields CH3 142 B7
Strawberry Gn CH66 95 A8
Strawberry La
Acton Bridge CW8 76 F3
Mollington CH1 94 D4
Wilmslow SK9 59 E6
Street Forest Walks The* SK17 90 E4
Street Hey La CH64 43 B1
Street La
Lower Whitley WA4 52 C3
Rode Heath ST7 176 F2
Skellorn Green SK10 62 D8
Street The
Mickle Trafford CH2 119 D8
Whaley Bridge SK10,SK17 90 C5
Streethead Cott WA14 20 F1
Stretton Ave WA3 3 E7
Stretton Cl CH62 43 E3
Stretton Hall Mews WA4 52 E8
Stretton Mill* SY14 198 A7
Stretton Rd WA4 26 E2
Stretton Way 3 SK9 34 D5
Stretton Wlk CW9 103 F4
Strickland Cl WA4 27 A7
Strines Rd SK6 38 D8
Stringer Ave CW11 175 C5
Stringer Cres WA4 16 E4
Stringer's La LL12,CH4 161 B4
Stroma Ave CH65 95 B8
Stromness Cl WA2 9 B3
Stuart Cl Chester CH3 119 C3
Winsford CW7 149 C5
Stuart Ct SK10 87 B2
Stuart Dr WA4 16 F2
Stuart Pl CH1 237 B3
Stuart Rd WA7 24 C4
Stubbs La
Lostock Gralam CW9 80 A2
Mobberley WA16 58 E4
Stubbs Pl CH1 117 E3
Stubbs Terr 17 SK11 112 E7
Stubby La SK10 84 E2
Sturgess St WA12 1 F3
Styal Cl 4 CW9 103 F4
Styal Cross SK9 33 E4
Styal Ctry Pk* SK9 33 E3
Styal Gn SK9 33 F3
Styal Prim Sch SK9 33 E3
Styal Rd Wilmslow SK9 60 B8
Woodhouse Park M22 33 F7
Styal Sta SK9 34 A4
Styal View SK9 34 B2
Styperson Way SK12 36 E3
Sudbrook Cl WA3 3 E8
Sudbury Dr SK8 34 C8
Sudbury Rd SK7 36 E8
Sudlow La
Knutsford WA16 56 D1
Plumley WA16 81 C7
Suez St Newton-le-W WA12 2 B3
Warrington WA1 16 B5
Suffolk Ave CH65 69 F5
Suffolk Cl
Congleton CW12 156 D4
Macclesfield SK10 86 F1
Warrington WA1 17 E6
Suffolk Dr SK9 34 C1
Suffolk Ho CH1 237 C3
Suffolk Pl WA8 22 C7
Suffolk St WA7 22 F3
Sugar La Bollington SK10 63 A3
Manley WA6 98 E5
Rainow SK10 88 D5
Sugar Pit La WA16 56 E3
Sugar St SK11 159 C2
Sulby Ave WA4 16 B3
Sulgrave Ave SK12 36 F4
Summer Cl WA7 23 F1
Summer La
Daresbury WA4 51 D7
Runcorn WA7 23 F1
Summercroft Cl WA3 3 A7
Summerfield ST7 195 B1
Summerfield Ave WA5 7 F2
Summerfield Cl CH4 139 A3
Summerfield Dr CW9 126 F8
Summerfield Ho CH3 119 F5
Summerfield Pl SK9 60 A5
Summerfield Rd
Guilden Sutton CH3 119 F5
Mobberley WA16 57 F4
Summerfields WA16 57 C3
Summerfields Ctr 11 SK9 34 D1
Summerhill Dr ST5 210 D1
Summerhill Rd SK10 86 F4
Summerlea SK8 35 B8
Summerlea Cl SK10 87 D1
Summers Cl WA16 82 A7
Summers Way WA16 82 A7
Summertrees Rd CH66 69 E3
Summerville Gdns WA4 16 F1
Summit Cl WA4 26 E1
Sumner Rd CH1 117 E4
Sumner St WA11 1 A6
Sumpter Pathway CH2 118 F3
Sunart Cl CW2 206 B6
Sunbank La WA15 32 E6
Sunbeam Cl WA7 22 F3
Sunbeam St WA12 2 C3
Sunbury Cl SK9 34 E2
Sunbury Cres 3 CH4 140 F6
Sunbury Gdns WA4 26 E7
Suncroft Cl WA1 17 E7
Suncroft Rd CH60 41 C7
Sundale Dr CW2 189 D4
Sunderland St SK11 112 D7
Sundial Ho WA3 4 F3
Sundown Cl SK22 39 A8
Sunfield Cl CH66 69 D3
Sunflower Cl WA9 6 A7
Sunningdale Ave WA8 12 B1
Sunningdale Cl
Burtonwood WA5 6 F6
Northwich CW9 104 E7
Winsford CW7 126 A2
Sunningdale Dr
Bebington CH63 43 B6
Bramhall SK7 36 A7
Sunningdale Rd
Cheadle Hulme SK8 35 A7
Macclesfield SK11 112 A6
Sunningdale Way CH64 66 E4
Sunninghey Ct SK9 59 F2
Sunny Bank
Macclesfield SK11 112 D5
Wilmslow SK9 59 D4
Wilmslow,Fulshaw Park SK9 60 B6
Sunny Bank Cl SK11 112 D5
Sunny Bank Cotts
Ashton Hayes CH3 121 E7
Warrington WA8 14 A4
Sunny Bank Rd WA14 31 C8
Sunny Lea Mews SK9 60 A6
Sunnybank Cl WA12 2 C4
Sunnybank Rd CW1,CW2 189 E5
Sunnymill Dr CW11 175 A6
Sunnyside Alsager ST7 193 A4
4 Ellesmere Port CH65 70 C6
Malpas SY14 212 F2
Warrington WA5 14 E6
Sunnyside La WA7 24 E4
Sunset Cotts CH64 67 A4
Surrey Dr CW12 156 E5
Surrey Rd Chester CH2 119 A5
Kidsgrove ST7 195 A2
Warren SK11 112 A4
Surrey St Crewe CW1 190 E4
9 Runcorn WA7 23 A2
Warrington WA4 16 D3
Surridge WA16 29 C5
Susan Dr WA5 14 D5
Susan St WA8 13 C2
Sussex Ave SK11 112 A5
Sussex Dr ST7 194 F2
Sussex Pl CW12 156 E5
Sussex Rd Chester CH2 118 F4
Irlam M44 11 C6
Partington M31 11 E2
Sussex St WA8 13 D1
Sussex Way CH2 118 F4
Sutch La WA13 19 A3
Sutherland Ct 5 WA7 23 B2
Sutherland Dr
Bebington CH62 43 D4
Macclesfield SK10 87 A1
Sutherland Way CH3 119 B3
Sutton Ave Culcheth WA3 4 F4
Neston CH64 66 E6
Sutton Cl Bebington CH62 43 E3
Higher Wincham CW9 79 F6
Macclesfield SK11 112 D5
Mickle Trafford CH2 119 F8
Nantwich CW5 204 C5
Sutton Cswy WA6,WA7 49 E2
Sutton Dr CH2 118 E5
Sutton Green Prim Sch CH66 69 C5
Sutton Hall Dr CH66 69 A6
Sutton Hall Gdns CH66 69 A6
Sutton High Sch CH66 69 E6
Sutton La CW10 151 C7
Sutton Quays Bsns Pk WA7 49 E3
Sutton Rd
Alderley Edge SK9 59 F2
Poynton SK12 37 A2
Sutton St Runcorn WA7 23 B2
Warrington WA1 16 C4
Sutton Way
Ellesmere Port CH66 69 E4
1 Handforth SK9 34 E5
Sutton's La WA8 23 B7
Swale Cl SK9 34 E2
Swale Rd CH65 70 A7
Swaledale Ave CW12 157 A5
Swaledale Cl
Bebington CH62 43 E5
Warrington WA5 14 F7
Swallow Cl
1 Kidsgrove ST7 195 B2
Macclesfield SK10 113 A7
Warrington WA3 9 F4
Swallow Ct Handforth SK9 34 B1
Winsford CW7 149 D5
Swallow Dr Alsager ST7 193 B3
Kelsall CW6 122 D5
Sandbach CW11 175 A8
Swallow Rd ST7 195 F1
Swallowfield Cl CW2 206 A8
Swallowfield Gdns WA4 26 F5
Swallowfields CH3 180 E2
Swallowmore View ST7 210 C8
Swan Ave WA9 1 A2
Swan Bank
Congleton CW12 156 D2
Talke ST7 210 D7
Swan Cl Poynton SK12 36 B4
Talke ST7 210 D8
Swan Ct CW8 101 E7
Swan Farm La CW3 232 B1
Swan Gr WA16 106 D7
Swan Ho ST7 210 D7
Swan La CW6 185 E8
Swan Rd WA12 1 E4
Swan St Congleton CW12 156 D2
Wilmslow SK9 60 B7
Swanage Cl WA4 16 E2
Swanage Ct 6 CW7 149 D6
Swanley La CW5 203 D4
Swanlow Ave CW7 149 D5
Swanlow Dr CW7 149 D6
Swanlow La CW7 149 E5
Swann Gr SK8 35 B8

Swann La SK8 . . . . . . 35 B8
Swanscoe Ave SK10 . . . 88 A7
Swanscoe Cl CW10 . . . 151 B8
Swanscoe La SK11 . . . 88 B3
Swanwick Cl CW4 . . . . 107 C1
Swanwick Gn SY13 . . . 215 C5
Swanwick Ho SK10 . . . 86 F6
Sweet Briar Cres CW2 . 189 F3
Sweet Brier Cl CW8 . . . 78 B4
Sweetfield Gdns CH66 . 69 D7
Sweetfield Rd CH66 . . . 69 D7
Sweettooth La CW11 . . 175 A7
Swettenham Cl
  Alsager ST7 . . . . 193 C3
  Sandbach CW11 . . . . 175 D7
Swettenham La CW12 . 131 E3
Swettenham Rd
  Handforth SK9 . . . . . 34 D5
  Swettenham CW12 . . . 132 B2
Swettenham St SK11 . . 112 E7
Swift Cl Kidsgrove ST7 . 195 B2
  Warrington WA2 . . . . . 8 E3
  Wistaston CW2 . . . . . 205 F8
Swinburne Dr CW1 . . . 190 F4
Swindale Ave WA2 . . . . 8 B3
Swinden Cl WA7 . . . . . 24 D2
Swine Market 2 CW5 . 204 E5
Swineyard La WA16 . . . 28 C4
Swinford Ave WA8 . . . . 13 E2
Swinley Chase SK9 . . . . 34 F1
Swinleys Hey CH3 . . . . 142 A7
Swinnerton St CW2 . . . 190 C2
Swinton Sq 17 WA16 . . 57 A2
Swireford Rd WA6 . . . . 73 B2
Swiss Cott
  Alderley Edge SK9 . . . 60 C1
  Macclesfield SK10 . . . 87 B2
Swiss Hill SK9 . . . . 60 B1
Swithin Rd M22 . . . . . . 33 E8
Swynnerton Way WA8 . 13 B5
Sycamore Ave
  Alsager ST7 . . . . 193 E2
  Congleton CW12 . . . . 155 F4
  Crewe CW1 . . . . 190 D6
  Haydock WA11 . . . . . . 1 A5
  Newton-le-W WA12 . . . 2 C3
  Rode Heath ST7 . . . . . 193 F7
  Widnes WA8 . . . . 13 B2
  Winsford CW7 . . . . . . 149 D8
Sycamore Cl
  Audlem CW3 . . . . 230 A4
  Biddulph ST8 . . . . 179 E2
  Handforth SK9 . . . . . 34 B2
  Holmes Chapel CW4 . 130 D3
  Nantwich CW5 . . . . . 204 F7
  Talke ST7 . . . . 210 E8
Sycamore Cres
  Barnton CW8 . . . . 78 B4
  Hollinfare WA3 . . . . . . 11 B2
  Macclesfield SK11 . . . 112 A7
Sycamore Dr
  Chester CH4 . . . . 140 F5
  Ellesmere Port CH66 . . 70 A1
  Lymm WA13 . . . . 18 D4
  Middlewich CW10 . . . 151 E5
  Sutton WA7 . . . . 50 B4
Sycamore Gr
  Broughton CH4 . . . . . 139 B3
  Sandbach CW11 . . . . 175 A8
Sycamore La WA5 . . . . . 15 B6
Sycamore Lane Com Prim
  Sch WA5 . . . . 15 B5
Sycamore Lo SK7 . . . . . 59 C5
Sycamore Rd
  Morley Green WA16,SK9 . 59 C5
  Partington M31 . . . . . . 11 E3
  Runcorn WA7 . . . . 49 D8
Sycamore Rise SK11 . . 112 B6
Sycamores The WA16 . . 58 E2
Syddal Cl SK7 . . . . 35 D5
Syddal Cres SK7 . . . . . . 35 D4
Syddal Gn SK7 . . . . 35 D5
Syddal Rd SK7 . . . . 35 D5
Syddall Ave SK8 . . . . . . 34 D8
Sydney Ave M90 . . . . . 33 A8
Sydney Rd Bramhall SK7 . 35 F5
  Chester CH1 . . . . 118 B3
  Crewe CW1 . . . . 190 F6
Sydney St
  Northwich CW8 . . . . . 103 C7
  Runcorn WA7 . . . . 48 D7
Syers Ct WA1 . . . . 16 E8
Sylvan Ave SK9 . . . . . . 59 B5
Sylvan Cl CW8 . . . . 103 C7
Sylvan Mews CH1 . . . . 117 E6
Sylvia Cres WA2 . . . . . . 8 D1
Symondley Rd SK11 . . 112 F2
Synge St WA2 . . . . 16 C7
Sytch Croft CH64 . . . . 66 E8

T

Tabley Ave WA8 . . . . . . 12 D2
Tabley Cl Knutsford WA16 . 56 E3
  Macclesfield SK10 . . . 112 A8
  Sandbach CW11 . . . . 174 E7
Tabley Cl WA16 . . . . . . 56 B4
Tabley Gr WA16 . . . . . . 56 E3
Tabley Hill La WA16 . . . 56 B2
Tabley Ho Knutsford WA16 . 81 B8
  * Knutsford WA16 . . . 81 B8
Tabley Rd Crewe CW2 . 189 E3
  Handforth WA16 . . . . 34 D5
  Knutsford WA16 . . . . 56 E3

Tabley St CW9 . . . . 79 A1
Tabley Stables WA16 . . 81 A8
Tabor St SK11 . . . . 112 E6
Tadgers La WA6 . . . . . . 73 D8
Tailors View CW5 . . . . 204 E6
Talbot Ave CH64 . . . . . 66 F6
Talbot Cl Neston CH64 . 66 F6
  Shavington CW2 . . . . 206 B4
  Warrington WA3 . . . . . 9 E3
Talbot Gdns CH64 . . . 66 F6
Talbot Rd
  Alderley Edge SK9 . . . 60 B1
  Dunham-on-t-H WA6 . . 97 E7
  Ellesmere Port CH66 . . 69 F3
Talbot St Chester CH1 . 237 B4
  Golborne WA3 . . . . 3 A8
Talbot Way CW5 . . . . . 205 A3
Talfryn Cl CH5 . . . . 91 D1
Talisman Cl WA7 . . . . . 50 D7
Talke Rd Alsager ST7 . . 193 E3
  High Carr ST5 . . . . . . 210 F2
Newcastle-u-Lyme ST7,
  ST5 . . . . 210 D4
Tall Ash Ave CW12 . . . 157 A4
Tall Chys CW11 . . . . . 175 D4
Tall Trees Cl CW8 . . . . 103 C6
Tally Ho La CW5 . . . . . 203 E3
Tamar Cl
  Congleton CW12 . . . . 156 F1
  Macclesfield SK10 . . . 86 E1
Tamar Rd Haydock WA11 . 1 C6
  Kidsgrove ST7 . . . . . . 195 B2
Tamar Wlk CW7 . . . . . 127 A2
Tame Cl Biddulph ST8 . 179 D1
  Sandbach CW11 . . . . 174 E8
Tame Wlk 8 SK9 . . . . 34 D2
Tamworth Cl SK7 . . . . 36 D8
Tamworth St WA12 . . . 2 A3
Tan House La
  Burtonwood WA5 . . . . 7 A5
  Widnes WA8 . . . . 23 D8
Tanhouse WA7 . . . . . . 23 E1
Tanhouse Ind Est WA8 . 23 C7
Tankersley Gr WA5 . . . 15 B6
Tanner St CW12 . . . . . 156 E2
Tanner's La WA3 . . . . . 3 B8
Tanners La WA2 . . . . . 16 A6
Tanners View CW5 . . . 204 E4
Tannery La Neston CH64 . 66 E8
  Warrington WA5 . . . . . 16 B3
Tanning Ct 3 WA1 . . . 16 C5
Tanyard Dr WA15 . . . . 32 C6
Tanyard La WA15 . . . . 32 A5
Tapley Ave SK12 . . . . . 36 E2
Taplow Cl WA4 . . . . . . 26 C5
Taporley War Meml Hospl
  CW6 . . . . 146 D2
Target Cl ST7 . . . . 210 E6
Target Rd CH60 . . . . . 40 C8
Tarn Cl WA7 . . . . 126 C3
Tarn Ct WA1 . . . . 17 F7
Tarn Mount SK11 . . . 112 A5
Tarnbeck WA7 . . . . . . 50 D8
Tarnway WA3 . . . . 3 F7
Tarporley Bsns Ctr
Tarporley CE Prim Sch
  CW6 . . . . 168 C8
Tarporley Com High Sch
  CW6 . . . . 146 D1
Tarporley Rd
  Duddon CH3 . . . . 144 E7
  Ellesmere Port CH66 . . 69 E4
  Little Budworth CW6,CW8 . 124 C5
  Lower Whitley WA4 . . . 52 C4
  Tarvin CH3 . . . . 121 C1
  Utkinton CW6 . . . . . . 146 E6
  Whitchurch SY13 . . . 225 F3
Tarporley Wlk SK9 . . . 34 E2
Tarrant Ct CH1 . . . . 94 F1
Tarvin Ave CW2 . . . . . 189 D4
Tarvin Bridge CH3 . . . 119 A2
Tarvin Cl
  Ellesmere Port CH65 . . 70 C4
  Golborne WA3 . . . . . . 3 E7
  Macclesfield SK11 . . . 112 E5
  Middlewich CW10 . . . 151 D5
  Northwich CW9 . . . . . 103 F5
  Runcorn WA7 . . . . 50 D7
Tarvin Prim Sch CH3 . 121 B1
Tarvin Rd Alvanley WA6 . 73 F4
  Bebington CH62 . . . . . 43 F3
  Chester, Boughton CH3 . 119 A2
  Chester,Vicarscross CH3 . 119 E2
  Christleton CH3 . . . . . 120 C3
  Manley WA6 . . . . 99 A4
Tarvin Rdbt CH3 . . . . 121 A2
Tarvin Sands Industries
  CH3 . . . . 121 B4
Tarvin Way
  1 Handforth SK9 . . . 34 D5
  Winsford CW7 . . . . . . 126 C2
Tasman Cl WA5 . . . . . . 15 C8
Tate Cl WA8 . . . . 12 D2
Tate Dr CW1 . . . . 191 C4
Tattenhall La
  Beeston CW6 . . . . . . 167 F2
  Tattenhall CH3 . . . . . 167 B3
Tattenhall Rd CH3 . . . 166 C4
Tatton Cl Alsager ST7 . 193 C3
  Chester CH4 . . . . 140 E5
  Northwich CW9 . . . . . 103 F4
  Winsford CW7 . . . . . . 126 C1
Tatton Ct
  4 Knutsford WA16 . . 57 A2
  Warrington WA1 . . . . . 9 D1
Tatton Dr CW11 . . . . . 175 C7
Tatton Hall* WA16 . . . 57 B8

Tatton Lodge 18 WA16 . 57 A2
Tatton Pk* WA16 . . . . 57 B7
Tatton Rd Crewe CW2 . 189 F2
  Handforth SK9 . . . . . 34 C5
Tatton St WA16 . . . . . 57 A2
Tatton Stile WA16 . . . 58 A4
Taurus Pk WA5 . . . . . . 7 D3
Tavener Cl CH63 . . . . 43 C5
Tavistock Rd WA5 . . . 14 E4
Tavlin Ave WA5 . . . . . . 7 F1
Tawney Cl ST7 . . . . . . 195 B2
Tawny Ct WA7 . . . . . . 49 E7
Taxal & Fernilee CE Prim Sch
  SK23 . . . . 65 D6
Taxal Moor Rd SK23 . . 65 C3
Taxmere Cl CW11 . . . 174 F7
Tay Cl ST8 . . . . 179 E1
Taylor Bsns Pk WA3 . . 4 F1
Taylor Dr CW5 . . . . . . 204 C5
Taylor Rd Altrincham WA14 . 20 F5
  Haydock WA11 . . . . . . 1 F7
Taylor St Warrington WA4 . 16 A1
  Widnes WA8 . . . . 13 C1
Taylor's La
  Oakhanger CW1 . . . . 192 C3
  Warrington WA5 . . . . . 14 A2
Taylors Row WA7 . . . 23 C2
Teal Ave Knutsford WA16 . 57 B2
  Poynton SK12 . . . . . . 36 A4
Teal Cl Warrington WA2 . 8 E3
  Winsford CW7 . . . . . . 149 D5
Teal Gr WA3 . . . . 9 F3
Tealby Cl CW9 . . . . . . 104 B8
Teals Way CH60 . . . . . 40 E8
Tebay Rd CH62 . . . . . 43 E8
Tedder Dr M22 . . . . . . 33 F7
Tedder Sq WA8 . . . . . 22 D8
Teddington Cl WA4 . . 26 E5
Tees Ct CH65 . . . . 70 A7
Teesdale Cl WA5 . . . . 14 F7
Teesdale Rd WA11 . . . 1 C7
Tegg's Nose Ctry Pk*
  SK11 . . . . 113 D6
Teggsnose La SK11 . . 113 C4
Tegid Way CH4 . . . . . 140 D5
Tegsnose Mount SK11 . 113 C4
Telegraph Rd CH60 . . 41 A7
Telfer Ct CW10 . . . . . 151 E6
Telford Cl
  Congleton CW12 . . . . 157 B2
  Macclesfield SK10 . . . 88 A1
  Talke ST7 . . . . 210 E8
  Widnes WA8 . . . . 12 C4
Telford Ct CH1 . . . . . . 94 D6
Telford Gdns CW11 . . 174 F7
Telford Pl CW5 . . . . . 204 C5
Telford Rd CH65 . . . . 70 F4
Telford Way
  Audlem CW3 . . . . 230 A3
  Chester CH4 . . . . 140 F6
  Middlewich CW10 . . . 128 E1
Telford's Quay CH65 . . 70 D7
Templeton Dr WA2 . . 9 A2
Tempest Rd SK9 . . . . . 59 C1
Templar Cl SK10 . . . . 87 A1
Temple Chambers CH1 . 237 B3
Temple Cl WA3 . . . . . . 9 E6
Templeton Dr WA2 . . 9 A3
Tenbury Cl WA5 . . . . . 15 A8
Tenby Cl WA5 . . . . 7 F2
Tenby Dr WA7 . . . . . . 23 D2
Tenby Rd SK11 . . . . . 111 F6
Tenchersfield CW5 . . 205 A4
Tennyson Ave CW1 . . 190 F4
Tennyson Cl Crewe CW2 . 190 A1
  Macclesfield SK11 . . . 111 E6
  Northwich CW9 . . . . . 104 C6
  Rode Heath ST7 . . . . . 193 E8
Tennyson Dr WA2 . . . 8 C2
Tennyson Rd
  Ellesmere Port CH65 . . 70 A4
  Widnes WA8 . . . . 13 A1
Tennyson Wlk CH1 . . 118 A5
Tensing Cl WA5 . . . . . 15 B8
Tenth Ave CH5 . . . . . . 92 D3
Terence Ave WA5 . . . 16 F6
Terminal Rd N M90 . . 33 B7
Terminal Rd S M90 . . 33 B7
Tern Ave ST7 . . . . 195 C4
Tern Cl WA8 . . . . 13 B4
Tern Dr SK12 . . . . 36 B4
Terra Nova Sch CW4 . 108 D1
Terrace Rd WA6 . . . . . 23 A5
Terrick Mews SY13 . . 226 B2
Terrick Rd SY13 . . . . 226 A2
Tetchill Cl
  Ellesmere Port CH66 . . 69 D2
  Runcorn WA7 . . . . 50 D8
Tetton Ct 9 CW12 . . 156 F1
Tetton La CW10 . . . . 151 E3
Tewkesbury Cl
  Cheadle Hulme SK8 . . 35 B6
  Chester CH2 . . . . 118 F7
  Ellesmere Port CH66 . . 94 E8
  Middlewich CW10 . . . 128 B1
  Poynton SK12 . . . . . . 36 D4
Tewkesbury Dr SK10 . 87 E4
Tewkesbury Rd WA3 . 3 B8
Thackeray Dr CH3 . . . 119 C3
Thackery Ct 6 CW11 . 174 D6
Thames Cl
  Congleton CW12 . . . . 156 F1
  Warrington WA2 . . . . . 8 E3
  Winsford CW7 . . . . . . 126 C1
Thames Ct
  2 Knutsford WA16 . . 57 A2
  Warrington WA1 . . . . . 9 D1
Thames Dr CW11 . . . 175 C7
Thames Pl CW7 . . . . 127 B1
Thames Rd WA3 . . . . 5 A2

Thames Side CH65 . . . 70 B3
Thames Trad Ctr M44 . 11 F7
Thamesdale CH65 . . . 70 B4
Thaxted Wlk M22 . . . 33 C8
The Verdin High Sch
  CW7 . . . . 126 C1
Theatre Ct CW9 . . . . 103 F8
Thelwall Com Inf Sch
  WA4 . . . . 17 C3
Thelwall Com Jun Sch
  WA4 . . . . 17 D3
Thelwall La
  Warrington WA4 . . . . 16 F3
  Warrington WA4 . . . . 17 D3
Thelwall New Rd WA4 . 17 C3
Thelwall New Rd Ind Est
  WA4 . . . . 17 C3
Thelwall Rd CH66 . . . 69 E4
Thetford Cl SK10 . . . 87 C3
Thetford Rd WA5 . . . 14 E6
Thewlis St WA5 . . . . . 15 E5
Third Ave
  Connah's Quay CH5 . . 92 F1
  Crewe CW1 . . . . 190 F1
  Kidsgrove ST7 . . . . . . 194 F1
  Poynton SK12 . . . . . . 36 D1
  Runcorn WA7 . . . . 49 F8
  Sandbach CW11 . . . . 175 A5
Thirlemere Cl SK11 . . 112 A5
Thirlmere SK11 . . . . . 111 F5
Thirlmere Ave WA2 . . 8 C3
Thirlmere Cl
  Alderley Edge SK9 . . . 59 F1
  Frodsham WA6 . . . . . 49 D1
  Holmes Chapel CW4 . 130 A3
  Winsford CW7 . . . . . . 126 F3
Thirlmere Ct CW12 . . 156 A2
Thirlmere Dr WA13 . . 18 F3
Thirlmere Lodge 5
  WA13 . . . . 18 E3
Thirlmere Rd
  Chester CH2 . . . . 119 A5
  Crewe CW2 . . . . 190 A2
  Ellesmere Port CH65 . . 70 C2
  Neston CH64 . . . . 66 E6
  Partington M31 . . . . . 11 E4
Thirlmere Way WA8 . . 22 C8
Thirsk Cl WA7 . . . . . . 49 C6
Thirsk Way SK10 . . . . 87 C3
Thurston Cl WA5 . . . . 15 D6
Thistle Cl WA15 . . . . 32 D8
Thistle Sq M31 . . . . . 11 E2
Thistle Wlk 4 M31 . . 11 E2
Thistleton Cl SK11 . . 112 D6
Thistlewood Dr SK9 . . 60 D8
Thomas Ave CW5 . . . 205 A3
Thomas Brassey Cl CH2 . 237 C4
Thomas Cl Alsager ST7 . 193 E4
  Blacon CH1 . . . . 117 F6
  Ellesmere Port CH65 . . 70 B2
  Mickle Trafford CH2 . 119 F8
Thomas Ct WA7 . . . . 49 F7
Thomas Ho CH1 . . . . 118 A5
Thomas Hodges Ct
  CW4 . . . . 130 D3
Thomas Row 8 CW5 . 204 E6
Thomas St Biddulph ST8 . 179 D1
  Congleton CW12 . . . . 156 E3
  Crewe CW1 . . . . 190 D4
  Golborne WA3 . . . . 3 A8
  Packmoor ST7 . . . . . . 195 F1
  Runcorn WA7 . . . . 23 B3
  Talke ST7 . . . . 210 D8
  2 Widnes WA8 . . . . . 23 A7
Thomas Wedge CE Jun Sch
  The CH1 . . . . 94 A3
Thomasons Bridge La
  WA4 . . . . 25 E6
Thompson Ave WA3 . . 4 E3
Thompson Cl WA12 . . 2 C1
Thomson Gdns CW12 . 156 A3
Thoresby Rd SK9 . . . . 9 E5
Thoresway Rd SK9 . . 59 E5
Thorley Rd WA3 . . . . 4 F3
Thorley Gr CW2 . . . . 190 A1
Thorley La M22 . . . . . 33 B8
Thorley Mews SK7 . . 35 F7
Thorn Cl Runcorn WA7 . 49 C7
  Warrington WA5 . . . . . 14 F3
Thorn Dr SK8 . . . . . . 34 A8
Thorn Gr SK8 . . . . 35 A7
Thorn Grove Prim Sch
  SK8 . . . . 35 A7
Thorn Ho CH4 . . . . . . 141 A5
Thorn La CW8 . . . . . . 103 C5
Thorn Rd Bramhall SK7 . 35 F7
  Runcorn WA7 . . . . 49 C7
Thorn Tree Cl J24 . . . 21 E2
Thorn Tree Dr CW1 . . 173 A1
Thorn Wlk 8 M31 . . . 11 E2
Thornberry Cl CH1 . . 117 E5
Thornbrook Way CW11 . 174 D5
Thornbury Ave WA3 . . 3 E7
Thorne Cl SK10 . . . . . 87 A5
Thorneycroft CW7 . . 126 A1
Thorney La SK10 . . . 87 A5
Thorneyholme Dr WA16 . 57 B2
Thornfield SK9 . . . . . 60 A4
Thornfield Cl WA3 . . . 9 C5
Thornfield Hey SK9 . . 60 E8
Thornfields CW1 . . . 173 B1
Thorngrove Dr SK9 . . 60 E8
Thorngrove Hill SK9 . . 60 C6
Thorngrove Rd SK9 . . 60 C6
Thornhills WA8 . . . . . 12 E5
Thornleigh Ave CH62 . 43 F3
Thornleigh Dr CH66 . . 69 E6
Thornley Cl 1 WA13 . 18 C3

Thornley Rd WA13 . . 18 C3
Thornsgreen Rd M22 . 33 D8
Thornton WA8 . . . . . 22 E8
Thornton Ave SK11 . . 112 A5
Thornton Bank CW5 . 169 D4
Thornton Cl CW7 . . . 127 A3
Thornton Common Rd
  CH63 . . . . 42 D7
Thornton Cres CH60 . 41 B6
Thornton Dr
  Chester CH2 . . . . 118 D5
  Handforth SK9 . . . . . 34 D3
  Wistaston CW2 . . . . . 206 A7
Thornton Green La CH2 . 71 E1
Thornton Ho
  Audlem CW3 . . . . 230 A5
  Thornton Hough CH63 . 42 B6
Thornton Hough Prim Sch
  CH63 . . . . 42 B7
Thornton Mews CH66 . 69 B8
Thornton Rd
  Ellesmere Port CH65 . . 70 E3
  Heald Green SK8 . . . . 34 C8
  Warrington WA5 . . . . . 15 B4
Thornton Sq SK11 . . 112 A5
Thorntondale Dr WA5 . 14 F7
Thorntree Bglws SK11 . 132 A8
Thorntree Gn WA4 . . 27 B5
Thornway Bollington SK10 . 88 A7
  Bramhall SK8 . . . . . . 35 C7
  High Lane SK6 . . . . . . 37 F7
Thornwythe Gr CH66 . 69 E4
Thornycroft CW7 . . . 126 A1
Thornycroft Cl SK8 . . 35 B7
Thornycroft St 7 SK11 . 112 E7
Thorp St SK10 . . . . . 112 D8
Thorpe Cl CW1 . . . . . 189 F8
Thowler La WA14 . . . 30 A6
Threaphurst La SK7 . . 37 C8
Three Acres La SK8 . . 34 E7
Three Fields Cl CW12 . 156 B3
Threeways CW8 . . . . 101 D4
Thresh Way CW7 . . . 126 F4
Thurlow WA3 . . . . . . 3 E7
Thursfield Ave ST7 . . 195 C3
Thursfield Ct CH1 . . . 118 B1
Thursfield Prim Sch
  ST7 . . . . 195 E3
Thurstaston Rd CH60 . 40 F8
Thurston Cl WA5 . . . 15 D6
Thurston Gn SK9 . . . 60 A1
Thurston Rd CH4 . . . 140 E5
Thynne St WA1 . . . . . 16 A4
Tibb St ST7 . . . . 209 F2
Tibbs Cross La WA8 . . 13 D8
Tidal La WA1 . . . . . . 16 F8
Tideswell Cl SK8 . . . 34 D8
Tideswell Rd SK7 . . . 36 E8
Tidnock Ave CW12 . . 156 E5
Tiffield Ct CW7 . . . . 127 A4
Tilbey Dr WA6 . . . . . 74 A8
Tilbury Pl WA7 . . . . . 50 E6
Tildsley Cres WA7 . . 48 F6
Tilewright Cl ST7 . . . 195 B2
Tilley St WA1 . . . . . . 16 C6
Tilling Ct WA11 . . . . 1 E3
Tilston Ave WA4 . . . 17 A4
Tilston CE Prim Sch
  SY14 . . . . 198 B3
Tilston Rd SY14 . . . 213 A5
Tilston Wlk 5 SK9 . . 34 E1
Tilstone Cl Hough CW2 . 206 E2
  Northwich CW9 . . . . . 104 A5
Tilston La 6 SY9 . . . 103 F8
Tilton St SK10 . . . . . 87 B2
Timberfields Rd CH1 . 117 A4
Timbersbrook Gr 5 SK9 . 34 D2
Timberscombe Gdns
  WA1 . . . . 17 E6
Timbrell Ave CW1 . . 190 A6
Timmis Cl WA2 . . . . 9 A3
Timmis La WA16 . . . 17 A4
Timperley Ave WA4 . . 17 A4
Tinkersfield CW5 . . . 205 A4
Tinkwood La SY14 . . 211 F1
Tinsley St WA4 . . . . 16 F3
Tintagel Cl
  Macclesfield SK10 . . . 111 E8
  Runcorn WA7 . . . . 50 B6
Tintern Ave CH2 . . . 118 F6
Tintern Cl Poynton SK12 . 36 D4
  Warrington WA5 . . . . . 7 E2
Tintern Rd SK8 . . . . 35 B6
Tipping Brow WA16 . . 58 C4
Tirley La CW6 . . . . . 123 A2
Tithebarn Cl CW6 . . 165 D6
Tithebarn Dr CH64 . . 41 B2
Tithebarn Rd WA15 . . 32 C8
Tithings The WA7 . . 50 C5
Tiverton Cl Chester CH2 . 118 F5
  Sandbach CW11 . . . . 175 C7
  Widnes WA8 . . . . 12 C3
Tiverton Ct 6 CW9 . . 103 E5
Tiverton Dr SK9 . . . . 34 D1
Tiverton Sq WA5 . . . 14 E4
Tiverton Cl CW9 . . . 103 F5
Tobermory Cl WA11 . . 1 A5
Todbrook Cl SK23 . . . 65 D6
Todds Rd WA8 . . . . . 23 A6
Toft Cl Chester CH4 . . 140 E5
  Widnes WA8 . . . . 12 F1
Toft Rd WA16 . . . . . . 82 B7
Toft Way SK9 . . . . . . 34 E4
Toll Bar Ave SK11 . . 112 D5
Toll Bar Pl WA2 . . . . 8 A3
Toll Bar Rd Chester CH3 . 142 C8
  Macclesfield SK11 . . . 111 F8
  Warrington WA2 . . . . 8 A3

Tolland La WA15 ....31 F8
Tollard Cl SK8 ....35 B6
Tollemache Cotts CW5 .203 C8
Tollemache Dr CW1 ....190 A8
Tollemache Terr CH2 ...118 F2
Tollgate Cl ST7 ....210 C8
Tollgate Dr CW3 ....229 F4
Tollitt St CW1 ....190 C4
Tom Brads Croft SK23 ..65 E8
Tom Fields ST7 ....209 F1
Tom La WA14 ....30 E6
Tomkinson Cl CW1 .....189 F7
Tomkinson St CH2 .....237 C4
Tomlins Terr CH1 ....117 E5
Tomlinson Ave WA2 ....16 D8
Tommy's La
Congleton CW12 ....156 F4
Crewe CW1 ....190 E2
Tonbridge Cl SK10 ......87 B2
Toogood Cl CH2 ....119 F8
Top Farm La CW7 ......170 F2
Top Rd Frodsham WA6 ..74 D5
Kingsley WA6 ....75 B1
Top Station Rd ST7 ....195 C7
Topgate Cl CH60 ....41 B8
Topping Ct WA3 ....9 B4
Torbrook Gr 1 SK9 .....34 D2
Torkington Rd SK9 ......60 D6
Toronto Ave M90 ....33 B7
Torr Dr CH62 ....44 A7
Torr Rd SK11 ....112 C4
Torr Rise CW6 ....16 D1
Torr Top St SK22 ....39 C7
Torridon Gr CH66 ......69 F3
Torrs Valley SK22 ....39 C7
Torrvale Rd SK22 ....39 B7
Totland Cl WA5 ....14 C7
Totland Gr CH2 ....118 E4
Totton Ct WA1 ....9 D1
Tourney Gn WA5 ....7 A2
Tower Hill SK10 ....88 D4
Tower Hill Rd ST7 .....195 F7
Tower Ho The 20 SK11 .112 C8
Tower La Lymm WA13 ..18 F2
Runcorn WA7 ....50 D7
Weaverham CW8 ....77 B1
Tower Rd CH1 ....118 B2
Tower Way CW1 ....190 C4
Towergate CH1 ....118 B1
Towers Cl Poynton SK12 .36 F5
Wistaston CW2 ....206 A7
Towers Ct WA5 ....15 E7
Towers La WA6 ....98 C7
Towers Rd SK12 ....36 F5
Towers The 6 SK10 ...111 F8
Town Farm La WA4 ....100 E7
Town Gn The WA4 .....52 D5
Town Hall WA1 ....16 B5
Town La Hale L24,WA8 ..21 E2
Mobberley WA16 ....58 B4
Neston CH64 ....66 F6
Town Sq
4 Northwich CW9 .....103 F8
6 Runcorn WA7 ....49 F7
Town Well WA6 ....75 C2
Town Wlk 8 WA7 ......49 F7
Townbridge Ct 15 CW8 .103 F8
Towneley St WA8 ....13 A1
Townfield Ave CH3 ....180 E2
Townfield Cl CW7 .....194 D2
Townfield Ct CW8 ......78 A3
Townfield La
Barnton CW8 ....78 A3
Blacon CH1 ....117 F8
Farndon CH3 ....180 D2
Frodsham WA6 ....74 D7
Lymm WA13 ....19 B7
Mollington CH1 ....94 D2
Swan Green WA16 ....106 E5
Tarvin CH3 ....121 B2
Tiverton CW6 ....168 C6
Townfield Rd
Mobberley WA16 ....58 A4
Runcorn WA7 ....24 C2
Townfield View WA7 ...24 C2
Townfield Villas CH2 ...72 B3
Townfields
Knutsford WA16 ....57 C2
Sandbach CW11 ....175 B5
Townfields Cotts 6
CW7 ....149 C7
Townfields Cres CW7 .149 D7
Townfields Dr CW7 ....149 C7
Townfields Gdns CW7 .149 D7
Townfields Rd CW7 ...149 C7
Townley Mill 8 SK11 .112 D7
Townley Pl 9 SK11 ...112 D7
Townley St 4 SK11 ...112 D7
Townsend Farm ST7 ...193 E2
Townsend La ST7 .....194 A8
Townsend Rd CW12 ...156 E2
Townsfield Dr CW6 ....147 F7
Townsfield La WA2 ......8 A5
Townshend Rd CW9 ...80 A3
Township Cl CH3 .....182 C1
Townwell Ct CW5 .....204 D5
Trackside Bsns Pk
CW11 ....174 C6
Tracy Dr WA12 ....2 E3
Trafalgar Ave SK12 ....37 A3
Trafalgar Cl
Northwich CW9 ....103 E3
Poynton SK12 ....37 A3
Trafalgar Ct
8 Macclesfield SK11 ..112 D7
Widnes WA8 ....23 A6
Trafford Ave WA5 ......15 F7
Trafford Cres WA7 .....49 C6

Trafford Pl SK9 ....60 D6
Trafford Rd
Alderley Edge SK9 .....60 B1
Handforth SK9 ....34 B1
Trafford St CH1 ......237 B3
Tragan Dr WA5 ....14 D3
Tramway M44 ....11 F7
Tramway St CH1 .....237 C3
Tranmere Dr SK9 ....34 E2
Trap Rd CW12 ....132 C3
Trap St SK11 ....132 B6
Travellers Rest Cvn Pk
CW7 ....150 C8
Travers' Entry WA9 .....6 A7
Travis St 10 WA8 ......23 B8
Treborth Rd CH1 ......117 D3
Tree Bank Cl WA7 ......49 A8
Tree Tops CH64 ....66 E4
Tree Way WA16 ....82 A7
Treen Cl SK10 ....86 D1
Treetops Cl WA1 ....16 F7
Trefoil Cl Huntington CH3 .142 B6
Warrington WA3 ....9 C5
Tregele Cl CH1 ....117 D3
Trenance Cl WA7 ....50 C5
Trenchard Dr M22 ......33 F7
Trent Ave CW7 ....127 B1
Trent Cl Bramhall SK7 ..35 C6
Widnes WA8 ....13 B4
Winsford CW7 ....127 B1
Trent Way CH60 ....41 C1
Trentdale CH65 ....70 B3
Trentham Cl WA8 ......13 B4
Trentham St WA7 ......22 F3
Tresham Dr WA4 ....27 A8
Trevithick Cl CW1 ....191 A4
Trevone Cl WA16 ......57 A1
Trickett La CW8 ......102 A3
Tricketts La CW5 .....205 E5
Tricketts Mews CW5 .205 E5
Trident Ind Est WA3 ....9 F6
Trident Ret Pk WA7 ....49 E7
Trident Way SK11 ....112 A5
Trinity Cl CW2 ....190 A1
Trinity Ct
Congleton CW12 ......157 B1
1 Knutsford WA16 .....57 A2
Warrington WA3 ....9 F5
Trinity Gdns 4 WA6 ...49 C1
Trinity La SK11 ....112 F3
Trinity Pl
Congleton CW12 ......179 B8
1 Widnes WA8 ....23 B7
Trinity Sq SK10 ....87 F1
Trinity St Chester CH1 .237 A2
Trinity Terr 2 CW8 ..103 E8
Troon Cl Bebington CH63 .43 C5
Bramhall SK7 ....36 A7
Haydock WA11 ....1 A5
Holmes Chapel CW4 ..130 C2
Trossach Cl WA2 ....8 E2
Troutbeck Ave
Congleton CW12 ......156 A2
Newton-le-W WA12 ......1 E4
Warrington WA5 ....15 F8
Troutbeck Cl WA7 .....50 A5
Troutbeck Gr CW7 ...126 D2
Trouthall La WA16 .....81 A2
Trubshaw Ct ST7 .....195 C3
Trubshaw Pl ST7 .....195 B3
Trumans La CH66 ......69 C2
Truro Cl Bramhall SK7 ..35 F7
Congleton CW12 ......178 E8
Ellesmere Port CH66 ..94 F8
Macclesfield SK10 ......86 E1
Runcorn WA7 ....50 C6
Warrington WA1 ....17 B8
Tudor Cl
Ellesmere Port CH66 ..94 F8
Northwich CW9 ....104 E6
Warrington WA4 ....17 A2
Winsford CW7 ....149 D6
Tudor Ct
Congleton CW12 ......156 D2
4 Warrington WA4 .....16 E1
Tudor Dr SK10 ....86 D7
Tudor Gn Blacon CH1 .117 E8
Handforth SK9 ....34 E1
Tudor Rd Handforth SK9 .34 E1
Runcorn WA7 ....24 C3
Tudor Way Chester CH3 .142 A7
Congleton CW12 ......156 D1
Nantwich CW5 ....204 E3
Tudorway CH60 ....41 B8
Tue La WA8 ....13 A6
Tulip Rd Haydock WA11 ..1 F6
Partington M31 ....11 E2
Tully Ave WA12 ....1 F3
Tulworth Rd SK12 ......36 D4
Tunbridge Cl
Warrington WA5 ....15 A8
Wistaston CW2 ....206 A8
Tunnel Rd CW8 ....78 B2
Tunnicliffe Rd SK11 ..112 F3
Tunnicliffe St 1 SK10 .112 D8
Tunstall Rd
Bosley CW12,SK11 ...158 C7
Congleton CW12,SK11 .157 F2
Turf La SK11 ....112 C3
Turnall Rd WA8 ....22 B7
Turnberry Cl Lymm WA13 ..18 F3
Macclesfield SK10 ......87 C4
Northwich CW7 ....104 E7
Winsford CW7 ....126 C2
Turnberry Dr SK9 ......60 D8
Turner Ave ST7 ....210 A1
Turner Cl Crewe CW1 .190 A8

Turner Cl continued
Widnes WA8 ....12 D3
Turner Rise SK10 ......88 C8
Turner St Bollington SK10 .88 B8
Nantwich CW5 ....204 F5
Turner's View CH64 ....41 D2
Turnhurst Rd ST7 ....195 F1
Turnock St SK11 ......112 E7
Turnstone Ave WA12 ...2 C4
Turret Hall Dr 1 WA3 ..3 E8
Turriff Dr CH63 ....43 C4
Turrocks Cl CH64 ......66 E5
Turrocks Croft CH64 ..66 E5
Turton Cl Hale L24 ....21 E1
Warrington WA3 ....9 F7
Turton St WA3 ....3 A8
Turville Ho SK9 ....34 D2
Tuscan Cl WA8 ....13 B5
Tushingham Cl CH3 ..142 B7
Tushingham-with-Grindley
CE Prim Sch SY13 ...214 C1
Tuson Dr WA8 ....12 F4
Tutor Bank Dr WA12 ...2 D3
Tweedsmuir CH3 ......119 A2
Tweedsmuir Cl WA2 ....9 A4
Twemlow Ave CW11 ..175 B7
Twemlow La CW4 .....130 D6
Twenty Acre Rd WA5 ..15 C8
Twinnies Rd SK9 ....34 B1
Twiss Green Com Prim Sch
WA3 ....4 E4
Twiss Green Dr WA3 ....4 E4
Twiss Green La WA3 ...4 E4
Twist Ave WA3 ....3 C8
Two Acre Gr CH66 .....69 F1
Twyford Cl WA8 ....13 B5
Twyford La WA8 ....13 D6
Tyldesley Way CW5 ..204 D6
Tyler St SK9 ....60 A1
Tyne Cl WA2 ....8 E2
Tynedale Ave CW2 ...190 C2
Tynedale Cl SK11 ....112 C8
Tynemouth Rd WA7 ...50 C6
Tynesdale CH65 ....70 B3
Tynwald Cres WA8 ....12 F5
Tynwald Dr WA4 ......26 C7
Tyrer Rd WA12 ....2 C1
Tyrer Wlk 2 WA3 ....3 F8
Tytherington Bsns Pk
SK10 ....87 D5
Tytherington Cl CW10 .151 C6
Tytherington Ct SK10 .87 D3
Tytherington Dr SK10 .87 E4
Tytherington Gr SK10 ..87 C4
Tytherington High Sch
SK10 ....87 D2
Tytherington La SK10 ..87 D5
Tytherington Park Rd
SK10 ....87 D3
Tytherington Sh Ctr 1
SK10 ....87 D3

U

Ullapool Cl CH66 ......68 F6
Ullswater Cl SK11 ....111 F5
Ullswater Ave
Crewe CW2 ....189 E3
Warrington WA2 ....8 D3
Winsford CW7 ....126 D2
Ullswater Cres CH2 ..119 A6
Ullswater Dr SK9 ....83 F7
Ullswater Gr WA7 ......49 D5
Ullswater Mans SK11 .111 F5
Ullswater Rd
Congleton CW12 ......156 A2
Ellesmere Port CH65 ..70 C2
Handforth SK9 ....34 C3
Ulverston Ave WA2 .....8 B4
Ulverston Cl WA11 ......1 A6
Ulviet Gate WA16 ......29 C4
Under Rainow Rd CW12 .157 E1
Underbridge La WA4 ...25 E6
Undercliffe Ho WA4 ....26 D8
Underway The WA7 ....49 F8
Underwood Cl SK10 ...86 D2
Underwood Ct CW1 ..190 B6
Underwood Dr CH65 ..70 C2
Underwood Ind Pk CW1 .190 A6
Underwood La CW1 ..190 B6
Underwood Rd SK9 ....60 C1
Underwood West Inf Sch
CW1 ....190 A5
Underwood West Jun Sch
CW1 ....190 A5
Unicorn Gateway 8
SK10 ....112 D8
Union Cl CW12 ....156 A2
Union Ind Est SK11 ..112 E7
Union Pl CH1 ....237 A2
Union Rd
Macclesfield SK11 ....112 E7
New Mills SK22 ....39 C7
Union St Chester CH1 .237 C3
Congleton CW12 ......156 D3
Crewe CW2 ....190 D3
Macclesfield SK11 ....112 D7
Runcorn WA7 ....23 B2
Sandbach CW11 ......175 B6
Union Terr CH1 ....237 B3
Union Wlk CH1 ....237 B3
Unity Way ST7 ....210 D8
Univ of Liverpool, Faculty of
Veterinary Science
(Leahurst) CH64 ....67 D8

University College Chester
CH1 ....237 A4
University Way CW1 ..191 B2
Unsworth Ct WA2 ......8 F1
Upcast La SK9 ....59 E3
Uplands CW8 ....101 D4
Uplands Rd CW9 ....78 E4
Uplands The
Biddulph ST8 ....179 E2
Macclesfield SK11 ....112 A8
Runcorn WA7 ....50 A7
Upper Cambrian Rd
CH1 ....118 B2
Upper Haigh St CW7 .149 C8
Upper Mersey Rd WA8 .23 A5
Upper Mersey St CH65 .70 C7
Upper Northgate St
CH1 ....237 A3
Upper Raby Rd CH64 ..42 A2
Upton Ave SK8 ....35 A8
Upton Bridle Path WA8 .12 F4
Upton Cl Golborne WA3 ..3 D8
Winsford CW7 ....126 F4
Upton Dr Chester CH2 .118 C6
Warrington WA5 ....14 F5
Upton Grange WA8 ...12 D4
Upton Heath CE Prim Sch
CH2 ....118 E8
Upton La Chester CH2 .118 D7
Widnes WA8 ....12 F4
Upton Mount SK10 .....87 A1
Upton Pk CH2 ....118 D6
Upton Priory Inf Sch
SK10 ....86 F2
Upton Priory Jun Sch
SK10 ....86 F2
Upton Rd CH66 ....69 D4
Upton Rocks Ave WA8 .12 E4
Upton Rocks Mews WA8 .12 E4
Upton Way 12 SK9 ....34 D5
Upton Westlea Prim Sch
CH2 ....118 E7
Upton-by-Chester High Sch
CH2 ....118 F6
Upwood Rd WA3 ....3 D7
Ure Ct CH65 ....70 A7
Urmston Ave WA12 .....2 B5
Utkinton Cl WA6 ......146 E7
Utkinton Rd CW6 .....146 C5
Utkinton St Paul's CE Prim
Sch CW6 ....146 B8

V

Vahler Terr WA7 ....23 C2
Vale Ave WA2 ....16 B8
Vale Bsns Ctr CW12 .156 D2
Vale Cl CH4 ....139 C3
Vale Ct WA4 ....16 A3
Vale Gdns Alsager ST7 .193 E4
Helsby WA6 ....73 C4
Vale Owen Rd WA2 .....8 D1
Vale Rd Alpraham CW6 .169 A4
Ellesmere Port CH65 ..70 B4
Hartford CW8 ....103 C4
Marston CW9 ....79 B6
Wilmslow SK9 ....59 E8
Vale Royal Ctyd CW8 ..126 B2
Vale Royal Dr CW8 ...126 A8
Vale Royal River Park Cvn
Site CW9 ....126 A6
Vale View CW9 ....79 D1
Vale Wlk CW12 ....156 D2
Valebrook Dr CW5 ....220 A8
Valentine Rd
Kidsgrove ST7 ....195 A1
Newton-le-W WA12 .....1 F3
Valiant Cl WA2 ....8 F2
Valley Brook Bsns Ctr
CW2 ....190 D1
Valley Cl Alsager ST7 .192 F3
Knutsford WA16 ....82 A7
Valley Ct WA2 ....8 F2
Valley Dr Chester CH2 .118 C5
Ellesmere Port CH66 ..69 D5
Newton-le-W WA12 .....2 B1
Northwich CW9 ....104 C7
Valley Way WA16 ......82 A7
Valleybrook Ave WA6 ..73 C4
Varden Rd SK12 ....36 E3
Varden Town Cotts SK10 .86 A4
Vardon Dr SK9 ....60 D6
Varey Rd CW1 ....156 F4
Vaudrey Cres CW12 ..156 F3
Vaudrey Dr WA1 ......17 D7
Vaughan Rd SK23 .....65 E5
Vaughans La CH3 ....142 A8
Vauxhall Cl WA5 ....14 F4
Vauxhall Rd CW9 ....104 C8
Vauxhall Way CW7 ...149 C6
Vearows Pl CH1 ......117 F4
Venable's Rd CH1 ....117 F4
Venables Rd CW9 ......79 A1

Venetian Marina Village
CW5 ....188 B8
Venns Rd WA2 ....16 D7
Ventnor Cl
Middlewich CW10 .....151 C8
Warrington WA5 ....14 D7
Venture Ho SK11 .....112 D6
Venture Way SK12 .....36 F3
Verbena Cl Partington M31 .11 F3
Verdin Ave CW8 ....78 F1
Verdin Cl Moulton CW9 .126 F7
Winsford CW7 ....126 C2
Verdin Ct CW1 ....190 A8
Verdin St CW9 ....104 C8
Vere St CW1 ....190 C5
Verity Cl CW1 ....191 C4
Vermont Cl WA5 ......15 C7
Vernay Gn CH4 ....141 B5
Vernon Ave Audley ST7 .209 D2
Congleton CW12 ......178 F8
Hooton CH66 ....44 A2
Vernon Cl Audley ST7 .209 D2
Poynton SK12 ....36 D2
Saughall CH1 ....117 A8
Vernon Dr CW3 ......230 D8
Vernon Jun Sch SK12 .36 E3
Vernon Lo SK12 ....36 E3
Vernon St Crewe CW1 .190 B5
Macclesfield SK10 ....112 F8
Warrington WA1 ......16 B4
Vernon Way CW1 ....190 D4
Veronica Way CH66 ...69 D7
Vetch Cl WA3 ....11 B5
Vetches The CH3 .....119 F5
Viaduct St WA12 ....2 A3
Vicar's Cl CH3 ....121 F7
Vicar's La CH1 ....237 B2
Vicarage Ave WA8 ....35 B7
Vicarage Cl
Guilden Sutton CH3 ..119 F5
Hale L24 ....21 E1
Vicarage Ct LL13 ....196 E8
Vicarage Dr WA11 ......1 B7
Vicarage Gdns CW11 .174 E8
Vicarage Hill WA6 .....73 C2
Vicarage La Audlem CW3 .230 A4
Bunbury CW6 ....168 F1
Burton CH64 ....67 D2
Frodsham WA6 ....74 C7
Vicarage Row WA6 .....44 A5
Vicarage Way 1 SK11 .111 F7
Vicarage Wlk
Northwich CW9 ....104 B7
Warrington WA4 ....26 C8
Vicars Cross Ct 2 CH3 .119 B2
Vicars Cross Rd CH3 ..119 C2
Vickers Rd WA8 ....22 F4
Vickery Way CW7 ....104 A7
Victoria Ave Crewe CW2 .190 A4
Newton-le-W WA12 .....1 F1
Widnes WA8 ....23 A7
Victoria Com Tech Sch
CW1 ....190 C5
Victoria Cres
Chester CH2 ....237 A4
Chester,Queen's Park
CH4 ....237 C1
Victoria Ct Chester CH2 .237 A4
2 Crewe CW1 ....190 C4
Haslington CW1 ......191 C4
8 Knutsford WA16 .....56 F1
Widnes WA8 ....23 A8
Victoria Gr WA8 ....13 A3
Victoria Inf Sch CH1 .237 A4
Victoria Infmry CW8 .103 E8
Victoria Mews CH65 ...70 B5
Victoria Mill Dr CW5 .205 D2
Victoria Pathway CH4 .237 C1
Victoria Pl Chester CH1 .237 B3
Warrington WA4 ....16 C1
Victoria Rd
Chester CH1,CH2 ....237 B3
Chester CH2 ....237 A4
Ellesmere Port CH65 ..70 C5
Macclesfield SK10 .....87 A1
Neston CH64 ....67 A6
Northwich CW9 ....104 B8

Victoria Rd continued
Runcorn WA7 ....23 A2
Runcorn WA7 ....23 B2
Saltney CH4 ....140 D5
Warrington WA4 ....16 F2
Warrington, Stockton Heath
WA4 ....16 D1
Warrington,Great Sankey
WA5 ....15 B4
Warrington,Penketh WA5 ..14 D4
Widnes WA8 ....23 A6
Wilmslow SK9 ....60 A6
Victoria Road Prim Sch
Northwich CW9 ....104 B8
Runcorn WA7 ....23 A2
Victoria Sq
Warrington WA4 ....16 C1
8 Widnes WA8 ....23 A7
Winsford CW7 ....149 A8
Victoria St
Congleton CW12 ....156 D2
Crewe CW1 ....190 C4
Knutsford WA16 ....56 F2
New Mills SK22 ....39 B6
Northwich CW9 ....79 E2
Sandbach CW11 ....175 B7
Warrington WA1 ....16 C5
Widnes WA8 ....23 B7
Victoria Stadium (Northwich
Victoria FC) CW9 .....79 D3
Victoria Trad Ctr WA8 ..23 A6
Victoria Way SK7 ....35 D6
Victoria Wlk SK10 .....112 E8
Victory Rd WA4 ....11 C4
Viewlands Dr SK9 .....34 D2
Villa Farm CW11 ....176 B8
Villa Rd CH5 ....116 B7
Village Cl
Lostock Green CW9 ....105 A8
Runcorn WA7 ....50 A8
Warrington WA4 ....17 E4
Village Ct 8 SK9 .....34 D1
Village Farm CW5 .....172 A5
Village La WA4 ....52 D4
Village Mews SK10 ....87 A6
Village Rd
Christleton CH3 ......142 E8
Great Barrow CH3 ....120 E6
Heswall CH60 ....40 F7
Waverton CH3 ....143 C4
Village St WA7 ....24 E2
Village Terr The 6 WA4 ..16 C1
Village The
Astbury CW12 ....178 B8
Burton CH64 ....67 D1
Prestbury SK10 ......86 F6
Village Way 12 SK9 ..34 D1
Villars St WA1 ....16 C5
Villas The CW4 ......131 A8
Villiers Russell Cl CW1 ..190 D5
Vincent Cl WA5 ....15 D8
Vincent Dr CH4 ......141 C6
Vincent St Crewe CW1 ..190 E4
Macclesfield SK11 ...112 D7
Vine Bank Rd ST7 ....195 A1
Vine Cl SK11 ....112 A6
Vine Cres WA5 ....14 F6
Vine Rd CH66 ....69 F1
Vine St Bollington SK10 ..88 B8
12 Runcorn WA7 .....23 A2
Widnes WA8 ....23 A7
Vine Terr WA8 ....12 A2
Vine Tree Ave
Crewe CW2 ....190 B1
Shavington CW2 .....206 B5
Vine Tree Prim Sch
CW2 ....190 A1
Violet Cl WA3 ....9 F5
Violet St WA8 ....23 A7
Virginia Chase SK8 ...34 F8
Virginia Dr CH1 .....117 C4
Virginia Gdns WA5 ...15 B8
Virginia Terr CH66 ..69 B8
Virtual Bsns Ctr CH1 ..117 E2
Viscount Dr
Heald Green SK8 ....34 D7
Woodhouse Park M90 ..32 F7
Viscount Rd WA2 .....8 E2
Vista Ave WA12 ......2 A4
Vista Rd
Newton-le-W WA11,WA12 ..2 A6
Runcorn WA7 ....49 A8
Vista The M44 ......11 C4
Vista Way WA12 .....2 A4
Vivian Gr WA8 ......12 F4
Volunteer Ave 7 CW5 ..204 E6
Volunteer Fields CW5 ..204 E6
Volunteer St
Chester CH1 ....237 B2
Frodsham WA6 ......49 D1
Vose Cl WA5 ....15 D6
Vulcan Cl
Newton-le-W WA12 ...2 C1
Warrington WA2 ....8 F2
Vulcan Ind Est WA12 ..2 D3
Vyrnwy Rd CH4 .....140 D6

W

Wadbrook Trad Est
CW9 ....104 C8
Waddington Cl
Golborne WA3 ....3 F8
Warrington WA2 ....8 F1

Wade Cres CW8 ....78 A3
Wade Ct ST7 ....195 A1
Wade Deacon High Sch
WA8 ....13 A2
Wade St CW9 ....79 B1
Wadebrook Gr 4 SK9 ..34 D1
Wades La CW7 ......126 D3
Wadeson Way WA3 ...9 B7
Wadsworth Cl SK9 ..34 E3
Wagg St CW12 ....156 D1
Waggon Cotts ST7 ..208 E1
Waggs Rd CW12 .....156 C1
Wagon La WA11 .....1 B6
Wain Ho CH1 ......94 A1
Wain Lee ST7 .....195 F4
Waine St CW1 .....190 D5
Wakefield Cl CW1 ..189 F7
Wakefield Ho WA5 ..15 F6
Wakefield Rd CH66 ..69 E1
Wakefield St WA3 ..3 A7
Wakeham Chase 8
SK11 ....111 F7
Wakes Mdw CW6 ...185 E8
Walden Cl WA4 ....17 D3
Walden Dr CH1 ...93 D8
Waldon Rd SK11 ..112 A5
Waldron Gdns CW2 ..189 F1
Waldron Rd CW1 ..191 D3
Waldron's La CW1 ..173 D1
Walfield Ave CW12 ..156 D5
Walford Dr CW2 ...190 B3
Walgrave Cl CW12 ..156 A3
Walker Cl CW1 ....191 D4
Walker Dr CW10 ..151 C8
Walker La WA16 ..112 E2
Walker St Chester CH2 ..237 C4
Crewe CW1 ....190 B5
2 Macclesfield SK10 ..112 C8
Warrington WA2 ...16 A6
Walkers La
Ellesmere Port CH66 ..69 C6
Farndon CH3 ......180 F2
Scholar Green ST7 ..177 B2
Tarporley CW6 ...146 D1
Warrington WA5 ..14 E3
Walkersgreen Rd ST5 ..210 D2
Wall Fields Rd CW5 ..204 E7
Wall Hill Way CW8 ..76 F3
Wall La CW5 ......204 E6
Wallace Ct CW7 ...127 D1
Wallace St
Northwich CW8 ...103 E7
Widnes WA8 .....23 A8
Wallcroft CH64 ...68 A7
Walled Gdn The CW10 ..127 D5
Waller St SK11 ..112 E6
Wallerscote Cl CW8 ..102 E8
Wallerscote Com Sch
CW8 ....102 E8
Wallerscote Rd CW8 ..102 E8
Walleys La CW5 ..203 C7
Wallfields Cl CW5 ..204 E7
Wallhill La CW11 ..177 D7
Wallingford Rd SK9 ..34 C5
Wallis St Crewe CW1 ..190 D4
Warrington WA4 ...16 B3
Wallrake CH60 ...40 F7
Walls Ave CH1 ...118 B1
Wallsend Ct WA8 ..12 F3
Wallworth Terr SK9 ..59 E8
Wallworth's Bank CW12 ..156 E2
Walmer Pl CW7 ...149 C6
Walmoor Pk CH3 ..119 A1
Walmsley St
Newton-le-W WA12 ..2 D4
Widnes WA8 .....23 C8
Walnut Ave CW8 ..102 D7
Walnut Cl Chester CH2 ..118 D7
Walnut Dr CW7 ...127 A1
Walnut Gr CH66 ..70 A1
Walnut La CW8 ...103 A5
Walnut Rd M31 ..11 D3
Walnut Rise CW12 ..156 B2
Walnut Tree La
Bradwall Green CW11 ..153 A4
Warrington WA1 ..26 F4
Walpole Cl CW1 ..191 C5
Walpole Gr WA2 ..8 C2
Walpole Rd WA7 ..49 C6
Walpole St CH1 ..237 A4
Walsh Cl WA12 ...2 C5
Walsingham Dr WA2 ..24 D2
Walsingham Rd WA5 ..14 F5
Walter St Chester CH1 ..237 B4
Warrington WA1 ..16 E7
Warrington WA3 ..13 D1
Walters Wood SK23 ..65 F5
Walthall St CW2 ..190 C2
Waltham Ave WA3 ..5 C7
Waltham Ct WA4 ..24 E4
Waltham Dr SK8 ..35 B6
Waltham Pl CH4 ..140 F5
Walton Ave WA5 ..14 E5
Walton Dr ST7 ..210 C8
Walton Hall* WA4 ..25 F7
Walton Hall Gdns* WA4 ..25 F6
Walton Heath Dr SK10 ..87 B4
Walton Heath Rd WA4 ..16 B1
Walton La WA3 ..9 E5
Walton Lea Rd WA4 ..26 B3
Walton New Rd WA4 ..26 B8
Walton Pl CH1 ..117 E4
Walton Rd Culcheth WA3 ..4 F3
Warrington WA4 ..26 C8

Walton St 15 WA7 ..23 A2
Walton Way ST7 ..210 C8
Waltons The CH4 ..141 E6
Wandsworth Way WA8* ..22 F5
Wansfell Pl WA2 ..8 A3
Warburton Bridge Rd
WA13,WA3 ....11 A1
Warburton Cl
Altrincham WA15 ..32 D6
Lymm WA13 ......19 A4
Warburton Dr WA15 ..32 D6
Warburton La M31,WA13 ..11 E2
Warburton Rd SK9 ..34 D4
Warburton St WA4 ..16 D1
Warburton View WA3 ..11 A2
Ward Ave SK10 ..88 A8
Ward Cl WA5 .....7 B1
Ward La SK12 ...38 F4
Ward's La CW11 ..153 C5
Ward's Terr CH2 ..118 F3
Wardle Ave CW5 ..187 C2
Wardle Cotts CW5 ..187 C2
Wardle Cres SK11 ..111 E1
Wardle Ind Est CW5 ..187 A7
Wardle Mews CW10 ..151 D8
Wardle St 3 SK11 ..112 D7
Wardley Rd WA4 ..16 B1
Wardour Cl 6 SK11 ..111 F7
Wardour St WA5 ..15 E6
Wards La CW12 ..179 E8
Wareham Cl Haydock WA11 ..1 C7
Warrington WA1 ..17 C8
Wareham Dr CW1 ..190 B8
Warford Ave SK9 ..59 E6
Warford Cres SK9 ..84 B7
Warford Hall Dr SK9 ..84 B6
Warford La WA16 ..59 B1
Warford Terr WA16 ..59 B2
Wargrave CE Prim Sch
WA12 ....2 C1
Wargrave Mews WA12 ..2 C1
Wargrave Rd WA12 ..2 C2
Warham St SK9 ..60 B7
Waring Ave St Helens WA9 ..1 B2
Warrington WA4 ..16 F5
Warkick Rd CH1 ..117 F5
Warkworth Cl WA8 ..12 C3
Warkworth Ct CH65 ..70 E3
Warmingham CE Prim Sch
CW11 ....173 E8
Warmingham Ct CW10 ..151 D7
Warmingham La
Middlewich CW10 ..151 D5
Sandbach CW11 ..174 B8
Warmingham Rd CW1 ..173 D4
Warnley Cl WA8 ..12 D3
Warren Ave
Knutsford WA16 ..56 E2
Lostock Gralam CW9 ..80 A3
Warren Cl Knutsford WA16 ..56 F2
Middlewich CW10 ..151 D8
Poynton SK12 ...36 B4
Warren Croft WA7 ..50 D7
Warren Ct
Ellesmere Port CH66 ..69 D3
Frodsham WA6 ..74 D6
Warren Dr
Altrincham WA15 ..32 D7
Broughton CH4 ..139 A3
Ellesmere Port CH66 ..69 E7
Newton-le-W WA12 ..2 F4
Warren St WA1 ..111 D1
Warrington WA4 ..26 D8
Warren Way 3 WA3 ..3 E8
Warrington WA1 ..17 D8
Warren Lea SK12 ..36 E5
Warren Rd
Warrington,Orford WA2 ..8 D1
Warren The CW8 ..101 D5
Warren Way CH6 ..168 D8
Warrilow Heath Rd ST5 ..210 C1
Warrington Ave
Crewe CW1 ....190 C6
Ellesmere Port CH65 ..70 B2
Warrington Bank Quay Sta
WA1 ....15 F4
Warrington Bsns ctr
WA2 ....16 A6
Warrington Bsns Pk WA2 ..8 C1
Warrington Central Sta
WA2 ....16 B6
Warrington Collegiate Inst
WA2 ....8 B1
Warrington Collegiate Inst
(Padgate Campus) WA2 ..9 B3
Warrington Hospl WA5 ..15 F6
Warrington La WA13 ..19 E2
Warrington Mus & Art
Gallery* WA1 ....16 A4
Warrington Rd
Bold Heath L35,WA8 ..13 D7
Comberbach CW9 ..78 D7
Cronton L35 .....12 F8
Cuddington CW8 ..102 A8
Fowley Common WA3,WN7 ..5 C5
Golborne WA3,WA12 ..3 A6
Hatton WA4 .....25 F4
Little Leigh CW8 ..77 A5
Lymm WA13 .....18 F6
Mickle Trafford CH2 ..119 E7
Runcorn,Castlefields WA7 ..23 E2
Runcorn, Manor Park WA7 ..49 D6

Warrington Rd continued
Warrington,Risley WA3 ..9 E7
Widnes WA8 .....13 D1
Warrington,Risley WA3 ..9 E7
Warrington St Ann's CE Prim
Sch WA2 ....16 C8
Warrington Trad Est
WA2 ....16 A6
Warton Cl Bramhall SK7 ..36 A7
Warrington WA5 ..15 A3
Warwick Ave
Newton-le-W WA12 ..2 E2
Warrington,Bewsey WA5 ..15 F7
Warrington,Great Sankey
WA5 ....14 D7
Warwick Cl
Kidsgrove ST7 ..195 A3
Knutsford WA16 ..57 C1
Macclesfield SK11 ..111 F6
Neston CH64 ....66 E5
Warwick Ct CH65 ..70 E2
Warwick Dr SK7 ..36 D8
Warwick Gr 1 WA7 ..23 F1
Warwick Pl CW7 ..149 C6
Warwick Rd Irlam M44 ..11 D5
Macclesfield SK11 ..111 E6
Warwick Wlk SK11 ..111 F6
Wasdale Gr CW1 ..173 B1
Wash La Allostock WA16 ..106 E3
Warrington WA4 ..16 E3
Washington Cl
Biddulph ST8 ...179 C2
Cheadle Hulme SK8 ..34 F8
Wasley Cl WA2 ...8 F3
Waste La
Cuddington CW8 ..101 E3
Delamere CW8 ...123 F6
Kelsall CW6 .....122 C7
Watch La CW11 ..174 A6
Water La SK9 ...60 A7
Water St Bollington SK10 ..88 B8
Macclesfield SK11 ..112 C8
Newcastle-u-Lyme ST5 ..210 D2
Newton-le-W WA12 ..2 C4
Northwich CW9 ..104 A7
Runcorn WA7 ....23 A3
Widnes WA8 .....23 A6
Water's Reach SK6 ..37 E7
Waterbank Row CW9 ..103 F7
Waterbridge Ct
2 Lymm WA13 ...18 C3
Warrington WA4 ..26 D8
Waterfoot La SK23 ..65 D6
Waterford Cl CH64 ..67 A7
Waterford Dr CH64 ..67 A7
Waterford Pl SK8 ..34 B8
Waterford Way WA7 ..50 F5
Waterfowl Sanctuary*
SY13 ....225 F6
Watergate Row N CH1 ..237 A2
Watergate Row S CH1 ..237 A2
Watergate St CH1 ..237 A2
Waterhouse Ave SK10 ..87 F8
Waterlode CW5 ..204 E5
Waterloo Cl SK11 ..112 A6
Waterloo Gr ST7 ..195 A2
Waterloo Ho 10 CH65 ..70 C5
Waterloo Ho 11 CW8 ..103 F8
Waterloo La WA6 ..73 D4
Waterloo Rd Bramhall SK7 ..35 F8
Chester CH2 .....118 C4
Haslington CW1 ..191 D4
Northwich CW8 ..103 E7
Poynton SK12 ...37 A2
8 Runcorn WA7 ..22 F2
Runcorn WA7 ...22 F3
Widnes WA8 .....23 A5
Waterloo St W SK11 ..112 C8
Watermead Dr WA7 ..50 F5
Watermill Dr SK11 ..112 F7
Waters Edge
Chester CH1 .....198 D3
Chester CH1 .....118 B2
Waters Edge Mews
CW10 ....151 C8
Waters Gn SK11 ..112 D8
Waters Reach SK12 ..36 F5
Waters Reams CH3 ..142 B8
Watersedge WA6 ..49 D2
Watersfield Cl SK8 ..34 D8
Waterside Disley SK12 ..38 E7
Macclesfield SK11 ..112 E7
Warrington WA4 ..26 D8
Watersmead Dr WA7 ..50 F5
Waterside Cotts CW5 ..216 E5
Waterside Dr WA6 ..49 D2
Waterside La WA8 ..22 D5
Waterside Mews CW1 ..173 F2
Waterside View
Chester CH1 .....237 B3
Northwich CW9 ..104 E6
Waterside Way CW10 ..128 B2
Watertower View CH3 ..119 B2
Waterway CH3 ....143 B5
Waterways WA5 ..15 D6
Waterworks La
Ellesmere Port CH66 ..68 E8
Hooton CH66 .....43 E1
Winwick WA2 .....8 F8
Watery La Astbury CW12 ..178 C5
Frodsham WA6 ..74 E6
Winwick WA2 .....7 E6
Watkin St WA1 ..16 B7
Watkins Ave WA12 ..1 F3
Watkinson Way WA8 ..13 C5

Watlands Rd ST7 ..209 E2
Watling Cres CH4 ..141 E7
Watling Ct Chester CH3 ..119 C2
Cuddington CW8 ..102 B2
Watling Dr CH6 ..123 C6
Watling St CW9 ..103 F8
Watson's Cl CH4 ..139 C3
Watton Cl WA4 ..17 C3
Wavell Ave WA8 ..22 D8
Wavells Way CH3 ..142 B5
Waverley Ave WA4 ..26 D8
Waverley Cl SK10 ..113 A8
Waverley Ct 1 CW2 ..190 D2
Waverley Dr SK8 ..35 B7
Waverley Terr CH2 ..118 E4
Waverton App CH3 ..164 E6
Waverton Bsns Pk CH3 ..142 F4
Waverton Cl Hough CW2 ..206 E2
Northwich CW9 ..103 A2
Waverton Com Prim Sch
CH3 ....143 A5
Waverton Mill Quays
CH3 ....143 B5
Waverton Pk CH3 ..143 B5
Waverton Rd CH66 ..69 E5
Wavertree Cl CH66 ..69 F7
Wavertree Dr CW10 ..151 B7
Wavertree Rd CH1 ..117 C5
Way's Gn CW7 ...149 E8
Waybutt La CW2 ..221 D8
Wayfarers Ct CW5 ..79 F7
Wayfarers Dr WA12 ..2 E2
Wayford Cl WA6 ..49 B1
Wayford Mews WA7 ..49 B1
Wayside Cl WA13 ..18 D2
Wayside Ct CH2 ..119 F8
Wayside Dr SK12 ..36 C4
Wayside Linley ST7 ..193 F2
Wayside Rd SK10 ..112 F8
Waystead Cl CW9 ..103 F4
Waywell Cl WA2 ..8 F3
Weald Dr CH66 ..69 A6
Wealstone Cl CH2 ..118 C6
Wealstone La CH2 ..118 C6
Wearhead Cl WA3 ..2 F7
Weates Cl WA8 ..12 F3
Weates La WA4 ..17 E2
Weathercock La CW12 ..157 E3
Weatherstones Cotts
CH64 ....67 D8
Weatherstones Mews
CH64 ....67 C8
Weaver Bank CW5 ..204 E5
Weaver Cl Alsager ST7 ..193 A3
Biddulph ST8 ...179 D1
Sandbach CW11 ..174 E7
Weaver Cres WA6 ..49 D1
Weaver Ct
Macclesfield SK11 ..112 C7
Northwich CW9 ..103 F8
Weaver Gr
Mickle Trafford CH2 ..119 F8
3 Winsford WA9 ..1 A3
Weaver Grange CW9 ..126 E8
Weaver Ho 18 CW8 ..103 F8
Weaver La WA6 ..49 B2
Weaver Park Ind Est
WA6 ....49 D2
Weaver Prim Sch CW5 ..204 E3
Weaverbank Cl CH3 ..5 A2
Weaver Rd CH65 ..70 C2
Frodsham WA6 ..49 D1
Moulton CW9 ...126 E2
Nantwich CW5 ..204 E6
Northwich CW8 ..103 E7
Weaver St Chester CH1 ..237 A2
Winsford CW7 ..126 E1
Weaver Valley Rd CW7 ..126 E3
Weaver View
Audlem CW3 ....229 E3
Church Minshull CW5 ..172 B6
Northwich CW8 ..103 F7
Weaverham CW8 ..77 D1
Weaver Way CW7 ..78 F1
Weaverhall La CW7 ..150 B5
Weaverham Forest Prim Sch
CW8 ....77 C1
Weaverham High Sch
CW8 ....102 C8
Weaverham Rd CW8 ..102 B4
Weaverham Way SK9 ..34 E4
Weavers Cotts 3 CW12 ..156 D3
Weavers La WA7 ..35 D6
Weaverside Ave WA7 ..49 F4
Weaverside Pk CW8 ..77 A6
Webb Dr WA5 ....6 F6
Webb's Ct CW9 ..103 F7
Webb's La CW10 ..128 C2
Webbs Orch SK23 ..65 D8
Webster Cl CH4 ..139 C3
Websters La CH66 ..69 F7
Weddell Cl WA5 ..15 D7
Wedge Ave WA11 ..1 A5
Wedgwood Ave ST7 ..210 A1
Wedgwood Dr WA8 ..13 C4
Wedgwood La ST8 ..179 C2
Wedgwood Rd ST7 ..210 D2
Wednesbury Dr WA5 ..14 F6
Weighbridge Rd
Connah's Quay CH5 ..92 B4
Connah's Quay CH5 ..92 C5
Weint The WA3 ..11 B3

Weir Gr ST7 .....195 B2
Weir La WA1 .....17 E6
Weir St Northwich CW9 .....103 F7
Warrington WA4 .....16 A1
Welbeck Ave WA12 .....2 D2
Welbeck Cl CW10 .....128 B1
Welford Ave WA3 .....3 C7
Welford Cl SK9 .....60 E8
Well Ave SY14 .....213 B3
Well Bank CW11 .....175 B6
Well Bank Cotts WA16 .....108 C8
Well Bank La WA16, SK11 .....108 C7
Well Cl CH64 .....67 A4
Well Farm Cl
Malpas SY14 .....213 B3
Warrington WA1 .....17 D8
Well Field Cl WA16 .....80 A7
Well La Alsager SK7 .....193 C3
Antrobus CW9 .....53 A4
Biddulph ST8 .....179 D3
Chester CH2 .....118 E5
Heswall CH60 .....41 B6
Kingsley WA6 .....75 C2
Little Budworth CW6 .....147 F7
Macclesfield SK10 .....88 B2
Manley WA6 .....98 F3
Mollington CH1 .....94 F2
Neston CH64 .....66 F5
Prestbury SK10 .....87 C8
Stretton WA4 .....52 E8
Warrington WA5 .....14 F3
Weaverham CW8 .....77 C2
Well St Malpas SY14 .....213 B3
Mow Cop ST7 .....195 D7
New Mills SK22 .....39 B8
Winsford CW7 .....126 C1
Welland Cl CW11 .....174 C5
Welland Rd SK9 .....34 E2
Wellbank Ct CW12 .....156 E2
Wellbrook Cl WA7 .....50 C5
Wellcroft Cl CW7 .....206 B7
Weller Ave SK12 .....36 D2
Weller Cl SK12 .....36 D2
Welles St CW11 .....175 B6
Wellesbourne Cl
Macclesfield SK10 .....86 F1
Neston CH64 .....66 D6
Wellesley Ave
Ellesmere Port CH65 .....70 C5
Haslington CW1 .....191 C4
Wellesley Cl WA12 .....2 B5
Wellesley Wlk [6] CH65 .....70 C5
Wellfield Runcorn WA7 .....50 E5
Widnes WA8 .....13 A3
Winsford CW7 .....127 A2
Wellfield Rd WA3 .....4 F4
Wellfield St
Warrington WA5 .....15 E5
Warrington WA5 .....15 E6
Wellfield Way SY13 .....225 F1
Wellington Cir SK10 .....112 E8
Wellington Cl
Congleton CW12 .....156 D4
[3] Ellesmere Port CH65 .....70 C5
Knutsford WA16 .....57 C4
Newton-le-W WA12 .....2 A3
Warrington WA2 .....8 F2
Wellington Gate CW1 .....21 E2
Wellington Gdns WA12 .....2 A3
Wellington Pl CH1 .....237 B3
Wellington Rd
Bollington SK10 .....87 F8
Broughton CH4 .....139 B4
Ellesmere Port CH65 .....70 B4
Ellesmere Port CH65 .....70 C5
Hazel Grove SK7 .....37 B8
Kidsgrove ST7 .....195 A2
Nantwich CW5 .....204 E4
Wellington Rd N CH65 .....70 C4
Wellington St
[8] Macclesfield SK11 .....112 D8
Newton-le-W WA12 .....2 A3
Northwich CW9 .....103 F7
[3] Runcorn WA7 .....23 A3
Warrington WA1 .....16 C5
Widnes WA8 .....23 B8
Wellington St Wrkshps [4]
WA1 .....16 C5
Wells Ave CW1 .....191 D5
Wells Cl
Ellesmere Port CH66 .....94 E8
Heald Green SK8 .....34 C7
Mickle Trafford CH2 .....119 F8
Warrington WA1 .....17 B8
Wellswood Dr CW2 .....205 F7
Wellswood Rd CH66 .....69 E7
Welsby Cl WA2 .....8 E3
Welsh La CW7 .....149 D6
Welsh Rd
Connah's Quay CH5 .....116 A7
Ellesmere Port CH66 .....68 E4
Hooton CH66 .....44 A1
Woodbank CH1 .....93 C6
Welsh Road Cotts CH1 .....93 D8
Welsh Row
Nantwich CW5 .....204 D5
Nether Alderley SK10 .....84 F6
Welshampton Cl CH66 .....69 D2
Welshmen's La CW5 .....204 C7
Welshpool Cl WA5 .....7 D2
Welton Cl SK9 .....59 E4
Welton Dr SK9 .....59 E4
Welton Gr SK9 .....59 E4
Welwyn Cl WA4 .....17 C3
Wem Gr ST5 .....210 E2
Wemyss Rd CH1 .....117 D4
Wendover Cl WA11 .....1 D7

Wenger Rd WA8 .....13 B5
Wenlock Cl
Macclesfield SK10 .....87 B2
Newcastle-u-Lyme ST5 .....210 E2
Warrington WA1 .....17 A8
Wenlock Gdns CH66 .....69 F2
Wenlock La CH66 .....69 F2
Wenlock Rd WA7 .....50 A4
Wenlock Way CH4 .....140 F6
Wensley Dr SK7 .....36 D7
Wensley Rd WA3 .....3 E7
Wensleydale Ave
Bebington CH62 .....43 E5
Congleton CW12 .....156 C3
Wensleydale Cl WA5 .....14 F8
Wentworth Ave
Macclesfield SK11 .....111 F6
Warrington WA1 .....17 B7
Wentworth Cl
Northwich CW9 .....104 C7
Widnes WA8 .....13 A5
Wentworth Dr
Bebington CH63 .....43 C5
Bramhall SK7 .....36 A7
Kidsgrove ST7 .....195 C3
Wentworth Gr CW7 .....126 A2
Wereton Rd ST7 .....209 D1
Wervin Rd CH2 .....96 A3
Wesley Ave Alsager ST7 .....193 D4
Haydock WA11 .....1 F7
[2] Sandbach CW11 .....175 B6
Wesley Cl Nantwich CW5 .....204 E5
Neston CH64 .....66 D8
Wesley Ct
Congleton CW12 .....156 D2
Winsford CW7 .....126 F1
Wesley Gdns [7] ST7 .....195 A2
Wesley Pl Crewe CW2 .....190 D2
[4] Northwich CW9 .....104 A8
Wesley St ST7 .....210 A1
Wessex Cl
Shavington CW2 .....206 C3
Warrington WA1 .....17 E7
Wessex Dr CW9 .....104 C6
West Ave Crewe CW1 .....190 B4
Kidsgrove ST7 .....194 C1
Middlewich CW10 .....128 C2
Northwich CW9 .....104 D7
Warrington WA2 .....16 B8
Warrington, Stockton Heath
WA4 .....16 C1
Weston CW2 .....207 B5
West Bank
Alderley Edge SK9 .....85 A8
Chester CH2 .....118 C4
West Bank Dock Est
WA8 .....22 C5
West Bank Prim Sch
WA8 .....23 A4
West Bank Rd SK10 .....87 B1
West Bank St WA8 .....23 A5
West Bond St WA8 .....23 A5
West Cheshire Coll CH65 .....70 B5
West Cheshire Coll
(Greenbank Ctr) CH4 .....141 D6
West Cheshire Coll
(Handbridge Ctr) CH4 .....141 D7
West Cl SK10 .....87 F7
West Dr Heswall CH60 .....41 A7
Neston CH64 .....66 E6
Warrington WA5 .....15 B4
Winsford CW7 .....126 C2
West Dudley St CW7 .....126 F1
West End CH3 .....121 C7
West End Cotts CW10 .....156 C2
West End Rd WA11 .....1 A6
West Gn CH5 .....116 A6
West Gr Alsager SK7 .....193 E4
Heswall CH60 .....40 F8
West Hall St WA6 .....29 C5
West Heath Gr WA13 .....18 C4
West Heath Sh Ctr
CW12 .....156 A3
West House St SK10 .....86 E1
West Hyde WA13 .....18 C3
West La Cuddington CW8 .....101 F3
High Legh WA16 .....29 C6
West Lorne St CH1 .....237 A3
West Mains L24 .....21 A3
West Park Ave SK10 .....63 A4
West Park Dr CH66 .....94 F8
West Park Mus* SK10 .....87 C1
West Quay Rd WA7 .....7 F3
West Rd Congleton CW12 .....156 C2
Ellesmere Port CH65 .....70 C3
Runcorn WA7 .....48 D7
Weaverham CW8 .....77 B1
West Side Ave WA11 .....1 A6
West St Alderley Edge SK9 .....60 A1
Chester CH2 .....237 C4
Congleton CW12 .....156 D3
Crewe CW1 .....190 B5
Haslington CW1 .....191 C5
Macclesfield SK11 .....112 B8
Middlewich CW10 .....128 C1
Mount Pleasant ST7 .....195 B6
Warrington WA2 .....16 B7
West Vale CW8 .....78 A4
West View
Ellesmere Port CH66 .....69 A8
Northwich CW9 .....104 B8
Warrington WA2 .....9 A1
Antrobus WA4 .....53 A5
West View Rd WA6 .....101 A6
West Way
Holmes Chapel CW4 .....130 B3

West Way continued
Sandbach CW11 .....174 F4
Shavington CW2 .....206 D5
West Wing The CW10 .....127 D5
Westage La CW9 .....79 B8
Westbourne Ave CW1 .....190 A6
Westbourne Dr [17] SK9 .....34 D1
Westbourne Ho CW12 .....156 B2
Westbourne Mews
CW12 .....156 B2
Westbourne Rd
Blacon CH1 .....118 A4
Warrington WA4 .....26 B7
Westbrook Ave WA4 .....16 D2
Westbrook Cres WA5 .....7 B2
Westbrook Ctr WA5 .....7 C1
Westbrook Dr SK10 .....87 C1
Westbrook Old Hall Prim Sch
WA5 .....15 D8
Westbrook Rd WA6 .....75 B2
Westbrook St WA5 .....7 C1
Westbury Cl Crewe CW2 .....206 C7
Middlewich CW10 .....151 B8
Warrington WA1 .....17 A8
Westbury Ct SK11 .....112 A7
Westbury Dr SK11 .....112 A7
Westbury Way CH4 .....140 F6
Westby Cl SK7 .....36 A7
Westcliffe Ct WA8 .....13 B4
Westcliffe Gdns WA4 .....26 E3
Westdale Rd WA1 .....17 A7
Westend St SK11 .....196 D8
Westerns Ave CH65 .....69 F6
Westerham Cl SK10 .....87 B2
Westerhope Way WA8 .....12 F3
Western App CW2 .....218 E4
Western Ave Blacon CH1 .....117 D4
Ellesmere Port CH65 .....69 F7
Macclesfield SK11 .....112 C5
Macclesfield SK11 .....112 D5
Milton Green CH3 .....165 C2
Nantwich CW5 .....204 E3
Western Ct CH2 .....118 E4
Western Dr SK11 .....112 C5
Western Pk CW11 .....191 F8
Westfield Ave SK7 .....209 C2
Winsford CW7 .....149 C5
Westfield Cres CW7 .....22 E1
Westfield Dr
Knutsford WA16 .....56 E1
Willaston CW8 .....205 E8
Westfield Gr CW8 .....77 F4
Westfield Inf Sch CW2 .....205 E8
Westfield Mews WA7 .....22 E1
Westfield Prim Sch WA7 .....22 E1
Westfield Rd
Cheadle Hulme SK8 .....34 F8
Mow Cop ST7 .....195 C7
Northwich CW9 .....104 B7
Runcorn WA7 .....22 E1
Westfields WA15 .....31 F8
Westfields Ave SK10 .....87 B1
Westfields Rise CW3 .....232 C1
Westford Rd WA4 .....26 A1
Westgate Widnes WA8 .....22 B7
Wilmslow SK9 .....60 A5
Westgate Ave CW7 .....126 A1
Westgate Pk CW7 .....206 E2
Westhay Cres WA3 .....10 A5
Westholme Cl
Congleton CW12 .....156 C3
Crewe CW2 .....206 C8
Westholme Ct SK9 .....60 A2
Westhouse Cl CH63 .....43 C5
Westland Cl CW12 .....156 C2
Westlands ST7 .....209 F2
Westlands Cl CH64 .....41 F1
Westlands Rd CW10 .....128 B1
Westlands The CW12 .....156 C2
Westmere Cl CW7 .....207 B5
Westmere Dr CW1 .....190 F2
Westminster Ave CH4 .....141 B6
Westminster Cl
Middlewich CW10 .....128 B1
Warrington WA4 .....17 C2
Widnes WA8 .....22 B8
Westminster Ct CH2 .....118 F2
Westminster Dr
Bebington CH62 .....43 D7
Cheadle Hulme SK8 .....35 B6
Haydock WA11 .....1 F7
Wilmslow SK9 .....60 A4
Westminster Gr
Ellesmere Port CH65 .....70 C6
[8] Winsford CW7 .....149 A8
Westminster Inf and Pk
CH65 .....70 C6
Westminster Pl [2] WA1 .....16 B5
Westminster Rd
Broughton CH4 .....139 B3
Chester CH4 .....118 F3
Ellesmere Port CH65 .....70 C6
[4] Macclesfield SK10 .....112 C8
Macclesfield SK10 .....87 C1
Westminster St
Crewe CW2 .....190 C2
[14] Macclesfield SK10 .....112 C8
Westminster Terr CH4 .....141 B7
Westmoreland WA14 .....31 B8
Westmorland Ave
Talke ST7 .....210 F7
Widnes WA8 .....13 B1
Westmorland Cl SK10 .....86 F2
Westmorland Rd M31 .....11 F2
Westmorland Terr CW4 .....130 B3

Weston Cl
Middlewich CW10 .....151 C7
Northwich CW9 .....103 F5
Weston Cres WA7 .....49 A6
Weston Ct Runcorn WA7 .....48 F7
Shavington CW2 .....206 C5
Weston Ctr The CW1 .....190 E1
Weston Gr Chester CH2 .....118 E7
Halewood L26 .....21 A6
Weston La CW2 .....206 A4
Weston Point Com Prim Sch
WA7 .....48 E7
Weston Point Expressway
Runcorn WA7 .....22 E2
Runcorn,Rocksavage WA7 .....49 B5
Runcorn WA7 .....48 E6
Weston Prim Sch WA7 .....49 A6
Weston Rd Crewe CW1 .....190 F1
Runcorn WA7 .....48 E7
Weston CW1,CW2 .....207 B7
Weston SK9 .....60 E6
Weston Sq SK11 .....111 F7
Weston View WA7 .....49 D4
Weston Village Prim Sch
CW2 .....207 C5
Westover Rd WA1 .....16 F8
Westrees CW8 .....101 D5
Westville Dr CW12 .....156 A2
Westward Rd
Chester CH3 .....142 B8
Wilmslow SK9 .....59 F6
Westway CH60 .....40 F6
Wilmslow WA7 .....24 C1
Westwood Cl CW2 .....207 B1
Westwood Cres WA4 .....16 F6
Westwood Ct CH64 .....41 E2
Westwood Rd SK8 .....34 B8
Westy La WA4 .....16 F4
Wet Gate La WA13 .....19 E4
Wetheral Rd SK10 .....87 B2
Wetherby Cl
Chester CH1 .....118 B2
Newton-le-W WA12 .....2 C5
Wetherby Way CH66 .....69 B5
Wetreins La SY14,CH3 .....197 D6
Wettenhall Rd CW5 .....188 B4
Wetton La WA6 .....76 E4
Wexford Ave L24 .....21 D2
Weybourne Cl CH4 .....140 E5
Weybridge Cl WA4 .....26 E7
Weygates Dr SK10 .....87 B3
Weygates Dr WA15 .....32 C7
Weymouth Cl WA7 .....50 E6
Weymouth Rd WA5 .....6 F6
Whaddon Dr CH4 .....140 F4
Whaley Bridge Prim Sch
SK23 .....65 E8
Whaley Bridge Sta SK23 .....65 E8
Whaley Cl CH1 .....117 A8
Whalley Ave WA3 .....5 C7
Whalley Dr CW7 .....147 B3
Whalley Gr WA8 .....13 D3
Whalley Hayes SK10 .....112 C8
Whalley La WA1 .....16 C6
Wharams Bank CW11 .....176 F5
Wharburton Cl CW8 .....101 F2
Wharf Cl SK23 .....65 E7
Wharf La CW12 .....178 B3
Wharf Mill CW12 .....156 F1
Wharf Rd
Collins Green WA12 .....1 E2
Whaley Bridge SK23 .....65 E7
Wharf St WA1 .....16 C4
Wharf The Chester CH1 .....118 B1
Runcorn WA7 .....50 F6
Wharf Works SK22 .....39 B6
Wharfdale Ave WA1 .....173 B1
Wharfdale Cl WA5 .....15 A7
Wharfdale Rd CW12 .....157 B1
Wharfe La CH65 .....70 A7
Wharfedale WA8 .....50 B6
Wharfedale Dr CH62 .....43 F5
Wharford La WA7 .....24 E3
Wharfside Ct [8] WA4 .....16 E1
Wharmby Rd WA11 .....1 B6
Wharton CE Jun Sch
CW7 .....126 F1
Wharton Cl CH2 .....118 F2
Wharton Gdns CW7 .....127 A3
Wharton Hall CW7 .....127 A3
Wharton Ind Est CW7 .....126 F2
Wharton Park Rd CW7 .....126 F2
Wharton Rd CW7 .....127 A2
Wharton Ret Pk CW7 .....126 F3
Whatcroft Cl WA7 .....49 D6
Whatcroft Hall La CW9 .....104 F1
Wheat Moss SK11 .....84 B3
Wheatcroft Cl WA5 .....15 C6
Wheatfield Cl
Barnton CW8 .....78 A4
Ellesmere Port CH66 .....69 C3
Macclesfield SK10 .....87 C3
Wheatland Cl WA7 .....50 C6
Wheatland Rd CH66 .....41 C2
Wheatlands ST7 .....209 F2
Wheatley Ave CW1 .....190 E6
Wheatsheaf Cl SK23 .....65 E6
Wheatsheaf La CW9 .....53 B3
Wheatsheaf Rd SK23 .....65 E6
Wheelman Rd CW1 .....190 E5
Wheelock Cl Alsager ST7 .....193 A3
Handforth SK9 .....34 D3
Wheelock Ct CW11 .....175 A2
Wheelock Dr CW7 .....127 B1

Wheelock Prim Sch
CW11 .....175 A4
Wheelock St CW10 .....128 C1
Wheelock Way [2] ST7 .....195 B2
Wheldon Cl CH2 .....118 E8
Wheldrake Cl CH2 .....118 E7
Wheldrake Cl CH66 .....69 B5
Whernside WA8 .....12 C3
Whetstone Hey CH66 .....69 D5
Whetstone Rd ST8 .....179 C2
Wheycroft Mews CW1 .....190 C5
Whickham Cl CH4 .....12 F3
Whimberry Cl WA12 .....2 C3
Whimbrel Cl WA7 .....49 F5
Whimbrel Ave WA12 .....2 C4
Whinchat Ave WA3 .....3 E7
Whinchat Dr WA3 .....9 F3
Whinfell Gr WA7 .....49 E5
Whipcord La CH1 .....118 B2
Whirley Cl CW10 .....151 C7
Whirley La SK10 .....85 F1
Whirley Prim Sch SK10 .....86 D1
Whirley Rd SK10 .....86 C1
Whirlow Rd CW2 .....206 B7
Whisterfield La SK11 .....109 E3
Whiston Cl
High Legh WA16 .....29 C4
Winsford CW7 .....127 A4
Whiston St SK11 .....112 C7
Whitbarrow Rd WA13 .....18 D4
Whitby Ave Chester CH2 .....118 D5
Warrington WA3 .....8 D2
Whitby Cl Crewe CW1 .....190 B8
Poynton SK12 .....36 D4
Whitby Heath Prim Sch
CH65 .....70 B3
Whitby High Sch The
CH66 .....70 A2
Whitby La CH1 .....95 B6
Whitby Rd
Ellesmere Port CH65 .....70 C5
Runcorn WA7 .....23 A1
Whitby's La CW7 .....126 B1
Whitchurch Gr ST5 .....210 E2
Whitchurch Rd
Audlem CW3 .....229 C3
Broxton CH3 .....183 A3
Chester CH3 .....119 B1
Christleton CH3 .....142 E7
Edge Green SY14,CH3 .....199 B4
Handley CH3 .....182 D8
Milton Green CH3 .....165 C4
Newhall CW5,SY13 .....228 A6
Royal's Green CW3,SY13 .....228 C2
Sound CW5 .....217 E3
Waverton CH3 .....143 A3
Whitchurch Way WA7 .....49 D7
White Ave CW7 .....189 F4
White Bear Yd [8] WA16 .....57 A2
White Broom WA13 .....19 B4
White Friars CH1 .....237 A2
White Hall La CW11 .....151 E1
White Hart Gdns CW8 .....102 F4
White Hart La CW2 .....205 E8
White House Cl WA11 .....1 B6
White House Dr WA1 .....17 E7
White Lodge Cl CH62 .....43 D8
White Lodge Mews
CW8 .....102 A3
White Park Cl CW10 .....128 D2
White St
Macclesfield SK11 .....112 D6
Warrington WA1 .....16 A5
Warrington, Stockton Heath
WA4 .....16 C1
Widnes WA8 .....23 A5
Whitebarn Rd SK9 .....85 B8
Whitebeam Ave [5] CH66 .....69 F1
Whitebeam Cl
Newcastle-u-Lyme ST5 .....210 D1
Runcorn WA7 .....24 C1
Whitebeam Row CW8 .....102 E7
Whitecroft Heath Rd
SK11 .....109 B3
Whitecroft Rd CH66 .....69 E2
Whitecroft Villas M31 .....11 E2
Whitecross Rd WA5 .....15 E5
Whitefield Ave WA3 .....19 A4
Whitefield Cl
Golborne WA3 .....3 A8
Lymm WA13 .....19 A5
Whitefield Gr WA13 .....19 A4
Whitefield Rd WA4 .....26 B8
Whitefields CH2 .....72 B3
Whitefriars Wlk M22 .....33 D8
Whitegate WA3 .....4 F2
Whitegate CE Prim Sch
CW8 .....125 F7
Whitegate Cl CW10 .....151 C6
Whitegate Fields LL13 .....180 D1
Whitegate La CH3 .....121 E7
Whitegate Rd CW7 .....125 F3
Whitegates CW12 .....179 D4
Whitegates Cres CH64 .....41 E1
Whitegates Ho CW2 .....189 E2
Whitehall Cl Barnton CW8 .....78 A4
Wilmslow SK9 .....60 A5
Whitehall Ct [3] CW5 .....204 D5

Whitehall Dr CW8 103 C5
Whitehall La CW6 124 E1
Whitehall Pl 5 WA6 74 B8
Whitehaven La CW5 203 A7
Whitehaven Rd SK7 35 C5
Whitehill Rd ST7 195 B2
Whitehouse Dr WA15 32 B8
Whitehouse Expressway WA7 50 B5
Whitehouse Ind Est WA7 50 E4
Whitehouse La
Nantwich CW5 204 F7
Partington WA14 20 D8
Plumley WA16 80 F5
Whitehouse Rd WA16 30 B3
Whiteleas Rd SK23 65 D3
Whitemere Ct CH65 70 C7
Whitemore Rd CW10 151 C6
Whiteridge Rd ST7 195 B2
Whites La CW2 207 B6
Whites Mdw CH3 142 A7
Whitesands Rd WA13 18 C4
Whiteside Rd WA11 1 B6
Whitesmead Cl SK12 38 D5
Whitethorn Ave WA5 14 F5
Whitethorn Way ST5 210 E1
Whitethroat Wlk WA3 9 F3
Whitewell Cl CW5 204 F5
Whitewood La SY14 212 D7
Whitfield Ave WA1 16 F7
Whitfield Gr WA11 1 A6
Whitfield Rd ST7 195 B2
Whitfields The SK10 87 A1
Whitley Ave Barnton CW8 78 B3
Warrington WA4 17 A4
Whitley Cl
Middlewich CW10 151 B7
Runcorn WA7 48 F8
Whitley Dr CW8 103 A4
Whitley La WA16 55 B8
Whitley Village Sch WA4 52 D4
Whitlow Ave CW5 204 F4
Whitlow La CW9 126 F8
Whitney Croft SK10 113 A8
Whitstable Pk WA8 12 E4
Whittaker Ave WA2 8 D2
Whittaker Cl CW1 190 A7
Whittington Gdns CW9 104 A2
Whittle Ave Haydock WA11 1 A5
Warrington WA5 15 A7
Whittle Cl CH5 116 A3
Whittle Hall La WA5 14 F6
Whittlewood Cl WA3 10 A5
Whitton Dr CH2 118 E5
Whitwell Cl WA5 14 D7
Whitworth Cl WA3 9 E3
Wicker La
Altrincham WA15 32 C8
Guilden Sutton CH3 120 A4
Wicklow Cl CH66 69 A6
Wickson La CH3,CW6 167 D3
Wickstead Cl CW5 205 A4
Wicksten Dr WA7 23 C2
Widdale Cl WA5 14 F7
Widgeon Cl SK12 36 B4
Widgeons Covert CH63 41 F5
Widnes & Runcorn Sixth Form Coll WA8 12 E5
Widnes Rd
Cuerdley Cross WA5,WA8 13 F2
Warrington WA5 14 C3
Widnes WA8 23 B8
Widnes Sta WA8 13 A3
Wiend The CH2 118 D4
Wight Cl CH65 70 C1
Wightman Ave WA12 2 C5
Wigmore Cl WA3 10 A6
Wigsey La WA13 19 A7
Wigshaw La WA3 4 D2
Wigwam Cl SK12 36 C4
Wilbraham Cl CW5 204 A7
Wilbraham Rd
Acton CW5 204 A7
Congleton CW12 156 F3
Weaverham CW8 77 E1
Wilbraham's Wlk ST7 209 D2
Wilbrahams Way ST7 193 D4
Wilcock Rd WA11 2 B8
Wilcote Cl WA8 13 C4
Wilcott Dr SK9 59 F4
Wild Arum Cl 8 WA3 3 E8
Wild Goose Ave ST7 195 D3
Wildenhall Cl WA5 15 B6
Wilderhope Cl CW2 206 C7
Wilderspool Cres WA4 16 B1
Wilderspool Cswy WA4 16 C3
Wilding Ave 8 WA7 23 B2
Wilding Bsns Pk CH3 119 C4
Wilding St CW1 190 E4
Wildings Old La WA3 9 A8
Wildmoor La CH3 97 D1
Wildwood Gr WA1 17 B7
Wilkin Croft 5 SK8 34 E8
Wilkins La SK9 33 E5
Wilkinson Ave WA1 16 F6
Wilkinson Cl WA8 23 A5
Wilkinson St
Ellesmere Port CH65 70 C6
Warrington WA2 16 C7
Wilkinson St N CH65 70 C6
Wilkinson Street Mews 1 CH65 70 C6
Willan Rd CH1 117 D4
Willaston CE Prim Sch CH64 67 F8
Willaston Dr L26 21 A6
Willaston Farm CH64 67 F8
Willaston Green Mews CH64 67 F8
Willaston Hall Gdns CW5 205 C6
Willaston Prim Sch CW5 205 D6
Willaston Rd CH63,CH64 42 D4
Willaston Way 8 SK9 34 D5
Willbank La CW5 202 D5
Willerby Cl 1 SK10 112 C8
Willeymoor La SY13 225 D8
William Beamont Com High Sch WA2 8 C1
William Ct CH64 41 F2
William Johnson Gdns CH65 70 C6
William Penn Cl WA5 14 E5
William Rd ST7 195 A2
William St Chester CH1 237 B3
Chester,Hoole Park CH2 118 F3
Congleton CW12 157 A4
Macclesfield SK10 112 F8
6 Northwich CW9 104 B8
Widnes WA8 13 C1
Winsford CW7 126 E1
William Stockton Com Sch CH65 70 B5
Williams Ave WA12 2 C5
Williams Cl CH2 118 C4
Williams Way
Frodsham WA6 74 A8
Henbury SK11 111 C8
Williamson Cres SK23 65 D8
Williamson Rd SK23 65 D8
Willington Ave CH62 43 E3
Willington La
Duddon CW6 145 E7
Kelsall CW6 122 D3
Willington Rd
Duddon CW6 145 B7
Kelsall CW6 122 C2
Willis St WA1 16 D6
Willmer Cres ST7 195 B6
Willotts Hill Rd ST5 210 D1
Willoughby Cl WA5 7 C1
Willow Ave
Newton-le-W WA12 2 E4
2 Widnes WA8 13 B2
Willow Bank
Cheadle Hulme SK8 35 A6
Helsby WA6 73 D2
Nantwich CW5 204 F6
Willow Bank Est WA12 2 F4
Willow Cl Chester CH2 118 D8
Lymm WA13 18 E4
Morley Green WA16 59 B5
Newcastle-u-Lyme ST5 210 D1
Poynton SK12 36 E3
Runcorn WA7 49 C7
Winsford CW7 126 D3
Willow Cres Chester CH2 119 A4
Crewe CW2 189 F2
Moore WA4 25 A7
Warrington WA1 17 B8
Willow Ct Alsager ST7 193 E4
Connah's Quay CH5 91 D1
Higher Kinnerton CH4 161 A7
Macclesfield SK10 87 B2
Middlewich CW10 128 C2
Nantwich CW5 204 F7
Newton-le-W WA12 2 D4
Winsford CW7 127 B2
Willow Dr Blacon CH1 117 D5
Bunbury CW6 185 E8
Handforth SK9 34 D3
Sandbach CW11 175 E7
Warrington WA4 16 E1
Willow Gn Knutsford WA16 56 F3
Weaverham CW8 102 D8
Willow Gr Barnton CW8 78 B4
Chester CH2 119 B4
Ellesmere Port CH66 95 A8
Elton CH2 72 A3
Willow Green La CW8 77 B5
Willow Hayes CH3 121 F7
Willow La Goostrey CW4 107 E1
Thornton Hough CH63,CH64 42 D3
Warrington WA4 26 E4
Willow Lea CH1 94 F2
Willow Rd Chester CH4 140 F6
Haydock WA11 1 E7
High Lane SK6 37 F7
Newton-le-W WA12 2 E4
Partington M31 11 E2
Willow Sq CW7 127 A2
Willow St CW12 156 E3
Willow Tree Gr ST7 193 F7
Willow Way Bramhall SK7 35 D7
Broughton CH4 139 B3
Prestbury SK10 87 A5
Willow Wood Inf Sch CW7 127 A2
Willow Wood Jun Sch CW7 127 B2
Willoway Rd CH3 119 B2
Willowbank Dr SK10 88 C8
Willowbrow Rd CH63, CH64 42 D3
Willowcroft Way ST7 195 E4
Willowdale WA12 2 E3
Willowdale Way CH66 94 F8
Willowherb Cl CH3 142 A6
Willowmead Dr SK10 87 A5
Willows SK9 59 F6
Willows Cl CW2 206 B7
Willows The
Frodsham WA6 74 C8
Higher Wincham CW9 79 F6
2 Northwich CW9 103 E6
Partington M31 11 F3
Sandbach CW11 175 B7
Warrington WA5 14 F5
Wilmere La WA8 13 A6
Wilmot Ave WA5 14 F6
Wilmot Dr WA3 2 F7
Wilmslow Ave CH66 69 E5
Wilmslow Cres WA4 17 D4
Wilmslow Ct SK9 34 D3
Wilmslow Dr CH66 69 E5
Wilmslow Grange Prim Sch SK9 34 C4
Wilmslow High Sch SK9 60 B6
Wilmslow Ho 6 SK9 60 B7
Wilmslow Old Rd
Mottram St Andrew SK10 61 A2
Woodhouse Park M90, WA15 33 A6
Wilmslow Park N SK9 60 D7
Wilmslow Park S SK9 60 C7
Wilmslow Prep Sch SK9 60 B7
Wilmslow Rd
Alderley Edge SK9 60 A2
Handforth SK9 34 D4
Heald Green SK8,SK9 34 C6
Mottram St Andrew SK10 61 A3
Mottram St Andrew SK10 61 D6
Mottram St Andrew, Greendale SK10 86 D8
Woodford SK7 35 C1
Woodhouse Park M90,SK9, WA15 32 F5
Wilmslow Sta SK9 60 C7
Wilmslow Wlk 13 SK11 112 E7
Wilsbury Grange CW8 103 A5
Wilsden Rd WA8 12 B1
Wilshaw Terr CH63 42 B6
Wilson Cl Warrington WA4 17 D3
4 Widnes WA8 13 D1
Wilson Cres CW9 80 B3
Wilson Dr CW9 126 F7
Wilson La WA3 9 E5
Wilson Patten St WA1 16 A4
Wilson St WA5 16 A7
Wilsons La CH65 70 A3
Wilton Ave SK8 34 C7
Wilton Cl CW9 103 E4
Wilton Cres
Alderley Edge SK9 59 F2
Macclesfield SK11 111 E6
Wilton Dr WA15 32 C8
Wilton La WA3 4 B5
Wiltshire Cl
Macclesfield SK10 86 E2
Warrington WA1 17 D6
Wiltshire Dr CW12 156 E4
Wiltshire Rd M31 11 E2
Wiltshire Wlk SK10 86 F2
Wilwick La SK11 111 F7
Wimberry Dr ST5 210 D1
Wimboldsley Com Prim Sch CW10 150 F4
Wincham Ave CW9 79 D3
Wincham Bsns Pk CW9 79 D3
Wincham Com Prim Sch CW9 79 E5
Wincham La CW9 79 D3
Wincham Park (Witton Albion FC) CW9 79 C2
Winchester Ave
Ellesmere Port CH65 70 D4
Warrington WA5 15 C5
Winchester Cl
Shavington CW2 206 B3
Wilmslow SK9 59 E5
Winchester Dr SK10 111 F8
Winchester Pl WA8 22 C8
Winchester Sq CH4 140 F5
Wincle Ave SK12 37 A2
Wincle CE Prim Sch SK11 136 F1
Windermere Ave
Chester CH2 119 A6
Warrington WA2 8 D3
Widnes WA8 13 B4
Windermere Cl CH64 66 F7
Windermere Dr
Alderley Edge SK9 59 F1
Congleton CW12 156 A2
Windermere Rd
Crewe CW2 189 E2
Ellesmere Port CH65 70 C2
Handforth SK9 34 C4
Haydock WA11 1 B6
High Lane SK6 37 E8
Winsford CW7 126 C2
Windermere St WA8 13 B4
Windfield Gdns CH66 69 D7
Windings The CW10 128 B2
Windle Ct Neston CH64 41 E2
Warrington WA3 9 C4
Windlehurst Ct SK6 37 D7
Windlehurst Rd SK6 37 D8
Windmill Cl
Buerton CW3 230 E4
Warrington WA4 26 C6
Windmill Ctr The WA8 23 B8
Windmill Dr CW3 229 F3
Windmill Hill Ave WA7 24 D2
Windmill Hill Ave E WA7 24 D1
Windmill Hill Ave N WA7 24 D3
Windmill Hill Ave S WA7 24 D2
Windmill Hill Ave W WA7 24 C2
Windmill Hill Prim Sch WA7 24 C2
Windmill La
Bollington SK10 88 B6
Christleton CH3 142 D8
Hankelow CW3 230 F4
Preston on t H WA4 51 A6
Warrington WA4 26 C6
Warrington,Penketh WA5 14 E5
Windmill Rise CH2 118 D7
Windmill St
Macclesfield SK11 112 E6
Runcorn WA7 23 B2
Windscale Rd WA2 9 A2
Windsor Ave Crewe CW1 190 B6
Nantwich CW5 204 F3
Newton-le-W WA12 2 D2
Tarporley CW6 146 D1
Wilmslow SK9 59 F7
Windsor Cl
Bollington SK10 87 E6
Cuddington CW8 101 F4
Poynton SK12 36 D4
Windsor Ct Chester CH1 237 B1
1 Warrington WA4 16 E1
Windsor Dr Alsager ST7 192 F4
Altrincham WA14 20 F1
Broughton CH4 139 A3
Ellesmere Port CH65 70 A3
Faddiley CW5 202 E7
Haydock WA11 2 A7
Helsby WA6 73 B2
Warrington WA4 17 B2
Winsford CW7 149 C5
Windsor Gdns SK7 35 E6
Windsor Gr
Cheadle Hulme SK8 34 F8
Runcorn WA7 49 B8
Windsor Ho
5 Northwich CW8 103 C5
Talke ST7 210 D6
Windsor Pl CW12 156 F2
Windsor Rd Chester CH4 140 F6
Golborne WA3 3 C8
Widnes WA8 13 A4
Wistaston CW2 205 E8
Windsor Sq SK11 112 D4
Windsor St WA5 15 E6
Windsor Way WA16 56 F2
Windways CH66 69 D7
Windy Bank Ave WA3 3 E8
Winfield Way WA8 23 B8
Winfrith Rd WA2 9 A2
Wingate Rd CH62 43 E5
Wingfield Ave SK9 59 E6
Wingfield Dr SK9 59 E6
Wingfield Pl CW7 149 B6
Winghay Rd ST7 195 B2
Winifred St WA2 16 C7
Winkwell Dr CH4 141 A5
Winlowe 18 SK11 112 E7
Winmarith Dr WA15 32 D7
Winmarleigh St WA1 16 A4
Winnington Ave CW8 103 C8
Winnington Ct 14 CW8 103 F8
Winnington Hill CW8 103 F8
Winnington La CW8 78 D1
Winnington Park Com Prim Sch CW8 103 D7
Winnington St
Northwich CW8 103 F8
Winsford CW7 126 E1
Winnows The WA7 23 D1
Winscombe Dr CH3 119 C2
Winsfield Rd SK7 36 E8
Winsford Cl WA11 1 F7
Winsford Cross Sh Ctr CW7 126 D1
Winsford Dr WA5 6 E7
Winsford Gr CH66 69 C3
Winsford High Street Com Sch CW7 126 D1
Winsford Ind Est CW7 127 C3
Winsford Rd CW7 170 F6
Winsford Sta CW7 127 C1
Winsford Way CH1 117 F2
Winslow Cl WA7 50 D8
Winstanley Cl WA5 15 C5
Winstanley Ho WA16 56 F2
Winstanley Ind Est WA2 8 B1
Winstanley Rd CH64 66 E5
Winston Ave Alsager ST7 193 C5
Newton-le-W WA12 2 C3
St Helens WA9 1 B2
Winston Ct CH2 119 A5
Winter Gr WA9 1 B3
Winterbottom La WA16 55 E8
Winterford La CW6 147 B2
Wintergreen Wlk 3 M31 11 F3
Winterley Dr L26 21 A6
Winterside Cl ST5 210 D1
Winterton Way SK11 112 D3
Winton Gr WA7 24 D1
Winton Rd WA3 3 E6
Winwick CE Prim Sch WA2 8 B6
Winwick La WA3 3 E3
Winwick Link Rd WA2, WA3 8 C6
Winwick Park Ave WA2 8 A5
Winwick Rd
Newton-le-W WA12 2 F1
Warrington WA2 8 A2
Winwick St WA2 16 B6
Winwick View WA5 1 D1
Wirksmoor Rd SK22 39 B7
Wirral Cl WA3 4 E4
Wirral Cres CH64 66 F5
Wirral Ctry Pk* CH64 67 C7
Wirral Ed Ctr CH62 43 D8
Wirral Metropolitan Coll CH62 44 A7
Wirswall Rd SY13 226 C8
Wisenholme Cl WA7 49 E5
Wistaston Ave CW2 189 F2
Wistaston Green Cl CW2 189 E2
Wistaston Green Inf Sch CW2 189 F2
Wistaston Green Jun Sch CW2 189 F2
Wistaston Green Rd CW2 189 E2
Wistaston Jun Sch CW2 205 E8
Wistaston Pk CW2 189 F1
Wistaston Rd
Crewe CW2 190 C3
Wistaston CW5 205 E6
Wistaston Road Bsns Ctr CW2 190 B4
Wisterdale Cl CW2 206 A7
Wisteria Way WA9 6 A7
Witchingham SK9 60 D6
Witham Cl CW2 206 A8
Witham Way ST8 179 E1
Withens Cl CW8 102 D8
Withens La CW8 102 D8
Withenshaw La SK11 136 E5
Wither's La
High Legh WA16 28 B4
High Legh WA16 28 C6
Withers Ave WA2 16 D8
Witherwin Ave WA4 26 F7
Within Way L24 21 E1
Withington Ave WA3 5 A4
Withington Cl
Northwich CW9 104 A6
Sandbach CW11 175 C7
Withinlee Rd SK10 86 D6
Withins Rd Culcheth WA3 4 F3
Haydock WA11 1 F8
Withnall Dr CW2 206 B4
Withy Cl WA6 74 C8
Withy Croft CH3 142 B7
Withycombe Rd WA5 14 E4
Withyfold Dr SK10 87 E1
Witney Gdns WA4 26 E6
Witney La SY14 213 D8
Witt Rd WA8 23 A7
Wittenham Ho SK9 34 D2
Witter Pl CH1 237 C3
Wittering La CH60 40 D7
Witterings The CH64 41 E1
Witton Church Walk CE Prim Sch CW9 104 A8
Witton St CW9 79 A1
Witton Wlk 5 CW9 103 F8
Wivern Pl WA7 23 B3
Wizard Country Pk SK10 85 D6
Woburn Ave WA12 2 D2
Woburn Cl Haydock WA11 1 F7
Macclesfield SK10 87 C2
Northwich CW9 103 E5
Woburn Ct SK12 36 F4
Woburn Dr Chester CH2 118 F7
Congleton CW12 179 B8
Cronton WA8 12 D6
Woburn Rd WA2 8 A4
Woking Rd SK8 35 A7
Wolfe Cl
Grappenhall Heys WA4 27 A8
Knutsford WA16 57 C3
Wolstanholme Cl CW12 156 F1
Wolverham Prim Sch CH65 70 D4
Wolverham Rd CH65 70 D3
Wolverton Dr
Handforth SK9 34 D1
Runcorn WA7 24 D1
Wolvesey Pl CW7 149 B6
Wood Croft CH3 119 F4
Wood Dr ST7 193 A4
Wood End Ct WA8 13 D2
Wood End La CH64 67 E4
Wood Farm CW2 189 B4
Wood Gdns SK9 60 B2
Wood Heath Way CH62 44 A7
Wood La Altrincham WA16 32 D1
Bradwall Green CW10, CW11 152 E3
Broughton CH4 139 B4
Burton CH64 67 C2
Duddon CW6 145 E7
Goostrey CW4 107 C1
Neston CH64 41 D2
Partington M31 11 D3
Runcorn WA7 49 F5
Runcorn, Brookvale WA7 50 C6
Sutton Weaver WA7 49 F4
Tattenhall CH3 167 A1
Warrington WA4 26 E8
Weaverham CW8 102 E8
Wood La E SK10 63 B8
Wood La N
Fourlane-ends SK10 63 B8
Wardsend SK10 37 B1
Wood La S SK10 63 B7
Wood La W
Fourlane-ends SK10 63 A8
Wardsend SK10 36 F1
Wood Lane Prim Sch ST7 210 A1
Wood Meml Sch CH4 140 F6
Wood Orchard La CW3 230 A2
Wood Sorrel Way WA3 3 E8
Wood St Audley ST7 209 E3

Wood St continued
Congleton CW12 ....156 D3
Crewe CW2 ....190 D2
Golborne WA3 ....3 B8
Macclesfield SK11 ....112 D7
Mow Cop ST7 ....195 D7
New Mills SK22 ....39 B7
Sandycroft CH5 ....116 A2
Warrington WA1 ....16 D6
Widnes WA8 ....13 C1
Wood View ST7 ....210 A1
Wood's Cl WA16 ....82 F6
Wood's La CW8 ....101 C5
Woodacre Gr CH66 ......69 F8
Woodacre Rd CH66 ......69 F8
Woodacres Ct SK9 ......59 F6
Woodale Cl WA5 ....14 E7
Woodall Ave CH4 .....140 E6
Woodall Dr WA7 ....23 B1
Woodavens Gr CW3 ....229 A2
Woodbank SK9 ....60 A2
Woodbank Cl CW2 ......206 A7
Woodbank La CH1 ....93 D5
Woodbank Rd
Ellesmere Port CH65 ....70 B2
Warrington WA5 ....15 A4
Woodbine La WA4 ......11 D4
Woodbine Rd WA13 ......19 B4
Woodbourne Rd SK22 ...39 A5
Woodbridge Cl WA4 .....26 E4
Woodbrook SK23 ....65 E8
Woodbrook Ct SK23 .....65 E8
Woodbrook Rd SK9 ......60 C1
Woodburn Dr CH60 ......40 F6
Woodchurch La CH66 ....69 E6
Woodclose WA4 ....44 A1
Woodcock La ST7 ......195 C6
Woodcocks' Well CE Prim
 Sch ST7 ....195 C6
Woodcote Ave CH65 .....70 B1
Woodcote Cl WA2 ....8 D1
Woodcote Pl CW11 .....191 F8
Woodcote View SK9 .....34 F1
Woodcotes The CH62 ...43 D6
Woodcott Ave CW7 .....126 B1
Woodcott Cl CW2 ......206 E2
Woodcott Gr 3 SK9 .....34 E1
Woodcotthill La CW5 ...217 B3
Woodcroft ST7 ....210 A1
Woodcroft Gdns WA4 ....26 E6
Woodend WA7 ....50 E7
Woodend Ct CW10 ......151 C6
Woodend La
Altrincham WA16 ....32 E1
Hollins Green WA3 ....10 D2
Mobberley WA16 ....58 E8
Woodend Rd CH65 ....69 F6
Woodfall Cl CH64 ....67 A6
Woodfall Gr CH64 ....67 A6
Woodfall Inf Sch CH64 ..67 A6
Woodfall Jun Sch CH64 ..67 A6
Woodfall La CH64 ....67 B6
Woodfield Cl CH4 ......139 A3
Woodfield Gr CH2 ......119 B5
Woodfield Ho CH2 .....119 A5
Woodfield Prim Sch
 CH2 ....119 A5
Woodfield Rd
Cheadle Hulme SK8 ......35 B7
Ellesmere Port CH65 ....70 C5
Woodfield Rd N 2 CH65 .70 C5
Woodfields CH3 ....142 E7
Woodfin Croft SK11 .....84 A3
Woodford Aerodrome
 SK7 ....36 A1
Woodford Ave WA3 ....3 D7
Woodford Cl Crewe CW2 .189 F2
Helsby WA6 ....73 B2
Runcorn WA7 ....49 B6
Warrington WA4 ....17 C2
Woodford Court Ind Est
 CW7 ....149 A8
Woodford La
Prestbury SK10 ....61 D7
Winsford CW7 ....149 B8
Woodford La W CW7 ....149 A7
Woodford Lodge High Sch
 CW7 ....149 A7
Woodford Park Ind Est
 CW7 ....148 F8
Woodford Rd
Bramhall SK7 ....35 E4
Poynton SK12 ....36 B6
Wilmslow SK9 ....61 B8
Woodgate Ave ST7 ......194 A5
Woodgreen La CW5 .....171 D5
Woodhall Cl Bramhall SK7 .35 E3
Warrington WA5 ....15 A8
Woodhall Rd ST7 ....195 C3
Woodham Cl CH4 ....103 C5
Woodham Gr CH64 ....66 F5
Woodhatch Rd WA7 ......50 B5
Woodhey Hall La CW5 ...202 B6
Woodhey La CW5 ....202 C5
Woodhouse Cl WA3 ....9 E3
Woodhouse End Rd
 SK11 ....135 C8
Woodhouse La
Biddulph ST8 ....179 F2
Buerton CW3 ....235 D8
Partington WA14 ....20 C1
Warren SK11 ....111 E1
Woodhouse Park M90 ....33 D7
Woodhouse Mid Sch
 ST8 ....179 E2
Woodhouse Rd M22 ......33 D8
Woodhouses Pk WA6 .....73 F5
Woodhouse Ct CW6 .....146 B6

Woodland Ave
Crewe CW1 ....190 F4
Lymm WA13 ....19 A2
Nantwich CW5 ....205 A5
Newton-le-W WA12 ....2 F3
Widnes WA8 ....12 F1
Woodland Bank CH2 .....96 F1
Woodland Cl SK11 ....84 A3
Woodland Ct ST7 ....193 D4
Woodland Dr WA13 ....19 A2
Woodland Gdns CW1 ....188 A3
Woodland Gdns CW1 ....190 D6
Woodland Rd
Ellesmere Port CH65 ....70 B2
Rode Heath ST7 ....193 E8
Woodland View
Ellesmere Port CH66 ....69 B8
Whaley Bridge SK23 .....65 F2
Woodland Wlk
Bebington CH62 ....43 C8
Runcorn WA7 ....24 A1
Woodlands
Hartford CW8 ....103 B5
Kidsgrove ST7 ....194 E3
Woodlands Ave
Chester CH1 ....118 B4
Congleton CW12 ....156 D4
Kidsgrove ST7 ....194 D1
Woodlands Cl
Cheadle Hulme SK8 ......35 A8
Eaton CW6 ....147 A8
Neston CH64 ....66 D8
Woodlands Cres WA16 ...29 C4
Woodlands Ct
Alderley Edge SK9 ....85 A8
2 Knutsford WA16 ....57 B2
Woodlands Cvn Pk
 WA16 ....106 E3
Woodlands Dr
Chester CH2 ....118 E4
Chorlton CW2 ....207 C3
Goostrey CW4 ....107 E1
Knutsford WA16 ....57 B2
Warrington WA4 ....17 D3
Woodlands Gr CW8 ......77 F3
Woodlands Ind Est WA12 ..2 C6
Woodlands Inf Sch CH66 .69 F2
Woodlands Jun Sch
 CH66 ....69 F2
Woodlands La CH3 .....119 A2
Woodlands Pk CW12 ....156 C3
Woodlands Rd
Chester CH4 ....141 A7
Handforth SK9 ....34 E3
High Lane SK6 ....38 A6
Huntington CH3 ....142 A6
Macclesfield SK11 .....112 C6
Neston CH64 ....66 D8
New Mills SK22 ....39 A8
Northwich CW8 ....103 C5
Wilmslow SK9 ....33 F1
Woodlands Rd E 1
 CW8 ....103 C5
Woodlands The
Higher Wincham CW9 ....80 A6
Winnington CW8 ....78 E1
Woodlands Way CW6 ...146 D2
Woodlark Cl CW7 ......150 A8
Woodlea Ave CH2 ......118 F7
Woodlea Cl CH62 ....43 D5
Woodlea Ct CW8 ....103 D7
Woodlea Dr SK10 ....87 E8
Woodleigh Ct SK9 ....60 A2
Woodley Fold WA5 ....14 F4
Woodnoth Dr CW2 ......206 C5
Woodpecker Cl WA3 ......9 F4
Woodpecker Dr
Northwich CW9 ....103 F4
Packmoor ST7 ....195 E1
Woodridge WA7 ....49 C8
Woodrow Way Irlam M44 ..11 F8
Newcastle-u-Lyme ST5 ..210 F7
Woodruff Cl ST7 ....195 F1
Woodruff Wlk 7 M31 ...11 F3
Woods Cl WA12 ....2 A3
Woods Gr SK8 ....35 B7
Woods La SK8 ....35 B7
Woods Rd M44 ....11 F8
Woodsfin La CH3 ......183 F7
Woodshutt's St ST7 ....194 E1
Woodside
Ellesmere Port CH65 ....70 C2
Knutsford WA16 ....57 B1
Lawton-gate ST7 ....194 E4
Siddington SK11 ....110 A3
Woodside Ave
Alsager ST7 ....193 E4
Crewe CW2 ....189 F2
Frodsham WA6 ....74 D7
Kidsgrove ST7 ....195 A1
Woodside Ct CH2 ......118 C4
Woodside Dr
High Lane SK6 ....37 F7
Sandbach CW11 ....175 C6
Woodside La Crewe CW2 .189 F1
Lymm WA13 ....19 A2
Poynton SK12 ....36 E4
Woodside Prim Sch WA7 .49 D7
Woodside Rd
Blacon CH1 ....117 C5
Haydock WA11 ....1 E7
Warrington WA5 ....14 F6
Woodside St SK22 ....39 B6
Woodsome Dr CH65 ......70 B1
Woodsome Dr CH65 ......70 B1
Woodstock Ave
Cheadle Hulme SK8 ......35 A7

Woodstock Ave continued
Newton-le-W WA12 ....2 D2
Woodstock Cl SK10 ......87 A2
Woodstock Ct 4 SK9 ....34 E5
Woodstock Dr CW10 ....151 E5
Woodstock Gdns WA4 ....26 F6
Woodstock Gr WA8 ......12 D2
Woodthorn Cl WA4 ......24 F4
Woodvale Cl WA4 ....8 E1
Woodvale Rd
Ellesmere Port CH66 ....69 D6
Knutsford WA16 ....82 A8
Woodview Cres WA8 .....22 A8
Woodview Rd WA8 ....22 A8
Woodville Pl WA8 ....12 D1
Woodward St CW8 ....77 D1
Woodward Wlk CH3 .....121 C3
Woodwards Cotts CH64 ..66 E7
Woodyear Rd CH62 .....43 E7
Woolacombe Cl WA4 .....16 D2
Woolaston Dr ST7 ......193 D3
Woolden Rd M44,WA3 ...11 B8
Woollam Dr CH66 ....69 D7
Woolley Ave SK12 ....36 D2
Woolley Cl WA6 ....49 D2
Woolston Ave CW12 .....3 A10
Woolston Ave CW12 ....157 A2
Woolston CE Prim Sch
 WA1 ....17 D8
Woolston Com High Sch
 WA1 ....17 B7
Woolston Com Prim Sch
 WA1 ....17 C7
Woolston Dr CW2 ......206 E2
Woolston Grange Ave
Warrington WA1 ....9 D1
Warrington,Woolston WA1 .17 B7
Woolston Hall WA1 ......17 D7
Woolston Rd WA11 ....1 C7
Woolton Ct CH66 ....69 F8
Woore Prim Sch CW3 ...232 C1
Woore Rd CW3 ....230 D3
Worcester Ave WA3 ......3 B8
Worcester Cl Talke ST7 .210 D7
Warrington WA5 ....15 C5
Worcester Pl CH1 ......118 A4
Worcester St CH65 ......70 C6
Worcester Wlk 6 CH65 ..70 C6
Wordsworth Ave
Crewe CW2 ....189 F1
7 Sandbach CW11 ......174 D6
Wordsworth Cres CH1 ..118 A5
Wordsworth Dr CW1 ....190 F4
Wordsworth Ho SK10 ....86 F1
Wordsworth Mews CH1 .118 A5
Wordsworth Sq CH1 ....118 A5
Wordsworth Way
Alsager ST7 ....193 D4
Ellesmere Port CH66 ....69 F1
Works Cotts WA7 ....49 E3
Works La CW9 ....79 E1
World Way M90 ....33 B8
Worleston Cl CW10 .....151 C6
Worley Ct CH3 ....183 A8
Worrall St CW12 ....156 E3
Worsborough Ave WA5 ..15 B5
Worsley Ave
Saughall CH1 ....117 A8
Warrington WA4 ....16 F4
Worsley Dr CW12 ....157 B1
Worsley Rd WA4 ....16 B1
Worsley St Golborne WA3 ..3 A8
Warrington WA5 ....16 C5
Worth Prim Sch SK12 ....36 F2
Worthing Ct WA8 ....13 D1
Worthing Rd WA5 ....14 C6
Worthington Ave 9 M31 .11 F3
Worthington Cl
Henbury SK11 ....111 C8
Nantwich CW5 ....205 A5
Runcorn WA7 ....50 E7
Worthington Ct CH2 ...118 D4
Wr Twr (Mus)* CH1 ....118 B2
Wr Twr Rd CH64 ....41 E1
Wr Twr St CH1 ....237 A3
Wrekin Ho 8 SK8 ....35 B8
Wrekin Way CH4 ....140 F6
Wren Ave CW4 ....129 C2
Wren Cl Macclesfield SK10 .87 A1
Runcorn WA7 ....50 A6
Warrington WA3 ....9 F4
Wrenbury Cl ST5 ......210 D1
Wrenbury Dr 3 CW9 ...103 E5
Wrenbury Frith CW5 ...216 B7
Wrenbury Hall Dr CW5 .217 A5
Wrenbury Heath Rd
 CW5 ....217 D5
Wrenbury Ind Est CW5 .217 A3
Wrenbury Prim Sch
 CW5 ....216 F4
Wrenbury Rd Aston CW5 .217 B3
Marbury SY13 ....226 E8
Marbury,Chorley Bank
 SY14 ....201 D1
Wrenbury SY13,CW5 ....216 B1
Wrenbury Sta CW5 .....217 A3
Wrenmere Cl CW11 .....174 E8
Wrenshot La WA16 ......29 D4
Wrexham Cl
Biddulph ST8 ....179 D1
Warrington WA5 ....14 F6
Wrexham Ind Est/Ystad
 Ddiwdiannol Wrecsam
 LL13 ....196 A1
Wrexham Rd
Bickerton SY14 ....200 A8

Wrexham Rd continued
Bulkeley SY14,CW6 .....184 E1
Burland CW5 ....203 C8
Chester CH4 ....141 B4
Faddiley CW5,CW6 .....202 D6
Holt LL13 ....196 B7
Malpas SY14 ....212 E2
Pulford CH4 ....162 E5
Roughhill CH4 ....140 F1
Worthenbury SY14 .....211 C1
Wright Ave CW9 ....104 D6
Wright Cres WA8 ....23 A5
Wright Ct CW5 ....204 F5
Wright Lodge 6 CW5 ...204 F5
Wright St ST7 ....194 D1
Wright Tree Villas M44 ..11 E5
Wright's La
Burtonwood WA5 ....6 E5
Sandbach CW11 ....175 D6
Wrights La WA5 ....13 F2
Wrigley La SK10 ....86 B3
Wrigley Rd WA11 ....1 E6
Wrinehill Rd CW5 ......220 E7
Wroxham Cl Chester CH2 .237 B4
Wroxham Rd WA5 ....14 C7
Wroxham Rd WA5 ....14 C6
Wrynose Rd CH62 ....43 E8
Wybersley Rd SK6 ....38 A8
Wybunbury Delves CE Prim
 Sch CW5 ....220 B7
Wybunbury La CW5 .....205 E3
Wybunbury Rd
Willaston CW5 ....205 D4
Wybunbury CW5 ....220 B7
Wybunbury CW5 ....220 B7
Wych House Bank CW5 ..204 D5
Wych La SK10 ....62 D5
Wych-House La CW10 ...128 C1
Wyche Ave CW5 ....204 D5
Wyche Cl CW9 ....104 E6
Wyche La CW5 ....185 F8
Wyche Prim Sch CW5 ..204 E6
Wyche Rd CW5 ....185 F8
Wychelm Rd M31 ....11 F3
Wychwood Ave WA13 ....18 C3
Wychwood Pk CW2 .....207 C1
Wycliffe Ave SK9 ....60 A7
Wycliffe Ct CH2 ....119 A2
Wycliffe Rd
Ellesmere Port CH65 ....69 F3
Haydock WA11 ....1 E7
Wyedale Cl CH65 ....70 B3
Wyedale Rd WA11 ....1 C6
Wyncroft Cl
Ellesmere Port CH65 ....70 B3
Widnes WA8 ....22 C7
Wyncroft Ct CW8 ....77 C1
Wyncroft Rd WA8 ....22 C7
Wynd The CW5 ....122 C4
Wyndham Cl Bramhall SK7 .35 E7
Northwich CW9 ....103 F5
Wyndham Cres CH66 ....69 E2
Wyndham Rd CH1 ......117 C4
Wynfield Ave M22 ....33 F7
Wyngate Rd WA15 ....31 F8
Wynnstay Rd CH4 ......139 C4
Wynter Cl CW9 ....198 B3
Wynter La SY14 ....198 B3
Wythburn Gr WA7 ....49 E5
Wythens Rd SK8 ....34 B8
Wythin St CW6 ....168 D1

Y

Y Berllan Geirios/Cherry
 Orch LL13 ....196 D8
Yardley Ave WA5 ....15 F8
Yarmouth Rd WA5 ....14 C6
Yarrow Cl CH4 ....139 C3
Yarwood Cl CW8 ....103 F7
Yarwoodheath La WA14 ..30 E7
Yatehouse La CW10 ....128 C1
Yates Cl WA5 ....15 C5
Yates Rd New Mills SK22 .39 C7
Thornton-le-M CH2 ......71 E1
Yates St CW2 ....190 C2
Yeald Brow WA13 ....18 B3
Yeardsley Ave SK23 .....39 D3
Yeardsley Gn SK23 ......65 D8
Yeardsley La SK23 ......39 D3
Yearsleys La WA6 ......101 A5
Yeld La CW6 ....122 E8
Yeoman Way CH66 ....69 F1
Yeovil Cl WA1 ....17 D8
Yerburgh St CH2 ....118 D4
Yew Tree Ave WA11 ......1 B6
Yew Tree Ave / Lon yr Ywen
 CH1 ....116 F7
Yew Tree Bank CW5 ....145 B5
Yew Tree Cl
Broughton CH4 ....139 C3
Bulkeley SY14 ....184 D2
Little Budworth CW6 ...147 F7
Lymm WA13 ....18 A6
Macclesfield SK11 .....112 A6
Middlewich CW10 ......128 B2
Prestbury SK10 ....87 B7
Thornton-le-M CH2 ......71 E1
Wilmslow SK9 ....60 D7
Yew Tree Ct Alsager ST7 .193 E2
Wimboldsley CW10 .....150 F3
Yew Tree Dr Barnton CW8 .78 B3
Nantwich CW5 ....204 D5
Yew Tree Farm Trad Est
 WA1 ....2 A8
Yew Tree La
Appleton Thorn WA4 .....27 C5
Astbury CW12 ....178 C3

Woodstock Ave continued

Yew Tree La continued
Bridgemere CW5 ....232 A6
Poynton SK12 ....36 F3
Yew Tree Park Rd SK8 ...35 B6
Yew Tree Rd
Wardsend SK10 ....37 B1
Wistaston CW2 ....206 A8
Yew Tree Way
Golborne WA3 ....3 B7
Prestbury SK10 ....87 C6
Yew Wlk 1 M31 ....11 E2
Yewdale Dr CH66 ....69 F1
Yewlands CW8 ....101 D5
Yewlands Dr WA16 ....57 C2
Yewtree Cl CH64 ....66 F7
Yewtree Rd WA16 ....80 F3
Yonne The CH1 ....237 A2
York Ave Culcheth WA3 ...4 F2
Warrington WA5 ....14 E7
York Cl Biddulph ST8 ...179 C2
Talke ST7 ....210 D7
York Cres SK9 ....60 D8
York Ct 1 WA4 ....16 E1
York Dr
Mickle Trafford CH2 ....119 E8
Warrington WA4 ....17 A2
Winsford CW7 ....149 D6
Woodhouse Park M90 ....32 F7
York Ho 4 CW8 ....103 C5
York Rd WA7 ....23 A2
York Rd
Connah's Quay CH5 .....91 C1
Ellesmere Port CH65 ....70 C5
Irlam M44 ....11 D5
Warrington WA4 ....17 A2
Widnes WA8 ....22 C8
York St Chester CH1 ...237 B3
Macclesfield SK10 .....112 E8
Runcorn WA7 ....23 A2
Warrington WA3 ....16 C4
Yorkshire Rd M31 ....11 E2
Yorston Lodge Sch WA16 .56 F1
Ysgol Derwen CH4 .....161 A7
Ystad Ddiwdiannol
Wrecsam/Wrexham Ind Est
 LL13 ....196 A1

Z

Zan Dr CW11 ....175 A3
Zan Ind Pk CW11 ......175 A3
Zara Ct WA11 ....1 C7
Zinnia Dr M44 ....11 E8
Zion St 3 CW8 ....103 E7

Addresses

Name and Address	Telephone	Page	Grid reference